Theory of Computation

Jones and Bartlett Books in Computer Science

Algorithms and Data Structures in Computer Engineering
E. Stewart Lee

Computer Architecture: Pipelined and Parallel Processor Design
Michael J. Flynn

Concurrency in Programming and Database Systems
Arthur J. Bernstein and Philip M. Lewis

Discrete Structures, Logic, and Computability
James L. Hein

Logic, Sets, and Recursion
Robert L. Causey

Introduction to Numerical Analysis
John Gregory and Don Redmond

An Introduction to Parallel Programming
K. Mani Chandy and Stephen Taylor

Laboratories for Parallel Computing
Christopher H. Nevison, Daniel C. Hyde, G. Michael Schneider, and Paul T. Tymann

The Limits of Computing
Henry M. Walker

Memory Systems and Pipelined Processors
Harvey G. Cragon

Theory of Computation: An Introduction
James L. Hein

Theory of Computation

An Introduction

James L. Hein

Department of Computer Science
Portland State University

Jones and Bartlett Publishers
Sudbury, Massachusetts

Boston   London   Singapore

Editorial, Sales, and Customer Service Offices
Jones and Bartlett Publishers
40 Tall Pine Drive
Sudbury, MA 01776
800-832-0034
508-443-5000

Jones and Bartlett Publishers International
7 Melrose Terrace
London W6 7RL
England

Library of Congress Cataloging-in-Publication Data

Hein, James L.
    Theory of computation : an introduction / James L. Hein
       p.   cm.
    Includes bibliographical references and index.
    ISBN 0-86720-497-4
    1. Machine theory.   I. Title.
  QA267.H45   1996
  511.3--dc20   95-45894
                                           CIP

Printed in the United States of America
99 98 97 96 95   10 9 8 7 6 5 4 3 2 1

In Memory of My Father

Lloyd Adolph Hein (1910–1991)

Late one Halloween night in rural Minnesota, he and some friends visited a neighboring farm where they dismantled a hay wagon. Then they hauled the parts of the wagon up to the top of a shed and put the wagon back together.

I hope that this book helps students put things together too.

Contents

Preface

*The last thing one discovers in writing a book
is what to put first.*
—Blaise Pascal (1623–1662)

This book is written for the prospective computer scientist, applied mathematician, or engineer who wants to learn about the theories that underlie computer science. I have attempted to give elementary introductions to those theoretical ideas—and resulting techniques—that are necessary to understand and practice the art and science of computing.

The choice of topics—and the depth and breadth of coverage—reflects the desire to provide students with the foundations needed to successfully complete courses at the upper division level in undergraduate computer science programs. The book can be read by anyone with a good background in high school mathematics and an introductory knowledge of computer programming. Although the book is intended for future computer scientists, applied mathematicians, or engineers, it may also be suitable for a wider audience. For example, it could be used in courses for students who intend to teach computer science.

This book differs in several ways from current books about the theory of computing. It presents an elementary and unified introduction to a collection of topics that, up to now, have not been available in a single source. The book starts off with two chapters that cover those areas of discrete mathematics that are used in the text. These chapters can be used for reference by those with some exposure to discrete mathematics. Chapter 3 is devoted to a formal presentation of logic, including equivalence proofs and inference-based proofs. Formal theories are discussed and then applied to proving correctness properties of programs. Chapter 4 introduces automatic reasoning and logic programming. Chapters 5, 6, 7, and 8 cover the traditional topics of languages, machines, and computability at a new—more elementary—level. Chapter 9 gives an elementary introduction to the field of computational complexity.

Special attention has been paid to the ACM/IEEE-CS Joint Curriculum Task Force report "Computing Curricula 1991." For example, the book covers the general areas of mathematical logic and theory of computation along with the following specific topics listed in the report:

AL3:   Recursive Algorithms
AL4:   Complexity Analysis
AL5:   Complexity Classes
AL7:   Computability and Undecidability
PL7:   Finite State Automata and Regular Expressions
PL8:   Context-Free Grammars and Pushdown Automata
PL11:   Programming Paradigms (functional and logical)
SE5:   Verification and Validation

Some Notes

- The writing style is intended to be informal. For example, the definitions and many of the examples are integrated into the prose.
- The book contains over 800 exercises. Answers are provided for about half of the exercises.
- Each chapter begins with a chapter guide, which gives a brief outline of the topics to be covered in each section.
- Each chapter ends with a chapter summary, which gives a brief description of the main ideas covered in the chapter.
- Most problems in computer science involve one of the following questions:

Can the problem be solved by a computer program?
If not, can you modify the problem so that it can be solved by a program?
If so, can you write a program to solve the problem?
Can you convince another person that your program is correct?
Can you convince another person that your program is efficient?

One goal of the book is that you obtain a better understanding of these questions together with a better ability to answer them. The book's ultimate goal is that you gain self-reliance and confidence in your own ability to solve problems, just like the self-reliance and confidence you have in your ability to ride a bike.

- Algorithms in the text are presented in a variety of ways. Some are simply a few sentences of explanation. Others are presented in a more traditional notation. For example, we use assignment statements like $x := t$ and control statements like **if** A **then** B **else** C **fi**, **while** A **do** B **od**, and **for** $i := 1$ **to** 10 **do** C **od**. We avoid the use of **begin-end** or {-} pairs by using indentation. We'll also present some algorithms as logic programs after logic programming has been introduced.

- The word "proof" makes some people feel uncomfortable. It shouldn't, but it does. Maybe words like "show" or "verify" make you cringe. Most of the time we'll discuss things informally and incorporate proofs as part of the prose. At times we'll start a proof with the word "Proof," and we'll end it with QED. QED is short for the Latin phrase *"quod erat demonstrandum,"* which means "which was to be proved." We'll formalize the idea of proof in the logic chapters.

- A laboratory component for a course is a natural way to motivate and study the topics of the book. The course at Portland State University has evolved into a laboratory course. The ideal laboratory uses an interactive, exploratory language such as Prolog or any of the various functional languages or symbolic computing systems. Labs have worked quite well when the lab experiments are short and specific. Interactive labs give students instant feedback in trying to solve a problem. A few handouts and a few sample problems usually suffice to get students started.

    I am engaged in a research effort to create a collection of declarative laboratory experiments for the topics in the book. Some samples of the current lab experiments can be found in the paper by Hein [1993].

- I wish to apologize in advance for any errors found in the book. They were not intentional, and I would appreciate hearing about them. As always, we should read the printed word with some skepticism.

Using the Book

Although the book is designed as a textbook, it can also be used as a reference book because it contains the background material for many computer science topics. As with most books, there are some dependencies among the topics. For example, all parts of the book depend on the introductory material contained in Chapter 1 and Sections 2.1–2.4. This material covers those topics from discrete mathematics that are used in the book. But you should feel free to jump into the book at whatever topic suits your fancy and then refer back to unfamiliar definitions. Here are the main topics of the book with associated dependencies:

Logic: Formal logic is covered in Chapter 3 and the sections should be read in order, except that Section 3.4 on higher-order logics is optional. Computational logic is covered in Chapter 4 and depends on propositional calculus and predicate calculus (Sections 3.1 and 3.2).

Languages and Automata: These ideas are covered in Chapters 5 and 6, which can be read after the introductory material on languages in Section 1.4. Chapter 6 depends on Section 5.2. Three examples use logic programming from Section 4.2 to construct interpreters. Algebra, as defined at the beginning of Section 2.5, is mentioned from time to time.

Computability: Chapters 7 and 8 should be read in order. There are a few references to topics in Sections 2.5 (algebra) and 4.2 (logic programming) and Chapters 5 and 6.

Complexity: Chapter 9 is almost independent. The last subsection of Section 9.3 discusses formal complexity theory in terms of Turing machines, which are introduced in Section 7.1.

Course Suggestions

The topics in the book can be presented in a variety of ways, depending on the length of the course, the emphasis, and student background. The major portion of the text has been taught for several years to sophomores at Portland State University. Parts of the text have also been used at Portland Community College. Here are a few suggestions for courses of various lengths and emphases.

Courses for Students with a Background in Discrete Mathematics

These courses include some emphasis on logic:

10-week course: Review 1, 2.1–2.4. Cover 3.1, 3.2, 4, 5.1, 5.2, 6.1, 6.2, 7.

15-week course: Review 1, 2.1–2.4. Cover 3.1, 3.2, 4, 5.1, 5.2, 6.1, 6.2, 7, 8.1, 8.2, 9.

20-week course: Review 1, 2. Cover 3.1, 3.2, 3.5, 3.6, 4, 5.1–5.3, 6.1, 6.2, 7, 8.1, 8.2, 9.

30-week course: Review 1, 2. Cover 3, 4, 5, 6.1, 6.2, 6.4, 7, 8.1, 8.2, 9, and either 6.3 or 8.3.

These courses do not emphasize logic:

10-week course: Review 1, 2.1–2.4. Cover 5, 6.1, 6.2, 6.4, 7.

15-week course: Review 1, 2.1–2.4. Cover 5, 6.1, 6.2, 6.4, 7, 8.1, 8.2, 9.

20-week course: Review 1, 2. Cover 5, 6.1, 6.2, 6.4, 7, 8.1, 8.2, 9, and either 6.3 or 8.3.

Courses for Students with No Background in Discrete Mathematics

These courses include some emphasis on logic:

10-week course: 1, 2.1–2.4, 3.1, 3.2, 5.1, 5.2, 6.1, 6.2, 7.

15-week course: 1, 2.1–2.4, 3.1, 3.2, 4, 5.1, 5.2, 6.1, 6.2, 7.

20-week course: 1, 2, 3.1, 3.2, 3.5, 3.6, 4, 5.1–5.3, 6.1, 6.2, 7, 8.1, 8.2, 9.

30-week course: 1, 2, 3, 4, 5, 6.1, 6.2, 6.4, 7, 8.1, 8.2, 9.

These courses do not emphasize logic:

10-week course: 1, 2.1–2.4, 5, 6.1, 6.2, 6.4, 7.

15-week course: 1, 2.1–2.4, 5, 6.1, 6.2, 6.4, 7, 8.1, 8.2, 9.

20-week course: 1, 2, 5, 6.1, 6.2, 6.4, 7, 8.1, 8.2, 9.

30-week course: 1, 2, 3.1, 3.2, 4.1, 5, 6.1, 6.2, 6.4, 7, 8.1, 8.2, 9, and either 6.3 or 8.3.

Acknowledgments

Many people helped me create this book. I received numerous suggestions and criticisms from the students and teaching assistants who used drafts of the manuscript. Five of these people—Janet Vorvick, Roger Shipman, Yasushi Kambayashi, Mike Eberdt, and Tom Hanrahan—deserve special mention for their help. Several reviewers of the manuscript gave very good suggestions that I incorporated into the text. In particular I would like to thank David Mix Barrington, Larry Christensen, Norman Neff, Karen Lemone, Michael Barnett, and James Crook. I also wish to thank Carl Hesler at Jones and Bartlett for his entrepreneurial spirit. Finally, I wish to thank my family—Janice, Gretchen, and Andrew—for their constant help and support.

J.L.H.
Portland, Oregon

1

Elementary Notions
and Notations

'Excellent!' I cried. 'Elementary,' said he.
—Watson in *The Crooked Man*
   by Arthur Conan Doyle (1859–1930)

To communicate, we sometimes need to agree on the meaning of certain terms. If the same idea is mentioned several times in a discussion, we often replace it with some shorthand notation. The choice of notation can help us avoid wordiness and ambiguity, and it can help us achieve conciseness and clarity in our written and oral expression.

Many problems of computer science, as well as other areas of thought, deal with reasoning about things and representing things. Since much of our communication involves reasoning about things, we'll begin the chapter with a short discussion about the notions of informal proof. Next we'll introduce the basic notions and notations for sets and other structures for representing information. Following this, we'll discuss the important concepts of functions. We'll close the chapter with a discussion about languages.

Chapter Guide

Section 1.1 introduces some informal proof techniques that are used throughout the book.

Section 1.2 introduces the basic notions and notations for sets, bags, tuples, lists, strings, graphs, and trees.

Section 1.3 introduces the basic facts about functions. We'll see how to compare the size (cardinality) of sets by using functions that are injective, surjective, or bijective.

Section 1.4 introduces the idea of a language. We'll see that languages can be combined in various ways. We'll introduce the concept of a grammar as the fundamental tool for describing a language.

1.1   A Proof Primer

For our purposes an *informal proof* is a demonstration that some statement is true. We normally communicate an informal proof in an Englishlike language that mixes everyday English with symbols that appear in the statement to be proved. In the next few paragraphs we'll discuss some basic techniques for doing informal proofs.

When we discuss proof techniques, we'll be giving sample proofs about numbers. The numbers that we'll be discussing are called *integers*, and we can list them as follows:

$$..., -3, -2, -1, 0, 1, 2, 3, ... \, .$$

For two integers m and n we say that m *divides* n if $m \neq 0$ and n can be written in the form $n = m \cdot k$ for some integer k. Sometimes we write $m \mid n$ to mean that m divides n. Any positive integer n has at least two positive divisors, 1 and n. For example, 9 has three positive divisors: 1, 3, and 9. The number 7 has exactly two positive divisors: 1 and 7. A positive integer p is said to be *prime* if $p > 1$ and its only positive divisors are 1 and p. For example, 9 is not prime because it has a positive divisor other than 1 and 9. The first eight prime numbers are

$$2, 3, 5, 7, 11, 13, 17, 19.$$

Logical Statements

For this primer we'll consider only statements that are either true or false. Let's look at some familiar ways to construct statements. If S represents some statement, then the *negation* of S is the statement "not S," whose truth value is opposite that of S. We can represent this relationship with a *truth table* in which each row gives a value for S and the corresponding value for not S:

S	not S
true	false
false	true

We often paraphrase the negation of a statement to make it more under-standable. For example, to negate the statement "x is odd," we normally write "x is not odd" or "it is not the case that x is odd" rather than "not x is odd."

The *conjunction* of A and B is the statement "A and B," which is true when both A and B are true. The *disjunction* of A and B is the statement "A or B," which is true if either or both of A and B are true. The truth tables for conjunction and disjunction are given in Table 1.1.

A	B	A and B	A or B
true	true	true	true
true	false	false	true
false	true	false	true
false	false	false	false

Table 1.1

Sometimes we paraphrase conjunctions and disjunctions. For example, instead of "x is odd and y is odd," we write "x and y are odd." Instead of "x is odd or y is odd," we might write "either x or y is odd." But we can't do much paraphrasing with a statement like "x is odd and y is even."

We can combine negation with either conjunction or disjunction to obtain alternative ways to write the same thing. For example, the two statements "not (A and B)" and "(not A) or (not B)" have the same truth tables. So they can be used interchangeably. We can state the rule as

> *The negation of a conjunction is a disjunction of negations.*

For example, the statement "it is not the case that x and y are odd" can be written as "either x is not odd or y is not odd."

Similarly, the two statements "not (A or B)" and "(not A) and (not B)" have the same truth tables. We can state this rule as

> *The negation of a disjunction is a conjunction of negations.*

For example, the statement "it is not the case that x or y is odd" can be writ-ten as "x is not odd and y is not odd."

Many statements are written in the general form "If A then B," where A and B are also logical statements. Such a statement is called a *conditional statement* in which A is the *hypothesis* and B is the *conclusion*. We can read "If A then B" in several other ways: "A is a sufficient condition for B," or "B is a necessary condition for A," or simply "A implies B." The truth table for the conditional is contained in Table 1.2.

A	B	if A then B
true	true	true
true	false	false
false	true	false
false	false	false

Table 1.2

Let's make a few comments about this table. Notice that the conditional is false only when the hypothesis is true and the conclusion is false. It's true in the other three cases. The conditional truth table gives some people fits because they interpret the statement "If A then B" to mean "B can be proved from A," which assumes that A and B are related in some way. But we've all heard statements like "If the moon is made of green cheese then $1 = 2$." We nod our heads and agree that the statement is true, even though there is no relationship between the hypothesis and conclusion. Similarly, we shake our heads and don't agree with a statement like "If $1 = 1$ then the moon is made of green cheese."

When the hypothesis of a conditional is false, we say that the conditional is *vacuously* true. For example, the statement "If $1 = 2$ then $39 = 12$" is vacuously true because the hypothesis is false. If the conclusion is true, we say that the conditional is *trivially* true. For example, the statement "If $1 = 2$ then $2 + 2 = 4$" is trivially true because the conclusion is true. We leave it to the reader to convince at least one person that the conditional truth table is defined properly.

The *converse* of "If A then B" is "If B then A." The converse does not always have the same truth value. For example, we know that the following statement about numbers is true:

If x and y are odd then $x + y$ is even.

The converse of this statement is

If $x + y$ is even then x and y are odd.

This converse is false because $x + y$ could be even with both x and y even.

The *contrapositive* of "If A then B" is "If not B then not A." These two statements have the same truth table. In other words, they can always be used interchangeably. For example, the following statement and its contra-positive are both true:

> If x and y are odd then $x + y$ is even.
>
> If $x + y$ is not even then not both x and y are odd.

Proof Techniques

Now we're in position to look at some proof techniques that offer a variety of ways to prove statements.

Proof by Example

When can an example prove something? Examples can be used to prove statements that claim the existence of an object. Suppose someone says, "There is a prime number between 80 and 88." This statement can be proved by observing that the number 83 is prime.

An example can also be used to disprove (show false) statements that assert that some property is true in many cases. Suppose someone says, "Every prime number is odd." We can disprove the statement by finding a prime number that is not odd. Since the number 2 is prime and even, it can't be the case that every prime number is odd. An example that disproves a statement is often called a *counterexample*.

Proof by Exhaustive Checking

Suppose we want to prove the statement "The sum of any two of the numbers 1, 3, and 5 is an even number." We can prove the statement by checking that each possible sum is an even number. In other words, we notice that each of the following sums represents an even number:

$$1 + 1, 1 + 3, 1 + 5, 3 + 3, 3 + 5, 5 + 5.$$

Of course, exhaustive checking can't be done if there are an infinity of things to check. But even in the finite case, exhaustive checking may not be feasible. For example, the statement "The sum of any two of the odd numbers ranging from 1 to 23195 is even" can be proved by exhaustive checking. But not many people are willing to do it.

Proof Using Variables

When proving a general statement like "The sum of any two odd integers is even," we can't list all possible sums of two odd integers to check to see whether they are even. So we must use variables and formulas to represent arbitrary odd integers.

For example, we can represent two arbitrary odd integers as expressions of the form $2k + 1$ and $2m + 1$, where k and m are arbitrary integers. Now we can use elementary algebra to compute the sum

$$(2k + 1) + (2m + 1) = 2(k + m + 1).$$

Since the expression on the right-hand side contains 2 as a factor, it represents an even integer. Thus we've proven that the sum of two odd integers is an even integer.

Direct Proofs

A *direct proof* of the conditional statement "If A then B" starts with the assumption that A is true. We then try to find another statement, say C, that is true whenever A is true. This means that the statement "If A then C" is true. If C happens to be B, then we're done. Otherwise, we try to find a statement D whose truth follows from that of C. This means that "If C then D" is true. From the truth of the two statements "If A then C" and "If C then D," we conclude that "If A then D" is true. If D happens to be B, then we're done. Otherwise, we continue the process until we eventually reach the goal B. When we're done, we have a direct chain of statements reaching from A to B.

It's often useful to work from both ends to find a direct proof of "If A then B." For example, we might find a sufficient condition C for B to be true. This gives us the true statement "If C then B." Now all we need is a proof of the statement "If A then C." We may be able to work forward from A or backward from C to finish constructing the proof.

Indirect Proofs

A proof is *indirect* if it contains an assumption that some statement is false. For example, since a conditional and its contrapositive have the same truth table, we can prove "If A then B" by proving its contrapositive statement "If not B then not A." In this case we assume that B is false and then try to show that A is false. This is called *proving the contrapositive*. For example, suppose we want to prove the following statement about integers:

If x^2 is even, then x is even.

Proof: We'll prove the contrapositive statement: If x is odd, then x^2 is odd. So assume that x is odd. Then x can be written in the form $x = 2k + 1$ for some integer k. Squaring x, we obtain

$$x^2 = (2k + 1)(2k + 1) = 4k^2 + 4k + 1 = 2(2k^2 + 2k) + 1.$$

The expression on the right side of the equation is an odd number. Therefore x^2 is odd.   QED.

The second indirect method is called *proof by contradiction*. A *contradiction* is a false statement. A proof by contradiction starts with the assumption that the entire statement to be proved is false. Then we argue until we reach a contradiction. Such an argument is often called a *refutation*. A contradiction often occurs in two parts. One part assumes or proves that some statement S is true. The second part proves that S is false. Since S can't be both true and false, a contradiction occurs.

We now have three different ways to prove the conditional "If A then B." We can use the direct method, or we can use either of the two indirect methods. Among the indirect methods, contradiction is often easier than proving the contrapositive because it allows us to assume more. We start by assuming that the whole statement "If A then B" is false. But this means that we can assume that A is true and B is false (from the truth table for conditional). Then we can wander wherever the proof takes us to find a contradiction.

If and Only If Proofs

The statement "A if and only if B" is shorthand for the two statements "If A then B" and "If B then A." The abbreviation "A iff B" is often used for "A if and only if B." Instead of "A iff B," some people write "A is a necessary and sufficient condition for B" or "B is a necessary and sufficient condition for A." Two separate proofs are required for an iff statement, one for each conditional.

For example, let's prove, for integers, that x is even if and only if x^2 is even. Since this is an iff statement, we must prove the following two statements:

(1) If x is even then x^2 is even.

(2) If x^2 is even then x is even.

Proof of (1): If x is even, then we can write x in the form $x = 2k$ for some integer k. Squaring x, we obtain $x^2 = (2k)^2 = 4k^2 = 2(2k^2)$. Thus x^2 is even. Proof of (2): We proved this statement in a preceding paragraph, so we won't repeat it here.   QED.

Exercises

1. See whether you can convince yourself, or a friend, that the conditional truth table is correct by making up English sentences of the form "If A then B."

2. Verify that the truth tables for each of the following pairs of statements are identical.

   a. "not (A and B)" and "(not A) or (not B)."

   b. "not (A or B)" and "(not A) and (not B)."

   c. "if A then B" and "if (not B) then (not A)."

3. Prove or disprove each of the following statements by giving an example or by exhaustive checking.

   a. There is a prime number between 45 and 54.

   b. The product of any two of the four numbers 2, 3, 4, and 5 is even.

   c. Every odd integer greater than 1 is prime.

   d. Every integer greater than 1 is either prime or the sum of two primes.

5. Prove each of the following statements about the integers.

   a. The sum of two even integers is even.

   b. The sum of an even integer and an odd integer is odd.

   c. If x and y are odd then $x - y$ is even.

6. Write down the converse of the following statement about integers:

   $$\text{If } x \text{ and } y \text{ are odd then } x - y \text{ is even.}$$

   Is the statement that you wrote down true or false? Prove your answer.

7. Prove that numbers having the form $3n + 4$, where n is any integer, are closed under multiplication. In other words, if two numbers of this form are multiplied, then the result is a number of the same form.

8. Prove that numbers having the form $3n + 2$, where n is any integer, are not closed under multiplication. In other words, if two numbers of this form are multiplied, then the result need not be of the same form.

9. Prove the following statement about the integers: x is odd if and only if x^2 is odd.

1.2 Sets and Other Structures

When we discuss ideas, we need some common ground for representing information concisely and clearly. In this section we'll present some common ground in the form of sets, bags, tuples, products, lists, strings, graphs, and trees.

Sets

Informally, a *set* is a collection of things called its *elements, members,* or *objects*. Sometimes the word *collection* is used in place of *set* to clarify a sentence. For example, "a collection of sets" seems clearer than "a set of sets." We say that a set contains its elements, or that the elements belong to the set, or that the elements are in the set. If S is a set and x is an element in S, then we write

$$x \in S.$$

If x is not an element of S, then we write $x \notin S$. If $x \in S$ and $y \in S$, we often denote this fact by the shorthand notation $x, y \in S$.

    A set is defined by describing its elements in some way. For example, a gaggle is a set whose members are geese. One way to define a set is to explicitly name its elements. A set defined in this way is denoted by listing its elements, separated by commas, and surrounding the listing with braces. For example, the set S consisting of the letters $x, y,$ and z is denoted by

$$S = \{x, y, z\}.$$

We often use the three-dot ellipsis, ..., to informally denote a sequence of elements that we do not wish to write down. For example, the set

$$\{1, 2, 3, 4, 5, 6, 7, 8, 9, 10, 11, 12\}$$

might be denoted by $\{1, 2, ..., 12\}$.

    The set with no elements is called the *empty set*—some people refer to it as the *null set*. The empty set is denoted by { } or more often by the symbol

$$\varnothing.$$

A set with one element is called a *singleton*. For example, $\{a\}$ is a singleton.

    Two sets A and B are *equal* if each element of A is an element of B and conversely each element of B is an element of A. We denote the fact that A and B are equal sets by writing

$$A = B.$$

If the sets A and B are not equal, we write

$$A \neq B.$$

We can use equality to demonstrate two important characteristics of sets:

> *There is no particular order or arrangement of the elements.*
> *There are no redundant elements.*

For example, the set whose elements are are g, h, and u can be represented in many ways, four of which are

$$\{u, g, h\} = \{h, u, g\} = \{h, u, g, h\} = \{u, g, h, u, g\}.$$

In other words, there are many ways to represent the same set.

Suppose we start counting the elements of a set S, one element per second of time with a stop watch. If $S = \varnothing$, then we don't need to start, because there are no elements to count. But if $S \neq \varnothing$, we agree to start the counting after we have started the timer. If a point in time is reached when all the elements of S have been counted, then we stop the timer, or in some cases we might need to have one of our descendants stop the timer. In this case we say that S is a *finite* set. If the counting never stops, then S is an *infinite* set.

Familiar infinite sets are sometimes denoted by listing a few of the elements followed by an ellipsis. We reserve some letters to denote specific sets that we'll refer to throughout the book. For example, the set of natural numbers will be denoted by $\mathbb{N}$[†] and the set of integers by $\mathbb{Z}$. So we can write

$$\mathbb{N} = \{0, 1, 2, 3, ...\} \quad \text{and} \quad \mathbb{Z} = \{..., -3, -2, -1, 0, 1, 2, 3, ...\}.$$

Many sets are hard to describe by a listing of elements. Examples that come to mind are the rational numbers, which we denote by $\mathbb{Q}$, and the real numbers, which we denote by $\mathbb{R}$. On the other hand, any set can be defined by stating a property that the elements of the set must satisfy. If P is some property, then there is a set S whose elements have property P, and we denote S by

$$S = \{x \mid x \text{ has property } P\},$$

which we read as "S is the set of all x such that x has property P." For example, we can write Gaggle $= \{x \mid x \text{ is a goose}\}$ and say that Gaggle is the set of all x such that x is a goose. The set Odd of odd integers can be defined by

$$\text{Odd} = \{x \mid x = 2k + 1 \text{ and } k \in \mathbb{Z}\}.$$

[†] Some people consider the natural numbers to be the set $\{1, 2, 3, ...\}$. If you are one of these people, then think of $\mathbb{N}$ as the Nonnegative integers.

Similarly, the set {1, 2, ..., 12} can be defined by writing

$$\{x \mid x \in \mathbb{N} \text{ and } 1 \leq x \leq 12\}.$$

If A and B are sets and every element of A is also an element of B, then we say that A is a *subset* of B and write

$$A \subset B.$$

For example, we have $\{a, b\} \subset \{a, b, c\}$, $\{0, 1, 2\} \subset \mathbb{N}$, and $\mathbb{N} \subset \mathbb{Z}$. It also follows from the definition that $A \subset A$ and $\emptyset \subset A$ for every set A.

If A is not a subset of B, we sometimes write

$$A \not\subset B.$$

For example, $\{a, b\} \not\subset \{a, c\}$ and $\{-1, -2\} \not\subset \mathbb{N}$.

If $A \subset B$ and there is some element in B that does not occur as an element in A, then A is called a *proper* subset of B. For example, $\{a, b\}$ is a proper subset of $\{a, b, c\}$.

In dealing with sets, it's often useful to draw a picture in order to visualize the situation. A *Venn diagram*—named after the logician John Venn (1834–1923)—consists of one or more closed curves in which the interior of each curve represents a set. For example, the Venn diagram in Figure 1.1 represents the fact that A is a proper subset of B and x is an element of B that does not occur in A.

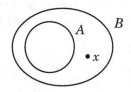

Figure 1.1 Venn diagram of proper subset $A \subset B$.

We can use the subset definition to give a precise definition of set equality. Two sets are equal if they are subsets of each other. In more concise form we can write

$$A = B \quad \text{means} \quad A \subset B \text{ and } B \subset A. \tag{1.1}$$

The collection of all subsets of a set S is called the *power set* of S, which we denote by power(S). For example, if $S = \{a, b, c\}$, then the power set of S can be written as follows:

$$power(S) = \{\varnothing, \{a\}, \{b\}, \{c\}, \{a, b\}, \{a, c\}, \{b, c\}, S\}.$$

Operations on Sets

If A and B are sets, then the *union* of A and B is the set of all elements that either are in A or in B or in both A and B. The union of A and B is denoted by $A \cup B$. So we can write

$$A \cup B = \{x \mid x \in A \text{ or } x \in B\}. \tag{1.2}$$

The use of the word "or" in the definition is taken to mean "either or both." For example, if $A = \{a, b, c\}$ and $B = \{c, d\}$, then $A \cup B = \{a, b, c, d\}$. The following properties give the basic facts about the union operation.

Properties of Union (1.3)

a) $A \cup \varnothing = A$.

b) $A \cup B = B \cup A$ ($\cup$ is commutative).

c) $A \cup (B \cup C) = (A \cup B) \cup C$ ($\cup$ is associative).

d) $A \cup A = A$.

e) $A \subset B$ if and only if $A \cup B = B$.

The union operation can be defined for any nonempty collection of sets. If C is a nonempty collection of sets, then the *union of the collection* C is the set of all elements that occur in some set of C, which we write as

$$\bigcup_{A \in C} A = \{x \mid x \in A \text{ for some } A \in C\}. \tag{1.4}$$

If I is a set of indices and A_i is a set for each $i \in I$, then we can write the union of the sets in the collection of sets $\{A_i \mid i \in I\}$ as

$$\bigcup_{i \in I} A_i.$$

If we have a finite collection of sets $\{A_1, ..., A_n\}$, then the union of the collection can be written in either of the following two ways:

$$\bigcup_{i=1}^{n} A_i \quad \text{or} \quad \bigcup_{1 \le i \le n} A_i \ .$$

If A and B are sets, then the *intersection* of A and B is the set of all elements that are in both A and B and is denoted by $A \cap B$. We can write

$$A \cap B = \{x \mid x \in A \text{ and } x \in B\}. \tag{1.5}$$

For example, if $A = \{a, b, c\}$ and $B = \{c, d\}$, then $A \cap B = \{c\}$. If $A \cap B = \varnothing$, then A and B are said to be *disjoint*. The basic facts about intersection are given next. The proofs are left as an exercise.

Properties of Intersection (1.6)

a) $A \cap \varnothing = \varnothing$.

b) $A \cap B = B \cap A$ ($\cap$ is commutative).

c) $A \cap (B \cap C) = (A \cap B) \cap C$ ($\cap$ is associative).

d) $A \cap A = A$.

e) $A \subset B$ if and only if $A \cap B = A$.

Intersection can be defined for any nonempty collection of sets. If C is a nonempty collection of sets, then the *intersection of the collection C* is the set of all elements that occur in every set in C, which we write as

$$\bigcap_{A \in C} A = \{x \mid x \in A \text{ for every } A \in C\}. \tag{1.7}$$

If I is a set of indices for a collection of sets $C = \{A_i \mid i \in I\}$, then we can write the intersection of the sets in the collection C as

$$\bigcap_{i \in I} A_i.$$

Two useful properties that combine the operations of union and intersection are the distributive properties.

Distributive Properties (1.8)

a) $A \cap (B \cup C) = (A \cap B) \cup (A \cap C)$ ($\cap$ distributes over $\cup$).

b) $A \cup (B \cap C) = (A \cup B) \cap (A \cup C)$ ($\cup$ distributes over $\cap$).

If A and B are sets, then the *difference* between A and B (also called the *relative complement* of B in A) is the set of elements in A that are not in B, and it is denoted by $A - B$. That is,

$$A - B = \{x \mid x \in A \text{ and } x \notin B\}. \tag{1.9}$$

For example, if $A = \{a, b, c\}$ and $B = \{c, d\}$, then $A - B = \{a, b\}$.

A natural extension of the difference $A - B$ is the *symmetric difference* of sets A and B, which is the union of $A - B$ with $B - A$ and is denoted by $A \oplus B$. We can define the symmetric difference by using the "exclusive" form of "or" as follows:

$$A \oplus B = \{x \mid x \in A \text{ or } x \in B \text{ but not both}\}. \tag{1.10}$$

As usual, there are many relationships to discover. For example, it's easy to see that

$$A \oplus B = (A \cup B) - (A \cap B).$$

Can you verify that $(A \oplus B) \oplus C = A \oplus (B \oplus C)$?

If the discussion always refers to sets that are subsets of a particular set U, then U is called the *universe of discourse*, and the difference $U - A$ is called the *complement* of A, which we denote by A'. The following properties give the basic facts about complement.

Properties of Complement $\tag{1.11}$

   a) $(A')' = A$.
   b) $\varnothing' = U$ and $U' = \varnothing$.
   c) $A \cap A' = \varnothing$ and $A \cup A' = U$.
   d) $A \subset B$ if and only if $B' \subset A'$.
   e) $(A \cup B)' = A' \cap B'$ and $(A \cap B)' = A' \cup B'$ (De Morgan's laws).

Bags (Multisets)

A *bag* (or *multiset*) is a collection of objects that may contain a finite number of redundant occurrences of elements. The two important characteristics of a bag are:

There is no particular order or arrangement of the elements.

There may be a finite number of redundant occurrences of elements.

To differentiate bags from sets, we'll use brackets to enclose the elements. For example, $[h, u, g, h]$ is a bag with four elements. Two bags A and B are *equal* if the number of occurrences of each element in A or B is the same in either bag. If A and B are equal bags, we write $A = B$. For example, $[h, u, g, h] = [h, h, g, u]$, but $[h, u, g, h] \neq [h, u, g]$.

We can define union and intersection for bags also (we will use the same symbols as for sets). Let A and B be bags, and let m and n be the number of times x occurs in A and B, respectively. Put the larger of m and n occurrences of x in $A \cup B$. Put the smaller of m and n occurrences of x in $A \cap B$. For example, we have

$$[2, 2, 3] \cup [2, 3, 3, 4] = [2, 2, 3, 3, 4]$$

and

$$[2, 2, 3] \cap [2, 3, 3, 4] = [2, 3] .$$

Tuples

Informally, a *tuple* is a collection of things, called its *elements,* where there is a first element, a second element, and so on. The elements of a tuple are also called *members*, *objects*, or *components*. We'll denote a tuple by writing down its elements, separated by commas, and surrounding everything with the two symbols "⟨" and "⟩." For example, the tuple $\langle 12, R, 9 \rangle$ has three elements. The first element is 12, the second element is the letter R, and third element is 9. The beginning sentence of this paragraph can be represented by the following tuple:

⟨When, we, write, down, ..., sequential, nature⟩.

If a tuple has n elements, we say that its *length* is n, and we call it an *n-tuple*. So the tuple $\langle 8, k, \text{hello} \rangle$ is a 3-tuple, and $\langle x_1, ..., x_8 \rangle$ is an 8-tuple. The 0-tuple is denoted by $\langle\ \rangle$, and we call it the *empty* tuple. A 2-tuple is often called an *ordered pair*, and a 3-tuple might be called an *ordered triple*. Other words used in place of the word *tuple* are *vector* and *sequence*, possibly modified by the word *ordered*. Some notations for a tuple use the two parentheses "(" and ")" in place of "⟨" and "⟩."

Two n-tuples $\langle x_1, ..., x_n \rangle$ and $\langle y_1, ..., y_n \rangle$ are said to be *equal* if $x_i = y_i$ for $1 \le i \le n$, and we denote this by $\langle x_1, ..., x_n \rangle = \langle y_1, ..., y_n \rangle$. Thus the ordered pairs $\langle 3, 7 \rangle$ and $\langle 7, 3 \rangle$ are not equal, and we write $\langle 3, 7 \rangle \neq \langle 7, 3 \rangle$. Since tuples convey the idea of order, they are different from sets and bags. Here are some examples:

Sets: $\{h, u, g, h\} = \{h, h, g, u\} = \{h, u, g\} = \{u, g, h\}.$

Bags: $[h, u, g, h] = [h, h, g, u] \neq [h, u, g] = [u, g, h].$

Tuples: $\langle h, u, g, h \rangle \neq \langle h, h, g, u \rangle \neq \langle h, u, g \rangle \neq \langle u, g, h \rangle.$

The two important characteristics of a tuple are

There is an order or arrangement of the elements.

There may be redundant occurrences of elements.

Products of Sets

We often need to represent information in the form of tuples, in which the elements in each tuple come from known sets. If A and B are sets, then the *product* of A and B is the set of all 2-tuples with first components from A and second components from B. The product is denoted by $A \times B$. So we can write

$$A \times B = \{\langle a, b \rangle \mid a \in A \text{ and } b \in B\}.$$

For example, if $A = \{x, y\}$ and $B = \{0, 1\}$, then we have

$$A \times B = \{\langle x, 0 \rangle, \langle x, 1 \rangle, \langle y, 0 \rangle, \langle y, 1 \rangle\}.$$

The product is sometimes called the *cross product* or the *Cartesian product*—after the mathematician René Descartes (1596–1650), who introduced the idea of graphing ordered pairs. The product of two sets is easily extended to any number of sets $A_1, ..., A_n$ by writing

$$A_1 \times \cdots \times A_n = \{\langle x_1, ..., x_n \rangle \mid x_i \in A_i\}.$$

If all the sets A_i in a product are the same set A, then we use the abbreviated notation $A^n = A \times \cdots \times A$. With this notation we have the following definitions for the sets A^1 and A^0:

$$A^1 = \{\langle a \rangle \mid a \in A\} \text{ and } A^0 = \{\langle \ \rangle\}.$$

So we must conclude that $A^1 \neq A$ and $A^0 \neq \varnothing$.

Lists

A *list* is a sequence of zero or more elements that can be redundant and that is ordered. In other words, a list is just like a tuple. In fact, we'll use tuple notation to represent lists. The *empty list* is $\langle \ \rangle$, and the number of elements in a list is called its *length*.

So what's the difference between tuples and lists? The difference is in what parts can be randomly accessed. In the case of tuples we can randomly access any component. In the case of lists we can randomly access only two things: the first component of a list, which is called its *head*, and the list made up of everything except the first component, which is called its *tail*. For example, given the list $\langle x, y, z \rangle$, its head is x, and its tail is the list $\langle y, z \rangle$.

An important property of lists is the ability to easily construct a new list from an element and another list. For example, given the element x and the list $\langle y, z \rangle$, we can easily construct the new list $\langle x, y, z \rangle$. This construction process can be done efficiently and dynamically during the execution of a program. We'll use this list construction operation by *cons*. For example,

$$\text{cons}(x, \langle y, z \rangle) = \langle x, y, z \rangle.$$

We often need to work with lists whose elements are from a single set A. A *list over the set A* is a finite sequence of elements from A. We'll denote the collection of all lists over A by Lists[A]. For example, if $A = \{a, b, c\}$, then three of the lists in Lists[A] are $\langle \ \rangle$, $\langle a, a, b \rangle$, and $\langle b, c, a, b, c \rangle$. If we forget that lists and tuples are accessed in different ways, then we can demonstrate an interesting relationship between the two ideas by writing the set Lists[A] as the union of the products A^0, A^1, A^2, ... So we have the following equation:

$$\text{Lists}[A] = A^0 \cup A^1 \cup \dots A^n \cup \dots. \tag{1.12}$$

The word *stream* (or infinite list, or infinite sequence) is often used in computer science to describe an infinite list of objects. We'll use the tuple notation to represent streams. For example, a program to compute the decimal expansion of pi would compute the following stream of integers:

$$\langle 3, 1, 4, 1, 5, 9, 2, 6, 5, 3, 5, 8, 9, 7, 9, 3, \dots \rangle.$$

Streams are useful in programming as inputs and outputs to computations. They normally have the same access and construction properties as lists. In other words, we can randomly access the first element and the stream consisting of everything except the first element. Similarly, if we are given an element and a stream, then we can construct a new stream.

Strings

A *string* is a finite sequence of zero or more elements that are placed next to each other in juxtaposition. The individual elements that make up a string are taken from a finite set called an *alphabet*. For example, the set $\{a, b, c\}$ is an alphabet for the string

aacabb.

The string with no elements is called the *empty string*, and we denote it by the Greek letter lambda

$$\Lambda.$$

The number of elements that occur in a string is called the *length* of the string. For example, over the alphabet $\{a, b, c\}$, the string $aacabb$ has length 6. We sometimes denote the length of a string s by $|s|$.

If A is an alphabet, then the set of all strings over A is denoted by A^*. In other words, A^* is the set of all possible strings made up from the elements of A. For example, if $A = \{a\}$, then we have

$$A^* = \{\Lambda, a, aa, aaa, ...\}.$$

For a natural number n and a string w we often let w^n denote the string of n w's. For example, we have

$$w^0 = \Lambda, w^1 = w, w^2 = ww, \text{ and } w^3 = www.$$

The exponent notation allows us to represent some sets of strings in a nice concise manner. For example, if $A = \{a\}$, then we can write

$$A^* = \{a^n \mid n \in \mathbb{N}\}.$$

We should note that if the empty string occurs as part of another string, then it does not contribute anything new to the string. In other words, for any string w, we have

$$w\Lambda = \Lambda w = w.$$

EXAMPLE 1 (*Numerals*). A *numeral* is a written number. In terms of strings, we can say that a numeral is a nonempty string of symbols that represents a number. Most of us are familiar with the following three numeral systems. The *Roman numerals* are used to represent the nonnegative integers by using the alphabet

$$\{I, V, X, L, C, D, M\}.$$

The *decimal numerals* represent the natural numbers by using the alphabet $\{0, 1, 2, 3, 4, 5, 6, 7, 8, 9\}$. The *binary numerals* represent the natural numbers by using the alphabet $\{0, 1\}$. For example, the Roman numeral MDCLXVI, the decimal numeral 1666, and the binary numeral 11010000010 all represent the same number.   ♦

Graphs

Informally, a *graph* is a set of objects in which some of the objects are connected to each other in some way. The objects are called *vertices* or *nodes*, and the connections are called *edges*. For example, the United States can be represented by a graph where the vertices are states and the edges are the common borders between adjacent states. In this case, Hawaii and Alaska would be vertices without any edges connected to them. We say that two vertices are *adjacent* if there is an edge connecting them.

We can picture a graph in several ways. For example, Figure 1.2 shows two ways to represent the graph with vertices 1, 2, and 3 and edges connecting 1 to 2 and 1 to 3.

Figure 1.2

A *directed graph* (*digraph* for short) is a graph where each edge points in one direction. For example, the vertices could be cities and the edges could be the one-way air routes between them. For digraphs we use arrows to denote the edges. For example, Figure 1.3 shows two ways to represent the digraph with three vertices a, b, and c and edges from a to b, c to a, and c to b.

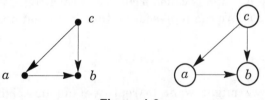

Figure 1.3

The *degree* of a vertex is the number of edges that it touches. For directed graphs the *indegree* of a vertex is the number of edges pointing at the vertex, while the *outdegree* of a vertex is the number of edges pointing away from the vertex. In a digraph a vertex is called a *source* if its indegree is zero and a *sink* if its outdegree is zero. For example, in the digraph of Figure 1.3, c is a source and b is a sink.

If a graph has more than one edge between some pair of vertices, the graph is called a *multigraph*, or a *directed multigraph* in case the edges point in the same direction. For example, there are usually two or more road routes between most cities. So a graph representing road routes between a set of cites is most likely a multigraph.

From a computational point of view, we need to represent graphs as data. This is easy to do because we can define a graph in terms of tuples, sets, and bags. For example, we can define a graph G as an ordered pair $\langle V, E \rangle$, where V is a set of vertices and E is a set or bag of edges. If G is a digraph, then the edges in E can be represented by ordered pairs, where $\langle a, b \rangle$ represents the edge with an arrow from a to b. For example, the digraph in Figure 1.3 has vertex set $\{a, b, c\}$ and edge set

$$\{\langle a, b \rangle, \langle c, b \rangle, \langle c, a \rangle\}.$$

If G is a directed multigraph, then we can represent the edges as a bag (or multiset) of ordered pairs. For example, the bag

$$[\langle a, b \rangle, \langle a, b \rangle, \langle b, a \rangle]$$

represents three edges: two from a to b and one from b to a.

If a graph is not directed, we have more ways to represent the edges. We could still represent an edge as an ordered pair $\langle a, b \rangle$ and agree that it represents an undirected line between a and b. But we can also represent an edge between vertices a and b by a set $\{a, b\}$. For example, the graph in Figure 1.2 has vertex set $\{1, 2, 3\}$ and edge set $\{\{1, 2\}, \{1, 3\}\}$.

We often encounter graphs that have information attached to each edge. For example, a good road map places distances along the roads between major intersections. A graph is called *weighted* if each edge is assigned a number, called a *weight*. We can represent an edge $\langle a, b \rangle$ that has weight w by the 3-tuple

$$\langle a, b, w \rangle.$$

In some cases we might want to represent an unweighted graph as a weighted graph. For example, if we have a multigraph in which we wish to distinguish between multiple edges that occur between two vertices, then we can assign a different weight to each edge, thereby creating a weighted multigraph.

Walks, Trails, and Paths

Some graph problems involve "walking" from one vertex to another by moving along a sequence of edges, where each edge shares a vertex with the next edge in the sequence. In formal terms, a *walk* from x_0 to x_n is a sequence of edges that we denote by a sequence of vertices $x_0, x_1, ..., x_n$ such that there is an edge from x_{i-1} to x_i for $1 \le i \le n$. A walk allows the possibility that some edge or some vertex occurs more than once. For example, in the graph of Figure 1.4, the sequence b, c, d, b, a is a walk that visits b twice and the sequence a, b, c, b, d is a walk that visits b twice and also uses the edge between b and c twice.

A *trail* is a walk in which no edge appears more than once. So vertices can be revisited in a trail, but edges cannot. For example, in the graph of Figure 1.4, the sequence b, c, d, b, a is a trail that visits b twice but the sequence a, b, c, b, d is not a trail.

A *path* is a walk in which no edge appears more than once and no vertex appears more than once, except possibly when the beginning vertex is also the ending vertex. For example, in the graph of Figure 1.4, the sequence a, b, c, d is a path, but the sequence a, b, c, d, b is not a path because the vertex b occurs twice. A *cycle* is a path whose beginning and ending vertices are equal. The sequence a, b, c, a is a cycle, but the sequence a, b, a is not a cycle because the edge from a to b occurs twice.

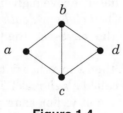

Figure 1.4

The *length* of a walk (also trail and path) is the number of edges on it. So the length of the walk $x_0, ..., x_n$ is n. For example, in the graph of Figure 1.4, the path a, b, d has length two and the cycle a, b, c, a has length three.

Let's emphasize here that the definitions for walk, trail, path, and cycle apply to both graphs and directed graphs. But now we come to an idea that needs a separate definition for each type of graph. A graph is *connected* if there is a path between any two vertices. A directed graph is *connected* if, when direction is ignored, the resulting undirected graph is connected. A graph with no cycles is called *acyclic*. A directed graph that is acyclic is sometimes referred to as a "DAG" to mean a directed acyclic graph.

Trees

From an informal point of view, a *tree* is a structure that looks like a real tree. For example, a family tree and an organizational chart for a business are both trees. In computer science, as well as many other disciplines, trees are usually drawn upside down, as in Figure 1.5. From a formal point of view we can say that a *tree* is a graph that is connected and has no cycles.

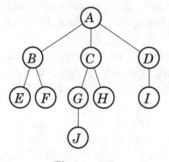

Figure 1.5

Trees have their own terminology. The elements of a tree are called *nodes*, and the lines between nodes are called *branches*. The node at the top is called the *root*. The nodes that hang immediately below a given node are its *children*, and the node immediately above a given node is its *parent*. If a node is childless, then it is a *leaf*. The *height* or *depth* of a tree is the length of the longest path from the root to the leaves. So the tree in Figure 1.5 has height 3.

If x is a node in a tree T, then x together with all its descendants forms a tree S with x as its root. S is called a *subtree* of T. If y is the parent of x, then S is sometimes called a subtree of y. For example, Figure 1.6 shows a tree that is a subtree of the tree in Figure 1.5. This tree is also called a subtree of node A.

Figure 1.6

If we don't care about the ordering of the children of a tree, then the tree is called an *unordered tree*. A tree is *ordered* if there is a unique ordering of the children of each node. Algebraic expressions have ordered tree representations. For example, the expression $x - y$ can be represented by a tree whose root is the minus sign and with two subtrees, one for x on the left and one for y on the right.

A *binary tree* is an ordered tree that may be empty or else has the property that each node has two subtrees, called the *left* and *right* subtrees of the node, which are binary trees. We can represent the empty binary tree by the empty tuple $\langle\,\rangle$. Since each node has two subtrees, we represent non-empty binary trees as 3-tuples of the form

$$\langle L, x, R\rangle, \tag{1.13}$$

where x is the root, L is the left subtree, and R is the right subtree. For example, the tree with one node x is represented by the tuple $\langle\langle\,\rangle, x, \langle\,\rangle\rangle$.

Exercises

1. Let $A = \{a, \varnothing\}$. Answer true or false for each of the following statements.

   a. $a \in A$.   b. $\{a\} \in A$.   c. $a \subset A$.   d. $\{a\} \subset A$.

   e. $\varnothing \subset A$.   f. $\varnothing \in A$.   g. $\{\varnothing\} \subset A$.   h. $\{\varnothing\} \in A$.

2. Show that $\varnothing \subset A$ for every set A.

3. Find two finite sets A and B such that $A \in B$ and $A \subset B$.

4. Write down the power set for each of the following sets.

   a. $\{x, y, z, w\}$.   b. $\{a, \{a, b\}\}$.   c. $\varnothing$.   d. $\{\varnothing\}$.   e. $\{\{a\}, \varnothing\}$.

5. For each collection of sets, find the smallest set A such that the collection is a subset of power(A).

   a. $\{\{a\}, \{b, c\}\}$.   b. $\{\{a\}, \{\varnothing\}\}$.   c. $\{\{a\}, \{\{a\}\}\}$.   d. $\{\{a\}, \{\{b\}\}, \{a, b\}\}$.

6. Show that power($A \cap B$) = power(A) $\cap$ power(B) by proving that each side is a subset of the other side.

7. Is power($A \cup B$) = power(A) $\cup$ power(B)?

8. Give a proof or a counterexample for each of the following statements.

   a. $A \cap (B \cup A) = A \cap B$?

   b. $A - (B \cap A) = A - B$?

   c. $A \cap (B \cup C) = (A \cup B) \cap (A \cup C)$?

   d. $A \oplus A = A$?

9. Find the union and intersection of each of the following pairs of bags.

   a. $[x, y]$ & $[x, y, z]$.   b. $[x, y, x]$ & $[y, x, y, x]$.

   c. $[a, a, a, b]$ & $[a, a, b, b, c]$.   d. $[1, 2, 2, 3, 3, 4, 4]$ & $[2, 3, 3, 4, 5]$.

   e. $[x, x, [a, a], [a, a]]$ & $[a, a, x, x]$.

   f. $[a, a, [b, b], [a, [b]]]$ & $[a, a, [b], [b]]$.

10. Find a bag B that solves the following two simultaneous bag equations.
$$B \cup [2, 2, 3, 4] = [2, 2, 3, 3, 4, 4, 5]$$
$$B \cap [2, 2, 3, 4, 5] = [2, 3, 4, 5].$$

11. How would you define the difference operation for bags? Try to make your definition agree with the difference operation for sets whenever the bags are like sets (without repeated elements).

12. Find a description of a set A satisfying the equation $A = \{a, A, b\}$. Notice in this case that $A \in A$.

13. Write down all possible 3-tuples over the set $\{x, y\}$.

14. Let $A = \{a, b, c\}$ and $B = \{a, b\}$. Compute each of the following sets.
    a. $A \times B$.   b. $B \times A$.   c. A^0.
    d. A^1.   e. A^2.   f. $A^2 \cap (A \times B)$.

15. Prove each of the following statements about the interaction of the set operations and the product.
    a. $(A \cup B) \times C = (A \times C) \cup (B \times C)$.
    b. $(A - B) \times C = (A \times C) - (B \times C)$.
    c. Find and prove a similar equality using the intersection operation.

16. Draw a picture of a graph that represents those states of the United States and provinces of Canada that touch the Atlantic Ocean or touch states or provinces that do.

1.3 Functional Notions

The idea of a function is perhaps the most common communication device used in science and engineering. In this section, we'll review the basic facts about functions. We'll also visit the notion of counting sets and we'll see how functions can help us find the size of sets.

Functions

Suppose A and B are sets and for each element in A we associate exactly one element in B. Such an association is called a *function* from A to B. The key point is that each element of A is associated with *exactly one* element of B. In other words, if $x \in A$ is associated with $y \in B$, then x is not associated with any other element of B.

Functions are normally denoted by letters like f, g, and h or other descriptive names or symbols. If f is a function from A to B and f associates an element $x \in A$ with $y \in B$, then we write $f(x) = y$ or $y = f(x)$. The notation $f(x)$ is read, "f of x," or "f at x," or "f applied to x." When $f(x) = y$, we often say, "f maps x to y." Some other words for "function" are *mapping, transformation,* and *operator.*

Functions can be described in many ways. Sometimes a formula will do the job. For example, if we want the function f to map every natural number x to its square, then we can define f by the formula $f(x) = x^2$ for all $x \in \mathbb{N}$. Other times, we'll have to write down all possible associations. For example, we can define a function g from $A = \{a, b, c\}$ to $B = \{1, 2, 3\}$ as follows:

$$g(a) = 1,\ g(b) = 1,\ \text{and}\ g(c) = 2.$$

To talk about functions, we need to introduce some more terminology. The symbol $A \to B$ denotes the set of all functions from A to B. If f is a function from A to B, we write

$$f : A \to B.$$

We also say that f has *type* $A \to B$. The set A is called the *domain* of f, and B is the *codomain* of f. If $f(x) = y$, then x is an *argument* of f, and y is a *value* of f.

If the domain of a function f is a product of n sets, then we say that f has *arity* n, or f has n *arguments*. For example, if the domain of f is $A \times B \times C$, then we say that f has arity 3, or f has 3 arguments. In this case, if $\langle a, b, c \rangle \in A \times B \times C$, then the expression $f(a, b, c)$ denotes the value of f at the three arguments a, b, and c.

A function f with two arguments is called a *binary* function. Binary functions give us the option of writing $f(x, y)$ in the popular *infix* form $x\ f\ y$. For example, $4 + 5$ is usually preferable to $+(4, 5)$ for representing values of the function $+ : \mathbb{R} \times \mathbb{R} \to \mathbb{R}$.

The *range* of f is the set of elements in B that are associated with some element of A. In other words, the range of f is the set of all values that f can take in B. We denote the range of f by range(f):

$$\text{range}(f) = \{f(a) \mid a \in A\}.$$

If $C \subset A$, then the *image* of C under f is the set of values in B associated with elements of C. We denote the image of C under f by $f(C)$:

$$f(C) = \{f(x) \mid x \in C\}.$$

We always have the special case $f(A) = \text{range}(f)$.

Now let's go in the other direction. If $D \subset B$, then the *pre-image* of D under f is the set of elements in A that associate with elements of D. The pre-image is also called the *inverse image*. We denote the pre-image of D under f by $f^{-1}(D)$:

$$f^{-1}(D) = \{a \in A \mid f(a) \in D\}.$$

We always have the special case $f^{-1}(B) = A$.

If f and g are both functions of type $A \rightarrow B$, then f and g are said to be *equal* if $f(x) = g(x)$ for all $x \in A$. If f and g are equal, we write

$$f = g.$$

For example, suppose f and g are functions of type $\mathbb{N} \rightarrow \mathbb{N}$ and they are defined by the formulas $f(x) = x + x$ and $g(x) = 2x$. It's easy to see that $f = g$.

Functions can often be defined by cases. For example, the absolute value function "abs" has type $\mathbb{R} \rightarrow \mathbb{R}$, and it can be defined by the following rule:

$$\mathrm{abs}(x) = \begin{cases} x & \text{if } x \geq 0 \\ -x & \text{if } x < 0. \end{cases}$$

A definition by cases can also be written in terms of the *if-then-else* rule. For example, we can write the preceding definition in the following form:

$$\mathrm{abs}(x) = \text{if } x \geq 0 \text{ then } x \text{ else } -x.$$

Let's look at some functions that are especially useful in computer science. These functions are used for tasks such as analyzing properties of data, analyzing properties of programs, and constructing programs.

The Floor and Ceiling Functions

Let's discuss two important functions that "integerize" real numbers by going down or up to the nearest integer. The *floor* function has type $\mathbb{R} \rightarrow \mathbb{Z}$ and is defined by setting floor(x) to the closest integer less than or equal to x. For example, floor(8) = 8, floor(8.9) = 8, and floor(−3.5) = −4. A useful shorthand notation for floor(x) is

$$\lfloor x \rfloor.$$

The *ceiling* function also has type $\mathbb{R} \rightarrow \mathbb{Z}$ and it is defined by setting ceiling(x) to the closest integer greater than or equal to x. For example, ceiling(8) = 8, ceiling(8.9) = 9, and ceiling(–3.5) = –3. The shorthand notation for ceiling(x) is

$$\lceil x \rceil.$$

The Mod Function

If a and b are integers and $b \neq 0$, then $a \bmod b$ is defined by

$$a \bmod b = a - b \left\lfloor \frac{a}{b} \right\rfloor.$$

We should note that $a \bmod b$ is the remainder upon division of a by b, where the remainder has the same sign as b. For example,

$$5 \bmod 4 = 1$$
$$5 \bmod -4 = -3.$$

If we agree to fix n as a positive integer constant, then we can define a function $f : \mathbb{Z} \to \mathbb{N}$ by $f(x) = x \bmod n$. The range of f is {0, 1, ..., $n - 1$}, which is the set of possible remainders obtained upon division of x by n. We sometimes let $\mathbb{N}_n$ denote the set

$$\mathbb{N}_n = \{0, 1, 2, ..., n - 1\}.$$

For example, $\mathbb{N}_0 = \varnothing$, $\mathbb{N}_1 = \{0\}$, and $\mathbb{N}_2 = \{0, 1\}$.

The Log Function

The *log* function—which is shorthand for logarithm—measures the size of exponents. If b is a positive real number, then $\log_b x = y$ means $b^y = x$, and we say, "log base b of x is y." Notice that x must be a positive real number. The base 2 log function $\log_2$ occurs frequently in computer science because many algorithms and data representations use a binary decision (two choices). For example, suppose we want to construct a binary search tree with 16 nodes that has the smallest possible depth. The smallest depth of such a tree is 4, which is the value of the expression $\log_2 16$.

For any positive real number b the function $\log_b$ is an increasing function with the positive real numbers as its domain and the real numbers as its range. The following list contains some of the most useful properties of the log function.

$$\log_b 1 = 0$$

$$\log_b b = 1$$

$$\log_b (b^x) = x$$

$$\log_b (x\,y) = \log_b x + \log_b y$$

$$\log_b (x^y) = y \log_b x$$

$$\log_b (x/y) = \log_b x - \log_b y$$

$$\log_a x = (\log_a b)\,(\log_b x) \quad \text{(change of base).}$$

Partial Functions

A *partial function* from A to B is like a function except that it might not be defined for some elements of A. In other words, some elements of A might not be associated with any element of B. But we still have the requirement that if $x \in A$ is associated with $y \in B$, then x can't be associated with any other element of B. For example, we know that division by zero is not allowed. Therefore $\div$ is a partial function of type $\mathbb{R} \times \mathbb{R} \to \mathbb{R}$ because $\div$ is not defined for all pairs of the form $\langle x, 0 \rangle$.

When discussing partial functions, to avoid confusion we use the term *total function* to mean a function that is defined on all its domain. Any partial function can be transformed into a total function. One simple technique is to shrink the domain to the set of elements for which the partial function is defined. For example, $\div$ is a total function of type $\mathbb{R} \times (\mathbb{R} - \{0\}) \to \mathbb{R}$.

A second technique keeps the domain the same but increases the size of the codomain. For example, suppose $f : A \to B$ is a partial function. Pick some symbol that is not in B, say $\# \notin B$, and assign $f(x) = \#$ whenever $f(x)$ is not defined. Then we can think of f as the total function of type $A \to B \cup \{\#\}$. In programming, the analogy would be to pick an error message to indicate that an incorrect input string has been received.

Composition and Tupling

The composition of functions is a natural process that we often use without even thinking. For example, the expression floor($\log_2(5)$) involves the composition of the two functions $\log_2$ and floor. To evaluate the expression, we first apply $\log_2$ to its argument 5, obtaining a value somewhere between 2 and 3. Then we apply the floor function to this number, obtaining the value 2.

To give a formal definition of composition, we start with two functions in which the domain of one is the codomain of the other:

$$f : A \to B \quad \text{and} \quad g : B \to C.$$

The *composition* of f and g is the function $g \circ f : A \to C$ defined by

$$(g \circ f)(x) = g(f(x)).$$

In other words, first apply f to x and then apply g to the resulting value. Composition also makes sense in the more general setting in which $f : A \to B$ and $g : D \to C$, and $B \subset D$. Can you see why?

Composition of functions is associative. In other words, if f, g, and h are functions, then $(f \circ g) \circ h = f \circ (g \circ h)$. This is easy to establish by noticing that the two expressions $((f \circ g) \circ h)(x)$ and $(f \circ (g \circ h))(x)$ are equal:

$$((f \circ g) \circ h)(x) = (f \circ g)(h(x)) = f(g(h(x))).$$

$$(f \circ (g \circ h))(x) = f(g \circ h)(x) = f(g(h(x))).$$

So we can feel free to write the composition of three or more functions without the use of parentheses. For example, the composition $f \circ g \circ h$ has exactly one meaning.

Notice that composition is usually not a commutative operation. For example, if f and g are defined by $f(x) = x + 1$ and $g(x) = x^2$, then

$$(g \circ f)(x) = g(f(x)) = g(x + 1) = (x + 1)^2$$

and

$$(f \circ g)(x) = f(g(x)) = f(x^2) = x^2 + 1.$$

The *identity* function "id" always returns its argument. For a particular set A we sometimes write "id_A" to denote the fact that $id_A(a) = a$ for all $a \in A$. If $f : A \to B$, then we certainly have the following equation:

$$f \circ id_A = f = id_B \circ f.$$

Another way to combine functions is to create a *tuple* of functions. For example, given the pair of functions $f : A \to B$ and $g . A \to C$, we can define the function $\langle f, g \rangle$ by

$$\langle f, g \rangle(x) = \langle f(x), g(x) \rangle.$$

The function $\langle f, g \rangle$ has type $A \to B \times C$. The definition for a tuple of two functions can be extended easily to an *n-tuple of functions*, $\langle f_1, f_2, ..., f_n \rangle$.

We can also compose tuples of functions with other functions. Suppose we are given the following three functions:

$$f : A \to B, \quad g : A \to C, \quad \text{and} \quad h : B \times C \to D.$$

We can form the composition $h \circ \langle f, g \rangle : A \to D$, where for $x \in A$ we have

$$(h \circ \langle f, g \rangle)(x) = h(\langle f, g \rangle(x)) = h(f(x), g(x)).$$

Properties of Functions

A function $f : A \to B$ is called *injective* (also *one-to-one*, or an *embedding*) if no two elements in A map to the same element in B. Formally, f is injective if for all $x, y \in A$, whenever $x \neq y$, then $f(x) \neq f(y)$. Another way to say this is that for all $x, y \in A$, if $f(x) = f(y)$, then $x = y$. An injective function is called an *injection*. For example, let $A = \{6k + 4 \mid k \in \mathbb{N}\}$ and $B = \{3k + 4 \mid k \in \mathbb{N}\}$. Define the function $f : A \to B$ by $f(x) = x + 3$. Then f is injective, since $x \neq y$ implies that $x + 3 \neq y + 3$.

A function $f : A \to B$ is called *surjective* (also *onto*) if each element $b \in B$ can be written as $b = f(x)$ for some element x in A. Another way to say this is that f is surjective if range$(f) = B$. A surjective function is called a *surjection*. For example, the floor function from $\mathbb{R}$ to $\mathbb{Z}$ is surjective. The function $f : \mathbb{Q} \to \mathbb{Z}$ defined by $f\left(\frac{m}{n}\right) = m$ is surjective.

A function is called *bijective* if it is both injective and surjective. Another term for bijective is "one to one and onto." A bijective function is called a *bijection* or a "one-to-one correspondence."

Whenever we have a bijection $f : A \to B$, then we always have an *inverse* function $g : B \to A$ defined by $g(b) = a$ if $f(a) = b$. The inverse is also a bijection and we always have the two equations $g \circ f = \text{id}_A$ and $f \circ g = \text{id}_B$. For example, the function $f : \text{Odd} \to \text{Even}$ defined by $f(x) = x - 1$ is a bijection, and its inverse is the function

$$g : \text{Even} \to \text{Odd defined by } g(x) = x + 1.$$

In this case we have $g \circ f = \text{id}_{\text{Odd}}$ and $f \circ g = \text{id}_{\text{Even}}$. For example, we have $g(f(3)) = g(3 - 1) = (3 - 1) + 1 = 3$. A function with an inverse is often called *invertible*. The inverse of f is often denoted by the symbol f^{-1}, which we should not confuse with the inverse image notation.

Counting

The size of a set S is called its *cardinality*, which we'll denote by

$$|S|.$$

For example, if $S = \{a, b, c\}$ then $|S| = |\{a, b, c\}| = 3$. We can say that "the cardinality of S is 3," or "3 is the cardinal number of S," or simply "S has three elements."

We say that two sets A and B have the *same cardinality* if there is a bijection between them. In other words, if there is a function $f : A \to B$ that is bijective, then A and B have the same cardinality. In this case we write

$$|A| = |B|.$$

The term *equipotent* is often used to indicate that two sets have the same cardinality. Since bijections might occur between infinite sets, the idea of equipotence applies not only to finite sets, but also to infinite sets.

For example, let Odd and Even denote the sets of odd and even natural numbers. Then $|\text{Odd}| = |\text{Even}|$ because the function $f : \text{Odd} \to \text{Even}$ defined by $f(x) = x - 1$ is a bijection. Similarly, $|\text{Even}| = |\mathbb{N}|$ because the function $g : \text{Even} \to \mathbb{N}$ defined by $g(y) = \frac{y}{2}$ is a bijection.

If there is an injection $f : A \to B$, then we say, "The cardinality of A is less than or equal to the cardinality of B," and we write

$$|A| \le |B|.$$

For example, let Even denote the set of even natural numbers. Then the function $f : \text{Even} \to \mathbb{N}$ defined by $f(x) = x$ is an injection from the even natural numbers to $\mathbb{N}$. So we can write $|\text{Even}| \le |\mathbb{N}|$.

If A and B are sets and $|A| \le |B|$ and $|A| \ne |B|$, then we say, "The cardinality of A is less than the cardinality of B," and we write

$$|A| < |B|.$$

In other words, $|A| < |B|$ means that there is an injection from A to B but no bijection between them.

Why can't we simply say that $|A| < |B|$ means that there is an injection from A to B that is not a bijection? To see why not, let Odd be the set of odd natural numbers, and let $g : \mathbb{N} \to \text{Odd}$ be defined by $g(x) = 4x + 1$. Then g is an injection, but g is not a bijection because $3 \in \text{Odd}$ and $g(x) \ne 3$ for any $x \in \mathbb{N}$. We surely don't want to conclude from this that $|\mathbb{N}| < |\text{Odd}|$. For example, the function $f : \mathbb{N} \to \text{Odd}$ defined by $f(x) = 2x + 1$ is a bijection. So $|\mathbb{N}| = |\text{Odd}|$. Thus we will stick with our definition of "more."

It's easy to find infinite sets having different cardinalities. Georg Cantor showed that any set A has less cardinality than its power set, which we can write as follows:

$$|A| < |\text{power}(A)|. \tag{1.14}$$

Proof: We know that this is true for finite sets. But it's also true for infinite sets. The easy part of the proof can be seen by observing that each element $x \in A$ corresponds to the singleton set $\{x\} \in \text{power}(A)$. This correspondence is an injection. Therefore $|A| \le |\text{power}(A)|$. For the other part, suppose, by way of contradiction, that $f : A \to \text{power}(A)$ is some mapping that is surjective. Now for the contradiction. Let's define the set $S = \{x \mid x \notin f(x)\}$. Since f is surjective, there some element $y \in A$ maps under f to the subset S. So we can write $f(y) = S$. Now we know that either $y \in S$ or $y \notin S$. If $y \in S$ then $y \notin f(y)$. But since $f(y) = S$, this implies that $y \notin S$. Now if $y \notin S$, then, since $S = f(y)$, it follows that $y \notin f(y)$, which says that $y \in S$. So we have the false statement that $y \in S$ if and only if $y \notin S$. So our assumption that f was a surjection was false. In other words, there are no surjections from A to $\text{power}(A)$. Therefore $|A| < |\text{power}(A)|$.   QED.

Countable and Uncountable

We want to describe those infinite sets that can be counted even if it takes forever to count them. A set C is *countable* if it's finite or if $|C| = |\mathbb{N}|$. In the case $|C| = |\mathbb{N}|$ we sometimes say that C is *countably infinite*. So $\mathbb{N}$ is the fundamental example of a countably infinite set. We could also define C to be countable if $|C| \le |\mathbb{N}|$. Thus we can show that a set C is countable by finding an injection from C to $\mathbb{N}$ or by finding a surjection from $\mathbb{N}$ to C. Can you see why? If a set is not countable, it is called *uncountable*. For example, (1.14) tells us that $|\mathbb{N}| < |\text{power}(\mathbb{N})|$. Since $\mathbb{N}$ is countable, it follows that $\text{power}(\mathbb{N})$ is uncountable.

The following result can often be used to show that a set is countable if it can be represented as a countable union of countable sets.

Counting Unions of Countable Sets   (1.15)

    If A is the union of a countable collection of sets, where each
    set in the collection is countable, then A is countable.

An important consequence of (1.15) is the following fact about the countability of the set of all strings over a finite alphabet:

    If A is a finite alphabet, then A^* is countably infinite.   (1.16)

As a result of (1.16) and (1.14), it follows that

    If A is a finite alphabet, then $\text{power}(A^*)$ is uncountable.   (1.17)

As another application of (1.16) we can answer the following question:

What is the cardinality of the set of all programs written in your favorite programming language?

The answer is countably infinite. One way to see this is to consider each program as a finite string of symbols over a fixed finite alphabet A. For example, A might consist of all characters that can be typed from a keyboard. Now we can proceed as in the proof of (1.16). For each natural number n, let P_n denote the set of all programs that are strings of length n over A. For example, the program {print(4)} is in P_{10} because it's a string of length 10. So the set of all programs is the union of the sets $P_0, P_1, ..., P_n, ...$. Since each P_n is finite, we can use (1.15) to give the following result:

> The set of all programs for a programming language   (1.18)
> is countably infinite.

We know that infinite sets can have different cardinalities. But some infinite sets have the same cardinality. Here is an example.

EXAMPLE 1. We'll show that the closed unit interval of real numbers [0, 1] has the same cardinality as power($\mathbb{N}$). To do this, we'll define a bijection between the two sets. Notice that any number in [0, 1] can be written in the binary form

$$0.d_0 d_1 ... d_i ...,$$

where each $d_i = 0$ or 1. Now define the function $h : \text{power}(\mathbb{N}) \to [0, 1]$ by $h(S) = 0.d_0 d_1 ... d_i ...$, where $d_i = 1$ if and only if $i \in S$. For example, the empty set corresponds to the binary form 0.000..., which is the number 0. The set of odd natural numbers corresponds to the binary form 0.010101.... $\mathbb{N}$ corresponds to the binary form 0.111..., which represents decimal number 1, just as the decimal form 0.999... represents the decimal number 1. The function h is a bijection (convince yourself). So $|\text{power}(\mathbb{N})| = |[0, 1]|$. ◆

It's not always easy to construct a bijection to show that two sets have the same cardinality. The following result—which was conjectured by Cantor, proved by Bernstein, and independently proved by Schröder—gives us a technique to show that two sets have the same cardinality without explicitly exhibiting a bijection between them:

$$\text{If } |A| \le |B| \text{ and } |B| \le |A|, \text{ then } |A| = |B|. \qquad (1.19)$$

In other words, to show that a bijection exists between sets A and B, it suffices to find two injections, one from A to B and one from B to A. Let's do some examples.

EXAMPLE 2. We'll use (1.19) to show that the two intervals $(0, 1)$ and $[0, 1]$ have the same cardinality. Since $(0, 1)$ is a subset of $[0, 1]$, the identity mapping from $(0, 1)$ to $[0, 1]$ is an injection. Now we need an injection from $[0, 1]$ to $(0, 1)$. Define $f : [0, 1] \to (0, 1)$ by $f(x) = \frac{x}{2} + \frac{1}{4}$. It follows that f is an injection. So we can apply (1.19) to conclude that $|[0, 1]| = |(0, 1)|$.   ◆

EXAMPLE 3. We'll show that $|\mathbb{R}| = |(0, 1)|$. Since $(0, 1) \subset \mathbb{R}$, we have $|(0, 1)| \le |\mathbb{R}|$. On the other hand, we can define an injection from $\mathbb{R}$ to $(0, 1)$ as follows. The mapping $f(x) = 2^x$ is an injection from $\mathbb{R}$ to the set of positive real numbers, and the mapping $g(x) = \frac{1}{x+1}$ is an injection (actually, it's a bijection) from the positive real numbers to $(0, 1)$. Therefore the composition $g \circ f$ is an injection from $\mathbb{R}$ to $(0, 1)$. Thus $|\mathbb{R}| \le |(0, 1)|$. Therefore $|\mathbb{R}| = |(0, 1)|$ by (1.19).   ◆

Now we can say that the following sets are uncountable and have the same cardinality:

$$|\text{power}(\mathbb{N})| = |[0, 1]| = |(0, 1)| = |\mathbb{R}|.$$

Let's show that not everything is computable. We'll do this by considering the computation of real numbers. The problem can be described as follows:

The Computable Number Problem   (1.20)

Compute a real number to any given number of decimal places.

Can any real number be computed? The answer is no. The reason is that there are "only" a countably infinite number of computer programs (1.18). Therefore there are only a countable number of computable numbers in $\mathbb{R}$ because each computable number needs a program to compute it. Since $\mathbb{R}$ is uncountable, most real numbers cannot be computed. The rational numbers can be computed, and there are also many irrational numbers that can be computed. Pi is the most famous example of a computable irrational number. In fact, there are countably infinitely many computable irrational numbers.

One way to show that a set is uncountable is to find another uncountable set and show that a bijection exists between them, as our examples have shown. Another way to proceed that works in some cases is to assume that the set is countable and come up with a contradiction. A general tool that can often be applied to this kind of problem is the technique of *diagonalization*, which was used by Cantor. We'll state the main result and introduce the technique in the proof.

Diagonalization   (1.21)

Suppose we have a countable listing of objects in which each object is represented as a stream (i.e., infinite list) over an alphabet A with at least two symbols. Then the listing is not exhaustive. In other words, there is some object that is represented as a stream over A but is NOT in the original listing.

Proof: We'll prove (1.21) for an alphabet with two symbols. Suppose we have a countable listing of objects in which each object can be represented as a stream over $A = \{x, y\}$. Then we can represent the listing as an infinite matrix M, where each row of M represents the stream for an object in the listing. For example, in Figure 1.7, row 0 represents the stream $\langle x, y, y, x, ...\rangle$, which represents the first object in the listing. Row 1 represents the second object, and so on. We've emphasized the main diagonal entries because they will be used to define a stream that is not in the listing.

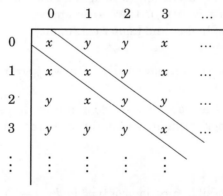

Figure 1.7

We'll define a new stream $\langle d_0, d_1, ...\rangle$ by using the diagonal entries of M as follows:

$$d_i = \text{if } M_{ii} = x \text{ then } y \text{ else } x.$$

For the example matrix we have the stream $\langle y, y, x, y, ...\rangle$. The new stream differs from the ith row of M at the ith position. So it can't occur as a row of M. Therefore we've defined a stream over A that represents an object that is NOT in the listing.   QED.

EXAMPLE 4 (*The Set of Functions of Type* $\mathbb{N} \to \mathbb{N}$ *is Uncountable*). Assume that the set of functions is countable. Then we can list all the functions as a countable sequence $f_0, f_1, f_2, ..., f_n, ...$. Each function f_n can be represented by its stream of values $\langle f_n(0), f_n(1), ...\rangle$. Therefore (1.21) implies that there is some function that is not in the original sequence. This contradiction gives the result. Another way to proceed is to actually construct a function that is not in the list, as outlined in the proof of (1.21). For example, we could define $g : \mathbb{N} \to \mathbb{N}$ as $g(n) = f_n(n) + 1$. g differs from each listed function f_n at its diagonal value $f_n(n)$. So g can't be in the list.   ◆

Let's find some more sets that have different infinite cardinalities. Since $|\mathbb{R}| = |(0, 1)|$ and $|(0, 1)| = |\text{power}(\mathbb{N})|$, we can apply (1.14) two times to obtain the following inequality:

$$|\mathbb{N}| < |\mathbb{R}| < |\text{power}(\text{power}(\mathbb{N}))|.$$

Is there any "well-known" set S such that $|S| = |\text{power}(\text{power}(\mathbb{N}))|$? Since the real numbers are hard enough to imagine, how can we comprehend all the elements in power(power($\mathbb{N}$))? If we keep applying (1.14), we can obtain an infinite set of sets of higher and higher cardinality:

$$|\mathbb{N}| < |\text{power}(\mathbb{N})| < |\text{power}(\text{power}(\mathbb{N}))| < |\text{power}(\text{power}(\text{power}(\mathbb{N})))| < \cdots$$

Luckily, in computer science we will seldom, if ever, have occasion to worry about sets having higher cardinality than the set of real numbers.

Exercises

1. Write down all possible functions of type $\{a, b, c\} \to \{1, 2\}$.

2. Suppose we have a function $f : \mathbb{N} \to \mathbb{N}$ defined by $f(x) = 2x + 1$. Describe each of the following sets, where E and O denote the even and odd natural numbers, respectively.
   a. range(f).   b. $f(E)$.   c. $f(O)$.   d. $f^{-1}(E)$.   e. $f^{-1}(O)$.

3. Evaluate each of the following expressions.
   a. $\lfloor -4.1 \rfloor$.   b. $\lceil -4.1 \rceil$.   c. $\lfloor 4.1 \rfloor$.   d. $\lceil 4.1 \rceil$.

4. Evaluate each of the following expressions.
   a. 15 mod 12.   b. −15 mod 12.   c. 15 mod (−12).   d. −15 mod (−12).

5. Let $f : \mathbb{N}_6 \to \mathbb{N}_6$ be defined by $f(x) = 2x \bmod 6$. Find the image and the pre- image for each of the following sets.
   a. {0, 2, 4}.   b. {1, 3}.   c. {0, 5}.

6. Given a function $f : A \to A$. An element $a \in A$ is called a *fixed point* of f if $f(a) = a$. Find the set of fixed points for each of the following functions.
   a. $f : A \to A$ where $f(x) = x$.
   b. $f : \mathbb{N} \to \mathbb{N}$ where $f(x) = x + 1$.
   c. $f : \mathbb{N}_6 \to \mathbb{N}_6$ where $f(x) = 2x \bmod 6$.
   d. $f : \mathbb{N}_6 \to \mathbb{N}_6$ where $f(x) = 3x \bmod 6$.

7. For each of the following types, compile some statistics: the number of functions of that type; the number that are injective; the number that are surjective; the number that are bijective; the number that are neither injective, surjective, nor bijective.
   a. $\{a, b, c\} \to \{1, 2\}$.
   b. $\{a, b\} \to \{1, 2, 3\}$.
   c. $\{a, b, c\} \to \{1, 2, 3\}$.

8. The fatherOf function from People to People is neither injective nor surjective. Why?

9. Show that each function is a bijection from the positive real numbers to the open interval (0, 1).
   a. $f(x) = \dfrac{1}{x + 1}$.   b. $g(x) = \dfrac{x}{x + 1}$.

10. Show that each function is a bijection from the open interval (0, 1) to the positive real numbers.
    a. $f(x) = \dfrac{x}{1 - x}$.   b. $g(x) = \dfrac{1 - x}{x}$.

11. Use diagonalization (1.21) to prove that the open unit interval (0, 1) is uncountable.

1.4 Languages

A *language* is a set of strings. If A is an alphabet, then a *language* over A is a collection of strings whose components come from A. Recall that A^* denotes the set of all strings over A. So A^* is the biggest possible language over A, and every other language over A is a subset of A^*. Four simple examples of languages over an alphabet A are the sets $\emptyset$, $\{\Lambda\}$, A, and A^*. For example, if A = $\{a\}$, then these four simple languages over A are

$$\emptyset, \quad \{\Lambda\}, \quad \{a\}, \quad \text{and} \quad \{\Lambda, a, aa, aaa, \ldots\}.$$

A string in a language is often called a *well-formed formula*—or *wff* for short (pronounce wff as "woof")—because the definition of the language usually allows only certain well-formed strings.

The natural operation of *concatenation* of strings places two strings in juxtaposition. For example, if $A = \{a, b\}$, then the concatenation of the two strings aab and ba is the string $aabba$. We will use the name "cat" to explicitly denote this operation. For example, we'll write cat(aab, ba) = $aabba$.

Combining Languages

Since languages are sets of strings, they can be combined by the usual set operations of union, intersection, difference, and complement. Another important way to combine two languages L and M is to form the set of all concatenations of strings in L with strings in M. This new language is called the *product* of L and M and is denoted by $L \cdot M$. A formal definition can be given as follows:

$$L \cdot M = \{\text{cat}(s, t) \mid s \in L \text{ and } t \in M\}.$$

For example, if $L = \{ab, ac\}$ and $M = \{a, bc, abc\}$, then the product $L \cdot M$ is the language

$$L \cdot M = \{aba, abbc, ababc, aca, acbc, acabc\}.$$

It's easy to see, from the definition of product, that the following simple properties hold for any language L:

$$L \cdot \{\Lambda\} = \{\Lambda\} \cdot L = L.$$
$$L \cdot \emptyset = \emptyset \cdot L = \emptyset.$$

But it's also easy to see that the product is not commutative in general. In other words, we can find two languages L and M such that $L \cdot M \neq M \cdot L$.

It's easy to see that the product is associative. In other words, if L, M, and N are languages, then $L \cdot (M \cdot N) = (L \cdot M) \cdot N$. So we can write down products without using parentheses. If L is a language, then the product $L \cdot L$ is denoted by L^2. In fact, we'll define the language product L^n for every $n \in \mathbb{N}$ as follows:

$$L^0 = \{\Lambda\},$$

$$L^n = L \cdot L^{n-1} \quad \text{if } n > 0.$$

For example, if $L = \{a, bb\}$, then the first few powers of L are

$L^0 = \{\Lambda\},$

$L^1 = L = \{a, bb\},$

$L^2 = L \cdot L = \{aa, abb, bba, bbbb\},$

$L^3 = L \cdot L^2 = \{aaa, aabb, abba, abbbb, bbaa, bbabb, bbbba, bbbbbb\}.$

If L is a language over A (i.e., $L \subset A^*$), then the *closure* of L is the language denoted by L^* and is defined as follows:

$$L^* = L^0 \cup L^1 \cup L^2 \cup \dots .$$

The *positive closure* of L is the language denoted by L^+ and defined as follows:

$$L^+ = L^1 \cup L^2 \cup L^3 \cup \dots .$$

It follows from the definition that $L^* = L^+ \cup \{\Lambda\}$. But it's not necessarily true that $L^+ = L^* - \{\Lambda\}$. For example, if we let our alphabet be $A = \{a\}$ and our language be $L = \{\Lambda, a\}$, then $L^+ = L^*$. Can you find a condition on a language L such that $L^+ = L^* - \{\Lambda\}$?

The closure of A coincides with our original definition of A^* as the set of all strings over A. In other words, we have a nice representation of A^* as follows:

$$A^* = A^0 \cup A^1 \cup A^2 \cup \dots ,$$

where A^n is the set of all strings over A having length n.

Some basic properties of the closure operation are given next. We'll leave the proofs as exercises.

Properties of Closure (1.22)

Let L and M be languages over the alphabet A. Then

a) $\{\Lambda\}^* = \varnothing^* = \{\Lambda\}.$

b) $L^* = L^* \cdot L^* = (L^*)^*.$

c) $\Lambda \in L$ if and only if $L^+ = L^*.$

d) $(L^* \cdot M^*)^* = (L^* \cup M^*)^* = (L \cup M)^*.$

e) $L \cdot (M \cdot L)^* = (L \cdot M)^* \cdot L.$

Grammars

Informally, a grammar is a set of rules used to define the structure of the strings in a language. Grammars are important in computer science not only to define programming languages, but also to define data sets for programs. Typical applications involve building algorithms to parse strings. To *parse* a string means to see whether it statisfies the rules of a grammar.

Let's describe the general structure of grammars for arbitrary languages. If L is a language over an alphabet A, then a grammar for L consists of a set of *grammar rules* of the following form:

$$\alpha \to \beta,$$

where α and β denote strings of symbols taken from A and from a set of grammar symbols that is disjoint from A. A grammar rule $\alpha \to \beta$ is often called a *production*, and it can be read in any of several ways as follows: "replace α by β," "α produces β," "α rewrites to β," or "α reduces to β."

Every grammar has a special grammar symbol called a *start symbol*, and there must be at least one production with left side consisting of only the start symbol. For example, if S is the start symbol for a grammar, then there must be at least one production of the form

$$S \to \beta.$$

Let's give an example of a grammar for a language and then discuss the process of deriving strings from the productions. Let $A = \{a, b, c\}$. Then a grammar for the language A^* can be described by the following four productions:

$$
\begin{aligned}
S &\to \Lambda \\
S &\to aS \\
S &\to bS \\
S &\to cS.
\end{aligned}
\tag{1.23}
$$

How do we know that this grammar describes the language A^*? We must be able to describe each string of the language in terms of the grammar rules. For example, let's see how we can use the productions (1.23) to show that the string *aacb* is in A^*. We'll begin with the start symbol S. Then we'll replace S by the right side of production $S \to aS$. We chose production $S \to aS$ because *aacb* matches the right hand side of $S \to aS$ by letting $S = acb$. The process of replacing S by aS is an example of a *derivation*, and we say, "S derives aS." We'll denote this derivation by writing

$$S \Rightarrow aS.$$

The symbol $\Rightarrow$ means "derives in one step." The right-hand side of this derivation contains the symbol S. So we again replace S by aS using the production $S \rightarrow aS$ a second time. This results in the derivation

$$S \Rightarrow aS \Rightarrow aaS.$$

The right-hand side of this derivation contains S. In this case we'll replace S by the right side of $S \rightarrow cS$. This gives the derivation

$$S \Rightarrow aS \Rightarrow aaS \Rightarrow aacS.$$

Continuing, we replace S by the right side of $S \rightarrow bS$. This gives the derivation

$$S \Rightarrow aS \Rightarrow aaS \Rightarrow aacS \Rightarrow aacbS.$$

Since we want this derivation to produce the string $aacb$, we now replace S by the right side of $S \rightarrow \Lambda$. This gives the desired derivation of the string $aacb$:

$$S \Rightarrow aS \Rightarrow aaS \Rightarrow aacS \Rightarrow aacbS \Rightarrow aacb\Lambda = aacb.$$

To indicate that a derivation of $aacb$ exists, we'll use the shorthand notation

$$S \Rightarrow^* aacb.$$

The symbol $\Rightarrow^*$ means "derives in zero or more steps."

A derivation can be represented by a tree called a *derivation tree* (or *parse tree*). For example, the derivation trees corresponding to the first three steps of our example are shown in Figure 1.8.

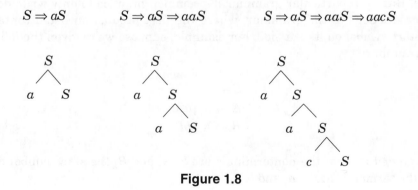

Figure 1.8

Now that we've introduced the idea of a grammar, let's take a minute to describe the four main ingredients of any grammar.

The Four Parts of a Grammar   (1.24)

1. An alphabet N of grammar symbols called *nonterminals*.

2. An alphabet T of symbols called *terminals*. The terminals are distinct from the nonterminals.

3. A specific nonterminal called the *start* symbol.

4. A finite set of productions of the form $\alpha \to \beta$, where α and β are strings over the alphabet $N \cup T$ with the restriction that α is not the empty string. There is at least one production with only the start symbol on its left side. Each nonterminal must appear on the left side of some production.

When two or more productions have the same left side, we can simplify the notation by writing one production with alternate right sides separated by the vertical line $|$. For example, the four productions (1.23) can be written in the following shorthand form:

$$S \to \Lambda \mid aS \mid bS \mid cS,$$

and we say, "S can be replaced by either Λ, or aS, or bS, or cS."

We can represent a grammar G as a 4-tuple $G = \langle N, T, S, P \rangle$, where P is the set of productions. For example, if P is the set of productions (1.23), then the grammar can be represented by the 4-tuple

$$\langle \{S\}, \{a, b, c\}, S, P \rangle.$$

The 4-tuple notation is useful for discussing general properties of grammars. But for a particular grammar it's common practice to only write down the productions of the grammar, where the first production listed contains the start symbol on its left side. For example, suppose we're given the following grammar:

$$S \to AB$$
$$A \to \Lambda \mid aA$$
$$B \to \Lambda \mid bB.$$

We can deduce that the nonterminals are S, A, and B, the start symbol is S, and the terminals are Λ, a, and b.

To discuss grammars further, we need to formalize things a bit. Suppose we're given some grammar. A string made up of terminals and/or nonterminals is called a *sentential form*. Now we can formalize the idea of a derivation. If x and y are sentential forms and $\alpha \to \beta$ is a production, then the replacement of α by β in $x\alpha y$ is called a *derivation*, and we denote it by writing

$$x\alpha y \Rightarrow x\beta y. \tag{1.25}$$

The following three symbols with their associated meanings are used quite often in discussing derivations:

$$\Rightarrow \quad \text{derives in one step,}$$
$$\Rightarrow^+ \quad \text{derives in one or more steps,}$$
$$\Rightarrow^* \quad \text{derives in zero or more steps.}$$

For example, suppose we have the following grammar:

$$S \to AB$$
$$A \to \Lambda \mid aA$$
$$B \to \Lambda \mid bB.$$

Let's consider the string aab. The statement $S \Rightarrow^+ aab$ means that there exists a derivation of aab that takes one or more steps. For example, we have

$$S \Rightarrow AB \Rightarrow aAB \Rightarrow aaAB \Rightarrow aaB \Rightarrow aabB \Rightarrow aab.$$

When a grammar contains more than one nonterminal—as the preceding grammar does—it may be possible to find several different derivations of the same string. Two kinds of derivations are worthy of note. A derivation is called a *leftmost derivation* if at each step the leftmost nonterminal of the sentential form is reduced by some production. Similarly, a derivation is called a *rightmost derivation* if at each step the rightmost nonterminal of the sentential form is reduced by some production. For example, the preceding derivation of aab is a leftmost derivation. Here's a rightmost derivation of aab:

$$S \Rightarrow AB \Rightarrow AbB \Rightarrow Ab \Rightarrow aAb \Rightarrow aaAb \Rightarrow aab.$$

Sometimes it's easy to write a grammar, and sometimes it can be quite difficult. The most important aspect of grammar writing is knowledge of the language under discussion. So we had better nail down the idea of the language associated with a grammar. If G is a grammar, then the *language of G*

is the set of terminal strings derived from the start symbol of G. The language of G is denoted by

$$L(G).$$

We can also describe $L(G)$ more formally. If G is a grammar with start symbol S and set of terminals T, then the language of G is the following set:

$$L(G) = \{s \mid s \in T^* \text{ and } S \Rightarrow^+ s\}. \tag{1.26}$$

When we're trying to write a grammar for a language, we should at least check to see whether the language is finite or infinite. If the language is finite, then a grammar can consist of all productions of the form $S \to w$ for each string w in the language. For example, the language $\{a, ba\}$ can be described by the grammar $S \to a \mid ab$.

If the language is infinite, then some production or sequence of productions must be used repeatedly to construct the derivations. To see this, notice that there is no bound on the length of strings in an infinite language. Therefore there is no bound on the number of derivation steps used to derive the strings. If the grammar has n productions, then any derivation consisting of $n + 1$ steps must use some production twice. For example, the infinite language $\{a^n b \mid n \geq 0\}$ can be described by the grammar

$$S \to b \mid aS .$$

To derive the string $a^n b$, we would use the production $S \to aS$ repeatedly—n times to be exact—and then stop the derivation by using the production $S \to b$. The production $S \to aS$ allows us to say "If S derives w, then it also derives aw."

A production is called *recursive* if its left side occurs on its right side. For example, the production $S \to aS$ is recursive. A production $S \to \alpha$ is *indirectly recursive* if S derives a sentential form that contains S. For example, suppose we have the following grammar:

$$S \to b \mid aA$$
$$A \to c \mid bS.$$

The productions $S \to aA$ and $A \to bS$ are both indirectly recursive because of the following derivations:

$$S \Rightarrow aA \Rightarrow abS,$$
$$A \Rightarrow bS \Rightarrow baA.$$

A grammar is *recursive* if it contains either a recursive production or an indirectly recursive production. We can make the following general statement about grammars for infinite languages:

> *A grammar for an infinite language must be recursive.*

We should note that a language can have more than one grammar. So we shouldn't be surprised when two people come up with two different grammars for the same language. The following list contains a few languages along with a grammar for each one.

Language	*Grammar*
$\{a, ab, abb, abbb\}$	$S \rightarrow a \mid ab \mid abb \mid abbb$
$\{\Lambda, a, aa, ..., a^n, ...\}$	$S \rightarrow \Lambda \mid aS$
$\{b, bbb, ..., b^{2n+1}, ...\}$	$S \rightarrow b \mid bbS$
$\{b, abc, aabcc, ..., a^nbc^n, ...\}$	$S \rightarrow b \mid aSc$
$\{ac, abc, abbc, ..., ab^nc, ...\}$	$S \rightarrow aBc$
	$B \rightarrow \Lambda \mid bB$

Sometimes a language can be written in terms of simpler languages, and a grammar can be constructed for the language in terms of the grammars for the simpler languages. We'll concentrate here on the operations of union, product, and closure.

Combining Grammars $\hfill$ (1.27)

Suppose M and N are languages whose grammars have disjoint sets of nonterminals. (Rename them if necessary.) Suppose also that the start symbols for the grammars of M and N are A and B, respectively. Then we have the following new languages and grammars:

Union Rule: The language $M \cup N$ starts with the two productions

$$S \rightarrow A \mid B.$$

Product Rule: The language $M \cdot N$ starts with the production

$$S \rightarrow AB.$$

Closure Rule: The language M^* starts with the production

$$S \rightarrow AS \mid \Lambda.$$

Let's see how we can use (1.27) to construct some grammars. For example, suppose we want to write a grammar for the following language:

$$L = \{\Lambda, a, b, aa, bb, ..., a^n, b^n, ...\}.$$

After a little thinking we notice that L is the union of the two languages $M = \{a^n \mid n \in \mathbb{N}\}$ and $N = \{b^n \mid n \in \mathbb{N}\}$. Thus we can write a grammar for L as follows:

$$S \to A \mid B \qquad \text{union rule,}$$
$$A \to \Lambda \mid aA \qquad \text{grammar for } M,$$
$$B \to \Lambda \mid bB \qquad \text{grammar for } N.$$

For another example, suppose we want to write a grammar for the following language:

$$L = \{a^m b^n \mid m, n \in \mathbb{N}\}.$$

After a little thinking we notice that L is the product of the two languages $M = \{a^m \mid m \in \mathbb{N}\}$ and $N = \{b^n \mid n \in \mathbb{N}\}$. Thus we can write a grammar for L as follows:

$$S \to AB \qquad \text{product rule,}$$
$$A \to \Lambda \mid aA \qquad \text{grammar for } M,$$
$$B \to \Lambda \mid bB \qquad \text{grammar for } N.$$

The closure rule in (1.27) describes the way we've been constructing grammars in some of our examples. For another example, suppose we want to construct the language L of all possible strings made up from zero or more occurrences of aa or bb. In other words, $L = \{aa, bb\}^*$. So we can write a grammar for L as follows:

$$S \to AS \mid \Lambda \qquad \text{closure rule,}$$
$$A \to aa \mid bb \qquad \text{grammar for } \{aa, bb\}.$$

We can simplify this grammar. Just replace the occurrence of A in $S \to AS$ by the right side of $A \to aa$ to obtain the production $S \to aaS$. Also replace A in $S \to AS$ by the right side of $A \to bb$ to obtain the production $S \to bbS$. This allows us to write the the grammar in simplified form as

$$S \to aaS \mid bbS \mid \Lambda.$$

Meaning and Ambiguity

Most of the time we attach a meaning or value to the strings in our lives. For example, the string 3+4 means 7 to most people. The string 3–4–2 may have two distinct meanings to two different people. One person might think that

$$3-4-2 = (3-4)-2 = -3,$$

while another person might think that

$$3-4-2 = 3-(4-2) = 1.$$

If we have a grammar, then we can define the *meaning* of any string in the grammar's language to be the parse tree produced by a derivation. We can often write a grammar so that each string in the grammar's language has exactly one meaning (i.e., one parse tree). A grammar is called *ambiguous* if its language contains some string that has two different parse trees. This is equivalent to saying that some string has two distinct leftmost derivations or, equivalently, some string has two distinct rightmost derivations.

To illustrate the ideas, we'll look at some grammars for simple arithmetic expressions. For example, suppose we define a set of arithmetic expressions by the grammar

$$E \rightarrow a \mid b \mid E\text{--}E.$$

The language of this grammar contains strings like a, b, b–a, a–b–a, and b–b–a–b. This grammar is ambiguous because it has a string, namely, a–b–a, that has two distinct leftmost derivations as follows:

$$E \Rightarrow E\text{--}E \Rightarrow a\text{--}E \Rightarrow a\text{--}E\text{--}E \Rightarrow a\text{--}b\text{--}E \Rightarrow a\text{--}b\text{--}a.$$
$$E \Rightarrow E\text{--}E \Rightarrow E\text{--}E\text{--}E \Rightarrow a\text{--}E\text{--}E \Rightarrow a\text{--}b\text{--}E \Rightarrow a\text{--}b\text{--}a.$$

These two derivations give us the two distinct parse trees in Figure 1.9.

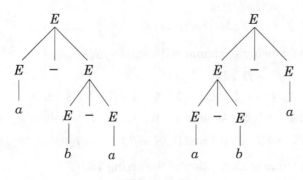

Figure 1.9

These two trees reflect the two ways that we could choose to evaluate the expression $a-b-a$. The first tree indicates that the second minus sign should be evaluated first. In other words, the first tree indicates the meaning

$$a-b-a = a-(b-a),$$

while the second tree indicates the meaning

$$a-b-a = (a-b)-a.$$

Exercises

1. Let $L = \{\Lambda, abb, b\}$ and $M = \{bba, ab, a\}$. Evaluate each of the following language expressions.
   a. $L \cdot M$.
   b. $M \cdot L$.
   c. L^2.

2. Use your wits to solve each of the following language equations for the unknown language.
   a. $\{\Lambda, a, ab\} \cdot L = \{b, ab, ba, aba, abb, abba\}$.
   b. $L \cdot \{a, b\} = \{a, baa, b, bab\}$.
   c. $\{a, aa, ab\} \cdot L = \{ab, aab, abb, aa, aaa, aba\}$.
   d. $L \cdot \{\Lambda, a\} = \{\Lambda, a, b, ab, ba, aba\}$

3. Let L and M be languages. Prove each of the following statements about the closure of languages.
   a. $\{\Lambda\}^* = \varnothing^* = \{\Lambda\}$.
   b. $L^* = L^* \cdot L^* = (L^*)^*$.
   c. $\Lambda \in L$ if and only if $L^+ = L^*$.
   d. $L \cdot (M \cdot L)^* = (L \cdot M)^* \cdot L$.
   e. $(L^* \cdot M^*)^* = (L^* \cup M^*)^* = (L \cup M)^*$.

4. Given the following grammar with start symbol S:

   $$S \rightarrow D \mid DS$$
   $$D \rightarrow 0 \mid 1 \mid 2 \mid 3 \mid 4 \mid 5 \mid 6 \mid 7 \mid 8 \mid 9.$$

   a. Find the productions used for the steps of the following derivation:

   $$S \Rightarrow DS \Rightarrow 7S \Rightarrow 7DS \Rightarrow 7DDS \Rightarrow 78DS \Rightarrow 780S \Rightarrow 780D \Rightarrow 7801.$$

   b. Find a leftmost derivation of the string 7801.
   c. Find a rightmost derivation of the string 7801.

5. Find a grammar for each of the following languages.

    a. $\{bb, bbbb, bbbbbb, ...\}$.

    b. $\{a, ba, bba, bbba, ...\}$.

    c. $\{\Lambda, ab, abab, ababab, ...\}$.

    d. $\{bb, bab, baab, baaab, ...\}$.

6. Find a grammar for each of the following languages.

    a. The set of decimal numerals that represent odd natural numbers.

    b. The set of binary numerals that represent odd natural numbers.

    c. The set of binary numerals that represent even natural numbers.

7. If w is a string, let w^R denote the *reverse* of w. For example, $aabc$ is the reverse of $cbaa$. Let $A = \{a, b, c\}$. Find a grammar to describe the language $\{w\, w^R \mid w \in A^*\}$.

8. Find a grammar for each of the following languages.

    a. $\{a^n b^n \mid n \geq 0\}$.

    b. $\{a^n b^m \mid n \geq 1 \text{ and } m \geq 1\}$.

    c. $\{a^n b c^n \mid n \geq 0\} \cup \{b^n a^m \mid n \geq 0 \text{ and } m \geq 0\}$.

9. Find a grammar to capture the precedence $\cdot$ over $+$ in the absence of parentheses. For example, the meaning of $a + b \cdot c$ should be $a + (b \cdot c)$.

10. The three questions below refer to the following grammar:

$$S \rightarrow S[S]S \mid \Lambda.$$

    a. Write down a sentence describing the language of this grammar.

    b. This grammar is ambiguous. Prove it.

    c. Find an unambiguous grammar that has the same language.

Chapter Summary

We normally prove things informally, and we use a variety of proof techniques: proof by example, proof by exhaustive checking, proof using variables, direct proofs, indirect proofs (e.g., proving the contrapositive and proof by contradiction), and iff proofs.

    Sets are characterized by lack of order and no redundant elements. There are easy techniques for comparing sets by subset and by equality. Sets can be combined by the operations of union, intersection, difference, and complement. Bags—also called multisets—are characterized by lack of order, and they may contain a finite number of redundant elements. Tuples are characterized by order, and they may contain a finite number of redundant elements. Many useful structures are related to tuples. Products of sets are collections of tuples. Lists are similar to tuples except that lists can be accessed only by head and tail. Strings are like lists except that elements from an alphabet are placed next to each other in juxtaposition.

Graphs are characterized by vertices and edges, where the edges may be undirected or directed, in which case they can be represented as tuples. Trees are special graphs that look like real trees.

Functions allow us to associate different sets of objects. They are characterized by associating each domain element with a unique codomain element. Two ways to combine functions are composition and tupling. Three important properties of functions that allow us to compare sets are injective, surjective, and bijective. These properties are also useful in comparing the cardinality of sets. Any set has smaller cardinality than its power set. Countable unions of countable sets are still countable. The diagonalization technique can be used to show that some countable listings are not exhaustive. It can also be used to show that some sets are uncountable, like the real numbers.

Three important properties of functions that allow us to compare sets are injective, surjective, and bijective. These properties are also useful in comparing the cardinality of sets. Any set has smaller cardinality than its power set, even when the set is infinite. Countable unions of countable sets are still countable. The diagonalization technique can be used to show that certain countable listings are not exhaustive.

A language is a sets of strings. We can combine existing languages into new langauges by applying the product (via concatenation of strings), the closure, or the usual set operations. A grammar is the most important way to describe a language. Grammar productions are used to derive strings of the language. Any grammar for an infinite language must contain at least one production that is recursive or indirectly recursive. Grammars for languages can be combined to form new grammars for unions, products, and closures of the languages. Some grammars are ambiguous.

2

Constructions and Structures

When we build, let us think that we build forever.
—John Ruskin (1819–1900)

To construct an object, we need some kind of description. If we're lucky, the description might include a technique to construct the object. This chapter is about construction techniques and structures that are useful in computer science. We'll begin by introducing the technique of inductive definition of sets. Then we'll discuss the technique of recursive definition of functions and procedures. We'll introduce the properties of binary relations that describe the intuitive notions of equivalence and order. We'll see how ordered structures are used to describe the technique of inductive proof. We'll discuss the structure of an algebra. We'll also see how the ideas of the chapter are used in computer science.

Chapter Guide

Section 2.1 introduces techniques for constructing inductively defined sets.

Section 2.2 introduces techniques for constructing recursively defined functions and procedures.

Section 2.3 introduces the idea of a relation. We'll see that the ideas of equivalence and order can be described by certain properties of binary relations.

Section 2.4 introduces inductive proof techniques that can be used to prove infinitely many statements in just two steps.

Section 2.5 introduces the idea of an algebra. We'll give some examples and we'll introduce the idea of a morphism to relate algebras with similar properties.

2.1 Inductively Defined Sets

When we write down an informal statement such as $A = \{3, 5, 7, 9, ...\}$, most of us will agree that we mean the set $A = \{2k + 3 \mid k \in \mathbb{N}\}$. Another way to describe A is to observe that $3 \in A$, that whenever $x \in A$, then $x + 2 \in A$, and that the only way an element gets in A is by the previous two steps. This description has three ingredients, which we'll state informally as follows:

1. There is a starting element (3 in this case).
2. There is a construction operation to build new elements from existing elements (addition by 2 in this case).
3. There is a statement that no other elements are in the set.

This process is an example of an *inductive definition* of a set. The set of objects defined is called an *inductive set*. An inductive set consists of objects that are constructed, in some way, from objects that are already in the set. So nothing can be constructed unless there is at least one object in the set to start the process. Inductive sets are important in computer science because the objects can be used to represent information, and the construction rules can often be programmed. We give the following formal definition:

> An *inductive definition* of a set S consists of three steps: (2.1)
>
> *Basis:*   List some specific elements of S (at least one element must be listed).
>
> *Induction:* Give one or more rules to construct new elements of S from existing elements of S.
>
> *Closure:*   State that S consists exactly of the elements obtained by the basis and induction steps. This step is usually assumed rather than stated explicitly.

The closure step is a very important part of the definition. Without it, there could be lots of sets satisfying the first two steps of an inductive definition. For example, the two sets $\mathbb{N}$ and $\{3, 5, 7, ...\}$ both contain the number 3, and if x is in either set, then so is $x + 2$. It's the closure statement that tells us that the only set defined by the basis and induction steps is $\{3, 5, 7, ...\}$. So the closure statement tells us that we're defining exactly one set, namely, the smallest set satisfying the basis and induction steps. We'll always omit the specific mention of closure in our inductive definitions.

The *constructors* of an inductive set are the basis elements and the rules for constructing new elements. For example, the inductive set {3, 5, 7, 9, ...} has two constructors, the number 3 and the operation of adding 2 to a number.

Examples

Now let's see how we can apply the technique of inductive definition to describe some different kinds of sets. We'll start with some sets of natural numbers.

EXAMPLE 1. The set of natural numbers $\mathbb{N}$ = {0, 1, 2, ...} is an inductive set. Its basis element is 0, and we can construct a new element from an existing one by adding the number 1. So we can write an inductive definition for $\mathbb{N}$ in the following way.

> *Basis:* $0 \in \mathbb{N}$.
>
> *Induction:*   If $n \in \mathbb{N}$, then $n + 1 \in \mathbb{N}$.

The constructors of $\mathbb{N}$ are the integer 0 and the operation that adds 1 to an element of $\mathbb{N}$. The operation of adding 1 to n is called the *successor* function, which we write as follows:

$$\text{succ}(n) = n + 1.$$

Using the successor function, we can rewrite the induction step in the above definition of $\mathbb{N}$ in the alternative form

$$\text{If } n \in \mathbb{N}, \text{ then succ}(n) \in \mathbb{N}.$$

Now we can say that $\mathbb{N}$ is an inductive set with constructors, 0 and succ.   ♦

EXAMPLE 2. Let A = {2, 3, 4, 7, 8, 11, 15, 16, ...}. Is A an inductive set? It might be easier if we think of A as the union of the two sets

$$B = \{2, 4, 8, 16, ...\} \text{ and } C = \{3, 7, 11, 15, ...\}.$$

Both of these sets are inductive. The constructors of B are the number 2 and the operation of multiplying by 2. The constructors of C are the number 3 and the operation of adding by 4. We can combine these definitions to give an inductive definition of A.

Basis: $2, 3 \in A$.

Induction: If $x \in A$ and x is odd, then $x + 4 \in A$ else $2x \in A$.

This example shows that there can be more than one basis element, and the induction step can include tests.   ♦

Lists

Let's try to find an inductive definition for the set of lists with elements from a set A. In Chapter 1 we denoted the set of all lists over A by Lists[A], and we'll continue to do so. We also mentioned that from a computational point of view the only parts of a nonempty list that can be accessed randomly are its *head* and its *tail*. Head and tail are sometimes called *destructors*, since they are used to destroy a list (take it apart). For example, the list $\langle x, y, z \rangle$ has x as its head and $\langle y, z \rangle$ as its tail, which we write as

$$\text{head}(\langle x, y, z \rangle) = x \quad \text{and} \quad \text{tail}(\langle x, y, z \rangle) = \langle y, z \rangle.$$

But we need to construct lists. The idea is to take an element h and a list t and construct a new list whose head is h and whose tail is t. We'll denote this newly constructed list by the expression

$$\text{cons}(h, t).$$

So *cons* is a constructor of lists. The operations cons, head, and tail work nicely together. For example, we can write

$$\langle x, y, z \rangle = \text{cons}(x, \langle y, z \rangle) = \text{cons}(\text{head}(\langle x, y, z \rangle), \text{tail}(\langle x, y, z \rangle)).$$

So if l is any nonempty list, then we have the equation

$$l = \text{cons}(\text{head}(l), \text{tail}(l)).$$

Now we have the proper tools, so let's get down to business and write an inductive definition for Lists[A]. The empty list, $\langle \, \rangle$, is certainly a basis element of Lists[A]. Using $\langle \, \rangle$ and cons as constructors, we can write the inductive definition of Lists[A] for any set A as follows:

Basis: $\langle\,\rangle \in \text{Lists}[A]$ (2.2)

Induction: If $x \in A$ and $t \in \text{Lists}[A]$, then $\text{cons}(x, t) \in \text{Lists}[A]$.

A popular infix notation for cons is the double colon symbol

$$:: \,.$$

Thus the infix form of $\text{cons}(x, t)$ is $x :: t$. For example, the list $\langle a, b, c\rangle$ can be constructed using cons as follows:

$$
\begin{aligned}
\text{cons}(a, \text{cons}(b, \text{cons}(c, \langle\,\rangle))) \quad &= \quad \text{cons}(a, \text{cons}(b, \langle c\rangle)) \\
&= \quad \text{cons}(a, \langle b, c\rangle) \\
&= \quad \langle a, b, c\rangle.
\end{aligned}
$$

Using the infix form, we construct $\langle a, b, c\rangle$ as follows:

$$a :: (b :: (c :: \langle\,\rangle)) = a :: (b :: \langle c\rangle) = a :: \langle b, c\rangle = \langle a, b, c\rangle.$$

The infix form of cons allows us to omit parentheses by agreeing that $::$ is right associative. In other words, $a :: b :: t = a :: (b :: t)$. Thus we can represent the list $\langle a, b, c\rangle$ by writing $a :: b :: c :: \langle\,\rangle$ instead of $a :: (b :: (c :: \langle\,\rangle))$.

Many programming problems involve processing data represented by lists. The operations cons, head, and tail provide basic tools for writing programs to create and manipulate lists. Thus they are necessary for programmers.

EXAMPLE 3. Suppose we need to define the set S of all lists over $\{a, b\}$ that begin with the single letter a followed by zero or more occurrences of b. We can describe S informally by writing a few of its elements:

$$S = \{\langle a\rangle, \langle a, b\rangle, \langle a, b, b\rangle, \langle a, b, b, b\rangle, \ldots\}.$$

It seems appropriate to make $\langle a\rangle$ the basis element of S. Then we can construct a new list from any list $x \in S$ by attaching the letter b on the right end of x. But cons places new elements at the left end of a list. We can overcome the problem by using the tail operation together with cons as follows:

$$\text{If } x \in S, \text{ then } \text{cons}(a, \text{cons}(b, \text{tail}(x))) \in S.$$

In infix form the statement reads as follows:

$$\text{If } x \in S, \text{ then } a :: b :: \text{tail}(x) \in S.$$

For example, if $x = \langle a \rangle$, then we construct the list

$$a :: b :: \text{tail}(\langle a \rangle) = a :: b :: \langle \; \rangle = a :: \langle b \rangle = \langle a, b \rangle.$$

So we have the following inductive definition of S:

> *Basis:* $\langle a \rangle \in S$.
>
> *Induction:*   If $x \in S$, then $a :: b :: \text{tail}(x) \in S$.   ◆

Strings

Suppose we want to give an inductive definition for a set of strings. To do so, we need to have some way to construct strings. The situation is similar to that of lists, in which the constructors are the empty list and cons (::). For strings the constructors are the empty string Λ together with the operation of *appending* a letter to the left end of a string in juxtaposition. We'll denote the append operation by the dot symbol. For example, to append the letter a to the string s, we'll use the following notation:

$$a \cdot s.$$

For example, if $s = aba$, then the evaluation of the expression $a \cdot s$ is given by

$$a \cdot s = a \cdot aba = aaba.$$

When a letter is appended to the empty string, the result is the letter. In other words, for any letter a we have

$$a \cdot \Lambda = a\Lambda = a.$$

To get along without parentheses, we'll agree that appending is right associative. For example, $a \cdot b \cdot \Lambda$ means $a \cdot (b \cdot \Lambda)$.

Now we have the tools to give inductive definitions for some sets of strings. For example, if A is an alphabet, then an inductive definition of A^* can be written as follows:

> *Basis:* $\Lambda \in A^*$.   (2.3)
>
> *Induction:*   If $a \in A$ and $s \in A^*$, then $a \cdot s \in A^*$.

For example, if $A = \{a, b\}$, then the string bab can be constructed as follows:

$$b \cdot a \cdot b \cdot \Lambda = b \cdot a \cdot b\Lambda = b \cdot a \cdot b = b \cdot ab = bab.$$

As we did with lists, we'll use the same two words *head* and *tail* to pick the appropriate parts of a nonempty string. For example, we have

$$\text{head}(abc) = a \quad \text{and} \quad \text{tail}(abc) = bc.$$

EXAMPLE 4. Let $A = \{a, b\}$, and let S be the following set of strings over A:

$$S = \{a, b, ab, ba, aab, bba, aaab, bbba, ...\}.$$

Suppose we start with a and b as basis elements. From a we can construct the element ba, from ba the element bba, and so on. Similarly, from b we construct ab, then aab, and so on. Another way to see this is to think of S as the union of two simpler sets

$$\{a, ba, bba, ...\}, \text{ and } \{b, ab, aab, ...\}.$$

To describe the construction, we can use the head function. Given a string $s \in S$, if $s = a$, then construct ba, while if $s = b$, then construct ab. Otherwise, if $\text{head}(s) = a$, then construct $a \cdot s$, and if $\text{head}(s) = b$, then construct $b \cdot s$. The definition of S can be written as follows:

Basis: $a, b \in S.$

Induction: Let $s \in S$. Construct a new element of S as follows:
   If $s = a$, then $b \cdot a \in S.$
   If $s = b$, then $a \cdot b \in S.$
   If $s \neq a$ and $\text{head}(s) = a$, then $a \cdot s \in S.$
   If $s \neq b$ and $\text{head}(s) = b$, then $b \cdot s \in S.$

Can you find another way to define S?   ♦

Languages

Recall that the language of a grammar is defined to be the set of all strings that can be derived from the grammar's start symbol. Now we can make the following interesting observation:

The language of a grammar is an inductively defined set.

In other words, for any grammar G, there is an inductive definition for $L(G)$, the language of G. The following inductive definition does the job, where S is the start symbol of G:

Inductive Definition of L(G)   (2.4)

Basis: For all strings w that can be derived from S without using a
                recursive or indirectly recursive production, put w in $L(G)$.

Induction: If $w \in L(G)$ and a derivation $S \Rightarrow^+ w$ contains a nonterminal
                from a recursive or indirectly recursive production, then
                modify the derivation by using the production to construct a
                new derivation $S \Rightarrow^+ x$, and put x in $L(G)$.

Proof: Let G be a grammar and let M be the inductive set defined by (2.4). We
need to show that $M = L(G)$. It's clear that $M \subset L(G)$ because all strings in M
are derived from the start symbol of G. Assume, by way of contradiction, that
$M \neq L(G)$. In other words, we have $L(G) - M \neq \varnothing$. Since S derives all the elements of $L(G) - M$, there must be some string $w \in L(G) - M$ that has the
shortest leftmost derivation among elements of $L(G) - M$. We can also assume
that this derivation uses a recursive or indirectly recursive production.
Otherwise, the basis case of (2.4) would force us to put $w \in M$, contrary to our
assumption that $w \in L(G) - M$. So the leftmost derivation of w must have the
following form, where s and t are terminal strings and α, β, and γ are sentential forms that don't include B:

$$S \Rightarrow^+ sB\gamma \Rightarrow^+ stB\beta\gamma \Rightarrow st\alpha\beta\gamma \Rightarrow^* w.$$

We can replace $sB\gamma \Rightarrow^+ stB\beta\gamma$ in this derivation with $sB\gamma \Rightarrow s\alpha\gamma$ to obtain the
following derivation of a string u of terminals:

$$S \Rightarrow^+ sB\gamma \Rightarrow s\alpha\gamma \Rightarrow^* u.$$

This derivation is shorter than the derivation of w. So we must conclude that
$u \in M$. Now we can apply the induction part of (2.4) to this latter derivation
of u to obtain the derivation of w. This tells us that $w \in M$, contrary to our assumption that $w \notin M$. The only think left for us to conclude is that our assumption that $M \neq L(G)$ was wrong. Therefore $M = L(G)$.   QED.

EXAMPLE 5. Suppose we're given the following grammar G:

$$S \to \Lambda \mid aB$$
$$B \to b \mid bB.$$

We want to give an inductive definition for $L(G)$. For the basis case there are
two derivations that don't contain recursive productions: $S \Rightarrow \Lambda$ and $S \Rightarrow aB$
$\Rightarrow ab$. This gives us the basis part of the definition for $L(G)$:

Basis: $\Lambda, ab \in L(G)$.

Now let's find the induction part of the definition. The only recursive production of G is $B \rightarrow bB$. So any element of $L(G)$ whose derivation contains an occurrence of B must have the general form $S \Rightarrow aB \Rightarrow^+ ay$ for some string y. So we can use the production $B \rightarrow bB$ to add one more step to the derivation as follows:

$$S \Rightarrow aB \Rightarrow abB \Rightarrow^+ aby.$$

This gives us the induction step in the definition of $L(G)$:

Induction: If $ay \in L(G)$, then put aby in $L(G)$.

For example, the basis case tells us that $ab \in L(G)$ and the derivation $S \Rightarrow aB \Rightarrow ab$ contains an occurrence of B. So we add one more step to the derivation using the production $B \rightarrow bB$ to obtain the derivation

$$S \Rightarrow aB \Rightarrow abB \Rightarrow abb.$$

So $ab \in L(G)$ implies that $abb \in L(G)$. Now we can use the fact that $abb \in L(G)$ to put $ab^3 \in L(G)$, and so on. We can conjecture with some confidence that $L(G) = \{ab^n \mid n \in \mathbb{N}\}$.   ◆

Binary Trees

Let's look at binary trees. In Chapter 1 we represented binary trees by tuples, where the empty binary tree is denoted by the empty tuple and a non-empty binary tree is denoted by a 3-tuple $\langle L, x, R \rangle$, in which x is the root, L is the left subtree, and R is the right subtree. Thus a new binary tree can be constructed from binary trees that already exist. This gives us the ingredients for an inductive definition of the set of all binary trees.

We'll let tree(L, x, R) denote the binary tree with root x, left subtree L, and right subtree R. If we still want to represent binary trees as tuples, then of course we can write

$$\text{tree}(L, x, R) = \langle L, x, R \rangle.$$

Now suppose A is any set. Let Trees[A] be the set of all binary trees whose nodes come from A. We can write down an inductive definition of BinTrees[A] using the two constructors $\langle \, \rangle$ and tree:

Basis: $\langle \, \rangle \in$ Trees[A].   (2.5)

Induction: If $x \in A$ and $L, R \in$ Trees[A], then tree$(L, x, R) \in$ Trees[A].

We also have destructor operations for binary trees. Suppose we let "left," "root," and "right" denote the operations that return the left subtree, the root, and the right subtree, respectively, of a nonempty tree. For example, if $t = \text{tree}(L, x, R)$, then $\text{left}(t) = L$, $\text{root}(t) = x$, and $\text{right}(t) = R$.

Product Sets

Let's see whether we can define some product sets inductively. For example, we know that $\mathbb{N}$ is inductive. Can the set $\mathbb{N} \times \mathbb{N}$ be inductively defined? Suppose we start by letting the tuple $\langle 0, 0 \rangle$ be the basis element. For the induction case, if a pair $\langle x, y \rangle \in \mathbb{N} \times \mathbb{N}$, then we can build the new pairs

$$\langle x + 1, y + 1 \rangle, \quad \langle x, y + 1 \rangle \quad \text{and} \quad \langle x + 1, y \rangle.$$

For example, we can construct $\langle 1, 1 \rangle$, $\langle 0, 1 \rangle$, and $\langle 1, 0 \rangle$ from the point $\langle 0, 0 \rangle$. It seems clear that this definition will define all elements of $\mathbb{N} \times \mathbb{N}$. Let's look at two general techniques to give an inductive definition for a product $A \times B$ of two sets A and B.

The first technique can be used if both A and B are inductively defined: For the basis case, put $\langle a, b \rangle \in A \times B$ whenever a is a basis element of A and b is a basis element of B. For the inductive part, if $\langle x, y \rangle \in A \times B$ and $x' \in A$ and $y' \in B$ are elements constructed from x and y, respectively, then put the elements $\langle x, y' \rangle$, $\langle x', y \rangle$ in $A \times B$.

The second technique can be used if only one of the sets, say A, is inductively defined: For the basis case, put $\langle a, b \rangle \in A \times B$ for all basis elements $a \in A$ and all elements $b \in B$. For the induction case, if $\langle x, y \rangle \in A \times B$ and $x' \in A$ is constructed from x, then put $\langle x', y \rangle \in A \times B$. A similar definition of $A \times B$ can also be made that uses only the fact that B is inductively defined. The choice of definition usually depends on how the product set will be used.

Exercises

1. Give an inductive definition for each of the following sets, under the assumption that the only known operation is the successor function, $\text{succ} : \mathbb{N} \to \mathbb{N}$.

   a. The set Odd, of odd natural numbers.

   b. The set Even, of even natural numbers.

   c. The set $S = \{4, 7, 10, 13, ...\} \cup \{3, 6, 9, 12, ...\}$.

2. Given a nonempty set A, find an inductive definition for each of the following subsets of Lists[A].

   a. The set Even of all lists that have an even number of elements.

   b. The set Odd of all lists that have an odd number of elements.

3. Given the set $A = \{a, b\}$, find an inductive definition for the set S of all lists over A that alternate a's and b's. For example, the lists $\langle \rangle$, $\langle a \rangle$, $\langle b \rangle$, $\langle a, b, a \rangle$, and $\langle b, a \rangle$ are in S. But $\langle a, a \rangle$ is not in S.

4. Give an inductive definition for the set B of all binary numerals containing an odd number of digits such that the only string with a leading (leftmost) 0 is 0 itself.

5. A *palindrome* is a string that reads the same left to right as right to left. For example, RADAR is a palindrome over the English alphabet. Let A be an alphabet. Give an inductive definition of the set P of all palindromes over A.

6. Given the following inductive definition for a subset B of $\mathbb{N} \times \mathbb{N}$:

   Basis: $\langle 0, 0 \rangle \in B$.
   Induction: If $\langle x, y \rangle \in B$, then $\langle \text{succ}(x), y \rangle$, $\langle \text{succ}(x), \text{succ}(y) \rangle\!\rangle \in B$.

   a. Describe the set B as a set of the form $\{\langle x, y \rangle \mid \text{some property holds}\}$.

   b. Describe those elements in B that get defined in more than one way.

7. Find two inductive definitions for each product set S. The first definition should use the fact that all components of S are inductive sets. The second definition should use only one inductive component set in S.
   a. $S = \text{Lists}[A] \times \text{Lists}[A]$ for some set A.
   b. $S = A^* \times A^*$ for some finite set A.
   c. $S = \mathbb{N} \times \text{Lists}[\mathbb{N}]$.
   d. $S = \mathbb{N} \times \mathbb{N} \times \mathbb{N}$.

8. Let A be a set. Suppose O is the set of binary trees over A that contain an odd number of nodes. Similarly, let E be the set of binary trees over A that contain an even number of nodes. Find inductive definitions for O and E. *Hint:* You can use O when defining E, and you can use E when defining O.

9. For each grammar G, use (2.4) to find an inductive definition for $L(G)$.
   a. $S \rightarrow \Lambda \mid aaS$.
   b. $S \rightarrow a \mid aBc, B \rightarrow b \mid bB$.

2.2 Recursively Defined Functions and Procedures

Since we're going to be constructing functions and procedures in this section, we'd better agree on the idea of a procedure. From a computer science point of view a *procedure* is a subprogram that carries out one or more actions, and it can also return any number of values—including none—through its arguments. For example, a statement like print(x, y) in a program will cause the print procedure to print the values of x and y on some output device. In this case, two actions are performed, and no values are returned. For another example, a statement like sort(L) might cause the sort procedure to carry out the action of sorting the list L in place. In this case, the action of sorting L is carried out, and the sorted list is returned as L. Or there might be a statement like sort(L, M) that leaves L alone but returns its sorted version as M.

A function or a procedure is said to be *recursively defined* if it is defined in terms of itself. In other words, a function f is recursively defined if at least one value $f(x)$ is defined in terms of another value $f(y)$, where $x \neq y$. Similarly, a procedure P is recursively defined if the actions of P for some argument x are defined in terms of the actions of P for another argument y, where $x \neq y$.

Many useful recursively defined functions have domains that are inductively defined sets. Similarly, many recursively defined procedures process elements from inductively defined sets. For these cases there are very useful construction techniques. Let's describe the two techniques.

Constructing a Recursively Defined Function   (2.6)

If S is an inductively defined set, we can construct a function f with domain S as follows:

Basis: For each basis element $x \in S$, specify a value for $f(x)$.

Induction: Give one or more rules that—for any inductively defined element $x \in S$—will define $f(x)$ in terms of previously defined values of f.

Any function constructed by (2.6) is recursively defined because it is defined in terms of itself by the induction part of the definition. In a similar way we can construct a recursively defined procedure to process the elements of an inductively defined set.

Constructing a Recursively Defined Procedure   (2.7)

If S is an inductively defined set, we can construct a procedure P to process the elements of S as follows:

Basis: For each basis element $x \in S$, specify a set of actions for $P(x)$.

Induction: Give one or more rules that—for any inductively defined element $x \in S$—will define the actions of $P(x)$ in terms of previously defined actions of P.

Examples

In the following examples we'll see how (2.6) and (2.7) can be used to construct recursively defined functions and procedures over a variety of inductively defined sets. Most of our examples will be functions. But we'll define a few procedures too. We'll also see some recursively defined stream functions that are not defined by (2.6).

Natural Numbers

Let $f : \mathbb{N} \to \mathbb{N}$ denote the function that, for each $n \in \mathbb{N}$, returns the sum of the odd numbers from 1 to $2n + 1$, as follows:

$$f(n) = 1 + 3 + \cdots + (2n + 1).$$

Notice that $f(0) = 1$. So we have a definition for f applied to the basis element $0 \in \mathbb{N}$. For the inductive part of the definition, notice how we can write $f(n + 1)$ in terms of $f(n)$ as follows:

$$
\begin{aligned}
f(n + 1) &= 1 + 3 + \cdots + (2n + 1) + [2(n + 1) + 1] \\
&= (1 + 3 + \cdots + 2n + 1) + 2n + 3 \\
&= f(n) + 2n + 3.
\end{aligned}
$$

This gives us the necessary ingredients for a recursive definition of f:

Basis: $f(0) = 1.$

Induction: $f(n + 1) = f(n) + 2n + 3.$

A definition like this is often called a *pattern-matching definition* because the evaluation of an expression $f(x)$ depends on $f(x)$ matching either $f(0)$ or $f(n + 1)$. For example, $f(3)$ matches $f(n + 1)$ with $n = 2$, so we would choose the second equation to evaluate $f(3)$.

An alternative form for the definition of f is the conditional form. One conditional form consists of equations with conditionals as follows:

Basis: $f(0) = 1.$

Induction: $f(n) = f(n - 1) + 2n + 1$ if $n > 0.$

A second conditional form is the familiar if-then-else equation as follows:

$$f(n) = \text{if } n = 0 \text{ then } 1 \text{ else } f(n - 1) + 2n + 1.$$

A recursively defined function can be easily evaluated by a technique called *unfolding* the definition. For example, to find the value of $f(4)$, we start by finding the appropriate expression to equate to $f(4)$ by using pattern matching or by using conditionals. Continue in this manner to unfold all expressions of the form $f(x)$ until none are left. The resulting expression can then be evaluated. Here is the sequence of unfoldings for the evaluation of $f(4)$ using the if-then-else definition:

$$
\begin{aligned}
f(4) &= f(3) + 2\cdot4+1 \\
&= f(2) + 2\cdot3+1 + 2\cdot4+1 \\
&= f(1) + 2\cdot2+1 + 2\cdot3+1 + 2\cdot4+1 \\
&= f(0) + 2\cdot1+1 + 2\cdot2+1 + 2\cdot3+1 + 2\cdot4+1 \\
&= 1 + 2\cdot1+1 + 2\cdot2+1 + 2\cdot3+1 + 2\cdot4+1 \\
&= 1 + 3 + 5 + 7 + 9 \\
&= 25.
\end{aligned}
$$

Sum and Product Notation

Many definitions and properties that we use without thinking are recursively defined. For example, given a sequence of numbers $\langle a_1, a_2, ..., a_n, ...\rangle$, we can represent the sum of the first n numbers of the sequence with summation notation using the symbol Σ as follows:

$$
\sum_{i=1}^{n} a_i = a_1 + a_2 + ... + a_n .
$$

This notation has a recursive definition, which makes the practical assumption that an empty sum is 0:

$$
\sum_{i=1}^{n} a_i = \text{if } n = 0 \text{ then } 0 \text{ else } a_n + \sum_{i=1}^{n-1} a_i .
$$

Similarly we can represent the product of the first n numbers in the sequence with the product notation, where the practical assumption is that an empty product is 1:

$$
\prod_{i=1}^{n} a_i = \text{if } n = 0 \text{ then } 1 \text{ else } a_n \cdot \prod_{i=1}^{n-1} a_i .
$$

In the special case in which $a_i = i$ this product defines the popular *factorial function*, which is denoted by $n!$ and is read "n factorial." In other words, we have $n! = n \cdot (n - 1) \cdots 1$. For example, $4! = 4 \cdot 3 \cdot 2 \cdot 1 = 24$, and $0! = 1$. So we can write $n!$ as follows:

$$n! = \text{if } n = 0 \text{ then } 1 \text{ else } n \cdot (n - 1)!.$$

The sum and product notations can be defined for any pair of indices $m \le n$. In fact, the symbols Σ and Π can be defined as functions if we consider a sequence to be a function. For example, the sequence $\langle a_1, a_2, ..., a_n, ... \rangle$ is a listing of functional values for the function $a : \mathbb{N} \to \mathbb{N}$, where we write a_i instead of $a(i)$. Then Π is a higher-order function of three variables

$$\prod(m, n, a) = \prod_{i=m}^{n} a(i) = a(m) \cdots a(n).$$

Many definitions and laws of exponents for arithmetic can be expressed recursively. For example,

$$a^n = \text{if } n = 0 \text{ then } 1 \text{ else } a \cdot a^{n-1}.$$

The law $a^m \cdot a^n = a^{m+n}$ for multiplication can be defined recursively by the equations that follow (where n is the induction variable):

$$a^m \cdot a^0 = a^m,$$
$$a^m \cdot a^{n+1} = a^{m+1} \cdot a^n.$$

For example, we can write $a^m \cdot a^2 = a^{m+1} \cdot a^1 = a^{m+2} \cdot a^0 = a^{m+2}$.

Lists

Suppose we need to define a function $f : \mathbb{N} \to \text{Lists}[\mathbb{N}]$ that computes a backwards sequence as follows:

$$f(n) = \langle n, ..., 1, 0 \rangle.$$

Notice that the list $\langle n, n - 1, ..., 1, 0 \rangle$ can also be written

$$\text{cons}(n, \langle n - 1, ..., 1, 0 \rangle) = \text{cons}(n, f(n - 1)).$$

Therefore f can be defined recursively by

   Basis: $f(0) = \langle 0 \rangle.$

   Induction: $f(n) = \text{cons}(n, f(n - 1))$ if $n > 0$.

This definition can be written in if-then-else form as

$$f(n) = \text{if } n = 0 \text{ then } \langle 0 \rangle \text{ else } \text{cons}(n, f(n-1)).$$

To see how the evaluation works, look at the unfolding that results when we evaluate $f(3)$:

$$
\begin{aligned}
f(3) &= \text{cons}(3, f(2)) \\
&= \text{cons}(3, \text{cons}(2, f(1))) \\
&= \text{cons}(3, \text{cons}(2, \text{cons}(1, f(0)))) \\
&= \text{cons}(3, \text{cons}(2, \text{cons}(1, \langle 0 \rangle))) \\
&= \text{cons}(3, \text{cons}(2, \langle 1, 0 \rangle)) \\
&= \text{cons}(3, \langle 2, 1, 0 \rangle) \\
&= \langle 3, 2, 1, 0 \rangle.
\end{aligned}
$$

We haven't given a recursively defined procedure yet. So let's give one for the problem we've been discussing. In the following procedure, $P(n)$ prints the numbers in the list $\langle n, n-1, ..., 0 \rangle$:

$$
\begin{aligned}
P(n)\!: \quad &\textbf{if } n = 0 \textbf{ then } \text{print}(0) \\
&\textbf{else} \\
&\qquad \text{print}(n); \\
&\qquad P(n-1) \\
&\textbf{fi.}
\end{aligned}
$$

Strings

If A is an alphabet, then the domain of the string concatenation function "cat" is $A^* \times A^*$. Since A^* is an inductively defined set, it follows that $A^* \times A^*$ is also inductively defined. We give a recursive definition of cat that uses only the fact that the first copy of A^* is inductively defined:

$$
\begin{aligned}
\text{cat}(\Lambda, s) \quad &= s, \\
\text{cat}(a \cdot t, s) \quad &= a \cdot \text{cat}(t, s).
\end{aligned}
$$

The if-then-else form of the definition can be written as follows:

$$\text{cat}(x, y) = \text{if } x = \Lambda \text{ then } y \text{ else } \text{head}(x) \cdot \text{cat}(\text{tail}(x), y).$$

For example, we evaluate the expression $\text{cat}(ab, cd)$ as follows:

$$\text{cat}(ab, cd) \;=\; a \cdot \text{cat}(b, cd)$$
$$=\; a \cdot b \cdot \text{cat}(\Lambda, cd)$$
$$=\; a \cdot b \cdot cd$$
$$=\; a \cdot bcd$$
$$=\; abcd.$$

EXAMPLE 1 (*Natural Numbers Represented as Binary Strings*). Recall that the division algorithm allows us to represent a natural number x in the form

$$x = 2 \cdot \text{floor}(x/2) + x \bmod 2.$$

For example, $27 = 2 \cdot 13 + 1$, and $48 = 2 \cdot 24 + 0$. This formula can be used to create a binary string representation of x because x mod 2 is the rightmost bit of the representation. The next bit is found by computing floor($x/2$) mod 2. The next bit is floor(floor($x/2$)/2) mod 2, and so on.

Let's try to use this idea to write a recursive definition for the function "bin" to compute the binary representation for a natural number. If $x = 0$, then x has 0 as a binary representation. So we can use this as a basis case: bin(0) = 0. If $x \neq 0$, then we should concatenate the binary string representation of floor($x/2$) with the bit x mod 2. The definition can be written in if-then-else form as follows:

$$\text{bin}(x) = \text{if } x = 0 \text{ then } 0 \text{ else } \text{cat}(\text{bin}(\text{floor}(x/2)), x \bmod 2). \tag{2.8}$$

For example, we unfold the definition to calculate the expression bin(13):

$$\begin{aligned}
\text{bin}(13) \;&=\; \text{cat}(\text{bin}(6), 1) \\
&=\; \text{cat}(\text{cat}(\text{bin}(3), 0), 1) \\
&=\; \text{cat}(\text{cat}(\text{cat}(\text{bin}(1), 1), 0), 1) \\
&=\; \text{cat}(\text{cat}(\text{cat}(\text{cat}(\text{bin}(0),1), 1), 0), 1) \\
&=\; \text{cat}(\text{cat}(\text{cat}(\text{cat}(0, 1), 1), 0), 1) \\
&=\; \text{cat}(\text{cat}(\text{cat}(01, 1), 0), 1) \\
&=\; \text{cat}(\text{cat}(011, 0), 1) \\
&=\; \text{cat}(0110, 1) \\
&=\; 01101.
\end{aligned}$$

Notice that bin always puts a leading 0 in front of the answer. Can you find an alternative definition that leaves off the leading 0? We'll leave this as an exercise. ◆

Binary Trees

Let's look at some functions that compute properties of binary trees. To start, suppose we need to know the number of nodes in a binary tree. Since the set of binary trees over a particular set can be defined inductively, we should be able to come up with a recursively defined function that suits our needs. Let "nodes" be the function that returns the number of nodes in a binary tree. Since the empty tree has no nodes, we have nodes($\langle\ \rangle$) = 0. If the tree is not empty, then the number of nodes can be computed by adding 1 to the number of nodes in the left and right subtrees. The equational definition of nodes can be written as follows:

$$\text{nodes}(\langle\ \rangle) = 0,$$
$$\text{nodes}(\text{tree}(L, a, R)) = 1 + \text{nodes}(L) + \text{nodes}(R).$$

If we want the corresponding if-then-else form of the definition, it looks like

$$\begin{aligned}
\text{nodes}(T) \quad &= \quad \text{if } T = \langle\ \rangle \text{ then } 0 \\
&\qquad \text{else } 1 + \text{nodes}(\text{left}(T)) + \text{nodes}(\text{right }(T)).
\end{aligned}$$

For example, we'll evaluate nodes(T) for $T = \langle\langle\langle\ \rangle, a, \langle\ \rangle\rangle, b, \langle\ \rangle\rangle$:

$$\begin{aligned}
\text{nodes}(T) \quad &= \quad 1 + \text{nodes}(\langle\langle\ \rangle, a, \langle\ \rangle\rangle) + \text{nodes}(\langle\ \rangle) \\
&= \quad 1 + 1 + \text{nodes}(\langle\ \rangle) + \text{nodes}(\langle\ \rangle) + \text{nodes}(\langle\ \rangle) \\
&= \quad 1 + 1 + 0 + 0 + 0 \\
&= \quad 2.
\end{aligned}$$

Traversing Binary Trees

There are several useful ways to list the nodes of a binary tree. The three most popular methods are called preorder, inorder, and postorder. The *preorder* listing of a binary tree has the root of the tree as its head, and its tail is the concatenation of the preorder listing of the left and right subtrees of the root, in that order. For example, the preorder listing of the nodes of the binary tree in Figure 2.1 is $\langle a, b, c, d, e\rangle$.

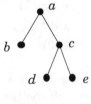

Figure 2.1

It's common practice to write the listing without any punctuation symbols as

$$a\ b\ c\ d\ e.$$

Since binary trees are inductively defined, we can easily write a recursively defined procedure to output the preorder listing of a binary tree. For example, the following recursively defined procedure prints the preorder listing of its argument T:

Preorder(T): **if** $T \neq \langle\ \rangle$ **then**
 print(root(T));
 Preorder(left(T));
 Preorder(right(T))
fi.

Now let's write a function to compute the preorder listing of a binary tree. Letting "preOrd" be the name of the preorder function, an equational definition can be written as follows:

preOrd($\langle\ \rangle$) = $\langle\ \rangle$,
preOrd(tree(L, x, R)) = x :: cat(preOrd(L), preOrd(R)).

The if-then-else form of preOrd can be written as follows:

preOrd(T) = if $T = \langle\ \rangle$ then $\langle\ \rangle$
 else root(T) :: cat(preOrd(left(T)), preOrd(right(T))).

We'll evaluate the expression preOrd(T) for the tree $T = \langle\langle\langle\ \rangle, a, \langle\ \rangle\rangle, b, \langle\ \rangle\rangle$:

preOrd(T) = b :: cat(preOrd($\langle\langle\ \rangle, a, \langle\ \rangle\rangle$), preOrd($\langle\ \rangle$))
 = b :: cat(a :: cat(preOrd($\langle\ \rangle$), preOrd($\langle\ \rangle$)), preOrd($\langle\ \rangle$))
 = b :: cat(a :: $\langle\ \rangle$, $\langle\ \rangle$)
 = b :: cat($\langle a\rangle, \langle\ \rangle$)
 = b :: $\langle a\rangle$
 = $\langle b, a\rangle$.

The definitions for inorder and postorder listings are similar. The *inorder* listing of a binary tree is the concatenation of the inorder listing of the left subtree of the root with the list whose head is the root of the tree and whose tail is the inorder listing of the right subtree of the root. For example, the inorder listing of the tree in Figure 2.1 is

$$b\ a\ d\ c\ e.$$

The *postorder* listing of a binary tree is the concatenation of the postorder listings of the left and right subtrees of the root, followed lastly by the root. The postorder listing of the tree in Figure 2.1 is

$$b\ d\ e\ c\ a.$$

We'll leave the construction of the inorder and postorder procedures and functions as exercises.

Exercises

1. Given the following definition for the nth Fibonacci number:

    fib$(n) =$ if $n = 0$ then 0 else if n $= 1$ then 1 else fib$(n - 1) +$ fib$(n - 2)$.

    Write down each unfolding step in the evaluation of fib(4).

2. Find a recursive definition for the function "small" to find the smallest number in a list.

3. Conway's challenge sequence is defined recursively as follows:

    Basis: $f(1) = f(2) = 1$.

    Induction: $f(n) = f(f(n - 1)) + f(n - f(n - 1))$ for $n > 2$.

    Calculate the first 17 elements $f(1)$, $f(2)$, ..., $f(17)$. The article by Mallows [1991] contains an account of this sequence.

4. Write a recursive definition for the function eq to check two lists for equality.

5. Write down a recursive definition for the function pal that tests a string to see whether it is a palindrome.

6. The conversion of a natural number to a binary string (2.8) placed a leading (leftmost) zero on each result. Modify the definition of the function to get rid of the leading zero.

7. Write down recursive definitions for each of the following procedures to print the nodes of a binary tree.

    a. In: prints the nodes of a binary tree from an inorder traversal.
    b. Post: prints the nodes of a binary tree from a postorder traversal.

8. Write a recursive definition for each of the following functions, in which the input arguments are sets represented as lists. Use the primitive operations of cons, head, and tail to build your functions (along with functions already defined):

   a. isMember. For example, isMember(a, $\langle b, a, c \rangle$) is true.

   b. isSubset. For example, isSubset($\langle a, b \rangle$, $\langle b, c, a \rangle$) is true.

   c. areEqual. For example, areEqual($\langle a, b \rangle$, $\langle b, a \rangle$) is true.

   d. union. For example, union($\langle a, b \rangle$, $\langle c, a \rangle$) = $\langle a, b, c \rangle$.

   e. intersect. For example, intersect($\langle a, b \rangle$, $\langle c, a \rangle$) = $\langle a \rangle$.

   f. difference. For example, difference($\langle a, b, c \rangle$, $\langle b, d \rangle$) = $\langle a, c \rangle$.

9. Write a function in if-then-else form to produce the product set of two finite sets. You may assume that the sets are represented as lists.

10. Suppose we define $f : \mathbb{N} \to \mathbb{N}$ by $f(x) = x - 10$ for $x > 10$ and $f(x) = f(f(x + 11))$ for $0 \leq x \leq 10$. This function is recursively defined even though it is not defined by (2.6). Give a simple definition of this function.

2.3 Relations

Ideas such as kinship, connection, and association of objects are key to the concept of a relation. Informally, a *relation* is a set of tuples in which the elements of each tuple are related in some way. For example, suppose we let "Family" be the relation whose tuples have the form

$$\langle \text{father, mother, } \langle \text{child1, child2, } \dots \rangle \rangle.$$

If we want to indicate that James and Janice are the parents of Gretchen and Andrew, we would write

$$\langle \text{James, Janice, } \langle \text{Gretchen, Andrew} \rangle \rangle \in \text{Family}.$$

If R is a relation, then the statement $\langle x_1, \dots, x_n \rangle \in R$ is also denoted by writing the prefix form $R(x_1, \dots, x_n)$. For example, we could write

$$\text{Family(James, Janice, } \langle \text{Gretchen, Andrew} \rangle).$$

A relation can usually be described as a subset of some product set. For example, using our definition for Family, we can see that

$$\text{Family} \subset \text{People} \times \text{People} \times \text{Lists[People]}.$$

A relation R may also be defined by giving a property that each tuple satisfies. When this is the case, we might use the names of the properties (*attributes*) of each part as the indices for a tuple. For example, if the attributes of a family are Father, Mother, and Children, then the components of the tuple

$$t = \langle \text{James, Janice}, \langle \text{Gretchen, Andrew} \rangle \rangle$$

might be accessed as

$$t(\text{Father}), t(\text{Mother}), \text{ and } t(\text{Children}).$$

They might also be accessd as

$$\text{Father}(t), \text{Mother}(t), \text{ and Children}(t).$$

We often use the term *n-ary relation* when referring to a relation R whose tuples are elements of a product set $A_1 \times \cdots \times A_n$. So an n-ary relation R over the product set $A_1 \times \cdots \times A_n$ is just a subset of $A_1 \times \cdots \times A_n$. Thus there are lots of n-ary relations over $A_1 \times \cdots \times A_n$, ranging from the smallest subset $\varnothing$, called the *empty relation*, to the largest subset $A_1 \times \cdots \times A_n$ itself, called the *universal relation*. The terms *unary*, *binary*, and *ternary* are often used instead of 1-ary, 2-ary, and 3-ary. If R is a subset of the product A^n, then R is called an *n-ary relation on A*.

If R is a binary relation and $\langle x, y \rangle \in R$, we often denote this fact by writing the following *infix expression*—the name appears between its two arguments:

$$x \, R \, y.$$

For example, we write $1 < 2$ instead of $\langle 1, 2 \rangle \in \, <$ and $<(1, 2)$. Suppose we define the "isParentOf" relation on People by letting isParentOf(a, b) mean "a is a parent of b." If Lloyd is a parent of Jim, then we can write "Lloyd isParentOf Jim."

We can observe from our discussion of graphs that any binary relation R on a set A can be thought of as a digraph $G = \langle A, R \rangle$ with vertices A and edges R. For example, let $A = \{1, 2, 3\}$ and $R = \{\langle 1, 2 \rangle, \langle 1, 3 \rangle, \langle 2, 3 \rangle, \langle 3, 3 \rangle\}$. Then the digraph corresponding to this binary relation is shown in Figure 2.2.

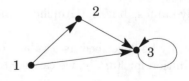

Figure 2.2

Properties of Binary Relations

Binary relations often satisfy certain special properties. Many useful binary relations satisfy at most three of five special properties that we are about to discuss. So let's get to it. The first three properties that we'll discuss are called *reflexive*, *symmetric*, and *transitive*, and they are defined as follows, where R is a binary relation over a set A:

Reflexive :	$a\,R\,a$	(for all $a \in A$).
Symmetric:	if $a\,R\,b$, then $b\,R\,a$	(for all $a, b \in A$).
Transitive:	if $a\,R\,b$ and $b\,R\,c$, then $a\,R\,c$	(for all $a, b, c \in A$).

Many well-known relations satisfy one or more of these three properties, and some relations don't satisfy any of them. For example, the "isParentOf" relation doesn't satisfy any of the three properties. The "isSiblingOf" relation is symmetric and transitive, and if we agree that people are self-siblings, then it's reflexive too. The relation "hasSameBirthdayAs" satisfies all three properties. The "less" relation on numbers is transitive but is neither reflexive nor symmetric. The relation $\{\langle n, n + 1 \rangle \mid n \in \mathbb{N}\}$ doesn't satisfy any of the three properties.

The simplest kind of equality on a set equates each element to itself. We'll call this *basic equality*. We can characterize basic equality on a set A by the relation

$$E = \{\langle x, x \rangle \mid x \in A\}.$$

Of course, E is often denoted by the popular symbol "=," and we write $x = x$ instead of either $x\,E\,x$ or $\langle x, x \rangle \in E$. Basic equality is reflexive, symmetric, and transitive. The reason that it's symmetric and transitive is that the if-then definitions of symmetric and transitive are vacuously satisfied.

The reflexive property has a corresponding opposite property, called *irreflexive*, which is defined as follows:

Irreflexive:	$a\,\not{R}\,a$	(for all $a \in A$).

The irreflexive property says that the reflexive property does not hold for every element $a \in A$. For example, the "isAncestorOf" relation and the "less" relation are both irreflexive and transitive.

The symmetric property has a corresponding opposite property, which we can define as follows:

Antisymmetric:	if $a \neq b$ and $a\,R\,b$, then $b\,\not{R}\,a$	(for all $a, b \in A$).

The antisymmetric property says that the symmetric property does not hold for every pair of elements. For example, the "isParentOf" relation is antisymmetric because if a is a parent of b, then b can't be a parent of a. We can write the antisymmetric property in an alternative form as follows:

Antisymmetric: if $a\,R\,b$ and $b\,R\,a$, then $a = b$ (for all $a, b \in A$).

For example, the "isParentOf" relation is antisymmetric by this definition because the hypothesis of the if-then statement is never satisfied. Therefore the antisymmetric property is vacuously true in this case.

Composition

Relations can often be defined in terms of other relations. For example, we can describe the "isGrandparentOf" relation in terms of the "isParentOf" relation by saying that $\langle a, c \rangle \in$ isGrandparentOf if and only if there is some b such that $\langle a, b \rangle$, $\langle b, c \rangle \in$ isParentOf. This example demonstrates the fundamental idea of composing binary relations.

Although we'll be dealing with binary relations over a single set, we'll define composition for general binary relations from one set to another set. If R is a binary relation from A to B and S is a binary relation from B to C, then the *composition* of R and S is the binary relation $R \circ S$ from A to C defined as follows:

$$a\,(R \circ S)\,c \text{ iff } a\,R\,b \text{ and } b\,S\,c \text{ for some } b \in B.$$

From the standpoint of ordered pairs this means that

$$\langle a, c \rangle \in R \circ S \text{ iff } \langle a, b \rangle \in R \text{ and } \langle b, c \rangle \in S \text{ for some } b \in B.$$

For example, we can compose the "isParentOf" relation with itself to construct the "isGrandparentOf" relation:

$$\text{isGrandparentOf} = \text{isParentOf} \circ \text{isParentOf}.$$

Since relations are just sets (of ordered pairs), it's clear that they can also be combined by the usual set operations of union, intersection, difference, and complement. For example, if we assume that "equal" and "less" are defined over the same set of numbers, then equal $\cap$ less = $\varnothing$.

An important property of composition, that follows easily from the definition, is that it is associative. In other words, $R \circ (S \circ T) = (R \circ S) \circ T$ for any binary relations R, S, and T. So we don't need to use parentheses when composing more than two relations.

If R is a binary relation on A, then we'll denote the composition of R with itself n times by writing R^n. For example, if we compose isParentOf with itself, we get some familiar names as follows:

$$\text{isParentOf}^2 = \text{isGrandparentOf},$$
$$\text{isParentOf}^3 = \text{isGreatGrandparentOf}.$$

We can give a precise definition of R^n as follows:

$$R^0 = \{\langle a, a\rangle \mid a \in A\} \quad \text{(basic equality)}$$
$$R^{n+1} = R^n \circ R.$$

We defined R^0 as the basic equality relation because we want to infer the equality $R^1 = R$ from the definition. To see this, notice the following evaluation of R^1:

$$R^1 = R^{0+1} = R^0 \circ R = \{\langle a, a\rangle \mid a \in A\} \circ R = R.$$

We also could have defined $R^{n+1} = R \circ R^n$ instead of $R^{n+1} = R^n \circ R$ because composition of binary operations is associative.

Let's note a few other interesting relationships between R and R^n. R^n inherits the reflexive, symmetric, and transitive properties from R. In other words, if R reflexive, then so is R^n. Similarly, if R is symmetric, then so is R^n. Also, if R is transitive, then so is R^n. On the other hand, if R is irreflexive, then it may not be the case that R^n is irreflexive. Similarly, if R is antisymmetric, it may not be the case that R^n is antisymmetric.

Closures

We've seen how to construct a new relation by composing two existing relations. Let's look at another way to construct a new relation from an existing relation. Here we'll start with a binary relation R and try to construct another relation containing R that also satisfies some particular property. For example, if we have the isParentOf relation, then we may want to use it to construct the isAncestorOf relation.

If R is a binary relation and p is some property, then the *p closure* of R is the smallest binary relation that contains R and satisfies property p. We'll denote the p closure of R by $p(R)$. If R already satisfies property p, then we have $R = p(R)$. We can state the relationship between R and $p(R)$ in several ways as follows: R is a *generator* of $p(R)$ or R *generates* $p(R)$ or $p(R)$ is *induced* by R.

We'll be concerned with the three properties reflexive, symmetric, and transitive. The *reflexive closure* of R is denoted by $r(R)$, the *symmetric closure* of R is denoted by $s(R)$, and the *transitive closure* of R is denoted by $t(R)$.

Our goal is to find some techniques to compute these closures. We'll start with a running example that will introduce the main ideas. Then we'll record the construction techniques. For our example we'll let $A = \{a, b, c\}$, and we'll let R be the following relation:

$$R = \{\langle a, a\rangle, \langle a, b\rangle, \langle b, a\rangle, \langle b, c\rangle\}.$$

Notice that R is neither reflexive nor symmetric nor transitive. We'll compute all three closures of R.

First we'll compute the reflexive closure $r(R)$. The two pairs missing from R are $\langle b, b\rangle$ and $\langle c, c\rangle$. So we can certainly compute $r(R)$ by forming the union of R and $\{\langle x, x\rangle \mid x \in A\}$. This gives us

$$r(R) = \{\langle a, a\rangle, \langle a, b\rangle, \langle b, a\rangle, \langle b, c\rangle, \langle b, b\rangle, \langle c, c\rangle\}.$$

Next we'll compute the symmetric closure $s(R)$. To create a symmetric relation, we need to add the pair $\langle c, b\rangle$. The *converse* of a binary relation R, which we denote by R^c, is defined as the following relation:

$$R^c = \{\langle x, y\rangle \mid \langle y, x\rangle \in R\}.$$

For example, the converse of "less" is "greater," and the converse of "equal" is itself. Notice that R is symmetric if and only if $R = R^c$. We can obtain $s(R)$ by simply forming the union of R with its converse R^c. For our example we have

$$s(R) = \{\langle a, a\rangle, \langle a, b\rangle, \langle b, a\rangle, \langle b, c\rangle, \langle c, b\rangle\}.$$

Lastly, we'll compute the transitive closure $t(R)$. For our example, R contains the pairs $\langle a, b\rangle$ and $\langle b, c\rangle$, but $\langle a, c\rangle$ is not in R. Similarly, R contains the pairs $\langle b, a\rangle$ and $\langle a, b\rangle$, but $\langle b, b\rangle$ is not in R. So $t(R)$ must contain the pairs $\langle a, c\rangle$ and $\langle b, b\rangle$. Is there some relation that we can union with R that will add the two needed pairs? The answer is yes, it's R^2. Notice that

$$R^2 = \{\langle a, a\rangle, \langle a, b\rangle, \langle b, b\rangle, \langle a, c\rangle\}.$$

It contains the two missing pairs along with two other pairs that are already in R. Thus we have

$$t(R) = R \cup R^2 = \{\langle a, a\rangle, \langle a, b\rangle, \langle b, a\rangle, \langle b, c\rangle, \langle a, c\rangle, \langle b, b\rangle\}.$$

The construction of the $t(R)$ may take more work for different values of R. For example, if $R = \{<a, b>, <b, c>, <c, d>\}$, then the pair $<a, d>$ belongs to $t(R)$ and we could get it from R^3. Here are the the general construction techniques for the three closures.

Constructing Closures (2.9)

If R is a binary relation over a set A, then:
a) $r(R) = R \cup R^0$ (R^0 is the equality relation).
b) $s(R) = R \cup R^c$ (R^c is the converse relation).
c) $t(R) = R \cup R^2 \cup R^3 \cup \ldots$.
d) If A is finite with n elements, then $t(R) = R \cup R^2 \cup \cdots \cup R^n$.

Equivalence Relations

The word "equivalent" is used in many ways. For example, we've all seen statements like "Two triangles are equivalent if their corresponding angles are equal." We want to find some general properties that describe the idea of "equivalence." We'll start by discussing the idea of "equality" because, to most people, "equal" things are examples of "equivalent" things, whatever meaning is attached to the word "equivalent."

Equality is important in computer science because programs use equality tests on data. If a programming language doesn't provide an equality test for certain data, then the programmer may need to implement such a test. Are there some fundamental properties that hold for any definition of equality on a set A? Certainly we want to have $x = x$ for each element x in A (the basic equality on A). Also, whenever $x = y$, it ought to follow that $y = x$. Lastly, if $x = y$ and $y = z$, then $x = z$ should hold. Of course, these are the three properties reflexive, symmetric, and transitive.

Most equalities are more than just basic equality. That is, they equate different syntactic objects that have the same meaning. In these cases the symmetric and transitive properties are needed to convey our intuitive notion of equality. For example, the following statements are true if we let "=" mean "has the same value as":

If $2 + 3 = 1 + 4$, then $1 + 4 = 2 + 3$.

If $2 + 5 = 1 + 6$ and $1 + 6 = 3 + 4$, then $2 + 5 = 3 + 4$.

Now we're ready to define equivalence. Any binary relation that is reflexive, symmetric, and transitive is called an *equivalence* relation. Sometimes people refer to an equivalence relation as an RST relation in order to remember the three properties.

Partitioning

An important property of any equivalence relation on a set is that it induces a partitioning of the set into a collection of subsets, each subset containing elements that are equivalent to each other. By a *partition* of a set we mean a collection of subsets that are disjoint from each other and whose union is the whole set. For example, the equality relation on the set $A = \{a, b, c\}$ induces a partitioning of A into the three singleton subsets $\{a\}$, $\{b\}$, and $\{c\}$. We write the partition as a set of sets as follows:

$$\{\{a\}, \{b\}, \{c\}\}.$$

On the other hand, if we start with a partition of a set, then we can define an equivalence relation on the set. We simply agree to say that two elements are equivalent whenever they are in the same subset of the partition. For example, suppose we have the following partition of the set $\{a, b, c, d, e\}$:

$$\{\{a, b\}, \{c, d, e\}\}.$$

This partition defines an equivalence relation in which each element is equivalent to itself, a is equivalent to b, and the three elements c, d, and e are equivalent to each other.

We can state the important connection between equivalence relations and partitions as follows:

Equivalence Relations and Partitions   (2.10)

   If R is an equivalence relation on the set S, then R induces a partition of S. Conversely, if P is a partition of a set S, then P induces an equivalence relation on S.

Let's introduce some notation for partitions and equivalence relations. Let R be an equivalence relation on a set S. If $x \in S$, then we use the symbol $[x]$ to denote the subset of S consisting of all elements that are equivalent to x. So $[x]$ is the following set:

$$[x] = \{y \mid y \in S \text{ and } x R y\}.$$

The set $[x]$ is called an *equivalence class*. We say, "the equivalence class of x," or simply "bracket x." Of course, we know that $x \in [x]$ because $x R x$. Notice also that any element of $[x]$ can be used to represent the set. For example, suppose we have an equivalence class $[x] = \{x, a, y, m\}$. Then we can also represent this set in any of the following ways:

$$[a] = \{x, a, y, m\},$$
$$[y] = \{x, a, y, m\},$$
$$[m] = \{x, a, y, m\}.$$

The partition of S consisting of the collection of all such equivalence classes is called the *partition* of S by R and is denoted by S/R. We also can say "S mod R," or "the quotient of S by R." We can write the partition S/R as the following set of sets:

$$S/R = \{[x] \mid x \in S\}.$$

Partitions help us simplify our thinking about sets of individuals by partitioning them into groups that are often easier to think about. For example, let S denote the set of all students at some university, and let M be the relation on S that pairs two students if they have the same major. (Assume here that every student has exactly one major.) M is clearly an equivalence relation on S, and it follows that S/M is the collection of sets of people sharing the same major. For example, one equivalence class in S/M is the set of computer science majors. So the partition S/M has the following general form:

$$S/M = \{\text{computer science majors, math majors, ...}\}.$$

The partition S/M can also be pictured by a Venn diagram as shown in Figure 2.3.

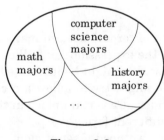

Figure 2.3

Generating Equivalence Relations

What is the smallest equivalence relation containing a relation R? Do we just take the reflexive closure of R, then the symmetric closure of $r(R)$, and finally the transitive closure of $sr(R)$, resulting in $tsr(R)$? Is the result an equivalence relation? As we shall see, the answer is yes to all these questions. Does it make any difference if we apply closures in another order? For example, what about $str(R)$?

An example will suffice to show that $str(R)$ need not be an equivalence relation. Let $A = \{a, b, c\}$ and $R = \{\langle a, b \rangle, \langle a, c \rangle, \langle b, b \rangle\}$. Then

$$str(R) = \{\langle a, a \rangle, \langle b, b \rangle, \langle c, c \rangle, \langle a, b \rangle, \langle b, a \rangle, \langle a, c \rangle, \langle c, a \rangle\}.$$

This relation is reflexive and symmetric, but it's not transitive. On the other hand, we have $tsr(R) = A \times A$, which is an equivalence relation. For any relation R, can it be that $tsr(R)$ is an equivalence relation? The answer is yes, and it is also the smallest equivalence relation containing R. We'll state the result as follows:

The Smallest Equivalence Relation   (2.11)

If R is a binary relation over A, then $tsr(R)$ is the smallest equivalence relation that contains R.

Proof: We'll leave the proof that $tsr(R)$ is an equivalence relation as an exercise. To see that it's the smallest equivalence relation containing R, we'll let T be an arbitrary equivalence relation containing R. So $R \subset T$. Apply tsr to both R and T to obtain $tsr(R) \subset tsr(T)$. But T is an equivalence relation. Therefore $tsr(T) = T$. Thus we have $tsr(R) \subset T$. So $tsr(R)$ is contained in every equivalence relation that contains R. Thus it's the smallest equivalence relation containing R.   QED.

Order Relations

Each day we see the idea of "order" used in many different ways. For example, we might encounter the expression $1 < 2$. We might notice that someone is older than someone else. We might be interested in the third component of the tuple $\langle x, d, c, m \rangle$. We might try to follow a recipe. Or we might see that the word "aardvark" resides at a certain place in the dictionary. The concept of order occurs in many different forms.

To have an ordering, we need a set of elements together with a binary relation having certain properties. What are these properties? Well, our intuition tells us that an ordering should be transitive. For example, if a, b, and c are natural numbers and $a < b$ and $b < c$, then we have $a < c$. Our intuition also tells us that an ordering should be antisymmetric because we don't want distinct elements "preceding" each other. For example, if $a \leq b$ and $b \leq a$, we certainly want $a = b$.

Some orders are reflexive, and some are not. For example, over the natural numbers we recognize that the relations $<$ and $\leq$ are orders because they are both transitive and antisymmetric, even though $<$ is irreflexive and $\leq$ is reflexive. So the two essential properties of any kind of order are antisymmetric and transitive.

EXAMPLE 1 (*Pancake Recipe*). Suppose we have the following recipe for making pancakes:

1. Mix the dry ingredients (flour, sugar, baking powder) in a bowl.
2. Mix the wet ingredients (milk, eggs) in a bowl.
3. Mix the wet and dry ingredients together.
4. Oil the pan. (It's an old pan.)
5. Heat the pan.
6. Make a test pancake and throw it away.
7. Make pancakes.

Steps 1 through 7 indicate an ordering for the steps of the recipe. But the steps could also be done in some other order. To help us discover some other orders, let's define a relation R on the seven steps of the pancake recipe as follows:

$$i R j \text{ means that step } i \text{ must be done before step } j.$$

Notice that R is antisymmetric and transitive. We can picture R as the digraph (without the transitive arrows) in Figure 2.4.

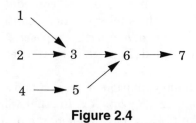

Figure 2.4

The graph helps us pick out different orders for the steps of the recipe. For example, the following ordering of steps will produce pancakes just as well:

$$4, 5, 2, 1, 3, 6, 7.$$

So there are several ways to perform the recipe. In fact, if three people were available, they could work in parallel doing tasks 1, 2, and 4 at the same time. ◆

This example demonstrates that different orderings for time-oriented tasks are possible whenever some tasks can be done at different times without changing the outcome. The orderings can be discovered by modeling the tasks by a binary relation R defined by

$i R j$ means that step i must be done before step j.

Notice that R is irreflexive because time-oriented tasks can't be done before themselves. If there are at least two tasks that are not related by R, as in Example 1, then there will be at least two different orderings of the tasks.

Now let's get down to business and discuss the basic ideas and techniques of ordering.

Partial Orders

A binary relation is called a *partial order* if it is antisymmetric and transitive. The set over which a partial order is defined is called a *partially ordered set*—or *poset* for short. If we want to emphasize the fact that R is the partial order that makes S a poset, we'll write the pair $\langle S, R \rangle$ and call it a poset. For example, in our pancake example we defined a partial order R on the set of recipe steps $\{1, 2, 3, 4, 5, 6, 7\}$. So we can say that $\langle \{1, 2, 3, 4, 5, 6, 7\}, R \rangle$ is a poset. There are many more examples of partial orders. For example, $\langle \mathbb{N}, < \rangle$ and $\langle \mathbb{N}, \leq \rangle$ are posets because the relations $<$ and $\leq$ are both antisymmetric and transitive.

The word "partial" is used in the definition because we include the possibility that some elements may not be related to each other, as in the pancake recipe example. For another example, consider the subset relation on power($\{a, b, c\}$). Certainly the subset relation is antisymmetric and transitive. So we can say that $\langle$power($\{a, b, c\}$), $\subset \rangle$ is a poset. Notice that there are some subsets that are not related. For example, the sets $\{a, b\}$ and $\{a, c\}$ are not related by $\subset$.

Suppose R is a binary relation on a set S and $x, y \in S$. We say that x and y are *comparable* if either $x R y$ or $y R x$. In other words, elements that are related are comparable. If every pair of elements in a partial order are comparable, then the order is called a *total* order (also called a *linear* order). If R is a total order on the set S, then we also say that S is a *totally ordered set* or a *linearly ordered set*. For example, the natural numbers are totally ordered by both "less" and "lessOrEqual." In other words, $\langle \mathbb{N}, < \rangle$ and $\langle \mathbb{N}, \leq \rangle$ are totally ordered sets.

We should note that the literature contains two different definitions of partial order. All definitions require the antisymmetric and transitive properties, but some authors also require the reflexive property. Since we require only the antisymmetric and transitive properties, if it's the case that a partial order is reflexive and we wish to emphasize it, we'll call it a *reflexive partial order*—or a RAT to remember the properties reflexive, antisymmetric, and transitive. For example, $\leq$ is a reflexive partial order on the integers. If a partial order is irreflexive and we wish to emphasize it, we'll call it an *irreflexive partial order*. For example, $<$ is an irreflexive partial order on the integers. When authors define partial order to mean RAT, they normally use the term quasi-order to mean irreflexive partial order.

When talking about partial orders, we'll often use the symbols $\prec$ and $\preceq$ to stand for an irreflexive partial order and a reflexive partial order, respectively. We can read $a \prec b$ as "a is less than b," and we can read $a \preceq b$ as "a is less than or equal to b." The two symbols can be defined in terms of each other. For example, if $\langle A, \prec \rangle$ is a poset, then we can define the relation $\preceq$ in terms of $\prec$ by writing

$$\preceq \; = \; \prec \cup \; \{\langle x, x \rangle \mid x \in A\}.$$

In other words, $\preceq$ is the reflexive closure of $\prec$. So $x \preceq y$ always means $x \prec y$ or $x = y$. Similarly, if $\langle B, \preceq \rangle$ is a poset, then we can define the relation $\prec$ in terms of $\preceq$ by writing

$$\prec \; = \; \preceq - \; \{\langle x, x \rangle \mid x \in B\}.$$

Therefore $x \prec y$ always means $x \preceq y$ and $x \neq y$. We also write the expression $y \succ x$ to mean the same thing as $x \prec y$.

A set of elements in a poset is called a *chain* if all the elements are comparable—linked—to each other. For example, any totally ordered set is itself a chain. A sequence of elements $x_1, x_2, x_3, \ldots$ in a poset is said to be *descending chain* if $x_i \succ x_{i+1}$ for each $i \geq 1$. We can write the descending chain in the following familiar form:

$$x_1 \succ x_2 \succ x_3 \succ \cdots .$$

For example, $4 > 2 > 0 > -2 > -4 > -6 > \ldots$ is a descending chain in $\langle \mathbb{Z}, < \rangle$. For another example, $\{a, b, c\} \supset \{a, b\} \supset \{a\} \supset \varnothing$ is a finite descending chain in $\langle \text{power}(\{a, b, c\}, \subset \rangle$. We can define an *ascending chain* of elements in a similar way.

If $x \prec y$, then we say that x is a *predecessor* of y, or y is a *successor* of x. Suppose that $x \prec y$ and there are no elements between x and y. In other words, suppose we have the following situation:

$$\{z \in A \mid x \prec z \prec y\} = \varnothing.$$

When this is the case, we say that x is an *immediate predecessor* of y, or y is an *immediate successor* of x. In a finite poset an element with a successor has an immediate successor. Some infinite posets also have this property. For example, every natural number x has an immediate successor $x + 1$ with respect to the "less" relation. But no rational number has an immediate successor with respect to the "less" relation.

A poset can be represented by a special graph called a *poset diagram* or a *Hasse diagram*—after the mathematician Helmut Hasse (1898–1979). Whenever $x \prec y$ and x is an immediate predecessor of y, then place an edge $\langle x, y \rangle$ in the poset diagram with x at a lower level than y. A poset diagram can often help us observe certain properties of a poset. For example, the two poset diagram in Figure 2.5 represents the pancake recipe poset from Example 1.

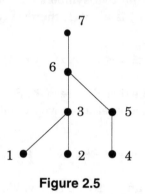

Figure 2.5

Bounds

When we have a partially ordered set, it's natural to use words like "minimal," "least," "maximal," and "greatest." Let's give these words some formal definitions.

Suppose that S is any nonempty subset of a poset P. An element $x \in S$ is called a *minimal element* of S if x has no predecessors in S. An element $x \in S$ is called the *least element* of S if x is minimal and $x \preceq y$ for all $y \in S$. For example, in the poset $\langle \text{power}(\{a, b, c\}), \subset \rangle$, the subset $\{\{a, b\}, \{a\}, \{b\}\}$ has two minimal elements, $\{a\}$ and $\{b\}$. The power set itself has least element $\varnothing$.

In a similar way we can define *maximal elements* and the *greatest element* of a subset of a poset. For example, in the poset $\langle \text{power}(\{a, b, c\}), \subset \rangle$, the subset $\{\varnothing, \{a\}, \{b\}\}$ has two maximal elements, $\{a\}$ and $\{b\}$. The power set itself has greatest element $\{a, b, c\}$.

Some sets may not have any minimal elements yet still be bounded below by some element. For example, the set of positive rational numbers has no least element yet is bounded below by the number 0. Let's introduce some standard terminology that can be used to discuss ideas like this.

If S is a nonempty subset of a poset P, an element $x \in P$ is called a *lower bound* of S if $x \preceq y$ for all $y \in S$. An element $x \in P$ is called the *greatest lower bound* (or *glb*) of S if x is a lower bound and $z \preceq x$ for all lower bounds z of S.

The expression glb(*S*) denotes the greatest lower bound of *S*, if it exists. For example, if we let $\mathbb{Q}^+$ denote the set of positive rational numbers, then over the poset $\langle \mathbb{Q}, \leq \rangle$ we have glb($\mathbb{Q}^+$) = 0.

In a similar way we define upper bounds for a subset *S* of the poset *P*. An element $x \in P$ is called an *upper bound* of *S* if $y \preceq x$ for all $y \in S$. An element $x \in P$ is called the *least upper bound* (or *lub*) of *S* if *x* is an upper bound and $x \preceq z$ for all upper bounds *z* of *S*. The expression lub(*S*) denotes the least upper bound of *S*, if it exists. For example, lub($\mathbb{Q}^+$) does not exist in the poset $\langle \mathbb{Q}, \leq \rangle$.

For another example, in the poset $\langle \mathbb{N}, \leq \rangle$, every finite subset has a glb—the least element—and a lub—the greatest element. Every infinite subset has a glb but no infinite subset has an upper bound.

Can subsets have upper bounds without having a least upper bound? Sure. Here's an example.

EXAMPLE 2. Suppose the set {1, 2, 3, 4, 5, 6} represents six time-oriented tasks. You can think of the numbers as chapters in a book, as processes to be executed on a computer, or as the steps in a recipe for making ice cream. In any case, suppose the tasks are partially ordered according to the poset diagram in Figure 2.6.

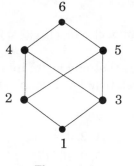

Figure 2.6

The subset {2, 3} is bounded above, but it has no least upper bound. Notice that 4, 5, and 6 are all upper bounds of {2, 3}, but none of them is a least upper bound. ◆

Well-Founded Orders

Let's look at a special property of the natural numbers. Suppose we're given a descending chain of natural numbers, starting at x_1, as follows:

$$x_1 > x_2 > x_3 > \cdots .$$

Can this descending chain continue forever? Of course not. We know that 0 is the least natural number, so the given chain must stop after only a finite number of terms. For example, if $x_1 = 4$, then there are at most five terms in any such chain. This is not an earthshaking discovery, but we'll state it anyway:

Every descending chain of natural numbers is finite in length.

Not all posets have such a property. The integers don't satisfy such a property, nor do the positive rational numbers, as the following examples show:

$$2 > 0 > -2 > -4 > \cdots$$

$$\frac{1}{2} > \frac{1}{3} > \frac{1}{4} > \frac{1}{5} > \cdots .$$

A poset is called a *well-founded set* if every descending chain of elements is finite. If a poset is well-founded, its partial order is called a *well-founded order*. Thus $\mathbb{N}$ is a well-founded set with respect to the usual "less" relation. Similarly, the power set of a finite set is well-founded by the subset relation. For example, the following expression displays a longest descending chain starting with the set $\{a, b, c\}$:

$$\{a, b, c\} \supset \{b, c\} \supset \{c\} \supset \varnothing.$$

For another example, notice that any set of integers with a least element is well-founded by the "less" relation. For example, the following sets of integers are well-founded:

$$\{1, 2, 3, 4, \ldots\},$$
$$\{5, 9, 13, 17, \ldots\}.$$

Another important property of well-founded sets is that every nonempty subset of a well-founded set has a minimal element. For example, the collection $\{\{a\}, \{b\}, \{a, b\}\}$ has two minimal elements with respect to the subset operation. The possession of minimal elements by nonempty subsets is equivalent to the property of well-foundedness, which we'll state as follows:

Descending Chains and Minimality   (2.12)

If A is a well-founded set, then every nonempty subset of A has a minimal element. Conversely, if every nonempty subset of A has a minimal element, then A is well-founded.

Proof: We'll prove the first half and leave the converse as an exercise. To prove this statement, suppose S is a nonempty subset a well-founded set W and x_1 is some element of S. If x_1 is a minimal element of S, then we are done. So assume that x_1 is not a minimal element of S. Then x_1 must have a predecessor x_2 in S —otherwise, x_1 would be a minimal element of S. If x_2 is a minimal element of S, then we are done. If x_2 is not a minimal element of S, then it has a predecessor x_3 in S, and so on. If we continue in this manner, we will obtain a descending chain of distinct elements in S:

$$x_1 \succ x_2 \succ x_3 \succ \cdots .$$

Since W is well-founded, this chain stops at some value, which must be a minimal element of S.   QED.

It follows from (2.12) that the property of finite descending chains is equivalent to the property of nonempty subsets having minimal elements. In other words, if a poset has one of the properties, then it also has the other property. Thus it is also correct to define a well-founded set to be a poset with the property that every nonempty subset has a minimal element. We will call this latter property the *minimum condition* on a poset.[†]

Whenever a well-founded set is totally ordered, then each nonempty subset has a single minimal element, the least element. Such a set is called a *well-ordered set*. So a well-ordered set is a totally ordered set such that every nonempty subset has a least element. For example, $\mathbb{N}$ is well-ordered by the "less" relation.

Constructing Well-Founded Orderings

Collections of strings, lists, trees, graphs, or other structures that programs process can usually be made into well-founded sets by defining an appropriate order relation. For example, any finite set can be made into a well-founded set—actually a well-ordered set—by simply listing its elements in any order we wish, letting the leftmost element be the least element.

Suppose we want to define a well-founded order on some infinite set S. A simple and useful technique is to associate each element of S with some element in an existing well-founded set. For example, the natural numbers are well-founded by $<$. So any function $f : S \to \mathbb{N}$ can be used to define a well-founded ordering on S by relating pairs of elements $x, y \in S$ as follows:

$$x \prec y \quad \text{means} \quad f(x) < f(y). \tag{2.13}$$

[†] Other names for well-founded set are *poset with minimum condition, poset with descending chain condition,* and *Artinian poset,* after Emil Artin, who studied algebraic structures with the descending chain condition. Some people use the term *Noetherian,* after Emmy Noether, who studied algebraic structures with the ascending chain condition.

Does the new relation $\prec$ make S into a well-founded set? Sure. Suppose we have a descending chain of elements in S as follows:

$$x_1 \succ x_2 \succ x_3 \succ \cdots .$$

The chain must stop because $x \succ y$ is defined to mean $f(x) > f(y)$, and we know that any descending chain of natural numbers must stop.

EXAMPLE 3. Let's look at a few more examples of well-founded orders.

    a) If L and M are lists, let $L \prec M$ mean length$(L) <$ length(M).

    b) If B and C are trees, let $B \prec C$ mean nodes$(B) <$ nodes(C), where nodes is the function that counts the number of nodes in a tree.

    c) If B and C are trees, let $B \prec C$ mean leaves$(B) <$ leaves(C), where leaves is the function that returns the number of leaves in a tree.

    d) For nonempty trees B and C, let $B \prec C$ mean depth$(B) <$ depth(C).
      ◆

Exercises

1. Draw a picture of the directed graph that corresponds to each of the following binary relations.

    a. $\{\langle a, a\rangle, \langle b, b\rangle, \langle c, c\rangle\}$.

    b. $\{\langle a, b\rangle, \langle b, b\rangle, \langle b, c\rangle, \langle c, a\rangle\}$.

    c. The relation $\leq$ on the set $\{1, 2, 3\}$.

2. Write down all the properties that each of the following relations satisfies from among the three properties reflexive, symmetric, and transitive.

    a. The relation R over the real numbers $R = \{\langle a, b\rangle \mid a^2 + b^2 = 1\}$.

    b. The relation R over the real numbers $R = \{\langle a, b\rangle \mid a^2 = b^2\}$.

    c. The relation $R = \{\langle x, y\rangle \mid x \bmod y = 0 \text{ and } x, y \in \{1, 2, 3, 4\}\}$.

3. Explain why the empty relation $\varnothing$ is symmetric and transitive.

4. Write down suitable names for each of the following compositions.

    a. isChildOf ∘ isChildOf.

    b. isSisterOf ∘ isParentOf.

    c. isSonOf ∘ isSisterOf.

    d. isChildOf ∘ isParentOf.

5. For each of the following conditions, find the smallest relation over the set $A = \{a, b, c\}$. Express each answer as a graph.

   a. Reflexive but not symmetric and not transitive.

   b. Symmetric but not reflexive and not transitive.

   c. Transitive but not reflexive and not symmetric.

   d. Reflexive and symmetric but not transitive.

   e. Reflexive and transitive but not symmetric.

   f. Symmetric and transitive but not reflexive.

   g. Reflexive, symmetric, and transitive.

6. What is the reflexive closure of the empty binary relation $\varnothing$ over a set A?

7. Find the symmetric closure of each of the following relations over the set $\{a, b, c\}$.

   a. $\varnothing$.

   b. $\{\langle a, b \rangle, \langle b, a \rangle\}$.

   c. $\{\langle a, b \rangle, \langle b, c \rangle\}$.

   d. $\{\langle a, a \rangle, \langle a, b \rangle, \langle c, b \rangle, \langle c, a \rangle\}$.

8. Find the transitive closure of each of the following relations over the set $\{a, b, c, d\}$.

   a. $\varnothing$.

   b. $\{\langle a, b \rangle, \langle a, c \rangle, \langle b, c \rangle\}$.

   c. $\{\langle a, b \rangle, \langle b, a \rangle\}$.

   d. $\{\langle a, b \rangle, \langle b, c \rangle, \langle c, d \rangle, \langle d, a \rangle\}$.

9. Find an appropriate name for the transitive closure of each of the following relations.

   a. IsParentOf.

   b. IsChildOf.

   c. $\{\langle x + 1, x \rangle \mid x \in \mathbb{N}\}$.

10. For each of the following relations, either prove that it is an equivalence relation or prove that it is not an equivalence relation.

   a. $a \sim b$ iff $a + b$ is even, over the set of integers.

   b. $a \sim b$ iff $a + b$ is odd, over the set of integers.

   c. $a \sim b$ iff $a \cdot b > 0$, over the set of nonzero rational numbers.

   d. $a \sim b$ iff a/b is an integer, over the set of nonzero rational numbers.

   e. $a \sim b$ iff $a - b$ is an integer, over the set of rational numbers.

   f. $a \sim b$ iff $|a - b| \leq 2$, over the set of natural numbers.

11. Let R be the relation on $\mathbb{N}$ defined by $a \, R \, b$ iff $a \bmod 4 = b \bmod 4$ and $a \bmod 6 = b \bmod 6$. Show that R is an equivalence relation, and describe the partition $\mathbb{N}/R$.

12. Let R be the relation on $\mathbb{N}$ defined by $a \, R \, b$ iff either $a \bmod 4 = b \bmod 4$ or $a \bmod 6 = b \bmod 6$. Show that R is not an equivalence relation on $\mathbb{N}$ and thus there is no partition of the form $\mathbb{N}/R$.

13. State whether each of the following relations is a partial order.
    a. isFatherOf.   b. isAncestorOf.   c. isOlderThan.
    d. isSisterOf   e. $\{\langle a, b\rangle, \langle a, a\rangle, \langle b, a\rangle\}$.   f. $\{\langle 2, 1\rangle, \langle 1, 3\rangle, \langle 2, 3\rangle\}$.

14. Draw a poset diagram for each of the following partially ordered relations.
    a. $\{\langle a, a\rangle, \langle a, b\rangle, \langle b, c\rangle, \langle a, c\rangle, \langle a, d\rangle\}$.
    b. power($\{a, b, c\}$), with the subset relation.
    c. Lists[$\{a, b\}$], where $L \prec M$ if length(L) < length(M).
    d. The set of all binary trees over the set $\{a, b\}$ that contain either one or two nodes. Let $s \prec t$ mean that s is either the left or right subtree of t.

15. For each set S, show that the given partial order on S is well-founded.
    a. Let S be a set of trees. Let $s \prec t$ mean that s has fewer nodes than t.
    b. Let S be a set of trees. Let $s \prec t$ mean that s has fewer leaves than t.
    c. Let S be a set of lists. Let $L \prec M$ mean that length(L) < length(M).

16. Suppose we define the relation R on $\mathbb{N} \times \mathbb{N}$ as follows:

    $$\langle a, b\rangle \prec \langle c, d\rangle \quad \text{if and only if} \quad \max\{a, b\} < \max\{c, d\}.$$

    Is $\mathbb{N} \times \mathbb{N}$ well-founded with respect to $\prec$?

2.4 Inductive Proof

This section concentrates on the inductive proof technique. We'll see that the technique provides us with a means to prove infinitely many statements in just two steps.

The Idea of Induction

Suppose we want to find the sum of numbers $1 + 2 + \cdots + n$ for any natural number n. Consider the following two programs, written by two different students, to calculate this sum:

$$f(n) = \text{if } n = 0 \text{ then } 0 \text{ else } n + f(n-1),$$

$$g(n) = \frac{n\,(n+1)}{2}.$$

Are these programs correct? That is, do they both compute the correct value of the sum $1 + 2 + \cdots + n$? We can test a few cases such as $n = 0, n = 1, n = 2$ until we feel confident that the programs are correct. Or maybe we just can't get any feeling of confidence in these programs. Is there a way to prove, once and for all, that these programs are correct for all natural numbers n? Let's look at the second program. If it's correct, then the following equation must be true for all natural numbers n:

$$1 + 2 + \cdots + n = \frac{n\,(n+1)}{2}.$$

Certainly we don't have the time to check it for the infinity of natural numbers. Is there some other way to prove it? Happily, we will be able to prove the infinitely many cases in just two steps with a technique called proof by induction, which we discuss next.

Interestingly, the technique that we present is based on the fact that any nonempty subset of the natural numbers has a least element. Recall that this is the same as saying that any descending chain of natural numbers is finite. In fact, this is just a statement that $\mathbb{N}$ is a well-founded set. In fact we can generalize a bit. Let m be an integer, and let W be the following set:

$$W = \{n \mid n \text{ is an integer and } n \geq m\}.$$

Every nonempty subset of W has a least element. Let's see whether this property can help us find a tool to prove infinitely many things in just two steps. The technique is called the principle of mathematical induction, which we state as follows:

The Principle of Mathematical Induction (2.14)

Let $m \in \mathbb{Z}$ and suppose that the following two statements are true:

1. $P(m)$ is true.
2. If $P(k)$ is true for an arbitrary $k \geq m$, then $P(k + 1)$ is true.

Then $P(n)$ is true for all $n \geq m$.

Proof: Let $S = \{n \mid n \geq m \text{ and } P(n) \text{ is false}\}$. If we can show that $S = \varnothing$, then we'll be done. Assume, by way of contradiction, that $S \neq \varnothing$. Then there is a least element $x \in S$. In other words, x is the smallest integer such that $x \geq m$

and $P(x)$ is false. Since the first statement of the hypothesis tells us that $P(m)$ is true, it must be the case that $x > m$. Therefore $x - 1 \geq m$. Now look at $P(x - 1)$. If $P(x - 1)$ is false, then $x - 1$ is be an element in S that is less than its least element x. This forces us to conclude that $P(x - 1)$ is true. Now we'll apply the first statement of the hypothesis. Since $P(x - 1)$ is true, it follows that $P(x - 1 + 1)$ is true. This tells us that $P(x)$ is true, which contradicts our assumption that $P(x)$ is false. Therefore $S = \varnothing$. So $P(n)$ is true for all $n \geq m$. QED.

The principle of mathematical induction contains a technique to prove that infinitely many statements are true in just two steps. Quite a savings in time. Let's look at an example. This proof technique is just what we need to prove our opening example about computing the sum of the first n natural numbers.

EXAMPLE 1 (*A Correct Closed Form*). Let's prove once and for all that the following equation is true for all natural numbers n:

$$1 + 2 + \cdots + n = \frac{n\,(n + 1)}{2}. \tag{2.15}$$

To see how to use (2.14), we can let $P(n)$ denote the above equation. Now we need to perform two steps. First, we have to show that $P(0)$ is true. Second, we have to assume that $P(k)$ is true and then prove that $P(k + 1)$ is true. When $n = 0$, equation (2.15) becomes the true statement

$$0 = \frac{0\,(0 + 1)}{2}.$$

Therefore $P(0)$ is true. Now assume that $P(k)$ is true. This means that we assume that the following equation is true:

$$1 + 2 + \cdots + k = \frac{k\,(k + 1)}{2}.$$

To prove that $P(k + 1)$ is true, start on the left side of the equation for the expression $P(k + 1)$:

$$
\begin{aligned}
1 + 2 + \cdots + k + (k + 1) &= (1 + \cdots + k) + (k + 1) &\text{(associate)} \\[2mm]
&= \frac{k\,(k + 1)}{2} + (k + 1) &\text{(assumption)} \\[2mm]
&= \frac{(k + 1)\,((k + 1) + 1)}{2} &\text{(arithmetic)}.
\end{aligned}
$$

The last term is the right-hand side of $P(k + 1)$. Therefore $P(k + 1)$ is true. So we have performed both steps of (2.14). It follows that $P(n)$ is true for all $n \in \mathbb{N}$. In other words, equation (2.15) is true for all natural numbers $n \geq 0$. QED. ◆

EXAMPLE 2 (*A Correct Summation Program*). We show that the following if-then-else program computes the sum $1 + 2 + \cdots + n$ for all natural numbers n:

$$f(n) = \text{if } n = 0 \text{ then } 0 \text{ else } f(n - 1) + n.$$

Proof: For each $n \in \mathbb{N}$, let $P(n) = $ "$f(n) = 1 + 2 + \cdots + n$." We want to show that $P(n)$ is true for all $n \in \mathbb{N}$. To start, notice that $f(0) = 0$. Thus $P(0)$ is true. Now assume that $P(k)$ is true for some $k \in \mathbb{N}$. Now we must furnish a proof that $P(k + 1)$ is true. Starting on the left side of the statement for $P(k + 1)$, we can proceed as follows:

$$
\begin{aligned}
f(k + 1) &= f(k + 1 - 1) + (k + 1) && \text{(definition of } f) \\
&= f(k) + (k + 1) \\
&= (1 + 2 + \cdots + k) + (k + 1) && \text{(induction assumption)} \\
&= 1 + 2 + \cdots + (k + 1).
\end{aligned}
$$

So if $P(k)$ is true, then $P(k + 1)$ is true. Therefore by (2.14), $P(n)$ is true for all $n \in \mathbb{N}$. In other words, $f(n) = 1 + 2 + \cdots + n$ for all $n \in \mathbb{N}$. QED. ◆

Here is a collection of closed forms for some elementary sums. We've already proven one of them. We'll leave the others as exercises.

Closed Forms of Elementary Finite Sums (2.16)

a) $\displaystyle\sum_{i=1}^{n} i = \frac{n(n + 1)}{2}.$

b) $\displaystyle\sum_{i=1}^{n} i^2 = \frac{n(n + 1)(2n + 1)}{6}.$

c) $\displaystyle\sum_{i=0}^{n} a^i = \frac{a^{n+1} - 1}{a - 1} \quad (a \neq 1).$

d) $\displaystyle\sum_{i=1}^{n} ia^i = \frac{a - (n + 1)a^{n+1} + na^{n+2}}{(a - 1)^2} \quad (a \neq 1).$

Sometimes, (2.14) does not have enough horsepower to do the job. For example, we might need to assume more than (2.14) will allow us, or we might be dealing with structures that are not numbers, such as lists, strings, or binary trees, and there may be no easy way to apply (2.14). The solution to many of these problems is a stronger version of induction based on well-founded sets. That's next.

Well-Founded Induction

Now we're going to extend the idea of induction to well-founded sets. Recall that a well-founded set is a poset whose nonempty subsets have minimal elements or, equivalently, every descending chain of elements is finite. We'll describe a technique for proving a collection of statements of the form $P(x)$ for each x in a well-founded set W. The technique is, of course, called well-founded induction.

Well-Founded Induction (2.17)

Let W be a well-founded set and let the following two statements be true:

1. $P(m)$ is true for all minimal elements $m \in W$.

2. If $P(k)$ is true for all elements k that are predecessors of an arbitrary element of n of W, then $P(n)$ is true.

Then $P(n)$ is true for all n in W.

Proof: Let $S = \{n \mid n \in W$ and $P(n) = $ false$\}$. If we can show that $S = \varnothing$, then we'll be done. The proof is very similar to the proof of (2.14).   QED.

Now we can state an important corollary of (2.17), which lets us make a bigger assumption than we were allowed in the princlple of mathematical induction (2.14):

Second Principle of Mathematical Induction (2.18)

Let $m \in \mathbb{Z}$ and assume that the following statements are true:

1. $P(m)$ is true.

2. If n is an arbitrary integer $n > m$ and $P(k)$ is true for $m \leq k < n$, then $P(n)$ is true.

Then $P(n)$ is true for all integers $n \geq m$.

EXAMPLE 3 (*Prime Number Theorem*). We want to prove that every natural number n ≥ 2 is a product of prime numbers. Proof: For $n \geq 2$, let $P(n)$ be the statement "n is a product of prime numbers." We need to show that $P(n)$ is true for all $n \geq 2$. Since 2 is prime, it follows that $P(2)$ is true. So Step 1 of (2.18) is finished. For Step 2 we'll assume that $n > 2$ and $P(k)$ is true for $2 \leq k < n$. With this assumption we must show that $P(n)$ is true. If n is prime, then $P(n)$ is true. So assume that n is not prime. Then $n = xy$, where $2 \leq x < n$ and $2 \leq y < n$. By our assumption, $P(x)$ and $P(y)$ are both true, which means that x and y are products of primes. Therefore n is a product of primes. So $P(n)$ is true. Now (2.18) implies that $P(n)$ is true for all $n \geq 2$. *Note*: We can't use (2.14) for this proof because its induction assumption is the single statement that $P(n - 1)$ is true. We need the stronger assumption that $P(k)$ is true for $2 \leq k < n$ to allow us to say that $P(x)$ and $P(y)$ are true.   QED.   ♦

Now let's do an example that does not involve numbers. Thus we'll be using well-founded induction (2.17). We should note that some people refer to well-founded induction as "structural induction" because well-founded sets can contain structures other than numbers, such as lists, strings, binary trees, and products of sets. Whatever it's called, let's see how to use it.

EXAMPLE 4 (*Correctness of MakeSet*). The following function is supposed to take any list K as input and return the list obtained by removing all redundant elements from K:

$$\text{makeSet}(\langle \, \rangle) = \langle \, \rangle,$$

$$\text{makeSet}(a :: L) = \begin{array}{l} \text{if isMember}(a, L) \text{ then makeSet}(L) \\ \text{else } a :: \text{makeSet}(L). \end{array}$$

We'll assume that isMember correctly checks whether an element is a member of a list. Let $P(K)$ be the statement "makeSet(K) is a list obtained from K by removing its redundant elements." We'll prove that $P(K)$ is true for all lists K.

Proof: We need a well-founded ordering for lists. For any lists K and M we'll define $K \prec M$ to mean length(K) < length(M). So the basis element is $\langle \, \rangle$. The definition of makeSet tells us that makeSet($\langle \, \rangle$) = $\langle \, \rangle$. Thus $P(\langle \, \rangle)$ is true. Next, we'll let K be an arbitrary nonempty list and assume that $P(L)$ is true for all lists $L \prec K$. In other words, we're assuming that makeSet(L) has no redundant elements for all lists $L \prec K$. We need to show that $P(K)$ is true. In other words, we need to show that makeSet(K) has no redundant elements. Since K is nonempty, we can write $K = a :: L$. Now there are two cases to consider. If isMember(a, L) is true, then the definition of makeSet gives

$$\text{makeSet}(K) = \text{makeSet}(a :: L) = \text{makeSet}(L).$$

Since $L \prec K$, it follows that $P(L)$ is true. Therefore $P(K)$ is true. If isMember(a, L) is false, then the definition of makeSet gives

$$\text{makeSet}(K) = \text{makeSet}(a :: L) = a :: \text{makeSet}(L).$$

Since $L \prec K$, it follows that $P(L)$ is true. Since isMember(a, L) is false, it follows that the list $a :: \text{makeSet}(L)$ has no redundant elements. Thus $P(K)$ is true. Therefore (2.17) implies that $P(K)$ is true for all lists K.   QED.   ◆

Multiple-Variable Induction

Up to this point, all our inductive proofs have involved claims and formulas with only a single variable. Often the claims that we wish to prove involve t.vo or more variables. For example, suppose we need to show that $P(x, y)$ is true for all $\langle x, y \rangle \in A \times B$. We saw earlier that $A \times B$ can be defined inductively in different ways. For example, it may be possible to emphasize only the inductive nature of the set A by defining $A \times B$ in terms of A. To show that $P(x, y)$ is true for all $\langle x, y \rangle$ in $A \times B$, we can perform the following steps (where y denotes an arbitrary element in B):

1. Show that $P(m, y)$ is true for minimal elements $m \in A$.
2. Assume that $P(a, y)$ is true for all predecessors a of x. Show that the statement $P(x, y)$ is true.

This technique is called "inducting on a single variable." The form of the statement $P(x, y)$ often gives us a clue to whether we can induct on a single variable. Here are some examples.

EXAMPLE 5. Suppose we want to prove that the following function computes the number y^{x+1} for any natural numbers x and y:

$$f(x, y) = \text{if } x = 0 \text{ then } y \text{ else } f(x - 1, y) * y.$$

In other words, we want to prove that $f(x, y) = y^{x+1}$ for all $\langle x, y \rangle$ in $\mathbb{N} \times \mathbb{N}$. We'll induct on the variable x because it's changing in the definition of f. Proof: For the basis case the definition of f gives $f(0, y) = y = y^{0+1}$. So the basis case is proved. For the induction case, assume that $x > 0$ and $f(n, y) = y^{n+1}$ for $n < x$. Now we must show that $f(x, y) = y^{x+1}$. From the definition of f and the induction assumption, we get the following equation:

$$\begin{aligned}
f(x, y) &= f(x - 1, y) * y && \text{(definition of } f) \\
&= y^{x-1+1} * y && \text{(induction assumption)} \\
&= y^{x+1}.
\end{aligned}$$

The result now follows from (2.17).   QED.   ◆

We often see induction proofs that don't mention the word "well-founded." For example, we might see a statement such as "We will induct on the depth of the trees." In such a case the induction assumption might be stated something like "Assume that $P(T)$ is true for all trees T with depth less than n." Then a proof is given that uses the assumption to prove that $P(T)$ is true for an arbitrary tree of depth n. Even though the term "well-founded" may not be mentioned in a proof, there is always a well-founded ordering lurking underneath the surface.

Exercises

1. Use induction to prove each of the following equations for all natural numbers $n \geq 1$.

   a. $1^2 + 2^2 + \cdots + n^2 = \dfrac{n\,(n + 1)\,(2n + 1)}{6}$.

   b. $(1 + 2 + \cdots + n)^2 = 1^3 + 2^3 + \cdots + n^3$.

   c. $1 + 3 + \cdots + (2n - 1) = n^2$.

2. The *Fibonacci numbers* are defined by $F_0 = 0$, $F_1 = 1$, and $F_n = F_{n-1} + F_{n-2}$ for $n \geq 2$. Use induction to prove the following statement for all natural numbers n:
$$F_0 + F_1 + \ldots + F_n = F_{n+2} - 1.$$

3. The *Lucas numbers* are defined by $L_0 = 2$, $L_1 = 1$, and $L_n = L_{n-1} + L_{n-2}$ for $n \geq 2$. The sequence begins as 2, 1, 3, 4, 7, 11, 18, ... These numbers are named after the mathematician Édouard Lucas (1842–1891). Use induction to prove each of the following statements.

   a. $L_0 + L_1 + \ldots + L_n = L_{n+2} - 1$.

   b. $L_n = F_{n-1} + F_{n+1}$ for $n \geq 1$, where F_n is the nth Fibonacci number.

4. Use induction to prove the following formula for the sum of a *geometric progression*:
$$a + ar + ar^2 + \ldots + ar^{n-1} = a\left(\frac{r^n - 1}{r - 1}\right) \qquad (r \neq 1).$$

5. Use induction to prove the following formula:

$$\sum_{i=1}^{n} i a^i = \frac{a - (n+1)a^{n+1} + n a^{n+2}}{(a-1)^2} \qquad (a \neq 1).$$

6. Use induction to prove that the sum of an *arithmetic progression* $a_1, \dots,$ a_n (i.e., the numbers differ by a constant) is given by the following formula:

$$a_1 + a_2 + \cdots + a_n = \frac{n}{2}(a_1 + a_n).$$

7. Use induction to prove that a finite set with n elements has 2^n subsets.

8. Suppose we have the following two procedures to write out the elements of a list. One claims to write the elements in the order listed, and one writes out the elements in reverse order. Prove that each is correct.

   a. forward(L): if $L \neq \langle\,\rangle$ then {print(head(L)); forward(tail(L))}.

   b. back(L): if $L \neq \langle\,\rangle$ then {back(tail(L)); print(head(L))}.

9. The following function "sort" takes a list of numbers and returns a sorted version of the list (from lowest to highest), where "insert" places an element correctly into a sorted list:

$$\text{sort}(\langle\,\rangle) = \langle\,\rangle,$$
$$\text{sort}(x :: L) = \text{insert}(x, \text{sort}(L)).$$

   a. Assume that the function insert is correct. That is, if S is sorted, then insert(x, S) is also sorted. Prove that sort is correct.

   b. Prove that the following definition for insert is correct. That is, prove that insert(x, S) is sorted for all sorted lists S.

$$\begin{aligned}
\text{insert}(x, S) \quad =\quad &\text{if } S = \langle\,\rangle \text{ then } \langle x\rangle \\
&\text{else if } x \leq \text{head}(S) \text{ then } x :: S \\
&\text{else head}(S) :: \text{insert}(x, \text{tail}(S)).
\end{aligned}$$

10. The following program computes a well-known function called *Acker-mann's function*. *Note:* If you try out this function, don't let x and y get too big.

$$\begin{aligned}
f(x, y) \quad =\quad &\text{if } x = 0 \text{ then } y + 1 \\
&\text{else if } y = 0 \text{ then } f(x-1, 1) \\
&\text{else } f(x-1, f(x, y-1)).
\end{aligned}$$

Prove that f is defined for all pairs $\langle x, y\rangle$ in $\mathbb{N} \times \mathbb{N}$. *Hint:* Use the lexicographic ordering on $\mathbb{N} \times \mathbb{N}$. This gives the single basis element $\langle 0, 0\rangle$. For the induction assumption, assume that $f(x', y')$ is defined for all $\langle x', y'\rangle$ such that $\langle x', y'\rangle \prec \langle x, y\rangle$. Then show that $f(x, y)$ is defined.

2.5 Algebraic Notions

The word "algebra" comes from the word "al-jabr" in the title of the textbook
Hisâb al-jabr w'al-muqâbala, which was written around 820 by the mathematician and astronomer al-Khowârizmî. The title translates roughly to
"calculations by restoration and reduction," where restoration—al-jabr—
refers to adding or subtracting a number on both sides of an equation, and reduction refers to simplification. We should also note that the word "algorithm" has been traced back to al-Khowârizmî because people used his
name—mispronounced of course—when referring to a method of calculating
with Hindu numerals that was contained in another of his books.

Having studied high school algebra, most of us probably agree that algebra has something to do with equations and simplification. In high school algebra we simplified a lot. In fact, we were often given the one word command
"simplify" in the exercises. So we tried to somehow manipulate a given expression into one that was simpler than the given one, although this was a bit
vague, and there always seemed to be a question about what "simplify"
meant. We also tried to describe word problems in terms of algebraic equations and then to apply our simplification methods to extract solutions.
Everything we did dealt with numbers and expressions for numbers.

In this section we'll clarify and broaden the idea of an algebra. We'll concentrate on those notions and notations of algebra that are used in computer
science.

What Is an Algebra?

Before we say just what an algebra is, let's see how an algebra is used in the
problem-solving process. An important part of problem solving is the process
of transforming informal word problems into formal things like equations,
expressions, or algorithms. Another important part of problem solving is the
process of transforming these formal things into solutions by solving equations, simplifying expressions, or implementing algorithms. For example, in
high school algebra we tried to describe certain word problems in terms of algebraic equations, and then we tried to solve the equations. An algebra
should provide tools and techniques to help us describe informal problems in
formal terms and to help us solve the resulting formal problems.

High School Algebra

A natural example of an algebra that we all know and love is the algebra of
numbers. We learned about it in school, and we probably had different ideas
about what it was. First we learned about arithmetic of the natural numbers
using the operation of addition. Soon we learned about the operation of

multiplication. We learned about the negative numbers and the integers. Somewhere along the line, we learned about division, the rational numbers $\mathbb{Q}$, and the fact that we could not divide by zero.

Then came the big leap. We learned to denote numbers by symbols such as the letters x and y and by expressions like $x^2 + y$. We spent much time transforming one expression into another, such as $x^2 + 4x + 4 = (x + 2)(x + 2)$. All this had something to do with algebra, perhaps because that was the name of the class.

There are two main ingredients to the algebra that we studied in high school. The first is a set of numbers to work with, such as the real numbers $\mathbb{R}$. The second is a set of operations on the numbers, such as $-$ and $+$. We learned about the general properties of the operations, such as $x + y = y + x$ and $x + 0 = x$. And we used the properties to solve word problems.

Now we are in position to discuss algebra from a more general point of view. We will see that high school algebra is just one of many different kinds of algebras.

Definition of an Algebra

An *algebra* is a structure consisting of one or more sets together with one or more operations on the sets. The sets are often called *carriers* of the algebra. This is a very general definition. If this is the definition of an algebra, how can it help us solve problems? As we will see, the utility of an algebra comes from knowing how to use the operations.

For example, high school algebra is an algebra with the single carrier $\mathbb{R}$, or maybe $\mathbb{Q}$. The operators of the algebra are $+$, $-$, $\cdot$, and $\div$. The constants 0 and 1 are also important to consider because they have special properties. Recall that a constant can be thought of as a nullary operation (having arity zero). Many familiar properties hold among the operations, such as the fact that multiplication distributes over addition: $a \cdot (b + c) = a \cdot b + a \cdot c$; and the fact that we can cancel: If $a \neq 0$, then $a \cdot b = a \cdot c$ implies $b = c$.

There are many algebras in computer science. For example, the Pascal data type INTEGER is an algebra. The carrier is a finite set of integers that changes from machine to machine. Some of the operators in this algebra are

$$\text{maxint}, +, -, *, \text{div}, \text{mod}, \text{succ}, \text{pred}.$$

Maxint is a constant that represents the largest integer in the carrier. Of course, there are many relationships that hold among the operations. For example, we know that for any $x \neq$ maxint the two operators pred and succ satisfy the equation $\text{pred}(\text{succ}(x)) = x$. The operators don't need to be total functions. For example, $\text{succ}(\text{maxint})$ is not defined.

An *algebraic expression* is a string of symbols that is used to represent an element in a carrier of an algebra. For example, in high school algebra the strings 3, $8 \div x$, and $x^2 + y$ are algebraic expressions. But the string $x + y +$ is not an algebraic expression. The set of algebraic expressions is a language. The symbols in the alphabet are the operators and constants from the algebra, together with variable names and grouping symbols, like parentheses and commas. For example, suppose x and y are variables and c is a constant. If g is a ternary operator, then the following five strings are algebraic expressions:

$$x, \quad y, \quad c, \quad g(x, y, c), \quad g(x, g(c, y, x), x).$$

Different algebraic expressions often mean the same thing. For example, the equation $2x = x + x$ makes sense to us because we look beyond the two strings $2x$ and $x + x$, which are not equal strings. Instead, we look at the possible values of the two expressions and conclude that they always have the same value, no matter what value x has. Two algebraic expressions are *equivalent* if they always evaluate to the same element in a carrier of the algebra. For example, the two expressions $(x + 2)^2$ and $x^2 + 4x + 4$ are equivalent in high school algebra. But $x + y$ is not equivalent to $5x$ because we can let $x = 1$ and $y = 2$, which makes $x + y = 3$ and $5x = 5$.

The set of operators in an algebra is called the *signature* of the algebra. When describing an algebra, we need to decide which operators to put in the signature. For example, we may wish to list only the primitive operators (the constructors) that are used to build all other operators. On the other hand, we might want to list all the operators that we know about.

Let's look at a convenient way to denote an algebra. We'll list the carrier or carriers first, followed by a semicolon. The operators in the signature are listed next. Then enclose the two listings with tuple markers. For example, this notation is used to denote the following four algebras:

$$\langle \mathbb{N}; \text{succ}, 0 \rangle \qquad \langle \mathbb{Z}; +, \cdot, -, 0, 1 \rangle$$
$$\langle \mathbb{Q}; +, \cdot, -, \div, 0, 1 \rangle \qquad \langle \mathbb{R}; +, \cdot, -, \div, 0, 1 \rangle$$

The constants 0 and 1 are listed as operations to emphasize the fact that they have special properties, such as $x + 0 = x$ and $x \cdot 1 = x$.

Let's look at some fundamental properties that may be associated with a binary operation. If $\circ$ is a binary operator on a set C, then an element $z \in C$ is called a *zero* for $\circ$ if the following condition holds:

$$z \circ x = x \circ z = z \quad \text{for all } x \in C.$$

For example, the number 0 is a zero for the multiply operation over the real numbers because $0 \cdot x = x \cdot 0 = 0$ for all real numbers x.

Continuing with the same binary operator ∘ and carrier C, we call an element $u \in C$ an *identity*, or *unit*, for ∘ if the following condition holds:

$$u \circ x = x \circ u = x \quad \text{for all } x \in C.$$

For example, the number 1 is a unit for the multiply operation over the real numbers because $1 \cdot x = x \cdot 1 = x$ for all numbers x. Similarly, the number 0 is a unit for the addition operation over real numbers because $0 + x = x + 0 = x$ for all numbers x.

Suppose u is an identity element for ∘, and $x \in C$. An element y in C is called an *inverse* of x if the following equation holds:

$$x \circ y = y \circ x = u.$$

For example, in the algebra $\langle \mathbb{Q}; \cdot, 1 \rangle$ the number 1 is an identity element. We also know that if $x \neq 0$, then

$$x \cdot \frac{1}{x} = \frac{1}{x} \cdot x = 1.$$

In other words, all nonzero rational numbers have inverses.

Each of the following examples presents an algebra together with some observations about its operators.

EXAMPLE 1. Let S be a set. Then the power set of S is the carrier for an algebra described as follows:

$$\langle \text{power}(S); \cup, \cap, \varnothing, S \rangle.$$

Notice that if $A \in \text{power}(S)$, then $A \cup \varnothing = A$, and $A \cap S = A$. So $\varnothing$ is an identity for $\cup$, and S is an identity for $\cap$. Similarly, $A \cap \varnothing = \varnothing$, and $A \cup S = S$. Thus $\varnothing$ is a zero for $\cap$, and S is a zero for $\cup$. This algebra has many well-known properties. For example, $A \cup A = A$ and $A \cap A = A$ for any $A \in \text{power}(S)$. We also know that $\cap$ and $\cup$ are commutative and associative and that they distribute over each other. ◆

EXAMPLE 2. Let $\mathbb{N}_n$ denote the set $\{0, 1, \ldots, n-1\}$, and let "max" be the function that returns the maximum of its two arguments. Consider the following algebra with carrier $\mathbb{N}_n$:

$$\langle \mathbb{N}_n; \max, 0, n-1 \rangle.$$

Notice that max is commutative and associative. Notice also that for any $x \in \mathbb{N}_n$ it follows that $\max(x, 0) = \max(0, x) = x$. So 0 is an identity for max. It's also easy to see that for any $x \in \mathbb{N}_n$,

$$\max(x, n - 1) = \max(n - 1, x) = n - 1.$$

So $n - 1$ is a zero for the operator max. ◆

EXAMPLE 3. Let S be a set, and let F be the set of all functions of type $S \to S$. If we let ∘ denote the operation of composition of functions, then F is the carrier of an algebra $\langle F; \circ, \text{id} \rangle$. The function id denotes the identity function. In other words, we have the equation $\text{id} \circ f = f \circ \text{id} = f$ for all functions f in F. Therefore id is an identity for ∘. This algebra has many properties. For example, the following property holds for all functions $f, g, h \in F$:

$$\langle f, g \rangle \circ h = \langle f \circ h, g \circ h \rangle.$$

Let's look at one more property. We can define the if-then function "if b then g else h" by

$$(\text{if } b \text{ then } g \text{ else } h)(x) = \text{if } b(x) \text{ then } g(x) \text{ else } h(x),$$

where $g, h \in F$ and $b : S \to \{\text{true, false}\}$. Now we can write the following property of composition:

$$f \circ (\text{if } b \text{ then } g \text{ else } h) = \text{if } b \text{ then } f \circ g \text{ else } f \circ h. \quad ◆$$

Notice that we used the equality symbol "=" in the above examples without explicitly defining it as a relation. The first example uses equality of sets, the second uses equality of numbers, and the third uses equality of functions. In our discussions we will usually assume an implicit equality theory on each carrier of an algebra. But, as we have said before, equality relations are operations that may need to be implemented when needed as part of a programming activity.

Suppose we consider the algebra $\langle S; s, a \rangle$, where s is a unary operator on S and a is a constant of S. We can use the operators s and a to construct the following algebraic expressions for elements of S:

$$a, s(a), s(s(a)), ..., s^n(a), ...$$

This is the most we can say about the elements of S. There might be other elements in S, but we have no way of knowing it. The elements of S that we know about can be represented by all possible algebraic expressions made up from the operator symbols in the signature together with left and right parentheses.

Interesting things can happen when we add axioms (i.e., assumptions or properties) to an algebra. For example, the algebra $\langle S; s, a \rangle$ changes its character when we add the single axiom $s^6(x) = x$ for all $x \in S$. All we can say about this algebra is that the algebraic expressions define a finite set of elements, which can be represented by the following six expressions:

$$a, \, s(a), \, s^2(a), \, s^3(a), \, s^4(a), \, s^5(a).$$

A complete definition of an algebra can be given by listing the carriers, operations, and axioms. For example, the algebra that we've been discussing can be defined as follows:

Carrier:	S
Operations:	$a \in S$
	$s : S \to S$
Axiom:	$s^6(x) = x.$

We assume that the variable x in the axiom is defined over all elements of S. The algebra $\langle \mathbb{N}_6; \mathrm{succ}_6, 0 \rangle$ is a concrete example of this algebra. But the algebra $\langle \mathbb{N}; \mathrm{succ}, 0 \rangle$ does not satisfy the axiom.

Here are some more algebras that might be familiar to you.

EXAMPLE 4 (*Polynomial Algebras*). Let $\mathbb{R}[x]$ denote the set of all polynomials over x with real numbers as coefficients. It's a natural process to add and multiply two polynomials. So we have an algebra $\langle \mathbb{R}[x]; +, \cdot, 0, 1 \rangle$, where $+$ and $\cdot$ represent addition and multiplication of polynomials and 0 and 1 represent themselves. ♦

EXAMPLE 5 (*Vector Algebras*). The algebra of n-dimensional vectors, with real numbers as components, can be described by listing two carriers $\mathbb{R}$ and $\mathbb{R}^n$. We can multiply a vector $\langle x_1, ..., x_n \rangle \in \mathbb{R}^n$ by number $b \in \mathbb{R}$ to obtain a new vector by multiplying each component of the vector by b, obtaining $\langle bx_1, ..., bx_n \rangle$. If we let $\cdot$ denote this operation, then we have

$$b \cdot \langle x_1, ..., x_n \rangle = \langle bx_1, ..., bx_n \rangle.$$

We can add vectors by adding corresponding components as follows:

$$\langle x_1, ..., x_n \rangle + \langle y_1, ..., y_n \rangle = \langle x_1 + y_1, ..., x_n + y_n \rangle.$$

Thus we have an algebra of n-dimensional vectors, which we can write in tuple form as $\langle \mathbb{R}, \mathbb{R}^n; \cdot, + \rangle$. Notice that the algebra has two carriers, $\mathbb{R}$ and $\mathbb{R}^n$. This is because they are both necessary to define the $\cdot$ operation, which has type $\mathbb{R} \times \mathbb{R}^n \to \mathbb{R}^n$. ◆

Boolean Algebras

Do the techniques of set theory and the techniques of logic have anything in common? Let's do an example to see that the answer is yes. When working with sets, we know that the following equation holds for all sets A, B, and C:

$$A \cup (B \cap C) = (A \cup B) \cap (A \cup C).$$

When working with statements that are true or false, it's easy to see that the following holds for all statements A, B, and C:

$$A \text{ or } (B \text{ and } C) = (A \text{ or } B) \text{ and } (A \text{ or } C).$$

Certainly these two examples have a similar pattern. As we'll see shortly, sets and logic have a lot in common. They can both be described as concrete examples of a Boolean algebra. The name "Boolean" comes from the mathematician George Boole (1815–1864), who studied relationships between set theory and logic. Let's get to the definition.

An algebra is a *Boolean algebra* if it has the structure

$$\langle B; +, \cdot, ^-, 0, 1 \rangle,$$

where the following properties hold:

1. The following properties hold for all $x, y, z \in B$:

    $$(x + y) + z = x + (y + z), \qquad (x \cdot y) \cdot z = x \cdot (y \cdot z),$$
    $$x + y = y + x, \qquad\qquad\quad x \cdot y = y \cdot x,$$
    $$x + 0 = x, \qquad\qquad\qquad\; x \cdot 1 = x.$$

2. $+$ and $\cdot$ distribute over each other. In other words, the following properties hold for all $x, y, z \in B$:

    $$x \cdot (y + z) = (x \cdot y) + (x \cdot z) \quad \text{and} \quad x + (y \cdot z) = (x + y) \cdot (x + z).$$

3. $x + \bar{x} = 1$ and $x \cdot \bar{x} = 0$ for all elements $x \in B$. The element $\bar{x}$ is called the *complement* of x or the *negation* of x.

EXAMPLE 6 (*Sets*). The algebra of sets in Example 1 is a Boolean algebra if we let union and intersection act as the operations + and ·, and we let X' be the complement of X, let $\varnothing$ act as 0, and let S act as 1. For example, the two properties in Part 3 of the definition are represented by the following two equations, where X is any subset of S:

$$X \cup X' = S \quad \text{and} \quad X \cap X' = \varnothing. \quad \blacklozenge$$

EXAMPLE 7 (*Logic*). Suppose we let B be the set of all statements that are true or false. Then B is the carrier of a Boolean algebra if we let "or" and "and" act as the operations + and ·, let not X be the complement of X, let false act as 0, and let true act as 1. $\blacklozenge$

Abstract Data Types

Programming problems involve data objects that are processed by a computer. To process data objects, we need operations to act on them. So algebra enters the programming picture. In computer science, an *abstract data type* consists of one or more sets of data objects together with one or more operations on the sets and some axioms to describe the operations. In other words, an abstract data type is an algebra. There is, however, a restriction on the carriers—the underlying sets—of abstract data types. The carriers must be able to be constructed in some way such that the data objects and operations can be implemented on a computer. So carriers must be countable sets. For example, any natural number can be constructed inductively from 0 and the successor function. So the set of natural numbers is an appropriate carrier for an abstract data type.

Programming languages normally contain some built-in abstract data types. But it's not possible for a programming language to contain all possible ways to represent and operate on data objects. So programmers often design and implement abstract data types as part of the programming process. In these cases the axioms are used by programmers as a guide to make sure that the operations are implemented correctly.

Natural Numbers

The naural numbers can be defined inductively by the number zero and the successor operation. An abstract data type for the natural numbers needs a few other operations in order to be a good platform for defining other functions. We'll also use the predecessor operation "pred" and we'll agree that pred(0) = 0. We also need an "is zero" test that occurs in the if-then-else form of definitions. So we'll also need the carrier Boolean = {true, false}. These notions are included in the following algebra that represents an abstract data type for processing natural numbers:

Carriers: $\mathbb{N}$, Boolean.

Operations: $0 \in \mathbb{N}$,
     isZero : $\mathbb{N} \to$ Boolean,
     succ : $\mathbb{N} \to \mathbb{N}$,
     pred : $\mathbb{N} \to \mathbb{N}$.

Axioms: isZero(0) = true,
     isZero(succ(x)) = false,
     pred(0) = 0,
     pred(succ(x)) = x.

The axioms provide important relationships among the operations that can be used as a basis for an implementation of the abstract data type. An abstract data type is useful only if its operations can be used to solve problems (i.e., define programs). Notice that we did not include the operations of addition and multiplication in our definition. We could have. But we want to demonstrate the power of the primitive operations of the algebra. For example, we can define the "add" operation for addition in terms of the given operations as follows:

$$\text{add}(x, y) = \text{if isZero}(x) \text{ then } y \text{ else succ(add(pred}(x), y)).$$

Now we can use this definition to define the "mult" operation of multiplication as follows:

$$\text{mult}(x, y) = \text{if isZero}(x) \text{ then } 0 \text{ else add(mult(pred}(x), y), y).$$

Lists

A list is a sequence of objects. We'll denote a list by placing angle brackets on either end. For example, $\langle b, a, b \rangle$ is a three-element list. We'll denote the set of all lists over a set A by Lists[A]. This set can be inductively defined by two constructors, the empty list $\langle\ \rangle$ and the operation *cons*, which takes an element and a list, and constructs a new list with the element attached to the front of the list. For example, cons(a, $\langle b, c \rangle$) = $\langle a, b, c \rangle$. Two useful list operations are *head* and *tail*. For example,

$$\text{head}(\langle a, b, c \rangle) = a \quad \text{and} \quad \text{tail}(\langle a, b, c \rangle) = \langle b, c \rangle.$$

Suppose we consider the following function f to compute the sum of a list of natural numbers:

$$f(x) = \text{if } x = \langle\,\rangle \text{ then } 0 \text{ else } \text{head}(x) + f(\text{tail}(x)).$$

This program will execute if the language knows how to test whether a list is empty, how to find the head and tail of a list, and how to add natural numbers. So the programmer must make sure that the language contains abstract data types for truth values, natural numbers, and lists.

The algebra of lists can be defined by the constructors $\langle\,\rangle$ and cons together with the operations isEmptyL, head, and tail. The operations head and tail are not defined on the empty list. One way to handle this situation is to return an error message when either head or tail is applied to the empty list. In this case, we'll let Error = {error}. Now we can define an abstract data type for lists over A as the following algebra:

Carriers: Lists[A], A, Boolean, Error.

Operations: $\langle\,\rangle \in$ Lists[A],

   isEmptyL : Lists[A] $\rightarrow$ Boolean,

   cons : $A \times$ Lists[A] $\rightarrow$ Lists[A],

   head : Lists[A] $\rightarrow A \cup$ Error,

   tail : Lists[A] $\rightarrow$ Lists[A] $\cup$ Error.

Axioms: isEmptyL($\langle\,\rangle$) = true,

   isEmptyL(cons(x, L)) = false,

   head($\langle\,\rangle$) = error,

   head(cons(x, L)) = x,

   tail($\langle\,\rangle$) = error,

   tail(cons(x, L)) = L.

Can all desired list functions be written in terms of the operations of this algebra? The answer depends on what "desired" means. For example, the following functions usually come in handy in programming with lists: *length* finds the length of a list; *member* tests for membership in a list; *last* finds the last element of a list; *concatenate* concatenates two lists; and *putLast* puts an element at the right end of a list. For example, the putLast function can be defined as follows:

$$\text{putLast}(a, L) \;=\; \text{if isEmptyL}(L) \text{ then cons}(a, \langle\,\rangle)$$
$$\text{else cons(head}(L), \text{putLast}(a, \text{tail}(L))).$$

Sometimes we need to use operations from more than one abstract data type. For example, the length function can be written as follows:

$$\text{length}(L) = \text{if isEmptyL}(L) \text{ then } 0$$
$$\text{else add}(1, \text{length}(\text{tail}(L))).$$

In this case we also need the natural numbers. We can define the member function as follows:

$$\text{member}(a, L) = \text{if isEmptyL}(L) \text{ then false}$$
$$\text{else if } a = \text{head}(L) \text{ then true}$$
$$\text{else member}(a, \text{tail}(L)).$$

In this case, the predicate "$a = \text{head}(L)$" must be computable. So an equality relation must be available for the carrier A; or else we must implement one.

Queues

A *queue* is a structure satisfying the FIFO property of first-in-first-out. In other words, the first element input is the first element output. So a queue is a fair waiting line. The main operations on a queue are the following: *addQ* adds a new element to a queue; *frontQ* examines the front element of a queue; and *delQ* deletes the front element from a queue.

To describe an abstract data type for queues, we'll let A be a set and $Q[A]$ be the set of queues over A. Let *emptyQ* denote the empty queue. Then we can construct queues with emptyQ and addQ. Now we can define an abstract data type for queues over A as the following algebra:

Carriers: A, $Q[A]$, Boolean, Error.

Operations: emptyQ $\in Q[A]$,
    isEmptyQ : $Q[A] \to$ Boolean,
    addQ : $A \times Q[A] \to Q[A]$,
    frontQ : $Q[A] \to A \cup$ Error,
    delQ : $Q[A] \to Q[A] \cup$ Error.

Axioms: isEmptyQ(emptyQ) = true,
    isEmptyQ(addQ(a, q)) = false,
    frontQ(emptyQ) = error,
    frontQ(addQ(a, q)) = if isEmptyQ(q) then a else frontQ(q),
    delQ(emptyQ) = error,
    delQ(addQ(a, q)) = if isEmptyQ(q) then q
            else addQ(a, delQ(q)).

We can implement this abstract data type by using list operations. For example, the list $\langle a, b \rangle$ will represent the queue with a at the front and b at the rear. If we add a new item c to this queue we obtain the queue $\langle a, b, c \rangle$. In other words, addQ($c, \langle a, b \rangle$) = $\langle a, b, c \rangle$. So addQ can be implemented as the putLast function on lists. The implementation of a queue algebra as a list algebra can be given as follows: Q[A] is Lists[A], emptyQ is $\langle \rangle$, isEmptyQ is isEmptyL, frontQ is head, delQ is tail, and addQ is putLast.

The proof of correctness of this implementation is interesting because two of the queue axioms are conditionals and putLast is written in terms of the list operations. For example, we'll prove that the implementation satisfies the fourth axiom by considering two cases:

Case 1. Assume q = emptyQ. Then we have the following equations:

$$
\begin{aligned}
\text{frontQ(addQ}(a, \text{emptyQ})) &= \text{head(putLast}(a, \langle \rangle)) \\
&= \text{head(cons}(a, \langle \rangle)) \\
&= a.
\end{aligned}
$$

Case 2: Assume $q \neq$ emptyQ. Then we have the following equations:

$$
\begin{aligned}
\text{frontQ(addQ}(a, q)) &= \text{head(putLast}(a, q)) \\
&= \text{head(cons(head}(q), \text{putLast}(a, \text{tail}(q)))) \\
&= \text{head}(q) \\
&= \text{frontQ}(q). \quad \text{QED.}
\end{aligned}
$$

Morphisms

This little discussion is about some tools that can be used to compare two different entities for common properties. For example, if A is an alphabet, then we know that a string over A is different from a list over A. In other words, we know that A^* and Lists[A] contain different kinds of objects. But we also know that A^* and Lists[A] have a lot in common. For example, we know that the operations on A^* are similar to the operations on Lists[A]. We know that the algebra of strings and the algebra of lists both have an empty object and that they construct new objects in a similar way. On the other hand, we know that A^* is quite different from the set of binary trees over A. For example, the construction of a string is not at all like the construction of a binary tree.

When two things are alike, we are often more familiar with one of the things. So we can apply our knowledge about the familiar one and learn something about the unfamiliar one. Whenever a light bulb goes on in our brain and we finally understand the meaning of some idea or object, we usually make statements like "Oh yes, I see it now" or "Yes, I understand." These statements usually mean that we have made a connection between the thing we're trying to understand and some other thing that is already familiar to us. So there is a transformation (i.e., a function) from the new idea to a familiar old idea.

For example, suppose we want to describe the meaning (semantics) of the binary numerals (i.e., nonempty strings of binary digits) and the Roman numerals in terms of natural numbers. Let m_{two} denote the semantics function for binary numerals and let m_{rom} denote the semantics function for Roman numerals. These functions have the following types:

$$m_{two} : \text{BinaryNumerals} \to \mathbb{N},$$

$$m_{rom} : \text{RomanNumerals} \to \mathbb{N}.$$

For example, we should have $m_{two}(1100) = 12$ and $m_{rom}(\text{XXV}) = 25$.

We can give formal definitions for these functions. For example, m_{two} can be defined as follows: If $d_k d_{k-1} \ldots d_1 d_0$ is a string of base 2 numerals, then

$$m_{two}(d_k d_{k-1} \ldots d_1 d_0) = 2^k d_k + \cdots + 2d_1 + d_0.$$

What properties, if any, should a semantics function possess? Certain operations defined on numerals should be, in some sense, "preserved" by the semantics function. For example, suppose we let $+_{bi}$ denote the usual binary addition defined on binary numerals. We would like to say that the meaning of the binary sum of two binary numerals is the same as the result obtained by adding the two individual meanings in the algebra $\langle \mathbb{N}; + \rangle$. In other words, for any binary numerals x and y the following equation holds:

$$m_{two}(x +_{bi} y) = m_{two}(x) + m_{two}(y).$$

The idea of a function preserving an operation can be defined in a general way. Let $f : A \to A'$ be a function between the carriers of two algebras. Suppose ω is an n-ary operation on A. We say that f *preserves* the operation ω if there is a corresponding operation ω' on A' such that for every $x_1, \ldots, x_n \in A$ the following equality holds:

$$f(\omega(x_1, \ldots, x_n)) = \omega'(f(x_1), \ldots, f(x_n)).$$

If ω is a binary operation, then, as in our example, we can write the above equation in its infix form as follows:

$$f(x \ \omega \ y)) = f(x) \ \omega' \ f(y).$$

Here's the thing to remember about an operation that is preserved by a function $f : A \rightarrow A'$: You can apply the operation to arguments in A and then use f to map the result to A', or you can use f to map each argument from A to A' and then apply the corresponding operation on A' to these arguments. In either case you get the same result.

We say that $f : A \rightarrow A'$ is a *morphism* (also called a *homomorphism*) if every operation in the algebra of A is preserved by f. If a morphism is injective, then it's called a *monomorphism*. If a morphism is surjective, then it's called an *epimorphism*. If a morphism is bijective, then it's called an *isomorphism*. If there is an isomorphism between two algebras, we say that the algebras are *isomorphic*. Two isomorphic algebras are very much alike, and, hopefully, one of them is easier to understand.

For example, m_{two} is a morphism from the algebra $\langle \text{BinaryNumerals}; +_{bi} \rangle$ to the algebra $\langle \mathbb{N}; + \rangle$. In fact, we can say that m_{two} is an epimorphism because it's surjective. Notice that distinct binary numerals like 011 and 11 both represent the number 3. Therefore m_{two} is not injective, so it is not a monomorphism, and thus it is not an isomorphism.

EXAMPLE 8. Suppose we define $f : \mathbb{Z} \rightarrow \mathbb{Q}$ by $f(n) = 2^n$. Notice that

$$f(n + m) = 2^{n+m} = 2^n \cdot 2^m = f(n) \cdot f(m).$$

Therefore f is a morphism from the algebra $\langle \mathbb{Z}; + \rangle$ to the algebra $\langle \mathbb{Q}; \cdot \rangle$. Notice that $f(0) = 2^0 = 1$. So f is a morphism from the algebra $\langle \mathbb{Z}; +, 0 \rangle$ to the algebra $\langle \mathbb{Q}; \cdot, 1 \rangle$. Notice that $f(-n) = 2^{-n} = (2^n)^{-1} = f(n)^{-1}$. Therefore f is a morphism from the algebra $\langle \mathbb{Z}; +, -, 0 \rangle$ to the algebra $\langle \mathbb{Q}; \cdot, ^{-1}, 1 \rangle$. It's easy to see that f is injective. It's also easy to see that f is not surjective. Therefore f is a monomorphism, but it is neither an epimorphism nor an isomorphism. ◆

EXAMPLE 9 (*Language Morphisms*). If A and B are alphabets, we call a function $f : A^* \rightarrow B^*$ a *language morphism* if $f(\Lambda) = \Lambda$ and $f(uv) = f(u)f(v)$ for any strings $u, v \in A^*$. In other words, a language morphism from A^* to B^* is a morphism from the algebra $\langle A^*; \text{cat}, \Lambda \rangle$ to the algebra $\langle B^*; \text{cat}, \Lambda \rangle$. Since concatenation must be preserved, a language morphism is completely determined by defining the values $f(a)$ for each $a \in A$. For example, we'll let $A = B = \{a, b\}$ and define a language morphism $f : \{a, b\}^* \rightarrow \{a, b\}^*$ by setting $f(a) = b$ and $f(b) = ab$. Then we can make statements like

$$f(bab) = f(b)f(a)f(b) = abbab \quad \text{and} \quad f(b^2) = (ab)^2.$$

Language morphisms can be used to help us transform one language into another language with a similar grammar. For example, the grammar

$$S \to aSb \mid \Lambda$$

defines the language $\{a^n b^n \mid n \in \mathbb{N}\}$. Since $f(a^n b^n) = b^n(ab)^n$ for $n \in \mathbb{N}$, the language $\{a^n b^n \mid n \in \mathbb{N}\}$ is transformed by f into the language $\{b^n(ab)^n \mid n \in \mathbb{N}\}$. This language can be generated by the grammar $S \to f(a)Sf(b) \mid f(\Lambda)$, which becomes $S \to bSab \mid \Lambda$. ♦

Exercises

1. Let m and n be two integers with $m < n$. Let $A = \{m, m + 1, ..., n\}$, and let "min" be the function that returns the smaller of its two arguments. Does min have a zero? Identity? Inverses? If so, describe them.

2. Recall that the product of two languages L and M is defined as follows:

$$L \cdot M = \{st \mid s \in L \text{ and } t \in M\}.$$

   Does the product operation have a zero? Identity? Inverses? If so, describe them.

3. Given the algebra $\langle S; f, a \rangle$, where f is a unary operation and a is a constant of S, suppose that all elements of S are described by algebraic expressions involving f and a. Suppose also that the axiom $f^5(x) = f^3(x)$ holds. Find a finite set of algebraic expressions that will represent the distinct elements of S.

4. The *monus* operation on natural numbers is like subtraction, except that it always gives a natural number as a result. An informal definition of monus can be written as follows:

$$\text{monus}(x, y) = \text{if } x \geq y \text{ then } x - y \text{ else } 0.$$

   Write down a recursive definition of monus that uses only the primitive operations isZero, succ, and pred.

5. Use the algebra of lists to write a definition of the function "reverse" to reverse the elements of a list. For example, $\text{reverse}(\langle x, y, z \rangle) = \langle z, y, x \rangle$.

6. For the list implementation of a queue, prove the correctness of the following axiom:
$$\text{delQ}(\text{addQ}(a, q)) = \text{if isEmptyQ}(q) \text{ then } q$$
$$\text{else addQ}(a, \text{delQ}(q)).$$

7. Find the three morphisms that transform the algebra $\langle \mathbb{N}_3; +_3, 0 \rangle$ to the algebra $\langle \mathbb{N}_6; +_6, 0 \rangle$.

8. Let A be an alphabet and $f : A^* \to \mathbb{N}$ be defined by $f(x) = \text{length}(x)$. Show that f is a morphism from the algebra $\langle A^*; \text{cat}, \Lambda \rangle$ to $\langle \mathbb{N}; +, 0 \rangle$, where cat denotes the concatenation of strings.

9. Give an example to show that the absolute value function abs : $\mathbb{Z} \to \mathbb{N}$ defined by $\text{abs}(x) = |x|$ is not a morphism from the algebra $\langle \mathbb{Z}; + \rangle$ to the algebra $\langle \mathbb{N}; + \rangle$.

10. Given the language morphism $f : \{a, b\}^* \to \{a, b\}^*$ defined by $f(a) = b$ and $f(b) = ab$, compute the value of each of the following expressions.

    a. $f(\{b^n a \mid n \in \mathbb{N}\})$.   b. $f(\{ba^n \mid n \in \mathbb{N}\})$.   c. $f^{-1}(\{b^n a \mid n \in \mathbb{N}\})$.

    d. $f^{-1}(\{ba^n \mid n \in \mathbb{N}\})$.   e. $f^{-1}(\{ab^{n+1} \mid n \in \mathbb{N}\})$.

Chapter Summary

Inductively defined sets are characterized by a basis case, an induction case, and a closure case that is always assumed without comment. The constructors of an inductively defined set are the elements listed in the basis case and the rules specified in the induction case. Many sets of objects used in computer science can be defined inductively—natural numbers, lists, strings, languages, binary trees, and products of sets.

A recursively defined function is defined in terms of itself. Most recursively defined functions have domains that are inductively defined sets. These functions are normally defined by a basis case and an induction case. The situation is similar for recursively defined procedures.

The basic properties that a binary relation may or may not possess are reflexive, symmetric, transitive, irreflexive, and antisymmetric. Binary relations can be constructed from other binary relations by composition, closure, and by the usual set operations.

Equivalence relations are characterized by being reflexive, symmetric, and transitive. These relations generalize the idea of basic equality by partitioning a set into classes of equivalent elements. Equivalence relations can be generated from other relations by taking the transitive symmetric reflexive closure.

Order relations are characterized by being transitive and antisymmetric. Sets with these properties are called posets—for partially ordered sets—because it may be the case that not all pairs of elements are related. The ideas of successor and predecessor apply to posets. A well-founded poset is characterized by the condition that no descending chain of elements can go on forever. This is equivalent to the condition that any nonempty subset has a minimal element.

Inductive proof is a powerful technique that can be used to prove infinitely many statements. The most basic inductive proof technique is the principle of mathematical induction. A useful inductive proof technique is well-founded induction. The important thing to remember about applying inductive proof techniques is to *make an assumption* and then *use the assumption* that you made. Inductive proof techniques can be used to prove properties of recursively defined functions and inductively defined sets.

An algebra consists of one or more sets, called carriers, together with operations on the sets. In high school algebra the carrier is the set of real numbers, and the operations are addition, multiplication, and so on. An algebra can be described by giving a set of axioms to describe the properties of its operations. Morphisms allow us to transform one algebra into another—often simpler—algebra and still preserve the meaning of the operations. Language morphisms can be used to build new languages along with their grammars.

3

Formal Logic

... if it was so, it might be; and if it were so, it would be:
but as it isn't, it ain't. That's logic.
—Tweedledee in *Through the Looking-Glass*
by Lewis Carroll (1832–1898)

Why is formalism so important in computer science? Because it allows us to study general concepts that apply to many specific instances. Of course, this is important in almost all endeavors. Why is it important to study logic? Two things that we continually try to accomplish are to understand and to be understood. We attempt to understand an argument given by someone so that we can agree with the conclusion or, possibly, so that we can say that the reasoning does not make sense. We also attempt to express arguments to others without making a mistake. A formal study of logic will help improve these fundamental communication skills.

Why should a student of computer science study logic? A computer scientist needs logical skills to argue whether or not a problem can be solved on a machine, to transform logical statements from everyday language to a variety of computer languages, to argue that a program is correct, and to argue that a program is efficient. Computers are constructed from logic devices and are programmed in a logical fashion. Computer scientists must be able to understand and apply new ideas and techniques for programming, many of which require a knowledge of the formal aspects of logic.

What Is a Calculus?

The Romans used small beads called "calculi" to perform counting tasks. The word "calculi" is the plural of the word "calculus." So it makes sense to think that "calculus" has something to do with calculating. Since there are many kinds of calculation, it shouldn't surprise us that "calculus" is used in many different contexts. Let's give a definition.

A *calculus* is a language of expressions of some kind, with definite rules for forming the expressions. There are values, or meanings, associated with the expressions, and there are definite rules to transform one expression into another expression having the same value.

In mathematics the word "calculus" usually means the calculus of real functions. For example, the two expressions

$$D_x[f(x)g(x)] \quad \text{and} \quad f(x)D_xg(x) + g(x)D_xf(x)$$

are equivalent in this calculus. The calculus of real functions satisfies our definition of a calculus because there are definite rules for forming the expressions and there are definite rules for transforming expressions into equivalent expressions.

We'll be studying some different kinds of "logical" calculi. In a logical calculus the expressions are defined by rules, the values of the expressions are related to the concepts of true and false, and there are rules for transforming one expression into another.

Chapter Guide

Section 3.1 introduces the formal notions and notations of logic as used in propositional calculus. We also discuss the basics of formal reasoning.

Section 3.2 introduces the predicate calulus, concentrating on the first-order predicate calculus.

Section 3.3 introduces the formal proof rules for manipulating quantifiers in the predicate calculus.

Section 3.4 introduces higher-order logics. We'll see how propositional calculus and first-order predicate calculus fit into the scheme of things.

Section 3.5 introduces the idea of a formal theory. We'll discuss the notion of equality in a first-order theory.

Section 3.6 introduces a formal theory for proving the correctness of imperative programs.

3.1   Propositional Calculus

A sentence that is either true or false is called a *proposition*. For this discussion we'll denote propositions by the letters P, Q, and R, possibly subscripted. Propositions can be combined to form more complicated propositions, just the way we combine sentences, using the words "not," "and," "or," and the phrase "if... then..." These combining operations are often called *connectives*. We'll denote them by the following symbols and words:

¬	not, negation.
∧	and, conjunction.
∨	or, disjunction.
→	conditional, implication.

Some common ways to read the expression $P \to Q$ are "if P then Q," "Q if P," "P implies Q," "P is a sufficient condition for Q," and "Q is a necessary condition for P." P is called the *antecedent*, *premise*, or *hypothesis*, and Q is called the *consequent* or *conclusion* of $P \to Q$.

Now that we have some symbols, we can denote propositions in symbolic form. For example, if P denotes the proposition "It is raining" and Q denotes the proposition "There are clouds in the sky," then $P \to Q$ denotes the proposition "If it is raining, then there are clouds in the sky." Similarly, $\neg P$ denotes the proposition "It is not raining."

The four logical operators are defined to reflect their usage in everyday English. Table 3.1, a *truth table*, defines the operators for all possible truth values of their operands.

P	Q	$\neg P$	$P \vee Q$	$P \wedge Q$	$P \to Q$
true	true	false	true	true	true
true	false	false	true	false	false
false	true	true	true	false	true
false	false	true	false	false	true

Table 3.1

A grammatically correct expression is called a *well-formed formula*, or wff for short, which can be pronounced "woof." To decide whether an expression is a wff, we need to define the rules for the formation of wffs in our language. As with any language, we must agree on a set of symbols to use as the alphabet. For our discussion we will use the following sets of symbols:

Truth symbols:	true, false
Connectives:	¬, →, ∧, ∨
Propositional variables:	Capital letters like P, Q, and R
Punctuation symbols:	(,).

Next we need to define those expressions (strings) that form the wffs of our language. We do this by giving the following informal inductive definition for the set of propositional wffs:

A wff is either a truth symbol, or a propositional letter, or the negation of a wff, or the conjunction of two wffs, or the disjunction of two wffs, or the implication of one wff from another, or a wff surrounded by parentheses.

This definition allows us to get some familiar-looking things as wffs. For example, the following expressions are wffs:

$$\text{true}, \quad \text{false}, \quad P, \quad \neg Q, \quad P \wedge Q, \quad P \to Q, \quad (P \vee Q) \wedge R, \quad P \wedge Q \to R.$$

Can we associate a truth table with each wff? Yes we can, once we agree on a hierarchy of precedence among the connectives. For example, $P \wedge Q \vee R$ is a perfectly good wff. But to find a truth table, we need to agree on which connective to evaluate first. We will define the following hierarchy of evaluation for the connectives of the propositional calculus:

$$\neg \quad \text{(highest, do first)}$$
$$\wedge$$
$$\vee$$
$$\to \quad \text{(lowest, do last)}$$

We also agree that the operations $\wedge$, $\vee$, and $\to$ are left associative. In other words, if the same operation occurs two or more times in succession, without parentheses, then evaluate the operations from left to right.

Now we can say that any wff has a unique truth table. This allows us to define the *meaning*, or *semantics*, of a wff by its truth table, as follows:

The meanings of the truth symbols true and false are true and false, respectively. Otherwise, the meaning of a wff is its truth table.

If all the truth table values for a wff are true, then the wff is called a *tautology*. For example, the wffs $P \vee \neg P$ and $P \to P$ are tautologies. If all the truth table values are false, then the wff is called a *contradiction*. The wff $P \wedge \neg P$ is a contradiction. If some of the truth values are true and some are false, then the wff is called a *contingency*. The wff P is a contingency.

We will often use capital letters to refer to arbitrary propositional wffs. For example, if we say, "A is a wff," we mean that A represents some arbitrary wff. We also use capital letters to denote specific propositional wffs. For example, if we want to talk about the wff $P \wedge (Q \vee \neg R)$ several times in a discussion, we might let $W = P \wedge (Q \vee \neg R)$. Then we can refer to W instead of always writing down the symbols $P \wedge (Q \vee \neg R)$.

Equivalence

Some wffs have the same meaning even though their expressions are different. For example, the wffs $P \wedge Q$ and $Q \wedge P$ have the same meaning because they have the same truth tables. Two wffs are said to be *equivalent* if they have the same meaning. In other words, two wffs are equivalent if their truth tables have the same values. If A and B are equivalent wffs, we denote this fact by writing

$$A \equiv B.$$

For example, we can write $P \wedge Q \equiv Q \wedge P$. The definition of equivalence also allows us to make the following formulation in terms of conditionals:

$$A \equiv B \quad \text{if and only if} \quad (A \rightarrow B) \wedge (B \rightarrow A) \text{ is a tautology.}$$

Before we go much further, let's list a few easy equivalences. All the equivalences in Table 3.2 are easily verified by truth tables.

Some Basic Equivalences (3.1)

Negation	Disjunction	Conjunction	Implication
$\neg \neg A \equiv A$	$A \vee \text{true} \equiv \text{true}$	$A \wedge \text{true} \equiv A$	$A \rightarrow \text{true} \equiv \text{true}$
	$A \vee \text{false} \equiv A$	$A \wedge \text{false} \equiv \text{false}$	$A \rightarrow \text{false} \equiv \neg A$
	$A \vee A \equiv A$	$A \wedge A \equiv A$	$\text{true} \rightarrow A \equiv A$
	$A \vee \neg A \equiv \text{true}$	$A \wedge \neg A \equiv \text{false}$	$\text{false} \rightarrow A \equiv \text{true}$
			$A \rightarrow A \equiv \text{true}$

Some Conversions	*Absorption laws*
$A \rightarrow B \equiv \neg A \vee B.$	$A \wedge (A \vee B) \equiv A$
$\neg (A \rightarrow B) \equiv A \wedge \neg B.$	$A \vee (A \wedge B) \equiv A$
$A \rightarrow B \equiv A \wedge \neg B \rightarrow \text{false}.$	$A \wedge (\neg A \vee B) \equiv A \wedge B$
$\wedge$ and $\vee$ are associative.	$A \vee (\neg A \wedge B) \equiv A \vee B$
$\wedge$ and $\vee$ are commutative.	
$\wedge$ and $\vee$ distribute over each other:	*De Morgan's laws*
$A \wedge (B \vee C) \equiv (A \wedge B) \vee (A \wedge C)$	$\neg (A \wedge B) \equiv \neg A \vee \neg B$
$A \vee (B \wedge C) \equiv (A \vee B) \wedge (A \vee C)$	$\neg (A \vee B) \equiv \neg A \wedge \neg B$

Table 3.2

Can we do anything with these equivalences? Sure. We can use them to show that other wffs are equivalent without checking truth tables. But first we need to observe two general properties of equivalence.

The first thing to observe is that equivalence is an "equivalence" relation. In other words, ≡ satisfies the reflexive, symmetric, and transitive properties. The transitive property is the most important property for our purposes. It can be stated as follows for any wffs W, X, and Y:

$$\text{If } W \equiv X \text{ and } X \equiv Y \text{ then } W \equiv Y.$$

This property allows us to write a sequence of equivalences and then conclude that the first wff is equivalent to the last wff, just the way we do it with ordinary equality of algebraic expressions.

The next thing to observe is the *replacement rule* of equivalences, which can be stated as follows:

Any subwff of a wff can be replaced by an equivalent wff without changing the truth value of the original wff.

It's just like the old phrase "Substituting equals for equals doesn't change the value of an expression." Can you see why this is OK for equivalences?

For example, suppose we want to simplify the wff $B \to (A \vee (A \wedge B))$. We might notice that one of the laws from (3.1) gives $A \vee (A \wedge B) \equiv A$. Therefore we can apply the replacement rule and write the following equivalence:

$$B \to (A \vee (A \wedge B)) \equiv B \to A.$$

Normal Forms

We're going to discuss some useful forms for propositional wffs. But first we need a little terminology. A *literal* is a propositional letter or its negation. For example, P, Q, $\neg P$, and $\neg Q$ are literals.

Conjunctive Normal Form

A *fundamental disjunction* is either a literal or the disjunction of two or more literals. For example, P and $P \vee \neg Q$ are fundamental disjunctions. A *conjunctive normal form* (CNF) is either a fundamental disjunction or a conjunction of two or more fundamental disjunctions. For example, the following wffs are CNFs:

$$P \wedge (\neg P \vee Q),$$
$$(P \vee Q) \wedge (\neg Q \vee P),$$
$$(P \vee Q \vee R) \wedge (\neg P \vee Q \vee R).$$

Sometimes the trivial cases are hardest to see. For example, try to explain why the following four wffs are CNFs: $P, \neg P, P \wedge \neg P$, and $\neg P \vee Q$.

The important point about CNFs is that any wff is equivalent to a CNF. We'll state the result and then show how to transform a wff into a CNF.

$$\textit{Every wff is equivalent to a CNF.} \qquad (3.2)$$

We can transform a wff into a CNF by using equivalences (3.1). First, remove all occurrences (if there are any) of the connective $\rightarrow$ by using the equivalence

$$A \rightarrow B \equiv \neg A \vee B.$$

Next, move all negations inside to create literals by using De Morgan's equivalences

$$\neg (A \wedge B) \equiv \neg A \vee \neg B \quad \text{and} \quad \neg (A \vee B) \equiv \neg A \wedge \neg B.$$

Finally, apply the distributive equivalences to obtain a CNF.

EXAMPLE 1. We'll construct a CNF for the wff $(P \vee Q \rightarrow R) \vee S$.

$$\begin{aligned}
(P \vee Q \rightarrow R) \vee S &\equiv (\neg (P \vee Q) \vee R) \vee S \\
&\equiv ((\neg P \wedge \neg Q) \vee R) \vee S \\
&\equiv (\neg P \wedge \neg Q) \vee (R \vee S) \\
&\equiv (\neg P \vee R \vee S) \wedge (\neg Q \vee R \vee S). \quad \blacklozenge
\end{aligned}$$

Disjunctive Normal Form

A *fundamental conjunction* is either a literal or a conjunction of two or more literals. For example, P and $P \wedge \neg Q$ are fundamental conjunctions. A *disjunctive normal form* (DNF) is either a fundamental conjunction or a disjunction of two or more fundamental conjunctions. For example, the following wffs are DNFs:

$$P \vee (\neg P \wedge Q),$$
$$(P \wedge Q) \vee (\neg Q \wedge P),$$
$$(P \wedge Q \wedge R) \vee (\neg P \wedge Q \wedge R).$$

Sometimes the trivial cases are hardest to see. For example, try to explain why the following four wffs are DNFs: $P, \neg P, P \vee \neg P$, and $\neg P \wedge Q$.

The important point about DNFs is that any wff is equivalent to a DNF.

We'll state the result and then show how to transform a wff into a DNF.

$$Every\ wff\ is\ equivalent\ to\ a\ DNF. \qquad (3.3)$$

We can transform a wff into a DNF by using equivalences (3.1). First, remove all occurrences (if there are any) of the connective $\rightarrow$ by using the equivalence

$$A \rightarrow B \equiv \neg A \vee B.$$

Next, move all negations inside to create literals by using De Morgan's equivalences. Finally, apply the distributive equivalences to obtain a DNF.

EXAMPLE 2. We'll construct a DNF for the wff $(P \wedge Q \rightarrow R) \wedge S$.

$$
\begin{aligned}
(P \wedge Q \rightarrow R) \wedge S \ &\equiv\ (\neg (P \wedge Q) \vee R) \wedge S \\
&\equiv\ (\neg P \vee \neg Q \vee R) \wedge S \\
&\equiv\ (\neg P \wedge S) \vee (\neg Q \wedge S) \vee (R \wedge S). \quad \blacklozenge
\end{aligned}
$$

Formal Reasoning

We have seen that truth tables are sufficient to find the truth of any proposition. However, if a proposition has three or more variables and contains several connectives, then a truth table can become quite complicated. When we use an equivalence proof, rather than truth tables, to decide the equivalence of two wffs, it seems somehow closer to the way we communicate with each other. Although there is no need to formally reason about the truth of propositions, it turns out that all other parts of logic need tools other than truth tables to reason about the truth of wffs. Thus we need to introduce the basic ideas of a formal reasoning system. We'll do it here because the techniques carry over to all logical systems. A formal reasoning system must have a set of well-formed formulas (wffs) to represent the statements of interest. But two other ingredients are required, and we'll discuss them next.

A reasoning system needs some rules to help us conclude things. An *inference rule* maps one or more wffs, called *premises, hypotheses,* or *antecedents*, to a single wff called the *conclusion*, or *consequent*. For example, the modus ponens rule maps the two wffs A and $A \rightarrow B$ to the wff B. A common way to represent an inference rule is to draw a horizontal line, place the premises above the line and place the conclusion below the line. The premises can be listed horizontally or vertically, and the conclusion is prefixed by the symbol $\therefore$ as follows:

$$P_1$$
$$\vdots$$

$$\frac{P_1, \ldots, P_k}{\therefore C} \quad \text{or} \quad \frac{\begin{array}{c} P_1 \\ \vdots \\ P_k \end{array}}{\therefore C} \, .$$

The symbol $\therefore$ can be read as any of the following words:

therefore, thus, whence, so, ergo, hence.

We can also say, "C is a direct consequence of P_1 and ... and P_k." For example, the modus ponens rule can be written as follows:

Modus ponens (*MP*)

$$\frac{A \rightarrow B, A}{\therefore B} \quad \text{or} \quad \frac{\begin{array}{c} A \\ A \rightarrow B \end{array}}{\therefore B} \, . \tag{3.4}$$

We would like our inference rules to preserve truth. In other words, if all the premises are tautologies, then we want the conclusion to be a tautology. So an inference rule with premises $P_1, \ldots, P_k$ and conclusion C preserves truth if the following wff is a tautology:

$$P_1 \wedge \ldots \wedge P_k \rightarrow C.$$

For example, the modus ponens rule preserves truth because whenever A and $A \rightarrow B$ are both tautologies, then B is also a tautology. We can prove this by showing that the following wff is a tautology:

$$A \wedge (A \rightarrow B) \rightarrow B.$$

Any conditional tautology of the form $C \rightarrow D$ can be used as an inference rule. For example, the tautology

$$(A \rightarrow B) \wedge \neg B \rightarrow \neg A$$

gives rise to the *modus tollens* inference rule (MT) for propositions:

Modus tollens (*MT*)

$$\frac{A \rightarrow B, \ \neg B}{\therefore \ \neg A} \, . \tag{3.5}$$

Now let's list a few more useful inference rules for the propositional calculus. Each rule can be easily verified by showing that $C \to D$ is a tautology, where C is the conjunction of the premises and D is the conclusion.

Conjunction (Conj)

$$\frac{A, B}{\therefore\ A \wedge B}.$$

(3.6)

Simplification (Simp)

$$\frac{A \wedge B}{\therefore\ A}.$$

(3.7)

Addition (Add)

$$\frac{A}{\therefore\ A \vee B}.$$

(3.8)

Disjunctive syllogism (DS)

$$\frac{A \vee B, \neg A}{\therefore\ B}.$$

(3.9)

Hypothetical syllogism (HS)

$$\frac{A \to B, B \to C}{\therefore\ A \to C}.$$

(3.10)

For any reasoning system to work, it needs some fundamental truths to start the process. An *axiom* is a wff that we wish to use as a basis from which to reason. So an axiom is usually a wff that we "know to be true" from our initial investigations (e.g., a proposition that has been shown to be a tautology by a truth table). When we apply logic to a particular subject, then an axiom might also be something that we "want to be true" to start out our discussion (e.g., "two points lie on one and only one line" for a geometry reasoning system).

We've introduced the three ingredients that make up any *formal reasoning system*:

A set of wffs,   a set of axioms,   and   a set of inference rules.

A formal reasoning system is often called a *formal theory*. How do we reason in such a system? Can we describe the reasoning process in some reasonable way? What is a proof? What is a theorem? Let's start off by describing a proof.

A *proof* is a finite sequence of wffs with the property that each wff in the sequence either is an axiom or can be inferred from previous wffs in the sequence. The last wff in a proof is called a *theorem*. For example, suppose the following sequence of wffs is a proof:

$$W_1, ..., W_n.$$

Then we know that W_1 is an axiom because there aren't any previous wffs in the sequence to infer it. We also know that for any $i > 1$, either W_i is an axiom or W_i is the conclusion of an inference rule, where the premises of the rule are taken from the set of wffs $\{W_1, ..., W_{i-1}\}$. We also know that W_n is a theorem. So when we say that a wff W is a theorem, we mean that there is a proof W_1, ..., W_n such that $W_n = W$.

Suppose we are unlucky enough to have a formal theory with a wff W such that both W and $\neg W$ can be proved as theorems. A formal theory exhibiting this bad behavior is said to be *inconsistent*. We probably would agree that inconsistency is a bad situation. A formal theory that doesn't possess this bad behavior is said to be *consistent*. We certainly would like our formal theories to be consistent. For the propositional calculus we'll get consistency if we choose our axioms to be tautologies and we choose our inference rules to map tautologies to tautologies. In this case, every theorem will have to be a tautology.

We'll write proofs in table format, where each line is numbered and contains a wff together with the reason it's there. For example, a proof sequence $W_1, ..., W_n$ will be written as follows:

Proof: 1. W_1 Reason for W_1

            2. W_2 Reason for W_2

          $\vdots$ $\vdots$ $\vdots$

          $n.$ W_n Reason for W_n.

The reason column for each line always contains a short indication of why the wff is on the line. If the line depends on previous lines because of an inference rule, then we'll always include the line numbers of those previous lines.

Now let's get down to business and study some formal proof techniques for the propositional calculus. The two techniques that we will discuss are conditional proof and indirect proof.

Conditional Proof

Most statements that we want to prove either are in the form of a conditional or can be restated in the form of a conditional. For example, someone might make a statement of the form "D follows from A, B, and C." The statement can be rephrased in many ways. For example, we might say, "From the premises A, B, and C we can conclude D." We can avoid wordiness by writing the statement as the conditional

$$A \wedge B \wedge C \to D.$$

Let's discuss a rule to help us prove conditionals in a straightforward manner. The rule is called the *conditional proof rule* (CP), and we can describe it as follows:

Conditional Proof Rule (CP) (3.11)

Suppose we wish to construct a proof for a conditional of the form

$$A_1 \wedge A_2 \wedge ... \wedge A_n \to B.$$

Start the proof by writing each of the premises A_1, A_2, ..., A_n on a separate line with the letter P in the reason column. Now treat these premises as axioms, and construct a proof of B.

Let's look at the structure of a typical conditional proof. For example, a conditional proof of the wff $A \wedge B \wedge C \to D$ will contain lines for the three premises A, B, and C. It will also contain a line for the conclusion D. Finally, it will contain a line for $A \wedge B \wedge C \to D$, with CP listed in the reason column along with the line numbers of the premises and conclusion. The following proof structure exhibits these properties:

Proof: 1. A P
        2. B P
        3. C P
        $\vdots$ $\vdots$ $\vdots$
        k. D ...
        $k+1$. $A \wedge B \wedge C \to D$ 1, 2, 3, k, CP.

Since many conditionals are quite complicated, it may be difficult to write them on the last line of a proof. Therefore we'll agree to write QED in place of the conditional on the last line of the proof, and we'll also omit the last line number. Thus the form of the above proof can be abbreviated to the following form:

Proof: 1. *A*   *P*
        2. *B*   *P*
        3. *C*   *P*
         ⋮ ⋮   ⋮
        k. *D*   ...
            QED   1, 2, 3, *k*, CP.

EXAMPLE 3. Let's do a real example to get the flavor of things. We'll give a conditional proof of the following statement:

$$(A \lor B) \land (A \lor C) \land \neg A \to B \land C.$$

The three premises are $A \lor B$, $A \lor C$, and $\neg A$. So we'll list them as premises to start the proof. Then we'll construct a proof of $B \land C$.

Proof: 1. $A \lor B$ *P*
        2. $A \lor C$ *P*
        3. $\neg A$ *P*
        4. *B*   1, 3, DS
        5. *C*   2, 3, DS
        6. $B \land C$ 4, 5, Conj
            QED   1, 2, 3, 6, CP.   ◆

Subproofs

Often a conditional proof will occur as part of another proof. We'll call a proof that is part of another proof a *subproof* of the proof. We'll always indicate a conditional subproof by indenting the wffs on its lines. We'll always write the conditional to be proved on the next line of the proof, without the indentation, because it will be needed as part of the main proof. Let's do an example to show the idea.

EXAMPLE 4. We'll give a proof of the following statement:

$$((A \lor B) \to (B \land C)) \to (B \to C) \lor D.$$

Notice that this wff is a conditional, where the conclusion $(B \to C) \lor D$ contains a second conditional $B \to C$. So we'll use a conditional proof that contains another conditional proof as a subproof. Here goes:

Proof: 1. $(A \vee B) \to (B \wedge C)$ P
        2. B P Start subproof of $B \to C$
        3. $A \vee B$ 2, Add
        4. $B \wedge C$ 1, 3, MP
        5. C 4, Simp
        6. $B \to C$ 2, 5, CP   Finish subproof of $B \to C$
        7. $(B \to C) \vee D$ 6, Add
        QED   1, 7, CP. ◆

An Important Rule about Conditional Subproofs

If there is a conditional proof as a subproof within another proof, as indicated by the indented lines, then these indented lines may not be used to infer some line that occurs after the subproof is finished. The only exception to this rule is if an indented line does not depend, either directly or indirectly, on any premise of the subproof. In this case the indented line could actually be placed above the subproof, with the indentation removed.

Simplifications in Conditional Proofs

We can make some simplifications in our proofs to reflect the way informal proofs are written. If W is a theorem, then we can use it to prove other theorems. We can put W on a line of a proof and treat it as an axiom. Or we can leave W out of the proof sequence but still use it as a reason for some line of the proof. Instead of writing down the specific tautology or theorem in the reason column, we'll usually write the symbol

$$T$$

to indicate that a tautology or theorem is being used.

EXAMPLE 5. We will give a conditional proof of the following wff:

$$A \wedge ((A \to B) \vee (C \wedge D)) \to (\neg B \to C).$$

Proof: 1. A P
        2. $(A \to B) \vee (C \wedge D)$ P
        3. $\neg B$ P
        4. $A \wedge \neg B$ 1, 3, Conj
        5. $\neg \neg A \wedge \neg B$ 4, T
        6. $\neg (\neg A \vee B)$ 5, T
        7. $\neg (A \to B)$ 6, T
        8. $C \wedge D$ 2, 7, DS

9.	C	8, Simp
10.	$\neg B \to C$	3, 9, CP
	QED	1, 2, 10, CP. ◆

EXAMPLE 6. Consider the following collection of statements:

> The team wins or I am sad. If the team wins, then I go to a movie. If I am sad, then my dog barks. My dog is quiet. Therefore I go to a movie.

Let's formalize these statements. Let W mean "The team wins;" let S mean "I am sad;" let M mean "I go to a movie;" and let B mean "My dog barks." Now we can symbolize the given statements by the wff

$$(W \vee S) \wedge (W \to M) \wedge (S \to B) \wedge \neg B \to M.$$

We'll show this wff is a theorem by giving a proof as follows:

Proof:	1.	$W \vee S$	P
	2.	$W \to M$	P
	3.	$S \to B$	P
	4.	$\neg B$	P
	5.	$\neg S$	3, 4, MT
	6.	W	1, 5, DS
	7.	M	2, 6, MP
		QED	1, 2, 3, 4, 7, CP. ◆

Indirect Proof

Suppose we want to prove a statement $A \to B$, but we just can't seem to find a way to get going using the conditional proof technique. Sometimes it may be worthwhile to try to prove the contrapositive of $A \to B$. In other words, we try a conditional proof of $\neg B \to \neg A$. Since we have the equivalence

$$A \to B \equiv \neg B \to \neg A,$$

we can start by letting $\neg B$ be the premise. Then we can try to find a proof that ends with $\neg A$.

What if we still have problems finding a proof? Then we might try another indirect method, called *proof by contradiction* or *reductio ad absurdum*. The idea is based on the following equivalence:

$$A \to B \equiv A \wedge \neg B \to \text{false}.$$

This indirect method gives us more information to work with than the contra-positive method because we can use both A and $\neg B$ as premises. We also have more freedom because all we need to do is find any kind of contradiction. You might try it whenever there doesn't seem to be enough information from the given premises or when you run out of ideas. You might also try it as your first method. Here's the formal description:

Indirect Proof Rule (IP)   (3.12)

Suppose we wish to construct an indirect proof of the conditional

$$A_1 \wedge A_2 \wedge ... \wedge A_n \rightarrow B.$$

Start the proof by writing each of the premises A_1, A_2, ..., A_n on a sepa-rate line with the letter P in the reason column. Then place the wff $\neg B$ on the next line, and write "P for IP" in the reason column to indicate that $\neg B$ is a premise for indirect proof. Now treat these premises as ax-ioms, and construct a proof of a false statement.

Let's look at the structure of a typical indirect proof. For example, an in-direct proof of the wff $A \wedge B \wedge C \rightarrow D$ will contain lines for the three premises A, B, and C, and for the IP premise $\neg D$. It will also contain a line for a false statement. Finally, it will contain a line for $A \wedge B \wedge C \rightarrow D$, with IP listed in the reason column along with the line numbers of the premises, the IP premise, and the false statement. The following proof structure exhibits these properties:

Proof: 1. A P

           2. B P

           3. C P

           4. $\neg D$ P for IP

            $\vdots$ $\vdots$ $\vdots$

           k. false   ...

    $k + 1$. $A \wedge B \wedge C \rightarrow D$ 1, 2, 3, 4, k, IP.

As with the case for conditional proofs, we'll agree to write QED in place the conditional on the last line of the proof, and we'll also omit the last line number. So the form of the above proof can be abbreviated as follows:

Proof: 1. A P

           2. B P

           3. C P

4. $\neg D$ P for IP

$\vdots$ $\vdots$ $\vdots$

$k.$ false   ...

QED   1, 2, 3, 4, k, IP.

EXAMPLE 7. Let's do a real example to get our feet wet. We'll give an indirect proof of the following statement, which is derived from the movies problem in Example 6:

$$(W \vee S) \wedge (W \to M) \wedge (S \to B) \wedge \neg B \to M.$$

Proof:
  1. $W \vee S$ P
  2. $W \to M$ P
  3. $S \to B$ P
  4. $\neg B$ P
  5. $\neg M$ P for IP
  6. $\neg W$ 2, 5, MT
  7. $\neg S$ 3, 4, MT
  8. $\neg W \wedge \neg S$ 6, 7, Conj
  9. $\neg (W \vee S)$ 8, T
10. $(W \vee S) \wedge \neg (W \vee S)$ 1, 9, Conj
11. false   10, T
     QED   1–4, 5, 11, IP.   ♦

Compare this proof to the earlier direct proof of the same statement. It's a bit longer, and it uses different rules. Sometimes a longer proof can be easier to create, using simpler steps. Just remember, there's more than one way to proceed when trying a proof.

Proof Notes

When proving something, we should always try to *tell the proof, the whole proof, and nothing but the proof*. Here are a few concrete suggestions that should make life easier for beginning provers.

Don't Use Unnecessary Premises

Sometimes beginners like to put extra premises in proofs to help get to a conclusion. But then they forget to give credit to these extra premises. For example, suppose we want to prove a conditional of the form $A \to C$. We start the proof by writing A as a premise. Suppose that along the way we decide to introduce another premise, say B, and then use A and B to infer C, either directly or indirectly. The result is not a proof of $A \rightarrow C$. Instead, we have given a proof of the statement $A \wedge B \rightarrow C$.

Remember: Be sure to use a premise only when it's the hypothesis of a conditional that you want to prove. Another way to say this is: If you use a premise to prove something, then the premise becomes part of the antecedent of the thing you proved. Still another way to say this is:

> The conjunction of all the premises that you use to prove something is precisely the antecedent of the conditional that you proved.

Don't Apply Inference Rules to Subexpressions

Beginners sometimes use an inference rule incorrectly by applying it to a subexpression of a larger wff. This violates the definition of a proof, which states that a wff in a proof either is an axiom or is inferred by previous wffs in the proof. In other words, an inference rule can be applied only to entire wffs that appear on previous lines of the proof. So

> Don't apply inference rules to subexpressions of wffs.

Exercises

1. Verify each of the following equivalences by writing an equivalence proof. That is, start on one side and use known equivalences to get to the other side.

   a. $(A \rightarrow B) \wedge (A \vee B) \equiv B$.

   b. $A \wedge B \rightarrow C \equiv (A \rightarrow C) \vee (B \rightarrow C)$.

   c. $A \wedge B \rightarrow C \equiv A \rightarrow (B \rightarrow C)$.

   d. $A \vee B \rightarrow C \equiv (A \rightarrow C) \wedge (B \rightarrow C)$.

   e. $A \rightarrow B \wedge C \equiv (A \rightarrow B) \wedge (A \rightarrow C)$.

   f. $A \rightarrow B \vee C \equiv (A \rightarrow B) \vee (A \rightarrow C)$.

2. Show that each of the following statements is not a tautology by finding truth values for the variables that make the premise true and the conclusion false.

   a. $(A \vee B) \rightarrow (C \vee A) \wedge (\neg C \vee B)$.

   b. $(A \rightarrow B) \wedge (B \rightarrow \neg A) \rightarrow A$.

   c. $(A \rightarrow B) \wedge (B \rightarrow C) \rightarrow (C \rightarrow A)$.

   d. $(A \vee B \rightarrow C) \wedge A \rightarrow (C \rightarrow B)$.

3. Use equivalences to transform each of the following wffs into a CNF.

    a. $(P \rightarrow Q) \rightarrow P$.

    b. $P \rightarrow (Q \rightarrow P)$.

    c. $Q \wedge \neg P \rightarrow P$.

    d. $(P \vee Q) \wedge R$.

    e. $P \rightarrow Q \wedge R$.

    f. $(A \wedge B) \vee E \vee F$.

    g. $(A \wedge B) \vee (C \wedge D) \vee (E \rightarrow F)$.

4. Use equivalences to transform each of the following wffs into a DNF.

    a. $(P \rightarrow Q) \rightarrow P$.

    b. $P \rightarrow (Q \rightarrow P)$.

    c. $Q \wedge \neg P \rightarrow P$.

    d. $(P \vee Q) \wedge R$.

    e. $P \rightarrow Q \wedge R$.

    f. $(A \vee B) \wedge (C \rightarrow D)$.

5. Give a formalized version of the following proof:

If I am dancing, then I am happy. There is a mouse in the house or I am happy. I am sad. Therefore there is a mouse in the house and I am not dancing.

6. Give formal proofs for each of the following tautologies by using the CP rule.

    a. $A \rightarrow (B \rightarrow (A \wedge B))$.

    b. $A \rightarrow (\neg B \rightarrow (A \wedge \neg B))$.

    c. $(A \vee B \rightarrow C) \wedge A \rightarrow C$.

    d. $(B \rightarrow C) \rightarrow (A \wedge B \rightarrow A \wedge C)$.

    e. $(A \vee B \rightarrow C \wedge D) \rightarrow (B \rightarrow D)$.

    f. $(A \vee B \rightarrow C) \wedge (C \rightarrow D \wedge E) \rightarrow (A \rightarrow D)$.

    g. $\neg (A \wedge B) \wedge (B \vee C) \wedge (C \rightarrow D) \rightarrow (A \rightarrow D)$.

    h. $(A \rightarrow (B \rightarrow C)) \rightarrow (B \rightarrow (A \rightarrow C))$.

    i. $(A \rightarrow C) \rightarrow (A \wedge B \rightarrow C)$.

    j. $(A \rightarrow C) \rightarrow (A \rightarrow B \vee C)$.

7. Give formal proofs for each of the following tautologies by using the IP rule.

    a. $A \rightarrow (B \rightarrow A)$.

    b. $(A \rightarrow B) \wedge (A \vee B) \rightarrow B$.

    c. $\neg B \rightarrow (B \rightarrow C)$.

    d. $(A \rightarrow B) \rightarrow (C \vee A \rightarrow C \vee B)$.

    e. $(A \rightarrow B) \rightarrow ((A \rightarrow \neg B) \rightarrow \neg A)$.

    f. $(A \rightarrow B) \rightarrow ((B \rightarrow C) \rightarrow (A \vee B \rightarrow C))$.

    g. $(A \rightarrow B) \wedge (B \rightarrow C) \rightarrow (A \rightarrow C)$. *Note:* This is the HS inference rule.

    h. $(C \rightarrow A) \wedge (\neg C \rightarrow B) \rightarrow (A \vee B)$.

8. Give formal proofs for each of the following tautologies by using the IP rule somewhere in each proof.

    a. $A \rightarrow (B \rightarrow (A \wedge B))$.

    b. $A \rightarrow (\neg B \rightarrow (A \wedge \neg B))$.

    c. $(A \vee B \rightarrow C) \wedge A \rightarrow C$.

    d. $(B \rightarrow C) \rightarrow (A \wedge B \rightarrow A \wedge C)$.

    e. $(A \vee B \rightarrow C \wedge D) \rightarrow (B \rightarrow D)$.

    f. $(A \vee B \rightarrow C) \wedge (C \rightarrow D \wedge E) \rightarrow (A \rightarrow D)$.

    g. $\neg (A \wedge B) \wedge (B \vee C) \wedge (C \rightarrow D) \rightarrow (A \rightarrow D)$.

    h. $(A \rightarrow B) \rightarrow ((B \rightarrow C) \rightarrow (A \vee B \rightarrow C))$.

    i. $(A \rightarrow (B \rightarrow C)) \rightarrow (B \rightarrow (A \rightarrow C))$.

    j. $(A \rightarrow C) \rightarrow (A \wedge B \rightarrow C)$.

    k. $(A \rightarrow C) \rightarrow (A \rightarrow B \vee C)$.

9. The following two inference rules, called *dilemmas,* can be useful in certain cases. Give a formal proof for each rule, showing that it maps tautologies to tautologies. In other words, prove that the conjunction of the premises implies the conclusion.

    a. *Constructive dilemma (CD):*

$$\frac{A \vee B, A \rightarrow C, B \rightarrow D}{\therefore\ C \vee D}.$$

    b. *Destructive dilemma (DD):*

$$\frac{\neg C \vee \neg D, A \rightarrow C, B \rightarrow D}{\therefore\ \neg A \vee \neg B}.$$

3.2 Predicate Calculus

The propositional calculus provides adequate tools for reasoning about propositional wffs, which are combinations of propositions. But a proposition is a sentence taken as a whole. With this restrictive definition, propositional calculus doesn't provide the tools to do everyday reasoning. For example, in the following argument it is impossible to find a formal way to test the correctness of the inference without further analysis of each sentence:

All computer science majors own a personal computer.

Socrates does not own a personal computer.

Therefore Socrates is not a computer science major.

To discuss such an argument, we need to break up the sentences into parts. The words in the set {All, own, not} are important to understand the argument. Somehow we need to symbolize a sentence so that the information needed for reasoning is characterized in some way. Therefore we will study the inner structure of sentences.

The statement "x owns a personal computer" is not a proposition because its truth value depends on x. If we give x a value, like x = Socrates, then the statement becomes a proposition because it has the value true or false. From the grammar point of view, the property "owns a personal computer" is a predicate, where a predicate is the part of a sentence that gives a property of the subject. A predicate usually contains a verb, like "owns" in our example. The word predicate comes from the Latin word *praedicare*, which means to proclaim.

From the logic point of view, a *predicate* is a relation, which of course we can also think of as a property. For example, suppose we let $p(x)$ mean "x owns a personal computer." Then p is a predicate that describes the relation (i.e., property) of owning a personal computer. Sometimes it's convenient to call $p(x)$ a predicate, although p is the actual predicate. If we replace the variable x by some definite value such as Socrates, then we obtain the proposition p(Socrates). For another example, suppose that for any two natural numbers x and y we let $q(x, y)$ mean "$x < y$." Then q is the predicate that we all know of as the "less than" relation. For example, the proposition $q(1, 5)$ is true, and the proposition $q(8, 3)$ is false.

Let $p(x)$ mean "x is an odd integer." Then the proposition $p(9)$ is true, and the proposition $p(20)$ is false. Similarly, the following proposition is true:

$$p(2) \vee p(3) \vee p(4) \vee p(5).$$

We can describe this proposition by saying, "There exists an element x in the set {2, 3, 4, 5} such that $p(x)$ is true." By letting D = {2, 3, 4, 5} the statement can be shortened to "There exists $x \in D$ such that $p(x)$ is true." If we don't care about the truth of the statement, then we can still describe the preceding disjunction by saying, "There exists $x \in D$ such that $p(x)$." Still more formally, we can write the expression

$$\exists x \in D : p(x).$$

Now if we want to consider the truth of the expression for a different set of numbers, say S, then we would write

$$\exists x \in S : p(x).$$

This expression would be true if S contained an odd integer. If we want to consider the statement without regard to any particular set of numbers, then we write

$$\exists x \, p(x).$$

This expression is not a proposition because we don't have a specific set of elements over which x can vary. Thus $\exists x \, p(x)$ cannot be given a truth value. If we don't know what p stands for, we can still say, "There exists an x such that $p(x)$." The symbol $\exists x$ is called an *existential quantifier*.

Now let's look at conjunctions rather than disjunctions. Suppose we have the following proposition:

$$p(1) \wedge p(3) \wedge p(5) \wedge p(7).$$

This conjunction can be represented by the expression $\forall x \in D : p(x)$, where $D = \{1, 3, 5, 7\}$. We say, "Every x in D is an odd integer." If we want to consider the statement without regard to any particular set of numbers, then we write

$$\forall x \, p(x).$$

The expression $\forall x \, p(x)$ is read, "For every $x \, p(x)$." The symbol $\forall x$ is called a *universal quantifier*.

These notions of quantification belong to a logic called *first-order predicate calculus*. The words "first-order" refer to the fact that quantifiers can quantify only variables that occur in predicates.

Syntax and Semantics

Now let's examine the structure (syntax) of the expressions that occur in first-order predicate calculus together with the meanings (semantics) that can be attached to these expressions.

Well-Formed Formulas

To give a precise description of a first-order predicate calculus, we need an alphabet of symbols. For this discussion we'll use several kinds of letters and symbols, described as follows:

Individual variables:	x, y, z
Individual constants:	a, b, c
Function constants:	f, g, h
Predicate constants:	p, q, r
Connective symbols:	$\neg, \rightarrow, \wedge, \vee$
Quantifier symbols:	$\exists, \forall$
Punctuation symbols:	$(,)$

From time to time we will use other letters, or strings of letters, to denote variables or constants. We'll also allow letters to be subscripted. The number of arguments for a predicate or function will normally be clear from the context. A predicate with no arguments is considered to be a proposition.

A *term* is either a variable, a constant, or a function applied to arguments that are terms. For example,

$$x, \quad a, \quad \text{and} \quad f(x, g(b))$$

are terms. An *atomic formula* (or simply *atom*) is a predicate applied to arguments that are terms. For example, $p(x, a)$ and $q(y, f(c))$ are atoms.

We can define the wffs—the well-formed formulas—of the first-order predicate calculus inductively as follows:

Basis: Any atom is a wff.

Induction: If W and V are wffs and x is a variable, then the following expressions are also wffs:

$$(W), \neg W, W \vee V, W \wedge V, W \rightarrow V, \exists x \, W, \text{ and } \forall x \, W.$$

To write formulas without too many parentheses and still maintain a unique meaning, we'll agree that the quantifiers have the same precedence as the negation symbol. We'll continue to use the same hierarchy of precedence for the operators $\neg, \wedge, \vee,$ and $\rightarrow$. Therefore the hierarchy of precedence now looks like the following:

$$\neg, \exists x, \forall y \qquad \text{(highest, do first)}$$
$$\wedge$$
$$\vee$$
$$\rightarrow \qquad \text{(lowest, do last)}$$

If any of the quantifiers or the negation symbol appear next to each other, then the rightmost symbol is grouped with the smallest wff to its right.

Here are a few wffs in both unparenthesized form and parenthesized form:

Unparenthesized Form	Parenthesized Form
$\forall x \neg \exists y \forall z\, p(x, y, z)$	$\forall x\, (\neg\, (\exists y\, (\forall z\, p(x, y, z))))$.
$\exists x\, p(x) \vee q(x)$	$(\exists x\, p(x)) \vee q(x)$.
$\forall x\, p(x) \rightarrow q(x)$	$(\forall x\, p(x)) \rightarrow q(x)$.
$\exists x \neg p(x, y) \rightarrow q(x) \wedge r(y)$	$(\exists x\, (\neg\, p(x, y))) \rightarrow (q(x) \wedge r(y))$.
$\exists x\, p(x) \rightarrow \forall x\, q(x) \vee p(x) \wedge r(x)$	$(\exists x\, p(x)) \rightarrow ((\forall x\, q(x)) \vee (p(x) \wedge r(x)))$.

Now let's discuss the relationship between the quantifiers and the variables that appear in a wff. When a quantifier occurs in a wff, it influences some occurrences of the quantified variable. The extent of this influence is called the scope of the quantifier, which we define as follows:

In the wff $\exists x\, W$, W is the *scope* of the quantifier $\exists x$.

In the wff $\forall x\, W$, W is the *scope* of the quantifier $\forall x$.

For example, the scope of $\exists x$ in the wff

$$\exists x\, p(x, y) \rightarrow q(x)$$

is $p(x, y)$ because the parenthesized version of the wff is $(\exists x\, p(x, y)) \rightarrow q(x)$. On the other hand, the scope of $\exists x$ in the wff $\exists x\, (p(x, y) \rightarrow q(x))$ is $p(x, y) \rightarrow q(x)$.

An occurrence of the variable x in a wff is said to be *bound* if it lies within the scope of either $\exists x$ or $\forall x$ or if it's the quantifier variable x itself. Otherwise, an occurrence of x is said to be *free* in the wff. For example, consider the following wff:

$$\exists x\, p(x, y) \rightarrow q(x).$$

The first two occurrences of x are bound because the scope of $\exists x$ is $p(x, y)$. The only occurrence y is free, and the third occurrence of x is free.

So every occurrence of a variable in a wff can be classified as either bound or free, and this classification is determined by the scope of the quantifiers in the wff. Now we're in position to discuss the meaning of wffs.

Semantics

Up to this point a wff is just a string of symbols with no meaning attached. For a wff to have a meaning, we must give an interpretation to its symbols so that the wff can be read as a statement that is true or false. For example, suppose we let $p(x)$ mean "x is an even integer" and we let x be the number 236. With this interpretation, $p(x)$ becomes the statement "236 is an even integer," which is true.

As another example, let's give an interpretation to the wff

$$\forall x \, \exists y \, s(x, y).$$

We'll let $s(x, y)$ mean that the successor of x is y, where the variables x and y take values from the set of natural numbers $\mathbb{N}$. With this interpretation the wff becomes the statement "For every natural number x there exists a natural number y such that the successor of x is y," which is true.

Before we proceed any further, we need to make a precise definition of an interpretation. Here's the definition:

Interpretations   (3.13)

An *interpretation* for a wff consists of a nonempty set D, called the *domain* of the interpretation, together with an assignment that associates the symbols of the wff to values in D as follows:

1. Each predicate letter must be assigned some relation over D. A predicate with no arguments is a proposition and must be assigned a truth value.

2. Each function letter must be assigned a function over D.

3. Each free variable must be assigned a value in D. All free occurrences of a variable x are assigned the same value in D.

4. Each constant must be assigned a value in D. All occurrences of the same constant are assigned the same value in D.

So there can be many interpretations for a wff. To describe the meaning of an interpreted wff, we need some notation. Suppose W is a wff, x is a free variable in W, and t is a term. Then the wff obtained from W by replacing all free occurrences of x by t is denoted by the expression

$$W(x/t).$$

The expression x/t is called a *binding* of x to t and can be read as "x gets t" or "x is bound to t" or "x has value t" or "x is replaced by t." We can read $W(x/t)$ as "W with x replaced by t" or "W with x bound to t." For example, suppose we have the following wff:

$$W = p(x) \vee \exists x \, q(x, y).$$

We can apply the binding x/a to W to obtain the wff

$$W(x/a) = p(a) \vee \exists x\, q(x, y).$$

We can apply the binding y/b to $W(x/a)$ to obtain the wff

$$W(x/a)\,(y/b) = p(a) \vee \exists x\, q(x, b).$$

We often want to emphasize the fact that a wff W contains a free variable x. In this case we'll use the notation

$$W(x).$$

When this is the case, we write $W(t)$ to denote the wff $W(x/t)$. For example, if $W = p(x) \vee \exists x\, q(x, y)$ and we want to emphasize the fact the x is free in W, we'll write

$$W(x) = p(x) \vee \exists x\, q(x, y).$$

Then we can apply the binding x/a to W by writing

$$W(a) = p(a) \vee \exists x\, q(x, y).$$

Now we have all the ingredients to define the *meaning*, or *semantics*, of wffs in first-order predicate calculus.

The Meaning of a Wff

Suppose we have an interpretation with domain D for a wff.

1. If the wff has no quantifiers, then its meaning is the truth value of the statement obtained from the wff by applying the interpretation.

2. If the wff contains quantifiers, then each quantified wff is evaluated as follows:

    $\exists x\, W$ is true if $W(x/d)$ is true for some $d \in D$. Otherwise $\exists x\, W$ is false.

    $\forall x\, W$ is true if $W(x/d)$ is true for every $d \in D$. Otherwise $\forall x\, W$ is false.

The meaning of a wff containing quantifiers can be computed by recursively applying this definition. For example, consider a wff of the form $\forall x\, \exists y\, W$, where W does not contain any further quantifiers. The meaning of $\forall x\, \exists y\, W$ is true if the meaning of $(\exists y\, W)(x/d)$ is true for every $d \in D$. We can write

$$(\exists y \ W)(x/d) = \exists y \ W(x/d).$$

So for each $d \in D$ we must find the meaning of $\exists y \ W(x/d)$. The meaning of $\exists y$ $W(x/d)$ is true if there is some element $e \in D$ such that $W(x/d)(y/e)$ is true.

Let's look at a few examples that use actual interpretations.

EXAMPLE 1. The meaning of the wff $\forall x \ \exists y \ s(x, y)$ is true with respect to the interpretation $D = \mathbb{N}$, and $s(x, y)$ means "the successor of x is y." The interpreted wff can be restated as "Every natural number has a successor." ◆

EXAMPLE 2. Let's look at some interpretations for $W = \exists x \forall y \ (p(y) \rightarrow q(x, y))$. For each of the following interpretations we'll let $q(x, y)$ denote the equality relation "$x = y$."

a. Let the domain $D = \{a\}$, and let $p(a) = $ true. Then W is true.

b. Let the domain $D = \{a\}$, and let $p(a) = $ false. Then W is true.

c. Let the domain $D = \{a, b\}$, and let $p(a) = p(b) = $ true. Then W is false.

d. Notice that W is true for any domain D for which $p(d) = $ true for at most one element $d \in D$. ◆

An interpretation for a wff W is a *model* for W if W is true with respect to the interpretation. Otherwise, the interpretation is a *countermodel* for W.

Validity

Can any wff be true for every possible interpretation? Although it may seem unlikely, this property holds for many wffs. The property is important enough to introduce some terminology. A wff is *valid* if it's true for all possible interpretations. So a wff is valid if every interpretation is a model. Otherwise, the wff is *invalid*. A wff is *unsatisfiable* if it's false for all possible interpretations. So a wff is unsatisfiable if all of its interpretations are countermodels. Otherwise, it is *satisfiable*. From these definitions we see that every wff satisfies exactly one of the following pairs of properties:

> valid and satisfiable,
> satisfiable and invalid,
> unsatisfiable and invalid.

In the propositional calculus the three words *tautology*, *contingency*, and *contradiction* correspond, respectively, to the preceding three pairs of properties for the predicate calculus.

EXAMPLE 3. The wff $\exists x \, \forall y \, (p(y) \rightarrow q(x, y))$ is satisfiable and invalid. To see that the wff is satisfiable, notice that the wff is true with respect to the following interpretation: The domain is the singleton $\{3\}$, and we define $p(3) =$ true and $q(3, 3) =$ true. To see that the wff is invalid, notice that it is false with respect to the following interpretation: The domain is still the singleton $\{3\}$, but now we define $p(3) =$ true and $q(3, 3) =$ false.   ♦

In the propositional calculus we can use truth tables to decide whether any propositional wff is a tautology. But how can we show that a wff of the predicate calculus is valid? We can't check the infinitely many interpretations of the wff to see whether each one is a model. This is the same as checking infinitely many truth tables, one for each interpretation. So we are forced to use some kind of reasoning to show that a wff is valid. Here's an example.

EXAMPLE 4. Let W denote the following wff:

$$\exists y \, \forall x \, p(x, y) \rightarrow \forall x \, \exists y \, p(x, y).$$

We'll give two proofs to show that W is valid—one direct and one indirect. In both proofs we'll let A be the antecedent and B be the consequent of W.

Direct Approach

Let M be an interpretation with domain D for W such that M is a model for A. Then there is an element $d \in D$ such that $\forall x \, p(x, d)$ is true. Therefore $p(e, d)$ is true for all $e \in D$. This says that M is also a model for B. Therefore W is valid.   QED.

Indirect Approach

Assume that W is invalid. Then it has a countermodel with domain D that makes A true and B false. Therefore there is an element $d \in D$ such that the wff $\exists y \, p(d, y)$ is false. Thus $p(d, e)$ is false for all $e \in D$. Now we are assuming that A is true. Therefore there is an element $c \in D$ such that $\forall x \, p(x, c)$ is true. In other words, $p(b, c)$ is true for all $b \in D$. In particular, this says that $p(d, c)$ is true. But this contradicts the fact that $p(d, e)$ is false for all elements $e \in D$. Therefore W is valid. QED.   ♦

There are two interesting transformations that we can apply to any wff containing free variables. One is to universally quantify each free variable, and that other is to existentially quantify each free variable. It seems reasonable to expect that these transformations will change the meaning of the original wff, as the following examples show:

$p(x) \wedge \neg p(y)$ is satisfiable, but $\forall x \, \forall y \, (p(x) \wedge \neg p(y))$ is unsatisfiable.

$p(x) \rightarrow p(y)$ is invalid, but $\exists x \, \exists y \, (p(x) \rightarrow p(y))$ is valid.

The interesting thing about the process is that validity is preserved if we universally quantify the free variables and unsatisfiability is preserved if we existentially quantify the free variables. To make this more precise, we need a little terminology.

Suppose W is a wff with free variables $x_1, \ldots, x_n$. The *universal closure* of W is the wff

$$\forall x_1 \cdots \forall x_n \, W.$$

The *existential closure* of W is the wff

$$\exists x_1 \cdots \exists x_n \, W.$$

For example, suppose $W = \forall x \, p(x, y)$. W has y as its only free variable. So the universal closure of W is

$$\forall y \, \forall x \, p(x, y),$$

and the existential closure of W is

$$\exists y \, \forall x \, p(x, y).$$

As we have seen, the meaning of a wff may change by taking either of the closures. But there are two properties that don't change, and we'll state them for the record as follows:

Closure Properties (3.14)

1. A wff is valid if and only if its universal closure is valid.
2. A wff is unsatisfiable iff its existential closure is unsatisfiable.

Proof of property 1: Let W be a wff and x be the only free variable of W. Let M be a model for W with domain D. Then $W(x/d)$ is true for every element $d \in D$. In other words, M is a model for $\forall x \, W$. On the other hand, let M be a model for $\forall x \, W$, where D is the domain. Then $W(x/d)$ is true for every element $d \in D$. Therefore M is a model for W. If there are more free variables in a wff, then apply the argument to each variable.   QED.

Equivalence

Two wffs A and B are *equivalent* if they both have the same truth value with respect to every interpretation of both A and B. By an interpretation of both A and B, we mean that all free variables, constants, functions, and predicates that occur in either A or B are interpreted with respect to a single domain. We denote the fact that A and B are equivalent by writing

$$A \equiv B.$$

We can describe equivalence in terms of a single valid wff as follows:

$$A \equiv B \quad \text{if and only if} \quad (A \to B) \wedge (B \to A) \text{ is a valid.}$$

To start things off, let's see how propositional equivalences give rise to predicate calculus equivalences. A wff W is an *instance* of a propositional wff V if W is obtained from V by replacing each propositional letter of V by a wff, where all occurrences of each propositional letter in V are replaced by the same wff. For example, the wff

$$\forall x\, p(x) \to \forall x\, p(x) \vee q(x)$$

is an instance of $P \to P \vee Q$ because Q is replaced by $q(x)$ and both occurrences of P are replaced by $\forall x\, p(x)$.

If W is an instance of a propositional wff V, then the truth value of W for any interpretation can be obtained by assigning truth values to the letters of V. For example, suppose we define an interpretation with domain $D = \{a, b\}$ and we set $p(a) = p(b) = \text{true}$ and $q(a) = q(b) = \text{false}$. For this interpretation, the truth value of the wff $\forall x\, p(x) \to \forall x\, p(x) \vee q(x)$ is the same as the truth value of the propositional wff $P \to P \vee Q$, where $P = \text{true}$ and $Q = \text{false}$.

So we can say that two wffs are equivalent if they are instances of two equivalent propositional wffs, where both instances are obtained by using the same replacement of propositional letters. For example, we have

$$\forall x\, p(x) \to q(x) \equiv \neg\, \forall x\, p(x) \vee q(x)$$

because the left and right sides are instances of the left and right sides of the propositional equivalence $P \to Q \equiv \neg P \vee Q$, where both occurrences of P are replaced by $\forall x\, p(x)$ and both occurrences of Q are replaced by $q(x)$. We'll state the result again for emphasis:

> *Two wffs are equivalent whenever they are instances of two equivalent propositional wffs, where both instances are obtained by using the same replacement of propositional letters.*

Let's see whether we can find some more equivalences to make our logical life easier. We'll start by listing two equivalences that relate the two quantifiers by negation. For any wff W we have the two equivalences

$$\neg\,(\forall x\; W) \equiv \exists x \neg\, W \quad \text{and} \quad \neg\,(\exists x\; W) \equiv \forall x \neg\, W. \tag{3.15}$$

It's easy to believe that these two equivalences are true. For example, we can illustrate the equivalence $\neg\,(\forall x\; W) \equiv \exists x \neg\, W$ by observing that the negation of the statement "Something is true for all possible cases" has the same meaning as the statement "There is some case for which the something is false." Similarly, we can illustrate the equivalence $\neg\,(\exists x\; W) \equiv \forall x \neg\, W$ by observing that the negation of the statement "There is some case for which something is true" has the same meaning as the statement "Every case of the something is false."

We'll prove the first equivalence, $\neg\,(\forall x\; W) \equiv \exists x \neg\, W$, of (3.15) and then use it to prove the second equivalence.

Proof: Let I be an interpretation with domain D for the two wffs $\neg\,(\forall x\; W)$ and $\exists x \neg\, W$. We want to show that I is a model for one of the wffs if and only if I is a model for the other wff. The following equivalent statements do the job:

I is a model for $\neg\,(\forall x\; W)$	iff	$\neg\,(\forall x\; W)$ is true for I
	iff	$\forall x\; W$ is false for I
	iff	$W(x/d)$ is false for some $d \in D$
	iff	$\neg\, W(x/d)$ is true for some $d \in D$
	iff	$\exists x \neg\, W$ is true for I
	iff	I is a model for $\exists x \neg\, W$.

This proves the equivalence $\neg\,(\forall x\; W) \equiv \exists x \neg\, W$. Now, since W is arbitrary, we can replace W by the wff $\neg\, W$ to obtain the following equivalence:

$$\neg\,(\forall x \neg\, W) \equiv \exists x \neg\, \neg\, W.$$

Now take the negation of both sides of this equivalence, and simplify the double negations to obtain the second equivalence of (3.15):

$$\forall x \neg\, W \equiv \neg\,(\exists x\; W). \quad \text{QED.}$$

Now let's look at two equivalences that allow us to interchange universal quantifiers if they are next to each other and similarly to interchange existential quantifiers if they are next to each other.

$$\forall x \; \forall y \; W \equiv \forall y \; \forall x \; W \quad \text{and} \quad \exists x \; \exists y \; W \equiv \exists y \; \exists x \; W. \qquad (3.16)$$

We leave the proofs of equivalences (3.16) as exercises. Let's look at another example.

EXAMPLE 5. We want to prove the following equivalence:

$$\exists x \; (p(x) \to q(x)) \equiv \forall x \; p(x) \to \exists x \; q(x). \qquad (3.17)$$

Proof: First, we'll prove $\exists x \; (p(x) \to q(x)) \to (\forall x \; p(x) \to \exists x \; q(x))$: Let I be a model for $\exists x \; (p(x) \to q(x))$ with domain D. Then $\exists x \; (p(x) \to q(x))$ is true for I, which means that $p(d) \to q(d)$ is true for some $d \in D$. Therefore

either $p(d) = $ false   or $p(d) = q(d) = $ true for some $d \in D$.

If $p(d) = $ false, then $\forall x \; p(x)$ is false for I; if $p(d) = q(d) = $ true, then $\exists x \; q(x)$ is true for I. In either case we obtain $\forall x \; p(x) \to \exists x \; q(x)$ is true for I. Therefore I is a model for $\forall x \; p(x) \to \exists x \; q(x)$.

Now we'll prove $(\forall x \; p(x) \to \exists x \; q(x)) \to \exists x \; (p(x) \to q(x))$: Let I be a model for $\forall x \; p(x) \to \exists x \; q(x)$ with domain D. Then $\forall x \; p(x) \to \exists x \; q(x)$ is true for I. Therefore

either $\forall x \; p(x)$ is false for I or   both $\forall x \; p(x)$ and $\exists x \; q(x)$ are true for I.

If $\forall x \; p(x)$ is false for I, then $p(d)$ is false for some $d \in D$. Therefore $p(d) \to q(d)$ is true. If both $\forall x \; p(x)$ and $\exists x \; q(x)$ are true for I, then there is some $c \in D$ such that $p(c) = q(c) = $ true. So $p(c) \to q(c)$ is true. So in either case, $\exists x \; (p(x) \to q(x))$ is true for I. Thus I is a model for $\exists x \; (p(x) \to q(x))$.   QED. $\blacklozenge$

Of course, once we know some equivalences, we can use them to prove other equivalences. For example, let's see how previous results can be used to prove the following equivalence:

$$\exists x \; (p(x) \vee q(x)) \equiv \exists x \; p(x) \vee \exists x \; q(x). \qquad (3.18)$$

Proof: $\begin{aligned} \exists x \; (p(x) \vee q(x)) \; &\equiv \; \exists x \; (\neg \, p(x) \to q(x)) \\ &\equiv \; \forall x \; \neg \, p(x) \to \exists x \; q(x) \qquad (3.17) \\ &\equiv \; \neg \, \exists x \; p(x) \to \exists x \; q(x) \qquad (3.15) \\ &\equiv \; \exists x \; p(x) \vee \exists x \; q(x) \qquad \text{QED.} \end{aligned}$

Next we'll look at some equivalences that hold under certain restrictions.

Restricted Equivalences

We'll start by considering the simple idea of replacing the names of variables. With certain restrictions we can rename the variables in a quantified wff without changing its meaning. For example, suppose we are given the following wff

$$\forall x \ (p(x) \rightarrow p(w)).$$

We can replace all occurrences of x by y to obtain the equivalence

$$\forall x \ (p(x) \rightarrow p(w)) \equiv \forall y \ (p(y) \rightarrow p(w)).$$

But we can't replace all occurrences of x by w because

$$\forall x \ (p(x) \rightarrow p(w)) \text{ is not equivalent to } \forall w \ (p(w) \rightarrow p(w)).$$

The key is to choose a new variable that doesn't occur in the wff and then be consistent with the replacement. Here's the rule:

Renaming Rule (3.19)

If y does not occur in $W(x)$, then the following equivalences hold:

a. $\exists x \ W(x) \equiv \exists y \ W(y)$.

b. $\forall x \ W(x) \equiv \forall y \ W(y)$.

Remember that $W(y)$ is obtained from $W(x)$ by replacing all free occurrences of x by y.

For example, let's use (3.19) to make all the quantifier variables distinct in the following wff:

$$\forall x \ \exists y \ (p(x, y) \rightarrow \exists x \ q(x, y) \lor \forall y \ r(x, y)).$$

Since the variables u and v don't occur in this wff, we can use (3.19) to write the equivalent wff

$$\forall u \ \exists v \ (p(u, v) \rightarrow \exists x \ q(x, v) \lor \forall y \ r(u, y)).$$

Now we'll look at some restricted equivalences that allow us to move a quantifier past a wff if the wff doesn't contain the quantified variable.

Equivalences with Restrictions

IF x does not occur in the wff C, THEN the following equivalences hold:

Disjunction (3.20)

$$\forall x\,(C \vee A(x)) \equiv C \vee \forall x\, A(x).$$
$$\exists x\,(C \vee A(x)) \equiv C \vee \exists x\, A(x).$$

Conjunction (3.21)

$$\forall x\,(C \wedge A(x)) \equiv C \wedge \forall x\, A(x).$$
$$\exists x\,(C \wedge A(x)) \equiv C \wedge \exists x\, A(x).$$

Implication (3.22)

$$\forall x\,(C \to A(x)) \equiv C \to \forall x\, A(x).$$
$$\exists x\,(C \to A(x)) \equiv C \to \exists x\, A(x).$$
$$\forall x\,(A(x) \to C) \equiv \exists x\, A(x) \to C.$$
$$\exists x\,(A(x) \to C) \equiv \forall x\, A(x) \to C.$$

The implication equivalences (3.22) are easily derived from the other equivalences. For example, the third equivalence of (3.22) can be proved as follows:

$$
\begin{aligned}
\forall x\,(A(x) \to C) &\equiv \forall x\,(\neg A(x) \vee C) \\
&\equiv \forall x\, \neg A(x) \vee C & (3.20)\\
&\equiv \neg\, \exists x\, A(x) \vee C & (3.15)\\
&\equiv \exists x\, A(x) \to C.
\end{aligned}
$$

The equivalences (3.20), (3.21), and (3.22) also hold under the weaker assumption that C does not contain a free occurrence of x. For example, if $C = \exists x\, p(x)$, then we can rename the variable x to y to obtain $\exists x\, p(x) \equiv \exists y\, p(y)$. Now x does not occur in the wff $\exists y\, p(y)$, and we can apply the rules as they are stated. For this example the first equivalence of (3.20) can be derived as follows:

$$
\begin{aligned}
\forall x\,(C \vee A(x)) &\equiv \forall x\,(\exists x\, p(x) \vee A(x)) \\
&\equiv \forall x\,(\exists y\, p(y) \vee A(x)) & (\text{rename})\\
&\equiv \exists y\, p(y) \vee \forall x\, A(x) & (3.20)\\
&\equiv \exists x\, p(x) \vee \forall x\, A(x) & (\text{rename})\\
&\equiv C \vee \forall x\, A(x).
\end{aligned}
$$

Now that we have some equivalences on hand, we can use them to prove other equivalences. In other words, we have a set of rules to transform wffs into other wffs having the same meaning. This justifies the word "calculus" in the name "predicate calculus."

Normal Forms

In the propositional calculus we know that any wff is equivalent to a wff in conjunctive normal form and to a wff in disjunctive normal form. Let's see whether we can do something similar with the wffs of the predicate calculus. We'll start with a definition. A wff W is in *prenex normal form* if all its quantifiers are on the left of the expression. In other words, a prenex normal form looks like the following:

$$Q_1 x_1 \dots Q_n x_n \, M,$$

where each Q_i is either $\forall$ or $\exists$, each x_i is distinct, and M is a wff without quantifiers. For example, the following wffs are in prenex normal form:

$$p(x),$$
$$\exists x \, p(x),$$
$$\forall x \, p(x, y),$$
$$\forall x \, \exists y \, (p(x, y) \rightarrow q(x)),$$
$$\forall x \, \exists y \, \forall z \, (p(x) \vee q(y) \wedge r(x, z)).$$

Is any wff equivalent to some wff in prenex normal form? Yes. In fact there's an easy algorithm to obtain the desired form. The idea is to make sure that variables have distinct names and then apply equivalences that send all quantifiers to the left end of the wff. Here's the algorithm:

Prenex Normal Form Algorithm   (3.23)

Any wff W has an equivalent prenex normal form, which can be constructed as follows:

1. Rename the variables of W so that no quantifiers use the same variable name and such that the quantified variable names are distinct from the free variable names.

2. Move quantifiers to the left by using equivalences (3.15), (3.20), (3.21), and (3.22).

The renaming of variables is important to the success of the algorithm. For example, we can't replace $p(x) \vee \forall x \, q(x)$ by $\forall x \, (p(x) \vee q(x))$ because they

aren't equivalent. But we can rename variables to obtain the following
equivalence:

$$p(x) \lor \forall x \; q(x) \equiv p(x) \lor \forall y \; q(y) \equiv \forall y \; (p(x) \lor q(y)).$$

EXAMPLE 6. Suppose we are given the following wff W:

$$A(x) \land \forall x \; (B(x) \to \exists y \; C(x, y) \lor \neg \exists y \; A(y)).$$

Let's put this wff in prenex normal form. First notice that y is used in two
quantifiers and x occurs both free and in a quantifier. After changing names,
we obtain the following version of W:

$$A(x) \land \forall z \; (B(z) \to \exists y \; C(z, y) \lor \neg \exists w \; A(w)).$$

Now each quantified variable is distinct, and the quantified variables are distinct from the free variable x. Now we'll apply equivalences to move all the
quantifiers to the left:

$$
\begin{aligned}
W \quad &\equiv \quad A(x) \land \forall z \; (B(z) \to \exists y \; C(z, y) \lor \neg \exists w \; A(w)) \\
&\equiv \quad \forall z \; (A(x) \land (B(z) \to \exists y \; C(z, y) \lor \neg \exists w \; A(w))) &&(3.21) \\
&\equiv \quad \forall z \; (A(x) \land (B(z) \to \exists y \; (C(z, y) \lor \neg \exists w \; A(w)))) &&(3.20) \\
&\equiv \quad \forall z \; (A(x) \land \exists y \; (B(z) \to C(z, y) \lor \neg \exists w \; A(w))) &&(3.22) \\
&\equiv \quad \forall z \; \exists y \; (A(x) \land (B(z) \to C(z, y) \lor \neg \exists w \; A(w))) &&(3.21) \\
&\equiv \quad \forall z \; \exists y \; (A(x) \land (B(z) \to C(z, y) \lor \forall w \; \neg A(w))) &&(3.15) \\
&\equiv \quad \forall z \; \exists y \; (A(x) \land (B(z) \to \forall w \; (C(z, y) \lor \neg A(w)))) &&(3.20) \\
&\equiv \quad \forall z \; \exists y \; (A(x) \land \forall w \; (B(z) \to C(z, y) \lor \neg A(w))) &&(3.22) \\
&\equiv \quad \forall z \; \exists y \; \forall w \; (A(x) \land (B(z) \to C(z, y) \lor \neg A(w))) &&(3.21).
\end{aligned}
$$

This wff is in the desired prenex normal form.   ◆

    There are two special prenex normal forms that correspond to the dis-
junctive normal form and the conjunctive normal form for propositional calculus. We define a *literal* in the predicate calculus to be an atom or the negation
of an atom. For example, $p(x)$ and $\neg \; q(x, y)$ are literals. A prenex normal form
is called a *prenex conjunctive normal form* if it has the form

$$Q_1 x_1 \ldots Q_n x_n \; (C_1 \land \ldots \land C_k),$$

where each C_i is a disjunction of one or more literals. Similarly, a prenex normal form is called a *prenex disjunctive normal form* if it has the form

$$Q_1 x_1 \dots Q_n x_n \, (D_1 \vee \dots \vee D_k),$$

where each D_i is a conjunction of one or more literals.

It's easy to construct either of these normal forms from a prenex normal form. Just eliminate conditionals, move $\neg$ inwards, and either distribute $\wedge$ over $\vee$ or distribute $\vee$ over $\wedge$. If we want to start with an arbitrary wff, then we can put everything together in a nice little algorithm. We can save some thinking by removing all conditionals at an early stage of the process. Then we won't have to remember the formulas (3.22). The algorithm can be stated as follows:

Prenex Conjunctive / Disjunctive Normal Form Algorithm (3.24)

Any wff W has an equivalent prenex disjunctive/conjunctive normal form, which can be constructed as follows:

1. Rename the variables of W so that no quantifiers use the same variable name and such that the quantified variable names are distinct from the free variable names.

2. Remove implications by using the equivalence

$$A \to B \equiv \neg A \vee B.$$

3. Move negations to the right to form literals by using the equivalences (3.15) and the equivalences

$$\neg (A \wedge B) \equiv \neg A \vee \neg B, \quad \neg (A \vee B) \equiv \neg A \wedge \neg B, \quad \text{and} \quad \neg \neg A \equiv A.$$

4. Move quantifiers to the left by using equivalences (3.20), and (3.21).

5. To obtain the conjunctive normal form, distribute $\vee$ over $\wedge$. To obtain the disjunctive normal form, distribute $\wedge$ over $\vee$.

EXAMPLE 7. Suppose W is the following wff:

$$\forall x \, A(x) \vee \exists x \, B(x) \to C(x) \wedge \exists x \, C(x).$$

We'll construct both the prenex disjunctive normal form and the prenex conjunctive normal form for W.

$$W \;=\; \forall x \, A(x) \vee \exists x \, B(x) \to C(x) \wedge \exists x \, C(x)$$

$$\equiv \; \forall y \, A(y) \vee \exists z \, B(z) \to C(x) \wedge \exists w \, C(w) \qquad \text{(rename variables)}$$

$$\equiv \; \neg \, (\forall y \, A(y) \vee \exists z \, B(z)) \vee (C(x) \wedge \exists w \, C(w)) \qquad \text{(remove} \to)$$

$$\equiv \; (\neg \, \forall y \, A(y) \wedge \neg \, \exists z \, B(z)) \vee (C(x) \wedge \exists w \, C(w)) \qquad \text{(move negation)}$$

$$\equiv \; (\exists y \, \neg \, A(y) \wedge \forall z \, \neg \, B(z)) \vee (C(x) \wedge \exists w \, C(w)) \qquad (3.15)$$

$$\equiv \; \exists y \, (\neg \, A(y) \wedge \forall z \, \neg \, B(z)) \vee (C(x) \wedge \exists w \, C(w)) \qquad (3.21)$$

$$\equiv \; \exists y \, ((\neg \, A(y) \wedge \forall z \, \neg \, B(z)) \vee (C(x) \wedge \exists w \, C(w))) \qquad (3.20)$$

$$\equiv \; \exists y \, (\forall z \, (\neg \, A(y) \wedge \neg \, B(z)) \vee (C(x) \wedge \exists w \, C(w))) \qquad (3.21)$$

$$\equiv \; \exists y \, \forall z \, ((\neg \, A(y) \wedge \neg \, B(z)) \vee (C(x) \wedge \exists w \, C(w))) \qquad (3.20)$$

$$\equiv \; \exists y \, \forall z \, ((\neg \, A(y) \wedge \neg \, B(z)) \vee \exists w \, (C(x) \wedge C(w))) \qquad (3.21)$$

$$\equiv \; \exists y \, \forall z \, \exists w \, ((\neg \, A(y) \wedge \neg \, B(z)) \vee (C(x) \wedge C(w))) \qquad (3.20).$$

This wff is in prenex disjunctive normal form. To obtain the prenex conjunctive normal form, we'll distribute $\vee$ over $\wedge$ to obtain the following equivalences:

$$\equiv \; \exists y \, \forall z \, \exists w \, ((\neg \, A(y) \wedge \neg \, B(z)) \vee C(x)) \wedge (\neg \, A(y) \wedge \neg \, B(z)) \vee C(w)))$$

$$\equiv \; \exists y \, \forall z \, \exists w \, ((\neg \, A(y) \vee C(x)) \wedge (\neg \, B(z) \vee C(x))$$

$$\wedge (\neg \, A(y) \vee C(w)) \wedge (\neg \, B(z)) \vee C(w))).$$

This wff is in prenex conjunctive normal form.   ◆

Summary of Equivalences

We collect here some equivalences, some restricted equivalences, and some conditionals that are not equivalences.

Some Useful Equivalences

1. $\neg \, \forall x \, W(x) \equiv \exists x \, \neg \, W(x).$ $\qquad\qquad$ (3.15)

2. $\neg \, \exists x \, W(x) \equiv \forall x \, \neg \, W(x).$ $\qquad\qquad$ (3.15)

3. $\exists x \, (A(x) \vee B(x)) \equiv \exists x \, A(x) \vee \exists x \, B(x).$ $\qquad$ (3.18)

4. $\forall x \, (A(x) \wedge B(x)) \equiv \forall x \, A(x) \wedge \forall x \, B(x).$

5. $\exists x \, (A(x) \to B(x)) \equiv \forall x \, A(x) \to \exists x \, B(x).$ $\qquad$ (3.17)

6. $\forall x \, \forall y \, W(x, y) \equiv \forall y \, \forall x \, W(x, y).$ $\qquad\qquad$ (3.16)

7. $\exists x \, \exists y \, W(x, y) \equiv \exists y \, \exists x \, W(x, y).$ $\qquad\qquad$ (3.16)

Some Restricted Equivalences

The following equivalences hold if x does not occur in the wff C:

Disjunction (3.20)
$$\forall x \, (C \vee A(x)) \equiv C \vee \forall x \, A(x).$$
$$\exists x \, (C \vee A(x)) \equiv C \vee \exists x \, A(x).$$

Conjunction (3.21)
$$\forall x \, (C \wedge A(x)) \equiv C \wedge \forall x \, A(x).$$
$$\exists x \, (C \wedge A(x)) \equiv C \wedge \exists x \, A(x).$$

Implication (3.22)
$$\forall x \, (C \rightarrow A(x)) \equiv C \rightarrow \forall x \, A(x).$$
$$\exists x \, (C \rightarrow A(x)) \equiv C \rightarrow \exists x \, A(x).$$
$$\forall x \, (A(x) \rightarrow C) \equiv \exists x \, A(x) \rightarrow C.$$
$$\exists x \, (A(x) \rightarrow C) \equiv \forall x \, A(x) \rightarrow C.$$

Some Conditionals That Are Not Equivalences

1. $\forall x \, A(x) \; \exists x \, A(x).$
2. $\exists x \, (A(x) \wedge B(x)) \rightarrow \exists x \, A(x) \wedge \exists x \, B(x).$
3. $\forall x \, A(x) \vee \forall x \, B(x) \rightarrow \forall x \, (A(x) \vee B(x)).$
4. $\forall x \, (A(x) \rightarrow B(x)) \rightarrow (\forall x \, A(x) \rightarrow \forall x \, B(x)).$
5. $\exists y \, \forall x \, W(x, y) \rightarrow \forall x \, \exists y \, W(x, y).$

Exercises

1. For each of the following wffs, label each occurrence of a variable as either bound or free.

   a. $p(x, y) \vee (\forall y \, q(y) \rightarrow \exists x \, r(x, y)).$
   b. $\forall y \, q(y) \wedge \neg \, p(x, y).$
   c. $\neg \, q(x, y) \vee \exists x \, p(x, y).$

2. Write down a single wff containing three variables x, y, and z, with the following properties: x occurs twice as a bound variable; y occurs once as a free variable; z occurs three times, once as a free variable and twice as a bound variable.

3. Given the wff $W = \exists x\, p(x) \to \forall x\, p(x)$.

   a. Find all possible interpretations of W over the domain $D = \{a\}$. Also give the truth value of W over each of the interpretations.

   b. Find all possible interpretations of W over the domain $D = \{a, b\}$. Also give the truth value of W over each of the interpretations.

4. Find a model for each of the following wffs.

   a. $p(c) \land \exists x\, \neg\, p(x)$.

   b. $\exists x\, p(x) \to \forall x\, p(x)$.

   c. $\exists y\, \forall x\, p(x, y) \to \forall x\, \exists y\, p(x, y)$.

   d. $\forall x\, \exists y\, p(x, y) \to \exists y\, \forall x\, p(x, y)$.

   e. $\forall x\, (p(x, f(x)) \to p(x, y))$.

5. Find a countermodel for each of the following wffs.

   a. $p(c) \land \exists x\, \neg\, p(x)$.

   b. $\exists x\, p(x) \to \forall x\, p(x)$.

   c. $\forall x\, (p(x) \lor q(x)) \to \forall x\, p(x) \lor \forall x\, q(x)$.

   d. $\exists x\, p(x) \land \exists x\, q(x) \to \exists x\, (p(x) \land q(x))$.

   e. $\forall x\, \exists y\, p(x, y) \to \exists y\, \forall x\, p(x, y)$.

   f. $\forall x\, (p(x, f(x)) \to p(x, y))$.

6. Given the wff $W = \forall x\, \forall y\, (p(x) \to p(y))$.

   a. Show that W is true for any interpretation whose domain is a singleton.

   b. Show that W is not valid.

7. Given the wff $W = \forall x\, p(x, x) \to \forall x\, \forall y\, \forall z\, (p(x, y) \lor p(x, z) \lor p(y, z))$.

   a. Show that W is true for any interpretation whose domain is a singleton.

   b. Show that W is true for any interpretation whose domain has two elements.

   c. Show that W is not valid.

8. Prove that each of the following wffs is valid. *Hint:* Either show that every interpretation is a model or assume that the wff is invalid and find a contradiction.

   a. $\forall x\, (p(x) \to p(x))$.

   b. $p(c) \to \exists x\, p(x)$.

   c. $\forall x\, p(x) \to \exists x\, p(x)$.

   d. $\exists x\, (A(x) \land B(x)) \to \exists x\, A(x) \land \exists x\, B(x)$.

e. $\forall x\, A(x) \vee \forall x\, B(x) \to \forall x\, (A(x) \vee B(x))$.

f. $\forall x\, (A(x) \to B(x)) \to (\exists x\, A(x) \to \exists x\, B(x))$.

g. $\forall x\, (A(x) \to B(x)) \to (\forall x\, A(x) \to \exists x\, B(x))$.

h. $\forall x\, (A(x) \to B(x)) \to (\forall x\, A(x) \to \forall x\, B(x))$.

9. Prove that each of the following wffs is unsatisfiable. *Hint:* Either show that every interpretation is a countermodel or assume that the wff is satisfiable and find a contradiction.

   a. $p(c) \wedge \neg p(c)$.

   b. $\exists x\, (p(x) \wedge \neg p(x))$.

   c. $\exists x\, \forall y\, (p(x, y) \wedge \neg p(x, y))$.

10. Prove each of the following equivalences with validity arguments (i.e., use interpretations and models).

   a. $\forall x\, (A(x) \wedge B(x)) \equiv \forall x\, A(x) \wedge \forall x\, B(x)$.

   b. $\exists x\, (A(x) \vee B(x)) \equiv \exists x\, A(x) \vee \exists x\, B(x)$.

   c. $\exists x\, (A(x) \to B(x)) \equiv \forall x\, A(x) \to \exists x\, B(x)$.

   d. $\forall x\, \forall y\, W(x, y) \equiv \forall y\, \forall x\, W(x, y)$.

   e. $\exists x\, \exists y\, W(x, y) \equiv \exists y\, \exists x\, W(x, y)$.

11. Assume that x does not occur in the wff C. Prove each of the following equivalences with validity arguments (i.e., argue using interpretations and models).

   a. $\forall x\, (C \wedge A(x)) \equiv C \wedge \forall x\, A(x)$.

   b. $\exists x\, (C \wedge A(x)) \equiv C \wedge \exists x\, A(x)$.

   c. $\forall x\, (C \vee A(x)) \equiv C \vee \forall x\, A(x)$.

   d. $\exists x\, (C \vee A(x)) \equiv C \vee \exists x\, A(x)$.

   e. $\forall x\, (C \to A(x)) \equiv C \to \forall x\, A(x)$.

   f. $\exists x\, (C \to A(x)) \equiv C \to \exists x\, A(x)$.

   g. $\forall x\, (A(x) \to C) \equiv \exists x\, A(x) \to C$.

   h. $\exists x\, (A(x) \to C) \equiv \forall x\, A(x) \to C$.

12. Construct a prenex conjunctive normal form for each of the following wffs.

   a. $\forall x\, (p(x) \vee q(x)) \to \forall x\, p(x) \vee \forall x\, q(x)$.

   b. $\exists x\, p(x) \wedge \exists x\, q(x) \to \exists x\, (p(x) \wedge q(x))$.

   c. $\forall x\, \exists y\, p(x, y) \to \exists y \forall x\, p(x, y)$.

   d. $\forall x\, (p(x, f(x)) \to p(x, y))$.

13. Construct a prenex disjunctive normal form for each of the following wffs.

   a. $\forall x \, (p(x) \vee q(x)) \rightarrow \forall x \, p(x) \vee \forall x \, q(x)$.

   b. $\exists x \, p(x) \wedge \exists x \, q(x) \rightarrow \exists x \, (p(x) \wedge q(x))$.

   c. $\forall x \, \exists y \, p(x, y) \rightarrow \exists y \forall x \, p(x, y)$.

   d. $\forall x \, (p(x, f(x)) \rightarrow p(x, y))$.

14. Prove that a wff is unsatisfiable if and only if its existential closure is unsatisfiable.

3.3 Formal Proofs in Predicate Calculus

To reason formally about wffs in the predicate calculus, we need some inference rules. It's nice to know that all the inference rules of the propositional calculus can still be used for the predicate calculus. We just need to replace "tautology" with "valid." In other words, if R is an inference rule for the propositional calculus that maps tautologies to a tautology, then R also maps valid wffs to a valid wff.

For example, let's take the modus ponens inference rule of the propositional calculus and prove that it also works for the predicate calculus. In other words, we'll show that modus ponens maps valid wffs to a valid wff.

Proof: Let A and $A \rightarrow B$ be valid wffs. We need to show that B is valid. Suppose we have an interpretation for B with domain D. We can use D to give an interpretation to A by assigning values to all the predicates, functions, free variables, and constants that occur in A but not B. This gives us interpretations for A, B, and $A \rightarrow B$ over the domain D. Since we are assuming that A and $A \rightarrow B$ are valid, it follows that A and $A \rightarrow B$ are true for these interpretations over D. Now we can apply the modus ponens rule for propositions to conclude that B is true with respect to the given interpretation over D. Since the given interpretation of B was arbitrary, it follows that every interpretation of B is a model. Therefore B is valid.   QED.

We can use similar arguments to show that all inference rules of the propositional calculus are also inference rules of the predicate calculus. So we have a built-in collection of rules to do formal reasoning in the predicate calculus. But we need more. We need to be able to remove quantifiers (instantiation) and to restore quantifiers (generalization). As luck would have it, there are conditions that must be met before these operations can occur. That's next.

Inference Rules

Universal Instantiation (UI)

It seems reasonable to say that if a property holds for everything, then it holds for any particular thing. In other words, we should be able to infer $W(x)$ from $\forall x \, W(x)$. Similarly, we should be able to infer $W(c)$ from $\forall x \, W(x)$ for any constant c. But we need to place a restriction on inferring $W(t)$ for an arbitrary term t. For example, suppose we let

$$W(x) = \exists y \; x < y.$$

Then a substitution of y for x in W yields

$$W(y) = \exists y \; y < y.$$

So we cannot infer $W(y)$ from $\forall x \, W(x)$ in this case.

The reason for the trouble is that y is a quantified variable in $W(x)$. So the substitution of y for x introduces a new bound occurrence of the variable y in the statement $W(y)$. We must restrict our inferences to wffs for which this kind of behavior doesn't happen. To make things precise, we'll make the following definition:

A term t is *free to replace* x in $W(x)$ if both $W(t)$ and $W(x)$ have the same bound occurrences of variables.

For example, we always have the following cases:

The variable x is free to replace x in $W(x)$.
Any constant is free to replace x in $W(x)$.
If y does not occur in $W(x)$, then y is free to replace x in $W(x)$.

We need to be careful only when the replacement term contains a variable that is bound in $W(x)$. For example, if $W(x) = \exists y \, p(x, y)$, then y is not free to replace x in $W(x)$ because $W(x)$ has two bound occurrences of y and $W(y) = \exists y \, p(y, y)$ has three bound occurrences of y. Now we're in position to state the *universal instantiation rule*:

Universal Instantiation Rule (UI)

$$\frac{\forall x \, W(x)}{\therefore \; W(t)} \qquad \text{if } t \text{ is free to replace } x \text{ in } W(x). \qquad (3.25)$$

The following special cases of (3.25) always satisfy the restriction, so they can be used any time:

$$\frac{\forall x\ W(x)}{\therefore\ W(x)} \quad \text{and} \quad \frac{\forall x\ W(x)}{\therefore\ W(c)}\ , \text{ where } c \text{ is any constant.} \qquad (3.26)$$

Existential Instantiation (EI)

It seems reasonable that whenever a property holds for some thing, then the property holds for a particular thing. In other words, from the statement

$$\exists x\ W(x),$$

we should be able to infer $W(c)$ for some constant c. But we must make sure that c is a new constant that has not yet occurred in the proof. For example, if $W(x)$ = "x is the mother of c," then $W(c)$ = "c is the mother of c," which can't be.

For another example, notice what happens in the following "attempted" proof when we don't introduce a new constant on line 5:

1.	$\exists x\ p(x) \wedge \exists x\ q(x)$	P
2.	$\exists x\ p(x)$	1, Simp
3.	$\exists x\ q(x)$	1, Simp
4.	$p(c)$	2, EI rule
5.	$q(c)$	3, Improper use of EI rule
6.	$p(c) \wedge q(c)$	4, 5, Conj.

If this proof is correct, then we have the conditional theorem

$$\exists x\ p(x) \wedge \exists x\ q(x) \rightarrow p(c) \wedge q(c).$$

But this wff is NOT valid. Consider the following interpretation: Let the domain be the natural numbers, and let $p(x)$ = "x is odd" and $q(x)$ = "x is even." Then $\exists x\ p(x) \wedge \exists x\ q(x)$ is true, since there is an odd number and there is an even number. But the consequent $p(c) \wedge q(c)$ is false, since no natural number c can be both odd and even. Therefore each time EI is used, we need to make sure a new constant is introduced. The *existential instantiation rule* is stated as follows:

Existential Instantiation Rule (EI)

$$\frac{\exists x\ W(x)}{\therefore\ W(c)} \qquad \text{if } c \text{ is a new constant in the proof.} \qquad (3.27)$$

EXAMPLE 1. We'll give an indirect formal proof of the following statement:

$$\forall x \neg W(x) \rightarrow \neg \exists x \, W(x).$$

Proof: 1. $\forall x \neg W(x)$ P
        2. $\neg \neg \exists x \, W(x)$ P for IP
        3. $\exists x \, W(x)$ $2, T$
        4. $W(c)$ 3, EI
        5. $\neg W(c)$ 1, UI
        6. $W(c) \wedge \neg W(c)$ 4, 5, Conj
        7. false $6, T$
          QED   1, 2, 7, IP.   ◆

Universal Generalization (UG)

We want to consider the possibility of generalizing a wff by attaching a universal quantifier. In other words, we want to consider the circumstances under which we can infer $\forall x \, W(x)$ from $W(x)$. There are some restrictions on the use of such an inference. For example, suppose we let $W(x)$ mean "x is a prime number." Most of us will agree that we can't infer $\forall x \, W(x)$ from $W(x)$. So the following attempted proof is wrong:

     1. $W(x)$ P
     2. $\forall x \, W(x)$ 1, proposed UG rule. It doesn't work!

We can't do Step 2 because $W(x)$ is a premise in which x occurs free. This leads us to our first restriction. To make things more precise, we'll make a definition.

> A variable x in a wff W is a *flagged variable* in W if x is free in W and either W is a premise or W is inferred by a wff containing x as a flagged variable.

If there are no free variables in any premise, then there are no flagged variables in the proof because the chain of flagged variables must start from free variables in premises. Now we can state our first restriction on universal generalization:

> *Do not infer $\forall x \, W(x)$ from $W(x)$ if x is a flagged variable.*

We can keep track of flagged variables in the reason column of each line where they appear. Here's an example proof segment that shows which variables are flagged.

1. $p(x)$ P   x is flagged
2. $\forall x\, q(x)$ P
3. $q(x)$ 2, UI
4. $p(x) \wedge q(x)$ 1, 3, Conj   x is flagged.

The restriction forbids us from making the following blunder:

5. $\forall x\, (p(x) \wedge q(x))$ 4, UG. NO because x is flagged on line 4.

If we had allowed such an inference, we would have proved the following invalid wff to be valid:

$$p(x) \wedge \forall x\, q(x) \rightarrow \forall x\, (p(x) \wedge q(x)).$$

There is one more restriction on our ability to infer $\forall x\, W(x)$ from $W(x)$. We'll illustrate it with the following proof sequence about the natural numbers:

1. $\forall x\, \exists y\, x < y$ P
2. $\exists y\, x < y$ 1, UI
3. $x < c$ 2, EI
4. $\forall x\, x < c$ 3, proposed UG rule. It doesn't work.

The statement $\forall x\, x < c$ on line 4 is certainly false, because it says that every natural number is less than a particular natural number c. What went wrong? Suppose we let $W(x) = $ "$x < c$" from line 3. Then the statement on line 4 can be written $\forall x\, W(x)$. In this case we cannot infer $\forall x\, W(x)$ from $W(x)$, even though x is not free in a premise. To see why things break down, we need to look back at line 2 of the proof. In line 2, x is a free variable, and the variable y depends on x. So in line 3 the constant c is not arbitrary. It depends on x.

When a constant c depends on x, we can think of c as a function of x and write down either $c(x)$ or c_x to denote the fact. This is the kind of situation that gets us into trouble when we try to perform UG with respect to x. Before we state the second restriction, we'll make the following definition:

A variable x is a *subscripted variable* of W if x is free in W and there is a constant c in W that was created by the EI rule, where c and x occur in the same predicate of W.

For example, if we apply EI to $\exists y\, p(x, y)$ and obtain $p(x, c)$, then x is subscripted in $p(x, c)$. If we apply EI to $\exists y\, p(f(x, y))$ and obtain $p(f(x, c))$, then x is subscripted in $p(f(x, c))$. But if we apply EI to $\exists y\ (q(x, z) \vee q(y, z))$ and obtain $q(x, z) \vee q(c, z)$, then z is subscripted and x is not subscripted in $q(x, z) \vee q(c, z)$ because c and x do not occur in the same predicate. In other words, c does not depend on x.

Now we can state our second restriction dealing with universal generalization:

Do not infer $\forall x\ W(x)$ from $W(x)$ if x is a subscripted variable.

We can keep track of a subscripted variable by writing something in the reason column of each line where such a variable occurs. Three possibilities are $c(x)$, c_x, or the statement "x is subscripted." We'll use all three ways to indicate the subscripted variables in the following proof segment:

1.	$\forall x\ \exists y\ p(x, y)$	P	
2.	$\exists y\ p(x, y)$	1, UI	
3.	$p(x, c)$	2, EI	$c(x)$, c_x, x is subscripted
4.	$p(x, c) \vee q(x, y)$	3, Add	$c(x)$, c_x, x is subscripted.

Since x is subscripted on lines 3 and 4, we cannot use $\forall x$ to generalize the wffs on these lines. In other words, we cannot infer $\forall x\ p(x, c)$ from line 3, and we cannot infer $\forall x\ (p(x, c) \vee q(x, y))$ from line 4. On the other hand, we can use line 4 to infer $\forall y\ (p(x, c) \vee q(x, y))$.

Now we're finally in position to state the *universal generalization rule* with its two restrictions:

Universal Generalization Rule (UG)

$$\frac{W(x)}{\therefore \forall x\ W(x)} \quad \text{if } x \text{ is not flagged AND } x \text{ is not subscripted.} \tag{3.28}$$

Although flagged and subscripted variables are a bit complicated, it's nice to know that the restrictions of the UG rule are almost always satisfied. For example, if the premises in the proof don't contain any free variables, then there can't be any flagged variables. And if the proof doesn't use the EI rule, then there can't be any subscripted variables. So go ahead and use the UG rule with abandon. After you have finished the proof, go back and check to make sure that the two restrictions are satisfied.

The UG inference rule has a natural use whenever we give an informal proof that a statement $W(x)$ is true for all elements x in a domain D. Such a proof goes something like the following:

First we let x be an arbitrary, but fixed, element of the domain D. After we've proved that $W(x)$ is true, we can then say that "Since x was arbitrary, it follows that $W(x)$ is true for all x in D."

Let's do an example that uses the UG rule in this way. We'll give a formal proof of the following statement:

$$\forall x \, (p(x) \rightarrow q(x) \lor p(x)).$$

Proof: 1. $p(x)$ P x is flagged
        2. $q(x) \lor p(x)$ 1, Add x is flagged
        3. $p(x) \rightarrow q(x) \lor p(x)$ 1, 2, CP
        4. $\forall x \, (p(x) \rightarrow q(x) \lor p(x))$ 3, UG
            QED.

We can use the UG rule to generalize the wff on line 3 because the variable x on line 3 is neither flagged nor subscripted. But suppose someone argues against this as follows:

The variable x is free in the premise on line 1, which is used to indirectly infer line 3. Thus x should be flagged on line 3, and so we can't use UG to generalize the wff on line 3.

This reasoning is wrong because it assumes that CP is an inference rule. But CP is a proof rule, not an inference rule. So x is flagged on lines 1 and 2. But x is not flagged on line 3. Therefore UG can be applied to line 3.

EXAMPLE 2. We'll prove the following general statement about swapping universal quantifiers: $\forall x \, \forall y \, W \rightarrow \forall y \, \forall x \, W$:

Proof: 1. $\forall x \, \forall y \, W$ P
        2. $\forall y \, W$ 1, UI
        3. W 2 , UI
        4. $\forall x \, W$ 3, UG
        5. $\forall y \, \forall x \, W$ 4, UG
            QED   1, 5, CP.

Of course, the converse of the statement can be proved in the same manner. Therefore we have a formal proof of the following equivalence in (3.16):

$$\forall x \, \forall y \, W \equiv \forall y \, \forall x \, W. \quad \blacklozenge$$

Existential Generalization (EG)

It seems to make sense that if a property holds for a particular thing, then the property holds for some thing. For example, we know that 5 is a prime number, and it makes sense to conclude that there is some prime number. If we let $p(x) =$ "x is a prime number," then we can infer $\exists x \, p(x)$ from $p(5)$. So far, so good. If W is a wff, can we infer $\exists x \, W(x)$ from $W(c)$ for a constant c? Can we infer $\exists x \, W(x)$ from $W(x)$? Can we infer $\exists x \, W(x)$ from $W(t)$ for any term t? The answers to these questions depend on whether certain restrictions hold.

Let's look at some examples to see why we need some restrictions. In the following proof, assume that we're talking about natural numbers:

$$
\begin{array}{lll}
1. & \forall x \, \exists y \, x < y & P \\
2. & \exists y \, x < y & 1, \text{UI} \\
3. & x < c & 2, \text{EI} \\
4. & \exists x \, x < x & 3, \text{proposed EG rule. It doesn't work.}
\end{array}
\qquad (3.29)
$$

The statement $\exists x \, x < x$ on line 4 is clearly false, since there is no natural number less than itself. How did we get it in the first place? Let the statement on line 3 be $W(c) =$ "$x < c$." Then the statement on line 4 has the form $\exists x \, W(x)$. So we can't always infer $\exists x \, W(x)$ from $W(c)$ for a constant c.

The same type of problem exhibited in (3.29) can occur with terms that are not constants. For example, look at the following proof about natural numbers:

$$
\begin{array}{lll}
1. & \forall x \, x < \mathrm{succ}(x) & P \\
2. & x < \mathrm{succ}(x) & 1, \text{UI} \\
3. & \exists x \, x < x & 2, \text{proposed EG rule. It doesn't work.}
\end{array}
\qquad (3.30)
$$

Line 3 is clearly false. We got it by letting $t = \mathrm{succ}(x)$ and $W(t) =$ "$x < t$" in line 2. Then line 3 becomes $\exists x \, W(x)$. So we can't always infer $\exists x \, W(x)$ from $W(t)$.

We need a restriction that will force us to make the right choices when introducing the existential quantifier. We'll state the restriction as follows and then discuss how it works:

To infer $\exists x \, W(x)$ from $W(t)$ for a term t, the following relationship must hold: $W(t) = W(x) \, (x/t)$.

In other words, $W(t)$ must equal the wff obtained from $W(x)$ by replacing all occurrences of x by t. When we check to see whether $W(t) = W(x)(x/t)$, we'll call this the *backwards check*, since $W(t)$ appears earlier in the proof.

For example, let's see why we can't use EG on line 4 of (3.29). We can write the wff on line 3 of (3.29) as $W(c) =$ "$x < c$." Then line 4 becomes $\exists x \, W(x)$, where $W(x) =$ "$x < x$." The backwards check fails because

$$W(x)(x/c) = \text{``}c < c\text{''} \text{ and } W(c) = \text{``}x < c.\text{''}$$

Since $W(x)(x/c) \neq W(c)$, we can't use EG to infer line 4.

There is one more restriction on the use of EG. It occurs if we try to infer $\exists x\, W(x)$ from $W(t)$ when t is not free to replace x during the backwards check. In other words, we have the following restriction:

To infer $\exists x\, W(x)$ from $W(t)$, *the term t must be free to replace x in* $W(x)$.

For example, look at the following proof segment about natural numbers:

1. $\forall y\, y < \text{succ}(y)$ P
2. $\exists x\, \forall y\, y < x$ 1, proposed EG rule. It doesn't work.

The statement of line 2 is clearly false. To see what's happening, let the statement in line 1 of the proof be $W(t) =$ "$\forall y\, y < t$," where $t = \text{succ}(y)$. Then the statement in line 2 has the form $\exists x\, W(x)$. When we apply the backwards check, it works! We get

$$W(x)\, (x/t) = W(t).$$

But t is NOT free to replace x. In other words, $W(t)$ contains two bound occurrences of the variable y, while $W(x)$ has only one bound occurrence of y.

Now we're in a position to state the *existential generalization rule* in its full generality.

Existential Generalization Rule (EG)

$$\frac{W(t)}{\therefore\ \exists x\, W(x)} \quad \text{if the following two restrictions hold:} \qquad (3.31)$$

a. $W(t) = W(x)(x/t)$.

b. t is free to replace x in $W(x)$.

The following special case of (3.31) always satisfies the two restrictions, so it can be used any time:

$$\frac{W(x)}{\therefore\ \exists x\, W(x)} . \qquad (3.32)$$

Examples of Formal Proofs

The following examples show the usefulness of the four quantifier rules. Notice in most cases that we can use the less restrictive forms of the rules.

EXAMPLE 3 (*Renaming Variables*). Let's give formal proofs of the equivalences that rename variables (3.19): Let $W(x)$ be a wff, and let y be a variable that does not occur in $W(x)$. Then the following renaming equivalences hold:

$$\exists x \ W(x) \equiv \exists y \ W(y),$$
$$\forall x \ W(x) \equiv \forall y \ W(y).$$

We'll start by proving the equivalence $\exists x \ W(x) \equiv \exists y \ W(y)$, which we'll do by proving the following two statements:

$$\exists x \ W(x) \to \exists y \ W(y) \quad \text{and} \quad \exists y \ W(y) \to \exists x \ W(x).$$

Proof of $\exists x \ W(x) \to \exists y \ W(y)$:

1. $\exists x \ W(x)$ P
2. $W(c)$ 1, EI
3. $\exists y \ W(y)$ 2, EG, since both EG conditions hold
    QED   1, 3, CP.

Proof of $\exists y \ W(y) \to \exists x \ W(x)$:

1. $\exists y \ W(y)$ P
2. $W(c)$ 1, EI
3. $\exists x \ W(x)$ 2, EG, since both EG conditions hold
    QED   1, 3, CP.

Next, we'll prove the equivalence $\forall x \ W(x) \equiv \forall y \ W(y)$ by proving the two statements $\forall x \ W(x) \to \forall y \ W(y)$ and $\forall y \ W(y) \to \forall x \ W(x)$. We'll combine the two proofs into one proof as follows:

Proof:
1. $\forall x \ W(x)$ P Start first proof
2. $W(y)$ 1, UI y is free to replace x
3. $\forall y \ W(y)$ 2, UG
4. $\forall x \ W(x) \to \forall y \ W(y)$ 1, 3, CP   Finish first proof
5. $\forall y \ W(y)$ P Start second proof
6. $W(x)$ 5, UI x is free to replace y
7. $\forall x \ W(x)$ 6, UG
8. $\forall y \ W(y) \to \forall x \ W(x)$ 5, 7, CP   Finish second proof
    QED   4, 8, T.   ♦

EXAMPLE 4. Let's consider the following argument:

> All computer science majors are people. Some computer science majors are logical thinkers. Therefore, some people are logical thinkers.

We'll give a formalization of this argument. Let $C(x)$ mean "x is a computer science major," $P(x)$ mean "x is a person," and $L(x)$ mean "x is a logical thinker." Now the statements can be represented by the following wff:

$$\forall x\ (C(x) \to P(x)) \wedge \exists x\ (C(x) \wedge L(x)) \to \exists x\ (P(x) \wedge L(x)).$$

We'll prove that this wff is valid as follows:

Proof:
1. $\forall x\ (C(x) \to P(x))$ P
2. $\exists x\ (C(x) \wedge L(x))$ P
3. $C(c) \wedge L(c)$ 2, EI
4. $C(c) \to P(c)$ 1, UI
5. $C(c)$ 3, Simp
6. $P(c)$ 4, 5, MP
7. $L(c)$ 3, Simp
8. $P(c) \wedge L(c)$ 6, 7, Conj
9. $\exists x\ (P(x) \wedge L(x))$ 8, EG
   QED   1, 2, 9, CP.   ◆

EXAMPLE 5. In Example 1 we gave a formal proof of the statement

$$\forall x \neg W(x) \to \neg \exists x\ W(x).$$

Now we're in a position to give a formal proof of its converse. Thus we'll have a formal proof of the following equivalence (3.15):

$$\forall x \neg W(x) \equiv \neg \exists x\ W(x).$$

The converse that we want to prove is the wff $\neg \exists x\ W(x) \to \forall x \neg W(x)$. To prove this statement, we'll divide the proof into two parts. First, we'll prove the statement $\neg \exists x\ W(x) \to \neg W(x)$. Our proof will be indirect.

Proof:
1. $\neg \exists x\ W(x)$ P
2. $W(x)$ P for IP x is flagged
3. $\exists x\ W(x)$ 2, EG

4. $\neg \exists x\, W(x) \wedge \exists x\, W(x)$ 1, 3, Conj
5. false   4, T
    QED   1, 2, 5, IP.

Now we can easily prove the statement $\neg \exists x\, W(x) \rightarrow \forall x \neg W(x)$.

Proof: 1. $\neg \exists x\, W(x)$ P
     2. $\neg \exists x\, W(x) \rightarrow \neg W(x)$ T, proved above
     3. $\neg W(x)$ 1, 2, MP
     4. $\forall x \neg W(x)$ 3, UG
     QED   1, 4, CP.   ♦

Summary of Quantifier Inference Rules

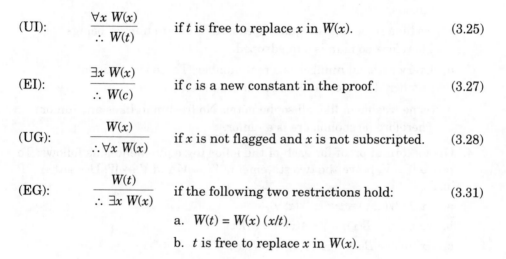

(UI): $\dfrac{\forall x\, W(x)}{\therefore\ W(t)}$ if t is free to replace x in $W(x)$.   (3.25)

(EI): $\dfrac{\exists x\, W(x)}{\therefore\ W(c)}$ if c is a new constant in the proof.   (3.27)

(UG): $\dfrac{W(x)}{\therefore \forall x\, W(x)}$ if x is not flagged and x is not subscripted.   (3.28)

(EG): $\dfrac{W(t)}{\therefore\ \exists x\, W(x)}$ if the following two restrictions hold: (3.31)

     a. $W(t) = W(x)\,(x/t)$.

     b. t is free to replace x in $W(x)$.

Exercises

1. Use the CP rule to prove that each of the following wffs is valid.
   a. $\forall x\, p(x) \rightarrow \exists x\, p(x)$.
   b. $\forall x\, (p(x) \rightarrow q(x)) \wedge \exists x\, p(x) \rightarrow \exists x\, q(x)$.
   c. $\exists x\, (p(x) \wedge q(x)) \rightarrow \exists x\, p(x) \wedge \exists x\, q(x)$.
   d. $\forall x\, (p(x) \rightarrow q(x)) \rightarrow (\exists x\, p(x) \rightarrow \exists x\, q(x))$.
   e. $\forall x\, (p(x) \rightarrow q(x)) \rightarrow (\forall x\, p(x) \rightarrow \exists x\, q(x))$.
   f. $\forall x\, (p(x) \rightarrow q(x)) \rightarrow (\forall x\, p(x) \rightarrow \forall x\, q(x))$.
   g. $\exists y\, \forall x\, p(x, y) \rightarrow \forall x\, \exists y\, p(x, y)$.
   h. $\exists x\, \forall y\, p(x, y) \wedge \forall x\, (p(x, x) \rightarrow \exists y\, q(y, x)) \rightarrow \exists y\, \exists x\, q(x, y)$.

2. Use the IP rule to prove each that each of the following wffs is valid.
   a. $\forall x\, p(x) \rightarrow \exists x\, p(x)$.
   b. $\forall x\, (p(x) \rightarrow q(x)) \wedge \exists x\, p(x) \rightarrow \exists x\, q(x)$.
   c. $\exists y\, \forall x\, p(x, y) \rightarrow \forall x\, \exists y\, p(x, y)$.
   d. $\exists x\, \forall y\, p(x, y) \wedge \forall x\, (p(x, x) \rightarrow \exists y\, q(y, x)) \rightarrow \exists y\, \exists x\, q(x, y)$.
   e. $\forall x\, p(x) \vee \forall x\, q(x) \rightarrow \forall x\, (p(x) \vee q(x))$.

3. Transform each informal argument into a formalized wff. Then give a formal proof of the wff, using either CP or IP.
   a. Every dog either likes people or hates cats. Rover is a dog. Rover loves cats. Therefore some dog likes people.
   b. Every committee member is rich and famous. Some committee members are old. Therefore some committee members are old and famous.
   c. No human beings are quadrupeds. All men are human beings. Therefore no man is a quadruped.
   d. Every rational number is a real number. There is a rational number. Therefore there is a real number.
   e. Some freshmen like all sophomores. No freshman likes any junior. Therefore no sophomore is a junior.

4. Give a formal proof for each of the following equivalences as follows: To prove $W \equiv V$, prove the two statements $W \rightarrow V$ and $V \rightarrow W$. Use either CP or IP.
   a. $\exists x\, \exists y\, W(x, y) \equiv \exists y\, \exists x\, W(x, y)$.
   b. $\forall x\, (A(x) \wedge B(x)) \equiv \forall x\, A(x) \wedge \forall x\, B(x)$.
   c. $\exists x\, (A(x) \vee B(x)) \equiv \exists x\, A(x) \vee \exists x\, B(x)$.
   d. $\exists x\, (A(x) \rightarrow B(x)) \equiv \forall x\, A(x) \rightarrow \exists x\, B(x)$.

5. Give a formal proof of the wff $A \rightarrow B$, where

   $$A = \forall x\, (\exists y\, (q(x, y) \wedge s(y)) \rightarrow \exists y\, (p(y) \wedge r(x, y))),$$
   $$B = \neg\, \exists x\, p(x) \rightarrow \forall x\, \forall y\, (q(x, y) \rightarrow \neg\, s(y)).$$

6. Give a formal proof of the wff $A \rightarrow B$, where

   $$A = \exists x\, (r(x) \wedge \forall y\, (p(y) \rightarrow q(x, y))) \wedge \forall x\, (r(x) \rightarrow \forall y\, (s(y) \rightarrow \neg\, q(x, y)))$$
   $$B = \forall x\, (p(x) \rightarrow \neg\, s(x)).$$

7. Each of the following proof segments contains an invalid use of a quantifier inference rule. In each case, state why the inference rule cannot be used.

a. 1. $x < 4$ P
    2. $\forall x \, (x < 4)$ 1, UG.

b. 1. $\exists x \, (y < x)$ P
    2. $y < c$ 1, EI
    3. $\forall y \, (y < c)$ 2, UG.

c. 1. $\forall y \, (y < f(y))$ P
    2. $\exists x \, \forall y \, (y < x)$ 1, EG.

d. 1. $q(x, c)$ P
    2. $\exists x \, q(x, x)$ 1, EG.

e. 1. $\exists x \, p(x)$ P
    2. $\exists x \, q(x)$ P
    3. $p(c)$ 1, EI
    4. $q(c)$ 2, EI.

f. 1. $\forall x \, \exists y \, x < y$ P
    2. $\exists y \, y < y$ 1, UI.

3.4 Higher-Order Logics

In first-order predicate calculus the only things that can be quantified are individual variables, and the only things that can be arguments for predicates are terms (i.e., constants, variables, or functional expressions with terms as arguments). If we loosen up a little and allow our wffs to quantify other things like predicates or functions, or if we allow our predicates to take arguments that are predicates or functions, then we move to a *higher-order logic*. Is higher-order logic necessary? The purpose of this section is to convince you that the answer is yes. After we do some examples we'll give a general definition that will allow us to discuss nth-order logic for any natural number n.

We often need higher-order logic to express simple statements about the things that interest us. For example, let's try to formalize the statement

"There is a function f such that $f(x) > \log x$ for all x."

This statement asserts the existence of a function. So if we want to formalize the statement, we'll need to use higher-order logic to quantify a function. We might formalize the statement as follows:

$$\exists f \, \forall x \, (f(x) > \log x).$$

This wff is an instance of the following more general wff, where > is an instance of p and log is an instance of g:

$$\exists f \ \forall x \ p(f(x), g(x)).$$

For another example, let's see whether we can formalize the notion of equality. Suppose we agree to say that x and y are identical if all their properties are the same. We'll signify this by writing $x = y$. Can we express this thought in formal logic? Sure. If P is some property, then we can think of P as a predicate, and we'll agree that $P(x)$ means that x has property P. Then we can define $x = y$ as the following higher-order wff:

$$\forall P \ ((P(x) \rightarrow P(y)) \wedge (P(y) \rightarrow P(x))).$$

This wff is higher-order because the predicate P is quantified.

Now that we have some examples, let's get down to business and discuss higher-order logic in a general setting that allows us to classify the different orders of logic.

Classifying Higher-Order Logics

To classify higher-order logics, we need to make an assumption about the relationship between predicates and sets. We'll assume that predicates are sets and that sets are predicates. Let's see why we can think of predicates and sets as the same thing. For example, if P is a predicate with one argument, we can think of P as a set in which $x \in P$ if and only if $P(x)$ is true. Similarly, if S is a set of 3-tuples, we can think of S as a predicate in which $S(x, y, z)$ is true if and only if $\langle x, y, z \rangle \in S$.

The relationship between sets and predicates allows us to look at some wffs in a new light. For example, consider the following wff:

$$\forall x \ (A(x) \rightarrow B(x)).$$

In addition to the usual reading of this wff as "For every x, if $A(x)$ is true, then $B(x)$ is true," we can now read it in terms of sets by saying, "For every x, if $x \in A$, then $x \in B$." In other words, we have a wff that represents the statement "A is a subset of B."

The identification of predicates and sets puts us in position to define higher-order logics. A logic is called *higher-order* if it allows sets to be quantified or if it allows sets to be elements of other sets. A wff that quantifies a set or has a set as an argument to a predicate is called a *higher-order wff*. For example, the following two wffs are higher-order wffs:

$\exists S\ S(x)$ — The set S is quantified.

$S(x) \wedge T(S)$ — The set S is an element of the set T.

Let's see how functions fit into the picture. Recall that a function can be thought of as a set of 2-tuples. For example, if $f(x) = 3x$ for all $x \in \mathbb{N}$, then we can think of f as the set

$$f = \{\langle x, 3x \rangle \mid x \in \mathbb{N}\}.$$

So whenever a wff contains a quantified function name, the wff is actually quantifying a set and thus is a higher-order wff by our definition. Similarly, if a wff contains a function name as an argument to a predicate, then the wff is higher-order. For example, the following two wffs are higher-order wffs:

$\exists f\ \forall x\ p(f(x), g(x))$ — The function f is a set and is quantified.

$p(f(x)) \wedge q(f)$ — The function f is a set and is an element of the set q.

Since we can think of a function as a set and we are identifying sets with predicates, we can also think of a function as a predicate. For example, let f be the function

$$f = \{\langle x, 3x \rangle \mid x \in \mathbb{N}\}.$$

We can think of f as a predicate with two arguments. In other words, we can write the wff $f(x, 3x)$ and let it mean "x is mapped by f to $3x$," which of course we usually write as $f(x) = 3x$.

Now let's see whether we can classify the different orders of logic. We'll start with the two logics that we know best. A propositional calculus is called a *zero-order logic* and a first-order predicate calculus is called a *first-order logic*. We want to continue the process by classifying the higher-order logics as second-order, third-order, and so on. To do this, we need to attach an order to each predicate and each quantifier that occurs in a wff. We'll define the *order of a predicate* as follows:

A predicate has *order* 1 if all its arguments are terms (i.e., constants, individual variables, or function values). Otherwise, the predicate has *order* $n + 1$, where n is the highest order among its arguments that are not terms.

For example, for each of the following wffs we've given the order of its predicates (i.e., sets):

$S(x) \wedge T(S)$ *S* has order 1, and *T* has order 2.

$p(f(x)) \wedge q(f)$ *p* has order 1, *f* has order 1, and *q* has order 2.

The reason that the function f has order 1 is that any function when thought of as a predicate takes only terms for arguments. Thus any function name has order 1. Remember to distinguish between $f(x)$ and f; $f(x)$ is a term, and f is a function (i.e., a set or a predicate).

We can also relate the order of a predicate to the level of nesting of its arguments, where we think of a predicate as a set. For example, if a wff contains the three statements $S(x)$, $T(S)$, and $P(T)$, then we have $x \in S$, $S \in T$, and $T \in P$. The orders of S, T, and P are 1, 2, and 3. So the order of a predicate (or set) is the maximum number of times the symbol $\in$ is used to get from the set down to its most basic elements.

Now we'll define the *order of a quantifier* as follows:

A quantifer has *order* 1 if it quantifies an individual variable. Otherwise, the quantifier has *order* $n + 1$, where n is the order of the predicate being quantified.

For example, let's find the orders of the quantifiers in the wff that follows. Try your luck before you read the answers.

$$\forall x \, \exists S \, \exists T \, \exists f \, (S(x, f(x)) \wedge T(S)).$$

The quantifier $\forall x$ has order 1 because x is an individual variable. $\exists S$ has order 2 because S has order 1. $\exists T$ has order 3 because T has order 2. $\exists f$ has order 2 because f is a function name, and all function names have order 1.

Now we can make a simple definition for the order of a wff. The *order of a wff* is the highest of the orders of its predicates and quantifiers. Here are a few examples:

Second-order wffs	Third-order wffs
$S(x) \wedge T(S)$	$S(x) \wedge T(S) \wedge P(T)$
$\exists S \, S(x)$	$\forall T \, (S(x) \wedge T(S))$
$\exists S \, (S(x) \wedge T(S))$	$\exists T \, (S(x) \wedge T(S) \wedge P(T))$
$P(x, f, f(x))$	

Now we can make the definition of a *n*th-order logic. A *nth-order logic* is a logic whose wffs have order *n* or less. Let's do an example that transforms a sentence into a higher-order wff.

EXAMPLE 1 (*Cities, Streets, and Addresses*). Suppose we think of a city as a set of streets and a street as a set of house addresses. We'll try to formalize the following statement:

> There is a city with a street named Main, and there is an address 1140 on Main Street.

Suppose C is a variable representing a city and S is a variable representing a street. If x is a name, then we'll let $N(S, x)$ mean that the name of S is x. A third-order logic formalization of the sentence can be written as follows:

$$\exists C \, \exists S \, (C(S) \wedge N(S, \text{Main}) \wedge S(1140)).$$

This wff is third-order because S has order 1, so C has order 2 and $\exists C$ has order 3. ◆

Semantics

How do we attach a meaning to a higher-order wff? The answer is that we construct an interpretation for the wff. We start out by specifying a domain D of individuals that we use to give meaning to the constants, the free variables, and the functions and predicates that are not quantified. The quantified individual variables, functions, and predicates are allowed to vary over all possible meanings in terms of D.

Let's try to make the idea of an interpretation clear with an example. We'll give an interpretation for the following second-order wff:

$$\exists S \, \exists T \, \forall x \, (S(x) \rightarrow \neg \, T(x)).$$

Suppose we let the domain be $D = \{a, b\}$. We observe that S and T are predicates of order 1, and they are both quantified. So S and T can vary over all possible single-argument predicates over D. For example, the following list shows the four possible predicate definitions for S together with the corresponding set definitions for S:

Predicate definitions for S	*Set definitions for S*
$S(a)$ and $S(b)$ are both true.	$S = \{a, b\}$.
$S(a)$ is true and $S(b)$ is false.	$S = \{a\}$.
$S(a)$ is false and $S(b)$ is true.	$S = \{b\}$.
$S(a)$ and $S(b)$ are both false.	$S = \varnothing$.

We can see from this list that there are as many possibilities for S as there are subsets of D. A similar statement holds for T. Now it's easy to see that our example wff is true for our interpretation. For example, if we choose $S = \{a, b\}$ and $T = \varnothing$, then S is always true and T is always false. Thus

$$S(a) \to \neg\, T(a) \quad \text{and} \quad S(b) \to \neg\, T(b)$$

are both true. So $\exists S\ \exists T\ \forall x\ (S(x) \to \neg\, T(x))$ is true for the interpretation.

EXAMPLE 2. We'll give an interpretation for the following third-order wff:

$$\exists T\ \forall x\ (T(S) \to S(x)).$$

We'll let $D = \{a, b\}$. Since S is not quantified, it is a normal predicate and we must give it a meaning. Suppose we let $S(a)$ be true and $S(b)$ be false. This is the same thing as setting $S = \{a\}$. Now T is an order 2 predicate because it takes an order 1 predicate as its argument. T is also quantified, so it is allowed to vary over all possible predicates that take arguments like S. From the standpoint of sets the arguments to T can be any of the four subsets of D. Therefore T can vary over any of the 16 subsets of $\{\varnothing, \{a\}, \{b\}, \{a, b\}\}$. For example, one possible value for T is $T = \{\varnothing, \{a\}\}$. If we think of T as a predicate, this means that $T(\varnothing)$ and $T(\{a\})$ are both true, while $T(\{b\})$ and $T(\{a, b\})$ are both false. This value of T makes the wff $\forall x\ (T(S) \to S(x))$ true. Thus the wff $\exists T\ \forall x\ (T(S) \to S(x))$ is true for our interpretation.   ◆

So we can give interpretations to higher-order wffs. This means that we can also use the following familiar terms in our discussions about higher-order wffs: model, countermodel, valid, invalid, satisfiable, and unsatisfiable.

Formal Proofs

To construct formal proofs in higher-order logic, we can proceed in much the same way as we do for first-order predicate calculus. All we have to do is make natural modifications to the inference rules for quantifiers. For example, from the statement $\exists L\ L(x)$, we can use EI to infer the existence of a particular constant l such that $l(x)$. Let's look at a familiar example to see how higher-order logic comes into play when we discuss elementary geometry.

EXAMPLE 3 (*Euclidean Geometry*). From an informal standpoint the wffs of Euclidean geometry are English sentences. For example, the following four statements describe part of Hilbert's axioms for Euclidean plane geometry:

1. On any two distinct points there is always a line.
2. On any two distinct points there is not more than one line.
3. Every line has at least two distinct points.
4. There are at least three points not on the same line.

Can we formalize these axioms? Let's assume that a line is a set of points. So two lines are equal if they have the same set of points. We'll also assume that points are denoted by the variables x, y, and z and by the constants a, b, and c. We'll denote lines by the variables L, M, and N and by the constants l, m, and n. We'll let the predicate $L(x)$ denote the fact that x is a point on line L or, equivalently, L is a line on the point x. Now we can write the four axioms as second-order wffs as follows:

1. $\forall x \, \forall y \, (x \neq y \rightarrow \exists L \, (L(x) \wedge L(y)))$.
2. $\forall x \, \forall y \, (x \neq y \rightarrow \forall L \, \forall M \, (L(x) \wedge L(y) \wedge M(x) \wedge M(y) \rightarrow L = M))$.
3. $\forall L \, \exists x \, \exists y \, (x \neq y \wedge L(x) \wedge L(y))$.
4. $\exists x \, \exists y \, \exists z \, (x \neq y \wedge x \neq z \wedge y \neq z \wedge \forall L \, (L(x) \wedge L(y) \rightarrow \neg L(z)))$.

Let's prove the following theorem: *There are at least two distinct lines.*

Informal proof: Axiom 4 tells us that there are three distinct points a, b, and c not on the same line. By axiom 1 there is a line l on a and b, and again by axiom 1 there is a line m on a and c. By Axiom 4, c is not on line l. Therefore $l \neq m$.   QED.

A formal version of the theorem and proof can be written as follows:

$$\exists L \, \exists M \, \exists x \, (\neg \, L(x) \wedge M(x)).$$

Proof:

1. $\exists x \, \exists y \, \exists z \, (x \neq y \wedge x \neq z \wedge y \neq z \wedge \forall L \, (L(x) \wedge L(y) \rightarrow \neg L(z)))$ Axiom 4
2. $a \neq b \wedge a \neq c \wedge b \neq c \wedge \forall L \, (L(a) \wedge L(b) \rightarrow \neg L(c))$ 1,EI, EI, EI
3. $\forall x \, \forall y \, (x \neq y \rightarrow \exists L \, (L(x) \wedge L(y)))$ Axiom 1
4. $a \neq b \rightarrow \exists L \, (L(a) \wedge L(b))$ 3, UI, UI
5. $a \neq b$ 2, Simp
6. $\exists L \, (L(a) \wedge L(b))$ 4, 5, MP
7. $l(a) \wedge l(b)$ 6, EI
8. $a \neq c \rightarrow \exists L \, (L(a) \wedge L(c))$ 3, UI, UI
9. $a \neq c$ 2, Simp
10. $\exists L \, (L(a) \wedge L(c))$ 8, 9, MP

11. $m(a) \wedge m(c)$	10, EI
12. $\forall L\ (L(a) \wedge L(b) \to \neg\, L(c))$	2, Simp
13. $l(a) \wedge l(b) \to \neg\, l(c)$	12, UI
14. $\neg\, l(c)$	7, 13, MP
15. $m(c)$	11, Simp
16. $\neg\, l(c) \wedge m(c)$	14, 15, Conj
17. $\exists x\ (\neg\, l(x) \wedge m(x))$	16, EG
18. $\exists M\ \exists x\ (\neg\, l(x) \wedge M(x))$	17, EG
19. $\exists L\ \exists M\ \exists x\ (\neg\, L(x) \wedge M(x)).$	18, EG
QED. ♦	

Exercises

1. State the minimal order of logic to which each of the following wffs belongs.

   a. $\forall x\ (Q(x) \to P(Q))$.

   b. $\exists x\ \forall g\ \exists p\ (q(c, g(x)) \wedge p(g(x)))$.

   c. $A(B) \wedge B(C) \wedge C(D) \wedge D(E) \wedge E(F)$.

   d. $\exists P\ (A(B) \wedge B(C) \wedge C(D) \wedge P(A))$.

   e. $S(x) \wedge T(S, x) \to U(T, S, x)$.

   f. $\forall x\ (S(x) \wedge T(S, x) \to U(T, S, x))$.

   g. $\forall x\ \exists S\ (S(x) \wedge T(S, x) \to U(T, S, x))$.

   h. $\forall x\ \exists S\ \exists T\ (S(x) \wedge T(S, x) \to U(T, S, x))$.

   i. $\forall x\ \exists S\ \exists T\ \exists U\ (S(x) \wedge T(S, x) \to U(T, S, x))$.

2. Formalize each of the following sentences as a wff in second-order logic.

   a. There are sets A and B such that $A \cap B = \varnothing$.

   b. There is a set S with two subsets A and B such that $S = A \cup B$.

3. Formalize each of the following sentences as a wff in an appropriate higher-order logic. Also figure out the order of the logic that you use in each case.

   a. Every state has a city named Springfield.

   b. There is a nation with a state that has a county named Washington.

   c. A house has a room with a bookshelf containing a book by Thoreau.

   d. There is a continent with a nation containing a state with a county named Lincoln, which contains a city named Central City that has a street named Broadway.

   e. Some set has a partition consisting of two subsets.

4. Find a formalization of the following statement upon which mathematical induction is based: If S is a subset of $\mathbb{N}$ and $0 \in S$ and whenever $x \in S$ then $\text{succ}(x) \in S$, then $S = \mathbb{N}$.

5. Show that each of the following wffs is valid by giving an informal validity argument.

    a. $\forall S\ \exists x\ S(x) \to \exists x\ \forall S\ S(x)$.

    b. $\forall x\ \exists S\ S(x) \to \exists S\ \forall x\ S(x)$.

    c. $\exists S\ \forall x\ S(x) \to \forall x\ \exists S\ S(x)$.

    d. $\exists x\ \forall S\ S(x) \to \forall S\ \exists x\ S(x)$.

6. Use the facts about geometry given in Example 3 to give an informal proof for each of the following statements. You may use any of these statements to prove a subsequent statement.

    a. For each line there is a point not on the line.

    b. Two lines cannot intersect in more than one point.

    c. Through each point there exist at least two lines.

    d. Not all lines pass through the same point.

7. Formalize each of the following statements as a wff in second-order logic, using the variable names from Example 3. Then provide a formal proof for each wff.

    a. Not all points lie on the same line.

    b. Two lines cannot intersect in more than one point.

    c. Through each point there exist at least two lines.

    d. Not all lines pass through the same point.

3.5 Formal Theories

When we reason, we usually do it in a particular domain of discourse. For example, we might reason about computer science, politics, mathematics, physics, automobiles, or cooking. But these domains are usually too large to do much reasoning. So we normally narrow our scope of thought and reason in domains such as imperative programming languages, international trade, plane geometry, optics, suspension systems, or pasta recipes.

No matter what the domain of discussion, we usually try to correctly apply inferences while we are reasoning. Since each of us has our own personal reasoning system, we sometimes find it difficult to understand one another. In an attempt to find common ground among the various ways that people reason, we introduced the propositional calculus and first-order predicate calculus. So we've looked at some formalizations of logic.

Can we go a step further and formalize the things that we talk about? Many subjects can be formalized by giving some axioms that define the properties of the objects being discussed. For example, when we reason about geometry, we make assumptions about points and lines. When we reason about automobile engines, we make certain assumptions about how they work. When we combine first-order predicate calculus with the formalization of some subject, we obtain a reasoning system called a *first-order theory*.

First-Order Theory with Equality

A first-order theory is called a *first-order theory with equality* if it contains a two-argument predicate, say e, that captures the properties of equality required by the theory. We usually denote $e(x, y)$ by the more familiar

$$x = y.$$

Similarly, we let $x \neq y$ denote $\neg e(x, y)$.

Let's try to describe some fundamental properties that all first-order theories with equality should satisfy. Of course, we want equality to satisfy the basic property that each term is equal to itself. The following axiom will suffice for this purpose:

Equality Axiom(EA)

$$t = t \text{ for all terms } t. \tag{3.33}$$

Now let's try to describe that well-known piece of folklore, *equals can replace equals*. Since this idea has such a wide variety of uses, it's hard to tell where to begin. So we'll start with a rule that describes the process of replacing some occurrence of a term in a predicate by an equal term. In this rule, p denotes an arbitrary predicate with one or more arguments. The letters t and u represent arbitrary terms:

Equals for Equals Rule (EE)

$$t = u \wedge p(\ldots t \ldots) \to p(\ldots u \ldots). \tag{3.34}$$

The notations $\ldots t \ldots$ and $\ldots u \ldots$ indicate that t and u occur in the same argument place of p. In other words, u replaces the indicated occurrence of t. Since (3.34) is an implication, we can use it as an inference rule in the following equivalent form:

Equals for Equals Rule (EE)

$$\frac{t = u, \, p(\ldots t \ldots)}{\therefore \, p(\ldots u \ldots)}.$$ (3.35)

The EE rule is sometimes called the *principle of extensionality*. Let's see what we can conclude from EE. We would like to conclude from EE that equals can replace equals in a term like $f(\ldots t \ldots)$. In other words, we would like the following wff to be valid:

$$t = u \rightarrow f(\ldots t \ldots) = f(\ldots u \ldots).$$

To prove that this wff is valid, we'll let $p(t, u)$ mean "$f(\ldots t \ldots) = f(\ldots u \ldots)$." Then the proof goes as follows:

Proof: 1. $t = u$ P
          2. $p(t, t)$ EA
          3. $p(t, u)$ 1, 2, EE
              QED   1, 3, CP.

Whenever we discuss equality of terms, we usually want the following two properties to hold for all terms:

Symmetric: $t = u \rightarrow u = t.$

Transitive: $t = u \wedge u = v \rightarrow t = v.$

We'll use the EE rule to prove the symmetric property in the next example and leave the transitive property as an exercise.

EXAMPLE 1. We'll prove the symmetric property $t = u \rightarrow u = t.$

Proof: 1. $t = u$ P
          2. $t = t$ EA
          3. $u = t$ 1, 2, EE
              QED   1, 3, CP.

To see why the statement on line 3 follows from the EE rule, let $p(x, y)$ mean "$x = y$." Then the proof can be rewritten in terms of the predicate p as follows:

Proof: 1. $t = u$ P
      2. $p(t, t)$ EA
      3. $p(u, t)$ 1, 2, EE
         QED   1, 3, CP.   ◆

When we're dealing with axioms for a theory, we sometimes write down more axioms than we really need. For example, some axiom might be deducible as a theorem from the other axioms. The practical purpose for this is to have a listing of the useful properties all in one place. For example, to describe equality for terms, we might write down the following five statements as axioms.

Equality Axioms for Terms   (3.36)

In these axioms the letters t, u, and v denote arbitrary terms, f is an arbitrary function, and p is an arbitrary predicate.

EA:	$t = t.$
Symmetric:	$t = u \rightarrow u = t.$
Transitive:	$t = u \wedge u = v \rightarrow t = v.$
EE (functional form):	$t = u \rightarrow f(\ldots t \ldots) = f(\ldots u \ldots).$
EE (predicate form):	$t = u \wedge p(\ldots t \ldots) \rightarrow p(\ldots u \ldots).$

The EE axioms in (3.36) allow only a single occurrence of t to be replaced by u. We may want to substitute more than one "equals for equals" at the same time. For example, if $x = a$ and $y = b$, we would like to say that $f(x, y) = f(a, b)$. It's nice to know that simultaneous use of equals for equals can be deduced from the axioms. For example, we'll prove the following statement:

$$x = a \wedge y = b \rightarrow f(x, y) = f(a, b).$$

Proof: 1. $x = a$ P
      2. $y = b$ P
      3. $f(x, y) = f(a, y)$ 1, EE
      4. $f(a, y) = f(a, b)$ 2, EE
      5. $f(x, y) = f(a, b)$ 3, 4, Transitive
         QED   1, 2, 5, CP.

This proof can be extended to substituting any number of equals for equals simultaneously in a function or in a predicate. In other words, we could have written the two EE axioms of (3.36) in the following form:

Multiple replacement EE (3.37)

EE (function): $t_1 = u_1 \wedge \cdots \wedge t_k = u_k \rightarrow f(t_1, ..., t_k) = f(u_1, ..., u_k)$.

EE (predicate): $t_1 = u_1 \wedge \cdots \wedge t_k = u_k \wedge p(t_1, ..., t_k) \rightarrow p(u_1, ..., u_k)$.

So the two axioms (8.1) and (3.34) are sufficient for us to deduce all the axioms in (3.36) together with those of (3.37).

Extending Equals for Equals

The EE rule for replacing equals for equals in a predicate can be extended to other wffs. For example, we can use the EE rule to prove the following more general statement about wffs without quantifiers:

If $W(x)$ is a wff without quantifiers, then the following wff is valid:

$$t = u \wedge W(t) \rightarrow W(u).$$ (3.38)

We assume in this case that $W(t)$ is obtained from $W(x)$ by replacing one or more occurrences of x by t and that $W(u)$ is obtained from $W(t)$ by replacing one or more occurrences of t by u.

For example, if $W(x) = p(x, y) \wedge q(x, x)$, then we might have $W(t) = p(t, y) \wedge q(x, t)$, where only two of the three occurrences of x are replaced by t. In this case we might have $W(u) = p(u, y) \wedge q(x, t)$, where only one occurrence of t is replaced by u. In other words, the following wff is valid:

$$t = u \wedge p(t, y) \wedge q(x, t) \rightarrow p(u, y) \wedge q(x, t).$$

What about wffs that contain quantifiers? Even when a wff has quantifiers, we can use the EE rule if we are careful not to introduce new bound occurrences of variables. Here is the full blown version of EE:

If $W(x)$ is a wff and t and u are terms that are free to replace x in $W(x)$, then the following wff is valid:

$$t = u \wedge W(t) \rightarrow W(u).$$ (3.39)

Again, we can assume in this case that $W(t)$ is obtained from $W(x)$ by replacing one or more occurrences of x by t and that $W(u)$ is obtained from $W(t)$ by replacing one or more occurrences of t by u.

For example, suppose $W(x) = \exists y\, p(x, y)$. Then for any terms t and u that do not contain occurrences of y, the following wff is valid:

$$t = u \wedge \exists y\, p(t, y) \rightarrow \exists y\, p(u, y).$$

A Partial Order Theory

Formal theories with equality often contain other axioms. For example, a *partial order theory* is a first-order theory with equality that also contains an ordering predicate. If the ordering predicate is reflexive, we denote it by $\leq$. Otherwise, we denote it by $<$. The three defining axioms for a reflexive partial order are as follows, for all x, y, and z:

Reflexive:	$x \leq x.$
Antisymmetric:	$x \leq y \wedge y \leq x \rightarrow x = y.$
Transitive:	$x \leq y \wedge y \leq z \rightarrow x \leq z.$

We can do formal reasoning in such a theory using the predicate calculus. For example, recall that $<$ and $\leq$ can be defined in terms of each other by using equality as follows:

$$x < y \text{ means } x \leq y \wedge x \neq y,$$
$$x \leq y \text{ means } x < y \vee x = y.$$

From either one of these statements we can write down a formal proof of the following well-known statement:

$$x < y \rightarrow x \leq y.$$

The two proofs of the statement are given as follows:

Proof:	1. $x < y$	P
	2. $x \leq y \wedge x \neq y$	1, T
	3. $x \leq y$	2, Simp
	4. $x < y \rightarrow x \leq y$	1, 3, CP
	QED.	

Proof:	1. $x < y$	P
	2. $x < y \vee x = y$	1, Addition
	3. $x \leq y$	2, T
	4. $x < y \rightarrow x \leq y$	1, 3, CP
	QED.	

What Is Logically Possible?

What is the job that we want done by a formal theory? Basically, we want two things. We want our proofs to yield theorems that are true (i.e., valid), and we want any valid wff to be provable as a theorem. These properties are converses of each other, and they have the following names:

Soundness: *All proofs yield theorems that are valid.*

Completeness: *All valid wffs are provable as theorems.*

To ensure soundness we must choose axioms that are valid and we must choose inference rules that map valid statements to valid statements. How do we ensure completeness? As we'll see, sometimes we can and sometimes we can't. We'll discuss it by starting with the propositional calculus.

Is there some simple formal system for the propositional calculus that is both sound and complete? Yes, there is. In fact, there are many of them. Each one specifies a fixed set of axioms and inference rules. We'll look at a system that is similar to a system introduced by the mathematician David Hilbert (1862–1943). Hilbert's system is described in Hilbert and Ackermann [1938]. So we'll call our system *Hilbert's system*. We'll use the connectives $\neg$, $\vee$, $\wedge$, and $\rightarrow$. Hilbert's system has the following axioms, where A, B, and C stand for arbitrary wffs:

Hilbert's Axioms

1. $A \vee A \rightarrow A$.
2. $A \rightarrow A \vee B$.
3. $A \vee B \rightarrow B \vee A$.
4. $(A \rightarrow B) \rightarrow (C \vee A \rightarrow C \vee B)$.
5. $A \rightarrow B \equiv \neg A \vee B \equiv \neg (A \wedge \neg B)$.

The first four axioms may appear a bit strange, but they can be verified by truth tables. Axiom 5 relates negation with the other operations, where an equivalence $D \equiv E$ is short for the two statements $D \rightarrow E$ and $E \rightarrow D$.

We'll use the modus ponens (MP) inference rule together with the conditional proof rule (CP). That's it. Everything that we do must be based only on the five axioms, MP, and CP. The remarkable thing is that this system is sound and complete. In other words, every proof yields a theorem that is a tautology, and there is a proof for every tautology of the propositional calculus.

There is a similar statement for the predicate calculus, which is due to the logician and mathematician Kurt Gödel (1906–1978). Gödel showed that the first-order predicate calculus is complete. In other words, there are formal systems for the first-order predicate calculus such that every valid wff can be proven as a theorem. The formal system presented by Gödel [1930] used fewer axioms and fewer inference rules than the system that we discussed in Section 3.2.

Gödel proved a remarkable result in 1931. He proved that if a formal theory is powerful enough to describe all the arithmetic formulas of the natural numbers and the system is consistent, then it is not complete. In other words, there is a valid wff that can't be proven as a theorem in the system. Even if additional axioms were added to make the wff provable, then there would exist a new valid wff that is not provable in the larger system. A very readable account of Gödel's proof is given by Nagel and Newman [1958].

The formulas of arithmetic can be described in a first-order theory with equality. So it follows from Gödel's result that first-order theories with equality are not complete. Similarly, we can represent the idea of equality with second-order predicate calculus. So it follows that second- and higher-order logics are not complete.

What does it really mean when we have a logic that is not complete? It means that we might have to leave the formalism of the logic to prove that some wffs are valid. In other words, we may need to argue informally—using only our wits and imaginations—to prove some logical statements. In some sense this is nice because it justifies our existence as reasoning beings. Since most theories cannot be captured by using only first-order logic, there will always be enough creative work for us to do—perhaps aided by computers.

Exercises

1. Use the EE rule to prove the double replacement rule

$$s = v \wedge t = w \wedge p(s, t) \rightarrow p(v, w).$$

2. Show that the transitive property of equality can be deduced from the other axioms for equality (3.36). In other words, use the other axioms to prove that

$$(t = u) \wedge (u = v) \rightarrow (t = v).$$

3. Let Ux mean "there exists a unique x." If $A(x)$ is a wff of the first-order predicate calculus, then $Ux\, A(x)$ means "There exists a unique x such that $A(x)$." Find a definition for $Ux\, A(x)$ as a wff from the first-order predicate calculus with equality.

4. Give a formal proof of the following statement about the integers:

$$c = a^i \wedge i \leq b \wedge \neg\, (i < b) \rightarrow c = a^b.$$

5. Use the the equality axioms (3.36) to prove each of the following versions of EE, where p and q are predicates, t and u are terms, and x, y, and z are variables.

   a. $t = u \wedge \neg\, p(\dots t \dots) \rightarrow \neg\, p(\dots u \dots)$.

   b. $t = u \wedge p(\dots t \dots) \wedge q(\dots t \dots) \rightarrow p(\dots u \dots) \wedge q(\dots u\dots)$.

   c. $t = u \wedge (p(\dots t \dots) \vee q(\dots t \dots)) \rightarrow p(\dots u \dots) \vee q(\dots u\dots)$.

   d. $x = y \wedge \exists z\, p(\dots x \dots) \rightarrow \exists z\, p(\dots y \dots)$.

   e. $x = y \wedge \forall z\, p(\dots x \dots) \rightarrow \forall z\, p(\dots y \dots)$.

6. Prove the validity of the wff $\forall x\, \exists y\, (x = y)$.

7. Prove each of the following equivalences.

   a. $p(x) \equiv \exists y\, (x = y \wedge p(y))$.

   b. $p(x) \equiv \forall y\, (x = y \rightarrow p(y))$.

3.6 Program Correctness

An important and difficult problem of computer science can be stated as follows:

$$\text{Prove that a program is correct.} \tag{3.40}$$

This takes some discussion. One major question to ask before we can prove that a program is correct is "What is the program supposed to do?" If we can state in English what a program is supposed to do, and English is the programming language, then the statement of the problem may itself be a proof of its correctness. Normally, a problem is stated in some language X, and its solution is given in some language Y. For example, the statement of the problem might use English mixed with some symbolic notation, while the solution might be in a programming language. How do we prove correctness in cases like this? Often the answer depends on the programming language. As an example, we'll look at a formal theory for proving the correctness of imperative programs.

Imperative Program Correctness

An imperative program consists of a sequence of statements that represent commands. The most important statement is the assignment statement. Other statements are used for control, such as looping and taking alternate paths. To prove things about such programs, we need a formal theory consisting of wffs, axioms, and inference rules.

Suppose we want to prove that a program does some particular thing. We must represent the thing that we want to prove in terms of a precondition P, which states what is supposed to be true before the program starts, and a postcondition Q, which states what is supposed to be true after the program halts. If S denotes the program, then we will describe this informal situation with the following wff:

$$\{P\}\ S\ \{Q\}.$$

The letters P and Q denote logical statements that describe properties of the variables that occur in S. P is called a *precondition* for S, and Q is called a *postcondition* for S. We assume that P and Q are wffs from a first-order theory with equality that depends on the program S. For example, if the program manipulates numbers, then the first-order theory must include the numerical operations and properties that are required to describe the problem at hand. If the program processes strings, then the first-order theory must include the string operations.

If we're going to have a logic, we need to assign a meaning to any wff of the form $\{P\}\ S\ \{Q\}$. In other words, we want to assign a truth value to $\{P\}\ S\ \{Q\}$.

Meaning of $\{P\}\ S\ \{Q\}$

The meaning of $\{P\}\ S\ \{Q\}$ is the truth value of the following statement:

> If P is true before S is executed and the execution of S halts, then Q is true after the execution of S halts.

If $\{P\}\ S\ \{Q\}$ is true, we can say that S is *correct* with respect to precondition P and postcondition Q.

For example, from our knowledge of the assignment statement, most of us will agree that the following wff is true:

$$\{x > 4\}\ x := x + 1\ \{x > 5\}.$$

On the other hand, most of us will also agree that the following wff is false:

$$\{x > 4\}\ x := x + 1\ \{x > 6\}.$$

A formal theory for proving correctness of these wffs needs some axioms and some inference rules. The axioms depend on the types of assignments allowed by the assignment statement. The inference rules depend on the control structures of the language. So we had better agree on a language before we go any further in our discussion. To keep things simple, we'll assume that the assignment statement has the following form, where x is a variable and t is a term:

$$x := t.$$

So the only thing we can do is assign a value to a variable. This effectively restricts the language so that it cannot use other structures, such as arrays and records. In other words, we can't make assignments like $a[i] := t$ or $a.b := t$.

Since our assignment statement is restricted to the form $x := t$, we need only one axiom. It's called the *assignment axiom*, and we'll motivate the discovery of the axiom by an example. Suppose we're told that the following wff is correct:

$$\{P\} \ x := 4 \ \{y > x\}.$$

In other words, if P is true before the execution of the assignment statement, then after its execution the statement $y > x$ is true. What should P be? From our knowledge of the assignment statement we might guess that P has the following definition:

$$P = \text{``}y > 4.\text{''}$$

This is about the most general statement we can make. Notice that P can be obtained from the postcondition $y > x$ by replacing x by 4. The assignment axiom generalizes this idea. We'll state it as follows:

Assignment Axiom (AA)

$$\{Q(x/t)\} \ x := t \ \{Q\}. \tag{3.41}$$

The notation $Q(x/t)$ denotes the wff obtained from Q by replacing all free occurrences of x by t. The axiom is often called the "backwards" assignment axiom because the precondition is constructed from the postcondition. When using AA, we always start by writing down the form of (3.41) with an empty precondition as follows:

$$\{ \qquad \} \ x := t \ \{Q\}.$$

Then we construct the precondition by replacing all free occurrences of x in Q by t.

For example, suppose we know that $x < 5$ is the postcondition for the assignment statement $x := x + 1$. We start by writing down the following partially completed version of AA:

$$\{ \quad \} \; x := x + 1 \; \{x < 5\}.$$

Then we use AA to construct the precondition. In this case we replace the x by $x + 1$ in the postcondition $x < 5$. This gives us the precondition $x + 1 < 5$, and we can write down the completed instance of the assignment axiom:

$$\{x + 1 < 5\} \; x := x + 1 \; \{x < 5\}.$$

It happens quite often that the precondition constructed by AA doesn't quite match what we're looking for. For example, most of us will agree that the following wff is correct:

$$\{x < 3\} \; x := x + 1 \; \{x < 5\}.$$

We've already seen that AA applied to this assignment statement gives

$$\{x + 1 < 5\} \; x := x + 1 \; \{x < 5\}.$$

Since the two preconditions don't match, we have some more work to do. In this case we know that for any number x we have $x < 3 \rightarrow x + 1 < 5$. So if $x < 3$ is true before the execution of $x := x + 1$, then we also know that $x + 1 < 5$ is true before execution of $x := x + 1$. Now AA tells us that $x < 5$ is true after execution of $x := x + 1$. So $\{x < 3\} \; x := x + 1 \; \{x < 5\}$ is correct.

This kind of argument happens so often that we have an inference rule to describe the situation for any program S. It's called the *consequence rule*:

Consequence Rule

$$\frac{P \rightarrow R \text{ and } \{R\} \, S \, \{Q\}}{\therefore \; \{P\} \, S \, \{Q\}} \quad \text{and} \quad \frac{\{P\} \, S \, \{T\} \text{ and } T \rightarrow Q}{\therefore \; \{P\} \, S \, \{Q\}} . \qquad (3.42)$$

Notice that each consequence rule requires two proofs: a proof of correctness and a proof of an implication.

Although assignment statements are the core of imperative programming, they can't do much without control structures. So let's look at a few fundamental control structures together with their corresponding inference rules.

The most basic control structure is the composition of two statements S_1 and S_2, which we denote by $S_1; S_2$. This means execute S_1 and then execute S_2. The *composition rule* can be used to prove the correctness of the composition of two statements.

Composition Rule

$$\frac{\{P\}\,S_1\,\{R\} \quad \text{and} \quad \{R\}\,S_2\,\{Q\}}{\therefore\ \{P\}\,S_1;\,S_2\,\{Q\}}.$$

(3.43)

The composition rule extends naturally to any number of program statements in a sequence. For example, suppose we prove that the following three wffs are correct:

$$\{P\}\,S_1\,\{R\},\ \{R\}\,S_2\,\{T\},\ \text{and}\ \{T\}\,S_3\,\{Q\}.$$

Then we can infer that $\{P\}\,S_1;\,S_2;\,S_3\,\{Q\}$ is correct.

For (3.43) to work, we need an intermediate condition R to place between the two statements. Intermediate conditions often appear naturally during a proof, as the next example shows.

EXAMPLE 2. We'll show the correctness of the following wff:

$$\{x > 2 \wedge y > 3\}\ x := x + 1;\ y := y + x\ \{y > 6\}.$$

This wff matches the bottom of the composition inference rule (3.43). Since the program statements are assignments, we can use the AA rule to move backward from the postcondition to find an intermediate condition to place between the two assignments. Then we can use AA again to move backward from the intermediate condition. The proof goes as follows:

Proof: First we'll use AA to work backward from the postcondition through the second assignment statement:

1. $\{y + x > 6\}\ y := y + x\ \{y > 6\}$ AA

Now we can take the new precondition and use AA to work backward from it through the first assignment statement:

2. $\{y + x + 1 > 6\}\ x := x + 1\ \{y + x > 6\}$ AA

Now we can use the composition rule (3.43) together with lines 1 and 2 to obtain line 3 as follows:

3. $\{y + x + 1 > 6\}\ x := x + 1;\ y := y + x\ \{y > 6\}$ 1, 2, Comp

At this point the precondition on line 3 does not match the precondition for the wff that we are trying to prove correct. Let's try to apply the consequence rule (3.42) to the situation:

4.	$x > 2 \land y > 3$	P
5.	$x > 2$	4, Simp
6.	$y > 3$	4, Simp
7.	$x + y > 2 + y$	5, T
8.	$2 + y > 2 + 3$	6, T
9.	$x + y > 2 + 3$	7, 8, Transitive
10.	$x + y + 1 > 6$	9, T
11.	$x > 2 \land y > 3 \rightarrow x + y + 1 > 6$	4, 10, CP

Now we're in position to apply the consequence rule to lines 3 and 11:

12.　$\{x > 2 \land y > 3\}\, x := x + 1;\, y := y + x\, \{y > 6\}$　　3, 11, Consequence
　　QED.　◆

Let's discuss a few more control structures. We'll start with the *if-then rule* for if-then statements. We should recall that the statement **if** C **then** S means that S is executed if C is true and S is bypassed if C is false. We obtain the following inference rule:

If-Then Rule

$$\frac{\{P \land C\}\, S\, \{Q\} \ \text{ and } \ P \land \neg C \rightarrow Q}{\therefore \ \{P\}\ \textbf{if } C \textbf{ then } S\ \{Q\}}. \qquad (3.44)$$

The two wffs in the hypothesis of (3.44) are of different type. The logical wff $P \land \neg C \rightarrow Q$ needs a proof from the predicate calculus. This wff is necessary in the hypothesis of (3.44) because if C is false, then S does not execute. But we still need Q to be true after C has been determined to be false during the execution of the if-then statement. Let's do an example.

EXAMPLE 3. We'll show that the following wff is correct:

$$\{\text{true}\}\ \textbf{if } x < 0 \textbf{ then } x := -x\ \{x \geq 0\}.$$

Proof: Since the wff fits the pattern of (3.44), all we need to do is prove the following two statements:

1. $\{\text{true} \wedge x < 0\}\ x := -x\ \{x \geq 0\}$.
2. $\text{true} \wedge \neg (x < 0) \rightarrow x \geq 0$.

The proofs are easy. We'll combine them into one formal proof:

Proof:	1.	$\{-x \geq 0\}\ x := -x\ \{x \geq 0\}$	AA
	2.	$\text{true} \wedge x < 0$	P
	3.	$x < 0$	2, Simp
	4.	$-x > 0$	3, T
	5.	$-x \geq 0$	4, Add
	6.	$\text{true} \wedge x < 0 \rightarrow -x \geq 0$	2, 5, CP
	7.	$\{\text{true} \wedge x < 0\}\ x := -x\ \{x \geq 0\}$	1, 6, Consequence
	8.	$\text{true} \wedge \neg (x < 0)$	P
	9.	$\neg (x < 0)$	8, Simp
	10.	$x \geq 0$	9, T
	11.	$\text{true} \wedge \neg (x < 0) \rightarrow x \geq 0$	8, 10, CP
	QED		7, 11, If-then. ◆

Next comes the *if-then-else rule* for the alternative conditional statement. The statement **if** C **then** S_1 **else** S_2 means that S_1 is executed if C is true and S_2 is executed if C is false. We obtain the following inference rule:

If-Then-Else Rule

$$\frac{\{P \wedge C\}\ S_1\ \{Q\}\ \text{ and }\ \{P \wedge \neg C\}\ S_2\ \{Q\}}{\therefore\ \{P\}\ \textbf{if } C \textbf{ then } S_1 \textbf{ else } S_2\ \{Q\}}. \tag{3.45}$$

EXAMPLE 4. Suppose we're given the following wff, where even(x) means that x is an even integer:

$$\{\text{true}\}\ \textbf{if } \text{even}(x) \textbf{ then } y := x \textbf{ else } y := x + 1\ \{\text{even}(y)\}.$$

We'll give a formal proof that this wff is correct. The wff matches the bottom of rule (3.45). Therefore the wff will be correct by (3.45) if we can show that the following two wffs are correct:

1. $\{\text{true} \wedge \text{even}(x)\}\ y := x\ \{\text{even}(y)\}$.
2. $\{\text{true} \wedge \text{odd}(x)\}\ y := x + 1\ \{\text{even}(y)\}$.

We'll combine the two proofs into the following formal proof:

Proof: 1. $\{even(x)\}\, y := x\, \{even(y)\}$ AA
     2. $true \wedge even(x)$ P
     3. $even(x)$ 2, Simp
     4. $true \wedge even(x) \to even(x)$ 2, 3, CP
     5. $\{true \wedge even(x)\}\, y := x\, \{even(y)\}$ 1, 4, Consequence
     6. $\{even(x + 1)\}\, y := x + 1\, \{even(y)\}$ AA
     7. $true \wedge odd(x)$ P
     8. $odd(x)$ 7, Simp
     9. $even(x + 1)$ 8, T
    10. $true \wedge odd(x) \to even(x + 1)$ 7, 9, CP
    11. $\{true \wedge odd(x)\}\, y := x + 1\, \{even(y)\}$ 6, 10, Consequence
       QED   5, 11, If-then-else.   ♦

The last inference rule that we will consider is the *while rule*. The statement **while** C **do** S means that S is executed if C is true, and if C is still true after S has executed, then the process is started over again. Since the body S may execute more than once, there must be a close connection between the precondition and postcondition for S. This can be seen by the appearance of P in all preconditions and postconditions of the rule:

While Rule

$$\frac{\{P \wedge C\}\, S\, \{P\}}{\therefore\ \{P\}\ \textbf{while}\ C\ \textbf{do}\ S\ \{P \wedge \neg C\}}. \tag{3.46}$$

The wff P is called a *loop invariant* because it must be true before and after each execution of the body S. Loop invariants can be tough to find in programs with no documentation. On the other hand, in writing a program, a loop invariant can be a helpful tool for specifying the actions of while loops.

To illustrate the idea of working with while loops, we'll work our way through an example that will force us to discover a loop invariant in order to prove the correctness of a wff. Suppose we want to prove the correctness of the following program to compute the power a^b of two natural numbers a and b, where $a > 0$ and $b \geq 0$:

$$\{a > 0 \wedge b \geq 0\}$$
$$i := 0;$$
$$p := 1;$$
$$\textbf{while}\ i < b\ \textbf{do}$$
$$\qquad p := p * a;$$
$$\qquad i := i + 1$$
$$\textbf{od}$$
$$\{p = a^b\}$$

The program consists of three statements. So we can represent the program and its precondition and postcondition in the following form:

$$\{a > 0 \wedge b \geq 0\}\ S_1;\ S_2;\ S_3\ \{p = a^b\}.$$

In this form, S_1 and S_2 are the first two assignment statements, and S_3 represents the while statement. The composition rule (3.43) tells us that we can prove that the wff is correct if we can find proofs of the following three statements for some wffs P and Q:

$$\{a > 0 \wedge b \geq 0\}\ S_1\ \{Q\},$$
$$\{Q\}\ S_2\ \{P\},$$
$$\{P\}\ S_3\ \{p = a^b\}.$$

Where do P and Q come from? If we know P, then we can use AA to work backward through S_2 to find Q. But how do we find P? Since S_3 is a while statement, P should be a loop invariant. So we need to do a little work.

From (3.46) we know that a loop invariant P for the while statement S_3 must satisfy the following form:

$$\{P\}\ \textbf{while}\ i < b\ \textbf{do}\ p := p * a;\ i := i + 1\ \textbf{od}\ \{P \wedge \neg\,(i < b)\}.$$

Let's try some possibilities for P. Suppose we set $P \wedge \neg\,(i < b)$ equivalent to the program's postcondition $p = a^b$ and try to solve for P. This won't work because $p = a^b$ does not contain the letter i. So we need to be more flexible in our thinking. Since we have the consequence rule, all we really need is an invariant P such that $P \wedge \neg\,(i < b)$ implies $p = a^b$.

After staring at the program, we might notice that the equation $p = a^i$ holds both before and after the execution of the two assignment statements in the body of the while statement. It's also easy to see that the inequality $i \leq b$ holds before and after the execution of the body. So let's try the following definition for P:

$$(p = a^i) \wedge (i \leq b).$$

This P has more promise. Notice that $P \wedge \neg\,(i < b)$ implies $i = b$, which gives us the desired postcondition $p = a^b$. Next, by working backward from P through the two assignment statements, we wind up with the statement

$$1 = a^0 \wedge 0 \leq b.$$

This statement can certainly be derived from the precondition $a \geq 0 \wedge b > 0$.

So P does OK from the start of the program down to the beginning of the while loop. All that remains is to prove the following statement:

$$\{P\} \textbf{ while } i < b \textbf{ do } p := p * a; i := i + 1 \textbf{ od } \{P \wedge \neg (i < b)\}.$$

By (3.46), all we need to prove is the following statement:

$$\{P \wedge i < b\}\, p := p * a; i := i + 1\, \{P\}.$$

This can be done easily, working backward from P through the two assignment statements.

Termination

Program correctness as we have been discussing it does not consider whether loops terminate. In other words, the correctness of the wff $\{P\}\, S\, \{Q\}$ includes the assumption that S halts. This kind of correctness is often called *partial correctness*. For *total correctness* we can't assume that loops terminate. We must prove that they terminate.

For example, suppose we're presented with the following while loop, and the only information we know is that the variables take integer values:

$$
\begin{aligned}
&x := a; \\
&y := b; \\
&\textbf{while } x \neq y \textbf{ do} \\
&\quad x := x - 1; \\
&\quad y := y + 1; \\
&\quad c := c + 1 \\
&\textbf{od}
\end{aligned}
\tag{3.47}
$$

We don't have enough information to be able to tell for certain whether the loop terminates. For example, if we initialize $a = 4$ and $b = 5$, then the loop will run forever. In fact the loop will run forever if $a < b$. If $a = 6$ and $b = 3$, the loop will run forever. After a little study and thought, we can see that the loop will terminate if $a \geq b$ and $a - b$ is an even number. The value of c doesn't affect the termination, but it probably has something to do with counting the number of times through the loop. In fact, if we initialize $c = 0$, then the value of c at the termination of the loop satisfies the equation $a - b = 2c$.

This example shows that the precondition for a loop must contain enough information to decide whether the loop terminates. We're going to present a formal condition that, if satisfied, will ensure the termination of a loop. But first we need to discuss a few preliminary ideas.

A *state* of a computation is a tuple representing the values of the variables at some point in the computation. For example, the tuple $\langle x, y, c \rangle$ denotes an arbitrary state of program (3.47), where we'll assume that a and b are constants. For our purposes the only time a state will change is when an assignment statement is executed.

For example, let the initial state of a computation for (3.47) be $\langle 10, 6, 0 \rangle$. For this state the loop condition is true because $10 \neq 6$. After the execution of the assignment statement $x := x - 1$ in the body of the loop, the state becomes $\langle 9, 6, 0 \rangle$. After one iteration of the loop the state will be $\langle 9, 7, 1 \rangle$. For this state the loop condition is true because $9 \neq 7$. After a second iteration of the entire loop the state becomes $\langle 8, 8, 2 \rangle$. For this state the loop condition is false, which causes the loop to terminate. We'll use "States" to represent the set of all possible states for a program's variables. For program (3.47) we have

$$\text{States} = \mathbb{Z} \times \mathbb{Z} \times \mathbb{Z}.$$

Program (3.47) terminates for the initial state $\langle 10, 6, 0 \rangle$ because the value $x - y$ gets smaller with each iteration of the loop, eventually equaling zero. In other words, $x - y$ takes on the sequence of values 4, 2, 0. This is the key point in showing loop termination. There must be some decreasing sequence of numbers that stops at some point. In more general terms, the numbers must form a decreasing sequence in some well-founded set. For example, in (3.47) the well-founded set is the natural numbers $\mathbb{N}$.

To show loop termination, we need to find a well-founded set $\langle W, \prec \rangle$ that we can use to associate an element $w_i \in W$ with the ith iteration of the loop such that the elements form a decreasing sequence as follows:

$$w_1 \succ w_2 \succ w_3 \cdots.$$

Since W is well-founded, the sequence must stop. Thus the loop must halt.

Let's put things together and describe in more detail the general process required to prove termination of the following while loop with respect to a precondition P:

$$\textbf{while } C \textbf{ do } S.$$

We'll assume that we already know, or we have already proven, that S halts. This reflects the normal process of working our way from the inside out when doing termination proofs.

We need to introduce a little terminology to precisely describe the termination condition. Let P be a precondition for the loop **while** C **do** S. For any state s, let $P(s)$ denote the wff obtained from P by replacing its variables by their corresponding values in s. Similarly, let $C(s)$ denote the wff obtained from C by replacing its variables by their corresponding values in s. Let s represent an arbitrary state prior to the execution of S, and let t be the state which follows that same execution of S.

Suppose we have a well-founded set $\langle W, \prec \rangle$ together with a function

$$f : \text{States} \to W,$$

where f may be a partial function. Now we can state the loop termination condition for the loop **while** C **do** S. The loop *terminates with respect to precondition P* if the following wff is valid:

Termination Condition

$$P(s) \wedge C(s) \wedge f(s) \in W \to f(t) \in W \wedge f(s) \succ f(t). \qquad (3.48)$$

Notice that (3.48) contains the two statements $f(s) \in W$ and $f(t) \in W$. Since f could be a partial function, these statements ensure that $f(s)$ and $f(t)$ are both defined and members of W in good standing. Therefore the statement $f(s) \succ f(t)$ will ensure that the loop terminates. For example, if s_i represents the state prior to the ith execution of S, then we can apply (3.48) to obtain the following decreasing sequence of elements in W:

$$f(s_1) \succ f(s_2) \succ f(s_3) \succ \cdots.$$

Since W is well-founded, the sequence must stop. Therefore the loop halts. Let's do an example to cement the idea.

EXAMPLE 5 (*A Termination Proof*). Let's see how the formal definition of termination relates to program (3.47). From our discussion it seems likely that P should be

$$x \geq y \wedge \text{even}(x - y).$$

We'll leave the proof that P is a loop invariant as an exercise. For a well-founded set W we'll choose $\mathbb{N}$. Then $f : \text{States} \to \mathbb{N}$ can be defined by

$$f(\langle x, y, c \rangle) = x - y.$$

If $s = \langle x, y, c \rangle$ represents the state prior to the execution of the loop body and t represents the state after execution of the loop body, then

$$t = \langle x - 1, y + 1, c + 1 \rangle.$$

In this case, $f(s)$ and $f(t)$ have the following values:

$$f(s) = f(x, y, c) = x - y,$$

$$f(t) = f(x - 1, y + 1, c + 1) = (x - 1) - (y + 1) = x - y - 2.$$

With these interpretations, (3.48) can be written as follows:

$$x \geq y \wedge \text{even}(x - y) \wedge x \neq y \wedge x - y \in \mathbb{N} \to x - y - 2 \in \mathbb{N} \wedge x - y > x - y - 2.$$

Now let's give a proof of this statement.

Proof:
1. $x \geq y \wedge \text{even}(x - y) \wedge x \neq y \wedge x - y \in \mathbb{N}$ P
2. $x \geq y \wedge x \neq y$ 1, Simp
3. $x > y$ 2, T
4. $\text{even}(x - y)$ 1, Simp
5. $x - y \in \mathbb{N}$ 1, Simp
6. $x - y \geq 2$ 3, 4, 5, T
7. $x - y - 2 \in \mathbb{N}$ 5, 6, T
8. $x - y > x - y - 2$ T
9. $x - y - 2 \in \mathbb{N} \wedge x - y > x - y - 2$ 7, 8, Conj
   QED   1, 9, CP.   ♦

As a final remark to this short discussion, we should remember the fundamental requirement that programs with loops need preconditions that contain enough restrictions to ensure that the loops terminate.

Note

Hopefully, this introduction has given you the flavor of proving properties of programs. There are many mechanical aspects to the process. For example, the backwards application of the AA rule is a simple substitution problem that can be automated. We've omitted many important results. For example, we did not discuss the problem of array assignment. If the programming language has other control structures, such as for-loops and repeat-loops, then new inference rules must be constructed. The original papers in these areas are by Hoare [1969] and Floyd [1967]. A good place to start reading more about this subject is the survey paper by Apt [1981].

Different languages usually require different formal theories to handle the program correctness problem. For example, declarative languages, in which programs can consist of recursive definitions, require methods of inductive proof in their formal theories for proving program correctness.

Exercises

1. Prove that the following wff is correct over the domain of integers:

$$\{true \wedge even(x)\} \; y := x + 1 \; \{odd(y)\}.$$

2. Prove that each of the following wffs is correct. Assume that the domain is the set of integers.

   a. $\{a > 0 \wedge b > 0\} \; x := a; y := b \; \{x + y > 0\}$.
   b. $\{a > b\} \; x := -a; y := -b \; \{x < y\}$.

3. Both of the following wffs claim to correctly perform the swapping process. The first one uses a temporary variable. The second does not. Prove that each wff is correct. Assume that the domain is the set of real numbers.

   a. $\{x < y\} \; temp := x; x := y; y := temp \; \{y < x\}$.
   b. $\{x < y\} \; y := y + x; x := y - x; y := y - x \; \{y < x\}$.

4. Prove that each of the following wffs is correct. Assume that the domain is the set of integers.

   a. $\{x < 10\}$ **if** $x \geq 5$ **then** $x := 4$ $\{x < 5\}$.
   b. $\{true\}$ **if** $x \neq y$ **then** $x := y$ $\{x = y\}$.
   c. $\{true\}$ **if** $x < y$ **then** $x := y$ $\{x \geq y\}$.
   d. $\{true\}$ **if** $x > y$ **then** $x := y + 1; y := x + 1$ **fi** $\{x \leq y\}$.

5. Prove that each of the following wffs is correct. Assume that the domain is the set of integers.

   a. $\{true\}$ **if** $x < y$ **then** $max := y$ **else** $max := x$ $\{max \geq x \wedge max \geq y\}$.
   b. $\{true\}$ **if** $x < y$ **then** $y := y - 1$ **else** $x := -x; y := -y$ **fi** $\{x \leq y\}$.

6. Show that each of the following wffs is NOT correct over the domain of integers.

   a. $\{x < 5\}$ **if** $x \geq 2$ **then** $x := 5$ $\{x = 5\}$.
   b. $\{true\}$ **if** $x < y$ **then** $y := y - x$ $\{y > 0\}$.

7. Prove that the following wff is correct, where x and y are integers:

$$\{x \geq y \wedge even(x - y)\}$$
$$\textbf{while } x \neq y \textbf{ do}$$
$$x := x - 1;$$
$$y := y + 1$$
$$\textbf{od}$$
$$\{x \geq y \wedge even(x - y) \wedge x = y\}.$$

8. Given a natural number n, the following program computes the sum of

the first n natural numbers. Prove that the wff is correct. *Hint:* For a loop invariant, try the conjunction $s = \frac{i(i+1)}{2} \wedge i \leq n$.

$$\{n \geq 0\}$$
$$i := 0;$$
$$s := 0;$$
$$\textbf{while } i < n \textbf{ do}$$
$$\qquad i := i + 1;$$
$$\qquad s := s + i$$
$$\textbf{od}$$
$$\left\{ s = \frac{n(n+1)}{2} \right\}.$$

9. Prove that each of the following loops terminates for the given precondition P. Assume that all variables take integer values. *Hint:* Find an appropriate well-founded set W and a function f : States $\rightarrow W$.

    a. **while** $i < x$ **do** $i := i + 1$ **od** and $P = i \leq x$.

    b. **while** $i < x$ **do** $x := x - 1$ **od** and $P = i \leq x$.

10. Prove that the following loop terminates with respect to the precondition P = true. Assume that all variables take values in the positive integers.

    while $x \neq y$ **do if** $x < y$ **then** $y := y - x$ **else** $x := x - y$ **od**.

Chapter Summary

The propositional calculus is the basic building block of formal logic. Each wff represents a statement that can be checked by truth tables to determine whether it is a tautology, a contradiction, or a contingency. There are basic equivalences (3.1) that allow us to simplify and transform wffs into other wffs. We can also use the equivalences to transform any wff into a CNF or a DNF. Propositional calculus also provides us with formal techniques for proving properties of wffs without using truth tables. A formal reasoning system has wffs, axioms, and inference rules.

The first-order predicate calculus extends propositional calculus by allowing wffs to contain predicates and quantifiers of variables. Meanings for these wffs are defined in terms of interpretations over nonempty sets called domains. A wff is valid if it's true for all possible interpretations. A wff is unsatisfiable if it's false for all possible interpretations. There are basic equivalences that allow us to simplify and transform wffs into other wffs. We can use equivalences to transform any wff into a prenex CNF or prenex DNF.

To decide whether a wff is valid, we can try to transform it into an equivalent wff that we know to be valid. But in general we must rely on some type of informal or formal reasoning. A formal reasoning system for the first-order predicate calculus can use all the inference rules of the propositional calculus. But we also need four quantifier inference rules: universal instantiation, existential instantiation, universal generalization, and existential generalization.

Higher-order logic extends first-order logic by allowing objects other than variables—such as predicates and function names—to be quantified and to be arguments in predicates. We can classify the order of a logic if we make the association that a predicate is a set. We can reason formally in higher-order logic just as we do in propositional logic and first-order logic.

A first-order theory is a formal treatment of some subject that uses first-order predicate calculus. For example, we often need the idea of equality when applying logic in a formal manner to a particular subject. Equality can be added to first-order logic in such a way that the following familiar notion is included: Equals can replace—be substituted for—equals.

We can prove elementary statements about imperative programs within a first-order theory where each program is bounded by two conditions—a precondition and a postcondition. The theory uses only one axiom—the assignment axiom. Some useful inference rules are the consequence rule and the rules for composition, if-then, if-then-else, and while statements. The termination of while loops can also be proven in a formal manner. The theory can be extended by adding axioms and inference rules for other items that are normally found in imperative languages, such as arrays and other loop forms.

Notes on Logic

The logical symbols that we've used in this chapter are not universal. So you should be flexible in your reading of the literature. From a historical point of view, Whitehead and Russell [1910] introduced the symbols $\supset$, $\vee$, $\cdot$, $\sim$, and $\equiv$ to stand for implication, disjunction, conjunction, negation, and equivalence, respectively. A prefix notation for the logical operations was introduced by Lukasiewicz [1929], where the letters C, A, K, N, and E stand for implication, disjunction, conjunction, negation, and equivalence, respectively. So in terms of our notation we have $Cpq = p \rightarrow q$, $Apq = p \vee q$, $Kpq = p \wedge q$, $Nq = \neg q$, and $Epq = p \equiv q$. This notation is called Polish notation; and its advantage is that each expression has a unique meaning without using parentheses and precedence. For example, $(p \rightarrow q) \rightarrow r$ and $p \rightarrow (q \rightarrow r)$ are represented by the expressions $CCpqr$ and $CpCqr$, respectively. The disadvantage of the notation is that it's harder to read. For example, $CCpqKsNr = (p \rightarrow q) \rightarrow (s \wedge \neg r)$.

The fact that a wff W is a theorem is often denoted by placing a turnstile in front of it as follows:

$$\vdash W.$$

So this means that there is a proof $W_1, ..., W_n$ such that $W_n = W$. Turnstiles are also used in discussing conditionals. For example, the notation

$$A_1, A_2, ..., A_n \vdash B$$

means that there is a conditional proof of the wff $A_1 \wedge A_2 \wedge ... \wedge A_n \to B$.

We should again emphasize that the logic that we are studying in this book deals with statements that are either true or false. This is sometimes called the *Law of the Excluded Middle*: Every statement is either true or false. If our logic does not assume the law of the excluded middle, then we can no longer use indirect proof because we can't conclude that a statement is false from the assumption that it is not true. A logic called *intuitionist logic* omits this law and thus forces all proofs to be direct. Intuitionists like to construct things in a direct manner.

Logics that assume the law of the excluded middle are called *two-valued logics*. Some logics take a more general approach and consider statements that may not be true or false. For example, a *three-valued logic* assigns one of three values to each statement: 0, .5, or 1, where 0 stands for false, .5 stands for unknown, and 1 stands for true. We can build truth tables for this logic by defining $\neg A = 1 - A$, $A \vee B = \max(A, B)$, and $A \wedge B = \min(A, B)$. We still use the equivalence $A \to B \equiv \neg A \vee B$. So we can discuss three-valued logic.

In a similar manner we can discuss *n-valued logic* for any natural number $n \geq 2$, where each statement takes on one of n specific values in the range 0 to 1. Some n-valued logics assign names to the values such as "necessarily true," "probably true," "probably false," and "necessarily false." For example, there is a logic called *modal logic* that uses two extra unary operators, one to indicate that a statement is necessarily true and one to indicate that a statement is possibly true. So modal logic can represent a sentence like "If P is necessarily true, then P is true."

Some logics assign values over an infinite set. For example, the term *fuzzy logic* is used to describe a logic in which each statement is assigned some value in the closed unit interval [0, 1].

All these logics have applications in computer science, but they are beyond our scope and purpose. However, it's nice to know that they all depend on a good knowledge of two-valued logic.

4

Computational Logic

Let us not dream that reason can ever be popular.
Passions, emotions, may be made popular, but
reason remains ever the property of the few.
—Johann Wolfgang von Goethe (1749–1832)

Can reasoning be automated? The answer is yes for some logics. In this chapter we'll discuss how to automate the reasoning process for first-order logic. We might start by automating the "natural deduction" proof techniques that we introduced in Chapter 3. A problem with this approach is that there are many inference rules that can be applied in many different ways. In this chapter we'll look at a more mechanical way to perform deduction.

We'll see that there is a single inference rule, called resolution, that can be applied automatically by a computer. We'll also see how the resolution rule is adapted to the execution of logic programs.

Chapter Guide

Section 4.1 introduces the resolution inference rule. To understand the rule, we'll need to discuss clauses, clausal forms, substitution, and unification. We'll see how the rule can be applied in a mechanical fashion to prove theorems.

Section 4.2 introduces logic programming and shows how resolution is applied to perform the computation of a logic program. We'll also give some elementary techniques for constructing logic programs.

4.1 Automatic Reasoning

Let's look at the mechanical side of logic. We're going to introduce an inference rule that can be applied automatically. As fate would have it, the rule must be applied while trying to prove that a wff is unsatisfiable. This is not

really a problem, because we know that a wff is valid if and only if its negation is unsatisfiable. In other words, if we want to prove that the wff W is
valid, then we can do so by trying to prove that $\neg W$ is unsatisfiable. For example, if we want to prove the validity of the conditional $A \rightarrow B$, then we can
try to prove the unsatisfiability of its negation $A \wedge \neg B$.

The new inference rule, which is called the *resolution rule*, can be applied over and over again in an attempt to show unsatisfiability. We can't
present the resolution rule yet because it can be applied only to wffs that are
written in a special form, called *clausal form*. So let's get to it.

Clauses and Clausal Forms

We need to introduce a little terminology before we can describe a clausal
form. Recall that a *literal* is either an atom or the negation of an atom. For
example, $p(x)$ and $\neg q(x, b)$ are literals. To distinguish whether a literal has a
negation sign, we may use the terms *positive literal* and *negative literal*. $p(x)$
is a positive literal, and $\neg q(x, b)$ is a negative literal.

A *clause* is a disjunction of zero or more literals. For example, the following wffs are clauses:

$$p(x),$$
$$\neg q(x, b),$$
$$\neg p(a) \vee p(b),$$
$$p(x) \vee \neg q(a, y) \vee p(a).$$

The clause that is a disjunction of zero literals is called the *empty clause*, and
it's denoted by the following special box symbol:

$$\square .$$

The empty clause is assigned the value false. We'll soon see why this makes
sense when we discuss resolution.

A *clausal form* is the universal closure of a conjunction of clauses. In
other words, a clausal form is a prenex conjunctive normal form, in which all
quantifiers are universal and there are no free variables. For ease of notation
we'll often represent a clausal form by the set consisting of its clauses. For
example, if $S = \{C_1, ..., C_n\}$, where each C_i is a clause, and if $x_1, ..., x_m$ are the
free variables in the clauses of S, then S denotes the following clausal form:

$$\forall x_1 \cdots \forall x_m (C_1 \wedge \cdots \wedge C_n).$$

For example, the following list shows five wffs in clausal form together with their corresponding sets of clauses:

Wffs in Clausal Form	*Sets of Clauses*
$\forall x \, p(x)$	$\{p(x)\}$
$\forall x \, \neg \, q(x, b)$	$\{\neg \, q(x, b)\}$
$\forall x \, \forall y \, (p(x) \wedge \neg \, q(y, b))$	$\{p(x), \neg \, q(y, b)\}$
$\forall x \, \forall y \, (p(y, f(x)) \wedge (q(y) \vee \neg \, q(a)))$	$\{p(y, f(x)), q(y) \vee \neg \, q(a)\}$
$(p(a) \vee p(b)) \wedge q(a, b)$	$\{p(a) \vee p(b), q(a, b)\}$

Notice that the last clausal form does not need quantifiers because it doesn't have any variables. In other words, it's a proposition. In fact, for propositions a clausal form is just a conjunctive normal form (CNF).

When we talk about an interpretation for a set S of clauses, we mean an interpretation for the clausal form that S denotes. Thus we can use the words "valid," "invalid," "satisfiable," and "unsatisfiable" to describe S because these words have meaning for the clausal form that S denotes.

It's easy to see that some wffs are not equivalent to any clausal form. For example, let's consider the following wff:

$$\forall x \, \exists y \, p(x, y).$$

This wff is not a clausal form, and it isn't equivalent to any clausal form because it has an existential quantifier. Since clausal forms are the things that resolution needs to work on, it's nice to know that we can associate a clausal form with each wff in such a way that the clausal form is unsatisfiable if and only if the wff is unsatisfiable. Let's see how to find such a clausal form for each wff.

To construct a clausal form for a wff, we can start by constructing a prenex conjunctive normal form for the wff. If there are no free variables and all the quantifiers are universal, then we have a clausal form. Otherwise, we need to get rid of the free variables and the existential quantifiers and still retain enough information to be able to detect whether the original wff is unsatisfiable. Luckily, there's a way to do this. The technique is due to the mathematician Thoralf Skolem (1887–1963), and it appears in his paper [1928].

Let's introduce Skolem's idea by considering the following example wff:

$$\forall x \, \exists y \, p(x, y).$$

In this case the quantifier $\exists y$ is inside the scope of the quantifier $\forall x$. So it may be that y depends on x. For example, if we let $p(x, y)$ mean "x has a successor y," then y certainly depends on x. If we're going to remove the quantifier $\exists y$ from $\forall x\, \exists y\, p(x, y)$, then we'd better leave some information about the fact that y may depend on x. Skolem's idea was to use a new function symbol, say f, and replace each occurrence of y within the scope of $\exists y$ by the term $f(x)$. After performing this operation, we obtain the following wff, which is now in clausal form:

$$\forall x\, p(x, f(x)).$$

We can describe the general method for eliminating existential quantifiers as follows:

Skolem's Rule   (4.1)

Let $\exists x\, W(x)$ be a wff or part of a larger wff. If $\exists x$ is not inside the scope of a universal quantifier, then pick a new constant c, and

$$\text{replace } \exists x\, W(x) \text{ by } W(c).$$

If $\exists x$ is inside the scope of universal quantifiers $\forall x_1, ..., \forall x_n$, then pick a new function symbol f, and

$$\text{replace } \exists x\, W(x) \text{ by } W(f(x_1, ..., x_n)).$$

The constants and functions introduced by the rule are called *Skolem functions*.

EXAMPLE 1. Let's apply Skolem's rule to the following wff:

$$\exists x\, \forall y\, \forall z\, \exists u\, \forall v\, \exists w\, p(x, y, z, u, v, w).$$

Since the wff contains three existential quantifiers, we'll use (4.1) to create three Skolem functions to replace the existentially quantified variables as follows:

replace x by b because $\exists x$ is not in the scope of a universal quantifier;

replace u by $f(y, z)$ because $\exists u$ is in the scope of $\forall y$ and $\forall z$;

replace w by $g(y, z, v)$ because $\exists w$ is in the scope of $\forall y$, $\forall z$, and $\forall v$.

Now we can apply (4.1) to eliminate the existential quantifiers by making the above replacements to obtain the following clausal form:

$$\forall y\, \forall z\, \forall v\, p(b, y, z, f(y, z), v, g(y, z, v)). \quad \blacklozenge$$

Now we have the ingredients necessary to construct clausal forms with the property that a wff and its clausal form are either both unsatisfiable or both satisfiable.

Skolem's Algorithm   (4.2)

Given a wff W, there exists a clausal form such that W and the clausal form are either both unsatisfiable or both satisfiable. The clausal form can be constructed from W as follows:

1. Construct the prenex conjunctive normal form of W.
2. Replace all occurrences of each free variable by a new constant.
3. Use Skolem's rule (4.1) to eliminate the existential quantifiers.

End Algorithm

Before we do some examples, let's make a couple of remarks about the steps of the algorithm. Step 2 could be replaced by the statement "Take the existential closure." But then Step 3 would remove these same quantifiers by replacing each of the newly quantified variables with a new constant name. So we saved time and did it all in one step. Step 2 can be done at any time during the process. We need Step 2 because we know that a wff and its existential closure are either both unsatisfiable or both satisfiable.

Step 3 can be applied during Step 1 after all implications have been eliminated and after all negations have been pushed to the right but before all quantifiers have been pushed to the left. Often this will reduce the number of variables in the Skolem function. Another way to simplify the Skolem function is to push all quantifiers to the right as far as possible before applying Skolem's rule. For example, suppose W is the following wff:

$$W = \forall x \, \neg \, p(x) \wedge \forall y \, \exists z \, q(y, z).$$

First, we'll apply (4.2) as stated. In other words, we calculate the prenex form of W by moving the quantifiers to the left to obtain

$$\forall x \, \forall y \, \exists z \, (\neg \, p(x) \wedge q(y, z)).$$

Next, we apply Skolem's rule (4.1), which says that we replace z by $f(x, y)$ to obtain the following clausal form for W:

$$\forall x \, \forall y \, (\neg p(x) \wedge q(y, f(x, y))).$$

Now let's start over with W and apply (4.1) during Step 1 before we move the quantifiers to the left. In this case the quantifier $\exists z$ is only within the scope of $\forall y$, so we replace z by $f(y)$ to obtain

$$\forall x \,\neg\, p(x) \wedge \forall y \, q(y, f(y)).$$

Now finish constructing the prenex form by moving the universal quantifiers to the left to obtain the following clausal form for W:

$$\forall x \, \forall y \, (\neg p(x) \wedge q(y, f(y))).$$

So we get a simpler clausal form for W in this case.

Let's look at a few examples that construct clausal forms with Skolem's algorithm (4.2).

EXAMPLE 2. Suppose we have a wff with no variables (i.e., a propositional wff). For example, let W be the wff

$$(p(a) \rightarrow q) \wedge ((q \wedge s(b)) \rightarrow r).$$

To find the clausal form for W, we need only apply equivalences from propositional calculus to find a CNF as follows:

$$
\begin{aligned}
(p(a) \rightarrow q) \wedge ((q \wedge s(b)) \rightarrow r) \;\equiv\; & (\neg p(a) \vee q) \wedge (\neg (q \wedge s(b)) \vee r) \\
\equiv\; & (\neg p(a) \vee q) \wedge ((\neg q \vee \neg s(b)) \vee r) \\
\equiv\; & (\neg p(a) \vee q) \wedge (\neg q \vee \neg s(b) \vee r). \quad \blacklozenge
\end{aligned}
$$

EXAMPLE 3. We'll use (4.2) to find a clausal form for the following wff:

$$\exists y \, \forall x \, (p(x) \rightarrow q(x, y)) \wedge \forall x \, \exists y \, ((q(x, x) \wedge s(y)) \rightarrow r(x)).$$

The first step is to find the prenex conjunctive normal form. Since there are two quantifiers with the same name, we'll do some renaming to obtain the following wff:

$$\exists y \, \forall x \, (p(x) \rightarrow q(x, y)) \wedge \forall w \, \exists z \, ((q(w, w) \wedge s(z)) \rightarrow r(w)).$$

Next, we eliminate the conditionals to obtain the following wff:

$$\exists y \, \forall x \, (\neg p(x) \vee q(x, y)) \wedge \forall w \, \exists z \, (\neg (q(w, w) \wedge s(z)) \vee r(w)).$$

Now, push negation to the right to obtain the following wff:

$$\exists y \, \forall x \, (\neg p(x) \vee q(x, y)) \wedge \forall w \, \exists z \, (\neg q(w, w) \vee \neg s(z) \vee r(w)).$$

Next, we'll apply Skolem's rule (4.1) to eliminate the existential quantifiers and obtain the following wff:

$$\forall x \, (\neg p(x) \vee q(x, a)) \wedge \forall w \, (\neg q(w, w) \vee \neg s(f(w)) \vee r(w)).$$

Lastly, we push the universal quantifiers to the left, obtaining the desired clausal form:

$$\forall x \, \forall w \, ((\neg p(x) \vee q(x, a)) \wedge (\neg q(w, w) \vee \neg s(f(w)) \vee r(w))). \quad \blacklozenge$$

EXAMPLE 4. We'll construct a clausal form for the following wff:

$$\forall x \, (p(x) \rightarrow \exists y \, \forall z \, ((p(w) \vee q(x, y)) \rightarrow \forall w \, r(x, w))).$$

The free variable w is also used in the quantifier $\forall w$, and the quantifier $\forall z$ is redundant. So we'll do some renaming, and we'll remove $\forall z$ to obtain the following wff:

$$\forall x \, (p(x) \rightarrow \exists y \, ((p(w) \vee q(x, y)) \rightarrow \forall z \, r(x, z))).$$

We remove the conditionals in the usual way to obtain the following wff:

$$\forall x \, (\neg p(x) \vee \exists y \, (\neg (p(w) \vee q(x, y)) \vee \forall z \, r(x, z))).$$

Next, we move negation inward to obtain the following wff:

$$\forall x \, (\neg p(x) \vee \exists y \, ((\neg p(w) \wedge \neg q(x, y)) \vee \forall z \, r(x, z))).$$

Now we can apply Skolem's rule (4.1) to eliminate $\exists y$ and replace the free variable w by b to get the following wff:

$$\forall x \, (\neg p(x) \vee ((\neg p(b) \wedge \neg q(x, f(x))) \vee \forall z \, r(x, z))).$$

Next, we push the universal quantifier $\forall z$ to the left, obtaining the following wff:

$$\forall x \, \forall z \, (\neg p(x) \vee ((\neg p(b) \wedge \neg q(x, f(x))) \vee r(x, z))).$$

Lastly, we distribute $\vee$ over $\wedge$ to obtain the following clausal form:

$$\forall x \, \forall z \, ((\neg p(x) \vee \neg p(b) \vee r(x, z)) \wedge (\neg p(x) \vee \neg q(x, f(x)) \vee r(x, z))). \quad \blacklozenge$$

So we can transform any wff into a wff in clausal form in which the two wffs are either both unsatisfiable or both satisfiable. Since the resolution rule tests clausal forms for unsatisfiability, we're a step closer to describing the idea of resolution. Before we introduce the general idea of resolution, we're going to pause and discuss resolution for the simple case of propositions.

A Primer of Resolution for Propositions

It's easy to see how resolution works for propositional clauses (i.e., clauses with no variables). The resolution inference rule works something like a cancellation process. It takes two clauses and constructs a new clause from them by deleting all occurrences of a positive literal p from one clause and all occurrences of $\neg p$ from the other clause. For example, suppose we are given the following two propositional clauses:

$$p \vee q,$$
$$\neg p \vee r \vee \neg p.$$

We obtain a new clause by first eliminating p from the first clause and eliminating the two occurrences of $\neg p$ from the second clause. Then we take the disjunction of the leftover clauses to form the new clause:

$$q \vee r.$$

Let's write down the resolution rule in a more general way. Suppose we have two propositional clauses of the following forms:

$$p \vee A,$$
$$\neg p \vee B.$$

Let $A - p$ denote the disjunction obtained from A by deleting all occurrences of p. Similarly, let $B - \neg p$ denote the disjunction obtained from B by deleting all occurrences of $\neg p$. The resolution rule allows us to infer the propositional clause

$$A - p \vee B - \neg p.$$

We'll write the rule as follows:

Resolution Rule for Propositions: (4.3)

$$\frac{p \vee A, \ \neg p \vee B}{\therefore \ A - p \vee B - \neg p}.$$

Although the rule may look strange, it's a good rule. That is, it maps tautologies to a tautology. To see this, we can suppose that $(p \vee A) \wedge (\neg p \vee B) =$ true. If p is true, then the equation reduces to $B =$ true. Since $\neg p$ is false, we can remove all occurrences of $\neg p$ from B and still have $B - \neg p =$ true. Therefore $A - p \vee B - \neg p =$ true. We obtain the same result if p is false. So the inference rule does its job.

A proof by resolution is a refutation that uses only the resolution rule. So we can define a *resolution proof* as a sequence of clauses, ending with the empty clause, in which each clause in the sequence either is a premise or is inferred by the resolution rule from two preceding clauses in the sequence. Notice that the empty clause is obtained from (4.3) when A either is empty or contains only copies of p and when B either is empty or contains only copies of $\neg p$. For example, the simplest version of (4.3) can be stated as follows:

$$\frac{p, \ \neg p}{\therefore \ \square}.$$

In other words, we obtain the well known tautology $p \wedge \neg p \rightarrow$ false.

For example, let's prove that the following clausal form is unsatisfiable:

$$(\neg p \vee q) \wedge (p \vee q) \wedge (\neg q \vee p) \wedge (\neg p \vee \neg q).$$

In other words, we'll prove that the following set of clauses is unsatisfiable:

$$\{\neg p \vee q, p \vee q, \neg q \vee p, \neg p \vee \neg q\}.$$

The following resolution proof does the job:

Proof:
1. $\neg p \vee q$ P
2. $p \vee q$ P
3. $\neg q \vee p$ P
4. $\neg p \vee \neg q$ P
5. $q \vee q$ 1, 2, Resolution
6. p 3, 5, Resolution
7. $\neg p$ 4, 5, Resolution
8. $\square$ 6, 7, Resolution

QED.

Now let's get back on our original track, which is to describe the resolution rule for clauses of the first-order predicate calculus.

Substitution and Unification

When we discuss the resolution inference rule for clauses that contain variables, we'll see that a certain kind of matching is required. For example, suppose we are given the following two clauses:

$$p(x, y) \lor q(y),$$
$$r(z) \lor \neg \, q(b).$$

The matching that we will discuss allows us to replace all occurrences of the variable y by the constant b, thus obtaining the following two clauses:

$$p(x, b) \lor q(b),$$
$$r(z) \lor \neg \, q(b).$$

Notice that one clause contains $q(b)$ and the other contains its negation $\neg \, q(b)$. Resolution will allow us to cancel them and construct the disjunction of the remaining parts, which is the clause $p(x, b) \lor r(z)$.

We need to spend a little time to discuss the process of replacing variables by terms. If x is a variable and t is a term, then the expression x/t is called a *binding* of x to t and can be read as "x gets t" or "x is bound to t" or "x has value t" or "x is replaced by t." Three typical bindings are written as follows:

$$x/a, \quad y/z, \quad w/f(b, v).$$

A *substitution* is a finite set of bindings $\{x_1/t_1, \ldots, x_n/t_n\}$, where variables $x_1, \ldots, x_n$ are all distinct and $x_i \neq t_i$ for each i. We use lowercase Greek letters to denote substitutions. The *empty substitution*, which is just the empty set, is denoted by the Greek letter ε.

What do we do with substitutions? We apply them to expressions, an *expression* being a finite string of symbols. Let E be an expression, and let θ be the following substitution:

$$\theta = \{x_1/t_1, \ldots, x_n/t_n\}.$$

Then the *instance* of E by θ, denoted $E\theta$, is the expression obtained from E by simultaneously replacing all occurrences of the variables $x_1, \ldots, x_n$ in E by the terms $t_1, \ldots, t_n$, respectively. We say that $E\theta$ is obtained from E by *applying* the substitution θ to the expression E. For example, if $E = p(x, y, f(x))$ and $\theta = \{x/a, y/f(b)\}$, then $E\theta$ has the following form:

$$E\theta = p(x, y, f(x))\{x/a, y/f(b)\} = p(a, f(b), f(a)).$$

If S is a set of expressions, then the *instance* of S by θ, denoted $S\theta$, is the set of all instances of expressions in S by θ. For example, if $S = \{p(x, y), q(a, y)\}$ and $\theta = \{x/a, y/f(b)\}$, then $S\theta$ has the following form:

$$S\theta = \{p(x, y), q(a, y)\}\{x/a, y/f(b)\} = \{p(a, f(b)), q(a, f(b)\}.$$

Now let's see how we can combine two substitutions θ and σ into a single substitution that has the same effect as applying θ and then applying σ to any expression. The *composition* of θ and σ, denoted by $\theta\sigma$, is a substitution that satisfies the following property: $E(\theta\sigma) = (E\theta)\sigma$ for any expression E. Although we have described the composition in terms of how it acts on all expressions, we can compute $\theta\sigma$ without any reference to an expression as follows:

Composition of Substitutions (4.4)

Given the two substitutions

$$\theta = \{x_1/t_1, ..., x_n/t_n\} \quad \text{and} \quad \sigma = \{y_1/s_1, ..., y_m/s_m\}.$$

The composition $\theta\sigma$ is constructed as follows:

1. Apply σ to the denominators of θ to form $\{x_1/t_1\sigma, ..., x_n/t_n\sigma\}$.
2. Delete all bindings x_i/x_i from line 1.
3. Delete from σ any binding y_i/s_i, where y_i is a variable in $\{x_1, ..., x_n\}$.
4. $\theta\sigma$ is the union of the two sets constructed on lines 2 and 3.

The process looks complicated, but it's really quite simple. It's just a formalization of the following construction: For each distinct variable v occurring in the numerators of θ and σ, apply θ and then σ to v, obtaining the expression $(v\theta)\sigma$. The composition $\theta\sigma$ consists of all bindings $v/(v\theta)\sigma$ such that $v \neq (v\theta)\sigma$.

It's also nice to know that we can always check whether we constructed a composition correctly. Just make up an example atom containing the distinct variables in the numerators of θ and σ, say $p(v_1, ..., v_k)$, and then check to make sure the following equation holds:

$$((p(v_1, ..., v_k)\theta)\sigma) = p(v_1, ..., v_k)(\theta\sigma).$$

EXAMPLE 5. Let $\theta = \{x/f(y),\, y/z\}$ and $\sigma = \{x/a,\, y/b,\, z/y\}$. To find the composition $\theta\sigma$, we first apply σ to the denominators of θ to form the following set:

$$\{x/f(y)\sigma,\, y/z\sigma\} = \{x/f(b),\, y/y\}.$$

Now remove the binding y/y to obtain $\{x/f(b)\}$. Next, delete the bindings x/a and y/b from σ to obtain $\{z/y\}$. Finally, compute $\theta\sigma$ as the union of these two sets $\theta\sigma = \{x/f(b),\, z/y\}$.

Let's check to see whether the answer is correct. For our example atom we'll pick

$$p(x, y, z)$$

because x, y, and z are the distinct variables occurring in the numerators of θ and σ. We'll make the following two calculations to see whether we get the same answer:

$$((p(x, y, z)\theta)\sigma) = p(f(y), z, z)\sigma = p(f(b), y, y),$$

$$p(x, y, z)(\theta\sigma) = p(f(b), y, y). \quad \blacklozenge$$

Three simple, but useful, properties of composition are listed next. The proofs are left as exercises.

Properties of Composition (4.5)

For any substitutions θ and σ and any expression E the following statements hold:

1. $E(\theta\sigma) = (E\theta)\sigma$.

2. $E\varepsilon = E$.

3. $\theta\varepsilon = \varepsilon\theta = \theta$.

A substitution θ is called a *unifier* of a finite set S of literals if $S\theta$ is a singleton set. For example, if we let $S = \{p(x, b), p(a, y)\}$, then the substitution $\theta = \{x/a, y/b\}$ is a unifier of S because

$$S\theta = \{p(a, b)\}, \text{ which is a singleton set.}$$

Some sets of literals don't have a unifier, while other sets have infinitely many unifiers. The range of possibilities can be shown by the following four simple examples:

$\{p(x), q(y)\}$ doesn't have a unifier.

$\{p(x), \neg\, p(x)\}$ doesn't have a unifier.

$\{p(x), p(a)\}$ has exactly one unifier $\{x/a\}$.

$\{p(x), p(y)\}$ has infinitely many unifiers: $\{x/y\}$, $\{y/x\}$, and $\{x/t, y/t\}$ for any term t.

Among the unifiers of a set there is always at least one unifier that can be used to construct every other unifier. To be specific, a unifier θ for S is called a *most general unifier* (mgu) for S if for every unifier α of S there exists a substitution σ such that $\alpha = \theta\sigma$. In other words, an mgu for S is a factor of every other unifier of S. Let's look at an example.

EXAMPLE 6. The set $S = \{p(x), p(y)\}$ has infinitely many unifiers:

$$\{x/y\}, \{y/x\}, \text{ and } \{x/t, y/t\} \text{ for any term } t.$$

The unifier $\{x/y\}$ is an mgu for S because we can write the other unifiers in terms of $\{x/y\}$ as follows: $\{y/x\} = \{x/y\}\{y/x\}$, and $\{x/t, y/t\} = \{x/y\}\{y/t\}$ for any term t. Similarly, $\{y/x\}$ is an mgu for S.   ◆

We want to find a way to construct an mgu for any set of literals. Before we do this, we need a little terminology. The *disagreement set* of S is a set of terms constructed from the literals of S in the following way:

Find the longest common substring that starts at the left end of each literal of S. The disagreement set of S is the set of all the terms that occur in the literals of S that are immediately to the right of the longest common substring.

For example, let's construct the disagreement set for the following set of literals:

$$S = \{p(x, f(x), y), p(x, y, z), p(x, f(a), b)\}.$$

The longest common substring for the literals in S is the string

$$\text{``}p(x,\text{''}$$

of length four. The terms in the literals of S that occur immediately to the right of this string are $f(x)$, y, and $f(a)$. Thus the disagreement set of S is

$$\{f(x), y, f(a)\}.$$

Now we have the tools to describe a very important algorithm of Robinson [1965]. The algorithm computes, for a set of atoms, a most general unifier, if one exists.

The Unification Algorithm   (4.6)

Input: A finite set S of atoms.

Output: Either a most general unifier for S or a statement
            that S is not unifiable.

1. Set $k = 0$ and $\theta_0 = \varepsilon$, and go to Step 2.

2. Calculate $S\theta_k$. If it's a singleton set, then stop (θ_k is the mgu for S).
    Otherwise, let D_k be the disagreement set of $S\theta_k$, and go to Step 3.

3. If D_k contains a variable v and a term t, such that v does not occur in
    t, then calculate the composition $\theta_{k+1} = \theta_k\{v/t\}$, set $k := k + 1$, and go to
    Step 2. Otherwise, stop (S is not unifiable).

End of Algorithm

The composition $\theta_k\{v/t\}$ in Step 3 is easy to compute for two reasons. The variable v doesn't occur in t, and v will never occur in the numerator of θ_k. Therefore the middle two steps of the composition construction (4.4) don't change anything. In other words, the composition $\theta_k\{v/t\}$ is constructed by applying $\{v/t\}$ to each denominator of θ_k and then adding the binding v/t to the result.

EXAMPLE 7. Let's try the algorithm on the set $S = \{p(x, f(y)), p(g(y), z)\}$. We'll list each step of the algorithm as we go:

1. Set $\theta_0 = \varepsilon$.

2. $S\theta_0 = S\varepsilon = S$ is not a singleton. $D_0 = \{x, g(y)\}$.

3. Variable x doesn't occur in term $g(y)$ of D_0.
    Put $\theta_1 = \theta_0 \{x/g(y)\} = \{x/g(y)\}$.

2. $S\theta_1 = \{p(g(y), f(y)), p(g(y), z)\}$ is not a singleton. $D_1 = \{f(y), z\}$.

3. Variable z does not occur in term $f(y)$ of D_1.
   Put $\theta_2 = \theta_1 \{z/f(y)\} = \{x/g(y), z/f(y)\}$.

2. $S\theta_2 = \{p(g(y), f(y))\}$ is a singleton. Therefore the algorithm terminates with the mgu $\{x/g(y), z/f(y)\}$ for the set S. ◆

EXAMPLE 8. Let's trace the algorithm on the set $S = \{p(x), p(g(x))\}$. We'll list each step of the algorithm as we go:

1. Set $\theta_0 = \varepsilon$.

2. $S\theta_0 = S\varepsilon = S$, which is not a singleton. $D_0 = \{x, g(x)\}$.

3. The only choices for a variable and a term in D_0 are x and $g(x)$. But the variable x occurs in $g(x)$. So the algorithm stops, and S is not unifiable.

This makes sense too. For example, if we were to apply the substitution $\{x/g(x)\}$ to S, we would obtain the set $\{p(g(x)), p(g(g(x)))\}$, which in turn gives us the same disagreement set $\{x, g(x)\}$. So the process would go on forever. Notice that a change of variables makes a big difference. For example, if we change the second atom in S to $p(g(y))$, then the algorithm unifies the set $\{p(x), p(g(y))\}$, obtaining the mgu $\{x/g(y)\}$. ◆

Resolution: The General Case

Now we've got the tools to discuss resolution of clauses that contain variables. Let's look at a simple example to help us see how unification comes into play. Suppose we're given the following two clauses:

$$p(x, a) \vee \neg q(x),$$

$$\neg p(b, y) \vee \neg q(a).$$

We want to cancel $p(x, a)$ from the first clause and $\neg p(b, y)$ from the second clause. But they won't cancel until we unify the two atoms $p(x, a)$ and $p(b, y)$. An mgu for these two atoms is $\{x/b, y/a\}$. If we apply this unifier to the original two clauses, we obtain the following two clauses:

$$p(b, a) \vee \neg q(b),$$

$$\neg p(b, a) \vee \neg q(a).$$

Now we can cancel $p(b, a)$ from the first clause and $\neg\, p(b, a)$ from the second clause and take the disjunction of what's left to obtain the following clause:

$$\neg\, q(b) \vee \neg\, q(a).$$

That's the way the resolution inference rule works when variables are present. Now let's give a detailed description of the rule.

The Resolution Inference Rule

The resolution inference rule takes two clauses and constructs a new clause. But *the rule can be applied only to clauses that possess the following two properties:*

1. The two clauses have no variables in common.

2. There are one or more atoms, L_1, ..., L_k, in one of the clauses and one or more literals, $\neg\, M_1$, ..., $\neg\, M_n$, in the other clause such that $\{L_1, ..., L_k, M_1, ..., M_n\}$ is unifiable.

The first property can always be satisfied by renaming variables. For example, the variable x is used in both of the following clauses:

$$q(b, x) \vee p(x), \quad \neg\, q(x, a) \vee p(y).$$

We can replace x in the second clause with a new variable z to obtain the following two clauses that satisfy the first property:

$$q(b, x) \vee p(x), \quad \neg\, q(z, a) \vee p(y).$$

Suppose we have two clauses that satisfy properties 1 and 2. Then they can be written in the following form, where C and D represent the other parts of each clause:

$$L_1 \vee ... \vee L_k \vee C \quad \text{and} \quad \neg\, M_1 \vee ... \vee \neg\, M_n \vee D.$$

Since the clauses satisfy the second property, we know that there is an mgu θ that unifies the set of atoms $\{L_1, ..., L_k, M_1, ..., M_n\}$. In other words, there is a unique atom N such that $N = L_i\theta = M_j\theta$ for any i and j. To be specific, we'll set

$$N = L_1\theta.$$

Now we're ready to do our cancelling. Let $C\theta - N$ denote the clause obtained from $C\theta$ by deleting all occurrences of the atom N. Similarly, let $D\theta - \neg N$ denote the clause obtained from $D\theta$ by deleting all occurrences of the atom $\neg N$. The clause that we construct is the disjunction of any literals that are left after the cancellation:

$$(C\theta - N) \vee (D\theta - \neg N).$$

Summing all this up, we can state the resolution inference rule as follows:

Resolution Rule (R) (4.7)

$$\frac{\begin{array}{c} L_1 \vee ... \vee L_k \vee C \\ \neg M_1 \vee ... \vee \neg M_n \vee D \end{array}}{\therefore (C\theta - N) \vee (D\theta - \neg N)}.$$

The clause constructed in the denominator of (4.7) is called a *resolvant* of the two clauses in the numerator. Let's describe how to use (4.7) to find a resolvant of the two clauses.

1. Check the two clauses for distinct variables (rename if necessary).
2. Find an mgu θ for the set of atoms $\{L_1, ..., L_k, M_1, ..., M_n\}$.
3. Apply θ to both clauses C and D.
4. Set $N = L_1\theta$.
5. Remove all occurrences of N from $C\theta$.
6. Remove all occurrences of $\neg N$ from $D\theta$.
7. Form the disjunction of the clauses in Steps 5 and 6. This is the resolvant.

Let's do some examples to get the look and feel of resolution before we forget everything.

EXAMPLE 9. We'll try to find a resolvant of the following two clauses:

$$q(b, x) \vee p(x) \vee q(b, a),$$
$$\neg q(y, a) \vee p(y).$$

We'll cancel the atom $q(b, x)$ in the first clause with the literal $\neg q(y, a)$ in the second clause. So we'll write the first clause in the form $L \vee C$, where L and C have the following values:

$$L = q(b, x) \quad \text{and} \quad C = p(x) \vee q(b, a).$$

The second clause can be written in the form $\neg M \vee D$, where M and D have the following values:

$$M = q(y, a) \quad \text{and} \quad D = p(y).$$

Now L and M, namely $q(b, x)$ and $q(y, a)$, can be unified by the mgu $\theta = \{y/b, x/a\}$. We can apply θ to either atom to obtain the common value $N = L\theta = M\theta = q(b, a)$. Now we can apply (4.7) to find the resolvant of the two clauses. First, compute the clauses $C\theta$ and $D\theta$:

$$C\theta = (p(x) \vee q(b, a))\{y/b, x/a\} = p(a) \vee q(b, a),$$

$$D\theta = p(y) \{y/b, x/a\} = p(b).$$

Next we'll remove all occurrences of $N = q(b, a)$ from $C\theta$ and remove all occurrences of $\neg N = \neg q(b, a)$ from $D\theta$:

$$C\theta - N = p(a) \vee q(b, a) - q(b, a) = p(a),$$

$$D\theta - \neg N = p(b) - \neg q(b, a) = p(b).$$

Lastly, we'll take the disjunction of the remaining clauses to obtain the desired resolvant: $p(a) \vee p(b)$.   ◆

EXAMPLE 10. In this example we'll consider cancelling two literals from one of the clauses. Suppose we have the following two clauses:

$$p(f(x)) \vee p(y) \vee \neg q(x),$$

$$\neg p(z) \vee q(w).$$

We'll pick the disjunction $p(f(x)) \vee p(y)$ from the first clause to cancel with the literal $\neg p(z)$ in the second clause. So we need to unify the set of atoms $\{p(f(x)), p(y), p(z)\}$. An mgu for this set is $\theta = \{y/f(x), z/f(x)\}$. The common value N obtained by applying θ to any of the atoms in the set is $N = p(f(x))$. To see how the cancellation takes place, we'll apply θ to both of the original clauses to obtain the clauses

$$p(f(x)) \vee p(f(x)) \vee \neg q(x),$$

$$\neg p(f(x)) \vee q(w).$$

We'll cancel $p(f(x)) \vee p(f(x))$ from the first clause and $\neg p(f(x))$ from the second clause, with no other deletions possible. Thus the resolvent of the original two clauses is the disjunction of the remaining parts of the preceding two clauses: $\neg q(x) \vee q(w)$.   ◆

What's so great about finding resolvents? Two things are great. One great thing is that the process is mechanical—it can be programmed. The other great thing is that the process preserves unsatisfiability. In other words, we have the following result:

> Let G be a resolvent of the clauses E and F. Then $\{E, F\}$ is unsatisfiable if and only if $\{E, F, G\}$ is unsatisfiable. $\qquad(4.8)$

Now we're almost in position to describe how to prove that a set of clauses is unsatisfiable. Let S be a set of clauses where—after possibly renaming some variables—distinct clauses of S have disjoint sets of variables. We define the *resolution* of S, denoted by $R(S)$, to be the set

$$R(S) = S \cup \{G \mid G \text{ is a resolvent of a pair of clauses in } S\}.$$

We can conclude from (4.8) that S is unsatisfiable if and only if $R(S)$ is unsatisfiable. Similarly, $R(S)$ is unsatisfiable if and only if $R(R(S))$ is unsatisfiable. We can continue on in this way. To simplify the notation, we'll define $R^0(S) = S$ and $R^{n+1}(S) = R(R^n(S))$ for $n > 0$. So for any n we can say that

$$S \text{ is unsatisfiable if and only if } R^n(S) \text{ is unsatisfiable.}$$

Let's look at some examples to demonstrate the calculation of the sequence of sets $S, R(S), R^2(S), \ldots$.

EXAMPLE 11. Suppose we start with the following set of clauses:

$$S = \{p(x), \neg p(a)\}.$$

To compute $R(S)$, we must add to S all possible resolvents of pairs of clauses. There is only one pair of clauses in S, and the resolvent of $p(x)$ and $\neg p(a)$, is the empty clause. Thus $R(S)$ is the following set:

$$R(S) = \{p(x), \neg p(a), \square\}.$$

Now let's compute $R(R(S))$. The only two clauses in $R(S)$ that can be resolved are $p(x)$ and $\neg p(a)$. Since their resolvent is already in $R(S)$, there's nothing new to add. So the process stops, and we have $R(R(S)) = R(S)$.   ◆

EXAMPLE 12. Consider the set of three clauses

$$S = \{p(x), q(y) \vee \neg p(y), \neg q(a)\}.$$

Let's compute $R(S)$. There are two pairs of clauses in S that have resolvents. The two clauses $p(x)$ and $q(y) \vee \neg p(y)$ resolve to $q(y)$. The clauses $q(y) \vee \neg p(y)$ and $\neg q(a)$ resolve to $\neg p(a)$. Thus $R(S)$ is the following set:

$$R(S) = \{p(x), q(y) \vee \neg p(y), \neg q(a), q(y), \neg p(a)\}.$$

Now let's compute $R(R(S))$. The two clauses $p(x)$ and $\neg p(a)$ resolve to the empty clause, and nothing new is added by resolving any other pairs from $R(S)$. Thus $R(R(S))$ is the following set:

$$R(R(S)) = \{p(x), q(y) \vee \neg p(y), \neg q(a), q(y), \neg p(a), \square\}.$$

It's easy to see that we can't get anything new by resolving pairs of clauses in $R(R(S))$. Thus we have $R^3(S) = R^2(S)$.   ◆

These two examples have something very important in common. In each case the set S is unsatisfiable, and the empty clause occurs in $R^n(S)$ for some n. This is no coincidence. The following result of Robinson [1965] allows us to test for the unsatisfiability of a set of clauses by looking for the empty clause in the sequence $S, R(S), R^2(S), \ldots$:

Resolution Theorem   (4.9)

A finite set S of clauses is unsatisfiable if and only if $\square \in R^n(S)$
for some $n \geq 0$.

The theorem provides us with an algorithm to prove that a wff is unsatisfiable. Let S be the set of clauses that make up the clausal form of the wff.

Start by calculating all the resolvants of pairs of clauses from S. The new resolvants are added to S to form the larger set of clauses $R(S)$. If the empty clause has been calculated, then we are done. Otherwise, calculate resolvants of pairs of clauses in the set $R(S)$. Continue the process until we find a pair of clauses whose resolvant is the empty clause. If we get to a point at which no new clauses are being created and we have not found the empty clause, then the process stops, and we conclude that the wff that we started with is satisfiable.

Theorem Proving with Resolution

Recall that a resolution proof is a sequence of clauses that ends with the empty clause, in which each clause either is a premise or can be inferred from two preceding clauses by the resolution rule. Recall also that a resolution proof is a proof of unsatisfiability. Since we normally want to prove that some wff is valid, we must first take the negation of the wff, then find a clausal form, and then attempt to do a resolution proof. We'll summarize the steps as follows:

Steps to Prove That W *Is Valid*

1. Form the negation $\neg W$. For example, if W is a conditional of the form $A \wedge B \wedge C \rightarrow D$, then $\neg W$ has the form $A \wedge B \wedge C \wedge \neg D$.

2. Use Skolem's algorithm (4.2) to convert line 1 into clausal form.

3. Take the clauses from line 2 as premises in the proof.

4. Apply the resolution rule (4.7) to derive the empty clause.

Let's look at a few examples to see how the process works.

EXAMPLE 13 (*The Family Tree Problem*). Suppose we let p stand for the isParentOf relation and let g stand for the isGrandParentOf relation. We can define g in terms of p as follows:

$$p(x, z) \wedge p(z, y) \rightarrow g(x, y).$$

In other words, if x is a parent of z and z is a parent of y, then we conclude that x is a grandparent of y. Suppose we have the following facts about parents, where we use the letters a, b, c, d, and e to denote names:

$$p(a, b) \wedge p(c, b) \wedge p(b, d) \wedge p(a, e).$$

Suppose someone claims that $g(a, d)$ is implied by the given facts. In other words, the claim is that the following wff is valid:

$$p(a, b) \wedge p(c, b) \wedge p(b, d) \wedge p(a, e) \wedge (p(x, z) \wedge p(z, y) \to g(x, y)) \to g(a, d).$$

If we're going to use resolution, the first thing we must do is negate the wff to obtain the following wff:

$$p(a, b) \wedge p(c, b) \wedge p(b, d) \wedge p(a, e) \wedge (p(x, z) \wedge p(z, y) \to g(x, y)) \wedge \neg g(a, d).$$

This wff will be in clausal form if we replace $p(x, z) \wedge p(z, y) \to g(x, y)$ by the following equivalent clause:

$$\neg p(x, z) \vee \neg p(z, y) \vee g(x, y).$$

Now we'll begin the proof by making each clause of the clausal form a premise, as follows:

Proof: 1. $p(a, b)$ P
         2. $p(c, b)$ P
         3. $p(b, d)$ P
         4. $p(a, e)$ P
         5. $\neg p(x, z) \vee \neg p(z, y) \vee g(x, y)$ P
         6. $\neg g(a, d)$ P Negation of conclusion

Now we can construct resolvants with the goal of obtaining the empty clause. In the following proof steps we've listed the mgu used for each application of resolution:

         7. $\neg p(a, z) \vee \neg p(z, d)$ 5, 6, R, $\{x/a, y/d\}$
         8. $\neg p(b, d)$ 1, 7, R, $\{z/b\}$
         9. $\square$ 3, 8, R, $\{\,\}$
           QED.

So we have a refutation. Therefore we can conclude that $g(a, d)$ is implied from the given facts.   ♦

EXAMPLE 14 (*Diagonals of a Trapezoid*). We'll give a resolution proof that the alternate interior angles formed by a diagonal of a trapezoid are equal. This problem is from Chang and Lee [1973]. Let $t(x, y, u, v)$ mean that x, y, u, and v are the four corner points of a trapezoid. Let $p(x, y, u, v)$ mean that edges xy

and uv are parallel lines. Let $e(x, y, z, u, v, w)$ mean that angle xyz is equal to angle uvw. We'll assume the following two axioms about trapezoids:

Axiom 1: $t(x, y, u, v) \rightarrow p(x, y, u, v)$.
Axiom 2: $p(x, y, u, v) \rightarrow e(x, y, v, u, v, y)$.

To prove: $t(a, b, c, d) \rightarrow e(a, b, d, c, d, b)$.

To prepare for a resolution proof, we need to write each axiom in its clausal form. This gives us the following two clauses:

Axiom 1: $\neg\, t(x, y, u, v) \lor p(x, y, u, v)$.

Axiom 2: $\neg\, p(x, y, u, v) \lor e(x, y, v, u, v, y)$.

Next, we need to negate the statement to be proved, which gives us the following two clauses:

$$t(a, b, c, d),$$

$$\neg\, e(a, b, d, c, d, b).$$

The resolution proof process begins by listing as premises the two axioms written as clauses together with the preceding two clauses that represent the negation of the conclusion. A proof follows:

Proof.
1. $\neg\, t(x, y, u, v) \lor p(x, y, u, v)$ P
2. $\neg\, p(x, y, u, v) \lor e(x, y, v, u, v, y)$ P
3. $t(a, b, c, d)$ P Antecedent
4. $\neg\, e(a, b, d, c, d, b)$ P Negation of consequent
5. $\neg\, p(a, b, c, d)$ $2, 4, R, \{x/a, y/b, v/d, u/c\}$
6. $\neg\, t(a, b, c, d)$ $1, 5, R, \{x/a, y/b, u/c, v/d\}$
7. $\square$ $3, 6, R, \{\,\}$
     QED.   ◆

Remarks

In the example proofs we didn't follow a specific strategy to help us choose which clauses to resolve. Strategies are important because they may help reduce the searching required to find a proof. Although a general discussion of strategy is beyond our scope, we'll present a strategy in the next section for the special case of logic programming.

The unification algorithm (4.6) is the original version given by Robinson [1965]. Other researchers have found algorithms that can be implemented more efficiently. For example, the paper by Paterson and Wegman [1978] presents a linear algorithm for unification.

There are also other versions of the resolution inference rule. One approach uses two simple rules, called *binary resolution* and *factoring*, which can be used together to do the same job as resolution. Another inference rule, called *paramodulation*, is used when the equality predicate is present to take advantage of substituting equals for equals. An excellent introduction to automatic reasoning is contained in the book by Wos, Overbeek, Lusk, and Boyle [1984].

Another subject that we haven't discussed is automatic reasoning in higher-order logic. In higher-order logic it's undecidable whether a set of atoms can be unified. Still there are many interesting results about higher-order unification and there are automatic reasoning systems for some higher-order logics. For example, in second-order monadic logic (*monadic logic* restricts predicates to at most one argument) there is an algorithm to decide whether two atoms can be unified. For example, if F is a variable that represents a function, then the two atoms $F(a)$ and a can be unified by letting F be the constant function that returns the value a or by letting F be the identity function. The paper by Snyder and Gallier [1989] contains many results on higher-order unification.

Automatic theorem-proving techniques are an important and interesting part of computer science, with applications to almost every area of endeavor. Probably the most successful applications of automatic theorem proving will be interactive in nature, the proof system acting as an assistant to the person using it. Typical tasks involve such things as finding ways to represent problems and information to be processed by an automatic theorem prover, finding algorithms that make proper choices in performing resolution, and finding algorithms to efficiently perform unification. We'll look at the programming side of theorem proving in the next section.

Exercises

1. Use Skolem's algorithm, if necessary, to transform each of the following wffs into a clausal form.

   a. $(A \wedge B) \vee C \vee D$.

   b. $(A \wedge B) \vee (C \wedge D) \vee (E \rightarrow F)$.

   c. $\exists y \, \forall x \, (p(x, y) \rightarrow q(x))$.

   d. $\exists y \, \forall x \, p(x, y) \rightarrow q(x)$.

   e. $\forall x \, \forall y \, (p(x, y) \vee \exists z \, q(x, y, z))$.

   f. $\forall x \, \exists y \, \exists z \, [(\neg p(x, y) \wedge q(x, z)) \vee r(x, y, z)]$.

2. What is the resolvent of the propositional clause $p \vee \neg p$ with itself? What is the resolvent of $p \vee \neg p \vee q$ with itself?

3. Find a resolution proof to show that each of the following sets of propositional clauses is unsatisfiable.

   a. $\{A \vee B, \neg A, \neg B \vee C, \neg C\}$.

   b. $\{p \vee q, \neg p \vee r, \neg r \vee \neg p, \neg q\}$.

   c. $\{A \vee B, A \vee \neg C, \neg A \vee C, \neg A \vee \neg B, C \vee \neg B, \neg C \vee B\}$.

4. Compute the composition $\theta\sigma$ of each of the following pairs of substitutions.

   a. $\theta = \{x/y\}$, $\sigma = \{y/x\}$.

   b. $\theta = \{x/y\}$, $\sigma = \{y/x, x/a\}$.

   c. $\theta = \{x/y, y/a\}$, $\sigma = \{y/x\}$.

   d. $\theta = \{x/f(z), y/a\}$, $\sigma = \{z/b\}$.

   e. $\theta = \{x/y, y/f(z)\}$, $\sigma = \{y/f(a), z/b\}$.

5. Use the unification algorithm to find a most general unifier for each of the following sets of atoms.

   a. $\{p(x, f(y, a), y), p(f(a, b), v, z)\}$.

   b. $\{q(x, f(x)), q(f(x), x)\}$.

   c. $\{p(f(x, g(y)), y), p(f(g(a), z), b)\}$.

   d. $\{p(x, f(x), y), p(x, y, z), p(w, f(a), b)\}$.

6. What is the resolvent of the clause $p(x) \vee \neg p(f(a))$ with itself? What is the resolvent of $p(x) \vee \neg p(f(a)) \vee q(x)$ with itself?

7. Use resolution to show that each of the following sets of clauses is unsatisfiable.

   a. $\{p(x), q(y, a) \vee \neg p(a), \neg q(a, a)\}$.

   b. $\{p(u, v), q(w, z), \neg p(y, f(x, y)) \vee \neg p(f(x, y), f(x, y)) \vee \neg q(x, f(x, y))\}$.

   c. $\{p(a) \vee p(x), \neg p(a) \vee \neg p(y)\}$

   d. $\{p(x) \vee p(f(a)), \neg p(y) \vee \neg p(f(z))\}$.

   e. $\{q(x) \vee q(a), \neg p(y) \vee \neg p(g(a)) \vee \neg q(a), p(z) \vee p(g(w)) \vee \neg q(w)\}$.

8. Prove that each of the following propositional statements is a tautology by using resolution to prove that its negation is a contradiction.

   a. $(A \vee B) \wedge \neg A \to B$.

   b. $(p \to q) \wedge (q \to r) \to (p \to r)$.

   c. $(p \vee q) \wedge (q \to r) \wedge (r \to s) \to (p \vee s)$.

   d. $[(A \wedge B \to C) \wedge (A \to B)] \to (A \to C)$.

9. Prove that each of the following statements is valid by using resolution to prove that its negation is unsatisfiable.

   a. $\forall x\, p(x) \rightarrow \exists x\, p(x)$.

   b. $\forall x\, (p(x) \rightarrow q(x)) \wedge \exists x\, p(x) \rightarrow \exists x\, q(x)$.

   c. $\exists y\, \forall x\, p(x, y) \rightarrow \forall x\, \exists y\, p(x, y)$.

   d. $\exists x\, \forall y\, p(x, y) \wedge \forall x\, (p(x, x) \rightarrow \exists y\, q(y, x)) \rightarrow \exists y\, \exists x\, q(x, y)$.

   e. $\forall x\, p(x) \vee \forall x\, q(x) \rightarrow \forall x\, (p(x) \vee q(x))$.

10. Translate each of the following arguments into first-order predicate calculus. Then use resolution to prove that the resulting wffs are valid by proving that the negations are unsatisfiable.

    a. All computer science majors are people. Some computer science majors are logical thinkers. Therefore some people are logical thinkers.

    b. Babies are illogical. Nobody is despised who can manage a crocodile. Illogical persons are despised. Therefore babies cannot manage crocodiles.

11. Translate each of the following arguments into first-order predicate calculus. Then use resolution to prove that the resulting wffs are valid by proving the negations are unsatisfiable.

    a. Every dog either likes people or hates cats. Rover is a dog. Rover loves cats. Therefore some dog likes people.

    b. Every committee member is rich and famous. Some committee members are old. Therefore some committee members are old and famous.

    c. No human beings are quadrupeds. All men are human beings. Therefore no man is a quadruped.

    d. Every rational number is a real number. There is a rational number. Therefore there is a real number.

    e. Some freshmen like all sophomores. No freshman likes any junior. Therefore no sophomore is a junior.

12. Let E be any expression, A and B two sets of expressions, and θ, σ, α any substitutions. Show that each of the following statements is true.

    a. $E(\theta\sigma) = (E\theta)\sigma$.

    b. $E\varepsilon = E$.

    c. $\theta\varepsilon = \varepsilon\theta = \theta$.

    d. $(\theta\sigma)\alpha = \theta(\sigma\alpha)$.

    e. $(A \cup B)\theta = A\theta \cup B\theta$.

4.2 Logic Programming

We'll introduce the idea of logic programming by considering some family tree problems.

Family Tree Problem

Given a set of parent-child relationships, find answers to family questions such as "Is x a second cousin of y?"

First of all, we need to decide what is meant by second cousin and the like. In other words, we need to define relationships such as the following:

> isGrandparentOf,
>
> isGrandchildOf,
>
> isNth-CousinOf,
>
> isNth-Cousin-Mth-RemovedOf,
>
> isNth-AncesterOf,
>
> isSiblingOf.

Let's do an example. We'll look at the isGrandParentOf relation. Let $p(a, b)$ mean "a is a parent of b," and let $g(x, y)$ mean "x is a grandparent of y." We often refer to a relational fact like $p(a, b)$ or $g(x, y)$ as an *atom* because it is an atomic formula in the first-order predicate calculus. To see what's going on, we'll do an example as we go. Our example will be a portion of the British royal family consisting of the following five facts:

> p(Edward VII, George V),
>
> p(Victoria, Edward VII),
>
> p(Alexandra, George V),
>
> p(George VI, Elizabeth II),
>
> p(George V, George VI).

We want to find all the grandparent relations. From our family knowledge we know that x is a grandparent of y if there is some z such that x is a parent of z and z is a parent of y. Therefore it seems reasonable to define the isGrandParentOf relation g as follows:

$$g(x, y) \text{ if } p(x, z) \text{ and } p(z, y).$$

For the five facts listed, it's easy to compute the isGrandParentOf relation by hand. It consists of the following four facts:

$$g(\text{Victoria, George V}),$$
$$g(\text{Edward VII, George VI}),$$
$$g(\text{Alexandra, George VI}),$$
$$g(\text{George V, Elizabeth II}).$$

But suppose the isParentOf relation contained 1000 facts and we wanted to list all possible grandparent relations. It would be a time-consuming process if we did it by hand. We could program a solution in almost any language. In fact, we can write a logic program to solve the problem by simply listing the parent facts and then giving the simple definition of the isGrandParentOf relation.

Can we discover how such a program does its computation? The answer is a big maybe. First, let's look at how we human beings get the job done. Somehow we notice the following two facts:

$$p(\text{Victoria, Edward VII}),$$
$$p(\text{Edward VII, George V}).$$

We conclude from these facts that Victoria is a grandparent of George V. A computation by a computer will have to do the same thing. Let's suppose we have an interactive system, in which we give commands to be carried out. To compute all possible grandparent relations, we give a command such as the following:

Find all pairs x, y such that x is a grandparent of y.

In a logic program this is usually represented by a statement such as the following, which is called a *goal*:

$$\leftarrow g(x, y).$$

The program executes by trying to carry out the goal. Upon termination a yes or no answer is output to indicate whether the goal was accomplished. Thus we can think of a goal as a question. For our example goal the system should eventually output something like the following:

"Yes, there are pairs x, y such that $g(x, y)$ is true, and here they are:"

$$x = \text{Victoria}, \qquad y = \text{George V};$$

$$x = \text{Edward VII}, \qquad y = \text{George VI};$$

$$x = \text{Alexandra}, \qquad y = \text{George VI};$$

$$x = \text{George V}, \qquad y = \text{Elizabeth II}.$$

As another example, suppose we want to know whether Victoria is a grandparent of Elizabeth II. In this case we write the following goal:

$$\leftarrow g(\text{Victoria, Elizabeth II}).$$

If the program does its job, it will output something like the following:

"No, Victoria is not a grandparent of Elizabeth II."

To get some insight into how the process works, let's introduce a little more terminology from logic programming. If $r(a, b, c)$ is a fact, then we denote it by writing a backwards arrow on its right side as follows:

$$r(a, b, c) \leftarrow.$$

For example, the fact $p(\text{Victoria, Edward VII})$ is written as follows:

$$p(\text{Victoria, Edward VII}) \leftarrow.$$

A conditional statement of the form "if A then B," where A and B are atoms, is written in logic programming as follows:

$$B \leftarrow A.$$

We read this statement as "B is true if A is true." A conditional statement of the form "if A and B then C" is written in logic programming as follows:

$$C \leftarrow A, B.$$

We read this statement as "C is true if A and B are true." For example, if g and p are the isGrandParentOf and isParentOf relations, respectively, then we have the conditional "if $p(x, z)$ and $p(z, y)$ then $g(x, y)$." We write this statement as follows:

$$g(x, y) \leftarrow p(x, z), p(z, y).$$

Now we're in a position to write down a logic program that solves our example problem. It consists of the five isParentOf facts together with the definition for the isGrandParentOf relation:

$$p(\text{Edward VII, George V}) \leftarrow \qquad\qquad (4.10)$$
$$p(\text{Victoria, Edward VII}) \leftarrow$$
$$p(\text{Alexandra, George V}) \leftarrow$$
$$p(\text{George VI, Elizabeth II}) \leftarrow$$
$$p(\text{George V, George VI}) \leftarrow$$
$$g(x, y) \leftarrow p(x, z), p(z, y)$$

How does this program's computation take place? Well, as we agreed, the computation starts with a command in the form of a goal. For example, suppose we want to find all grandparent-grandchild pairs. We'll do this by giving the following goal, where v and w are variables:

$$\leftarrow g(v, w).$$

The computation proceeds by trying to unify the atom $g(v, w)$ with some program fact on the left side of an arrow. Notice that $g(v, w)$ unifies with $g(x, y)$ in the program by the substitution $\{v/x, w/y\}$. But $g(x, y)$ has an antecedent consisting of the two atoms $p(x, z)$ and $p(z, y)$. These atoms have to be unified with some facts before we can return the answer yes. If we start searching from the top of the list, we see that the atom $p(x, z)$ unifies with the first fact, $p(\text{Edward VII, George V})$, by the substitution $\{x/\text{Edward VII}, z/\text{George V}\}$.

Before we try to process the second atom, $p(z, y)$, we need to apply the binding $z/\text{George V}$. Thus we try to find a fact to unify with the atom

$$p(\text{George V}, y).$$

This atom unifies with $p(\text{George V, George VI})$ by $\{y/\text{George VI}\}$. Therefore the computation returns the following answer:

Yes, $x = $ Edward VII and $y = $ George VI.

If necessary the computation can continue by trying to find other "yes" answers.

In the next few paragraphs we'll define what a logic program is, and we'll show how logic program computations are performed. After the general discussion about logic programming we'll finish with some examples of logic programming techniques.

Definition of a Logic Program

Let's start by introducing the notation for logic programs. A logic program consists of clauses that have a special form—they contain exactly one positive literal. So a *logic program clause* takes one of the following two forms, where $A, B_1, ..., B_n$ are atoms:

$$A \vee \neg B_1 \vee \cdots \vee \neg B_n \quad \text{(one positive and some negative literals),}$$

$$A \qquad\qquad\qquad\qquad \text{(one positive and no negative literals).}$$

The computation of a logic program begins after it has been given a *goal*, which is a clause containing only negative literals. So a goal clause takes the following form, where $B_1, ..., B_n$ are atoms:

$$\neg B_1 \vee \cdots \vee \neg B_n \qquad \text{(no positive and all negative literals).}$$

The program clauses and goal clauses of a logic program are often called Horn clauses because a *Horn clause* is a clause containing at most one positive literal. So a program clause is a Horn clause with one positive literal, and a goal clause is a Horn clause with no positive literals. There's a simple notation for Horn clauses that is used in logic programming. To see where the notation comes from, notice how we can use equivalences to write a program clause as an implication:

$$A \vee \neg B_1 \vee \cdots \vee \neg B_n \equiv A \vee \neg (B_1 \wedge \cdots \wedge B_n) \equiv B_1 \wedge \cdots \wedge B_n \to A.$$

In logic programming the implication $B_1 \wedge \cdots \wedge B_n \to A$ is denoted by writing it backwards and replacing the conjunction symbols by commas, as follows:

$$A \leftarrow B_1, ..., B_n.$$

We can read this program clause as "A is true if $B_1, ..., B_n$ are all true." In a similar manner we denote the clause consisting of a single atom A as follows:

$$A \leftarrow .$$

We read this program clause as "A is true."

Now let's consider goal clauses. A goal clause like $\neg B_1 \vee \cdots \vee \neg B_n$ is denoted as follows:

$$\leftarrow B_1, ..., B_n.$$

We can interpret this goal clause as the question "Are $B_1, ..., B_n$ all true?" However, since a goal is supposed to relate to a program, a more complete interpretation of the goal clause is "Are $B_1, ..., B_n$ inferred by the program?" We'll make more sense out of this shortly.

Let's summarize. A *logic program* is a finite set of program clauses of the following forms:

$$A \leftarrow B_1, ..., B_n$$
$$A \leftarrow .$$

A *goal* for a logic program has the following form:

$$\leftarrow B_1, ..., B_n.$$

EXAMPLE 1. Let P be the logic program consisting of the following three clauses:

$$q(a) \leftarrow$$
$$r(a) \leftarrow$$
$$p(x) \leftarrow q(x), r(x).$$

Suppose we give P the following goal:

$$\leftarrow p(a).$$

We can read this goal as "Is $p(a)$ true?" or "Is $p(a)$ inferred from P?" The answer to these goal questions is yes. We can argue informally. The three program clauses tell us that $q(a)$ and $r(a)$ are both true and the implication $p(a) \leftarrow q(a), r(a)$ is also true. Therefore we infer that $p(a)$ is true by modus ponens. In the next paragraph we'll see how the answer follows from resolution.   ♦

Resolution and Logic Programming

Let's make a closer examination of goals to see why things are set up to use resolution. For this little discussion we'll suppose that P is a logic program and

$$G \text{ is the goal} \leftarrow B_1, ..., B_n.$$

We can read this goal clause as the following question:

"Does P imply $B_1 \wedge \cdots \wedge B_n$?"

Now remember that the goal $\leftarrow B_1, \ldots, B_n$ is just shorthand for the following equivalent expressions:

$$\neg B_1 \vee \cdots \vee \neg B_n \equiv \neg (B_1 \wedge \cdots \wedge B_n).$$

So the goal is actually represented as the negation of the thing we want to infer from the program. This is exactly what we want because we will be performing resolution. In other words, we will prove the validity of a statement by showing that its negation is unsatisfiable. For example, to prove that $P \rightarrow B$ is valid, we negate the conditional to obtain $P \wedge \neg B$. Then we apply resolution to obtain a contradiction—the empty clause. In other words, we prove the validity of the statement $P \wedge \neg B \rightarrow$ false.

Let's continue our detailed examination of the goal G. First, remember that clauses are written under the assumption that all variables are universally quantified. For this discussion we'll use the notation

$$\forall (\neg B_1 \vee \cdots \vee \neg B_n)$$

to emphasize this fact. Thus we can write the following equivalences for the goal G:

$$\forall (\neg B_1 \vee \cdots \vee \neg B_n) \equiv \forall \neg (B_1 \wedge \cdots \wedge B_n) \equiv \neg \exists (B_1 \wedge \cdots \wedge B_n).$$

This allows us to give the following more detailed version of the question we need answered for G:

"Does P imply $\exists (B_1 \wedge \cdots \wedge B_n)$?"

To prove "P implies $\exists (B_1 \wedge \cdots \wedge B_n)$" by resolution, we need to negate the statement and then use resolution to show that the negation is unsatisfiable. In other words, we want to prove that the following set of clauses is unsatisfiable (we're using sets because P is a set of clauses):

$$P \cup \{\neg \exists (B_1 \wedge \cdots \wedge B_n)\}.$$

Of course, we have the following equivalences and equalities:

$$
\begin{aligned}
\neg \exists (B_1 \wedge \cdots \wedge B_n) &\equiv \forall \neg (B_1 \wedge \cdots \wedge B_n) \\
&\equiv \forall (\neg B_1 \vee \cdots \vee \neg B_n) \\
&= \leftarrow B_1, \ldots, B_n \\
&= G.
\end{aligned}
$$

So to answer the question "Does P imply $\exists\,(B_1 \wedge \cdots \wedge B_n)$?" we must show that the following set of clauses is unsatisfiable:

$$P \cup \{G\}.$$

What's the point of all this? The point is that if P is a logic program and G is a goal, then the goal question can be answered in the affirmative if there is a proof that the set of clauses $P \cup \{G\}$ is unsatisfiable.

When we give a goal to a logic program, we usually want more than just the answer yes or no. If the answer is yes, we might want to know the values of any of the variables appearing in the goal. So a more technically accurate reading of the goal statement "Does P imply $\exists\,(B_1 \wedge \cdots \wedge B_n)$?" is the following:

"Does there exist a substitution θ such that P implies $(B_1 \wedge \cdots \wedge B_n)\theta$?"

Let's look at an example to see how the notation for logic program clauses makes it easy to find answers to goal questions.

EXAMPLE 2. Suppose we have a logic program P consisting of the following two clauses:

$$q(a) \leftarrow$$
$$p(f(x)) \leftarrow q(x).$$

Let G be the goal $\leftarrow p(y)$. This means that we want an answer to the question "Does P imply $\exists y\ p(y)$?" In other words, "Is there is a substitution θ such that $p(y)\theta$ is inferred from P?" Let's give the answer first and then see how we got it. The answer is yes. Letting $\theta = \{y/f(a)\}$, we can evaluate $p(y)\theta$ as follows:

$$p(y)\theta = p(y)\{y/f(a)\} = p(f(a)).$$

We claim that $p(f(a))$ is inferred from P. This is easy to see from an informal standpoint. Just apply θ to the second clause. This transforms the two clauses of P into the following:

$$q(a) \leftarrow$$
$$p(f(a)) \leftarrow q(a).$$

Now, since $q(a)$ is a fact, we can apply modus ponens to conclude that $p(f(a))$ is true.

So much for the informal discussion. Now let's give a resolution proof showing that $P \cup \{G\}$ is unsatisfiable. We'll convert the logic program notation for the clauses and the goal into normal clausal notation, and we'll keep track of the most general unifiers as we go.

Proof:
  1. $q(a)$ P program clause: $q(a) \leftarrow$
  2. $p(f(x)) \vee \neg q(x)$ P program clause: $p(f(x)) \leftarrow q(x)$
  3. $\neg p(y)$ P goal clause: $\leftarrow p(y)$
  4. $\neg q(x)$ $2, 3, R, \{y/f(x)\}$
  5. $\square$ $1, 4, R, \{x/a\}$
        QED.

Therefore by the resolution theorem, $P \cup \{G\}$ is unsatisfiable. So the answer to the goal question is yes. What value of y does the job? The y that does the job can be obtained by composing the mgu's obtained during the resolution process and then applying the result to y, as follows:

$$y \; \{y/f(x)\} \; \{x/a\} = y \; \{y/f(a)\} = f(a).$$

Therefore $p(f(a))$ is a logical consequence of program P.   ◆

There are three important advantages to the notation that we are using for logic programs:

1. The notation is easy to write down because we don't have to use the symbols $\neg$, $\wedge$, and $\vee$.

2. The notation allows us to interpret a program in two different ways. For example, suppose we have the clause $A \leftarrow B_1, ..., B_n$. This clause has the usual logical interpretation "A is true if $B_1, ..., B_n$ are all true." The clause also has the procedural interpretation "A is a procedure that is executed by executing the procedures $B_1, ..., B_n$ in the order they are written." Most logic programming systems allow this procedural interpretation.

3. The notation makes it easy to apply the resolution rule. We'll discuss this next.

Whenever we apply the resolution rule, we have to do a lot of choosing. We have to choose two clauses to resolve, and we have to choose literals to "cancel" from each clause. Since there are many choices, it's easy to understand why we can come up with many different proof sequences. When resolution is used with logic program clauses, we can specialize the rule.

The specialized rule always picks one clause to be the most recent line of the proof, which is always a goal clause. Start the proof by picking the initial goal. Select the leftmost atom in the goal clause as the literal to "cancel." For the second clause, pick a program clause whose head unifies with the atom selected from the goal clause. The resolvant of these two clauses is created by first replacing the leftmost atom in the goal clause by the body atoms of the program clause and then applying the unifier to the resulting goal. Here is a formal description of the rule, which is called the *SLD-resolution* rule:[†]

SLD-Resolution Rule   (4.11)

Resolve the goal $\leftarrow B_1, ..., B_k$ with the program clause $A \leftarrow A_1, ..., A_n$ by first unifying B_1 with A via mgu θ. Then replace B_1 in the goal by the body $A_1, ..., A_n$ and apply θ to the resulting goal to obtain the resolvant

$$\leftarrow (A_1, ..., A_n, B_2, ..., B_k)\theta.$$

To construct a logic program proof, we start by listing each program clause as a premise. Then we write the goal clause as a premise. Now we use (4.11) repeatedly to add new resolvants to the proof, each new resolvant being constructed from the goal on the previous line together with some program clause. We can summarize the application of (4.11) with the following four-step procedure:

1. Pick the goal clause on the last line of the partial proof, and select its leftmost atom, say B_1.

2. Find a program clause whose head unifies with B_1, say by θ. Be sure the two clauses have distinct sets of variables (rename if necessary).

3. Replace B_1 in the goal clause with the body of the program clause.

4. Apply θ to the goal constructed on line 3 to get the resolvant, which is placed on a new line of the proof.

We'll introduce the use of the SLD-resolution rule with an example. Suppose we are given the following logic program, where p means isParentOf and g means isGrandparentOf:

$$p(a, b) \leftarrow$$
$$p(d, b) \leftarrow$$
$$p(b, c) \leftarrow$$
$$g(x, y) \leftarrow p(x, z), p(z, y).$$

[†] SLD-resolution means Selective Linear resolution of Definite clauses. In our case we always "select" the leftmost atom of the goal clause.

We'll execute the program by giving it the following goal:

$$\leftarrow g(w, c).$$

Since there is a variable w in this goal, we can read the goal as the question

"Is there a grandparent for c?"

The resolution proof starts by letting the program clauses and the goal clause be premises. For this example we have the following five lines:

Proof: 1. $p(a, b) \leftarrow$ P
     2. $p(d, b)\leftarrow$ P
     3. $p(b, c) \leftarrow$ P
     4. $g(x, y) \leftarrow p(x, z), p(z, y).$ P
     5. $\leftarrow g(w, c)$ P Initial goal

The proof starts by resolving the initial goal on line 5 with some program clause. The atom $g(w, c)$ from the initial goal unifies with $g(x, y)$, the head of the program clause on line 4, by the mgu

$$\theta_1 = \{w/x, y/c\}.$$

Therefore we can use (4.11) to resolve the two clauses on lines 4 and 5. So we replace the goal atom $g(w, c)$ on line 5 with the body of the clause on line 4 and then apply the mgu θ_1 to the result to obtain the following resolvant goal clause:

$$\leftarrow p(x, z), p(z, c).$$

Let's compare what we've just done for logic program clauses using (4.11) to the case for regular clauses using (4.7). The following two lines are copies of lines 4 and 5 in which we've included the clausal notation for each logic program clause:

Logic Program Notation	*Clausal Notation*
4. $g(x, y) \leftarrow p(x, z), p(z, y)$	$g(x, y) \vee \neg p(x, z) \vee \neg p(z, y)$
5. $\leftarrow g(w, c)$	$\neg g(w, c)$

We apply (4.11) to the logic program notation clauses, and we apply (4.7) to the clauses in clausal notation. This gives the following pair of resolvants:

Logic Program Notation	*Clausal Notation*
$\leftarrow p(x, z), p(z, c)$	$\neg p(x, z) \vee \neg p(z, c)$

So we get the same answer with either method.

Now let's continue the proof. We'll write down the new resolvant on line 6 of our proof, in which we've added the mgu to the reason column:

$$6. \quad \leftarrow p(x, z), p(z, c) \qquad 4, 5, R, \theta_1 = \{w/x, y/c\}$$

To continue the proof according to (4.11), we must choose this new goal on line 6 for one of the clauses, and we must choose its leftmost atom $p(x, z)$ for "cancellation." For the second clause we'll choose the clause on line 1 because its head $p(a, b)$ unifies with our chosen atom by the mgu

$$\theta_2 = \{x/a, z/b\}.$$

To apply (4.11), we must replace $p(x, z)$ on line 6 by the body of the clause on line 1 and then apply θ_2 to the result. Since the clause on line 1 does not have a body, we simply delete $p(x, z)$ from line 6 and apply θ_2 to the result, obtaining the resolvant

$$\leftarrow p(b, c).$$

Let's compute this result in terms of both (4.11) and (4.7). The clauses on lines 1 and 6 take the following forms, in which we've added the regular clausal notation for each clause:

Logic Program Notation	*Clausal Notation*
1. $p(a, b) \leftarrow$	$p(a, b)$
6. $\leftarrow p(x, z), p(z, c)$	$\neg p(x, z) \vee \neg p(z, c)$

After applying (4.11) and (4.7) to the respective notations on lines 1 and 6, we obtain the following pair of resolvants:

Logic Program Notation	*Clausal Notation*
$\leftarrow p(b, c)$	$\neg p(b, c)$

So we can continue the proof by writing down the new resolvant on line 7 as follows:

$$7. \quad \leftarrow p(b, c) \qquad 1, 6, R, \theta_2 = \{x/a, z/b\}$$

To continue the proof using (4.11), we must choose the goal clause on line 7 together with its only atom $p(b, c)$. It unifies with the head $p(b, c)$ of the clause on line 3 by the empty unifier

$$\theta_3 = \{\ \}.$$

Since there is only one atom in the goal clause of line 7 and there is no body in the clause on line 3, it follows that the resolvant of the clauses on these two lines is just the empty clause. Thus our proof is completed by writing this information on line 8 as follows:

8. □ $3, 7, R, \theta_3 = \{\ \}$
    QED.

To finish things off, we'll collect the eight steps of the proof and rewrite them as a single unit:

Proof: 1. $p(a, b) \leftarrow$ P
        2. $p(d, b) \leftarrow$ P
        3. $p(b, c) \leftarrow$ P
        4. $g(x, y) \leftarrow p(x, z), p(z, y)$ P
        5. $\leftarrow g(w, c)$ P Initial goal
        6. $\leftarrow p(x, z), p(z, c)$ $4, 5, R, \theta_1 = \{w/x, y/c\}.$
        7. $\leftarrow p(b, c)$ $1, 6, R, \theta_2 = \{x/a, z/b\}$
        8. □ $3, 7, R, \theta_3 = \{\ \}$
            QED.

Since □ was obtained, the answer to the question for the goal

$$\leftarrow g(w, c)$$

is yes. Now, what about the variable w in the goal statement? The only reason we got the answer yes is because w was bound to some term. We can recover the value of that binding by composing the three unifiers θ_1, θ_2, and θ_3 and then applying the result to w:

$$w\theta_1\theta_2\theta_3 = a.$$

So the goal question "Is there a grandparent for c?" is answered as follows:

$$\text{Yes}$$

$$w = a.$$

We should notice for this example that there is another possible yes answer to the goal $\leftarrow g(w, c)$. Namely,

$$\text{Yes}$$
$$w = d.$$

Can this answer be computed? Sure. Keep the first six lines of the proof as they are. Then resolve the goal on line 6 with the clause on line 2 instead of the clause on line 1. The goal atom $p(x, z)$ on line 6 unifies with the head $p(d, b)$ from line 1 by mgu

$$\theta_2 = \{x/d, z/b\}.$$

This θ_2 is different from the previous θ_2. So we get a new line 7 and, in this case, the same line 8 as follows:

7. $\leftarrow p(b, c)$ 2, 6, R, $\theta_2 = \{x/d, z/b\}$
8. $\square$ 3, 7, R, $\theta_3 = \{\ \}$
 QED.

With this proof we obtain the answer yes, and we calculate a new value of w as follows:

$$w \theta_1 \theta_2 \theta_3 = d.$$

Computation Trees

Now that we have an example under our belts, let's look again at the general picture. The preceding proof had two possible yes answers. We would like to find a way to represent all possible answers (i.e., proof sequences) for a goal. For our purposes a tree will do the job.

A *computation tree* for a goal is an ordered tree whose root is the goal. The children of any parent node are all the possible goals (i.e., resolvants) that can be obtained by resolving the parent goal with a program clause. We agree to order the children of each node from left to right in terms of the top-to-bottom ordering of the program clauses that are used with the parent to create the children. Each parent-child branch is labeled with the mgu obtained to create the child. A leaf may be the empty clause or a goal. If the empty clause occurs as a leaf, we write "yes" together with the values of any variables that occur in the original goal at the root of the tree. If a goal occurs as a leaf, this means that it can't be resolved with any program clause, so we write "failure." The computation tree will always show all possible answers for the given goal at its root.

For example, the computation tree for the goal $\leftarrow g(w, c)$ with respect to our example program can be pictured as shown in Figure 4.1.

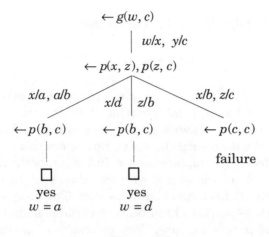

Figure 4.1

Notice that the tree contains all possible answers to the goal question.

A logic programming system needs a strategy to search the computation tree for a leaf with a yes answer. The strategy used by most Prolog systems is the *depth-first* search strategy, which starts by traversing the tree down to the leftmost leaf. If the leaf is the empty clause, then the yes answer is reported. If the leaf is a failure leaf, then the search returns to the parent of the leaf. At this point a depth-first search is started at the next child to the right. If there is no next child, then the search returns to the parent of the parent, and a depth-first search starts with its next child to the right, and so on. If this process eventually returns to the root of the tree and there are no more paths to search, then failure is reported.

It might be desirable for a logic programming system to attempt to find all possible answers to a goal question. One strategy for attempting to find all possible answers is called *backtracking*. For example, with depth-first search we perform backtracking by continuing the depth-first search process from the point at which the last yes answer was found. In other words, when a yes answer is found, the system reports the answer and then continues just as though a failure leaf was encountered.

In the next few examples we'll construct some computation trees and discuss the problems that can arise in trying to find all possible answers to a goal question.

EXAMPLE 3. Let's consider the following two-clause program:

$$p(a) \leftarrow$$

$$p(\text{succ}(x)) \leftarrow p(x).$$

Suppose we give the following goal to the program:

$$\leftarrow p(x).$$

This goal will resolve with either one of the program clauses. So the root of the computation tree has two children. One child, the empty clause, results from the resolution of $\leftarrow p(x)$ with $p(a) \leftarrow$. The other child results from the resolution of $\leftarrow p(x)$ with $p(\text{succ}(x)) \leftarrow p(x)$. But before this happens, we need to change variables. We'll replace x by x_1 in the program clause to obtain $p(\text{succ}(x_1)) \leftarrow p(x_1)$. Resolving $\leftarrow p(x)$ with this clause produces the clause $\leftarrow p(x_1)$, which becomes the second child of the root. The process starts all over again with the goal $\leftarrow p(x_1)$. To keep track of variable names, we'll replace x by x_2 in the second program clause. Then resolve $\leftarrow p(x_1)$ with $p(\text{succ}(x_2)) \leftarrow p(x_2)$ to obtain the clause $\leftarrow p(x_2)$. This process continues forever.

The computation tree for this example is shown in Figure 4.2. It is an infinite tree, which continues the indicated pattern forever.

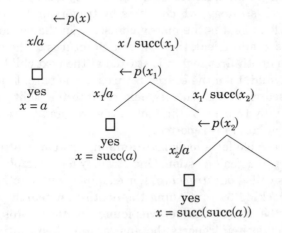

Figure 4.2

If we use the depth-first search rule, the first answer is "yes, $x = a$." If we force backtracking, the next answer we'll get is "yes, $x = \text{succ}(a)$." If we force backtracking again, we'll get the answer "yes, $x = \text{succ}(\text{succ}(a))$." Continuing in this way, we can generate the following infinite sequence of possible values for x:

$$a, \text{succ}(a), \text{succ}(\text{succ}(a)), ..., \text{succ}^k(a), ... \quad \blacklozenge$$

EXAMPLE 4. Consider the following three-clause program, in which the third clause has more than one atom in its body:

$$q(a) \leftarrow$$
$$p(a) \leftarrow$$
$$p(f(x)) \leftarrow p(x), q(x).$$

Figure 4.3 shows a few levels of the computation tree for the goal $\leftarrow p(x)$. Notice that as we travel down the rightmost path from the root, the number of goal atoms at each node is increased by one for each new level.

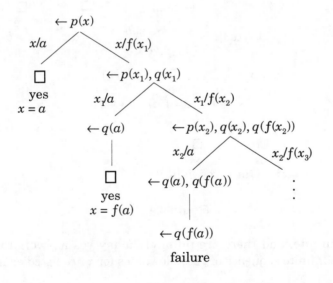

Figure 4.3

Using the depth-first search rule, we obtain the answer "yes, $x = a$." Backtracking works one time to give the answer "yes, $x = f(a)$." If we force backtracking again, then the computation takes an infinite walk down the tree, failing at each leaf. $\blacklozenge$

EXAMPLE 5. Suppose we're given the following three-clause program:

$$p(f(x)) \leftarrow p(x)$$
$$p(a) \leftarrow$$
$$p(b) \leftarrow .$$

If we start with the goal

$$\leftarrow p(x),$$

then the computation tree will be a ternary tree because there are three "p" clauses that match each goal. The first few levels of the tree are given in Figure 4.4.

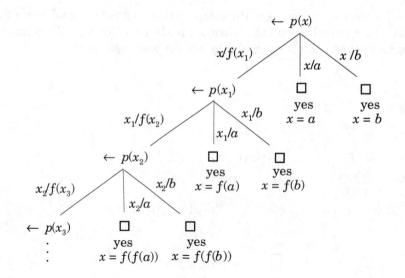

Figure 4.4

The tree is infinite, and there are infinitely many yes answers to the goal question. The infinite sequence of possible values for x are listed as follows:

$$a, b, f(a), f(b), f(f(a)), f(f(b)), ..., f^k(a), f^k(b), ...$$

Notice that if we used the depth-first search strategy, then the computation would take an infinite walk down the left branch of the tree. So although there are infinitely many answers, the depth-first search strategy won't find even one of them.   ◆

In the preceding example, depth-first search did not find any answers to the goal $\leftarrow p(x)$. Suppose we reordered the three program clauses as follows:

$$p(a) \leftarrow$$
$$p(b) \leftarrow$$
$$p(f(x)) \leftarrow p(x).$$

The computation tree corresponding to these three clauses can be searched in a depth-first fashion with backtracking to generate all the answers to the goal $\leftarrow p(x)$. Suppose we write the three clauses in the following order:

$$p(a) \leftarrow$$
$$p(f(x)) \leftarrow p(x)$$
$$p(b) \leftarrow.$$

The computation tree for these three clauses, when searched with depth-first and backtracking, will yield some, but not all, of the possible answers.

So when a logic programming language uses depth-first search, two problems can occur when the computation tree for a goal is infinite:

1. The yes answers found may depend on the order of the clauses.

2. Backtracking might not find all possible yes answers to a goal.

Many logic programming systems use the depth-first search strategy because it's efficient to implement and because it reflects the procedural interpretation of a clause. For example, the clause $A \leftarrow B, C$ represents a procedure named A that is executed by first calling procedure B and then calling procedure C.

Another search strategy is called *breadth-first search*. It looks for a yes answer by examining all the children of a node before it looks at the next level of the tree. This strategy will find all possible answers to a goal question. But it will carry on forever looking for more answers if the computation tree is infinite.

Some implementation strategies for searching the computation tree use breadth-first search with a twist. All children of a node are searched in parallel. A search at a particular node is started only when the goal atom has not already occurred at a higher level in the tree. If the goal atom matches a goal at a higher level in the tree, then the process waits for the answer to the other goal. When it receives the answer, then it continues with its search. This technique requires a table containing previous goal atoms and answers.

It has proved useful in detecting certain kinds of loops that give rise to infinite computation trees. In some cases the search process won't take an infinite walk. An introduction to these ideas is given in Warren [1992].

Logic Programming Techniques

Let's spend some time discussing a few elementary techniques to construct logic programs. First we'll see how to construct logic programs that process relations. Then we'll discuss logic programs that process functions. The clauses in our examples are ordered to take advantage of the depth-first search strategy. This strategy is used by most Prolog systems.

Techniques for Relations

Logic programming allows us to easily process many relations because relations are just predicates. For example, we've already seen an example of how to find the isGrandparentOf relation if we're given the isParentOf relation. The technique is to write down the isParentOf relation as a set of facts of the form

$$p(a, b) \leftarrow .$$

We read this clause as "a is a parent of b." Then we define the isGrandparentOf relation as the following clause:

$$g(x, y) \leftarrow p(x, z), p(z, y).$$

This clause is read as "x is a grandparent of y if x is a parent of z and z is a parent of y."

Suppose we want to write the isAncestorOf relation in terms of the isParentOf relation, where an ancestor is either a parent, or a grandparent, or a great-grandparent, and so on. The next example discusses this problem in general terms.

EXAMPLE 6 (*Transitive Closure*). The isAncestorOf relation is the transitive closure of the isParentOf relation. In general terms, suppose we're given a binary relation r and we need to compute the transitive closure of r. If we let tc denote the transitive closure of r, the following two-clause program does the job:

$$tc(x, y) \leftarrow r(x, y)$$
$$tc(x, y) \leftarrow r(x, z), tc(z, y).$$

For example, suppose r is the isParentOf relation. Then tc is the isAncestorOf relation. The first clause can be read as "x is an ancestor of y if x is a parent of y," and the second clause can be read as "x is an ancestor of y if x is a parent of z and z is an ancestor of y." ◆

Techniques for Functions

Now let's see whether we can find a technique to construct logic programs to compute functions. Actually, it's pretty easy. The major thing to remember in translating a function definition to a logic definition is the following:

The functional equation $f(x) = y$ can be represented by a predicate expression as follows:

$$\text{pf}(x, y).$$

The predicate name "pf" can remind us that we have a "predicate for f." The predicate expression $\text{pf}(x, y)$ can still be read as "f of x is y."

Now let's discuss a technique to construct a logic program for a recursively defined function. If f is defined recursively, then there is at least one part of the definition that defines $f(x)$ in terms of some $f(y)$. In other words, some part of the definition of f has the following form, where $E(f(y))$ denotes an expression containing $f(y)$:

$$f(x) = E(f(y)).$$

Using our technique to create a predicate for this functional equation, we get the following expression:

$$\text{pf}(x, E(f(y))).$$

But we aren't done yet because the recursive definition of f causes $f(y)$ to occur as an argument in the predicate. Since we're trying to compute f by the predicate pf, we need to get rid of $f(y)$. The solution is to replace $f(y)$ by a new variable z. We can represent this replacement by writing down the following version of the expression:

$$\text{pf}(x, E(z)) \text{ where } z = f(y).$$

Now we have a functional equation $z = f(y)$, which we can replace by $\text{pf}(y, z)$.

So we obtain the following expression:

$$\text{pf}(x, E(z)) \text{ where pf}(y, z).$$

The transformation to a logic program is now simple: Replace the word "where" by the symbol ← to obtain a logic program clause as follows:

$$\text{pf}(x, E(z)) \leftarrow \text{pf}(y, z).$$

Thus we have a general technique to transform a functional equation into a logic program. Here are the steps, all in one place:

$f(x) = E(f(y))$	The given functional equation.
$\text{pf}(x, E(f(y)))$	Create a predicate expression.
$\text{pf}(x, E(z))$ where $z = f(y)$	Let $z = f(y)$.
$\text{pf}(x, E(z))$ where $\text{pf}(y, z)$	Create a predicate expression.
$\text{pf}(x, E(z)) \leftarrow \text{pf}(y, z)$	Create a clause.

Of course, there may be more work to do, depending on the complexity of the expression $E(z)$. Let's do some examples to help get the look and feel of this process.

EXAMPLE 7. Suppose we want to write a logic program to compute the factorial function. Letting $f(x) = x!$, we have the following recursive definition of f:

$$f(0) = 1$$
$$f(x) = x * f(x - 1).$$

To implement f as a logic program, we'll let "fact" be the predicate to compute f. Then the two equations of the recursive definition become the following two predicate expressions:

$$\text{fact}(0, 1)$$
$$\text{fact}(x, x * f(x - 1)).$$

The second statement contains the argument $f(x - 1)$, which we'll replace by a new variable y to obtain the following version of the two expressions:

$$\text{fact}(0, 1)$$
$$\text{fact}(x, x * y) \text{ where } y = f(x - 1).$$

Now we can change the functional equation $y = f(x - 1)$ into a predicate expression to obtain the following version:

$$fact(0, 1)$$
$$fact(x, x * y) \text{ where } fact(x - 1, y).$$

Therefore the desired logic program has the following two clauses:

$$fact(0, 1) \leftarrow$$
$$fact(x, x * y) \leftarrow fact(x - 1, y). \quad \blacklozenge$$

EXAMPLE 8. Suppose we want to write a logic program to compute the length of a list. Let's start with the following recursively defined function L that does the job:

$$L(\langle \, \rangle) = 0.$$
$$L(x :: y) = L(y) + 1.$$

We can start by writing down two predicate expressions to represent these two functional equations. We'll use the predicate name "length" as follows:

$$length(\langle \, \rangle, 0)$$
$$length(x :: y, L(y) + 1).$$

The second expression contains an occurrence of the function L, which we're trying to define. So we'll replace $L(y)$ by a new variable z to obtain the following version:

$$length(\langle \, \rangle, 0)$$
$$length(x :: y, z + 1) \text{ where } z = L(y).$$

Now replace the functional equation $z = L(y)$ by the predicate expression $length(y, z)$ to obtain the following version:

$$length(\langle \, \rangle, 0)$$
$$length(x :: y, z + 1) \text{ where } length(y, z).$$

Lastly, convert the expressions to the following logic program clauses:

$$length(\langle \, \rangle, 0) \leftarrow$$
$$length(x :: y, z + 1) \leftarrow length(y, z). \quad \blacklozenge$$

EXAMPLE 9. Suppose we want to delete the first occurrence of an element from a list. A recursively defined function to do the job can be written as follows:

$$\text{delete}(x, L) \;=\; \begin{aligned}[t] &\text{if } L = \langle\,\rangle \text{ then } \langle\,\rangle \\ &\text{else if } \text{head}(L) = x \text{ then } \text{tail}(L) \\ &\text{else } \text{head}(L) :: \text{delete}(x, \text{tail}(L)). \end{aligned}$$

Let's construct a logic program to compute this function. It's much easier to write a logic program for a function described as a set of equations. So we'll rewrite the functional definition as three functional equations in the following way:

$$\text{delete}(x, \langle\,\rangle) = \langle\,\rangle$$
$$\text{delete}(x, x :: T) = T$$
$$\text{delete}(x, y :: T) = y :: \text{delete}(x, T).$$

First we'll convert each equation to a predicate expression using the predicate named "remove" as follows:

$$\text{remove}(x, \langle\,\rangle, \langle\,\rangle)$$
$$\text{remove}(x, x :: T, T)$$
$$\text{remove}(x, y :: T, y :: \text{delete}(x, T)).$$

Since the functional value delete(x, T) occurs in the third expression, we'll replace it by a new variable U to obtain the following version:

$$\text{remove}(x, \langle\,\rangle, \langle\,\rangle)$$
$$\text{remove}(x, x :: T, T)$$
$$\text{remove}(x, y :: T, y :: U) \text{ where } U = \text{delete}(x, T).$$

Now replace the functional equation $U = \text{delete}(x, T)$ by the predicate expression remove(x, T, U) as follows:

$$\text{remove}(x, \langle\,\rangle, \langle\,\rangle)$$
$$\text{remove}(x, x :: T, T)$$
$$\text{remove}(x, y :: T, y :: U) \text{ where } \text{remove}(x, T, U).$$

Finally, transform these three expressions into the following three-clause logic program:

$$\text{remove}(x, \langle \, \rangle, \langle \, \rangle) \leftarrow$$
$$\text{remove}(x, x :: T, T) \leftarrow$$
$$\text{remove}(x, y :: T, y :: U) \leftarrow \text{remove}(x, T, U).$$

Exercises

1. Suppose you are given an isParentOf relation. Find a definition for each of the following relations.

   a. isChildOf.

   b. isGrandchildOf.

   c. isGreatGrandparentOf.

2. Suppose you are given an isParentOf relation. Try to find a definition for each of the following relations. *Hint:* You might want to consider some kind of test for equality.

   a. isSiblingOf.

   b. isCousinOf.

   c. isSecondCousinOf.

   d. isFirstCousinOnceRemovedOf.

3. Suppose we're given the following logic program:

$$p(a, b) \leftarrow$$
$$p(a, c) \leftarrow$$
$$p(b, d) \leftarrow$$
$$p(c, e) \leftarrow$$
$$g(x, y) \leftarrow p(x, z), p(z, y).$$

   a. Find a resolution proof for the goal $\leftarrow g(a, w)$.

   b. Draw a picture of the computation tree for the goal $\leftarrow g(a, w)$.

4. Suppose we're given the following logic program:

$$p(a) \leftarrow$$
$$p(g(x)) \leftarrow p(x)$$
$$p(b) \leftarrow.$$

   a. Draw at least three levels of the computation tree for the goal $\leftarrow p(x)$.

   b. What are the possible yes answers for the goal $\leftarrow p(x)$?

   c. Describe the values of x that are generated by backtracking with the depth-first search strategy for the goal $\leftarrow p(x)$.

5. The following logic program claims to test an integer to see whether it is a natural number, where pred(x, y) means that the predecessor of x is y:

$$\text{isNat}(0) \leftarrow$$
$$\text{isNat}(x) \leftarrow \text{isNat}(y), \text{pred}(x, y).$$

   a. What happens when the goal is $\leftarrow$ isNat(2)?
   b. What happens when the goal is $\leftarrow$ isNat(−1)?

6. Let r denote a binary relation. Write logic programs to compute each of the following relations.
   a. The symmetric closure of r.
   b. The reflexive closure of r.

7. Translate each of the following functional definitions into a logic program. *Hint:* First, translate the if-then-else definitions into equational definitions.
   a. The function f computes the nth Fibonacci number:

   $$f(n) = \text{if } n = 0 \text{ then } 1 \text{ else if } n = 1 \text{ then } 1 \text{ else } f(n-1) + f(n-2).$$

   b. The function "cat" computes the concatenation of two lists:

   $$\text{cat}(x, y) = \text{if } x = \langle\,\rangle \text{ then } y \text{ else head}(x) :: \text{cat(tail}(x), y).$$

   c. The function "nodes" computes the number of nodes in a binary tree:

   $$\text{nodes}(t) = \text{if } t = \langle\,\rangle \text{ then } 0 \text{ else } 1 + \text{nodes(left}(t)) + \text{nodes(right}(t)).$$

8. Find a logic program to implement each of the following functions, where the variables represent elements or lists.
   a. equalLists(x, y) tests whether the lists x and y are equal.
   b. member(x, y) tests whether x is an element of the list y.
   c. all(x, y) is the list obtained from y by removing all occurrences of x.
   d. makeSet(x) is the list obtained from x by deleting redundant elements.
   e. subset(x, y) tests whether x, considered as a set, is a subset of y.
   f. equalSets(x, y) tests whether x and y, considered as sets, are equal.
   g. subBag(x, y) tests whether x, considered as a bag, is a subbag of y.
   h. equalBags(x, y) tests whether the bags x and y are equal.

9. Suppose we have a schedule of classes with each entry having the form class(i, s, t, p), which means that class i section s meets at time t in place p. Find a logic program to compute the possible schedules available for a given list of classes.

10. Write a logic program to test whether a propositional wff is a tautology. Assume that the wffs use the four operators in the set $\{\neg, \wedge, \vee, \rightarrow\}$. *Hint:* Use the fact that if A is a wff containing a letter p, then A is a tautology iff $A(p/\text{true})$ and $A(p/\text{false})$ are both tautologies. To assist in finding the propositional letters, assume that the predicate atom(x) means that x is a propositional letter.

Chapter Summary

The major component of automatic reasoning for the first-order predicate calculus is the resolution inference rule. Resolution proofs work by showing that a wff is unsatisfiable. So to prove that a wff is valid, we can use resolution to show that its negation is unsatisfiable. Resolution requires wffs to be represented as sets of clauses, which can be constructed by Skolem's algorithm. Before each step of a resolution proof involving predicates, the unification algorithm must calculate a substitution—a most general unifier—that will unify a set of atoms. The process of applying the resolution rule can be programmed to perform automatic reasoning.

Logic programs consist of clauses that have one positive literal and zero or more negative literals. A logic program goal is a clause consisting of one or more negative literals. Logic program goals are computed by a modification of resolution called SLD-resolution. Each goal of a logic program has an associated computation tree that can be searched in a variety of ways. The depth-first search strategy is used by most logic programming languages. Elementary techniques for logic programming include the implementation of relations and recursively defined functions.

5

Regular Languages and Finite Automata

Unlearn'd, he knew no schoolman's subtle art,
No language, but the language of the heart.
—Alexander Pope (1688–1744)

Can a machine recognize a language? The answer is yes for some machines and some languages. In this chapter we'll study an elementary class of languages called regular languages and an elementary class of machines called finite automata. We'll see that regular languages can be represented by certain kinds of algebraic expressions, by finite automata, and by certain grammars.

To start things off, let's look at a familiar problem for most programmers. The problem is to check for correctly formed input. We'll state the problem as follows:

The Recognition Problem

Write an algorithm to recognize input strings with a certain property.

For example, suppose we represent rational numbers in either decimal form or scientific notation. Can we write an algorithm to recognize strings of symbols represented in this way? Most of us will answer yes after we have the answers to a few more questions. For example, do we want to allow leading + signs? What is scientific notation? This example is an instance of a general class of problems that can be solved by some special techniques that we'll discuss in this chapter.

Chapter Guide

Section 5.1 introduces the regular languages that we'll be discussing in this chapter. We'll see that these languages can be represented algebraically by "regular" expressions. We'll also see some techniques for simplifying regular expressions.

Section 5.2 introduces finite automata as machines to recognize regular languages. We'll present algorithms to transform between finite automata and regular expressions. We'll also introduce finite automata as output devices, and we'll present interpreters for finite automata.

Section 5.3 introduces algorithms to help construct efficient finite automata. We'll see how to start with a regular expression and end up with a minimum-state deterministic finite automaton.

Section 5.4 introduces grammars for regular languages. We'll see how to transform between regular grammars and nondeterministic finite automata. We'll introduce some properties of regular languages given by pumping lemmas, set operations, and morphisms. We'll also see examples of languages that are not regular.

5.1   Regular Languages

Recall that a language over a finite alphabet A is a set of strings of letters from A. So a language over A is a subset of A^*. If we are given a language L and a string w, can we tell whether w is in L? The answer depends on our ability to describe the language L. Some languages are easy to describe, and others are not so easy to describe. In this section we'll introduce a class of languages that are easy to describe and for which algorithms can be found to solve the recognition problem.

The languages that we are talking about can be constructed from the letters of an alphabet by using the language operations of union, concatenation, and closure. These languages are called regular languages. Let's give a specific definition and then some examples. The collection of *regular languages* over A is defined inductively as follows:

Basis: $\emptyset$, $\{\Lambda\}$, and $\{a\}$ are regular languages for all $a \in A$.

Induction: If L and M are regular languages, then the following languages are also regular: $L \cup M$, $M \cdot L$, and L^*.

For example, the basis case of the definition gives us the following four regular languages over the alphabet $A = \{a, b\}$:

$$\varnothing, \quad \{\Lambda\}, \quad \{a\}, \quad \{b\}.$$

Now let's use the induction part of the definition to construct some more regular lanagues over $\{a, b\}$. Is the language $\{\Lambda, b\}$ regular? Sure. We can write it as the union of the two regular languages $\{\Lambda\}$ and $\{b\}$:

$$\{\Lambda, b\} = \{\Lambda\} \cup \{b\}.$$

Is the language $\{a, ab\}$ regular? Yes. We can write it as the product of the two regular languages $\{a\}$ and $\{\Lambda, b\}$:

$$\{a, ab\} = \{a\} \cdot \{\Lambda, b\}.$$

Is the language $\{\Lambda, b, bb, ..., b^n, ...\}$ regular? Sure. It's just the closure of the regular language $\{b\}$:

$$\{b\}^* = \{\Lambda, b, bb, ..., b^n, ...\}.$$

Here are two more regular languages over $\{a, b\}$, along with factorizations to show the reasons why:

$$\{a, ab, abb, ..., ab^n, ... \} = \{a\} \cdot \{\Lambda, b, bb, ..., b^n, ... \} = \{a\} \cdot \{b\}^*,$$

$$\{\Lambda, a, b, aa, bb, ..., a^n, b^n, ...\} = \{a\}^* \cup \{b\}^*.$$

This little example demonstrates that there are many regular languages to consider. From a computational point of view we want to find algorithms that can recognize whether a string belongs to a regular language. To accomplish this task, we'll introduce a convenient algebraic notation for regular languages.

Regular Expressions

A regular language is often described by means of an algebraic expression called a regular expression. We'll define the regular expressions and then relate them to regular languages. The set of *regular expressions* over an alphabet A is defined inductively as follows, where $+$ and $\cdot$ are binary operations and $*$ is a unary operation:

Basis: $\Lambda, \varnothing$, and a are regular expressions for all $a \in A$.

Induction: If R and S are regular expressions, then the following expressions are also regular: $(R), R + S, R{\cdot}S$, and R^*.

For example, here are a few of the infinitely many regular expressions over the alphabet $A = \{a, b\}$:

$$\Lambda, \quad \varnothing, \quad a, \quad b, \quad \Lambda + b, \quad b^*, \quad a + (b \cdot a), \quad (a + b) \cdot a, \quad a \cdot b^*, \quad a^* + b^*.$$

To avoid using too many parentheses, we assume that the operations have the following hierarchy:

$$* \qquad \text{highest (do it first)},$$

$$\cdot$$

$$+ \qquad \text{lowest (do it last)}.$$

For example, the regular expression

$$a + b \cdot a^*$$

can be written in fully parenthesized form as

$$(a + (b \cdot (a^*))).$$

We'll often use juxtaposition instead of $\cdot$ whenever no confusion arises. For example, we can write the preceding expression as

$$a + ba^*.$$

At this point in the discussion a regular expression is just a string of symbols with no specific meaning or purpose. For each regular expression E we'll associate a regular language $L(E)$ as follows, where A is an alphabet and R and S are any regular expressions:

$$
\begin{aligned}
L(\varnothing) \quad &= \quad \varnothing, \\
L(\Lambda) \quad &= \quad \{\Lambda\}, \\
L(a) \quad &= \quad \{a\} \quad \text{for each } a \in A, \\
L(R + S) \quad &= \quad L(R) \cup L(S), \\
L(R \cdot S) \quad &= \quad L(R) \cdot L(S) \qquad \text{(language product)}, \\
L(R^*) \quad &= \quad L(R)^* \qquad \text{(language closure)}.
\end{aligned}
$$

From this association it is clear that each regular expression represents a regular language and, conversely, each regular language is represented by a regular expression.

EXAMPLE 1. Let's find the language of the regular expression $a + bc^*$. We can evaluate the expression $L(a + bc^*)$ as follows:

$$
\begin{aligned}
L(a + bc^*) &= L(a) \cup L(bc^*) \\
&= L(a) \cup (L(b) \cdot L(c^*)) \\
&= L(a) \cup (L(b) \cdot L(c)^*) \\
&= \{a\} \cup (\{b\} \cdot \{c\}^*) \\
&= \{a\} \cup (\{b\} \cdot \{\Lambda, c, c^2, ..., c^n, ...\}) \\
&= \{a\} \cup \{b, bc, bc^2, ..., bc^n, ...\} \\
&= \{a, b, bc, bc^2, ..., bc^n, ...\}. \quad \blacklozenge
\end{aligned}
$$

Regular expressions give nice descriptive clues to the languages that they represent. For example, the regular expression $a + bc^*$ represents the language containing the single letter a or strings of the form b followed by zero or more occurrences of c.

Sometimes it's an easy matter to find a regular expression for a regular language. For example, the language

$$\{a, b, c\}$$

is represented by the regular expression $a + b + c$. In fact it's easy to find a regular expression for any finite language. Just form the regular expression consisting of the strings in the language separated by + symbols.

Infinite languages are another story. An infinite language might not be regular. We'll see an example of a nonregular language later in this chapter. But many infinite languages are easily seen to be regular. For example, the language

$$\{a, aa, aaa, ..., a^n, ...\}$$

is regular because it can be written as the regular language $\{a\} \cdot \{a\}^*$, which is represented by the regular expression aa^*. The slightly more complicated language

$$\{\Lambda, a, b, ab, abb, abbb, ..., ab^n, ...\}$$

is also regular because it can be represented by the regular expression

$$\Lambda + b + ab^*.$$

Do distinct regular expressions always represent distinct languages? The answer is no. For example, the regular expressions $a + b$ and $b + a$ are different, but they both represent the same language,

$$L(a + b) = L(b + a) = \{a, b\}.$$

We want to equate those regular expressions that represent the same language. We say that regular expressions R and S are *equal* if $L(R) = L(S)$, and we denote this equality by writing the following familiar relation:

$$R = S.$$

For example, we know that $L(a + b) = \{a, b\} = \{b, a\} = L(b + a)$. Therefore we can write $a + b = b + a$. We also have the equality

$$(a + b) + (a + b) = a + b.$$

On the other hand, we have $L(ab) = \{ab\}$ and $L(ba) = \{ba\}$. Therefore $ab \neq ba$. Similarly, $a(b + c) \neq (b + c)a$. So although the expressions might make us think of high school algebra, we must remember that we are talking about regular expressions and languages, not numbers.

There are many general equalities for regular expressions. We'll list a few simple equalities together with some that are not so simple. All the properties can be verified by using properties of languages and sets. We'll assume that R, S, and T denote arbitrary regular expressions.

Properties of Regular Expressions (5.1)

1. (+ properties) $R + T = T + R,$
   $R + \varnothing = \varnothing + R = R,$
   $R + R = R,$
   $(R + S) + T = R + (S + T).$

2. (· properties) $R\varnothing = \varnothing R = \varnothing,$
   $R\Lambda = \Lambda R = R,$
   $(RS)T = R\,(ST).$

3. (Distributive properties) $R(S + T) = RS + RT,$
   $(S + T)R = SR + TR.$

   (Closure properties)

4. $\varnothing^* = \Lambda^* = \Lambda.$

5. $R^* = R^*R^* = (R^*)^* = R + R^*,$
   $R^* = \Lambda + R^* = (\Lambda + R)^* = (\Lambda + R)R^* = \Lambda + RR^*,$
   $R^* = (R + ... + R^k)^*$ \qquad for any $k \geq 1,$
   $R^* = \Lambda + R + ... + R^{k-1} + R^kR^*$ \qquad for any $k \geq 1.$

6. $R^*R = RR^*$.

7. $(R + S)^* = (R^* + S^*)^* = (R^*S^*)^* = (R^*S)^*R^* = R^*(SR^*)^*$.

8. $R(SR)^* = (RS)^*R$.

9. $(R^*S)^* = \Lambda + (R + S)^*S$,
    $(RS^*)^* = \Lambda + R\ (R + S)^*$.

Proof: We'll prove three of the properties and leave the rest as exercises. First we'll prove $R + R = R$ by noticing the following equalities:

$$L(R + R) = L(R) \cup L(R) = L(R).$$

Next, let's prove the distributive property $R\ (S + T) = RS + RT$. The following series of equalities will do the job:

$$
\begin{aligned}
L(R\ (S + T)) &= L(R)\ L(S + T) \\
&= L(R)\ (L(S) \cup L(T)) \\
&= L(R)\ L(S) \cup L(R)\ L(T) \quad \text{(language property)} \\
&= L(RS) \cup L(RT) \\
&= L(RS + RT).
\end{aligned}
$$

Lastly, we'll prove that $R^* = R^*R^*$. Since $L(R^*) = L(R)^*$, we need to show that $L(R)^* = L(R)^*L(R)^*$. Let $x \in L(R)^*$. Then $x = x\ \Lambda \in L(R)^*\ L(R)^*$. Therefore $L(R)^* \subset L(R)^*L(R)^*$. For the other way, suppose $x \in L(R)^*\ L(R)^*$. Then $x = yz$, where $y \in L(R)^*$ and $z \in L(R)^*$. Thus $y \in L(R)^k$ and $z \in L(R)^n$ for some k and n. Therefore $yz \in L(R)^{k+n}$, which says that $x = yz \in L(R)^*$. So $L(R)^*L(R)^* \subset L(R)^*$. Thus $L(R)^* = L(R)^*L(R)^*$, so $R^* = R^*R^*$.   QED.

The properties (5.1) can be used to simplify regular expressions and to prove the equality of two regular expressions. So we have an algebra of regular expressions. For example, suppose that we want to prove the following equality:

$$ba^*(baa^*)^* = b(a + ba)^*.$$

Since both expressions start with the letter b, we'll be done if we prove the simpler equality obtained by cancelling b from both sides:

$$a^*(baa^*)^* = (a + ba)^*.$$

But this equality is an instance of property 7 of (5.1). To why, we'll let $R = a$ and $S = ba$. Then we have

$$(a + ba)^* = (R + S)^* = R^*(SR^*)^* = a^*(baa^*)^*.$$

Therefore the example equation is true. Let's look at a few more examples.

EXAMPLE 2. We'll show that $(\emptyset + a + b)^* = a^*(ba^*)^*$ by starting with the left side as follows:

$$
\begin{aligned}
(\emptyset + a + b)^* &= (a + b)^* & \text{(property 1)} \\
&= a^*(ba^*)^* & \text{(property 7).} \quad \blacklozenge
\end{aligned}
$$

EXAMPLE 3. We'll show that

$$b^*(abb^* + aabb^* + aaabb^*)^* = (b + ab + aab + aaab)^*$$

by starting with the left side and proceeding to the right side.

$$
\begin{aligned}
b^*(abb^* + aabb^* + aaabb^*)^* &= b^*((ab + aab + aaab)b^*)^* & \text{(property 3)} \\
&= (b + ab + aab + aaab)^* & \text{(property 7).} \quad \blacklozenge
\end{aligned}
$$

EXAMPLE 4. We'll show that $R + RS^*S = a^*bS^*$, where $R = b + aa^*b$ and S is any regular expression:

$$
\begin{aligned}
R + RS^*S &= R\Lambda + RS^*S & \text{(property 2)} \\
&= R(\Lambda + S^*S) & \text{(property 3)} \\
&= R(\Lambda + SS^*) & \text{(property 6)} \\
&= RS^* & \text{(property 5)} \\
&= (b + aa^*b)S^* & \text{(definition of } R) \\
&= (\Lambda + aa^*)bS^* & \text{(properties 2 and 3)} \\
&= a^*bS^* & \text{(property 5).} \quad \blacklozenge
\end{aligned}
$$

Exercises

1. Describe the language for each of the following regular expressions.

   a. $a + b$.   b. $a + bc$.   c. $a + b^*$.

   d. $ab^* + c$.   e. $ab^* + bc^*$.   f. $a^*bc^* + ac$.

2. Find a regular expression to describe each of the following languages.

   a. $\{a, b, c\}$.

   b. $\{aa, ab, ac\}$.

c. $\{a, b, ab, ba, abb, baa, ..., ab^n, ba^n, ...\}$.

d. $\{a, aaa, aaaaa, ..., a^{2n+1}, ...\}$.

e. $\{ \Lambda, a, abb, abbbb, ..., ab^{2n}, ...\}$.

f. $\{\Lambda, a, b, c, aa, bb, cc, ..., a^n, b^n, c^n, ...\}$.

g. $\{\Lambda, a, b, ca, bc, cca, bcc, ..., c^na, bc^n, ...\}$.

h. $\{a^{2k} \mid k \in \mathbb{N}\} \cup \{b^{2k+1} \mid k \in \mathbb{N}\}$.

i. $\{a^mbc^n \mid m, n \in \mathbb{N}\}$.

3. Find a regular expression over the alphabet $\{0, 1\}$ to describe the set of all binary numerals without leading zeros (except 0 itself). So the language is the set $\{0, 1, 10, 11, 100, 101, 110, 111, ...\}$.

4. Find a regular expression for each of the following languages over the alphabet $\{a, b\}$.

   a. Strings with even length.

   b. Strings whose length is a multiple of 3.

   c. Strings containing the substring aba.

   d. Strings with an odd number of a's.

5. Simplify each of the following regular expressions.

   a. $\Lambda + ab + abab(ab)^*$.

   b. $aa(b^* + a) + a(ab^* + aa)$.

   c. $a(a + b)^* + aa(a + b)^* + aaa(a + b)^*$.

6. Prove each of the following equalities of regular expressions.

   a. $b + ab^* + aa^*b + aa^*ab^* = a^*(b + ab^*)$.

   b. $a^*(b + ab^*) = b + aa^*b^*$.

   c. $ab^*a(a + bb^*a)^*b = a(b + aa^*b)^*aa^*b$.

7. Prove each of the following properties of regular expressions.

   a. $\varnothing^* = \Lambda^* = \Lambda$.

   b. $R^* = (R^*)^* = R + R^*$.

   c. $R^* = \Lambda + R^* = (\Lambda + R)^* = (\Lambda + R)R^* = \Lambda + RR^*$.

   d. $R^* = (R + ... + R^k)^*$ for any $k \geq 1$.

   e. $R^* = \Lambda + R + ... + R^{k-1} + R^kR^*$ for any $k \geq 1$.

   f. $(R + S)^* = (R^* + S^*)^* = (R^*S^*)^* = (R^*S)^*R^* = R^*(SR^*)^*$.

   g. $R(SR)^* = (RS)^*R$.

   h. $(R^*S)^* = \Lambda + (R + S)^*S$.

8. Answer each of the following questions for the algebra of regular expressions over an alphabet A.

    a. Is there an identity for the + operation?

    b. Is there an identity for the · operation?

    c. Is there a zero for the · operation?

    d. Is there a zero for the + operation?

9. Find regular expressions for each of the following languages over the alphabet $\{a, b\}$.

    a. No string contains the substring aa.

    b. No string contains the substring aaa.

    c. No string contains the substring $aaaa$.

10. Find regular expressions to show that the following statement about cancellation is false: If $R \neq \varnothing$, $S \neq \Lambda$, $T \neq \Lambda$, and $RS = RT$, then $S = T$.

11. Let R and S be regular expressions, and let X represent a variable in the following equation:

$$X = RX + S.$$

    a. Show that $X = R^*S$ is a solution to the given equation.

    b. Find two distinct solutions to the equation $X = a^*X + ab$.

    c. Show that if $\Lambda \notin L(R)$, then the solution in part (a) is unique.

5.2 Finite Automata

We've described regular languages in terms of regular expressions. Now let's see whether we can solve the recognition problem for regular languages. In other words, let's see whether we can find algorithms to recognize the strings from a regular language. To do this, we need to discuss some basic computing machines called finite automata.

Deterministic Finite Automata

Informally, a *deterministic finite automaton* over a finite alphabet A can be thought of as a finite directed graph with the property that each node emits one labeled edge for each distinct element of A. The nodes are called *states*. There is one special state called the *start* or *initial state*, and there is at least one state called a *final state*. We use the abbreviation DFA to stand for deterministic finite automaton.

For example, the labeled graph in Figure 5.1 represents a DFA over the alphabet $A = \{a, b\}$ with start state 0 and final state 3. We'll always indicate the start state by writing the word *Start* with an arrow pointing at it. Final states are indicated by a double circle.

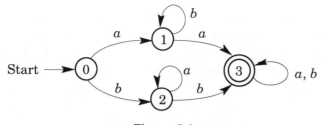

Figure 5.1

The single arrow out of state 3 labeled with a, b is shorthand for two arrows from state 3 going to the same place, one labeled a and one labeled b. It's easy to check that this digraph represents a DFA over $\{a, b\}$ because there is a start state and a final state, and each state emits exactly two arrows, one labeled with a and one labeled with b.

At this point in the discussion a DFA is just a syntactic object without any semantics. We need to say what it means for a DFA to accept or reject a string in A^*. A DFA *accepts* a string w in A^* if there is a path from the start state to some final state such that w is the concatenation of the labels on the edges of the path. Otherwise, the DFA *rejects* w. The set of all strings accepted by a DFA M is called the *language* of M and is denoted by

$$L(M).$$

For example, in the DFA in Figure 5.1 has a path 0, 1, 1, 3 with edges labeled a, b, a. Since 0 is the start state and 3 is a final state, we conclude that the DFA accepts the string aba. The DFA also accepts the string $baaabab$ by traveling along the path 0, 2, 2, 2, 2, 3, 3, 3. It's easy to see that the DFA accepts infinitely many strings because we can traverse the loop out of and into states 1, 2, or 3 any number of times. The DFA also rejects infinitely many strings. For example, any string of the form ab^n is rejected for any natural number n.

Now we're in position to state a remarkable result that is due to the mathematician and logician Stephen Kleene. Kleene [1956] showed that the languages recognized by DFAs are exactly the regular languages. We'll state the result for the record:

> The class of regular languages is exactly the same as the   (5.2)
> class of languages accepted by DFAs.

In fact, there is an algorithm to transform any regular expression into a DFA, and there is an algorithm to transform any DFA into a regular expression. We'll get to them soon enough. But for now let's look at some examples.

EXAMPLE 1. We'll give DFAs to recognize the regular languages represented by the regular expressions $(a + b)^*$ and $a(a + b)^*$ over the alphabet $A = \{a, b\}$. The language for the regular expression $(a + b)^*$ is the set $\{a, b\}^*$ of all strings over $\{a, b\}$, and it can be recognized by the following DFA:

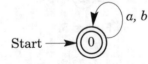

The language for the regular expression $a(a + b)^*$ is the set of all strings over A that begin with a, and it can be recognized by the following DFA:

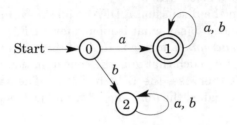

Notice that state 2 acts as an error state. It's necessary because of the requirement that each state of a DFA must emit one labeled arrow for each symbol of the alphabet.

Some programming languages define an *identifier* as a string beginning with a letter followed by any number of letters or digits. If we let a and b stand for letter and digit, respectively, then the set of all identifiers can be described by the regular expression $a(a + b)^*$ and thus be recognized by the preceding DFA.   ♦

EXAMPLE 2. Suppose we want to build a DFA to recognize the regular language represented by the regular expression $(a + b)^*abb$ over the alphabet $A = \{a, b\}$. The language is the set of strings that begin with anything, but must end with the string abb. The diagram in Figure 5. 2 shows a DFA to recognize this language. Try it out on a few strings. For example, does it recognize abb and $bbaabb$?   ♦

Example 2 brings up two questions: How was the DFA in Figure 5.2 created? How do we know that its language is represented by $(a + b)^*abb$? At this point it's a hit-or-miss operation to answer these questions. But we will

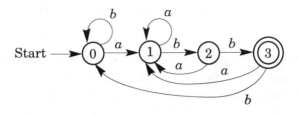

Figure 5.2

soon see that there is an algorithm to construct a DFA, and there is also an algorithm to find the language of a DFA.

The graphical definition of a DFA is an important visual aid to help us understand finite automata. But we can also represent a DFA by a *state transition function*, which we'll denote by T, where any state transition of the form

$$i \xrightarrow{\;a\;} j$$

is represented by

$$T(i, a) = j.$$

When a DFA is represented in this form, it can be easily programmed as a recognizer of strings. In fact, we'll soon give an interpreter for DFAs that are written in this form.

Nondeterministic Finite Automata

A machine that is similar to a DFA, but less restrictive, is a *nondeterministic finite automaton* (NFA for short). An NFA over an alphabet A is a finite directed graph with each node having zero or more edges, where each edge is labeled either with a letter from A or with Λ. Repetitions are allowed on edges emitted from the same node, so nondeterminism can occur. If an edge is labeled with the empty string Λ, then we can travel the edge without consuming an input letter. There is a single start state and one or more final states. Acceptance and rejection are defined as for DFAs. That is, an NFA *accepts* a string w in A^* if there is a path from the start state to some final state such that w is the concatenation of the labels on the edges of the path. Otherwise, the NFA *rejects* w.

NFAs are usually simpler than DFAs because they don't need an edge out of each node for each letter of the alphabet. Now we're in position to state a remarkable result of Rabin and Scott [1959], which tells us that NFAs recognize a very special class of languages—the regular languages:

The class of regular languages is exactly the same as the   (5.3)
class of languages accepted by NFAs.

Combining (5.3) with Kleene's result (5.2), we can say that NFAs and DFAs recognize the same class of languages, the regular languages. In other words, we have the following statements about regular languages:

Regular expressions represent the regular languages.
DFAs recognize the regular languages.
NFAs recognize the regular languages.

If we examine the definitions for DFA and NFA, it's easy to see that any DFA is an NFA. Later on, we'll give an algorithm that transforms any NFA into a DFA that recognizes the same regular language.

For now, let's get an idea of the utility of NFAs by considering the simple regular expression $a*a$. An NFA for $a*a$ can be drawn as follows:

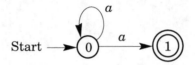

This NFA is certainly not a DFA because two edges are emitted from state 0, both labeled with the letter a. Thus there is nondeterminism. Another reason this NFA is not a DFA is that state 1 does not emit any edges.

We can also draw a DFA for $a*a$. If we remember the equality $a*a = aa*$, then it's an easy matter to construct the following DFA:

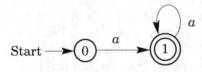

Sometimes it's much easier to find an NFA for a regular expression than it is to find a DFA for the expression. The next example should convince you.

EXAMPLE 3. We'll draw two NFAs to recognize the language of the regular expression $ab + a*a$. The NFA in Figure 5.3 has a Λ edge, which allows us to travel to state 2 without consuming an input letter. Thus $a*a$ will be recognized on the path from state 0 to state 2 to state 3.

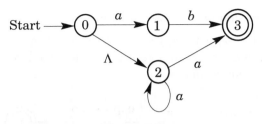

Figure 5.3

The NFA in Figure 5.4 also recognizes the same language. Perhaps it's easier to see this by considering the equality $ab + a^*a = ab + aa^*$.

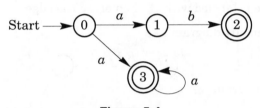

Figure 5.4

Both NFAs are simple and easy to construct from the given regular expression. Now try to construct a DFA for the regular expression $ab + a^*a$.   ◆

As with DFAs, we can represent an NFA by a *state transition function*. Since there may be nondeterminism, we'll let the values of the function be sets of states. For example, if there are no edges from state k labeled with a, we'll write

$$T(k, a) = \varnothing.$$

If there are three edges from state k, all labeled with a, going to states i, j, and k, we'll write

$$T(k, a) = \{i, j, k\}.$$

We'll soon give an interpreter for NFAs that are written in this form.

Transforming Regular Expressions into Finite Automata

Now we're going to look at a simple algorithm that we can use to transform any regular expression into a finite automaton that accepts the regular language of the given regular expression.

Regular Expression to Finite Automaton   (5.4)

Given a regular expression, we start the algorithm with a machine that has a start state, a single final state, and an edge labeled with the given regular expression as follows:

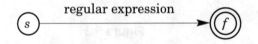

Now transform this machine into a DFA or an NFA by applying the following rules until all edges are labeled with either a letter or Λ:

1. If an edge is labeled with ∅, then erase the edge.

2. Transform any diagram like

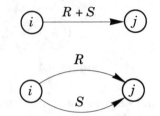

into the diagram

3. Transform any diagram like

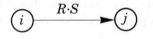

into the diagram

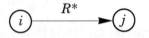

4. Transform any diagram like

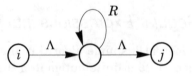

into the diagram

End of Algorithm

EXAMPLE 4. To construct an NFA for $a^* + ab$, we'll start with the diagram

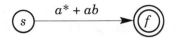

Next we apply rule 2 to obtain the following NFA:

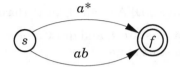

Next we'll apply rule 4 to a^* to obtain the following NFA:

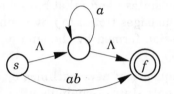

Finally, we apply rule 3 to ab to obtain the desired NFA for $a^* + ab$:

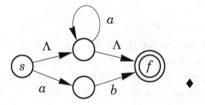

Algorithm (5.4) has a shortcoming when it comes to implementation because rule 2 can cause many edges to be emitted from the same state. For example, if the algorithm is applied to an edge labeled with $(a + b) + c$, then two applications of rule 2 cause three new edges to be emitted from the same state. So it's easy to see that there is no bound on the number of edges that might be emitted from NFA states constructed by using (5.4). In Section 5.3 we'll give an alternative algorithm that's easy to implement because it limits the number of edges emitted from each node to at most 2.

Transforming Finite Automata into Regular Expressions

Now let's look at the opposite problem of transforming a finite automaton into a regular expression that represents the regular language accepted by the machine. Starting with either a DFA or an NFA, the algorithm performs a series of transformations into new machines, where these new machines have edges that may be labeled with regular expressions. The algorithm stops when a machine is obtained that has two states, a start state and a final state, and there is a single edge between them labeled with the regular expression that represents the language of the original automaton.

Finite Automaton to Regular Expression   (5.5)

Assume that we have a DFA or an NFA. Perform the following steps:

1. Create a new start state s, and draw a new edge labeled with Λ from s to the original start state.

2. Create a new final state f, and draw new edges labeled with Λ from all the original final states to f.

3. For each pair of states i and j that have more than one edge from i to j, replace all the edges from i to j by a single edge labeled with the regular expression formed by the sum of the labels on each of the edges from i to j.

4. Construct a sequence of new machines by eliminating one state at a time until the only states remaining are s and the f. As each state is eliminated, a new machine is constructed from the previous machine as follows:

Eliminate State k

For convenience we'll let old(i, j) denote the label on edge $\langle i, j \rangle$ of the current machine. If there is no edge $\langle i, j \rangle$, then set old$(i, j) = \varnothing$. Now for each pair of edges $\langle i, k \rangle$ and $\langle k, j \rangle$, where $i \neq k$ and $j \neq k$, calculate a new edge label, new(i, j), as follows:

$$\text{new}(i, j) = \text{old}(i, j) + \text{old}(i, k)\, \text{old}(k, k)^*\, \text{old}(k, j).$$

For all other edges $\langle i, j \rangle$ where $i \neq k$ and $j \neq k$, set

$$\text{new}(i, j) = \text{old}(i, j).$$

The states of the new machine are those of the current machine with state k eliminated. The edges of the new machine are the edges $\langle i, j \rangle$ for which label new(i, j) has been calculated.

After eliminating all states except s and f, we wind up with a two-state machine with the single edge $\langle s, f \rangle$ labeled with the regular expression new(s, f), which represents the regular language accepted by the original finite automaton.

End of Algorithm

Let's walk through a simple example to demonstrate the algorithm. Suppose we start with the DFA in Figure 5.5.

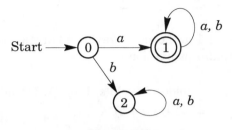

Figure 5.5

The first three steps of (5.5) transform this machine into the following machine, where s is the start state and f is the final state:

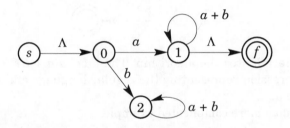

Now let's eliminate the states 0, 1, and 2. We can eliminate state 2 without any work because there are no paths passing through state 2 between states that are adjacent to state 2. In other words, new(i, j) = old(i, j) for each pair of states $\langle i, j \rangle$, where $i \neq 2$ and $j \neq 2$. This gives us the machine

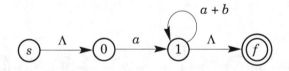

Now we'll eliminate state 0 from this machine by adding a new edge $\langle s, 1 \rangle$ that is labeled with the following regular expression:

$$
\begin{aligned}
\text{new}(s, 1) &= \text{old}(s, 1) + \text{old}(s, 0)\,\text{old}(0, 0)^*\,\text{old}(0, 1) \\
&= \varnothing + \Lambda\,\varnothing^*\,a \\
&= a.
\end{aligned}
$$

Therefore we delete state 0 and add the new edge $\langle s, 1 \rangle$ labeled with a to obtain the following machine:

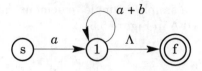

Next we eliminate state 1 in the same way by adding a new edge $\langle s, f \rangle$ labeled with the following regular expression:

$$
\begin{aligned}
\text{new}(s, f) &= \text{old}(s, f) + \text{old}(s, 1)\, \text{old}(1, 1)^*\, \text{old}(1, f) \\
&= \varnothing + a(a + b)^*\Lambda \\
&= a(a + b)^*.
\end{aligned}
$$

Therefore we delete state 1 and label the edge $\langle s, f \rangle$ with $a(a + b)^*$ to obtain the following machine:

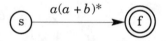

This machine terminates the algorithm. The label $a(a + b)^*$ on edge $\langle s, f \rangle$ is the regular expression representing the regular language of the original DFA given in Figure 5.5.

Now let's do a more complicated example.

EXAMPLE 5. We'll verify that the regular expression $(a + b)^*abb$ does indeed represent the regular language accepted by the DFA in Figure 5.2 from Example 2. We start the algorithm by attaching start state s and final state f to the DFA in Figure 5.2 to obtain the following machine:

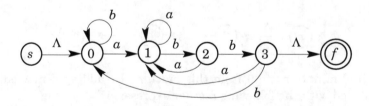

Now we need to eliminate the internal states. As we construct new edge labels, we'll simplify the regular expressions as we go. First we'll eliminate the state 0. To eliminate state 0, we construct the following new edges:

$$
\text{new}(s, 1) = \varnothing + \Lambda b^*a = b^*a,
$$
$$
\text{new}(3, 1) = a + bb^*a = (\Lambda + bb^*)a = b^*a.
$$

With these new edges we eliminate state 0 and obtain the following machine:

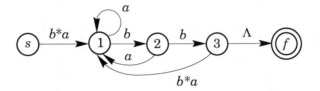

The states can be eliminated in any order. For example, we'll eliminate state 3 next, which forces us to create the following new edges:

$$\text{new}(2, f) = \varnothing + b\; \varnothing^*\Lambda = b,$$
$$\text{new}(2, 1) = a + b\; \varnothing^*b^*a = a + bb^*a = (\Lambda + bb^*)a = b^*a.$$

With these new edges we eliminate state 3 and obtain the following machine:

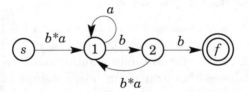

Next, we'll eliminate state 2, which forces us to create the following new edges:

$$\text{new}(1, f) = \varnothing + b\; \varnothing^*b = bb,$$
$$\text{new}(1, 1) = a + b\; \varnothing^*b^*a = a + bb^*a = (\Lambda + bb^*)a = b^*a.$$

With these new edges we eliminate state 2 and obtain the following machine:

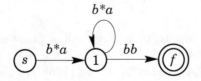

Finally we remove state 1 by creating a new edge

$$
\begin{aligned}
\text{new}(s, f) \;&=\; \varnothing + b^*a(b^*a)^*bb \\
&=\; b^*(ab^*)^*abb \qquad \text{(by 8 of (5.1))} \\
&=\; (a + b)^*abb \qquad \text{(by 7 of (5.1)).}
\end{aligned}
$$

So we obtain the last machine with the desired regular expression for the DFA in Figure 5.2:

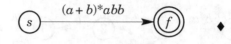

The process of constructing a regular expression from a finite automaton can produce some complex regular expressions. If we remove the states in different orders, then we might obtain different regular expressions, some of which might be more complex than others. So the algebraic properties of regular expressions (5.1) are nice tools to simplify these complex regular expressions. As we've indicated in the example, it's better to simplify the regular expressions at each stage of the process to keep things manageable.

Finite Automata as Output Devices

The automata that we've discussed so far have only a limited output capability to indicate the acceptance or rejection of an input string. We want to introduce two classic models for finite automata that have output capability. We'll consider machines that transform input strings into output strings. These machines are like DFAs, except that we associate an output symbol with each state or with each state transition, and there are no final states because we are not interested in acceptance or rejection.

The first model, invented by Mealy [1955], is called a *Mealy machine*. It associates an output letter with each transition. For example, if the output associated with the edge labeled with the letter a is x, we'll write a/x on that edge. A state transition for a Mealy machine can be pictured as follows:

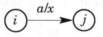

In a Mealy machine an output always takes place during a transition of states.

The second model, invented by Moore [1956], is called a *Moore machine*. It associates an output letter with each state. For example, if the output associated with state i is x, we'll always write i/x inside the state circle. A typical state transition for a Moore machine can be pictured as follows:

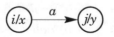

Each time a state is entered, an output takes place. So the first output always occurs as soon as the machine is started.

One way to remember the output structure of the two machines is to associate the word "mean" with "Mealy," where the output occurs at the "mean" or "middle" of two states. It turns out that Mealy and Moore machines are equivalent. In other words, any problem that is solvable by one type of machine can also be solved by the other type of machine.

Let's look at an example problem, which we'll solve both with a Mealy machine and with a Moore machine. Suppose we want to compute the number of substrings of the form

$$bab$$

that occur in an arbitrary input string over the alphabet {a, b}. For example, there are three such substrings in the string

$$ababababaababb.$$

A Mealy machine to solve this problem is given by the following graph:

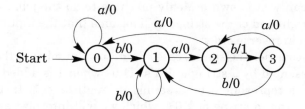

The output of any Mealy machine has the same length as the input string. For example, the output of this Mealy machine for the sample string

$$ababab aababb$$

is

$$0\ 0\ 0\ 1\ 0\ 1\ 0\ 0\ 0\ 0\ 1\ 0.$$

The problem can also be solved by the following Moore machine:

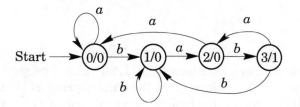

Since the start state always causes an initial output, the length of the output string for a Moore machine is always one more than the length of the input string. For example, the output for the sample string

$$abababaababb$$

is

$$0\,0\,0\,0\,1\,0\,1\,0\,0\,0\,0\,1\,0.$$

We can count the number of 1's in the output string to obtain the number of occurrences of the substring *bab*.

From a practical point of view we might wish to let some output symbol mean that no output takes place. For example, if we replaced the output symbol 0 with Λ in the preceding machines, then the output for the sample string would be the string 111. Let's look at a few more examples.

EXAMPLE 6 (*The Successor Function for Binary Numbers*). Suppose we represent a natural number in the form of a binary string. To compute the successor, we need to add 1. Using the standard addition algorithm, which involves carrying, we can write down a Mealy machine to do the job. Since addition starts on the right end of the string, we'll assume that the input is the binary representation in reverse order.

We must consider the special case of a natural number of the form $2^k - 1$, which is represented by a string of k 1's. Thus when 1 is added to $2^k - 1$, we get 2^k, which is represented by a string of length $k + 1$. In this case our machine will output a string of k 0's, which we will interpret as the number 2^k. With this assumption the Mealy machine looks like the following, where state 1 is the carry state and state 2 is the no-carry state:

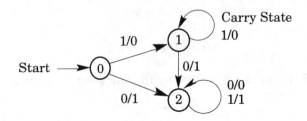

For example, let's find the successor of 13. The binary representation of 13 is 1101. So we take its reverse, which is 1011, as input. The sequence of states for this input is 1, 2, 2, 2, which gives the output string 0111. The reverse of this string is 1110, which is the binary representation of 14.   ◆

EXAMPLE 7 (*A Simple Vending Machine*). Suppose we have a simple vending machine that allows the user to pick from two 10-cent items A and B. To simplify things, the slot will accept only dimes. There are four inputs to the machine: d (dime), a (select item A), b (select item B), and r (return coins). The outputs will be n (do nothing), A (vend item A), B (vend item B), and d (dime). A Mealy machine to model this simple vending machine can be pictured as follows:

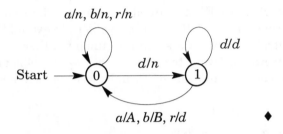

EXAMPLE 8 (*A Simple Traffic Signal*). Suppose we have a simple traffic intersection, where a north-south highway intersects with an east-west highway. We'll assume that the east-west highway always has a green light unless some north-south traffic is detected by sensors. When north-south traffic is detected, after a certain time delay the signals change and stay that way for a fixed period of time. The input symbols will be 0 (no traffic detected) and 1 (traffic detected). Let G, Y, and R mean green, yellow, and red, respectively. The output symbols will be GR, YR, RG, and RY, where the first letter is the color of the east-west light and the second letter is the color of the north-south light. A Moore machine to model this simple traffic intersection can be described as follows:

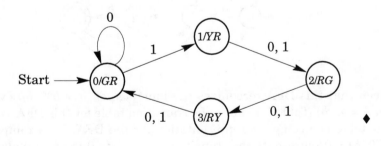

Mealy machines appear to be more useful than Moore machines. But problems like traffic signal control have nice Moore machine solutions because each state is associated with a new output configuration. The exercises include some more problems.

Representing and Executing Finite Automata

We've seen that the graphical definition of finite automata is an important visual aid to help us understand and construct the machines. In the next few paragraphs we'll introduce some other ways to represent finite automata that will help us describe algorithms to execute DFAs and NFAs.

DFA Representation and Execution

We've seen that when a DFA has an edge from i to j labeled with a, we can denote it by writing $T(i, a) = j$. It will be convenient to extend this idea so that T takes an arbitrary string as a second argument rather than just a single letter. In other words, we want to define $T(i, w)$, where w is any string. A recursive definition of this extension of T can be written as follows:

> *Basis:* $T(i, \Lambda) = i.$
>
> *Induction:* $T(i, a \cdot s) = T(T(i, a), s).$

This gives us an easy way to see whether a string w is accepted by a DFA. Just evaluate $T(i, w)$, where i is the start state of the DFA. If the resulting state is final, then w is accepted by the DFA. Otherwise, w is rejected.

   To construct a program to execute a DFA, it's useful represent the transition function in a tabular form called a *transition table*. The rows are labeled with the states and the columns are labeled with the elements of the alphabet. The start state and the final states are also labeled.

   For example, suppose we have the following DFA, which is the same as the DFA in Figure 5.2:

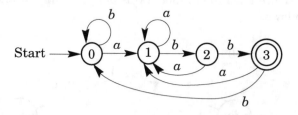

We've seen that this DFA recognizes the language of $(a + b)^*abb$ over the alphabet $A = \{a, b\}$. Table 5.1 shows the transition table for this DFA.

   This table is a complete representation for the DFA. For example, the value $T(0, b) = 0$ represents the transition from state 0 to state 0 along the edge labeled with b. Of course, we can also use the table to compute values of the extended transition function. For example, we can compute $T(0, aab)$ as follows:

$$T(0, aab) = T(T(0, a), ab) = T(1, ab) = T(T(1, a), b) = T(1, b) = 2.$$

	T	a	b
start	0	1	0
	1	1	2
	2	1	3
final	3	1	0

Table 5.1   Transition Table

Since state 2 is not a final state, it follows that *aab* is rejected by the DFA.

When we discuss DFAs in general terms, it is sometimes convenient to represent a DFA by listing five things: the set of states, the alphabet, the transition function or graph, the start state, and the set of final states. Traditionally, these five items are listed as a 5-tuple as follows:

⟨states, alphabet, transition function, start state, final states⟩.

For example, someone may say, "Let ⟨S, A, T, s, F⟩ be a DFA." We can then assume that S is the set of states, A is the alphabet, T is the transition function, s is the start state, and F is the set of final states. We can also use the 5-tuple notation to represent a particular DFA. For example, we can represent the DFA described in Table 5.1 by the 5-tuple

$$\langle \{0, 1, 2, 3\}, \{a, b\}, T, 0, \{3\} \rangle,$$

where T represents the transition function.

We can also represent any DFA as an algebraic structure. This kind of representation can help us discover a general algorithm for executing any DFA. Suppose we have a DFA ⟨S, A, T, s, F⟩. We can represent this DFA as an algebra as follows:

Carriers: A, A^*, S, Boolean.   (5.6)

Operations: $s \in S$,
                        $F \subset S$,
                        $T : S \times A \to S$,
                        accept : $A^* \to$ Boolean,
                        path : $S \times A^* \to$ Boolean.

Axioms: accept(w)   =   path(s, w),
                  path(k, Λ)   =   **if** k is a final state **then** true **else** false,
                  path($k, a{\cdot}t$)   =   path($T(k, a), t$).

The axioms are the important part because they form the basis for an algorithm to recognize the language of any DFA. In other words, for any DFA and any string w the value accept(w) is true if w is accepted by the DFA and false if w is rejected. Let's look at a particularly simple implementation of the algorithm as a logic program.

EXAMPLE 9 (*A Logic Program Interpreter for DFAs*). We'll write a logic program to compute any DFA. The axioms in (5.6) return Boolean values, which makes it easy to write them as logic program clauses. We'll represent the transition function T by facts of the following form:

$$t(\text{state, letter, nextstate}) \leftarrow$$

where $T(\text{state, letter}) = \text{nextstate}$. To denote that a state is final we'll write

$$\text{final(state)} \leftarrow.$$

For example, Table 5.1 can be represented by the following facts:

$$t(0, a, 1) \leftarrow$$
$$t(0, b, 0) \leftarrow$$
$$t(1, a, 1) \leftarrow$$
$$t(1, b, 2) \leftarrow$$
$$t(2, a, 1) \leftarrow$$
$$t(2, b, 3) \leftarrow$$
$$t(3, a, 1) \leftarrow$$
$$t(3, b, 0) \leftarrow$$
$$\text{final}(3) \leftarrow.$$

The main part of the logic program for a DFA consists of the following three clauses, where all arguments beginning with capital letters are variables:

$$\text{accept}(W) \leftarrow \text{path}(0, W)$$
$$\text{path}(K, \Lambda) \leftarrow \text{final}(K)$$
$$\text{path}(K, \text{Head} \cdot \text{Tail}) \leftarrow t(K, \text{Head}, M), \text{path}(M, \text{Tail}).$$

For example, to test whether the string $aaab$ is accepted by the DFA, we would write the following goal:

$$\leftarrow \text{accept}(aaab).$$

If the logic language does not support strings, then we could use lists to represent each string. In this case the second and third clauses of the program would be written as follows:

$$\text{path}(K, \langle \rangle) \leftarrow \text{final}(K)$$
$$\text{path}(K, \text{Head} :: \text{Tail}) \leftarrow t(K, \text{Head}, M), \text{path}(M, \text{Tail}).$$

Then the goal to test the string *aaab* would be written as follows:

$$\leftarrow \text{accept}(\langle a, a, a, b \rangle). \quad \blacklozenge$$

NFA Representation and Execution

Just as we did with DFAs, we can associate a transition table with any NFA. Recall that the transition function for an NFA returns a set of states because of the nondeterminism. For example, $T(k, b) = \varnothing$ if there are no edges from state k labeled with b. The notation $T(k, a) = \{i, j, k\}$ means that three edges are emitted from state k, all labeled with a, pointing at states i, j, and k.

Now we can construct a transition table for any NFA. For example, suppose we have the following NFA:

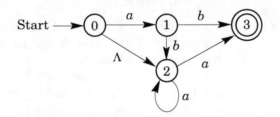

The transition table for this NFA is pictured as follows:

T		a	b	Λ
start	0	{1}	$\varnothing$	{2}
	1	$\varnothing$	{2,3}	$\varnothing$
	2	{2,3}	$\varnothing$	$\varnothing$
final	3	$\varnothing$	$\varnothing$	$\varnothing$

For example, we have $T(2, a) = \{2, 3\}$ because state 2 emits two edges labeled with a, one going to state 2 and one going to state 3.

We can represent an NFA as a 5-tuple having the same form as a DFA:

⟨states, alphabet, transition function, start state, final states⟩.

The only difference is that the transition function for an NFA returns values that are sets of states because there may be nondeterminism.

We can also represent any NFA as an algebraic structure. This kind of representation can help us discover a general algorithm for executing any NFA. Suppose we have an NFA ⟨S, A, T, s, F⟩. We can represent this NFA as an algebra as follows:

Carriers:	A, A^*, S, power(S), Boolean.
Operations:	$s \in S$,
	$F \subset S$,
	$T : S \times A \cup \{\Lambda\} \rightarrow$ power(S),
	accept : $A^* \rightarrow$ Boolean,
	path : $S \times A^* \rightarrow$ Boolean,

Axioms: accept(w) = path(s, w),

path(k, Λ) = **if** k is final **or** a final state is reachable from k by
following Λ edges
then true **else** false,

path($k, a \cdot t$) = **if** there is $m \in T(k, a)$ such that path(m, t) = true
or there is $m \in T(k, \Lambda)$ such that path($m, a \cdot t$) = true
then true **else** false.

The rather complicated-looking equation for path($k, a \cdot t$) is necessary to allow for the nondeterminism that may take place either by having more than one edge labeled with the same letter emitted from state k or by traversing a Λ edge from state k without consuming an input letter.

The next example shows how an NFA interpreter can be implemented with a very simple logic program.

EXAMPLE 10 (*A Logic Program Interpreter for NFAs*). It's almost as easy to program an NFA in logic as a DFA. We'll represent the transition function T by facts of the form

t(state, letter, nextstate) ←,

where nextstate ∈ T(state, letter). To denote that a state is final, we'll write

final(state) ←.

For example, suppose we have the following NFA table:

	T	a	b	Λ
start	0	{1, 2}	$\varnothing$	{1}
	1	$\varnothing$	{2}	$\varnothing$
final	2	{2}	$\varnothing$	$\varnothing$

The facts to represent this table are listed as follows, where there are two facts to take care of the table value $T(0, a) = \{1, 2\}$:

$$t(0, a, 1) \leftarrow$$
$$t(0, a, 2) \leftarrow$$
$$t(0, \Lambda, 1) \leftarrow$$
$$t(1, b, 2) \leftarrow$$
$$t(2, a, 2) \leftarrow$$
$$\text{final}(2) \leftarrow.$$

The main part of the logic program for any NFA consists of the following four clauses, where all arguments beginning with capital letters are variables:

$$\text{accept}(W) \leftarrow \text{path}(0, W)$$
$$\text{path}(K, \Lambda) \leftarrow \text{final}(K)$$
$$\text{path}(K, \text{Head} \cdot \text{Tail}) \leftarrow t(K, \text{Head}, M), \text{path}(M, \text{Tail})$$
$$\text{path}(K, X) \leftarrow t(K, \Lambda, M), \text{path}(M, X).$$

The last clause is necessary to follow a Λ edge without consuming any input. For example, the letter b is accepted by the NFA by traveling along a Λ edge. So the fourth clause does the trick. The computation to recognize b consists of the following sequence of goals:

$$\leftarrow \text{accept}(b)$$
$$\leftarrow \text{path}(0, b)$$
$$\leftarrow t(0, \Lambda, M), \text{path}(M, b)$$
$$\leftarrow \text{path}(1, b)$$
$$\leftarrow t(1, b, M), \text{path}(M, \Lambda)$$
$$\leftarrow \text{path}(2, \Lambda)$$
$$\text{Yes.}$$

If the logic language doesn't support strings, then we could use lists to represent each string. In this case we can replace all occurrences of Λ by ⟨ ⟩ and all occurrences of Head · Tail by Head :: Tail. Then the goal to test the string *abaa* would look something like the following:

$$\leftarrow \text{accept}(\langle a, b, a, a \rangle). \quad \blacklozenge$$

Exercises

1. Write down the transition function for the following DFA:

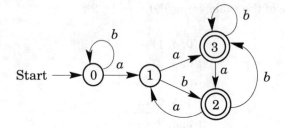

2. Use your wits to construct a DFA for each of the following regular expressions.

    a. *a + b*.   b. *a + bc*.   c. *a + b**.

    d. *ab* + c*.   e. *ab* + bc**.   f. *a*bc* + ac*.

3. Suppose we need a DFA to recognize decimal representations of rational numbers with no repeating decimal patterns. We can represent the strings by the following regular expression, where *d* represents a decimal digit and the vertical line "|" denotes the usual + for regular expressions, since + is now used as the arithmetic plus sign:

$$(- \mid \Lambda \mid +)dd^*.dd^*.$$

    Find a DFA for this regular expression.

4. Write down the transition function for the following NFA:

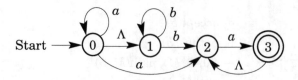

5. Use your wits to construct an NFA for each of the following regular expressions.

    a. *a*bc* + ac*.   b. *(a + b)*a*.   c. *a* + ab*.

6. For each of the following regular expressions, use (5.4) to construct an NFA.

   a. $(ab)^*$.   b. a^*b^*.   c. $(a + b)^*$.   d. $a^* + b^*$.

7. Show why Step 4 of (5.4) can't be simplified to the following: Transform any diagram like

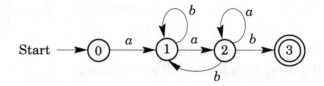

   into

   Hint: Look at the NFA obtained for the regular expression a^*b^*.

8. Given the following NFA:

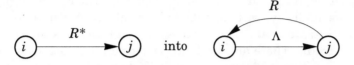

   Use algorithm (5.5) to find two regular expressions for the language accepted by the NFA as follows.

   a. Delete state 1 before deleting state 2.

   b. Delete state 2 before deleting state 1.

   c. Prove that the regular expressions obtained in parts (a) and (b) are equal.

9. Use algorithm (5.5) to find a regular expression for the language accepted by the following NFA:

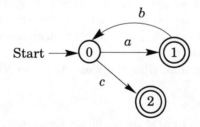

10. Suppose we have a vending machine with two kinds of soda pop, A and B, costing 20 cents each. (It's an old fashioned machine from the 1970s.) Use the following input alphabet: n (nickel), d (dime), q (quarter), a (select A), b (select B), and r (return coins). For the output, use strings over the alphabet $\{c, n, d, q, A, B, \Lambda\}$, where c denotes the coins inserted so far and Λ denotes no output. Assume also that the message "correct

change only" is off. For example, if the input is qa, then the output should be a string like An, which represents a can of A soda and five cents change. Construct a Mealy machine to model the behavior of this machine.

11. Suppose there are traffic signals at the intersection of two highways, an east-west highway and a north-south highway. The east-west highway is the major highway, with signals for through traffic and left-turn lanes with left-turn signals. The north-south highway has signals only for through traffic. There are two kinds of sensors to indicate left turn traffic on the east-west highway and to indicate regular traffic on the north-south highway. Once a signal light turns green in response to a sensor, it stays green for only a finite period of time. Priority is given to the left-turn lanes when there is left-turn traffic and north-south traffic. Construct a Moore machine to model the behavior of the traffic lights.

5.3   Constructing Efficient Finite Automata

In this section we'll see how any regular expression can be automatically transformed into an efficient DFA that recognizes the regular language of the given expression. The construction will be in three parts. First, we transform a regular expression into an NFA. Next, we transform the NFA into a DFA. Finally, we transform the DFA into an efficient DFA having the minimum number of states. So let's begin.

Another Regular Expression to NFA Algorithm

In the preceding section we gave an algorithm to transform a regular expression into an NFA. The algorithm was easy to understand but not so easy to implement efficiently. Here we'll give a more mechanical algorithm that has an efficient implementation.

The following algorithm will always construct an NFA with the following properties:

> There is exactly one final state with no edges emitted.
> Every nonfinal state emits either one or two edges.

These properties allow the algorithm to be efficiently implemented because each entry of the transition table for an NFA constructed by the algorithm is a set consisting of at most two states. Let's get to the algorithm, which is due to Thompson [1968]:

Regular Expression to NFA (5.7)

Apply the following rules inductively to any regular expression.
The letters s and f represent the start state and the final state.

1. Construct an NFA of the following form for each occurrence of the symbol $\emptyset$ in the regular expression:

   The final state can never be reached. Thus the empty language is accepted by this NFA.

2. Construct an NFA of the following form for each occurrence of the symbol Λ in the regular expression:

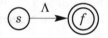

3. Construct an NFA of the following form for each occurrence of a letter x in the regular expression:

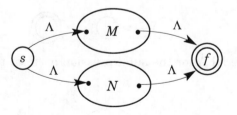

4. Let M and N be NFAs constructed by this algorithm for the regular expressions R and S, respectively. The next three rules show how to construct the NFAs for the regular expressions $R + S$, $R{\cdot}S$, and R^*.

   a. The NFA for $R + S$ has the following form, where the dots indicate the previous start and final states of M and N:

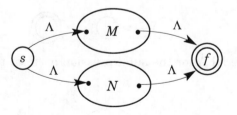

   b. The NFA for $R{\cdot}S$ has the following form, where the dot combines the final state of M and the start state of N into a single state, s is the start state of M, and f is the final state of N:

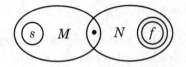

c. The NFA for R^* has the following form, where the dots are the start and final states of M:

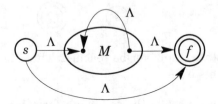

End of Algorithm

The key to applying algorithm (5.7) is to construct the little NFAs first and work in a bottom-up fashion to the bigger ones. Here's an example.

EXAMPLE 1. We'll use (5.7) to construct an NFA for the regular expression a^* $+ ab$. Since the letter a occurs twice and b occurs once in the expression, we need to construct three little NFAs as follows:

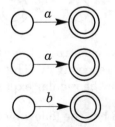

We construct the NFA for the subexpression ab from the latter two little NFAs as follows:

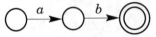

We construct the NFA for the subexpression a^* from the first little NFA as follows:

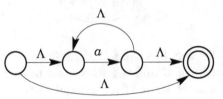

Now we construct the NFA for the expression $a^* + ab$ from the preceding two NFAs to get the desired result:

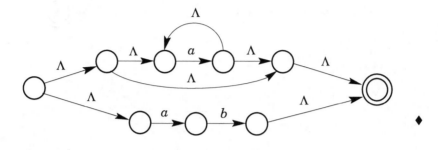

Transforming an NFA into a DFA

We now have an automatic process to transform any regular expression into an NFA. Since NFAs have fewer restrictions than DFAs, it's also easier to create an NFA by using our wits. But no matter how we construct an NFA, it may be inefficient to execute because of nondeterminism. So it's nice to know that we can automatically transform any NFA into a DFA. Let's describe the process.

The key idea is that each state of the new DFA will actually be a certain subset of the NFA's states. That's why some people call the process "subset construction." We'll use two kinds of building blocks to construct the new subsets:

1. The sets of states that occur in the NFA transition table.

2. Certain sets of NFA states that are reachable by traversing Λ edges.

Let's describe the meaning of "reachable by traversing Λ edges." If s is an NFA state, then the *lambda closure of s* , denoted $\lambda(s)$, is the set of states that can be reached from s by traversing zero or more Λ edges. We can define $\lambda(s)$ inductively as follows for any state s in an NFA:

Basis: $s \in \lambda(s)$.

Induction: If $p \in \lambda(s)$ and there is a Λ edge from p to q, then $q \in \lambda(s)$.

EXAMPLE 2. Lambda closures are easy to construct. For example, suppose we have the following NFA, which we've described in graphical form as well as table form:

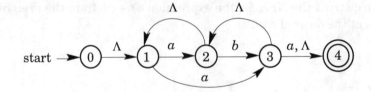

T_N	a	b	Λ
start 0	$\varnothing$	$\varnothing$	$\{1\}$
1	$\{2, 3\}$	$\varnothing$	$\varnothing$
2	$\varnothing$	$\{3\}$	$\{1\}$
3	$\{4\}$	$\varnothing$	$\{2, 4\}$
final 4	$\varnothing$	$\varnothing$	$\varnothing$

The lambda closures for the five states of the NFA are as follows:

$$\lambda(0) = \{0, 1\},$$
$$\lambda(1) = \{1\},$$
$$\lambda(2) = \{1, 2\},$$
$$\lambda(3) = \{1, 2, 3, 4\},$$
$$\lambda(4) = \{4\}. \quad \blacklozenge$$

Let's extend the definition of lambda closure to a set of states. If S is a set of states, then the *lambda closure of S*, denoted $\lambda(S)$, is the set of states that can be reached from states in S by traversing zero or more Λ edges. A useful property of lambda closure involves taking unions. If C and D are any sets of states, then we have

$$\lambda(C \cup D) = \lambda(C) \cup \lambda(D).$$

This property extends easily to the union of two or more sets of states. So the lambda closure of a union of sets is the union of the lambda closures of the sets. Therefore we can compute the lambda closure of a set by calculating the union of the lambda closures of the individual elements in the set. In other words, if $S = \{s_1, ..., s_n\}$, then

$$\lambda(S) = \lambda(\{s_1, ..., s_n\}) = \lambda(s_1) \cup ... \cup \lambda(s_n).$$

For example, the lambda closure of the set {0, 2, 4} for the NFA in Example 2 can be computed as follows:

$$\lambda(\{0, 2, 4\}) = \lambda(0) \cup \lambda(2) \cup \lambda(4) = \{0, 1\} \cup \{1, 2\} \cup \{4\} = \{0, 1, 2, 4\}.$$

Now that we have the tools, let's describe the algorithm for transforming any NFA into a DFA that recognizes the same language. Here's the algorithm in all its glory:

NFA to DFA Algorithm (5.8)

Input: An NFA over alphabet A with transition function T_N.

Output: A DFA over A with transition function T_D that accepts the same language as the NFA. The states of the DFA are subsets of NFA states.

1. The DFA start state is $\lambda(s)$, where s is the NFA start state.

2. For each DFA state $\{s_1, ..., s_n\}$ and for each $a \in A$, construct the following entry for the DFA table in either of two ways:

$$T_D(\{s_1, ..., s_n\}, a)$$
$$= \lambda(T_N(s_1, a) \cup ... \cup T_N(s_n, a)) \quad \text{(closure of union)}$$
$$= \lambda(T_N(s_1, a)) \cup ... \cup \lambda(T_N(s_n, a)) \quad \text{(union of closure)}.$$

3. A DFA state is final if one of its elements is an NFA final state.

End of Algorithm

Let's work through an example to show how to use the algorithm. We'll transform the NFA of Example 2 into a DFA by constructing the transition table for the DFA. The first step of (5.8) computes the DFA's start state: $\lambda(0)$ = {0, 1}. So we can begin constructing the transition table T_D for the DFA as follows:

T_D	a	b
start {0, 1}		

Our next step is to fill in the table entries for the first row. In other words, we want to compute $T_D(\{0, 1\}, a)$ and $T_D(\{0, 1\}, b)$. Using the closure of union formula from Step 2 of (5.8), we calculate $T_D(\{0, 1\}, a)$ as follows:

$$T_D(\{0, 1\}, a) = \lambda(T_N(0, a) \cup T_N(1, a))$$
$$= \lambda(\varnothing \cup \{2, 3\})$$
$$= \lambda(\{2, 3\})$$
$$= \lambda(2) \cup \lambda(3)$$
$$= \{1, 2\} \cup \{1, 2, 3, 4\}$$
$$= \{1, 2, 3, 4\}.$$

We can describe this process in terms of the NFA table as follows: Using the state $\{0, 1\}$, we enter the NFA table at rows 0 and 1. To construct the entry in column a of T_D, we take the union of the sets in column a rows 0 and 1 to get $\varnothing \cup \{2, 3\} = \{2, 3\}$. Then we compute the lambda closure of $\{2, 3\}$, obtaining $\{1, 2, 3, 4\}$. Similarly, we obtain $T_D(\{0, 1\}, b) = \varnothing$. In terms of the table, we take the union of the sets in column b rows 0 and 1 to get $\varnothing \cup \varnothing = \varnothing$. The lambda closure of $\varnothing$ is $\varnothing$. So the table for T_D now looks like the following:

	T_D	a	b
start	$\{0, 1\}$	$\{1, 2, 3, 4\}$	$\varnothing$

Next, we check to see whether any new states have been added to the new table. Both $\{1, 2, 3, 4\}$ and $\varnothing$ are new states. So we choose one of them and make it a new row label:

	T_D	a	b
start	$\{0, 1\}$	$\{1, 2, 3, 4\}$	$\varnothing$
	$\{1, 2, 3, 4\}$		

Now, we apply the same process to fill in the entries for this new row. In this case we get $T_D(\{1, 2, 3, 4\}, a) = \{1, 2, 3, 4\}$ and also $T_D(\{1, 2, 3, 4\}, b) = \{1, 2, 3, 4\}$. Therefore the table for T_D looks like the following:

	T_D	a	b
start	$\{0, 1\}$	$\{1, 2, 3, 4\}$	$\varnothing$
	$\{1, 2, 3, 4\}$	$\{1, 2, 3, 4\}$	$\{1, 2, 3, 4\}$

The state $\varnothing$ is in the table and is not yet a row label. So we add $\varnothing$ as a new row label to create the following table:

T_D		a	b
start	$\{0, 1\}$	$\{1, 2, 3, 4\}$	$\varnothing$
	$\{1, 2, 3, 4\}$	$\{1, 2, 3, 4\}$	$\{1, 2, 3, 4\}$
	$\varnothing$		

Now we continue the process by filling in the row labeled with $\varnothing$. We'll use the convention that an empty union is empty (there are no states in $\varnothing$). So we get $T_D(\varnothing, a) = \varnothing$ and $T_D(\varnothing, b) = \varnothing$. Therefore the table looks like the following:

T_D		a	b
start	$\{0, 1\}$	$\{1, 2, 3, 4\}$	$\varnothing$
	$\{1, 2, 3, 4\}$	$\{1, 2, 3, 4\}$	$\{1, 2, 3, 4\}$
	$\varnothing$	$\varnothing$	$\varnothing$

Now every entry in the table is also a row label. Therefore we've completed the definition of T_D. To finish things off, we note that state $\{1, 2, 3, 4\}$ contains a final state of the NFA. Therefore we mark it as final in the DFA and obtain the following table for T_D:

T_D		a	b
start	$\{0,1\}$	$\{1,2,3,4\}$	$\varnothing$
final	$\{1,2,3,4\}$	$\{1,2,3,4\}$	$\{1,2,3,4\}$
	$\varnothing$	$\varnothing$	$\varnothing$

Since the states of the constructed DFA are sets, it's awkward to draw a picture. So we'll make the following changes to simplify the process:

> Replace $\{0, 1\}$ by the symbol 0.
>
> Replace $\{1, 2, 3, 4\}$ by the symbol 1.
>
> Replace $\varnothing$ by the symbol 2.

With these replacements the table for T_D can be written in the following form:

T_D	a	b
start 0	1	2
1	1	1
final 2	2	2

The graph version of the DFA for table T_D can be drawn as follows:

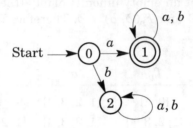

It's easy to see that the regular expression for this DFA is $a(a + b)^*$. Therefore $a(a + b)^*$ is also the regular expression for the NFA of Example 2.

If an NFA does not have any Λ edges, then the lambda closure of a set is just the set itself. In this case, (5.8) simplifies to the following:

NFA (without Λ edges) to DFA

1. The DFA start state is $\{s\}$, where s is the NFA start state.

2. For each DFA state $\{s_1, ..., s_n\}$ and each $a \in A$, construct the following entry for the DFA table:

$$T_D(\{s_1, ..., s_n\}, a) = T_N(s_1, a) \cup ... \cup T_N(s_n, a).$$

3. A DFA state is final if one of its elements is an NFA final state.

End of Algorithm

Let's summarize the situation as it now stands. We can start with a regular expression and use (5.4) or (5.7) to construct an NFA for the expression. Next we can use (5.8) to transform the NFA into a DFA. Since the NFAs constructed by (5.4) or (5.7) might have a large number of states, it follows that the DFA constructed by (5.8) might have a large number of states. In the next few paragraphs we'll see that any DFA can be automatically transformed into a DFA with the minimum number of states. Then, putting everything together, we'll have an automatic process for constructing the most efficient DFA for any regular expression.

Minimum-State DFAs

One way to try and simplify the DFA for some regular expression is to algebraically transform the regular expression into a simpler one before starting construction of the DFA. For example, from the properties (5.1) we have

$$\Lambda + a + aaa^* = a^*.$$

If we used our wits, most of us would construct a simpler DFA for a^* than for $\Lambda + a + aaa^*$. If we used the algorithms, we would also obtain a simpler DFA for a^* than for $\Lambda + a + aaa^*$. But we still might not have obtained the simplest DFA.

It's nice to know that no matter what DFA we come up with, we can always transform it into a DFA with the minimum number of states that recognizes the same language. The basic result is given by the following theorem, which is named after Myhill [1957] and Nerode [1958]:

Every regular expression has a unique minimum-state DFA.   (5.9)

The word "unique" in (5.9) means that the only difference that can occur between any two minimum-state DFAs for a regular expression is not in the number of states, but rather in the names given to the states. So we could rename the states of one DFA so that it becomes the same as the other DFA.

We already know how to transform a regular expression into an NFA and then into a DFA. Now let's see how to transform a DFA into a minimum-state DFA. The key idea is to define two states s and t to be *equivalent* if for every string w, the transitions

$$T(s, w) \text{ and } T(t, w) \text{ are either both final or both nonfinal.}$$

In other words, to say that s and t are equivalent means that whenever the execution of the DFA reaches either s or t with the same string w left to consume, then the DFA will consume w and, in either case, enter the same type of state—either both reject or both accept.

It's easy to see that equivalence is an equivalence relation. Stop and check it out. So once we know the equivalent pairs of states, we can partition the states of the DFA into a collection of subsets, where each subset contains states that are equivalent to each other. These subsets become the states of the new minimum-state DFA.

Before we present the algorithm, let's try to make the idea more precise with a very simple example. Suppose we're given the four-state DFA in Figure 5.6, which is represented in graphical form and as a transition table.

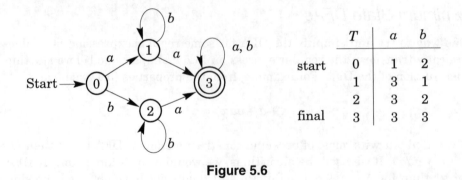

T	a	b
start 0	1	2
1	3	1
2	3	2
final 3	3	3

Figure 5.6

It's pretty easy to see that states 1 and 2 are equivalent. For example, if the DFA is in either state 1 or 2 with any string starting with a, then the DFA will consume a and enter state 3. From this point the DFA stays in state 3. On the other hand, if the DFA is in either state 1 or 2 with any string starting with b, then the DFA will consume b and stay in the same two states, both of which are reject states. So for any string w, both $T(1, w)$ and $T(2, w)$ are either both final or both nonfinal.

It's also pretty easy to see that no other distinct pairs of states are equivalent. For example, states 0 and 1 are not equivalent because $T(0, a) = 1$, which is a reject state, and $T(1, a) = 3$, which is an accept state. Since the only distinct equivalent states are 1 and 2, we can partition the states of the DFA into the subsets

$$\{0\}, \quad \{1, 2\}, \quad \text{and} \quad \{3\}.$$

These three subsets form the states of the minimum-state DFA. This minimum-state DFA can be represented by either one of the two forms shown in Figure 5.7.

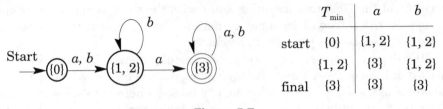

$T_{\min}$	a	b
start {0}	{1, 2}	{1, 2}
{1, 2}	{3}	{1, 2}
final {3}	{3}	{3}

Figure 5.7

There are several methods to compute the equivalence relation and its corresponding partition. The method that we'll present is easy to understand,

and it can be programmed. We start the process by forming the set

$$E_0$$

of distinct pairs of the form $\{s, t\}$, where s and t are either both final or both nonfinal. This collection contains the possible equivalent pairs.

Next we construct a new collection E_1 from E_0 by throwing away any pair $\{s, t\}$ if there is some letter a such that $\{T(s, a), T(t, a)\}$ is a distinct pair that does not occur in E_0. This means that the pair $\{T(s, a), T(t, a)\}$ contains two states of different types. So we must throw $\{s, t\}$ away.

The process continues by constructing a new collection E_2 from E_1 by throwing away $\{s, t\}$ if there is some letter a such that $\{T(s, a), T(t, a)\}$ is a distinct pair that does not occur in E_1. This means that there is a string of length 2 such that the DFA, if started from either s or t, consumes the string and enters two different types of states. So we must throw $\{s, t\}$ out of E_1.

We continue the process by constructing a descending sequence

$$E_0 \supset E_1 \supset E_2 \supset \ldots \supset E_n \supset \ldots .$$

Each set E_n in the sequence has been constructed to have the property that for each pair $\{s, t\}$ in E_n and for any string of length less than or equal to n, the DFA, if started from either s or t, will consume the string and enter the same type of states—either both reject or both accept. Since E_0 is a finite set, the sequence of sets must eventually stop with some set E_k such that

$$E_{k+1} = E_k.$$

This means E_k is the desired set of equivalent pairs of states, because for any pair $\{s, t\}$ in E_k and any length string, the DFA, if started from either s or t, will consume the string and enter the same type of states—either both reject or both accept.

For example, from the DFA in Figure 5.6 we start with

$$E_0 = \{\{0, 1\}, \{0, 2\}, \{1, 2\}\}.$$

To construct E_1 from E_0, we throw away $\{0, 1\}$ because

$$\{T(0, a), T(1, a)\} = \{1, 3\},$$

which is not in E_0. We must also throw away $\{0, 2\}$ because

$$\{T(0, a), T(2, a)\} = \{1, 3\},$$

which is not in E_0. This leaves us with the set

$$E_1 = \{\{1, 2\}\}.$$

We can't throw away any pairs from E_1. Therefore $E_2 = E_1$, which says that the desired set of equivalent pairs is $E_1 = \{\{1, 2\}\}$. Notice that $\{1, 2\}$ is a state in the minimum-state DFA shown in Figure 5.7.

Now we're ready to present the actual algorithm to transform a DFA into a minimum-state DFA.

Algorithm to Construct a Minimum-State DFA   (5.10)

Given: A DFA with set of states S and transition table T. Assume
           that all states can be reached from the start state.

Output: A minimum-state DFA recognizing the same regular lan-
           guage as the input DFA.

1. Construct the equivalent pairs of states by calculating the descending
   sequence of sets of pairs $E_0 \supset E_1 \supset ...$ defined as follows:

   $E_0 = \{\{s, t\} \mid s$ and t are distinct and either both states are final or
   both states are nonfinal$\}$.

   $E_{i+1} = \{\{s, t\} \mid \{s, t\} \in E_i$ and for every $a \in A$ either $T(s, a) = T(t, a)$
   or $\{T(s, a), T(t, a)\} \in E_i\}$.

   The computation stops when $E_k = E_{k+1}$ for some index k. E_k is the desired set of equivalent pairs.

2. Use the equivalence relation generated by the pairs in E_k to partition
   S into a set of equivalence classes. These equivalence classes are the
   states of the new DFA.

3. The *start state* is the equivalence class containing the start state of
   the input DFA.

4. A *final state* is any equivalence class containing a final state of the
   input DFA.

5. The transition table $T_{\min}$ for the minimum-state DFA is defined as follows, where $[s]$ denotes the equivalence class containing s and a is
   any letter: $T_{\min}([s], a) = [T(s, a)]$.

End of Algorithm

Now let's do two examples to get the look and feel of the algorithm.

EXAMPLE 3. We'll compute the minimum-state DFA for the following DFA:

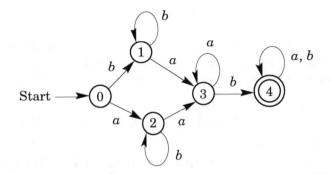

The set of states is $S = \{0, 1, 2, 3, 4\}$. For Step 1 we'll start by calculating E_0 as the set of pairs $\{s, t\}$, where s and t are both final or both nonfinal:

$$E_0 = \{\{0, 1\}, \{0, 2\}, \{0, 3\}, \{1, 2\}, \{1, 3\}, \{2, 3\}\}.$$

E_0 contains pairs that might be equivalent. Now we'll compute E_1 from E_0 by keeping a pair $\{s, t\}$ if for each letter x, either

$$\{T(s, x), T(t, x)\} \in E_0 \quad \text{or} \quad T(s, x) = T(t, x).$$

So we must throw away $\{0, 3\}$ because $\{T(0, b), T(3, b)\} = \{1, 4\}$, which is not in E_0. We also must throw away $\{1, 3\}$ and $\{2, 3\}$. That leaves us with

$$E_1 = \{\{0, 1\}, \{0, 2\}, \{1, 2\}\}.$$

Next we'll compute E_2 from E_1. In this case we must throw away $\{0, 2\}$ because $\{T(0, a), T(2, a)\} = \{2, 3\}$, which is not in E_1. That leaves us with

$$E_2 = \{\{1, 2\}\}.$$

Next we'll compute E_3 from E_2. In this case we don't throw anything away. So we have our stopping condition

$$E_3 = E_2 = \{\{1, 2\}\}.$$

So E_3 is our set of equivalent pairs. In other words, the only distinct equivalence pair is $\{1, 2\}$. The equivalence relation generated by this equivalence partitions S into the following four equivalence classes:

$$\{0\}, \{1, 2\}, \{3\}, \{4\}.$$

These are the states for the new DFA. The start state is $\{0\}$, and the final state is $\{4\}$. Using the standard notation for equivalence classes—where any element in a class can name the class—we have

$$[0] = \{0\}, \quad [1] = [2] = \{1, 2\}, \quad [3] = \{3\}, \quad \text{and} \quad [4] = \{4\}.$$

Thus we can apply Step 5 to construct the table for $T_{\min}$. For example, we'll compute $T_{\min}(\{0\}, a)$ and $T_{\min}(\{1, 2\}, b)$ as follows:

$$T_{\min}(\{0\}, a)= T_{\min}([0], a) = [T(0, a)] = [2] = \{1, 2\},$$

$$T_{\min}(\{1, 2\}, b)= T_{\min}([1], b) = [T(1, b)] = [1] = \{1, 2\}.$$

Similar computations yield the table for $T_{\min}$, which is listed as follows:

	$T_{\min}$	a	b
start	$\{0\}$	$\{1, 2\}$	$\{1, 2\}$
	$\{1, 2\}$	$\{3\}$	$\{1, 2\}$
	$\{3\}$	$\{3\}$	$\{4\}$
final	$\{4\}$	$\{4\}$	$\{4\}$

Of course, we can simplify the table by assigning a single number to each set of states. For example, if we let the numbers 0, 1, 2, and 3 represent the states $\{0\}$, $\{1, 2\}$, $\{3\}$, and $\{4\}$, then the preceding table can be written in the following familiar form:

	$T_{\min}$	a	b
start	0	1	1
	1	2	1
	2	2	3
final	3	3	3

Be sure to draw a picture of this minimum-state DFA.   ◆

EXAMPLE 4. We'll compute the minimum-state DFA for the DFA given by the following transition table:

	T	a	b
start	0	1	2
	1	4	1
	2	4	3
	3	4	3
final	4	4	5
final	5	5	5

The set of states is $S = \{0, 1, 2, 3, 4, 5\}$. For Step 1 we get the following sequence of relations:

$$E_0 = \{\{0, 1\}, \{0, 2\}, \{0, 3\}, \{1, 2\}, \{1, 3\}, \{2, 3\}, \{4, 5\}\},$$

$$E_1 = \{\{1, 2\}, \{1, 3\}, \{2, 3\}, \{4, 5\}\},$$

$$E_2 = E_1.$$

Therefore the equivalence relation is generated by the four equivalent pairs $\{1, 2\}$, $\{1, 3\}$, $\{2, 3\}$, and $\{4, 5\}$. Thus we obtain a partition of S into the following three equivalence classes:

$$\{0\}, \{1, 2, 3\}, \{4, 5\}.$$

These are the states for the new DFA. The start state is $\{0\}$, and the final state is $\{4, 5\}$. Using the standard notation for equivalence classes, we have

$$[0] = \{0\}, \quad [1] = [2] = [3] = \{1, 2, 3\}, \quad \text{and} \quad [4] = [5] = \{4, 5\}.$$

So we can apply Step 5 to construct the table for $T_{\min}$. For example, we can compute $T_{\min}(\{1, 2, 3\}, b)$ and $T_{\min}(\{4, 5\}, a)$ as follows:

$$T_{\min}(\{1, 2, 3\}, b) = T_{\min}([1], b) = [T(1, b)] = [1] = \{1, 2, 3\},$$

$$T_{\min}(\{4, 5\}, a) = T_{\min}([4], a) = [T(4, a)] = [4] = \{4, 5\}.$$

Similar computations will yield the table for $T_{\min}$. We'll leave these calculations as an exercise. ◆

Exercises

1. Use (5.7) to build an NFA for each of the following regular expressions.

    a. $a*b*$.   b. $(a + b)*$.   c. $a* + b*$.

2. Construct a DFA table for the following NFA in two ways using (5.8):

		a	b	Λ
start	0	$\varnothing$	$\{1, 2\}$	$\{1\}$
	1	$\{2\}$	$\varnothing$	$\varnothing$
final	2	$\varnothing$	$\{2\}$	$\{1\}$

    a. Take unions of lambda closures of the NFA entries.

    b. Take lambda closures of unions of the NFA entries.

3. Suppose we are given the following NFA over the alphabet $\{a, b\}$:

    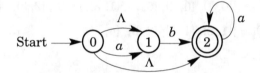

    a. Find a regular expression for the language accepted by the NFA.

    b. Write down the transition table for the NFA.

    c. Use (5.8) to transform the NFA into a DFA.

    d. Draw a picture of the resulting DFA.

4. Transform each of the following NFAs into a DFA.

    a. $T(0, a) = \{0, 1\}$, where 0 is start and 1 is final.

    b. $T(0, a) = \{1, 2\}$, $T(1, b) = \{1, 2\}$, where 0 is start and 2 is final.

5. Transform each of the following regular expressions into a DFA by using (5.7) and (5.8). Note that the NFAs obtained by (5.7) are the answers to Exercise 1.

    a. $a*b*$.   b. $(a + b)*$.   c. $a* + b*$.

6. Let the set of states for a DFA be $S = \{0, 1, 2, 3, 4, 5\}$, where the start state is 0 and the final states are 2 and 5. Let the equivalence relation on S for a minimum-state DFA be generated by the following set of equivalent pairs of states:

$$\{\{0, 1\}, \{0, 4\}, \{1, 4\}, \{2, 5\}\}.$$

    Write down the states of the minimum-state DFA.

7. Finish Example 4 by calculating the transition table for the new minimum-state DFA.

8. Given the following DFA table, use algorithm (5.10) to compute the minimum-state DFA. Answer parts (a), (b), and (c) as you proceed through the algorithm.

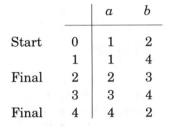

		a	b
Start	0	1	2
	1	1	4
Final	2	2	3
	3	3	4
Final	4	4	2

   a. Write down the set of equivalent pairs.
   b. Write down the states of the minimum-state DFA.
   c. Write down the transition table for the minimum-state DFA.

9. For each of the following DFAs, use (5.10) to find the minimum-state DFA.

   a.

		a	b
Start	0	1	2
Final	1	1	2
	2	3	2
Final	3	4	2
Final	4	1	2

   b.

		a	b
Start	0	1	2
Final	1	4	4
Final	2	3	4
Final	3	3	4
	4	4	4

10. For each of the following regular expressions, start by writing down the NFA obtained by algorithm (5.7). Then use (5.8) to transform the NFA into a DFA. Then use (5.10) to find the minimum-state DFA.
    a. $a^* + a^*$ (don't simplify).   b. $(a + b)^* a$.
    c. $a^* b^*$.   d. $(a + b)^*$.

11. Suppose we're given the following NFA table:

		a	b	Λ
start	0	{1}	{1}	{2}
	1	{1, 2}	$\varnothing$	$\varnothing$
final	2	$\varnothing$	{0}	{1}

Find a simple regular expression for the regular language recognized by this NFA. *Hint:* Transform the NFA into a DFA, and then find the minimum-state DFA.

12. What can you say about the regular language accepted by a DFA in which all states are final?

5.4 Regular Language Topics

We've already seen characterizations of regular languages by regular expressions, languages accepted by DFAs, and languages accepted by NFAs. In this section we'll introduce still another characterization of regular languages in terms of certain restricted grammars. We'll discuss some properties of regular languages that can be used to find languages that are not regular.

Regular Grammars

A regular language can be described by a special kind of grammar in which the productions take a certain form. A grammar is called a *regular grammar* if each production takes one of the following forms, where the capital letters are nonterminals and w is a nonempty string of terminals:

$$S \to \Lambda,$$
$$S \to w,$$
$$S \to T,$$
$$S \to wT.$$

The thing to keep in mind here is that only one nonterminal can appear on the right side of a production, and it must appear at the right end of the right side. For example, the productions $A \to aBc$ and $S \to TU$ are are not part of a regular grammar. But the production $A \to abcA$ is OK.

The most important aspect of grammar writing is knowledge of the language under discussion. We should also remember that grammars are not unique. So we shouldn't be surprised when two people come up with two different grammars for the same language.

To start things off, we'll look at a few regular grammars for some simple regular languages. Each line of the following list describes a regular language in terms of a regular expression and a regular grammar. As you look through the following list, cover up the grammar column with your hand and try to discover your own version of a regular grammar for the regular language of each regular expression.

Regular Expression	Regular Grammar
$a*$	$S \to \Lambda \mid aS$
$(a + b)*$	$S \to \Lambda \mid aS \mid bS$
$a* + b*$	$S \to \Lambda \mid A \mid B$
	$A \to a \mid aA$
	$B \to b \mid bB$
$a*b$	$S \to b \mid aS$
$ba*$	$S \to bA$
	$A \to \Lambda \mid aA$
$(ab)*$	$S \to \Lambda \mid abS$

The last three examples in the preceding list involve products of languages. Most problems occur in trying to construct a regular grammar for a language that is the product of languages. Let's look at an example to see whether we can get some insight into constructing such grammars.

Suppose we want to construct a regular grammar for the language of the regular expression $a*bc*$. First we observe that the strings of $a*bc*$ start with either the letter a or the letter b. We can represent this property by writing down the following two productions, where S is the start symbol:

$$S \to a\,S \mid b\,C.$$

These productions allow us to derive strings of the form bC, abC, $aabC$, and so on. Now all we need is a definition for C to derive the language of $c*$. The following two productions do the job:

$$C \to \Lambda \mid c\,C.$$

Therefore a regular grammar for $a*bc*$ can be written as follows:

$$S \to a\,S \mid b\,C$$
$$C \to \Lambda \mid c\,C.$$

EXAMPLE 1. We'll consider some regular languages, all of which consist of strings of a's followed by strings of b's. The largest language of this form is the language $\{a^m b^n \mid m, n \in \mathbb{N}\}$, which is represented by the regular expression $a*b*$. A regular grammar for this language can be written as follows:

$$S \to \Lambda \mid aS \mid B$$
$$B \to b \mid bB.$$

Let's look at four sublanguages of $\{a^m b^n \mid m, n \in \mathbb{N}\}$ that are defined by whether each string contains occurrences of a or b. The following list shows each language together with a regular expression and a regular grammar.

Language	Expression	Regular Grammar
$\{a^m b^n \mid m \geq 0 \text{ and } n > 0\}$	$a*bb*$	$S \to aS \mid B$ $B \to b \mid bB.$
$\{a^m b^n \mid m > 0 \text{ and } n \geq 0\}$	$aa*b*$	$S \to aA$ $A \to aA \mid B$ $B \to \Lambda \mid bB.$
$\{a^m b^n \mid m > 0 \text{ and } n > 0\}$	$aa*bb*$	$S \to a A$ $A \to aA \mid B$ $B \to b \mid bB.$
$\{a^m b^n \mid m > 0 \text{ or } n > 0\}$	$aa*b* + a*bb*$	$S \to aA \mid bB$ $A \to \Lambda \mid aA \mid B$ $B \to \Lambda \mid b B.$ ♦

Any regular language has a regular grammar; conversely, any regular grammar generates a regular language. To see this, we'll give two algorithms: one to transform an NFA to a regular grammar and the other to transform a regular grammar to an NFA, where the language accepted by the NFA is identical to the language generated by the regular grammar.

NFA to Regular Grammar (5.11)

Perform the following steps to construct a regular grammar that generates the language of a given NFA:

1. Rename the states to a set of capital letters.
2. The start symbol is the NFA's start state.
3. For each state transition from I to J labeled with a, create the production $I \to aJ$.
4. For each state transition from I to J labeled with Λ, create the production $I \to J$.
5. For each final state K, create the production $K \to \Lambda$.

End of Algorithm

It's easy to see that the language of the NFA and the language of the constructed grammar are the same. Just notice that each state transition in the NFA corresponds exactly with a production in the grammar so that the acceptance path in the NFA for some string corresponds to a derivation by the grammar for the same string. Let's do an example.

EXAMPLE 2. Let's see how (5.11) transforms the following NFA into a regular grammar:

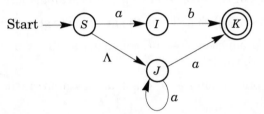

The algorithm takes this NFA and constructs the following regular grammar with start symbol S:

$$S \to aI \mid J$$
$$I \to bK$$
$$J \to aJ \mid aK$$
$$K \to \Lambda.$$

For example, to accept the string aa, the NFA follows the path S, J, J, K with edges labeled Λ, a, a, respectively. The grammar derives this string with the following sequence of productions:

$$S \to J, \quad J \to aJ, \quad J \to aK, \quad K \to \Lambda. \quad \blacklozenge$$

Now let's look at the converse problem of constructing an NFA from a regular grammar. For the opposite transformation we'll first take a regular grammar and rewrite it so that all the productions have one of two forms $S \to w$ or $S \to wT$, where w is either Λ or a single letter. Let's see how to do this so that we don't lose any generality. For example, if we have a production like

$$A \to bcB,$$

we can replace it by the following two productions, where C is a new nonterminal:

$$A \to bC \quad \text{and} \quad C \to cB.$$

Now let's look at an algorithm that does the job of transforming a regular grammar into an NFA.

Regular Grammar to NFA   (5.12)

Perform the following steps to construct an NFA that accepts the language of a given regular grammar:

1. If necessary, transform the grammar so that all productions have the form $A \rightarrow x$ or $A \rightarrow xB$, where x is either a single letter or Λ.

2. The start state of the NFA is the grammar's start symbol.

3. For each production $I \rightarrow aJ$, construct a state transition from I to J labeled with the letter a.

4. For each production $I \rightarrow J$, construct a state transition from I to J labeled with Λ.

5. If there are productions of the form $I \rightarrow a$ for some letter a, then create a single new state symbol F. For each production $I \rightarrow a$, construct a state transition from I to F labeled with a.

6. The final states of the NFA are F together with all I for which there is a production $I \rightarrow \Lambda$.

End of Algorithm

It's easy to see that the language of the NFA is the same as the language of the given regular grammar because the productions used in the derivation of any string correspond exactly with the state transitions on the path of acceptance for the string. Here's an example.

EXAMPLE 3. Let's use (5.12) to transform the following regular grammar into an NFA:

$$S \rightarrow aS \mid bI$$
$$I \rightarrow a \mid aI.$$

Since there is a production $I \rightarrow a$, we need to introduce a new state F, which then gives us the following NFA:

Properties of Regular Languages

We need to face the fact that not all languages are regular. To see this, let's look at a classic example. Suppose we want to find a DFA or NFA to recognize the following language:

$$\{a^n b^n \mid n > 0\}.$$

After a few attempts at trying to find a DFA or an NFA or a regular expression or a regular grammar, we might get the idea that it can't be done. But how can we be sure that a language is not regular? We can try to prove it. A proof usually proceeds by assuming that the language is regular and then trying to find a contradiction of some kind. For example, we might be able to find some property of regular languages that the given language doesn't satisfy. So let's look at a few properties of regular languages.

A useful property of regular languages comes from the observation that any DFA for an infinite regular language must contain a cycle to recognize infinitely many strings. For example, suppose we have a DFA with n states that recognizes an infinite language. Since the language is infinite, we can pick a string with more than n letters. To accept the string, the DFA must enter some state twice (by the pigeonhole principle). So any DFA for an infinite regular language must contain a subgraph that is a cycle. We can symbolize the situation as follows, where each arrow represents a path that may contain other states of the DFA and x, y, and z are the strings of letters along each path:

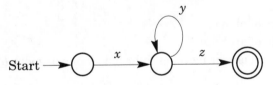

This means that the DFA must accept strings that have the the form $xy^k z$ for all $k \geq 0$. We can also observe this property by looking at the grammar for an infinite regular language. The grammar must contain a production that is recursive or indirectly recursive. For example, consider the following regular grammar fragment:

$$S \to xN$$
$$N \to yN \mid z.$$

This grammar accepts all strings of the form $xy^k z$ for all $k \geq 0$. For example, the string $xy^3 z$ can be derived as follows:

$$S \Rightarrow xN \Rightarrow xyN \Rightarrow xyyN \Rightarrow xyyyN \Rightarrow xyyyz.$$

The property that we've been discussing is called the *pumping property* because the string y can be pumped up to y^k by traveling through the same loop k times. Our discussion serves as an informal proof of the following pumping lemma:

Pumping Lemma (Regular Languages) (5.13)

Let L be an infinite regular language over the alphabet A. Then there exist strings $x, y, z \in A^*$, where $y \neq \Lambda$, such that $xy^k z \in L$ for all $k \geq 0$.

If an infinite language does not satisfy the conclusion of (5.13), then it can't be regular. So we can sometimes use this fact to prove that a language is not regular. Here's an example.

EXAMPLE 4. Let's show that the language $L = \{a^n b^n \mid n \geq 0\}$ is not regular. We'll assume, by way of contradiction, that L is regular. Then we can use the pumping lemma (5.13) to assert the existence of strings x, y, z $(y \neq \Lambda)$ such that $xy^k z \in L$ for all $k \geq 0$. Let's choose $k = 1$and see if we can find some kind of contradiciton. In this case, there is some n such that

$$xyz = a^n b^n.$$

Since $y \neq \Lambda$, there are three possibilities for y:

1. y consists of all a's.
2. y consists of all b's.
3. y consists of one or more a's followed by one or more b's.

In cases 1 and 2 we obtain a contradiction because the pumping lemma implies that $xy^2 z$ is in the language. This can't be true because in case 1 there would be more a's than b's in the string $xy^2 z$. In case 2 there would be more b's than a's. A contradiction also results in case 3 (an exercise). Therefore there are contradictions in all possible cases. Thus the original assumption is false, and the language cannot be regular.   ♦

Sometimes we can't use (5.13) to show the nonregularity of a language. For example, the language of all palindromes over an alphabet with two or more letters is not regular. But we can't prove it by using (5.13) to obtain a contradiction from an assumption that the language is regular. The reason is that palindromes satisfy the conclusion of (5.13). For example, over the alphabet $\{a, b\}$, suppose we let $x = a$, $y = aba$, and $z = a$. Then certainly $xy^n z$ is a palindrome for all $n \geq 0$.

There is another version of the pumping lemma for infinite regular languages. It can sometimes be used when (5.13) does not do the job, because it specifies some additional properties of infinite regular languages. We'll state this second pumping lemma as follows:

Second Pumping Lemma (Regular Languages) (5.14)

Let L be an infinite regular language over the alphabet A, and suppose that L can be accepted by a DFA with m states. Then for any string $s \in L$ such that $|s| > m$ there exist strings $x, y, z \in A^*$, where $y \neq \Lambda$, such that $s = xyz$ and $|xy| \leq m$ and $xy^k z \in L$ for all $k \geq 0$.

The proof of (5.14) is a refinement of the discussion preceding (5.13), and we'll leave it as an exercise. Let's see how (5.14) can be used to prove that the language consisting of all palindromes over an alphabet with two or more letters is not regular.

EXAMPLE 5. Suppose P is the language of palindromes over the alphabet of two letters a and b. To prove that P is not regular, we'll assume that P is regular and try for a contradiction. If P is regular, then there is a DFA with m states to recognize P. Let's choose a palindrome of the following form:

$$s = a^{m+1}ba^{m+1}.$$

Now apply (5.14) to assert the existence of strings x, y, z such that $y \neq \Lambda$ and

$$xyz = s = a^{m+1}ba^{m+1},$$

where $|xy| \leq m$. Therefore x and y are both strings of a's. Thus z has the form $a^i ba^{m+1}$, where $i > 0$. Since $y \neq \Lambda$, we can pump y up to y^2 and obtain the form

$$xy^2z = a^n ba^{m+1},$$

where it must be the case that $n > m+1$. Therefore $a^n ba^{m+1}$ cannot be a palindrome. This contradicts the fact that it must be a palindrome according to (5.14). Therefore P is not regular. ◆

If we're trying to find out whether a language is regular, it may help to know how regular languages can be combined or transformed to form new regular languages. We know by definition that regular languages can be combined by union, language product, and closure to form new regular languages. We'll list these three properties along with two others.

Properties of Regular Languages   (5.15)

1. The union of two regular languages is regular.
2. The language product of two regular languages is regular.
3. The closure of a regular language is regular.
4. The complement of a regular language is regular.
5. The intersection of two regular languages is regular.

Proof: We'll prove statement 4 and leave statement 5 as an exercise.If D is a DFA for the regular language L, then construct a new DFA, say D', from D by making all the final states nonfinal and by making all the nonfinal states final. If we let A be the alphabet for L, it follows that D' recognizes the complement $A^* - L$. Thus the complement of L is regular.   QED.

EXAMPLE 6. Suppose L is the language over alphabet $\{a, b\}$ consisting of all strings with an equal number of a's and b's. For example, the strings *abba*, *ab*, and *babbaa* are all in L. Is L a regular language? To see that the answer is no, consider the following argument:

Let M be the language of the regular expression a^*b^*. It follows that

$$L \cap M = \{a^n b^n \mid n \geq 0\}.$$

Now we're in position to use (5.15). Suppose on the contrary that L is regular. We know that M is regular because it's the language of the regular expression a^*b^*. Therefore $L \cap M$ must be regular by (5.15). In other words, the language $\{a^n b^n \mid n \geq 0\}$ must be regular. But we know that $\{a^n b^n \mid n \geq 0\}$ is NOT regular. Therefore our assumption that L is regular leads to a contradiction. Thus L is not regular.   ◆

We'll finish by listing two interesting properties of regular languages that can also be used to determine nonregularity.

Regular Language Morphisms   (5.16)

Let $f : A^* \to A^*$ be a language morphism. In other words, $f(\Lambda) = \Lambda$ and $f(uv) = f(u)f(v)$ for all strings u and v. Let L be a language over A.

1. If L is regular, then $f(L)$ is regular.
2. If L is regular, then $f^{-1}(L)$ is regular.

Proof: We'll prove statement 1 and leave statement 2 as an exercise. Since L is regular, it has a regular grammar. We'll create a regular grammar for $f(L)$

as follows: Transform productions like $S \to w$ and $S \to wT$ into new productions of the form $S \to f(w)$ and $S \to f(w)T$. The new grammar is regular, and any string in $f(L)$ is derived by this new grammar.   QED.

EXAMPLE 7. Let's use (5.16) to show that the language $L = \{a^n bc^n \mid n \in \mathbb{N}\}$ is not regular. We can define a morphism $f : \{a, b, c\}^* \to \{a, b, c\}^*$ by $f(a) = a$, $f(b) = \Lambda$, and $f(c) = b$. Then $f(L) = \{a^n b^n \mid n \geq 0\}$. If L is regular, then we must also conclude by (5.16) that $f(L)$ is regular. But we know that $f(L)$ is not regular. Therefore L is not regular.   ◆

There are some very simple nonregular languages. For example, we know that the language $\{a^n b^n \mid n \geq 0\}$ is not regular. Therefore finite automata are not powerful enough to recognize it. Therefore finite automata can't recognize some simple programming constructs, such as nested begin-end pairs, nested open and closed parentheses, brackets, and braces. We'll see in the next chapter that there are more powerful machines to recognize such constructs.

Exercises

1. Find a regular grammar for each of the following regular expressions.

    a. $a + b$.

    b. $a + bc$.

    c. $a + b^*$.

    d. $ab^* + c$.

    e. $ab^* + bc^*$.

    f. $a^* bc^* + ac$.

    g. $(aa + bb)^*$.

    h. $(aa + bb)(aa + bb)^*$.

    i. $(ab)^* c(a + b)^*$.

2. Find a regular grammar to describe each of the following languages.

    a. $\{a, b, c\}$.

    b. $\{aa, ab, ac\}$.

    c. $\{a, b, ab, ba, abb, baa, \ldots, ab^n, ba^n, \ldots\}$.

    d. $\{a, aaa, aaaaa, \ldots, a^{2n+1}, \ldots\}$.

    e. $\{\Lambda, a, abb, abbbb, \ldots, ab^{2n}, \ldots\}$.

    f. $\{\Lambda, a, b, c, aa, bb, cc, \ldots, a^n, b^n, c^n, \ldots\}$.

    g. $\{\Lambda, a, b, ca, bc, cca, bcc, \ldots, c^n a, bc^n, \ldots\}$.

    h. $\{a^{2k} \mid k \in \mathbb{N}\} \cup \{b^{2k+1} \mid k \in \mathbb{N}\}$.

    i. $\{a^m bc^n \mid m, n \in \mathbb{N}\}$.

3. Find a regular grammar for each of the following languages over the alphabet $\{a, b\}$.

    a. All strings have even length.

    b. All strings have length a multiple of 3.

c. All strings contain the substring *aba*.

d. All strings have an odd number of *a*'s.

4. Any regular language can also be defined by a grammar with productions of the following form, where *w* is a nonempty string of terminals:

$$S \rightarrow w, \quad S \rightarrow w, \quad S \rightarrow T, \quad \text{or} \quad S \rightarrow Tw.$$

Find a grammar of this form for the language of each of the following regular expressions.

a. $a(ab)^*$.   b. $(ab)^*a$.   c. $(ab)^*c(a + b)^*$.

5. It's easy to see that the regular expression $(a + b)^*abb$ represents the language recognized by the following NFA:

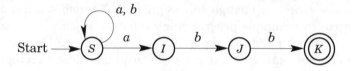

Use (5.11) to find a grammar for the language represented by the NFA.

6. Use (5.12) to construct an NFA to recognize the language of the following regular grammar:

$$S \rightarrow aI \mid bJ$$
$$I \rightarrow bI \mid \Lambda$$
$$J \rightarrow aJ \mid \Lambda.$$

7. The language $\{a^n b^n \mid n \in \mathbb{N}\}$ is not regular. If it is regular, the pumping lemma asserts the existence of strings x, y, z $(y \neq \Lambda)$ such that $xy^k z$ is in the language for all $k \geq 0$. Let $k = 1$. Then there is some n such that

$$xyz = a^n b^n.$$

Show that it is impossible for *y* to have the form of one or more *a*'s followed by one or more *b*'s.

8. Show that each of the following languages is not regular by using (5.13).

a. $\{a^n ba^n \mid n \in \mathbb{N}\}$.

b. $\{a^p \mid p \text{ is a prime number}\}$.

9. Prove that the intersection of two regular languages is regular.

10. Prove the second pumping lemma (5.14). *Hint:* Extend the discussion preceding (5.13).

11. Let $f : A^* \rightarrow A^*$ be a language morphism (i.e., $f(\Lambda) = \Lambda$ and $f(uv) = f(u)f(v)$ for all strings *u* and *v*), and let *L* be a regular language over *A*.

Prove that $f^{-1}(L)$ is regular. *Hint:* Construct a DFA for $f^{-1}(L)$ from a DFA for L.

12. Show that the language $\{a^n ba^n \mid n \in \mathbb{N}\}$ is not regular by performing the following tasks:

 a. Given the morphism $f : \{a, b, c\}^* \to \{a, b, c\}^*$ defined by

$$f(a) = a, \quad f(b) = b, \quad \text{and} \quad f(c) = a,$$

 describe $f^{-1}(\{a^n ba^n \mid n \in \mathbb{N}\})$.

 b. Show that

$$f^{-1}(\{a^n ba^n \mid n \in \mathbb{N}\}) \cap \{a^m bc^n \mid m,n \in \mathbb{N}\} = \{a^n bc^n \mid n \in \mathbb{N}\}.$$

 c. Define a morphism $g : \{a, b, c\}^* \to \{a, b, c\}^*$ such that

$$g(\{a^n bc^n \mid n \in \mathbb{N}\}) = \{a^n b^n \mid n \in \mathbb{N}\}.$$

 d. Argue that $\{a^n ba^n \mid n \in \mathbb{N}\}$ is not regular by using parts (a), (b), and (c) together with (5.15) and (5.16).

Chapter Summary

This chapter introduced several formulations for regular languages. Regular expressions are algebraic representations of regular languages. Finite automata—DFAs and NFAs—are machines that recognize regular languages. Regular grammars derive regular languages. The most important point is that there are algorithms to transform from any one of these formulations into any other one. In other words, each formulation is equivalent to any of the other formulations. There is also an algorithm to transform any DFA into a minimum-state DFA. Therefore we can start with a regular language as either a regular expression or a regular grammar and automatically transform it into a minimum-state DFA to recognize the regular language.

We also observed some other things. Finite automata can be used as output devices—Mealy and Moore machines. There are some very simple interpreters for DFAs and NFAs. There are some basic properties of regular languages given by the pumping lemmas, set operations, and morphisms. Many simple languages are not regular. For example, the nonregularity of the language $\{a^n b^n \mid n \geq 0\}$ tells us that finite automata can't recognize some simple programming constructs such as nested begin-end pairs and nested open and closed parentheses.

6

Context-Free Languages and Pushdown Automata

If it keeps up, man will atrophy all his limbs but
the pushbutton finger.
—Frank Lloyd Wright (1869–1959)

We want to go beyond regular languages and the finite automata that recognize them to larger classes of languages and machines. In this chapter we'll study the context-free languages and the pushdown automata that recognize them. We'll also look at some classical parsing methods for context-free languages.

Chapter Guide

Section 6.1 introduces context-free languages and the grammars that describe them. We'll see some techniques for combining context-free languages.

Section 6.2 introduces pushdown automata as machines to recognize context-free languages. We'll see how to transform between context-free grammars and pushdown automata. We'll also present an interpreter for pushdown automata.

Section 6.3 gives an informal introduction to two basic parsing techniques for context-free languages: LL(k) parsing and LR(k) parsing.

Section 6.4 introduces some properties of context-free languages. We'll look at some restricted grammars for context-free languages. We'll discuss properties of context-free languages given by a pumping lemma, set operations, and morphisms. We'll also see examples of languages that are not context-free.

6.1 Context-Free Languages

In Chapter 5 we studied the class of regular languages and their representations via regular expressions, regular grammars, and finite automata. We also noticed that not all languages are regular. So it's time again to consider the recognition problem and find out whether we can solve it for a larger class of languages.

We know that there are nonregular languages. In Example 4 of Section 5.4 we showed that the following language is not regular:

$$\{a^n b^n \mid n \geq 0\}. \tag{6.1}$$

Therefore we can't describe this language by any of the four representations of regular languages: regular expressions, DFAs, NFAs, and regular grammars.

Language (6.1) can be easily described by the nonregular grammar:

$$S \to \Lambda \mid a\,S\,b. \tag{6.2}$$

This grammar is an example of a more general kind of grammar, which we'll now define.

A *context-free grammar* is a grammar whose productions are of the form

$$S \to w,$$

where S is a nonterminal and w is any string over the alphabet of terminals and nonterminals. For example, the grammar (6.2) is context-free. Also, any regular grammar is context-free. A language is *context-free* if it is generated by a context-free grammar. So language (6.1) is a context-free language. Regular languages are context-free. On the other hand, we know language (6.1) is context-free but not regular. Therefore the set of all regular languages is a proper subset of the set of all context-free languages.

The term "context-free" comes from the requirement that all productions contain a single nonterminal on the left. When this is the case, any production $S \to w$ can be used in a derivation without regard to the "context" in which S appears. For example, we can use this rule to make the following derivation step:

$$aS \Rightarrow aw.$$

A grammar that is not context-free must contain a production whose left side is a string of two or more symbols. For example, the production $Sc \to w$ is not part of any context-free grammar. A derivation that uses this production can replace the nonterminal S only in a "context" that has c on the right. For example, we can use this rule to make the following derivation step:

$$aSc \Rightarrow aw.$$

We'll see some examples of languages that are not context-free later.

Most programming languages are context-free. For example, a grammar for some typical statements in an imperative language might look like the following, where the words in boldface are considered to be single terminals:

$$S \rightarrow \textbf{while } E \textbf{ do } S \mid \textbf{if } E \textbf{ then } S \textbf{ else } S \mid \{ S L \} \mid I := E$$
$$L \rightarrow ; S L \mid \Lambda$$
$$E \rightarrow ... \quad \text{(description of an expression)}$$
$$I \rightarrow ... \quad \text{(description of an identifier)}.$$

We can combine context-free languages by union, language product, and closure to form new context-free languages. This follows from (1.27), which we'll reproduce here in terms of context-free languages.

Combining Context-Free Languages $\hfill$ (6.3)

Suppose M and N are context-free languages whose grammars have disjoint sets of nonterminals (rename them if necessary). Suppose also that the start symbols for the grammars of M and N are A and B, respectively. Then we have the following new languages and grammars:

1. The language $M \cup N$ is context-free, and its grammar starts with the two productions
   $$S \rightarrow A \mid B.$$

2. The language $M \cdot N$ is context-free, and its grammar starts with the production
   $$S \rightarrow AB.$$

3. The language M^* is context-free, and its grammar starts with the production
   $$S \rightarrow \Lambda \mid AS.$$

Now let's get back to our main topic of discussion. Since there are context-free languages that aren't regular and thus can't be recognized by DFAs and NFAs, we have a natural question to ask: Are there other kinds of automata that will recognize context-free languages? The answer is yes! We'll discuss them in the next section.

Exercises

1. Find a context-free grammar for each of the following languages over the alphabet $\{a, b\}$.

   a. $\{a^n b^{2n} \mid n \geq 0\}$.

   b. $\{a^n b^{n+2} \mid n \geq 0\}$.

   c. The palindromes of even length.

   d. The palindromes of odd length.

   e. All palindromes.

   f. All strings with the same number of a's and b's.

2. Find a context-free grammar for each of the following languages.

   a. $\{a^n b^n \mid n \geq 0\} \cup \{a^n b^{2n} \mid n \geq 0\}$.

   b. $\{a^n b^n \mid n \geq 0\} \cdot \{a^n b^{2n} \mid n \geq 0\}$.

   c. $\{a^n b^n \mid n \geq 0\}^*$.

   d. $\{a^n b^m \mid n \geq m \geq 0\}$.

6.2 Pushdown Automata

From an informal point of view a *pushdown automaton* is a finite automaton with a stack. A *stack* is a structure with the LIFO property of last in, first out. In other words, the last element put into a stack is the first element taken out. We'll let PDA stand for pushdown automaton. We can imagine a pushdown automaton as a machine with the ability to read input symbols and perform stack operations. A PDA has a single starting state and one or more final states.

The execution of a PDA always begins with one symbol on the stack. So we must

always specify the initial symbol on the stack.

We could eliminate this specification by simply assuming that a PDA always begins execution with a particular symbol on the stack, but we'll designate whatever symbol we please as the starting stack symbol. A PDA will use three stack operations as follows:

The *pop* operation reads the top symbol and removes it from the stack.

The *push* operation writes a designated symbol onto the top of the stack.

The *nop* operation does nothing to the stack.

We can represent a pushdown automaton as a digraph in which each edge is labeled with an input symbol, a stack symbol, and a stack operation to perform. There is no restriction on the number of edges that can be emitted from each node. The following diagram shows a labeled edge between two states, where b is an input symbol, C is a stack symbol, and pop is the operation to perform:

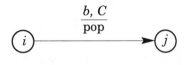

We'll interpret this picture as follows:

> If the machine is in state i, the current input symbol is b, and the symbol on top of the stack is C, then pop the stack and place the machine in state j.

Since it takes five pieces of information to describe a labeled edge, we'll also represent labeled edges by 5-tuples. For example, the labeled edge in the previous diagram is represented by the following 5-tuple:

$$\langle i, b, C, \text{pop}, j \rangle.$$

We allow a PDA to move from one state to another without consuming any input by writing Λ as the current input symbol. For example, the execution of the following 5-tuple will cause the PDA to pop the stack, change state, and NOT consume any input letter:

$$\langle i, \Lambda, C, \text{pop}, j \rangle.$$

A PDA is *deterministic* if—for the current input symbol and stack symbol—there is at most one move possible from each state. Otherwise, the PDA is *nondeterministic*. There are two types of nondeterminism that may occur. One kind of nondeterminism occurs when a state emits two or more edges labeled with the same input symbol and the same stack symbol. In other words, there are two 5-tuples with the same first three components. For example, the following two 5-tuples represent nondeterminism:

$$\langle i, b, C, \text{pop}, j \rangle,$$
$$\langle i, b, C, \text{push}(D), k \rangle.$$

The second kind of nondeterminism occurs when a state emits two edges labeled with the same stack symbol, where one input symbol is Λ and the other input symbol is not. For example, the following two 5-tuples represent nondeterminism because the machine has the option of consuming the input letter b or leaving it alone:

$$\langle i, \Lambda, C, \text{pop}, j \rangle,$$
$$\langle i, b, C, \text{push}(D), k \rangle.$$

We will always use the designation PDA to mean a pushdown automaton that may be either deterministic or nondeterministic.

A string is *accepted* by a PDA if the machine is in a final state and all letters of the string have been consumed (i.e., the input string is exhausted). Otherwise, the string is *rejected* by the PDA.

Before we do an example, let's discuss a way to represent the computation of a PDA. We'll represent a computation as a sequence of 3-tuples of the following form:

⟨current state, unconsumed input, stack contents⟩.

Such a 3-tuple is called an *instantaneous description*, or ID for short. For example, the ID

$$\langle i, abc, XYZW \rangle$$

means that the PDA is in state i, reading the letter a, where X is at the top of the stack. Let's do an example.

EXAMPLE 1. The language $\{a^n b^n \mid n \geq 0\}$ can be accepted by a PDA. We'll keep track of the number of a's in an input string by pushing the symbol Y onto the stack for each a. A second state will be used to pop the stack for each b encountered. The following PDA will do the job, where X is the initial symbol on the stack:

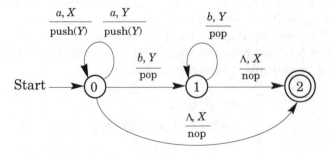

This PDA can be represented by the following six instructions:

$\langle 0, \Lambda, X, \text{nop}, 2 \rangle,$

$\langle 0, a, X, \text{push}(Y), 0 \rangle,$

$\langle 0, a, Y, \text{push}(Y), 0 \rangle,$

$\langle 0, b, Y, \text{pop}, 1 \rangle,$

$\langle 1, b, Y, \text{pop}, 1 \rangle,$

$\langle 1, \Lambda, X, \text{nop}, 2 \rangle.$

This PDA is nondeterministic because either of the first two instructions in the list can be executed if the first input letter is a and X is on top of the stack. Let's see how a computation proceeds. For example, a computation sequence for the input string $aabb$ can be written as follows:

$\langle 0, aabb, X \rangle$	Start in state 0 with X on the stack.
$\langle 0, abb, YX \rangle$	Consume a and push Y.
$\langle 0, bb, YYX \rangle$	Consume a and push Y.
$\langle 1, b, YX \rangle$	Consume b and pop.
$\langle 1, \Lambda, X \rangle$	Consume b and pop.
$\langle 2, \Lambda, X \rangle$	Move to final state. ◆

Equivalent Forms of Acceptance

We defined acceptance of a string by a PDA in terms of final-state acceptance. That is, a string is accepted if it has been consumed and the PDA is in a final state. But there is an alternative definition of acceptance called *empty stack acceptance*, which requires the input string to be consumed and the stack to be empty, with no requirement that the machine be in any particular state. These definitions of acceptance are equivalent. In other words, the class of languages accepted by PDAs that use empty stack acceptance is the same class of languages accepted by PDAs that use final-state acceptance.

EXAMPLE 2. Let's consider the language $\{a^n b^n \mid n \geq 0\}$. The PDA that follows will accept this language by empty stack, where X is the initial symbol on the stack:

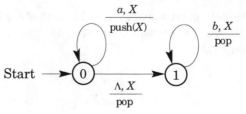

This PDA can be represented by the following three instructions:

$$\langle 0, a, X, \text{push}(X), 0 \rangle,$$
$$\langle 0, \Lambda, X, \text{pop}, 1 \rangle,$$
$$\langle 1, b, X, \text{pop}, 1 \rangle.$$

This PDA is nondeterministic. Can you see why? Let's see how a computation proceeds. For example, a computation sequence for the input string *aabb* can be written as follows:

$\langle 0, aabb, X \rangle$	Start in state 0 with X on the stack.
$\langle 0, abb, XX \rangle$	Consume a and push X.
$\langle 0, bb, XXX \rangle$	Consume a and push X.
$\langle 1, bb, XX \rangle$	Pop.
$\langle 1, b, X \rangle$	Consume b and pop.
$\langle 1, \Lambda, \Lambda \rangle$	Consume b and pop (stack is empty). ◆

Acceptance by final state is more common than acceptance by empty stack. But we need to consider empty stack acceptance when we discuss why the context-free languages are exactly the class of languages accepted by PDAs. So let's convince ourselves that we get the same class of languages with either type of acceptance.

Equivalence of Acceptance by Final State and Empty Stack

We'll give two algorithms. One algorithm transforms a final-state acceptance PDA into an empty stack acceptance PDA, and the second algorithm does the reverse, where both PDAs accept the same language.

Transforming a Final-State PDA into an Empty Stack PDA (6.4)

1. Create a new start state s, a new "empty stack" state e, and a new stack symbol Y that is at the top of the stack when the new PDA starts its execution.

2. Connect the new start state to the old start state by an edge labeled with the following expression, where X is the starting stack symbol for the given PDA:

$$\frac{\Lambda, Y}{\text{push}(X)}.$$

3. Connect each final state to the new "empty stack" state e by an edge labeled with the following expressions, where Z denotes any stack symbol, including Y:

$$\frac{\Lambda, Z}{\text{pop}}.$$

4. Add new edges from e to e labeled with the same expressions described in Step 3.

End of Algorithm

We can observe from the algorithm that *if the final-state PDA is deterministic, then the empty stack PDA might be nondeterministic.*

EXAMPLE 3. We'll consider the little language $\{\Lambda, a\}$. A deterministic PDA to accept $\{\Lambda, a\}$ by final state is given as follows, where X is the initial stack symbol:

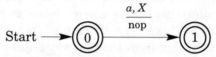

After applying algorithm (6.4) to this PDA, we obtain the following PDA, which accepts $\{\Lambda, a\}$ by empty stack, where Y is the initial stack symbol:

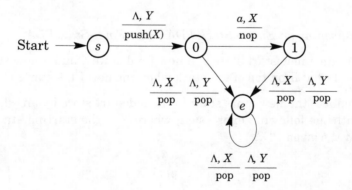

Notice that this PDA is nondeterministic even though the given PDA is deterministic. ◆

As the example shows, we don't always get pretty-looking results. Sometimes we can come up with simpler results by using our wits. For example, the following PDA also accepts—by empty stack—the language $\{\Lambda, a\}$, where X is the initial stack symbol:

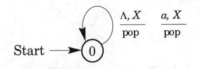

$$
\begin{array}{cc}
\dfrac{\Lambda,\,X}{\text{pop}} & \dfrac{a,\,X}{\text{pop}}
\end{array}
$$

Start $\longrightarrow$ ⓪

This PDA is also nondeterministic because either of the two instructions can be executed when a is the input letter. In fact, all PDAs that accept $\{\Lambda, a\}$ by empty stack must be nondeterministic. To see this, remember that a PDA must start with an initial symbol on the stack. If the letter a is the input symbol, then there must be a transition that eventually causes the stack to become empty. But if there is no input, then another transition from the same state must also cause the stack to become empty. Thus there is a nondeterministic choice at that state. This argument holds whenever the language under consideration contains Λ and at least one other string.

Now we'll discuss the other direction of our goal, which is to transform a PDA that accepts by empty stack into a final-state-accepting PDA. The idea is to create a new final state that can be entered when an empty stack occurs in the given PDA. We can do this by creating a new start state with a new stack symbol Y. Then add a Λ edge from the new start state to the old start state that pushes the old start stack symbol X onto the stack. Now an empty stack of the given PDA will be detected whenever Y appears at the top of the stack. Here is the algorithm to construct a final-state PDA from an empty stack PDA.

Transforming an Empty Stack PDA into a Final-State PDA   (6.5)

1. Create a new start state s, a new final state f, and a new stack symbol Y that is on top of the stack when the new PDA starts executing.

2. Connect the new start state to the old start state by an edge labeled with the following expression, where X is the starting stack symbol for the given PDA:

$$
\frac{\Lambda,\,Y}{\text{push}(X)}.
$$

3. Connect each state of the given PDA to the new final state f, and label each of these new edges with the expression

$$
\frac{\Lambda,\,Y}{\text{nop}}.
$$

End of Algorithm

We can also observe from this algorithm that *if the empty stack PDA is deterministic, then the final-state PDA is deterministic*. This is easy to see because the new edges created by the algorithm are all labeled with the new stack symbol Y, which doesn't occur in the original PDA.

Let's do a simple example.

EXAMPLE 4. The following PDA accepts $\{\Lambda\}$ by empty stack, where X is the initial stack symbol:

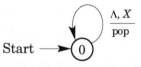

The algorithm creates the following PDA that accepts $\{\Lambda\}$ by final state:

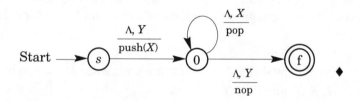

As the example shows, algorithm (6.5) doesn't always give the simplest results. For example, a simpler PDA to accept $\{\Lambda\}$ by final state can be written as follows:

Context-Free Grammars and Pushdown Automata

Now we're in the proper position to state the main result that connects context-free languages to pushdown automata.

The context-free languages are exactly the languages accepted by PDAs.   (6.6)

The proof of (6.6) consists of two algorithms. One algorithm transforms a context-free grammar into a PDA, and the other algorithm transforms a PDA into a context-free grammar. In each case the grammar generates the same language that the PDA accepts. Let's look at the algorithms.

Transforming a Context-Free Grammar into a PDA

We'll give here an algorithm to transform any context-free grammar into a PDA such that the PDA recognizes the same language as the grammar. For convenience we'll allow the operation field of a PDA instruction to hold a list of stack instructions. For example, the 5-tuple

$$\langle i, a, C, \langle \text{pop, push}(X), \text{push}(Y)\rangle, j\rangle$$

is executed by performing the three operations

$$\text{pop, push}(X), \text{push}(Y).$$

We can implement these actions in a "normal" PDA by placing enough new symbols on the stack at the start of the computation to make sure that any sequence of pop operations will not empty the stack if they are followed by a push operation. For example, we can execute the example instruction by the following sequence of normal instructions, where k and l are new states:

$$\langle i, a, C, \text{pop}, k\rangle,$$
$$\langle k, \Lambda, ?, \text{push}(X), l\rangle \qquad \text{(? represents some stack symbol)},$$
$$\langle l, \Lambda, X, \text{push}(Y), j\rangle.$$

Here's the algorithm to transform any context-free grammar into a PDA that accepts by empty stack.

Context-Free Grammar to PDA (Empty Stack Acceptance)   (6.7)

The PDA will have a single state 0. The stack symbols will be the set of terminals and nonterminals. The initial symbol on the stack will be the grammar's start symbol. Construct the PDA instructions as follows:

1. For each terminal symbol a, create the instruction $\langle 0, a, a, \text{pop}, 0\rangle$.

2. For each production $A \to B_1 B_2 \ldots B_n$, where each B_i represents either a terminal or a nonterminal, create the instruction

$$\langle 0, \Lambda, A, \langle \text{pop, push}(B_n), \text{push}(B_{n-1}), \ldots, \text{push}(B_1)\rangle, 0\rangle.$$

3. For each production $A \to \Lambda$, create the instruction $\langle 0, \Lambda, A, \text{pop}, 0\rangle$.

End of Algorithm

The PDA built by the algorithm accepts the language of the grammar because each state transition of the PDA corresponds exactly to one derivation step in a derivation. Let's do an example to get the idea.

EXAMPLE 5. Suppose we have the following context-free grammar for the language $\{a^n b^n \mid n \geq 0\}$:

$$S \to aSb \mid \Lambda.$$

We can apply algorithm (6.7) to this grammar to construct a PDA. From the terminals a and b we'll use rule 1 to create the two instructions

$$\langle 0, a, a, \text{pop}, 0 \rangle,$$
$$\langle 0, b, b, \text{pop}, 0 \rangle.$$

From the production $S \to \Lambda$ we'll use rule 3 to create the instruction

$$\langle 0, \Lambda, S, \text{pop}, 0 \rangle.$$

From the production $S \to aSb$, we'll use rule 2 to create the instruction

$$\langle 0, \Lambda, S, \langle \text{pop}, \text{push}(b), \text{push}(S), \text{push}(a) \rangle, 0 \rangle.$$

For example, let's write down the PDA computation sequence for the input string $aabb$:

ID	PDA Instruction to Obtain ID
$\langle 0, aabb, S \rangle$	Initial ID
$\langle 0, aabb, aSb \rangle$	$\langle 0, \Lambda, S, \langle \text{pop}, \text{push}(b), \text{push}(S), \text{push}(a) \rangle, 0 \rangle$
$\langle 0, abb, Sb \rangle$	$\langle 0, a, a, \text{pop}, 0 \rangle$
$\langle 0, abb, aSbb \rangle$	$\langle 0, \Lambda, S, \langle \text{pop}, \text{push}(b), \text{push}(S), \text{push}(a) \rangle, 0 \rangle$
$\langle 0, bb, Sbb \rangle$	$\langle 0, a, a, \text{pop}, 0 \rangle$
$\langle 0, bb, bb \rangle$	$\langle 0, \Lambda, S, \text{pop}, 0 \rangle$
$\langle 0, b, b \rangle$	$\langle 0, b, b, \text{pop}, 0 \rangle$
$\langle 0, \Lambda, \Lambda \rangle$	$\langle 0, b, b, \text{pop}, 0 \rangle$

See whether you can tell which steps of this computation correspond to the steps in the following derivation of $aabb$:

$$S \Rightarrow aSb \Rightarrow aaSbb \Rightarrow aabb. \quad \blacklozenge$$

Transforming a PDA into a Context-Free Grammar

Now let's go in the other direction and transform any PDA into a context-free grammar that accepts the same language. We will assume that the PDA accepts strings by empty stack. The idea is to construct a grammar so that a leftmost derivation for a string w corresponds to a computation sequence of the PDA that accepts w. To do this, we'll define the nonterminals of the grammar in terms of the stack symbols of the PDA. Here's the algorithm:

PDA (Empty Stack Acceptance) to Context-Free Grammar   (6.8)

For each stack symbol B and each pair of states i and j of the PDA, we construct a nonterminal of the grammar and denote it by B_{ij}. We can think of B_{ij} as deriving all strings that cause the PDA to move, in one or more steps, from state i to state j in such a way that the stack at state j is obtained from the stack at state i by popping B. We create one additional nonterminal S to denote the start symbol for the grammar.

1. For each state j of the PDA, construct a production of the following form, where s is the start state and E is the starting stack symbol:

$$S \to E_{sj}.$$

2. For each instruction of the form $\langle p, a, B, \text{pop}, q \rangle$, construct a production of the following form:

$$B_{pq} \to a.$$

3. For each instruction of the form $\langle p, a, B, \text{nop}, q \rangle$, construct a production of the following form for each state j:

$$B_{pj} \to aB_{qj}.$$

4. For each instruction of the form $\langle p, a, B, \text{push}(C), q \rangle$ construct productions of the following form for all states i and j:

$$B_{pj} \to aC_{qi}B_{ij}.$$

End of Algorithm

Note: This algorithm normally produces many useless productions that can't derive terminal strings. For example, if a nonterminal occurs on the right side of a production but not on the left side of any production, then the production can't derive a string of terminals. Similarly, if a recursive production doesn't have a basis case, then it can't derive a terminal string. We can safely discard these productions

Let's do an example to get the idea.

EXAMPLE 6. The following PDA accepts the language $\{a^n b^{n+2} \mid n \geq 1\}$ by empty stack, where X is the starting stack symbol:

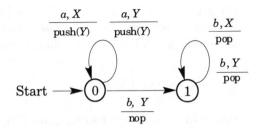

We can apply algorithm (6.8) to this PDA to construct the following context-free grammar; we've omitted the productions that can't derive terminal strings:

$$S \to X_{01}$$
$$X_{01} \to aY_{01}X_{11}$$
$$Y_{01} \to aY_{01}Y_{11} \mid bY_{11}$$
$$X_{11} \to b$$
$$Y_{11} \to b.$$

We'll do a sample derivation of the string $aabbbb$ as follows:

$$S \;\Rightarrow X_{01} \Rightarrow aY_{01}X_{11} \Rightarrow aaY_{01}Y_{11}X_{11} \Rightarrow aabY_{11}Y_{11}X_{11}$$
$$\Rightarrow aabbY_{11}X_{11} \Rightarrow aabbbX_{11} \Rightarrow aabbbb.$$

We should note from this example that the algorithm doesn't always construct the nicest-looking grammar. For example, the constructed grammar can be transformed into the following grammar for $\{a^n b^{n+2} \mid n \geq 1\}$:

$$S \to aBb$$
$$B \to aBb \mid bb. \quad \blacklozenge$$

Nondeterministic PDAs Are More Powerful

Recall that DFAs accept the same class of languages as NFAs, namely, the regular languages. We know by (6.6) that the context-free languages coincide with the languages accepted by PDAs. But we haven't said anything about determinism versus nondeterminism with respect to PDAs. In fact, there are some context-free languages that can't be recognized by any deterministic PDA. We'll state the result for the record as follows:

There are some context-free languages that are accepted   (6.9)
only by nondeterministic PDAs.

Although we won't prove (6.9), we'll give an indication of the kind of property that requires nondeterminism. For example, the language of even palindromes over $\{a, b\}$ can be generated by the following context-free grammar:

$$S \to aSa \mid bSb \mid \Lambda.$$

So by (6.6) the even palindromes can be recognized by a PDA. But this language can't be recognized by any deterministic PDA. In other words, every PDA to accept the even palindromes over $\{a, b\}$ must be nondeterministic. To see why this is the case, notice that we can describe the even palindromes over $\{a, b\}$ as follows, where w^R is the reverse of w:

$$\{ww^R \mid w \in \{a, b\}^*\}.$$

We can recognize a string of the form ww^R by stacking the letters of w and then unstacking the letters of w^R. This is a nondeterministic algorithm because it is impossible to know when the middle of the string has been reached. This is the underlying reason why no deterministic PDA can recognize even palindromes over $\{a, b\}$.

Since we've been discussing the fact that even palindromes over $\{a, b\}$ can be recognized only by nondeterministic PDAs, let's give an example.

EXAMPLE 7. We'll find a PDA—necessarily nondeterministic—for the even palindromes over $\{a, b\}$. The start state is 0, the final state is 2, and X is the initial stack symbol. To simplify things, we'll let "?" stand for any stack symbol. With these assumptions the instructions for the PDA can be written as follows:

$\langle 0, a, ?, \text{push}(a), 0 \rangle$ (push string w on the stack),

$\langle 0, b, ?, \text{push}(b), 0 \rangle$,

$\langle 0, \Lambda, ?, \text{nop}, 1 \rangle$,

$\langle 1, a, a, \text{pop}, 1 \rangle$ (pop string w^R off the stack),

$\langle 1, b, b, \text{pop}, 1 \rangle$,

$\langle 1, \Lambda, X, \text{nop}, 2 \rangle$.

How many instructions does the PDA have if we don't allow question marks? For practice, draw the graphical version of the PDA.   ♦

Representing and Executing Pushdown Automata

When we talk about PDAs, it's sometimes convenient to represent them by listing seven things: the set of states, the alphabet, the stack alphabet, the instructions, the starting stack symbol, the start state, and set of final states. Traditionally, these seven items are listed as a 7-tuple. For example, if someone says, "Let $\langle S, A, B, I, E, s, F \rangle$ be a PDA," then we can assume that S is the set of states, A is the alphabet, B is the set of stack symbols, I is the instruction set, E is the starting stack symbol, s is the start state, and F is the set of final states.

We can also represent any PDA as an algebraic structure, which will help us discover a general algorithm for a PDA interpreter. To start things off, suppose we have a PDA represented as the 7-tuple $\langle S, A, B, I, E, s, F \rangle$. Assume that we also have an algebra of stacks, where "Stacks" is the set of stacks whose elements are from the set of stack symbols B and "StkCalls" is the set of stack operations. We can describe the algebra for a PDA as follows:

Carriers: $S, A, A^*, B,$ Stacks, StkCalls, Boolean.

Operations: $s \in S,$
                $F \subset S,$
                $I \subset S \times A \cup \{\Lambda\} \times B \times \text{StkCalls} \times S,$
                path : $S \times A^* \times \text{Stacks} \rightarrow \text{Boolean},$
                accept : $A^* \rightarrow \text{Boolean}.$

Axioms: To simplify the presentation of the axioms, we'll represent a stack as a list of the form $X :: Y$, where X is the top of the stack. If we have a stack $X :: Y$ and an instruction $\langle k, \Lambda, X, O, j \rangle$, then newStack denotes the stack obtained by applying operation O to the stack $X :: Y$. With these assumptions we can write the axioms as follows, where w is an input string and E is the starting stack symbol:

accept(w) =   path$(s, w, \langle E \rangle)$.

path$(k, \Lambda, X :: Y)$ =   **if** k is a final state **then** true
                            else if there is an instruction $\langle k, \Lambda, X, O, n \rangle$
                               then path$(n, \Lambda, \text{newStack})$ **else** false.

path$(k, a{\cdot}t, X :: Y)$ =   **if** there is an instruction $\langle k, a, X, O, n \rangle$
                              and path$(n, t, \text{newStack})$ = true
                          or there is an instruction $\langle k, \Lambda, X, O, n \rangle$
                              and path$(n, a{\cdot}t, \text{newStack})$ = true
                          then true **else** false.

The axioms give us the basic information we need to build an interpreter for PDAs. We'll give a logic program version in the next example.

EXAMPLE 8 (*A Logic Program Interpreter for PDAs*). Suppose we write a PDA as a set of logic program facts taking one of the following forms:

$$t(\text{state, letter, top, operation, nextState}) \leftarrow,$$
$$\text{final(state)} \leftarrow.$$

To write a simple interpreter for PDAs, we'll make a few assumptions. We will require that every PDA start in state 0. The stack is a list that is initialized with the value $\langle e \rangle$, which means that e is always the starting stack symbol. We'll reserve the letters p and n for the operations pop and nop, and we'll agree to let the push instruction be represented by the symbol that is to be pushed. For example, in the instruction

$$t(0, a, e, b, 1) \leftarrow$$

the letter b means push b. For example, a PDA to recognize the language $\{a^n b^n \mid n \geq 0\}$ can be written as follows:

$$t(0, a, e, a, 0) \leftarrow$$
$$t(0, a, a, a, 0) \leftarrow$$
$$t(0, b, a, p, 1) \leftarrow$$
$$t(0, \Lambda, e, n, 2) \leftarrow$$
$$t(1, b, a, p, 1) \leftarrow$$
$$t(1, \Lambda, e, n, 2) \leftarrow$$
$$\text{final}(2) \leftarrow.$$

To test whether the string *aabb* is accepted, we would write the goal

$$\leftarrow \text{accept}(aabb).$$

This goal starts the execution of the PDA interpreter, which we'll now describe.

The interpreter executes a computation sequence, where the "path" predicate represents an ID containing the current state, the current input string, and the current stack. If the input is empty and the current state is final, then the computation ends successfully. Otherwise, if the input is not empty, the computation continues by looking up an appropriate instruction.

The predicate oper(Stack, O, NewStack) means "perform stack operation O on Stack, resulting in NewStack." Recall that $A \cdot B$ denotes the string whose head is A and whose tail is B, and $H :: T$ denotes the list whose head is H and whose tail is T. The interpreter can be written as follows, where S is the input string, and all variables start with capital letters:

$$\text{accept}(S) \leftarrow \text{path}(0, S, \langle e \rangle)$$

$$\text{path}(K, \Lambda, \text{Stack}) \leftarrow \text{final}(K)$$

$$\text{path}(K, A{\cdot}B, H::T) \leftarrow \quad t(K, A, H, O, N),$$
$$\text{oper}(H::T, O, \text{NewStack}),$$
$$\text{path}(N, B, \text{NewStack})$$

$$\text{path}(K, \text{String}, H::T) \leftarrow \quad t(K, \Lambda, H, O, N),$$
$$\text{oper}(H::T, O, \text{NewStack}),$$
$$\text{path}(N, \text{String}, \text{NewStack})$$

$$\text{oper}(H::T, p, T) \leftarrow$$

$$\text{oper}(\text{Stack}, n, \text{Stack}) \leftarrow$$

$$\text{oper}(\text{Stack}, A, A::\text{Stack}) \leftarrow.$$

If we need to represent input strings as lists, then some minor modifications need to be made. Then to test whether the string *aabb* is accepted we would write the goal

$$\leftarrow \text{accept}(\langle a, a, b, b \rangle). \quad \blacklozenge$$

Exercises

1. Find a pushdown automaton for each of the following languages.
    a. $\{ab^ncd^n \mid n \geq 0\}$.
    b. All strings over $\{a, b\}$ with the same number of a's and b's.
    c. $\{wcw^R \mid w \in \{a, b\}^*\}$.
    d. The palindromes of odd length over $\{a, b\}$.
    e. $\{a^nb^{n+2} \mid n \geq 0\}$.

2. Find a single state PDA to recognize the language $\{a^nb^m \mid n, m \in \mathbb{N}\}$.

3. For each of the following languages, find a deterministic PDA that accepts by final state.
    a. $\{a^nb^n \mid n \geq 0\}$.
    b. $\{a^nb^{2n} \mid n \geq 0\}$.

4. If we allow each PDA instruction to contain any finite sequence of stack operations, then we can reduce the number of states required for any PDA. Let $L = \{a^nb^n \mid n \in \mathbb{N}\}$. Find PDAs that accept L by final state with the given restrictions.

a. A two-state PDA that contains one or more Λ instructions.

b. A two-state PDA that does not contain any Λ instructions.

5. Use (6.4) to transform the final state PDA from Example 1 into an empty stack PDA.

6. Use (6.5) to transform the empty stack PDA from Example 2 into a final state PDA.

7. In each of the following cases, use (6.7) to construct a PDA that accepts the language of the given grammar.

   a. $S \to c \mid aSb$.

   b. $S \to \Lambda \mid aSb \mid aaS$.

8. Use (6.8) to construct a grammar for the language of the following PDA that accepts by empty stack, where 0 is the start state and X is the initial stack symbol: $\langle 0, a, X, \text{push}(X), 0 \rangle, \langle 0, \Lambda, X, \text{pop}, 1 \rangle$, $\langle 1, b, X, \text{pop}, 1 \rangle$.

9. Suppose we're given the following PDA that accepts by empty stack, where X is the initial stack symbol:

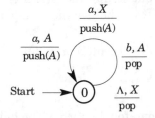

   a. Use your wits to describe the language recognized by the PDA.

   b. Use (6.8) to construct a grammar for the language of the PDA.

   c. Do your answers to parts (a) and (b) describe the same language?

10. Give an argument to show that the following context-free language is not accepted by any deterministic PDA: $\{a^n b^n \mid n \geq 0\} \cup \{a^n b^{2n} \mid n \geq 0\}$.

6.3 Parsing Techniques

An important part of compiler construction for programming languages is the study of techniques to construct parsers. Virtually all programming language constructs can be represented by context-free grammars. Since the context-free languages are exactly those that can be recognized by PDAs, it follows that parsers can be constructed for these languages (i.e., a parser is a PDA). Context-free languages that are not regular don't have algebraic representations like the regular expressions that represent regular languages. Therefore the grammar is the important factor in trying to construct parsers for programming languages.

One goal of the compiler writer is to build a parser that is efficient. If a parser is nondeterministic, then time can be wasted by backtracking to find a proper derivation path. It's nice to know that most programming language constructs have deterministic parsers. In other words, the languages are recognized by deterministic PDAs. If a context-free language can be recognized by a deterministic PDA by final state, then the language is said to be a *deterministic context-free* language. We'll confine our remarks to deterministic context-free languages.

When a parse tree for a string is constructed by starting at the root and proceeding downward toward the leaves, the construction is called *top-down parsing*. A top-down parser constructs a derivation by starting with the grammar's start symbol and working toward the string. Another type of parsing is *bottom-up parsing*, in which the parse tree for a string is constructed by starting with the leaves and working up to the root of the tree. A bottom-up parser constructs a derivation by starting with the string and working backwards to the start symbol.

LL(k) Parsing

Many deterministic context-free languages can be parsed top-down if they can be described by a special kind of grammar called an LL(k) grammar. An LL(k) *grammar* has the property that a parser can be constructed that scans an input string from left to right and builds a leftmost derivation of the string by examining the next k symbols of the input string. In other words, the next k input symbols of a string are enough to determine the unique production to be used at each step of the derivation. The next k symbols of the input string are often called *lookahead symbols*. LL(k) grammars were introduced by Lewis and Stearns [1968]. The first letter L stands for the left-to-right scan of input, and the second letter L stands for the leftmost derivation.

It's often quite easy to inspect a grammar and determine whether it's an LL(k) grammar for some k. So we'll spend a little time discussing LL(k) grammars. Let's get our feet wet with some examples.

EXAMPLE 1 (*An LL(1) Grammar*). Let's consider the following language:

$$\{a^n b c^n \mid n \in \mathbb{N}\}. \tag{6.10}$$

A grammar for this language can be written as follows:

$$S \to aSc \mid b. \tag{6.11}$$

This grammar is LL(1) because the right sides of the two S productions begin with distinct letters a and b. Therefore each step of a leftmost derivation is uniquely determined by examining the current input symbol (i.e., one lookahead symbol). In other words, if the lookahead symbol is a, then the production $S \to aSc$ is used; if the lookahead symbol is b, then the production $S \to b$ is used. For example, the derivation of the string

$$aabcc$$

can be constructed as follows, where we've written a reason for each step:

$$\begin{aligned} S &\Rightarrow aSc & &\text{Use } S \to aSc \text{ because } aabcc \text{ begins with } a. \\ &\Rightarrow aaScc & &\text{Use } S \to aSc \text{ because } abcc \text{ begins with } a. \\ &\Rightarrow aabcc & &\text{Use } S \to b \text{ because } bcc \text{ begins with } b. \end{aligned}$$

This derivation is a leftmost derivation by default because there is only one nonterminal to replace in each *sentential form* (i.e., string of terminals and/or nonterminals).   ◆

EXAMPLE 2 (*An* LL(2) *Grammar*). Let's consider the following language:

$$\{a^m b^n c \mid m \geq 1 \text{ and } n \geq 0\}. \tag{6.12}$$

A grammar for this language can be written as follows:

$$\begin{aligned} S &\to AB & &\tag{6.13} \\ A &\to aA \mid a \\ B &\to bB \mid c. \end{aligned}$$

This grammar is not LL(1) because the right sides of the two A productions begin with the same letter a. For example, the first letter of the string abc is not enough information to choose the correct A production to continue the following leftmost derivation:

$$\begin{aligned} S &\Rightarrow AB & &\text{No other choice.} \\ &\Rightarrow ? & &\text{Don't know which } A \text{ production to choose.} \end{aligned}$$

After some thought we can see that (6.13) is LL(2) because a string starting with aa causes the production $A \to aA$ to be chosen, and a string starting with either ab or ac forces the production $A \to a$ to be chosen. For example, the leftmost derivation of the string $aabbc$ can be constructed as follows:

S	$\Rightarrow AB$	No other choice.
	$\Rightarrow aAB$	Use $A \to aA$ because $aabbc$ begins with aa.
	$\Rightarrow aaB$	Use $A \to a$ because $abbc$ begins with ab.
	$\Rightarrow aabB$	Use $B \to bB$ because bbc begins with b.
	$\Rightarrow aabbB$	Use $B \to bB$ because bc begins with b.
	$\Rightarrow aabbc$	Use $B \to c$ because c begins with c. ◆

Suppose we have a grammar that contains two productions—where one or both right sides begin with nonterminals—like the two S productions in the following grammar:

$$S \to A \mid B \tag{6.14}$$
$$A \to aA \mid \Lambda$$
$$B \to bB \mid c.$$

Is this an LL(k) grammar? The answer is yes. In fact it's an LL(1) grammar. The A and B productions are clearly LL(1). The only problem is to figure out which S production should be chosen to start a derivation. If the first letter of the input string is a or if the input string is empty, we use production $S \to A$. Otherwise, if the first letter is b or c, then we use the production $S \to B$. In either case, all we need is one lookahead symbol. So we might have to chase through a few productions to check the LL(k) property. Most programming constructs can be described by LL(1) grammars that are easy to check.

Grammar Transformations

Just because we write down an LL(k) grammar for some language doesn't mean we've found an LL grammar with the smallest such k. For example, grammar (6.13) is an LL(2) grammar for $\{a^m b^n c \mid m \geq 1 \text{ and } n \geq 0\}$. But it's easy to see that the following grammar is an LL(1) grammar for this language:

$$S \to aAB \tag{6.15}$$
$$A \to aA \mid \Lambda$$
$$B \to bB \mid c.$$

Sometimes it's possible to transform an LL(k) grammar into an LL(n) grammar for some $n < k$ by a process called *left factoring*. An example should suffice to describe the process. Suppose we're given the following LL(3) grammar fragment:

$$S \to abcC \mid abdD.$$

Since the two right sides have the common prefix ab, we can "factor out" the string ab to obtain the following equivalent productions, where B is a new nonterminal:

$$S \to abB$$
$$B \to cC \mid dD.$$

This grammar fragment is LL(1). So an LL(3) grammar fragment has been transformed into an LL(1) grammar fragment by left factoring.

Sometimes we can transform a grammar that is not LL(k) into an LL(k) grammar for the same language. A grammar is *left-recursive* if for some non-terminal A there is a derivation of the form $A \Rightarrow \dots \Rightarrow Aw$ for some nonempty string w. An LL(k) grammar can't be left-recursive because there is no way to tell how many times a left-recursive derivation may need to be repeated before an alternative production is chosen to stop the recursion. Here's an example of a grammar that is not LL(k) for any k.

EXAMPLE 3 (*A Non*-LL(k) *Grammar*). The language $\{ba^n \mid n \in \mathbb{N}\}$ has the following left-recursive grammar:

$$A \to Aa \mid b.$$

We can see that this grammar is not LL(1) because if the string ba is input, then the first letter b is not enough to determine which production to use to start the leftmost derivation of ba. Similarly, the grammar is not LL(2) because if the input string is baa, then the first two-letter string ba is enough to start the derivation of baa with the production $A \to Aa$. But the letter b of the input string can't be consumed because it doesn't occur at the left of Aa. Thus the same two-letter string ba must determine the next step of the derivation, causing $A \to Aa$ to be chosen. This goes on forever, obtaining an infinite derivation. The same idea can be used to show that the grammar is not LL(k) for any k. ◆

Sometimes we can remove the left recursion from a grammar and the resulting grammar is an LL(k) grammar for the same language. A simple form of left recursion that occurs frequently is called *immediate* left recursion. This type of recursion occurs when the grammar contains a production of the form $A \to Aw$. In this case there must be at least one other A production to stop the recursion. Thus the simplest form of immediate left recursion takes the following form, where w and y are strings:

$$A \to Aw \mid y.$$

But there may be more than one A production that is left-recursive. For example, three of the following A productions are left-recursive, where u, v, w, x, and y denote arbitrary strings of symbols:

$$A \to Aw \mid Au \mid Av \mid x \mid y.$$

It's easy to remove this immediate left recursion. Notice that any string derived from A must start with either x or y and is followed by any combination of w's, u's, and v's. We replace the A productions by the following productions, where B is a new nonterminal:

$$A \to xB \mid yB$$
$$B \to wB \mid uB \mid vB \mid \Lambda.$$

This grammar may or may not be LL(k). It depends on the value of the strings x, y, w, u, and v. For example, if they all are single distinct terminals, then the grammar is LL(1). Here are two examples.

EXAMPLE 4. Let's look again at the language $\{ba^n \mid n \in \mathbb{N}\}$ and the following left-recursive grammar:

$$A \to Aa \mid b.$$

We saw in Example 3 that this grammar is not LL(k) for any k. But we can remove the immediate left recursion in this grammar to obtain the following LL(1) grammar for the same language:

$$A \to bB$$
$$B \to aB \mid \Lambda. \quad \blacklozenge$$

EXAMPLE 5. Let's look at an example that occurs in programming languages that process arithmetic expressions. Suppose we want to parse the set of all arithmetic expressions described by the following grammar:

$$E \to E+T \mid T$$
$$T \to T*F \mid F$$
$$F \to (E) \mid a.$$

This grammar is not LL(k) for any k because it's left-recursive. For example, the expression $a*a*a+a$ requires a scan of the first six symbols to determine that the first production in a derivation is $E \to E+T$.

Let's remove the immediate left recursion for the nonterminals E and T. The result is the following LL(1) grammar for the same language of expressions:

$$E \rightarrow TR$$
$$R \rightarrow +TR \mid \Lambda$$
$$T \rightarrow FV$$
$$V \rightarrow *FV \mid \Lambda$$
$$F \rightarrow (E) \mid a.$$

For example, we'll construct a leftmost derivation of $(a+a)*a$. Check the LL(1) property by verifying that each step of the derivation is uniquely determined by the single current input symbol:

$$E \Rightarrow TR \Rightarrow FVR \Rightarrow (E)VR \Rightarrow (TR)VR \Rightarrow (FVR)VR$$
$$\Rightarrow (aVR)VR \Rightarrow (aR)VR \Rightarrow (a+TR)VR$$
$$\Rightarrow (a+FVR)VR \Rightarrow (a+aVR)VR$$
$$\Rightarrow (a+aR)VR \Rightarrow (a+a)VR \Rightarrow (a+a)*FVR$$
$$\Rightarrow (a+a)*aVR \Rightarrow (a+a)*aR \Rightarrow (a+a)*a. \quad \blacklozenge$$

The other kind of left recursion that can occur in a grammar is called *indirect* left recursion. This type of recursion occurs when at least two nonterminals are involved in the recursion. For example, the following grammar is left-recursive because it has indirect left recursion:

$$S \rightarrow Bb$$
$$B \rightarrow Sa \mid a.$$

To see the left recursion in this grammar, notice the following derivation:

$$S \Rightarrow Bb \Rightarrow Sab.$$

We can remove indirect left recursion from this grammar in two steps. First, replace B in the S production by the right side of the B production to obtain the following grammar:

$$S \rightarrow Sab \mid ab.$$

Now remove the immediate left recursion in the usual manner to obtain the following LL(1) grammar:

$$S \to abT$$
$$T \to abT \mid \Lambda.$$

This idea can be generalized to remove all left recursion in many context-free grammars.

Top-Down Methods

LL(k) grammars have top-down parsing algorithms because a leftmost derivation can be constructed by starting with the start symbol and proceeding through sentential forms until the desired string is obtained. We'll illustrate the ideas of top-down parsing with examples. One method of top-down parsing, called *recursive descent*, can be accomplished by associating a procedure with each nonterminal. The parse begins by calling the procedure associated with the start symbol.

For example, suppose we have the following LL(1) grammar fragment for two statements in a programming language:

$$S \to \text{id} = E \mid \textbf{while } E \textbf{ do } S.$$

We'll assume that any program statement can be broken down into "tokens," which are numbers that represent the syntactic objects. For example, the statement

while $x < y$ **do** $x = x + 1$

might be represented by the following string of tokens, which we've represented by capitalized words:

WHILE ID LESS ID DO ID EQ ID PLUS CONSTANT

To parse a program statement, we'll assume that there is a variable "lookahead" that holds the current input token. Initially, lookahead is given the value of the first token, which in our case is the WHILE token. We'll also assume that there is a procedure "match," where match(x) checks to see whether x matches the lookahead value. If a match occurs, then lookahead is given the next token value in the input string. Otherwise, an error message is produced. The match procedure can be described as follows:

procedure match(x)
  if lookahead = x **then**
    lookahead := next input token
  else
    error
  fi

For example, if lookahead = WHILE and we call match(WHILE), then a match occurs, and lookahead is given the new value ID. We'll assume that the procedure for the nonterminal E, to recognize expressions, is already written. Now the procedure for the nonterminal S can be written as follows:

procedure S
    if lookahead = ID **then**
        match(ID);
        match(EQ);
        E
    else if lookahead = WHILE **then**
        match(WHILE);
        E;
        match(DO);
        S
    else
        error
fi

This parser is a deterministic PDA in disguise: The "match" procedure consumes an item of input; the state transitions are statements in the then and else clauses; and the stack is hidden because the procedures are recursive. In an actual implementation, procedure S would also contain output statements that could be used to construct the machine code to be generated by the compiler. Thus an actual parser is a PDA with output. A PDA with output is often called a *pushdown transducer*. So we can say that parsers are pushdown transducers.

Another top-down parsing method uses a parse table and an explicit stack instead of the recursive descent procedures. We'll briefly describe the idea for LL(1) grammars. Each parse table entry is either a production or an error message. The entries in the parse table are accessed by two symbols— the symbol on top of the stack and the current input symbol. We pick a non-grammar symbol such as

$$\$$$

and place one $\$$ on the bottom of the stack and one $\$$ at the right end of the input string.

The parsing algorithm begins with the grammar's start symbol on top of the stack. The algorithm consists of a loop that stops when either the input string is accepted or an error is detected. An input string is accepted when the top of the stack is $\$$ and the current input symbol is $\$$. The actions in the loop are guided by the top of the stack T and the current input symbol c. The loop can be described as follows, where P is the parse table and $P[T, c]$ denotes the entry in row T and column c:

> **loop**
>> Let T be the top symbol on the stack;
>> Let c be the current input symbol;
>> **if** $T = c = \$$ **then** "accept"
>> **else if** T is a terminal or $T = \$$ **then**
>>> **if** $T = c$ **then** pop T and consume the input c
>>> **else** call an error routine
>> **else if** $P[T, c]$ is the production $T \to w$ **then**
>>> pop T and push the symbols of w onto the stack in reverse order
>>> **else** call an error routine
>
> **pool**

The construction of the parse table is the major task for this parsing method. We'll give a brief overview. To describe the table-building process we need to introduce two functions—*First* and *Follow*—that construct certain sets of terminals.

We'll start with the *First* sets. If x is any string, then First(x) is the set of terminals that appear at the left end of any string derived from x. We also put Λ in First(x) if x derives Λ. We can compute First inductively by applying the following rules, where a is a terminal, A is a nonterminal, and w denotes any string of grammar symbols that may include terminals and/or nonterminals:

1. First(Λ) = {Λ}.
2. First(aw) = First(a) = {a}.
3. If $A \to w_1 \mid ... \mid w_n$, then First($A$) = First($w_1$) $\cup$ ... $\cup$ First(w_n).
4. If $w \neq \Lambda$, then we can compute First(Aw) as follows:
   If $\Lambda \notin$ First(A) then First(Aw) = First(A).
   If $\Lambda \in$ First(A) then First(Aw) = (First(A) − {Λ}) $\cup$ First(w).

EXAMPLE 6. Suppose we have the following grammar:

$$S \to ASb \mid C \qquad\qquad (6.16)$$
$$A \to a$$
$$C \to cC \mid \Lambda.$$

Let's compute the First sets for some strings that occur in the grammar.

Make sure you can follow each calculation by referring to one of the four First rules.

First(Λ) = {Λ},

First(a) = {a}, First(b) = {b}, and First(c) = {c},

First(cC) = First(c) = {c},

First(C) = First(cC) $\cup$ First(Λ) = {c} $\cup$ {Λ} = {c, Λ},

First(A) = First(a) = {a},

First(ASb) = First(A) = {a},

First(S) = First(ASb) $\cup$ First(C) = {a} $\cup$ {c, Λ} = {a, c, Λ},

First(Sb) = (First(S) $-$ {Λ}) $\cup$ First(b) = ({a, c, Λ} $-$ {Λ}) $\cup$ {b} = {a, b, c}. ◆

Now let's define the *Follow* sets. If A is a nonterminal, then Follow(A) is the set of terminals that can appear to the right of A in some sentential form of a derivation. To calculate Follow we apply the following rules until they can't be applied any longer, where capital letters denote nonterminals and x and y denote arbitrary strings of grammar symbols that may include terminals and/or nonterminals:

1. If S is the start symbol, then put \$ $\in$ Follow(S).
2. If $A \to xB$, then put Follow(A) $\subset$ Follow(B).
3. If $A \to xBy$, then put (First(y) $-$ {Λ}) $\subset$ Follow(B).
4. If $A \to xBy$ and $\Lambda \in$ First(y), then put Follow(A) $\subset$ Follow(B).

EXAMPLE 7. We'll compute the Follow sets for the three nonterminals in the following grammar, which is grammar (6.16) of Example 6:

$$S \to ASb \mid C$$
$$A \to a$$
$$C \to cC \mid \Lambda.$$

We'll also need to use some of the First sets for this grammar that we computed in Example 6.

Follow(S):

By rule 1, we have \$ $\in$ Follow(S). By rule 3 applied to $S \to ASb$, we have (First(b) $-$ {Λ}) $\subset$ Follow(S). This says that $b \in$ Follow(S). Since no other rules apply, we have Follow(S) = {$b,$ \$}.

Follow(A):

By rule 3 applied to $S \rightarrow ASb$, we have (First(Sb) − {Λ}) $\subset$ Follow(A). Since First(Sb) = {a, b, c}, we have {a, b, c} $\subset$ Follow(A). Since no other rules apply, we have Follow(A) = {a, b, c}.

Follow(C):

By rule 2 applied to $S \rightarrow C$, we have Follow(S) $\subset$ Follow(C). Rule 2 applied to $C \rightarrow cC$ says that Follow(C) $\subset$ Follow(C). Since no other rules apply, we have Follow(C) = Follow(S) = {$b, \$$}.

So the three Follow sets for the grammar are

$$\text{Follow}(S) = \{b, \$\},$$
$$\text{Follow}(A) = \{a, b, c\},$$
$$\text{Follow}(C) = \{b, \$\}. \quad \blacklozenge$$

Once we know how to compute First and Follow sets, it's an easy matter to construct an LL(1) parse table. Here's the algorithm:

Construction of LL(1) *Parse Table*

The parse table P for an LL(1) grammar can be constructed by performing the following three steps for each production $A \rightarrow w$:

1. For each terminal $a \in$ First(w), put $A \rightarrow w$ in $P[A, a]$.

2. If $\Lambda \in$ First(w), then for each terminal $a \in$ Follow(A), put $A \rightarrow w$ in $P[A, a]$.

3. If $\Lambda \in$ First(w) and $\$ \in$ Follow(A), then put $A \rightarrow w$ in $P[A, \$]$.

End of Algorithm

This algorithm also provides a check to see whether the grammar is LL(1). If some entry of the table contains more than one production, then the grammar is not LL(1). Here's an example.

EXAMPLE 8. We'll apply the algorithm to grammar (6.16) of Example 6:

$$S \rightarrow ASb \mid C$$
$$A \rightarrow a$$
$$C \rightarrow cC \mid \Lambda.$$

Using the First and Follow sets from Examples 6 and 7 we obtain the following parse table for the grammar:

	a	b	c	$\$$
S	$S \to ASb$	$S \to C$	$S \to C$	$S \to C$
A	$A \to a$			
C		$C \to \Lambda$	$C \to cC$	$C \to \Lambda$

Let's do a parse of the string *aaccbb* using this table. We'll represent each step of the parse by a line containing the stack contents and the unconsumed input, where the top of the stack is at the right end of the stack string and the current input symbol is at the left end of the input string. The third column of each line contains the actions to perform to obtain the next line, where consume means get the next input symbol.

Stack	*Input*	*Actions to Perform*
$\$S$	$aaccbb\$$	Pop, push b, push S, push A
$\$bSA$	$aaccbb\$$	Pop, push a
$\$bSa$	$aaccbb\$$	Pop, consume
$\$bS$	$accbb\$$	Pop, push b, push S, push A
$\$bbSA$	$accbb\$$	Pop, push a
$\$bbSa$	$accbb\$$	Pop, consume
$\$bbS$	$ccbb\$$	Pop, push C
$\$bbC$	$ccbb\$$	Pop, push C, push c
$\$bbCc$	$ccbb\$$	Pop, consume
$\$bbC$	$cbb\$$	Pop, push C, push c
$\$bbCc$	$cbb\$$	Pop, consume
$\$bbC$	$bb\$$	Pop
$\$bb$	$bb\$$	Pop, consume
$\$b$	$b\$$	Pop, consume
$\$$	$\$$	Accept ◆

LL(*k*) Facts

An important result about LL(*k*) grammars is that they describe a proper hierarchy of languages. In other words, for any $k \in \mathbb{N}$ there is a proper containment of languages as follows:

$$LL(k) \text{ languages} \subset LL(k + 1) \text{ languages.} \tag{6.17}$$

This result is due to Kurki-Suonio [1969]. In particular, Kurki-Suonio showed that for each $k > 1$ the following grammar is an $LL(k)$ grammar whose language has no $LL(k - 1)$ grammar:

$$S \to aSA \mid \Lambda \tag{6.18}$$
$$A \to a^{k-1}bS \mid c.$$

We should emphasize that the $LL(k)$ grammars can't describe every deterministic context-free language. This result was shown by Rosenkrantz and Stearns [1970]. For example, consider the following language:

$$\{a^n \mid n \ge 0\} \cup \{a^n b^n \mid n \ge 0\}.$$

This is a classic example of a deterministic context-free language that is not $LL(k)$ for any k. It is deterministic context-free because it can be accepted by the following deterministic PDA, where X is the starting stack symbol:

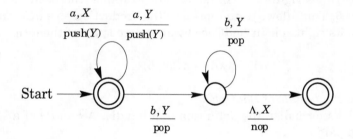

Let's see why the language is not $LL(k)$ for any k. Any grammar for the language needs two productions, such as $S \to A \mid C$, where A generates strings of the form a^n and C generates strings of the form $a^n b^n$. Notice that the two strings a^{k+1} and $a^{k+1}b^{k+1}$ both start with $k + 1$ a's. Therefore k symbols of lookahead are not sufficient to decide whether to use $S \to A$ or $S \to C$.

Next we'll discuss a bottom-up technique for parsing any deterministic context-free language.

LR(k) Parsing

A powerful class of grammars whose languages can be parsed bottom-up is the set of $LR(k)$ grammars, which were introduced by Knuth [1965]. These grammars allow a string to be parsed in a bottom-up fashion by constructing a rightmost derivation in reverse.

To describe these grammars and the parsing technique for their languages, we need to define an object called a *handle*. We'll introduce the idea with an example and then give the formal definition. Suppose the production $A \to aCb$ is used to make the following derivation step in some rightmost derivation, where we've underlined the occurrence of the production's right side in the derived sentential form:

$$BaAbc \Rightarrow Ba\underline{aCb}bc.$$

The problem of bottom-up parsing is to perform this derivation step in reverse. In other words, we must discover this derivation step from our knowledge of the grammar and by scanning the sentential form

$$BaaCbbc.$$

By scanning $BaaCbbc$ we must find two things: The production $A \to aCb$ and the occurrence of its right side in $BaaCbbc$. With these two pieces of information we can reduce $Ba\underline{aCb}bc$ to $BaAbc$.

We'll denote the occurrence of a substring within a string by the position of the substring's rightmost character. For example, the position of aCb in $BaaCbbc$ is 5. This allows us to represent the production $A \to aCb$ and the occurrence of its right side in $BaaCbbc$ by an ordered pair of the form

$$\langle A \to aCb \, , 5 \rangle,$$

which we call a *handle* of $BaaCbbc$.

Now let's formalize the definition of a handle. A *handle* of a sentential form w is a pair

$$\langle A \to y, p \rangle,$$

where w can be written in the form $w = xyz$, p is the length of the string xy, and z is a string of terminals. This allows us to say that there is a rightmost derivation step

$$xAz \Rightarrow xyz = w.$$

EXAMPLE 9 (*A Bottom-Up Parse*). Suppose we have the following grammar for arithmetic expressions, where a stands for an identifier:

$$E \to E{+}T \mid T$$
$$T \to T{*}F \mid F$$
$$F \to (E) \mid a.$$

We'll perform a bottom-up parse of the string $a+a*a$ by constructing a rightmost derivation in reverse. Each row of the following table represents a step of the reverse derivation by listing a sentential form together with the handle used to make the reduction for the next step.

Sentential Form	Handle
$a+a*a$	$\langle F \to a, 1 \rangle$
$F+a*a$	$\langle T \to F, 1 \rangle$
$T+a*a$	$\langle E \to T, 1 \rangle$
$E+a*a$	$\langle F \to a, 3 \rangle$
$E+F*a$	$\langle T \to F, 3 \rangle$
$E+T*a$	$\langle F \to a, 5 \rangle$
$E+T*F$	$\langle T \to T*F, 5 \rangle$
$E+T$	$\langle E \to E+T, 3 \rangle$
E	

So we've constructed the following rightmost derivation in reverse:

$$E \ \Rightarrow E+T \Rightarrow E+T*F \Rightarrow E+T*a \Rightarrow E+F*a \Rightarrow E+a*a$$
$$\Rightarrow T+a*a \Rightarrow F+a*a \Rightarrow a+a*a. \quad \blacklozenge$$

Now let's get down to business and discuss LR(k) grammars and parsing techniques. An LR(k) *grammar* has the property that every string has a unique rightmost derivation that can be constructed in reverse order, where the handle of each sentential form is found by scanning the form's symbols from left to right, including up to k symbols past the handle. By "past the handle" we mean: If $\langle A \to y, p \rangle$ is the handle of xyz, then we can determine it by a left-to-right scan of xyz, including up to k symbols in z. We should also say that the L in LR(k) means a left-to-right scan of the input and the R means construct a rightmost derivation in reverse.

For example, in an LR(0) grammar we can't look at any symbols beyond the handle to find it. Knuth showed that the number k doesn't affect the collection of languages defined by such grammars for $k \geq 1$. He also showed that the deterministic context-free languages are exactly the languages that can be described by LR(1) grammars. Thus we have the following relationships for all $k \geq 1$:

LR(k) languages = LR(1) languages

= deterministic context-free languages.

EXAMPLE 10 (*An* LR(0) *Grammar*). Let's see whether we can convince ourselves that the following grammar is LR(0):

$$S \to aAc$$
$$A \to Abb \mid b.$$

This grammar generates the language $\{ab^{2n+1}c \mid n \geq 0\}$. We need to see that the handle of any sentential form can be found without scanning past it. There are only three kinds of sentential forms, other than the start symbol, that occur in any derivation:

$$ab^{2n+1}c, \quad aAb^{2n}c, \quad \text{and} \quad aAc.$$

For example, the string *abbbbbc* is derived as follows:

$$S \Rightarrow aAc \Rightarrow aAbbc \Rightarrow aAbbbbc \Rightarrow abbbbbc.$$

Scanning the prefix *ab* in $ab^{2n+1}c$ is sufficient to conclude that the handle is $\langle A \to b, 2\rangle$. So we don't need to scan beyond the handle to discover it. Similarly, scanning the prefix *aAbb* of $aAb^{2n}c$ is enough to conclude that its handle is $\langle A \to Abb, 4\rangle$. Here, too, we don't need to scan beyond the handle to find it. Lastly, scanning all of *aAc* tells us that its handle is $\langle S \to aAc, 3\rangle$ and we don't need to scan beyond the *c*.

Since we can determine the handle of any sentential form in a rightmost derivation without looking at any symbols beyond the handle, it follows that the grammar is LR(0). ◆

To get some more practice with LR(*k*) grammars, let's look at a grammar for the language of Example 10 that is not LR(*k*) for any *k*.

EXAMPLE 11. In the preceding example we gave an LR(0) grammar for the language $\{ab^{2n+1}c \mid n \geq 0\}$. Here's an example of a grammar for the same language that is not LR(*k*) for any *k*:

$$S \to aAc$$
$$A \to bAb \mid b.$$

For example, the handle of *abbbc* is $\langle A \to b, 3\rangle$, but we can discover this fact only by examining the entire string, which includes two symbols beyond the handle. Similarly, the handle of *abbbbbc* is $\langle A \to b, 4\rangle$, but we can discover this fact only by examining the entire string, which in this case includes three symbols beyond the handle. In general, the handle for any string $ab^{2n+1}c$ with $n > 0$ is $\langle A \to b, n + 2 \rangle$, and we can discover it only by examining all symbols of the string, including $n + 1$ symbols beyond the handle. Since n can be any positive integer, we can't constrain the number of symbols that need to be examined past a handle to find it. Therefore the grammar is not LR(k) for any natural number k. ◆

EXAMPLE 12 (*An* LR(1) *Grammar*). Let's consider the following grammar:

$$S \to aCd \mid bCD$$
$$C \to cC \mid c$$
$$D \to d.$$

To see that this grammar is LR(1), we'll examine the possible kinds of sentential forms that can occur in a rightmost derivation. The following two rightmost derivations are typical:

$$S \Rightarrow aCd \Rightarrow acCd \Rightarrow accCd \Rightarrow acccd.$$
$$S \Rightarrow bCD \Rightarrow bCd \Rightarrow bcCd \Rightarrow bccCd \Rightarrow bcccd.$$

So we can say with some confidence that any sentential form in a rightmost derivation looks like one of the following forms, where $n \geq 0$:

$$aCd, ac^{n+1}Cd, ac^{n+1}d, bCD, bCd, bc^{n+1}Cd, bc^{n+1}d.$$

It's easy to check that for each of these forms the handle is determined by at most one symbol to its right. In fact, for most these forms the handles are determined with no lookahead. In the following table we've listed each sentential form together with its handle and the number of lookahead symbols to its right that are necessary to determine it.

Sentential Form	Handle	Lookahead
aCd	$\langle S \to aCd, 3 \rangle$	0
$ac^{n+1}Cd$	$\langle C \to cC, n + 3 \rangle$	0
$ac^{n+1}d$	$\langle C \to c, n + 2 \rangle$	1
bCD	$\langle S \to bCD, 3 \rangle$	0
bCd	$\langle D \to d, 3 \rangle$	0
$bc^{n+1}Cd$	$\langle C \to cC, n + 3 \rangle$	0
$bc^{n+1}d$	$\langle C \to c, n + 3 \rangle$	1

So each handle can be determined by observing at most one character to its right. The only situation in which we need to look beyond the handle is when the substring cd occurs in a sentential form. In this case we must examine the d to conclude that the handle's production is $C \to c$. Therefore the grammar is LR(1).   ♦

Now let's discuss LR(k) parsing. Actually, we'll discuss only LR(1) parsing, which is sufficient for all deterministic context-free languages. The goal of an LR(1) parser is to build a rightmost derivation in reverse by using one symbol of lookahead to find handles. To make sure that there is always one symbol of lookahead available to be scanned, we'll attach an end-of-string symbol $ to the right end of the input string. For example, to parse the string abc, we input the string $abc$$.

An LR(1) parser is a table-driven algorithm that uses an explicit stack that always contains the part of a sentential form to the left of the currently scanned symbol. We'll describe the parse table and the parsing process with an example. The grammar of Example 12 is simple enough for us to easily describe the possible sentential forms with handles at the right end. There are eight possible forms, where we've also included S itself:

$$S, aCd, ac^{n+1}C, ac^{n+1}, bCD, bCd, bc^{n+1}C, bc^{n+1}.$$

The next task is to construct a DFA that accepts all strings having these eight forms. The diagram in Figure 6.1 represents such a DFA, where any missing edges go to an error state that we've also omitted.

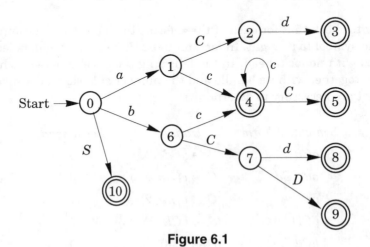

Figure 6.1

Here's the connection between the DFA and the parser: Any path that is traversed by the DFA is represented as a string of symbols on the stack. For example, the path whose symbols concatenate to bC is represented by the stack

$$0\ b\ 6\ C\ 7.$$

The path whose symbols concatenate to $accc$ is represented by the stack

$$0\ a\ 1\ c\ 4\ c\ 4\ c\ 4.$$

The state on top of the stack always represents the current state of the DFA. The parsing process starts with 0 on the stack.

The two main actions of the parser are shifting input symbols onto the stack and reducing handles, which is why this method of parsing is often called *shift-reduce* parsing. The best thing about the parser is that when a handle has been found, its symbols are sitting on the topmost portion of the stack. So a reduction can be performed by popping these symbols off the stack and pushing a nonterminal onto the stack.

Now let's describe the parse table. The rows are indexed by the states of the DFA, and the columns are indexed by the terminals and nonterminals of the grammar, including $. For example, Table 6.1 is the LR(1) parse table for the grammar of Example 12.

	a	b	c	d	$\$$	S	C	D
0	shift 1	shift 6				10		
1			shift 4				2	
2				shift 3				
3					$S \to aCd$			
4			shift 4	$C \to c$			5	
5				$C \to cC$				
6			shift 4				7	
7				shift 8				9
8					$D \to d$			
9					$S \to bCD$			
10					accept			

Table 6.1

The entries in the parse table represent the following actions to be accomplished by the parser:

Entry	Parser Action
shift j	Shift the current input symbol *and* state j onto the stack.
$A \to w$	Reduce the handle by popping the symbols of w from the stack, leaving state k on top. Then push A, and push state table$[k, A]$ onto the stack.
j	Push state j onto the stack during a reduction.
accept	Accept the input string.
blank	This represents an error condition.

Let's use the Table 6.1 to guide the parse of the input string *bccd*. The parse starts with state 0 on the stack and *bccd*$ as the input string. Each step of the parse starts by finding the appropriate action in the parse table indexed by the state on top of the stack and the current input symbol. Then the action is performed, and the parse continues in this way until an error occurs or until an accept entry is found in the table. The following table shows each step in the parse of *bccd*:

Stack	Input	Action to Perform
0	*bccd*$	Shift 6
0 *b* 6	*ccd*$	Shift 4
0 *b* 6 *c* 4	*cd*$	Shift 4
0 *b* 6 *c* 4 *c* 4	*d*$	Reduce by $C \to c$
0 *b* 6 *c* 4 *C* 5	*d*$	Reduce by $C \to cC$
0 *b* 6 *C* 7	*d*$	Shift 8
0 *b* 6 *C* 7 *d* 8	$	Reduce by $D \to d$
0 *b* 6 *C* 7 *D* 9	$	Reduce by $S \to bCD$
0 *S* 10	$	Accept

There are two main points about LR(1) grammars. They describe the class of deterministic context-free languages, and they produce efficient parsing algorithms to perform rightmost derivations in reverse. It's nice to know that there are algorithms to automatically construct LR(1) parse tables. We'll give a short description of the process next.

Constructing an LR(1) Parse Table

To describe the process of constructing a parse table for an LR(1) grammar, we need to introduce a thing called an *item*, which is an ordered pair consisting of a production with a dot placed somewhere on its right side and a terminal symbol or $ or a set of these symbols. For example, the production

$$A \to aBC$$

and the symbol

$$d$$

give rise to the following four items:

$$\langle A \to \cdot bBC, d \rangle,$$
$$\langle A \to b \cdot BC, d \rangle,$$
$$\langle A \to bB \cdot C, d \rangle,$$
$$\langle A \to bBC \cdot, d \rangle.$$

The production $A \to \Lambda$ and the symbol d combine to define the single item

$$\langle A \to \cdot, d \rangle.$$

We're going to use items as states in a finite automaton that accepts strings that end in handles. The position of the dot in an item indicates how close we are to finding a handle. If the dot is all the way to the right end and the currently scanned input symbol (the lookahead) coincides with the second component of the item, then we've found a handle, and we can reduce it by the production in the item. Otherwise, the portion to the left of the dot indicates that we've already found a substring of the input that can be derived from it, and it's possible that we may find another substring that is derivable from the portion to the right of the dot.

For example, if the item is $\langle A \to bBC \cdot, d \rangle$ and the current input symbol is d, then we can use the production $A \to bBC$ to make a reduction. On the other hand, if the item is $\langle A \to bB \cdot C, d \rangle$, then we've already found a substring of the input that can be derived from bB, and it's possible that we may find another substring that is derivable from C.

We can construct an LR(1) parse table by first constructing an NFA whose states are items. Then convert the NFA to a DFA. From the DFA we can read off the LR(1) table entries. We always augment the grammar with a new start symbol S' and a new production $S' \to S$. This ensures that there is only one accept state, as we shall soon see. The algorithm to construct the

NFA consists of applying the following five rules until no new transitions are created:

1. The start state is the item $\langle S' \to \cdot S, \$ \rangle$, which we'll picture graphically as follows:

$$\text{Start} \longrightarrow \boxed{S' \to \cdot S, \$}$$

2. Make the following state transition for each production $B \to w$:

$$\boxed{A \to x \cdot By, d} \xrightarrow{\Lambda} \boxed{B \to \cdot w, \text{First}(yd)}$$

   Note: This transition is a convenient way to represent all transitions of the following form, where $c \in \text{First}(yd)$:

$$\boxed{A \to x \cdot By, d} \xrightarrow{\Lambda} \boxed{B \to \cdot w, c}$$

3. Make the following state transition when B is a nonterminal:

$$\boxed{A \to x \cdot By, d} \xrightarrow{B} \boxed{A \to xB \cdot y, d}$$

4. Make the following state transition when b is a terminal:

$$\boxed{A \to x \cdot by, d} \xrightarrow{b} \boxed{A \to xb \cdot y, d}$$

5. The final states are those items that have the dot at the production's right end.

The NFAs that are constructed by this process can get very large. So we'll look at a very simple example to illustrate the idea. We'll construct a parse table for the grammar

$$S \to aSb \mid \Lambda,$$

which of course generates the language $\{a^n b^n \mid n \geq 0\}$. The NFA for the parse table is shown in Figure 6.2.

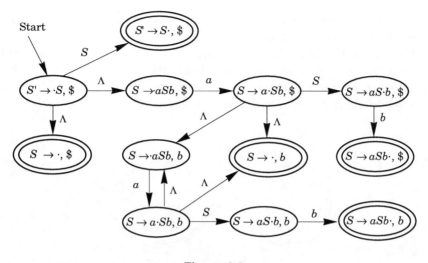

Figure 6.2

Next we transform this NFA into a DFA using the method of Chapter 5. The resulting DFA is shown in Figure 6.3.

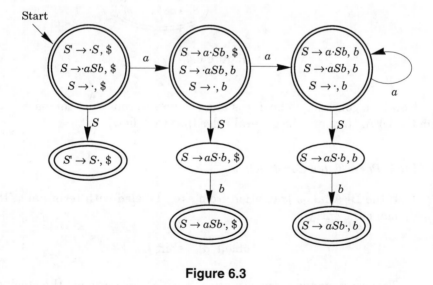

Figure 6.3

At this point we can use the DFA to construct an LR(1) parse table for the grammar. The parse table will have a row for each state of the DFA. We can often reduce the size of the parse table by reducing the number of states in the DFA. We can apply the minimum-state DFA technique from Chapter 5 *if we add the additional condition that equivalent states may not contain distinct productions that end in a dot.*

The reason for this is that productions ending with a dot either cause a reduction to occur or cause acceptance if the item is $\langle S' \to S\cdot, \$\rangle$. With this restriction we can reduce the number of states occurring in the DFA shown in Figure 6.3 from eight to five as shown in Figure 6.4.

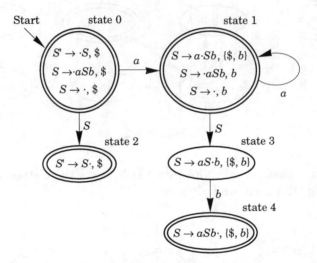

Figure 6.4

Now let's get down to business and see how to construct the parse table from the DFA. Here are the general rules that we follow:

LR(1) *Parse Table Construction*

1. If the DFA has a transition from i to j labeled with terminal a, then make the entry

$$\text{table}[i, a] = \text{shift } j.$$

This corresponds to the situation in which i is on top of the stack and a is the current input symbol. The table entry "shift j" says that we must consume a and push state j onto the stack.

2. If the DFA has a transition from i to j labeled with nonterminal A, then make the entry

$$\text{table}[i, A] = j.$$

This entry is used to find the state j to push onto the stack after some handle has been reduced to A.

3. If i is the final state containing the item $\langle S' \rightarrow S\cdot, \$ \rangle$, then make the entry

$$\text{table}[i, \$] = \text{accept}.$$

Otherwise, if i is a final state containing the item $\langle A \rightarrow w\cdot, a \rangle$, then make the entry

$$\text{table}[i, a] = A \rightarrow w.$$

This means that a reduction must be performed. To perform the reduction, we pop the symbols of w from the stack and observe the state k left sitting on top. Then push A and the state table$[k, A]$ onto the stack. In effect we've backtracked in the DFA along the path of w and then traveled to a new state along the edge labeled with A.

4. Any table entries that are blank at this point are used to signal error conditions about the syntax of the input string.

End of Algorithm

EXAMPLE 13. We can apply the algorithm to the five-state DFA in Figure 6.4 to obtain the LR(1) parse table shown in Table 6.2.

	a	b	$\$$	S
0	shift 1		$S \rightarrow \Lambda$	2
1	shift 1	$S \rightarrow \Lambda$		3
2			accept	
3		shift 4		
4		$S \rightarrow aSb$	$S \rightarrow aSb$	

Table 6.2

Here's a parse of the string $aabb$ that uses the parse table in Table 6.2. Make sure you can follow each step:

Stack	Input	Action to Perform
0	$aabb\$$	Shift 1
$0\,a\,1$	$abb\$$	Shift 1
$0\,a\,1\,a\,1$	$bb\$$	Reduce by $S \to \Lambda$
$0\,a\,1\,a\,1\,S\,3$	$bb\$$	Shift 4
$0\,a\,1\,a\,1\,S\,3\,b\,4$	$b\$$	Reduce by $S \to aSb$
$0\,a\,1\,S\,3$	$b\$$	Shift 4
$0\,a\,1\,S\,3\,b\,4$	$\$$	Reduce by $S \to aSb$
$0\,S\,2$	$\$$	Accept ◆

For even the simplest grammars it can be a tedious process to construct an LR(1) parse table. But as we've noted, the process is automatic. You'll find all the details about the algorithms to construct LR(1) parsers in any book about compilers.

Exercises

1. Find an LL(1) grammar for each of the following languages.
   a. $\{a, ba, bba\}$.
   b. $\{a^n b \mid n \in \mathbb{N}\}$.
   c. $\{a^{n+1} bc^n \mid n \in \mathbb{N}\}$.
   d. $\{a^m b^n c^{m+n} \mid m, n \in \mathbb{N}\}$.

2. Find an LL(k) grammar for the language $\{aa^n \mid n \in \mathbb{N}\} \cup \{aab^n \mid n \in \mathbb{N}\}$. What is k for your grammar?

3. For each of the following grammars, perform the left-factoring process, where possible, to find an equivalent LL(k) grammar where k is as small as possible.
   a. $S \to abS \mid a$.
   b. $S \to abA \mid abcA, A \to aA \mid \Lambda$.

4. For each of the following grammars, find an equivalent grammar with no left recursion. Are the resulting grammars LL(k)?
   a. $S \to Sa \mid Sb \mid c$.
   b. $S \to SaaS \mid ab$.

5. Write down the recursive descent procedures to parse strings in the language of expressions defined by the following grammar:

$$E \to TR$$
$$R \to +TR \mid \Lambda$$
$$T \to FV$$
$$V \to *FV \mid \Lambda$$
$$F \to (E) \mid a.$$

6. For each of the following grammars, do the following three things:

   Construct First sets for strings on either side of each production.

   Construct Follow sets for the nonterminals.

   Construct the LL(1) parse table.

   a. $S \to aSb \mid \Lambda$.

   b. $S \to aSB \mid C$
   $B \to b$
   $C \to c$.

   c. $E \to TR$
   $R \to +TR \mid \Lambda$
   $T \to FV$
   $V \to *FV \mid \Lambda$
   $F \to (E) \mid a$.

7. Show that each of the following grammars is LR(0).

   a. $S \to aA \mid bB$
   $A \to cA \mid d$
   $B \to cB \mid d$.

   b. $S \to aAc \mid b$
   $A \to aSc \mid b$.

8. Show that the following grammar is LR(1): $S \to aSb \mid \Lambda$.

9. The language $\{a^n b^n \mid n \geq 0\} \cup \{a^n b^{2n} \mid n \geq 0\}$ is not deterministic context-free. So it doesn't have any LR(k) grammars for any k. For example, give an argument to show that the following grammar for this language is not LR(k) for any k:

   $$S \to A \mid B \mid \Lambda$$
   $$A \to aAb \mid ab$$
   $$B \to aBbb \mid ab.$$

10. Construct an LR(1) parse table for each of the following grammars.

    a. $S \to Sa \mid b$.

    b. $S \to A \mid B$
    $A \to a$
    $B \to b$.

    c. $S \to AB$
    $A \to a$
    $B \to b$.

6.4 Context-Free Language Topics

In this section we'll look at a few properties of context-free grammars and languages. We'll start by discussing some restricted grammars that still generate all the context-free languages. Then we'll discuss a tool that can be used to show that some languages are not context-free.

Context-free grammars appear to be very general because the right side of a production can be any string of any length. It's interesting and useful to know that we can put more restrictions on the productions and still generate the same context-free languages. We'll see that for languages that don't contain Λ, we can modify their grammars so that the productions don't contain Λ. Then we'll introduce two classic special grammars that have many applications.

Removing Λ-Productions

A context-free language that does not contain Λ can be written with a grammar that does not contain Λ on the right side of any production. For example, suppose we have the following grammar:

$$S \to aDaE$$
$$D \to bD \mid E$$
$$E \to cE \mid \Lambda.$$

Although Λ appears in this grammar, it's clear that Λ does not occur in the language generated by the grammar. After some thought, we can see that this grammar generates all strings of the form $ab^k c^m ac^n$, where k, m, and n are nonnegative integers. Since the language does not contain Λ, we can write a grammar whose productions don't contain Λ. Try it on your own, and then look at the following three-step algorithm:

1. Find the set of all nonterminals N such that N derives Λ.

2. For each production of the form $A \to w$, create all possible productions of the form $A \to w'$, where w' is obtained from w by removing one or more occurrences of the nonterminals found in Step 1.

3. The desired grammar consists of the original productions together with the productions constructed in Step 2, minus any productions of the form $A \to \Lambda$.

EXAMPLE 1. Let's try this algorithm on our example grammar. Step 1 gives us two nonterminals D and E because they both derive Λ as follows:

$$E \Rightarrow \Lambda \quad \text{and} \quad D \Rightarrow E \Rightarrow \Lambda.$$

For Step 2 we'll list each original production together with all new productions that it creates:

Original Productions	New Productions
$S \to aDaE$	$S \to aaE \mid aDa \mid aa$
$D \to bD$	$D \to b$
$D \to E$	$D \to \Lambda$
$E \to cE$	$E \to c$
$E \to \Lambda$	None

For Step 3, we take the originals together with the new productions and throw away those containing Λ to obtain the following grammar:

$$S \to aDaE \mid aaE \mid aDa \mid aa$$
$$D \to bD \mid b \mid E$$
$$E \to cE \mid c. \quad \blacklozenge$$

Chomsky Normal Form

Any context-free grammar can be written in a special form called *Chomsky normal form*, which appears in Chomsky [1959]. In this form the right side of each production is either a single terminal or a string of exactly two nonterminals, with the exception that $S \to \Lambda$ is allowed, where S is the start symbol. The production $S \to \Lambda$ occurs only when Λ is in the language of the grammar. The Chomsky normal form has several uses. For example, any string of length $n > 0$ can be derived in $2n - 1$ steps. Also, the derivation trees are binary trees. Here's the algorithm:

1. If the grammar contains Λ in a production whose left side is not the start symbol, then use the preceding algorithm to transform the grammar into one that does not contain Λ, but keep $S \to \Lambda$, where S is the start symbol.

2. Replace each production of the form $A \to B$ with $A \to w_1 \mid \ldots \mid w_n$, where $B \to w_1 \mid \ldots \mid w_n$ represents all productions with B on the left.

3. For each production, if the right side has two or more symbols and also contains a terminal a, then replace all occurrences of a with a new nonterminal A, and also add the new production $A \to a$.

4. For each production of the form $B \to C_1C_2\ldots C_n$, where $n > 2$, replace the production by the following two productions, where D is a new nonterminal:
$$B \to C_1D \quad \text{and} \quad D \to C_2\ldots C_n.$$

Continue this step until all productions with nonterminal strings on the right side have length 2.

EXAMPLE 2. Let's write the following grammar in Chomsky normal form:

$$S \to aSa \mid b.$$

First we replace the letter a by A and add the rule $A \to a$ to obtain the grammar

$$S \to ASA \mid b$$
$$A \to a.$$

Now replace $S \to ASA$ by $S \to AB$, where $B \to SA$. This gives us the Chomsky normal form

$$S \to AB \mid b$$
$$B \to SA$$
$$A \to a. \quad \blacklozenge$$

Greibach Normal Form

Any context-free grammar can be written in a special form called *Greibach normal form*, which appears in Greibach [1965]. In this form the right side of each production is a single terminal followed by zero or more nonterminals, with the exception that $S \to \Lambda$ is allowed, where S is the start symbol. The production $S \to \Lambda$ occurs only when Λ is in the language of the grammar. The Greibach normal form has several uses. For example, any string of length $n > 0$ can be derived in n steps, which makes parsing quite efficient.

The algorithm to transform any context-free grammar into Greibach normal form is quite involved. Instead of describing all the details, we'll give an informal description.

Remove Λ from all productions except possibly $S \to \Lambda$.

Get rid of all left recursion.

Make substitutions to transform the grammar into the proper form.

Let's do a "simple" example to get the general idea. Suppose we have the following grammar:

$$S \to AB \mid B$$
$$A \to Aa \mid b$$
$$B \to Ab \mid c.$$

The grammar has a left-recursive production $A \to Aa$. We can get rid of this left recursion by replacing the rules $A \to Aa \mid b$ with the productions

$$A \rightarrow b \mid bD$$
$$D \rightarrow aD \mid a.$$

With these replacements our grammar takes the form

$$S \rightarrow AB \mid B$$
$$A \rightarrow b \mid bD$$
$$D \rightarrow aD \mid a$$
$$B \rightarrow Ab \mid c.$$

Now we can make some substitutions. We can replace B in the production $S \rightarrow B$ by the right side of the productions $B \rightarrow Ab \mid c$. In other words, $S \rightarrow B$ is replaced by $S \rightarrow Ab \mid c$. Now our grammar takes the form

$$S \rightarrow AB \mid Ab \mid c$$
$$A \rightarrow b \mid bD$$
$$D \rightarrow aD \mid a$$
$$B \rightarrow Ab \mid c.$$

Now we can replace the leftmost occurrences of A in $S \rightarrow AB \mid Ab$ by the right side of $A \rightarrow b \mid bD$. In other words, $S \rightarrow AB \mid Ab$ is replaced by

$$S \rightarrow bB \mid bDB \mid bb \mid bDb \mid c.$$

Similarly, we can replace A in $B \rightarrow Ab$ by the right side of $A \rightarrow b \mid bD$ to give

$$B \rightarrow bb \mid bDb.$$

This gives us the following grammar, which no longer needs $A \rightarrow b \mid bD$:

$$S \rightarrow bB \mid bDB \mid bb \mid bDb \mid c$$
$$D \rightarrow aD \mid a$$
$$B \rightarrow bb \mid bDb \mid c.$$

This grammar is almost in Greibach normal form. The only problem is with the following productions that contain the terminal b on the right end of each right side:

$$S \rightarrow bb \mid bDb$$
$$B \rightarrow bb \mid bDb.$$

We can solve this problem by creating a new production $E \to b$ and then rewriting the preceding productions into the following form:

$$S \to bE \mid bDE$$
$$B \to bE \mid bDE.$$

Finally, we obtain the Greibach normal form of the original grammar:

$$S \to bB \mid bDB \mid bE \mid bDE \mid c$$
$$B \to bE \mid bDE \mid c$$
$$D \to aD \mid a$$
$$E \to b.$$

Non-Context-Free Languages

Although most languages that we encounter are context-free languages, we need to face the fact that not all languages are context-free. For example, suppose we want to find a PDA or a context-free grammar for the language $\{a^n b^n c^n \mid n \geq 0\}$. After a few attempts we might get the idea that the language is not context-free. How can we be sure? In some cases we can use a pumping argument similar to the one used to show that a language is not regular. So let's discuss a pumping lemma for context-free languages.

If a context-free language has an infinite number of strings, then any grammar for the language must be recursive. In other words, there must be a production that is recursive or indirectly recursive. For example, a grammar for an infinite context-free language will contain a fragment similar to the following:

$$S \to uNy$$
$$N \to vNx \mid w.$$

Notice that either v or x must be nonempty. Otherwise, the language derived is finite, consisting of the single string uwy. The grammar allows us to derive infinitely many strings having a certain pattern. For example, the derivation to recognize the string uv^3wx^3y can be written as follows:

$$S \Rightarrow uNy \Rightarrow uvNxy \Rightarrow uvvNxxy \Rightarrow uvvvNxxxy \Rightarrow uv^3wx^3y.$$

This derivation can be shortened or lengthened to obtain the set of all strings of the form $uv^k wx^k y$ for all $k \geq 0$. This example illustrates the main result of the pumping lemma for context-free languages, which we'll state in all its detail as follows:

Pumping Lemma for Context-Free Languages (6.19)

Let L be an infinite context-free language. There is a positive integer m such that for all strings $z \in L$ with $|z| \geq m$, z can be written in the form $z = uvwxy$, where the following properties hold:

$$|vx| \geq 1,$$
$$|vwx| \leq m,$$
$$uv^k wx^k y \in L \text{ for all } k \geq 0.$$

The positive integer m in the (6.19) depends on the grammar for the language L. Without going into the proof, suffice it to say that m is large enough to ensure a recursive derivation of any string of length m or more. Let's use the lemma to show that a particularly simple language is not context-free.

EXAMPLE 3. We'll show that the language $L = \{a^n b^n c^n \mid n \geq 0\}$ is not context-free by assuming that it is context-free and trying to find a contradiction.

Proof: If L is context-free, then by (6.19) we can pick a string $z = a^m b^m c^m$ in L, where m is the positive integer mentioned in the lemma. Since $|z| \geq m$, we can write it in the form $z = uvwxy$, such that $|vx| \geq 1$, $|vwx| \leq m$, and such that $uv^k wx^k y \in L$ for all $k \geq 0$.

Now we need to come up with a contradiction. One thing to observe is that the pumped variable v can't contain two distinct letters. For example, if the substring ab occurs in v, then the substring $ab...ab$ occurs in v^2, which means that the pumped string $uv^2 wx^2 y$ can't be in L, contrary to the the pumping lemma conclusion. Therefore v is a string of a's, or v is a string of b's, or v is a string of c's. A similar argument shows that x can't contain two distinct letters.

Since $|vx| \geq 1$, we know that at least one of v and x is a nonempty string of the form a^i, or b^i, or c^i for some $i > 0$. Therefore the pumped string $uv^2 wx^2 y$ can't contain the same number of a's, b's, and c's because one of the three letters a, b, and c does not get pumped up. For example, if $v = a^i$ for some $i > 0$, and $x = \Lambda$, then $uv^2 wx^2 y = a^{m+i} b^m c^m$, which is not in L. The other cases for v and x are handled in a similar way. Thus $uv^2 wx^2 y$ can't be in L, which contradicts the pumping lemma (6.19). So it follows that the language L is not context-free.   QED.   ♦

In (6.3) we saw that the operations of union, product, and closure can be used to construct new context-free languages from other context-free languages. Now that we have an example of a language that is not context-free, we're in position to show that the operations of intersection and complement can't always be used in this way. Here's the first statement:

$$\text{Context-free languages are not closed under intersection.} \qquad (6.20)$$

For example, we know from Example 3 that the language $L = \{a^n b^n c^n \mid n \geq 0\}$ is not context-free. It's easy to see that L is the intersection of the two languages

$$L_1 = \{a^n b^n c^k \mid n, k \in \mathbb{N}\} \quad \text{and} \quad L_2 = \{a^k b^n c^n \mid n, k \in \mathbb{N}\}.$$

It's also easy to see that these two languages are context-free. Just find a context-free grammar for each language. Thus we have an example of two context-free languages whose intersection is not context-free.

Now we're in position to prove the following result about complements:

$$\text{Context-free languages are not closed under complement.} \qquad (6.21)$$

Proof: Suppose, by way of contradiction, that complements of context-free languages are context-free. Then we can take the two languages L_1 and L_2 from the proof of (6.20) and make the following sequence of statements: Since L_1 and L_2 are context-free, it follows that the complements L_1' and L_2' are context-free. We can take the union of these two complements to obtain another context-free language. Further, we can take the complement of this union to obtain the following context-free language:

$$(L_1' \cup L_2')'.$$

Now let's describe a contradiction. Using De Morgan's laws, we have the following statement:

$$(L_1' \cup L_2')' = L_1 \cap L_2.$$

So we're forced to conclude that $L_1 \cap L_2$ is context-free. But we know that

$$L_1 \cap L_2 = \{a^n b^n c^n \mid n \geq 0\},$$

and we've shown that this language is not context-free. This contradiction proves (6.21).   QED.

Although (6.20) says that we can't expect the intersection of context-free languages to be context-free, we can say that the intersection of a regular language with a context-free language is context-free. We won't prove this, but we'll include it with the closure properties that we do know about. Here is a listing of them:

Properties of Context-Free Languages (6.22)

1. The union of two context-free languages is context-free.
2. The language product of two context-free languages is context-free.
3. The closure of a context-free language is context-free.
4. The intersection of a regular language with a context-free language is context-free.

We'll finish with two more properties of context-free languages that can be quite useful in showing that a language is not context-free:

Context-Free Language Morphisms (6.23)

Let $f : A^* \to A^*$ be a language morphism. In other words, $f(\Lambda) = \Lambda$ and $f(uv) = f(u)f(v)$ for all strings u and v. Let L be a language over A.

1. If L is context-free, then $f(L)$ is context-free.
2. If L is context-free, then $f^{-1}(L)$ is context-free.

Proof: We'll prove statement 1 (statement 2 is a bit complicated). Since L is context-free, it has a context-free grammar. We'll create a context-free grammar for $f(L)$ as follows: Transform each production $A \to w$ into a new production of the form $A \to w'$, where w' is obtained from w by replacing each terminal a in w by $f(a)$. The new grammar is context-free, and any string in $f(L)$ is derived by this new grammar.   QED.

EXAMPLE 4. Let's use (6.23) to show that $L = \{a^n b c^n d e^n \mid n \geq 0\}$ is not context-free. We can define a morphism $f : \{a, b, c, d, e\}^* \to \{a, b, c, d, e\}^*$ by

$$f(a) = a, \quad f(b) = \Lambda, \quad f(c) = b, \quad f(d) = \Lambda, \quad f(e) = c.$$

Then $f(L) = \{a^n b^n c^n \mid n \geq 0\}$. If L is context-free, then we must also conclude by (6.22) that $f(L)$ is context-free. But we know that $f(L)$ is not context-free. Therefore L is not context-free.   ◆

It might occur to you that the language $\{a^n b^n c^n \mid n \geq 0\}$ could be recognized by a pushdown automaton with two stacks available rather than just one stack. For example, we could push the a's onto one stack. Then we pop the a's as we push the b's onto the second stack. Finally, we pop the b's from the second stack as we read the c's.

So it might make sense to take the next step and study pushdown automata with two stacks. Instead, we're going to switch gears and discuss another type of device, called a Turing machine, which is closer to the idea of a computer. The interesting thing is that Turing machines are equivalent in power to pushdown automata with two stacks. In fact, Turing machines are equivalent to pushdown automata with n stacks for any $n \geq 2$. We'll discuss them in the next chapter.

Exercises

1. For each of the following grammars, find a grammar without Λ productions that generates the same language.

   a. $S \to aA \mid aBb$
      $A \to aA \mid \Lambda$
      $B \to aBb \mid \Lambda.$

   b. $S \to aAB$
      $A \to aAb \mid \Lambda$
      $B \to bB \mid \Lambda.$

2. Find a Chomsky normal form for each of the following grammars.

   a. $S \to aSa \mid bSb \mid c.$

   b. $S \to abC \mid babS \mid de$
      $C \to aCa \mid b.$

3. Find a Greibach normal form for the following grammar:

   $$S \to AbC \mid D$$
   $$A \to Aa \mid \Lambda$$
   $$C \to cC \mid c$$
   $$D \to d.$$

4. Use the pumping lemma (6.19) to show that each of the following languages is not context-free.

   a. $\{a^n b^n a^n \mid n \geq 0\}$. *Hint:* Look at Example 3.

   b. $\{a^i b^j c^k \mid 0 < i < j < k\}$. *Hint:* Let $z = a^m b^{m+1} c^{m+2} = uvwxy$, and consider the following two cases: (1) There is at least one a in either v or x. (2) Neither v nor x contains any a's.

   c. $\{a^p \mid p$ is a prime number$\}$. *Hint:* Let $z = a^p = uvwxy$, where p is a prime and $p > m$.

5. Show that the language $\{a^n b^n a^n \mid n \in \mathbb{N}\}$ is not context-free by performing the following tasks:

   a. Given the morphism $f : \{a, b, c\}^* \to \{a, b, c\}^*$ defined by $f(a) = a$, $f(b) = b$, and $f(c) = a$, describe $f^{-1}(\{a^n b^n a^n \mid n \in \mathbb{N}\})$.

b. Show that

$$f^{-1}(\{a^n b^n a^n \mid n \in \mathbb{N}\}) \cap \{a^k b^m c^n \mid k, m, n \in \mathbb{N}\} = \{a^n b^n c^n \mid n \in \mathbb{N}\}.$$

c. Argue that $\{a^n b^n a^n \mid n \in \mathbb{N}\}$ is not context-free by using parts (a) and (b) together with (6.22) and (6.23).

Chapter Summary

This chapter introduced context-free languages as languages derived by context-free grammars, which are grammars in which every production contains exactly one nonterminal on its left side. Context-free grammars can be easily constructed for unions, products, and closures of context-free languages.

A pushdown automaton (PDA) is like a finite automaton with a stack attached. PDAs can accept strings by final state or by empty stack. Either form of acceptance is equivalent to the other. PDAs are equivalent to context-free grammars. The important point is that there are algorithms to transform back and forth between PDAs and context-free grammars. Therefore we can start with a context-free grammar and automatically transform it into a PDA that recognizes the context-free language. Deterministic PDAs are less powerful than nondeterministic PDAs, which means that deterministic PDAs recognize a proper subcollection of the context-free languages. A simple interpreter can be constructed for PDAs.

A deterministic context-free language is a context-free language that is recognized by a deterministic PDA using final-state acceptance. Most programming language constructs can be recognized by efficient deterministic parsers. LL(k) parsing is an efficient top-down technique for parsing many— but not all—deterministic context-free languages. LR(k) parsing is an efficient bottom-up technique for parsing any deterministic context-free language.

We observed some other things too. Although context-free grammars have few restrictions, any context-free grammar can be transformed into either of two special restricted forms—Chomsky normal form and Greibach normal form. There are some basic properties of context-free languages given by a pumping lemma, set operations, and morphisms. Many simple languages, including $\{a^n b^n c^n \mid n \geq 0\}$, are not context-free.

7

Turing Machines and Equivalent Models

*Machines are worshipped because they are beautiful
and valued because they confer power; they are hated
because they are hideous and loathed because they
impose slavery.*
—Bertrand Russell (1872–1970)

Is there a computing device more powerful than any other computing device?
What does "powerful" mean? Can we easily compare machines to see whether
they have the same power? In this chapter we try to answer these questions
by studying Turing machines and the Church-Turing thesis, which claims
that there are no models of computation more powerful than Turing machines.

Chapter Guide

Section 7.1 introduces Turing machines. We'll see that Turing machines are
more powerful than pushdown automata. We'll also see that Turing machines can do general-purpose computation. We'll look at alternative definitions for a Turing machine, and we'll present an interpreter for
Turing machines.

Section 7.2 discusses a variety of computational models that can simulate the
action of each other and of Turing machines. Thus there is much support
for the Church-Turing thesis.

7.1 Turing Machines

It's time to discuss a simple yet powerful computing device that was invented by the mathematician and logician Alan Turing (1912–1954). The machine is described in the paper by Turing [1936]. It models the actions of a person doing a primitive calculation on a long strip of paper divided up into contiguous individual cells, each of which contains a symbol from a fixed alphabet. The person uses a pencil with an eraser. Starting at some cell, the person observes the symbol in the cell and decides either to leave it alone or to erase it and write a new symbol in its place. The person can then perform the same action on one of the adjacent cells. The computation continues in this manner, moving from one cell to the next along the paper in either direction. We assume that there is always enough paper to continue the computation in either direction as far as we want. The computation can stop at some point or continue indefinitely.

Let's give a more precise description of this machine, which is named after its creator. A *Turing machine* consists of two major components, a tape and a control unit. The *tape* is a sequence of cells that extends to infinity in both directions. Each cell contains a symbol from a finite alphabet. There is a tape head that reads from a cell and writes into the same cell. The *control unit* contains a finite set of instructions, which are executed as follows: Each instruction causes the tape head to read the symbol from a cell, to write a symbol into the same cell, and either to move the tape head to an adjacent cell or to leave it at the same cell. Here is a picture of a Turing machine:

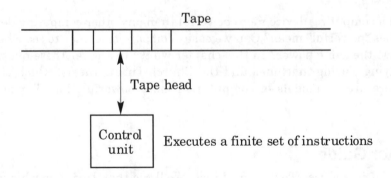

Each Turing machine instruction contains the following five parts:

The current machine state.
A tape symbol read from the current tape cell.
A tape symbol to write into the current tape cell.
A direction for the tape head to move.
The next machine state.

We'll agree to let the letters L, S, and R mean "move left one cell," "stay at the current cell," and "move right one cell," respectively. We can represent an instruction as a 5-tuple or in graphical form. For example, the 5-tuple

$$\langle i, a, b, L, j \rangle$$

is interpreted as follows:

> If the current state of the machine is i, and if the symbol in the current tape cell is a, then write b into the current tape cell, move left one cell, and go to state j.

We can also write the instruction in graphical form as follows:

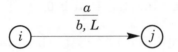

The tape is used much like the memory in a modern computer, to store the input, to store data needed during execution, and to store the output. To describe a Turing machine computation, we need to make a few more assumptions:

> An input string is represented on the tape by placing the letters of the string in contiguous tape cells. All other cells of the tape contain the blank symbol, which we'll denote by Λ.

> The tape head is positioned at the leftmost cell of the input string unless specified otherwise.

> There is one *start state*.

> There is one *halt state*, which we denote by "Halt."

The execution of a Turing machine stops when it enters the Halt state or when it enters a state for which there is no valid move. For example, if a Turing machine enters state i and reads a in the current cell, but there is no instruction of the form $\langle i, a, ... \rangle$, then the machine stops in state i.

We say that an input string is *accepted* by a Turing machine if the machine enters the Halt state. Otherwise, the input string is *rejected*. There are two ways to reject an input string: Either the machine stops by entering a state other than the Halt state from which there is no move, or the machine runs forever. The *language of a Turing machine* is the set of all input strings accepted by the machine.

It's easy to see that Turing machines can solve all the problems that PDAs can solve because a stack can be maintained on some portion of the tape. In fact a Turing machine can maintain any number of stacks on the tape by allocating some space on the tape for each stack.

Let's do a few examples to see how Turing machines are constructed.

EXAMPLE 1. Suppose we want to write a Turing machine to recognize the language $\{a^n b^m \mid m, n \in \mathbb{N}\}$. Of course this is a regular language, represented by the regular expression $a*b*$. So there is a DFA to recognize it. Of course there is also a PDA to recognize it. So there had better be a Turing machine to recognize it.

The machine will scan the tape to the right, looking for the empty symbol and making sure that no a's are scanned after any occurrence of b. Here are the instructions, where the start state is 0:

$\langle 0, \Lambda, \Lambda, S, \text{Halt} \rangle$	The string is Λ.
$\langle 0, a, a, R, 0 \rangle$	Scan a's.
$\langle 0, b, b, R, 1 \rangle$	
$\langle 1, b, b, R, 1 \rangle$	Scan b's.
$\langle 1, \Lambda, \Lambda, S, \text{Halt} \rangle$	

For example, to accept the string abb, the machine enters the following sequence of states: 0, 0, 1, 1, Halt. This Turing machine also has the following graphical definition, where H stands for the Halt state:

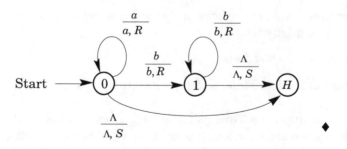

EXAMPLE 2. To show the power of Turing machines, we'll construct a Turing machine to recognize the following language:

$$\{a^n b^n c^n \mid n \geq 0\}.$$

We've already shown that this language cannot be recognized by a PDA. A

Turing machine to recognize the language can be written from the following informal algorithm:

> If the current cell is empty, then halt with success. Otherwise, if the current cell contains an a, then write an X in the cell and scan right, looking for a corresponding b to the right of any a's, and replace it by Y. Then continue scanning to the right, looking for a corresponding c to the right of any b's, and replace it by Z. Now scan left to the X and see whether there is an a to its right. If so, then start the process again. If there are no a's, then scan right, making sure there are no b's and no c's.

Now let's write a Turing machine to implement this algorithm. The state 0 will be the initial state. The instructions for each state are preceded by a prose description. In addition, each line contains a short comment.

> If Λ is found, then halt. If a is found, then write X and scan right. If Y is found, then scan over Y's and Z's to find the right end of the string.

$\langle 0, a, X, R, 1 \rangle$	Replace a by X and scan right.
$\langle 0, Y, Y, R, 0 \rangle$	Scan right.
$\langle 0, Z, Z, R, 4 \rangle$	Go make the final check.
$\langle 0, \Lambda, \Lambda, S, \text{Halt} \rangle$	Success.

Scan right, looking for b. If found, replace it by Y.

$\langle 1, a, a, R, 1 \rangle$	Scan right.
$\langle 1, b, Y, R, 2 \rangle$	Replace b by Y and scan right.
$\langle 1, Y, Y, R, 1 \rangle$	Scan right.

Scan right, looking for c. If found, replace it by Z.

$\langle 2, c, Z, L, 3 \rangle$	Replace c by Z and scan left.
$\langle 2, b, b, R, 2 \rangle$	Scan right.
$\langle 2, Z, Z, R, 2 \rangle$	Scan right.

Scan left, looking for X. Then move right and repeat the process.

$\langle 3, a, a, L, 3 \rangle$	Scan left.
$\langle 3, b, b, L, 3 \rangle$	Scan left.
$\langle 3, X, X, R, 0 \rangle$	Found X. Move right one cell.
$\langle 3, Y, Y, L, 3 \rangle$	Scan left.
$\langle 3, Z, Z, L, 3 \rangle$	Scan left.

Scan right, looking for Λ. Then halt.

$\langle 4, Z, Z, R, 4 \rangle$	Scan right.
$\langle 4, \Lambda, \Lambda, S, \text{Halt} \rangle$	Success. ◆

Turing Machines with Output

Turing machines can also be used to compute functions. As usual, the input is placed on the tape in contiguous cells. We usually specify the form of the output along with the final position of the tape head when the machine halts. Here are a few examples.

EXAMPLE 3 (*Adding 2 to a Natural Number*). Let a natural number be represented in unary form. For example, the number 4 is represented by the string 1111. We'll agree to represent 0 by the empty string Λ. Now it's easy to construct a Turing machine to add 2 to a natural number. The initial state is 0. When the machine halts, the tape head will point at the left end of the string. There are just three instructions. Comments are written to the right of each instruction.

$$\langle 0, 1, 1, L, 0 \rangle \qquad \text{Move left to blank cell.}$$
$$\langle 0, \Lambda, 1, L, 1 \rangle \qquad \text{Add 1 and move left.}$$
$$\langle 1, \Lambda, 1, S, \text{Halt} \rangle \qquad \text{Add 1 and halt.}$$

The following diagram is a graphical picture of this Turing machine:

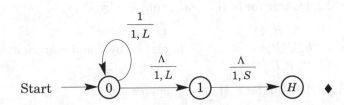

EXAMPLE 4 (*Adding 1 to a Binary Natural Number*). Here we'll represent natural numbers as binary strings. For example, the number 5 will be represented as the string 101 placed in three tape cells. The algorithm can be described as follows:

Move to right end of string;
repeat
      If current cell contains 1, write 0 and move left
until current cell contains 0 or Λ;
Write a 1;
Move to left end of string and halt.

A Turing machine to implement this algorithm follows:

$\langle 0, 0, 0, R, 0 \rangle$	Scan right.
$\langle 0, 1, 1, R, 0 \rangle$	Scan right.
$\langle 0, \Lambda, \Lambda, L, 1 \rangle$	Found right end of string.
$\langle 1, 0, 1, L, 2 \rangle$	Write 1, done adding.
$\langle 1, 1, 0, L, 1 \rangle$	Write 0 and move left with carry bit.
$\langle 1, \Lambda, 1, S, \text{Halt} \rangle$	Write 1, done and in proper position.
$\langle 2, 0, 0, L, 2 \rangle$	Move to left end and halt.
$\langle 2, 1, 1, L, 2 \rangle$	
$\langle 2, \Lambda, \Lambda, R, \text{Halt} \rangle$ ◆	

EXAMPLE 5 (*An Equality Test*). Let's write a Turing machine to test the equality of two natural numbers, representing the numbers as unary strings separated by #. We'll assume that the number 0 is denoted by a blank cell. For example, the string Λ#11 represents the two numbers 0 and 2. The two numbers 3 and 4 are represented by the string 111#1111. The idea is to repeatedly cancel leftmost and rightmost 1's until none remain. The machine will halt with a 1 in the current cell if the numbers are not equal and Λ if they are equal. A Turing machine program to accomplish this follows:

$\langle 0, 1, \Lambda, R, 1 \rangle$	Cancel leftmost 1.
$\langle 0, \Lambda, \Lambda, R, 4 \rangle$	Left number is zero.
$\langle 0, \#, \#, R, 4 \rangle$	Finished with left number.
$\langle 1, 1, 1, R, 1 \rangle$	Scan right.
$\langle 1, \Lambda, \Lambda, L, 2 \rangle$	Found the right end.
$\langle 1, \#, \#, R, 1 \rangle$	Scan right.
$\langle 2, 1, \Lambda, L, 3 \rangle$	Cancel rightmost 1.
$\langle 2, \#, 1, S, \text{Halt} \rangle$	Not equal, first > second.
$\langle 3, 1, 1, L, 3 \rangle$	Scan left.
$\langle 3, \Lambda, \Lambda, R, 0 \rangle$	Found left end.
$\langle 3, \#, \#, L, 3 \rangle$	Scan left.
$\langle 4, 1, 1, S, \text{Halt} \rangle$	Not equal, first < second.
$\langle 4, \Lambda, \Lambda, S, \text{Halt} \rangle$	Equal.
$\langle 4, \#, \#, R, 4 \rangle$	Scan right.

If the two numbers are not equal, then it's easy to modify the Turing machine so that it can detect the inequality relationship. For example, the second instruction of state 2 could be modified to write the letter G to mean that the first number is greater than the second number. Similarly, the first instruction of state 4 could write the letter L to mean that the first number is less than the second number.   ◆

Alternative Definitions

We should point out that there are many different definitions of Turing machines. Our definition is similar to the machine originally defined by Turing. Some definitions allow the tape to be infinite in one direction only. In other words, the tape has a definite left end and extends infinitely to the right. A *multihead* Turing machine has two or more tape heads positioned on the tape. A *multitape* Turing machine has two or more tapes with corresponding tape heads. It's important to note that all these Turing machines are *equivalent* in power. In other words, any problem solved by one type of Turing machine can also be solved on any other type of Turing machine.

Let's give an informal description of how a multitape Turing machine can be simulated by a single-tape Turing machine. For our description we'll assume that we have a Turing machine T that has two tapes, each with a single tape head. We'll describe a new single-tape, single-head machine M that will start with its tape containing the two nonblank portions taken from the tapes of T, separated by a new tape symbol

$$@.$$

Whenever T executes an instruction (which is actually a pair of instructions, one for each tape), M simulates the action by performing two corresponding instructions, one instruction for the left side of @ and the other instruction for the right side of @.

Since M has only one tape head, it must chase back and forth across @ to execute instructions. So it needs to keep track of the positions of the two tape heads that it is simulating. One way to do this is to place a position marker · in every other tape cell. To indicate a current cell, we'll write the symbol

$$\wedge$$

in place of · in the adjacent cell to the right of the current cell for the left tape and to the adjacent cell to the left of the current cell for the right tape. For example, if the two tapes of T contain the strings abc and $xyzw$, with tape heads pointing at b and z, then the tape for M has the following form, where the symbol # marks the left end and the right end of the relevant portions of the tape:

$$... \Lambda \cdot \# \cdot a \cdot b \wedge c \cdot @ \cdot x \cdot y \wedge z \cdot w \cdot \# \cdot \Lambda ....$$

Suppose now that T writes a into the current cell of its abc tape and then moves right and that it writes w into the current cell of its $xyzw$ tape and then moves left. These actions would be simulated by M to produce the following tape:

$$... \Lambda \cdot \# \cdot a \cdot a \cdot c \wedge @ \cdot x \wedge y \cdot w \cdot w \cdot \# \cdot \Lambda ....$$

A problem can occur if the movement of one of T's tape heads causes M's tape head to bump into either @ or #. In either case we need to make room for a new cell. If M's tape head bumps into @, then the entire representation on that side of @ must be moved to make room for a new tape cell next to @. This is where the # is needed to signal the end of the relevant portion of the tape. If M's tape head bumps into #, then # must be moved farther out to make room for a new tape cell.

Multitape Turing machines are usually easier to construct because distinct data sets can be stored on distinct tapes. This eliminates the tedious scanning back and forth required to maintain different data sets. An instruction of a multitape Turing machine is still a 5-tuple. But now the elements in positions 2, 3, and 4 are tuples. For example, a typical instruction for a 3-tape Turing machine looks like the following:

$$\langle i, \langle a, b, c \rangle, \langle x, y, z \rangle, \langle R, L, S \rangle, j \rangle.$$

This instruction is interpreted as follows:

If the machine state is i and if the current three tape cells contain the symbols a, b, and c, respectively, then overwrite the cells with x, y, and z. Then move the first tape head right, move the second tape head left, and keep the third tape head stationary. Then go to state j.

The same instruction format can also be used for multihead Turing machines. In the next example, we'll use a multitape Turing machine to multiply two natural numbers.

EXAMPLE 6 (*Multiplying Natural Numbers*) Suppose we want to construct a Turing machine to multiply two natural numbers, each represented as a unary string of ones. We'll use a three-tape Turing machine, where the first two tapes hold the input numbers and the third tape will hold the answer. If either number is zero, the product is zero. Otherwise, the the machine will use the first number as a counter to repeatedly add the second number to itself, by repeatedly copying it onto the third tape.

For example, the diagrams in Figure 7.1 show the contents of the three tapes before the computation of 3·4 and before the start of the second of the three additions:

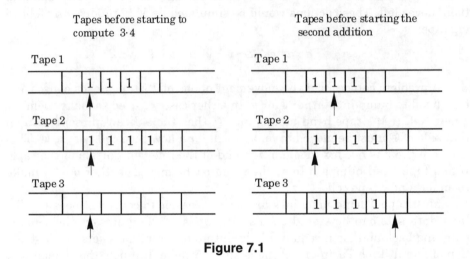

Tapes before starting to compute 3·4

Tapes before starting the second addition

Figure 7.1

The following three-tape Turing machine will perform the multiplication of two natural numbers by repeated addition, where 0 is the start state.

Start by checking to see whether either number is zero:

$\langle 0, \langle \Lambda, \Lambda, \Lambda \rangle, \langle \Lambda, \Lambda, \Lambda \rangle, \langle S, S, S \rangle, \text{Halt} \rangle$ Both are zero.

$\langle 0, \langle \Lambda, 1, \Lambda \rangle, \langle \Lambda, 1, \Lambda \rangle, \langle S, S, S \rangle, \text{Halt} \rangle$ First is zero.

$\langle 0, \langle 1, \Lambda, \Lambda \rangle, \langle 1, \Lambda, \Lambda \rangle, \langle S, S, S \rangle, \text{Halt} \rangle$ Second is zero.

$\langle 0, \langle 1, 1, \Lambda \rangle, \langle 1, 1, \Lambda \rangle, \langle S, S, S \rangle, 1 \rangle$ Both are nonzero.

Add the number on second tape to the third tape:

$\langle 1, \langle 1, 1, \Lambda \rangle, \langle 1, 1, 1 \rangle, \langle S, R, R \rangle, 1 \rangle$ Copy.

$\langle 1, \langle 1, \Lambda, \Lambda \rangle, \langle 1, \Lambda, \Lambda \rangle, \langle S, L, S \rangle, 2 \rangle$ Done copying.

Move the tape head of second tape back to left end of the number, and also move the tape head of the first number one cell to the right:

$\langle 2, \langle 1, 1, \Lambda \rangle, \langle 1, 1, \Lambda \rangle, \langle S, L, S \rangle, 2 \rangle$ Move to the left end.

$\langle 2, \langle 1, \Lambda, \Lambda \rangle, \langle 1, \Lambda, \Lambda \rangle, \langle R, R, S \rangle, 3 \rangle$ Move both tape heads to the right one cell.

Check the first tape head to see whether all the additions have been performed:

$$\langle 3, \langle \Lambda, 1, \Lambda \rangle, \langle \Lambda, 1, \Lambda \rangle, \langle S, S, L \rangle, \text{Halt} \rangle \qquad \text{Done.}$$

$$\langle 3, \langle 1, 1, \Lambda \rangle, \langle 1, 1, \Lambda \rangle, \langle S, S, S \rangle, 1 \rangle \qquad \text{Do another add.} \quad \blacklozenge$$

Nondeterminism

We haven't yet classified Turing machines as deterministic or nondeterministic. Let's do so now. If a Turing machine has at least two instructions with the same state and input letter, then the machine is *nondeterministic*. Otherwise, it's *deterministic*. For example, the following two instructions are nondeterministic:

$$\langle i, a, b, L, j \rangle,$$
$$\langle i, a, a, R, j \rangle.$$

All our preceding examples are deterministic Turing machines. It's natural to wonder whether nondeterministic Turing machines are more powerful than deterministic Turing machines. We've seen that nondeterminism is more powerful than determinism for pushdown automata. But we've also seen that the two ideas are equal in power for finite automata.

For Turing machines we don't get any more power by allowing nondeterminism. In other words, we have the following result:

If a nondeterministic Turing machine accepts a language L, $\qquad$ (7.1)
then there is a deterministic Turing machine that also accepts L.

We'll give an informal idea of the proof. Suppose N is a nondeterministic Turing machine that accepts language L. We define a deterministic Turing machine D that simulates the execution of N by exhaustively executing all possible paths caused by N's nondeterminism. But since N might very well have an input that leads to an infinite computation, we must be careful in the way D simulates the actions of N. First D simulates all possible computations of N that take one step. Next D simulates all possible computations of N that take two steps. This process continues, with three steps, four steps, and so on. If during this process D simulates the action of N entering the Halt state, then D enters its Halt state. So N halts on an input string if and only if D halts on the same input string.

The problem is to write D so that it does all these wonderful things in a deterministic manner. The usual approach is to define D as a three-tape machine. One tape holds a permanent copy of the input string for N. The second tape keeps track of the next computation sequence and the number of steps of

N that must be simulated by D. The third tape is used repeatedly by D to simulate the computation sequences for N that are specified on the second tape.

The computation sequences on the second tape are the interesting part of D. Since N is nondeterministic, there may be more than one instruction of the form ⟨state, input, ?, ?, ?⟩. Let m be the maximum number of instructions for any ⟨state, input⟩ pair. For purposes of illustration, suppose $m = 3$. Then for any ⟨state, input⟩ pair there are no more than three instructions of the form ⟨state, input, ?, ?, ?⟩, and we can number them 1, 2, and 3. If some ⟨state, input⟩ pair doesn't have three nondeterministic instructions, then we'll simply write down extra copies of one instruction to make the total three. This gives us exactly three choices for each ⟨state, input⟩ pair. For convenience we'll use the letters a, b, and c rather than 1, 2, and 3.

Each simulation by D will be guided by a string over $\{a, b, c\}$ that is sitting on the second tape. For example, the string $ccab$ tells D to simulate four steps of N because length($ccab$) = 4. For the first simulation step we pick the third of the possible instructions because $ccab$ starts with c. For the second simulation step we also pick the third of the possible instructions because the second letter of $ccab$ is c. The third letter of $ccab$ is a, which says that the third simulation step should choose the first of the possible instructions. And the fourth letter of $ccab$ is b, which says that the fourth simulation step should choose the second of the possible instructions.

To make sure D simulates all possible computation sequences, it needs to generate all the strings over $\{a, b, c\}$. One way to do this is to generate the non-empty strings in standard order, where $a \prec b \prec c$. Recall that this means that strings are ordered by length, and strings of equal length are ordered lexicographically. For example, here are the first few strings in the standard ordering, not including Λ:

$$a, b, c, aa, ab, ac, ba, bb, bc, ca, cb, cc, aaa, aab, \ldots.$$

So D needs to generate a new string in this ordering before it starts a new simulation. We've left the job of finding a Turing machine to compute the successor as an exercise.

A Universal Turing Machine

In the examples that we've seen up to this point, each problem required us to build a special-purpose Turing machine to solve only that problem. Is there a more general Turing machine that acts like a general-purpose computer? The answer is yes. We'll see that a Turing machine can be built to interpret any other Turing machine. In other words, there is a Turing machine that can take as input an arbitrary Turing machine M together with an arbitrary input for M and then perform the execution of M on its input. Such a machine is called a *universal Turing machine*. A universal Turing machine acts like a general purpose computer that stores a program and its data in memory and then executes the program.

We'll give a description of a universal Turing machine U. Since U can have only a finite number of instructions and a finite alphabet of tape cell symbols, we have to discuss the representation of any Turing machine in terms of the fixed symbols of U. We begin by selecting a fixed infinite set of states, say $\mathbb{N}$, and a fixed infinite set of tape cell symbols, say $L = \{a_i \mid i \in \mathbb{N}\}$. Now we require that every Turing machine must use states from the set $\mathbb{N}$ and tape cell symbols from L. This is easy to do by simply renaming the symbols used in any Turing machine.

Now we select a fixed finite alphabet A for the machine U and find a way to encode any Turing machine (i.e., the instructions for any Turing machine) into a string over A. Similarly, we encode any input string for a Turing machine into a string over A.

Now that we have the two strings over A, one for the Turing machine and one for its input, we can get down to business and describe the action of machine U. We'll describe U as a three-tape Turing machine. We use three tapes because it's easier to describe the machine's actions. Recall that any k-tape machine can be simulated by a one-tape machine.

Before U starts its execution, we place the two strings over A on tapes 1 and 2, where tape 1 holds the representation for a Turing machine and tape 2 holds the representation of an input string. We also place the start state on tape 3. The action of U repeatedly performs the following actions: If the state on tape 3 is the halt state, then halt. Otherwise, get the current state from tape 3 and the current input symbol from tape 2. With this information, find the proper instruction on tape 1. Write the next state at the beginning of tape 3, and then perform the indicated write and move operations on tape 2.

It's much easier to build an interpreter for Turing machines by using a programming language than to build a universal Turing machine. We'll do so in the next example, where we'll write a logic program version of an interpreter for Turing machines. Our representation of the input tape in the logic program should give you an indication of the difficult problem a universal Turing machine has in maintaining the input portion of its tape.

EXAMPLE 7 (*A Logic Program Interpreter for Turing Machines*). We'll make a few assumptions about the interpreter. The start state is 0, and the input is a nonempty list representing the tape, which we denote by Head :: Tail. The tape will be represented by three quantities, "Left," "Cell," and "Right," where Cell denotes the current letter in the tape cell pointed at by the tape head, and Left and Right denote the lists of symbols to the left and right of Cell. When the halt state is reached, the tape is reconstructed as a single list. A typical instruction will be represented as a fact as follows:

$$t(\text{state, letterToRead, letterToWrite, move, nextState}) \leftarrow .$$

We'll assume that the three moves of the tape head are represented by the three letters l, s, and r. The symbol # will denote a blank tape entry.

The interpreter starts by calling the predicate "compute" with the input string as the first argument and a variable to receive the output tape as the second argument. The predicate "find" tries to find and execute an instruction. Its first argument is the state. The next three arguments are the representation of the tape, and the last argument holds the variable for the output tape. The "move" predicate makes a move and returns a new representation of the tape in variables A, B, and C. The "continue" predicate checks for the halt state. If it's found, the output tape is constructed and placed in the last variable. Otherwise, the "find" predicate is called to execute another instruction. The clauses for the interpreter are listed as follows:

compute(⟨ ⟩, OutTape)   (blank input tape)
    ← find(0, ⟨ ⟩, #, ⟨ ⟩, OutTape)

compute(Head::Tail, OutTape)   (nonblank input tape)
    ← find(0, ⟨ ⟩, Head, Tail, OutTape)

find(State, Left, Cell, Right, OutTape)
    ← t(State, Cell, Write, Move, Next),
      move(Move, Left, Write, Right, A, B, C),
      continue(Next, A, B, C, OutTape)

continue(halt, Left, Cell, Right, OutTape)
    ← cat(Left, Cell :: Right, OutTape)

continue(State, Left, Cell, Right, OutTape)
    ← find(State, Left, Cell, Right, OutTape)

move(l, ⟨ ⟩, Cell, Right, ⟨ ⟩, #, Cell :: Right) ←

move(l, ⟨Head⟩, Cell, Right, ⟨ ⟩, Head, Cell :: Right) ←

move(l, Head :: Tail, Cell, Right, Head :: X, Y, Cell :: Right)
    ← tailLeft(Tail, X), last(Tail, Y)

move(s, Left, Cell, Right, Left, Cell, Right) ←

move(r, Left, Cell, $\langle\,\rangle$, A, #, $\langle\,\rangle$)
      $\leftarrow$ cat(Left, $\langle$Cell$\rangle$, A)

move(r, Left, Cell, Head :: Tail, A, Head, Tail)
      $\leftarrow$ cat(Left, $\langle$Cell$\rangle$, A).

The predicate "cat(X, Y, Z)" sets Z to the concatenation of the two lists X and Y. The predicate "tailLeft(X, Y)" sets Y to the string obtained from X by removing its rightmost element. The predicate "last(X, Y)" sets Y to the rightmost element of the string X.

We can use the interpreter to test an arbitrary Turing machine. For example, the Turing machine to add 1 to a binary number can be written as the following set of facts:

$$t(0, 0, 0, r, 0) \leftarrow$$
$$t(0, 1, 1, r, 0) \leftarrow$$
$$t(0, \#, \#, l, 1) \leftarrow$$
$$t(1, 0, 1, s, \text{halt}) \leftarrow$$
$$t(1, 1, 0, l, 1) \leftarrow$$
$$t(1, \#, 1, s, \text{halt}) \leftarrow.$$

For example, to add 1 to the binary number 11011, we represent 11011 as a list and write the following goal:

$$\leftarrow \text{compute}(\langle 1, 1, 0, 1, 1 \rangle, \text{Out}).$$

The Turing machine interpreter should answer "yes" and output the value

$$\text{Out} = \langle 1, 1, 1, 0, 0, \# \rangle,$$

which signifies the binary number 11100.   ◆

We'll finish this introduction to Turing machines with an example of Turing machines that work hard.

EXAMPLE 8 (*Busy Beavers*). The Turing machines in this example are deterministic, can write either Λ or 1 on a tape cell, and must shift left or right after each move. Such a Turing machine is called a *busy beaver* if it accepts the empty string and, before it halts, it writes the largest number of 1's that can be written by Turing machines with the same number of states that accept the empty string. In other words, a busy beaver starts with a blank tape and halts after writing the maximum number of 1's possible by Turing machines with the same number of states that halt after starting with a blank tape. So a busy beaver is a hard-working Turing machine.

Let $b(n)$ denote the number of 1's that can be written by a busy beaver with n states, not including the halt state. It's pretty easy to see that $b(1) = 1$. For example, the following 1-state Turing machine prints a 1 and then halts:

$$\langle 0, \Lambda, 1, S, \text{Halt} \rangle.$$

If we try to build a 1-state machine that prints two or more 1's, then our machine would need an instruction like

$$\langle 0, \Lambda, 1, R, 0 \rangle \quad \text{or} \quad \langle 0, \Lambda, 1, L, 0 \rangle.$$

But this causes the machine to loop forever without halting. So $b(1) = 1$.

Busy beavers and the problem of finding the values of $b(n)$ were introduced by Rado [1962], where he observed that $b(1) = 1$ and $b(2) = 4$. For example, the following Turing machine is a busy beaver that satisfies $b(2) = 4$. In other words, the machine has two states (not including the halt state) and it writes four 1's before halting.

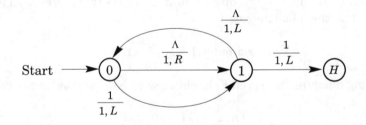

Rado proved that the function b cannot be computed by any algorithm. We'll discuss this further in the next chapter. So there will never be a formula to compute b Yet, some progress has been made. Lin and Rado [1965] proved that $b(3) = 6$. Brady [1983] proved that $b(4) = 13$. For $n \geq 5$, things get out of hand quickly. Marxen and Buntrock [1990] constructed a 5-state Turing machine that prints 4,098 1's before it halts. This is the best known result at this writing. Therefore we can say that $b(5) \geq 4,098$.

So it is not easy to discover busy beavers. An interpreter—such as the one given in Example 7—can be helpful in testing busy beaver candidates. The interpreter can be modified so that it stops after executing a given number of the candidates instructions. Thus you can experiment without worrying about whether the busy beaver candidate halts.   ♦

Exercises

1. Construct a Turing machine to recognize the language of all palindromes over {a, b}.

2. Construct a Turing machine that starts with the the symbol # in one cell, where all other tape cells are blank. The beginning position of the tape head is not known. The machine should halt with the tape head pointing at the cell containing #, all other tape cells being blank.

3. Construct a Turing machine to move an input string over {a, b} to the right one cell position. Assume that the tape head is at the left end of the input string if the string is nonempty. The rest of the tape cells are blank. The machine moves the entire string to the right one cell position, leaving all remaining tape cells blank.

4. Construct a Turing machine to implement each function. The inputs are pairs of natural numbers represented as unary strings and separated by the symbol #. Where necessary, represent zero by Λ.

   a. Add two natural numbers, neither of which is zero.

   b. Add two natural numbers, either of which may be zero.

5. Construct Turing machines to perform each task.

   a. Complement the binary representation of a natural number, and then add 1 to the result.

   b. Add 2 to a natural number represented as a binary string.

   c. Add 3 to a natural number represented as a binary string.

6. Construct a Turing machine to test for equality of two strings over the alphabet {a, b}, where the strings are separated by a cell containing #. Output a 0 if the strings are not equal and a 1 if they are equal.

7. Construct a three-tape Turing machine to add two binary numbers, where the first two tapes hold the input strings and the tape heads are positioned at the right end of each string. The third tape will hold the output.

8. Construct a single-tape Turing machine that inputs any string over the alphabet {a, b, c} and outputs its successor in the standard ordering, where we assume that $a \prec b \prec c$. Recall that in the standard ordering, strings are ordered by length, strings of the same length being ordered lexicographically.

9. In Example 8 we introduced busy beavers. It is known that $b(3) = 6$, which means that 3-state busy beavers print six 1's before halting. Try to construct a 3-state busy beaver.

7.2   The Church-Turing Thesis

The word "computable" is meaningful to most of us because we have a certain intuition about it, and we actually feel quite comfortable with it. We might even say something like, "A thing is computable if it can be computed." Or we might say, "A thing is computable if there is some computation that computes it." Of course, we might also say, "A thing is computable if it can be described by an algorithm."

So the word "computable" is defined by using words like "computation" and "algorithm." We can relate these two words by saying that a computation is the execution of an algorithm. So we can say that "computable" has something to do with a formal process (execution) and a formal description (algorithm). Let's list some examples of formal processes and formal descriptions that have something to do with our intuitive notion of computable:

The derivation process associated with grammars.

The evaluation process associated with functions.

The state transition process associated with machines.

The execution process associated with programs and programming languages.

For example, we can talk about the strings derived by regular grammars or the strings derived by context-free grammars. We can talk about the evaluation of a certain class of functions. We can discuss the state transitions of Turing machines, or pushdown automata, or real computers. We can also discuss the execution of programs written in our favorite programming language.

So when we think of computability, we most often try to formalize it in some way. For our purposes, a *model* is a formalization of an idea. So we'll use the word "model" instead of "formalization." Since there are many ways to model the idea of computability, the following two questions need to be answered:

Is one model more powerful than another? That is, does one model solve all the problems of another model and also solve some problem that is not solvable by the other model?

Is there a most powerful model?

We've already seen some answers to the first question. For example, we know that Turing machines are more powerful than pushdown automata and that pushdown automata are more powerful than deterministic finite automata. We also know that nondeterministic finite automata have the same power as deterministic finite automata.

What about the second question? One of the goals of these paragraphs is to convince you that the answer is yes. In fact there are many equivalent most powerful models. In particular, we would like to convince you that the following statement is true:

Church-Turing Thesis

Anything that is intuitively computable can be computed by a Turing machine.

The Church-Turing thesis says that any problem that is intuitively solvable in some way can also be solved by a Turing machine. Now let's discuss why the word "thesis" is used instead of the word "theorem." Each of us has some idea of what it means to be computable, even though the idea is informal. On the other hand, the idea of a Turing machine is formal and precise. So there is no possibility of ever proving that everyone's idea of computability is equivalent to the formal idea of a Turing machine. That's why the statement is a thesis rather than a theorem.

The Church-Turing thesis is important because no one has ever invented a computational model more powerful than a Turing machine! The name Church in the Church-Turing thesis belongs to the mathematician and logician Alonzo Church. He proposed a formalization—different from that of Turing—for the informal notion of algorithm. The account is contained in the paper by Church [1936]. We'll introduce the formalization in Chapter 8 when we discuss the lambda calculus.

Equivalence of Computational Models

In these paragraphs we'll discuss some computational models, each of which is equal in power to the Turing machine model. To say that two computational models are *equivalent* (i.e., *equal in power*) means that they both solve the same class of problems. Once we know that some computational model, say M, is equivalent to the Turing machine model, then we have an alternative form of the Church-Turing thesis:

Church-Turing Thesis for M

Anything that is intuitively computable can be computed by the M computational model.

For example, a normal task of any programming language designer is to make sure that the new language being developed—call it X—has the same power as a Turing machine. Is this hard to do? Maybe yes and maybe no. If we already know that some other language, say Y, is equivalent in power to a Turing machine, then we don't need to concern ourselves with Turing machines. All we need to do is show that languages X and Y are equal in power.

We'll see that a programming language does not need to be sophisticated to be powerful. In fact, we'll see that there are just a few properties that need to be present in any language. At first glance it may be hard to accept the Church-Turing thesis. Most of the results of this chapter should help convince the skeptic. If we accept the Church-Turing thesis, then we can associate "computable" with the phrase "computed by a Turing machine." If we don't want to make the leap of assuming the Church-Turing thesis, then we can refer to a thing being *Turing-computable* if it can be computed by a Turing machine.

Gödel Numbering

If two computational models process different kinds of data, then we need some method of representing the data of one model in terms of the data of the other. No matter what data are being processed, we can think of the data as strings of symbols that represent numbers, words, lists, signals, pulses, pictures, and so on.

A nice thing about symbols is that they can be represented by numbers. For example, each character in an alphabet can be represented as a binary string of digits representing a natural number. Thus each string of characters can be represented as a string of binary digits, which again represents a natural number. So the set $\mathbb{N}$ of natural numbers is a common denominator when discussing the representation of objects.

We must take some care when we represent strings as numbers because each string must be represented by a distinct number. In other words, the mapping from strings to numbers must be an injection. Gödel was the first person to define such a correspondence. Thus the name *Gödel numbering* has been given to any correspondence that associates a unique natural number with each string from a set.

We'll briefly describe a numbering similar to the one given by Gödel. Suppose we have an infinite set S of symbols that will be used as an alphabet for strings. For example, let S be the following set of symbols:

$$S = \{s_1, s_2, ..., s_n, ...\}.$$

We want to associate a unique natural number with each nonempty string over S. Recall that S^+ denotes the set of nonempty strings over S. In other words, we want to define a function $g : S^+ \to \mathbb{N}$ such that g (for Gödel) is an injection. We'll let g map each string to a product of primes. Let p_n denote the nth prime number, where $p_1 = 2$, $p_2 = 3$, and so on. If $s_{i_1} s_{i_2} \ldots s_{i_k}$ is a string of length k over S, then we'll define g as follows:

$$g(s_{i_1} s_{i_2} \ldots s_{i_k}) = p_1^{i_1} p_2^{i_2} \ldots p_k^{i_k}.$$

Each symbol in S corresponds to a power of 2:

$$g(s_1) = 2, \quad g(s_2) = 2^2, \quad g(s_3) = 2^3, \quad \text{and so on.}$$

The function g is an injection because prime factorization is unique for natural numbers greater than 1. For example,

$$g(s_7 s_1 s_4) = 2^7 \cdot 3^1 \cdot 5^4 = 240{,}000,$$

and $s_7 s_1 s_4$ is the only string over S that g maps to the number 240,000. The function g is not a surjection because, for example, the only prime number in the range of g is 2.

What's the point of all this? The point is that we want to compare computational models that process different types of data. For example, suppose we're comparing two classes of functions, one of which maps strings to natural numbers and the other of which maps natural numbers to natural numbers. Suppose we're interested in finding out whether we can model any function in one of these classes by a function in the other class.

For example, the "length" function maps strings to natural numbers. Let's see whether we can model this function by a computable function whose domain and codomain are the natural numbers. We already have a Gödel numbering that associates each string x with a unique natural number $g(x)$. So all we need to do is find a function f such that

$$\text{length}(x) = f(g(x)).$$

We can define such a function f by letting $f(n)$ be the number of distinct primes in the prime factorization of n. The function f is computable because there are algorithms to compute the prime factorization of a positive natural number. See whether you can find one. Here are some sample calculations:

$$\text{length}(s_7 s_1 s_4) = 3 \quad \text{and} \quad f(g(s_7 s_1 s_4)) = f(2^7 \cdot 3^1 \cdot 5^4) = 3,$$
$$\text{length}(s_5) = 1 \quad \text{and} \quad f(g(s_5)) = f(2^5) = 1.$$

We can go in the other direction too. In other words, we can represent any computable natural number function by a string-processing function. To do this, we must represent every natural number as a string. We've already seen several encodings of natural numbers as strings.

For example, suppose we want to model the function $h(n) = n + 2$ by a computable function from strings to natural numbers. We'll agree to represent a natural number n by a string of n a's, which we'll denote by $s(n)$. Now we need to find a string function k such that $h(n) = k(s(n))$. This again is easy to do. Just let $k(x) = \text{length}(x) + 2$. Then for any natural number n we have the equation $h(n) = k(s(n))$. For example, $h(4) = 6$, and we can also calculate $k(s(4))$ as follows:

$$k(s(4)) = k(aaaa) = \text{length}(aaaa) + 2 = 4 + 2 = 6.$$

Some Gödel numberings are bijections. When this is the case, we can use the encoding and its inverse to go back and forth between strings and natural numbers. For our purposes, we just need to know that there are encodings that will allow the comparison of computational models that process different kinds of data. Now let's look at some computational models that are equivalent in power to the Turing machine model.

A Simple Programming Language

Let's look at a little imperative language containing a small set of commands and a few other minimal features. The language that we present is a slight variation of a formalism called an unbounded register machine (URM), which was introduced by Shepherdson and Sturgis [1963]. An informal description of the language, which we'll call the *simple language*, can be given as follows:

1. There are variables that take values in the set $\mathbb{N}$.

2. There is a while statement of the form

    while $X \neq 0$ **do** statement **od**.

3. There is an assignment statement taking one of the three forms

    $X := 0, \quad X := \text{succ}(Y), \quad \text{and} \quad X := \text{pred}(Y).$

4. A statement can be a sequence of two or more statements separated by semicolons.

5. A program is a sequence of one or more statements separated by semicolons.

A formal description of the syntax for a simple program can be given as follows, where P stands for a program statement:

$P \to S \mid S\ T$

$T \to\ ;\ S\ T \mid \Lambda$

$S \to V := 0 \mid V := \mathrm{succ}(V) \mid V := \mathrm{pred}(V) \mid$ **while** $V \neq 0$ **do** P **od**

$V \to$ identifier.

The language doesn't have any input or output statements. We'll take care of this problem by assuming that all the variables in a program have been given initial values. Similarly, we'll assume that the output consists of the collection of values of the variables at program termination. The statements

$$X := \mathrm{succ}(Y) \text{ and } X := \mathrm{pred}(Y)$$

assign to X the value of the successor of Y and the predecessor of Y, respectively. We'll agree that $\mathrm{pred}(0) = 0$ because variables take values in $\mathbb{N}$.

Let's see whether this language can do anything. The language doesn't have an assignment statement like "$X := Y$." But we can accomplish the same action by the following program:

$$X := \mathrm{succ}(Y); X := \mathrm{pred}(X).$$

Thus we can let the statement "$X := Y$" be a macro for the above code.

Similarly, the language doesn't allow a statement like "$X := 3$." But we can accomplish the same action with the following program:

$$X := 0; X := \mathrm{succ}(X); X := \mathrm{succ}(X); X := \mathrm{succ}(X).$$

So if n is a natural number, we can let the statement "$X := n$" be a macro for the appropriate piece of code.

What about a statement like "$X := X + Y$?" Again, the grammar does not allow such a statement. But we can use the statement as a macro for the following piece of code:

$$I := Y; \textbf{while } I \neq 0 \textbf{ do } X := \mathrm{succ}(X); I := \mathrm{pred}(I) \textbf{ od}.$$

With the aid of macros, we can construct some familiar-looking programs. We'll leave some more macro problems as exercises.

This simple language has the same power as a Turing machine. In other words, any problem that can be solved by a Turing machine can be solved with a simple program; conversely, any problem that can be solved by a simple program can be solved by a Turing machine. The details can be found in many books, so we'll gladly omit them.

Partial Recursive Functions

If we believe anything, we most likely believe that functions like the following are computable:

$$f(x) = 0, \quad g(x) = x + 1, \quad \text{or} \quad h(x, y, z) = x.$$

We intuitively believe that these functions are computable because they are simple, and we can easily implement them in most programming languages. It also makes sense to say that the composition of two computable functions is computable. Similarly, the idea of recursive definition gives us a simple way to construct a computable function.

We're going to describe a collection of intuitively computable functions, called the *partial recursive functions*. We'll define the collection inductively by four rules (7.2)–(7.5). The first rule is the basis case, which gives us some initial functions to start the collection:

Initial Functions   (7.2)

There are three types of initial functions, as follows:

1. The *zero* function always returns zero:

    $$\text{zero}(x) = 0 \quad \text{for all } x \in \mathbb{N}.$$

2. The *successor* function returns the next natural number:

    $$\text{succ}(x) = x + 1 \quad \text{for all } x \in \mathbb{N}.$$

3. The *projection* functions pick an argument from one or more arguments:

    $$p_i(x_1, ..., x_n) = x_i \quad \text{for } 1 \le i \le n.$$

For example, the familiar identity function is a projection function as follows: $\text{id}(x) = p_1(x) = x$. Now let's look at the second rule, which combines partial recursive functions by composition:

Composition Rule   (7.3)

If h and $g_1, ..., g_m$ are partial recursive functions, then we can form a new partial recursive function f by composition:

$$f(x) = h(g_1(x), ..., g_m(x)).$$

Note: We can replace x by any number of arguments. For example, a composition may take the form

$$f(x, y) = h(g_1(x, y), ..., g_m(x, y)).$$

We can use the composition rule to construct many familiar partial recursive functions. For example, any constant function is partial recursive because it's a composition of initial functions. We can show the idea for the constant function $f(x, y) = 2$ as follows:

$$f(x, y) = p_1(\text{succ}(\text{succ}(\text{zero}(x))), \text{id}(y)) = \text{succ}(\text{succ}(\text{zero}(x))) = 2.$$

Now we'll look at the third rule, which constructs partial recursive functions by recursion:

Primitive Recursion Rule (7.4)

A new partial recursive function f can be constructed from the two partial recursive functions h and g as follows, where we'll assume that f takes two arguments:

$$f(x, 0) = h(x),$$
$$f(x, \text{succ}(y)) = g(x, y, f(x, y)).$$

Note: If f takes more than two arguments, then x can be replaced by the extra arguments. If f takes only a single argument, then x is removed, and the definition becomes

$$f(0) = h \qquad (h \text{ is a fixed constant in } \mathbb{N}),$$
$$f(\text{succ}(y)) = g(y, f(y)).$$

Let's do some examples to see how some familiar functions can be defined by primitive recursion.

EXAMPLE 1. We can define the function "plus" to perform addition as follows:

$$\text{plus}(x, 0) = x,$$
$$\text{plus}(x, \text{succ}(y)) = \text{succ}(\text{plus}(x, y)).$$

To see that this definition fits the form of the primitive recursion rule, let's see how the right sides of the two equations fit the pattern for the functions h and g of (7.4). We can transform the right sides of the plus definition into the following equations:

$$\text{plus}(x, 0) = x = \text{id}(x),$$
$$\text{plus}(x, \text{succ}(y)) = \text{succ}(\text{plus}(x, y)) = \text{succ}(p_3(x, y, \text{plus}(x, y))).$$

If we let h = id and g = succ $\circ$ p_3, then h and g are partial recursive functions because id is partial recursive and g is the composition of two partial recursive functions. With these simplifications we get the following definition of plus, which fits the form of the primitive recursion rule (7.4):

$$\text{plus}(x, 0) = h(x),$$
$$\text{plus}(x, \text{succ}(y)) = g(x, y, \text{plus}(x, y)). \quad \blacklozenge$$

As this example shows, it can be a tedious process showing how a nice recursive definition fits the form of (7.4). We won't go through this process again. Instead, we'll write clear, easy-to-understand right sides, with the assumption that we can always come up with h and g if required.

EXAMPLE 2. The predecessor function "pred" is defined as follows, where we assume that the predecessor of 0 is 0:

$$\text{pred}(0) = 0,$$
$$\text{pred}(\text{succ}(x)) = x.$$

For another example, the "sign" function—also called "signum"—returns 0 if its argument is zero and 1 for nonzero arguments:

$$\text{sign}(0) = 0,$$
$$\text{sign}(\text{succ}(x)) = 1. \quad \blacklozenge$$

We can write any function defined by primitive recursion in if-then-else form. For example, a typical definition using the primitive recursion rule looks like the following:

$$f(x, 0) = h(x),$$
$$f(x, \text{succ}(y)) = g(x, y, f(x, y)).$$

To write the if-then-else form of f, we need the predecessor function and a Boolean "test for zero" function:

$$f(x, y) = \text{if } y = 0 \text{ then } h(x) \text{ else } g(x, \text{pred}(y), f(x, \text{pred}(y))).$$

EXAMPLE 3. The predecessor function is also useful in defining the "monus" function, which has the following informal definition:

$$\text{monus}(x, y) = \text{if } x \geq y \text{ then } x - y \text{ else } 0.$$

We can define monus using the primitive recursion rule as follows:

$$\text{monus}(x, 0) = x,$$
$$\text{monus}(x, \text{succ}(y)) = \text{pred}(\text{monus}(x, y)).$$

For example, we'll compute monus(2, 1) and monus(1, 2):

$$\text{monus}(2, 1) = \text{pred}(\text{monus}(2, 0)) = \text{pred}(2) = 1.$$

$$
\begin{aligned}
\text{monus}(1, 2) &= \text{pred}(\text{monus}(1, 1)) \\
&= \text{pred}(\text{pred}(\text{monus}(1, 0))) \\
&= \text{pred}(\text{pred}(1)) \\
&= \text{pred}(0) \\
&= 0. \quad \blacklozenge
\end{aligned}
$$

EXAMPLE 4. Let's implement the "less than" relation on the natural numbers. Since we don't have the values true and false available, we need to represent these notions. We'll assume that 0 means false and 1 means true. So we can give an informal description of the "less than" relation as the following function:

$$\text{less}(x, y) = \text{if } x < y \text{ then } 1 \text{ else } 0.$$

How can we construct this function using the rules of partial recursive functions? First we'll notice the following relationship between less and monus:

$$\text{less}(x, y) = 1 \text{ iff monus}(y, x) \neq 0.$$

So we can write less in terms of monus as follows:

$$\text{less}(x, y) = \text{if monus}(y, x) = 0 \text{ then } 0 \text{ else } 1.$$

This definition tests the monus function for zero. The sign function gives us the tool we need to define less as a partial recursive function by the composition rule:

$$\text{less}(x, y) = \text{sign}(\text{monus}(y, x)).$$

For example, the value of the expression less(1, 3) is computed as follows:

$$\text{less}(1, 3) = \text{sign}(\text{monus}(3, 1)) = \text{sign}(2) = 1. \quad \blacklozenge$$

A great many useful functions can be defined by using one or more of the first three rules (7.2)–(7.4). It's always nice to be able to build complex things with simple tools like these three rules. Any function defined by the rules (7.2)–(7.4) is called a *primitive recursive function*. After studying these rules, it's easy to see that the primitive recursive functions are total functions (i.e, they are defined for all argument values in $\mathbb{N}$). So if we want to construct partial functions that are not total, we need another rule. Here's the last rule for constructing partial recursive functions:

Minimalization Rule   (7.5)

If g is partial recursive, then f is partial recursive, where f is defined as follows:

$$f(x) = \min_y(g(x, y) = 0).$$

We say "$f(x)$ is the minimum y such that $g(x, y) = 0$." If there is no such value, then $f(x)$ is undefined. The condition $g(x, y) = 0$ is more general than it looks. For example, we can use the condition $x + y = 2$ because it can be rewritten in the form $x + y - 2 = 0$.

EXAMPLE 5. Let's consider the function f defined as follows:

$$f(x) = \min_y(x + y = 2).$$

We have $f(0) = 2$, $f(1) = 1$, and $f(2) = 0$. But $f(x)$ is undefined for any natural number $x \geq 3$.   ◆

EXAMPLE 6. Let's consider the function h defined as follows:

$$h(x, y) = \min_z(x = y + z).$$

For example, we have $h(5, 2) = 3$, and $h(2, 5)$ is undefined. After a few more examples it's easy to see that if $x \geq y$, then $h(x, y) = x - y$. Otherwise, $h(x, y)$ is undefined.   ◆

As we said at the beginning, any function defined by one or more of the four rules (7.2)–(7.5) is called a *partial recursive function*. We know there are an uncountable number of natural number functions, and it's easy to see that the collection of partial recursive functions is countable. We've also seen that the primitive recursive functions form a proper subcollection of the partial recursive functions. The nice thing about the collection of partial recursive functions is that they are exactly the class of functions that are computed by Turing machines. This fact was proven by Kleene [1936]. So the partial recursive functions are also equivalent to the functions computed by simple programs. It's an easy exercise to implement the four rules for partial recursive functions in most programming languages.

An interesting fact about the partial recursive functions is that some are total yet they are not primitive recursive. That is, they can't be defined by using the first three rules. In other words, there are partial recursive functions that are total and not primitive recursive. A famous example of a partial recursive function that is total and not primitive recursive is *Ackermann's function*:

$$A(x, y) \;=\; \text{if } x = 0 \text{ then } y + 1$$
$$\text{else if } y = 0 \text{ then } A(x - 1, 1)$$
$$\text{else } A(x - 1, A(x, y - 1)).$$

Since A is presented as an algorithm, we can use the Church-Turing thesis to conclude that it can be represented as a Turing machine, a simple program, or a partial recursive function. We might like to conclude that A is primitive recursive because it's defined recursively. But it can't be defined by using the first three rules. The proof is based on the fact (which we won't prove) that for any primitive recursive function $f(x, y)$ there is a number n such that $f(x, y) < A(n, \max\{x, y\})$ for all $x, y \in \mathbb{N}$. Now, if A were primitive recursive, then there would exist a number n such that $A(x, y) < A(n, \max\{x, y\})$ for all $x, y \in \mathbb{N}$. Letting $x = y = n$, we get the contradiction $A(n, n) < A(n, n)$.

So Ackermann's function is an example of a partial recursive function that is total but not primitive recursive. We can picture the situation with the Venn diagram of proper subsets shown in Figure 7.2.

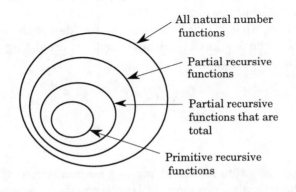

All natural number functions

Partial recursive functions

Partial recursive functions that are total

Primitive recursive functions

Figure 7.2

Machines That Transform Strings

Let's turn our attention to some powerful models for processing strings rather than numbers.

Markov Algorithms

A *Markov algorithm* over an alphabet A is a finite ordered sequence of productions $x \rightarrow y$, where $x, y \in A^*$. Some productions may be labeled with the word "halt," although this is not a requirement. A Markov algorithm transforms an input string into an output string. In other words, a Markov algorithm computes a function from A^* to A^*. Here's how the execution proceeds:

> Given an input string w, the productions are scanned, starting at the beginning of the ordered sequence. If there is a production $x \rightarrow y$ such that x occurs as a substring of w, then the leftmost occurrence of x in w is replaced by y to obtain a transformed string. If $x \rightarrow y$ is a halt production, then the process halts with the transformed string as output. Otherwise, the process starts all over again with the transformed string, where again the scan starts at the beginning of the ordered sequence of productions. If a scan of the instructions occurs without any new replacements of the current string, then the process halts with the current string as output.

If a production has the form $\Lambda \rightarrow y$, then it transforms any string w into the string yw. For example, suppose we wish to transform any string of the form a^i into the string a^{i+1}. The following single production Markov algorithm will do the job:

$$\Lambda \rightarrow a \quad (\text{halt}).$$

This production causes the letter a to be appended to the left of any input string, after which the process halts.

Let's look at another example to get a better idea of the execution process. Suppose M is the Markov algorithm over $\{a, *\}$ consisting of the following sequence of three productions:

$$a*a \rightarrow *$$

$$*a \rightarrow *$$

$$* \rightarrow \Lambda.$$

We'll execute the algorithm for the string $w = aa*aaa$. When M is applied to w, we obtain the following sequence of transformations, where the reasons are listed to the right:

1. $aa*aaa$	input string
2. $a*aa$	$a*a \rightarrow *$
3. $*a$	$a*a \rightarrow *$
4. $*$	$*a \rightarrow *$
5. Λ	$* \rightarrow \Lambda$

It's easy to see that M computes Λ for all strings of the form a^i*a^j, where $i \leq j$. It's also easy to see that M computes a^{i-j} for all input strings of the form a^i*a^j, where $i \geq j$. So if we think of a^i as a representation of the natural number i, then M transforms a^i*a^j into a representation of the monus operation applied to i and j. Let's look at another example.

EXAMPLE 7 (*Reversing a String*). Let's write a Markov algorithm to reverse any string over the alphabet $\{a, b, c\}$. For example, if the input string is abc, then the output string is cba. The algorithm will move the leftmost letter of a string to the right end of the string by swapping adjacent letters. Then it will move the leftmost letter of the transformed string to its proper position, and so on. We'll use the symbol X to keep track of the swapping process, and we'll use the symbol Y to help remove the X's after all swapping has been completed. The algorithm follows:

1. $XX \rightarrow Y$	(clean up instructions)
2. $Ya \rightarrow aY$	
3. $Yb \rightarrow bY$	
4. $Yc \rightarrow cY$	
5. $YX \rightarrow Y$	
6. $Y \rightarrow \Lambda$ (halt)	
7. $Xaa \rightarrow aXa$	(swapping instructions)
8. $Xab \rightarrow bXa$	
9. $Xac \rightarrow cXa$	
10. $Xba \rightarrow aXb$	
11. $Xbb \rightarrow bXb$	
12. $Xbc \rightarrow cXb$	
13. $Xca \rightarrow aXc$	
14. $Xcb \rightarrow bXc$	
15. $Xcc \rightarrow cXc$	
16. $\Lambda \rightarrow X$	(introduce X at left).

For example, the string abc gets transformed into cba as follows (fill in the appropriate production used for each step):

$$abc \to Xabc \to bXac \to bcXa \to XbcXa \to cXbXa \to XcXbXa \to XXcXbXa$$
$$\to YcXbXa \to cYXbXa \to cYbXa \to cbYXa \to cbYa \to cbaY \to cba. \quad \blacklozenge$$

Markov algorithms are described in Markov [1954]. Are Markov algorithms as powerful as Turing machines? The answer is yes, they are equivalent in power. So now we have the following equivalent models of computation: Turing machines, simple programs, partial recursive functions, and Markov algorithms.

Post Algorithms

Let's look at another string processing model—due to the mathematician Emil Post (1897–1954)—which appears in Post [1943]. A *Post algorithm* over an alphabet A is a finite set of productions that are used to transform strings. So a Post algorithm computes a function from A^* to A^*. The productions have the form $s \to t$, where s and t are strings made up of symbols from A and possibly some variables. A variable X occurs in s if and only if it occurs in t. There is no particular ordering of the productions in a Post algorithm, unlike the ordering of productions in Markov algorithms. Some productions may be labeled with the word "halt," although this is not required.

The computation of a Post algorithm proceeds by string pattern matching. If the input string matches the left side of some production, then we construct a new string to match the right side of the same production. If the production is a halt production, then the computation halts, and the new string is output. Otherwise, the process continues by trying to match the new string with the left side of some production. If no matches can be found, then the process halts, and the output is the current string.

A Post algorithm can be deterministic or nondeterministic depending on whether the current string matches the left side of more than one production or whether the current string matches the left side of a production in more than one way. Any nondeterministic Post algorithm can be rewritten as a deterministic Post algorithm. So no additional power is obtained by nondeterminism.

Let's start off with a simple example. The following single production makes up a Post algorithm over the alphabet $\{a, *\}$:

$$aX* \to X.$$

We'll execute the algorithm for the string $aa*$. Execution starts by matching $aa*$ with $aX*$, where $X = a$. Thus $aa*$ is transformed into the string a. Since a

doesn't match the left side the production, the computation halts. Notice that X can match the empty string too. For example, if the input string is $a*$, then it matches $aX*$, where $X = \Lambda$. So $a*$ gets transformed to Λ. It's easy to see that this Post algorithm transforms any string a^i* to a^{i-1} for $i > 0$.

EXAMPLE 8. Suppose we want to replace all occurrences of a by b in any string over $\{a, b, c\}$. We'll construct two Post algorithms to solve the problem. The first is nondeterministic, consisting of the single production

$$XaY \rightarrow XbY.$$

For example, the string $acab$ is transformed to $bcbb$ in two different ways as follows, depending on which a is matched:

$$acab \rightarrow bcab \rightarrow bcbb,$$
$$acab \rightarrow acbb \rightarrow bcbb.$$

Now we'll write a deterministic Post algorithm. We'll use the symbol # to mark the current position in a left to right scan of a string, and we'll use the symbol @ to mark the left end of the string so exactly one instruction can be used at each step:

$$aX \rightarrow @b\#X$$
$$bX \rightarrow @b\#X$$
$$cX \rightarrow @c\#X$$
$$@X\#aY \rightarrow @Xb\#Y$$
$$@X\#bY \rightarrow @Xb\#Y$$
$$@X\#cY \rightarrow @Xc\#Y$$
$$@X\# \rightarrow X \text{ (halt).}$$

For example, for the input string $acab$ the algorithm makes the following unique sequence of transformations:

$$acab \rightarrow @b\#cab \rightarrow @bc\#ab \rightarrow @bcb\#b \rightarrow @bcbb\# \rightarrow bcbb. \quad \blacklozenge$$

Are Post algorithms as powerful as Turing machines? The answer is yes, they have equivalent power. So now we have the following equivalent models of computation: Turing machines, simple programs, partial recursive functions, Markov algorithms, and Post algorithms.

Post Systems

Now let's look at systems that generate sets of strings. A *Post system* over the alphabet A (actually it's called a Post canonical system) is a finite set of inference rules and a finite set of strings in A^* that act as axioms to start the process. The inference rules are like the productions of a Post algorithm, except that an inference rule may contain more than one string on the left side. For example, a rule might have the form

$$s_1, s_2, s_3 \rightarrow t.$$

Computation proceeds by finding axioms to match the patterns on the left side of some inference rule and then constructing a new string from the right side of the same rule. The new string can then be used as an axiom. In this way, each Post system generates a set of strings over A consisting of the axioms and all strings inferred by the axioms.

EXAMPLE 9. Let's write a Post system to generate the set of all balanced parentheses. The alphabet will be the two symbols (and). The axioms and inference rules have the following form:

Axiom: Λ.

Inference rules: $X \rightarrow (X),$
$\qquad\qquad\qquad X, Y \rightarrow XY.$

We'll do a few computations. The axiom Λ matches the left side of the first rule. Thus we can infer the string ( ). Now the string ( ) matches the left side of the same rule, which allows us to infer the string (( )). If we let $X =$ ( ) and $Y =$ (( )), the second rule allows us to infer the string ( )(( )). So the set of strings generated by this Post system is

$$\{\Lambda, (\,), ((\,)), (\,)((\,)), \dots \}. \quad \blacklozenge$$

EXAMPLE 10. We can generate the set of all palindromes over the alphabet $\{a, b\}$ by the Post system with the following axioms and inference rules:

Axioms: Λ, a, b.

Inference rules: $X \rightarrow aXa,$
$\qquad\qquad\qquad X \rightarrow bXb. \quad \blacklozenge$

If A is an alphabet and $f : A^* \to A^*$ is a function, then f is said to be *Post-computable* if there is a Post system that computes the following set of pairs that define the function:

$$\{\langle x, f(x) \rangle \mid x \in A^*\}.$$

To simplify things, we'll agree to represent the pair $\langle x, f(x) \rangle$ as the string $x\#f(x)$, where # is a new symbol not in A.

For example, the function $f(x) = xa$ over the alphabet $\{a\}$ is Post-computable by the Post system consisting of the axiom $\#a$ together with the following rule:

$$X \,\#X\, a \to Xa \,\#X\, a\, a.$$

This Post system computes f as the set $\{\#a, a\#aa, aa\#aaa, \dots \}$.

Are Post systems as powerful as Turing machines? The answer is yes, they have equivalent power. So now we have the following equivalent models of computation: Turing machines, simple programs, partial recursive functions, Markov algorithms, Post algorithms, and Post systems.

Logic Programming Languages

Are logic programming languages as powerful as Turing machines? In other words, is the set of functions that can be computed by logic programs the same as the set of functions computed by Turing machines? The answer is yes. We'll show that logic programs compute the set of partial recursive functions, which are equivalent in power to Turing machines.

First, it's easy to see that the initial functions can be computed by logic programs: The program with single clause

$$\text{zero}(x, 0) \leftarrow$$

computes the zero function. Next, if we agree that $s(x)$ denotes the successor of a natural number x, then the program

$$\text{succ}(x, s(x)) \leftarrow$$

computes the successor function. Lastly, there is a predicate for each projection function. For example, the program

$$\text{proj3}(x_1, x_2, x_3, x_4, x_5, x_3) \leftarrow$$

computes the projection of a 5-tuple onto its third argument.

This takes care of the initial functions. Now we must show that any function defined by composition, primitive recursion, or minimalization can be computed by a logic program. To keep things simple, we'll illustrate the proof using single variable functions. We can proceed by induction on the number n of applications of the three rules, composition, primitive recursion, or minimalization, needed to define a function f.

The case for $n = 0$ is completed already because the initial functions don't use any occurrences of the three rules. So let $n > 0$, and assume (the induction assumption) that any partial recursive function using fewer than n applications of the three rules can be computed by a logic program. Now, let f be a partial recursive function that uses n applications of the three rules. We need to show that f can be computed by a logic program. There are three cases to consider based on how f is defined: by composition, by primitive recursion, or by minimalization.

For the case of composition, f has the form $f(x) = h(g(x))$, where h and g are partial recursive functions. Since h and g use fewer than n applications of the three rules, the induction assumption implies that there are logic programs to compute h and g. Call the programs H and G, where "ph" and "pg" are the names of the predicates to compute h and g. The logic program to compute f is the union of G, H, and the singleton set containing the following clause, where "pf" is the predicate to compute f:

$$\text{pf}(x, z) \leftarrow \text{pg}(x, y), \text{ph}(y, z).$$

For example, let's compute the goal $\leftarrow \text{pf}(4, z)$. This goal causes two goals to be executed. The goal $\leftarrow \text{pg}(4, y)$ returns $y = g(4)$. Then the goal $\leftarrow \text{ph}(y, z)$ becomes $\leftarrow \text{ph}(g(4), z)$, which returns $z = h(g(4)) = f(4)$.

For the case of primitive recursion, we'll assume that f has the following form:

$$f(0) = c,$$
$$f(\text{succ}(x)) = g(x, f(x)),$$

where g is partial recursive. Since g uses fewer than n applications, the induction assumption implies that there is a logic program to compute g. Let G be the program to compute g, where "pg" is the predicate to compute g. The logic program to compute f is the union of the set G and the set consisting of the following two clauses, where "pf" is the predicate to compute f:

$$\text{pf}(0, c) \leftarrow,$$
$$\text{pf}(\text{succ}(x), z) \leftarrow \text{pf}(x, y), \text{pg}(x, y, z).$$

For example, let's compute the goal $\leftarrow \text{pf}(\text{succ}(0), z)$. This goal causes the evaluation of the two goals $\leftarrow$ pf(0, y) and $\leftarrow$ pg(0, y, z). The goal $\leftarrow$ pf(0, y) returns $y = f(0)$. So the goal $\leftarrow$ pg(0, y, z) becomes $\leftarrow$ pg(0, f(0), z), which returns $z = g(0, f(0))$. Therefore $f(\text{succ}(0)) = g(0, f(0))$ as expected.

For the case of minimalization we'll assume that f has the following form, where g is partial recursive:

$$f(x) = \min_y(g(x, y) = 0).$$

Again, g uses fewer than n applications. So the induction assumption implies that g can be computed by a logic program. Let G be the program to compute g, where "pg" is the predicate that computes g. The logic program F to compute f can be defined as the union of G with the set consisting of the following three clauses, where "pf" is the predicate to compute f:

$$\text{pf}(x, y) \leftarrow \text{pmin}(x, 0, y),$$
$$\text{pmin}(x, y, y) \leftarrow \text{pg}(x, y, 0),$$
$$\text{pmin}(x, y, z) \leftarrow \text{pmin}(x, \text{succ}(y), z).$$

For example, suppose we let $g(x, y) = x$. Then the goal $\leftarrow$ pf(0, y) will return $y = 0$, which means that $f(0) = 0$. But the goal $\leftarrow$ pf(succ(0), y) will cause the program to loop forever, which signifies that $f(\text{succ}(0))$ is undefined.

So logic programs are equal in power to partial recursive functions. Therefore our list of equivalent models of computation includes Turing machines, simple programs, partial recursive functions, Markov algorithms, Post algorithms, Post systems, and logic programs.

Some Notes

Of course, there are many other computational models that have the same power as a Turing machine. For example, most modern programming languages are as powerful as a Turing machine if we assume that they can handle numbers of arbitrary size and if we assume that enough memory is always available. A model that we haven't discussed yet is called the lambda calculus. We'll introduce it in Section 8.3.

Some models of computation may seem to be more powerful than others. For example, a parallel computation may speed up the solution to a problem. But a parallel language is no more powerful than a nonparallel language. That is, if some problem can be solved by using n processors running in parallel, then the same problem can be solved by using one processor, by simulating the use of n processors.

We'll end this section by reasserting the fact that every computational model invented so far has no more power than that of the Turing machine model. So it's easy to see why most people believe the Church-Turing thesis.

Exercises

1. Write *simple* programs to perform the actions indicated by each of the following macros. *Hint:* Each problem can be solved with the aid of a macro in a previous problem or a macro defined in the text.

   a. $Z := X + Y$.

   b. $Z := X * Y$.

   c. **if** $X \neq 0$ **then** S **fi**.

   d. **if** $X \neq 0$ **then** S **else** T **fi**.

   e. $Z := X$ monus Y, where X monus $Y =$ if $X \geq Y$ then $X - Y$ else 0.

   f. **while** $X < Y$ **do** S **od**.

   g. **while** $X \leq Y$ **do** S **od**.

   h. $Z :=$ absoluteDiff(X, Y), which is the absolute value of the difference between X and Y.

   i. **while** $X \neq Y$ **do** S **od**.

   j. **while** $X \neq 0$ and $Y \neq 0$ **do** S **od**.

   k. **while** $X \neq 0$ or $Y \neq 0$ **do** S **od**.

2. For each of the following definitions, find the functions h and g to make the definition conform exactly to the primitive recursive rule.

   a. pred$(0) = 0$,

   pred$(\text{succ}(x)) = x$.

   b. sign$(0) = 0$,

   sign$(\text{succ}(x)) = 1$.

3. Give an informal description of each of the following functions.

   a. $f(x) = \min_y(x = y - 1)$.

   b. $f(x) = \min_y(x = y + 1)$.

   c. $f(x, y) = \min_z(x = y - z)$.

   d. $f(x, y) = \min_z(x = y * z)$.

4. Let $f(x) = \min_y(g(x, y) = 0)$. Assume that there is an algorithm to compute g. Find a *simple* program to compute f.

5. Let LE stand for the "less than or equal to" function on natural numbers. In other words, LE can be defined informally as

$$\text{LE}(x, y) = \text{if } x \leq y \text{ then } 1 \text{ else } 0.$$

   Find a definition for LE as a partial recursive function. *Hint:* Write LE in terms of the "less" function.

6. For each of the following Markov algorithms over $\{a, *\}$, describe the form that the output takes in terms of an input string of the form $a^i * a^j$. Each algorithm is a permutation of the three productions

$$a*a \rightarrow *, \quad *a \rightarrow *, \quad \text{and} \quad * \rightarrow \Lambda.$$

   a. $*a \rightarrow *, a*a \rightarrow *, * \rightarrow \Lambda$.

   b. $* \rightarrow \Lambda, *a \rightarrow *, a*a \rightarrow *$.

   c. $*a \rightarrow *, * \rightarrow \Lambda, a*a \rightarrow *$.

7. Write Markov algorithms to accomplish each of the following actions.

   a. An infinite loop occurs when the input is the letter a.

   b. Delete the leftmost occurrence of b in any string over $\{a, b, c\}$.

   c. For inputs of the form $a^i * a^j$ the output is a^{i+j}.

   d. Transform strings of the form $a^n b c^n$ to $c^n b^2 a^n$ for any $n \in \mathbb{N}$.

   e. Interchange all a's and b's in any string over $\{a, b\}$.

8. Write Post algorithms to accomplish each of the following actions.

   a. An infinite loop occurs when the input is the letter a.

   b. Add 1 to a unary string of 1's.

   c. For inputs of the form $a^i * a^j$ the output is a^{i+j}.

   d. Transform strings of the form $a^n b c^n$ to $c^n b^2 a^n$ for any $n \in \mathbb{N}$.

   e. Interchange all a's and b's in any string over $\{a, b\}$.

   f. Delete the leftmost occurrence of b in any string over $\{a, b, c\}$.

9. Write a Post system to generate each of the following sets of strings.

   a. The even palindromes over the alphabet $\{a, b\}$.

   b. The odd palindromes over the alphabet $\{a, b, c\}$.

   c. $\{a^n * b^n \# c^n \mid n \in \mathbb{N}\}$.

   d. The binary strings that represent the natural numbers, where each string except 0 begins with 1 on the left end.

Chapter Summary

This chapter discussed Turing machines and other equivalent computational models. Turing machines may be defined with multiple tapes, multiple heads, and having either two-way infinite tapes or one-way infinite tapes. All formulations are equivalent. Turing machines can recognize languages, and they can generate output. They are general-purpose computation devices that are more powerful that pushdown automata. Deterministic Turing machines have the same power as nondeterministic Turing machines. A simple interpreter can be constructed for Turing machines.

The Church-Turing thesis says that anything that is intuitively computable can be computed by a Turing machine. We can compare computational models that process different types of data because there are encodings between the different types of data. We discussed a variety of computational models that are equal in power to the Turing machine model: simple programs, partial recursive functions, Markov algorithms, Post algorithms, Post systems, and logic programs. All known computational models are no more powerful than the Turing machine model. So there is much support for the Church-Turing thesis.

8

Computational Notions

Give us the tools, and we will finish the job.
—Winston Churchill (1874–1965)

Some problems can't be solved by machines. In this chapter we look at the limits of computation by discussing some classic problems that are not solvable by any machine. But we also look at some classic problems that are solvable, and we look at some classic computational techniques for evaluating expressions.

Chapter Guide

Section 8.1 discusses some general problems that can't be solved by any machine. We'll also see examples of unsolvable problems that are partially solvable, and we'll see examples of unsolvable problems that can be modified to create solvable problems.

Section 8.2 presents a hierarchy of languages, some that can be recognized by machines and others that can't be recognized by any machine.

Section 8.3 returns to the positive side of the discussion by introducing some basic computational techniques for evaluating expressions. We'll introduce a computational model called the lambda calculus, whose evaluation rules can be efficiently implemented. We'll also introduce the famous Knuth-Bendix procedure for finding evaluation rules.

8.1 Computability

It's fun when we solve a problem, and it's not fun when we can't solve a problem. If we can't solve a problem, we can sometimes alter it in some way and then solve the modified problem. If no one can solve a problem, then it could mean that the problem can't be solved, but it could also mean that the problem is hard and a solution will eventually be found. We want to introduce some classic problems that cannot be solved by any machine. But first, we need to discuss a few preliminaries.

If something is computable, the Church-Turing thesis tells us that it can be computed by a Turing machine. A Turing machine or any other equivalent model of computation can be described by a finite number of symbols. So each Turing machine can be considered as a finite string. If we let S be a countable set of symbols, then any Turing machine can be coded as a finite string of symbols over S. Since there are a countable number of strings over S, it follows that there are a countable number of Turing machines. We can make the same statement for any computational model: There are a countable number of instances of the model. The word "countable" as we've used it means "countably infinite." So there are a countably infinite number of problems that can be solved by computational models. This is nice to know because we won't ever run out of work trying to find algorithms to solve problems. That's good. But we should also be aware that some problems are too general to be solvable by any machine.

Since the inputs and outputs of any computation can be represented by natural numbers, we'll restrict our discussion to functions that have natural numbers as arguments and as values. It follows from Example 4 of Section 1.3 that this set of functions is uncountable. If we assume the Church-Turing thesis, which we do, then there are only countably many of these functions that are "computable," which means that they can be computed by Turing machines or other equivalent computational models.

Effective Enumerations

To discuss computability, we need to define the idea of an effective enumeration of a set. An *effective enumeration* of a set is a listing of its elements by an algorithm. There is no requirement that an effective enumeration list the elements in any particular way, and it's OK for an effective enumeration to output redundant values.

For example, the evaluation of the expression odds(1) will enumerate all the odd natural numbers, where odds(x) is defined by

$$\text{odds}(x) = (\text{if } x \text{ is odd then } x + 2 \text{ else } x - 1) :: \text{odds}(x + 1).$$

We'll unfold the expression odds(1) for a few steps to get the idea:

$$odds(1) = 3 :: odds(2)$$
$$= 3 :: (1 :: odds(3))$$
$$= 3 :: (1 :: (5 :: odds(4)))$$
$$= 3 :: (1 :: (5 :: (3 :: odds(5))))$$
$$= 3 :: (1 :: (5 :: (3 :: (7 :: odds(6))))).$$

In other words, the evaluation of odds(1) effectively enumerates the set of odd natural numbers as the following stream:

$$\langle 3, 1, 5, 3, 7, 5, 9, 7, ... \rangle.$$

Let's get to the important part of the discussion. We want to be able to effectively enumerate all instances of any particular computational model. For example, we want to be able to effectively enumerate the set of all Turing machines, or the set of all Simple programs, or the set of all partial recursive functions, and so on. Since any instance of a computational model can be thought of as a string of symbols, we'll associate each natural number with an appropriate string of symbols.

One way to accomplish this is to let $b(n)$ denote the binary representation of a natural number n. For example,

$$b(7018) = 1101101101010.$$

Next we'll partition $b(n)$ into seven bit blocks by starting at the right end of the string. If necessary we can add leading zeros to the left end of the string to make sure that all blocks contain seven bits. For example, $b(7018)$ gets partitioned into the two seven bit blocks

$$0110110 \text{ and } 1101010.$$

Recall that each character in the ASCII character set is represented by a block of seven bits. For example, the block 0110110 represents the character 6 and the block 1101010 represents the character j. Let $a(b(n))$ denote the string of ASCII characters represented by the partitioning of $b(n)$ into seven bit blocks. For example, we have

$$a(b(7018)) = 6j.$$

Now we're in position to effectively enumerate all of the instances of any computational model. Here's the general idea: If the string $a(b(n))$ represents a syntactically correct definition for an instance of the model, then we'll use it as the nth instance of the model. If $a(b(n))$ doesn't make any sense, we set the nth instance of the model to be some specifically chosen instance. We observed in our little example that $a(b(7018)) = 6j$. So n will have to be a very large number before $a(b(n))$ has a chance of being a syntactically correct instance of the model. But that's OK. All we're interested in is effectively enumerating all instances of a computational model. Since we have forever, we'll eventually get them all.

Here are a few examples to clarify the discussion.

Turing machines: For each natural number n, let T_n denote the Turing machine defined as follows: If $a(b(n))$ represents a string of valid Turing machine instructions, then let $T_n = a(b(n))$. Otherwise, let T_n be the simple machine $T_n = $ "$\langle 0, a, a, S, \text{Halt} \rangle$." Now we can effectively enumerate all the Turing machines by evaluating the expression Turing(0), where Turing(n) = T_n :: Turing($n + 1$).

Simple programs: For each natural number n, let S_n denote the Simple program defined as follows: If $a(b(n))$ represents a string of valid Simple program instructions, then let $S_n = a(b(n))$. Otherwise, let $S_n = $ "$X := 0$." Now we can effectively enumerate all the simple programs by evaluating the expression Simple(0), where Simple(n) = S_n :: Simple($n + 1$).

Partial recursive functions: For each natural number n, let P_n denote the partial recursive function defined as follows: If $a(b(n))$ represents a string defining a partial recursive function, then let $P_n = a(b(n))$. Otherwise, let $P_n = $ "zero(x) = 0." Now we can effectively enumerate the set of all partial recursive functions by evaluating the expression ParRecur(0), where ParRecur(n) = P_n :: ParRecur($n + 1$).

We most likely have the idea by now. We can effectively enumerate all possible instances of any computational model. Therefore, by the Church-Turing thesis, we can effectively enumerate all possible computable functions. For our discussion, we'll assume that we have an effective enumeration of all the computable functions as follows:

$$f_0, f_1, f_2, ..., f_n, ... \tag{8.1}$$

If we like Turing machines, we can think of f_n as the function computed by T_n. If we like partial recursive functions, we can think of f_n as P_n. If we like algorithms expressed in English mixed with other symbols, then we can think of f_n in this way too. The important point is that we can effectively enumerate all the computable functions. Thus the list (8.1) contains all the usual functions that we think of as computable, such as successor, addition, multiplication, and others like

$$p(k) = \text{the } k\text{th prime number.}$$

The list (8.1) also contains many functions that we might not even think about. For example, suppose we define the following simple function:

$$g(x) = \text{if the fifth digit of } \pi \text{ is 7 then 1 else 0.}$$

Since we know $\pi = 3.14159...$, it follows that g is the constant function $g(x) = 0$. So g is clearly computable. Now let's define the following simple function:

$$f(x) = \text{if the googolth digit of } \pi \text{ is 7 then 1 else 0.}$$

This function is computable because we know that the condition "the googolth digit of π is 7," is either true or false. Therefore either f is the constant function 1 or f is the constant function 0. We just don't know the value of f because no one has computed π to a googol places.

The list (8.1) also contains functions that are partially defined, such as the following samples:

$$f(n) = \text{if } n \text{ is odd then } n + 1 \text{ else error,}$$
$$h(k) = \text{if } k \text{ is even then 1 else loop forever.}$$

At times we'll want to talk about all the computable functions that take a single argument. Can they be effectively enumerated? Sure. For example, suppose we are enumerating partial recursive functions. If $a(b(n))$ represents a valid string for a partial recursive function of a single variable, then set $P_n = a(b(n))$. Otherwise, set $P_n = $ "zero$(x) = 0$."

Now we're prepared to study a few classic problems. For convenience of expression, we will only consider decision problems. A *decision problem* is a problem that asks a question that has a yes or no answer. A decision problem is *solvable* (or *decidable*) if there is an algorithm that can input any arbitrary instance of the problem and halt with the correct answer. If no such algorithm exists, then the problem is *unsolvable* (or *undecidable*). A decision problem is *partially solvable* (or *partially decidable*) if there is an algorithm that halts with the answer yes for those instances of the problem that have yes answers, but that may run forever for those instances of the problem whose answers are no.

The Halting Problem

Can we tell by examining a program whether its execution halts on an arbitrary input? Depending on the program, we might be able to do it. For example, suppose we're given the function $f : \mathbb{N} \to \mathbb{N}$ defined by $f(x) = 2x + 1$, and we're given the input value 17. We can certainly say that f halts on input 17. In fact we can see that f halts for all natural numbers x. For another example, suppose we're given the function h defined by

$$h(x) = \text{if } x = 7 \text{ then } 2 \text{ else loop forever.}$$

In this case we can see that $h(7)$ halts. We can also see that $h(x)$ does not halt for all $x \neq 7$.

In these two examples we were able to tell whether the programs halted on arbitrary inputs. Now let's consider a more general question. The *halting problem* asks the following question about programs:

> Is there an algorithm that can decide whether the execution   (8.2)
> of an arbitrary program halts on an arbitrary input?

The answer to the question is no. In other words, the halting problem is unsolvable. The halting problem was introduced and proved unsolvable by Turing [1936]. He considered the problem in terms of Turing machines rather than programs. Of course, we can replace "Turing machine" by any equivalent computational model. If we assume the Church-Turing thesis, then we can replace "algorithm" by any computational model that is equivalent to the Turing machine model. For example, we can state the halting problem in terms of computable functions as follows:

> Is there a computable function that can decide whether   (8.3)
> the execution of an arbitrary computable function halts
> on an arbitrary input?

We'll prove that the answer to version (8.3) of the halting problem is no.

Proof: Suppose, by way of contradiction, that the answer is yes. Then we can define the following "halt" function, where we're assuming that the functions f_x in (8.1) take single arguments:

$$\text{halt}(x) = \text{if } f_x \text{ halts on input } x \text{ then } 1 \text{ else } 0.$$

We must conclude that "halt" is computable because we are assuming that a

computable function exists to compute the condition, "f_x halts on input x."
Now we need to find some kind of contradiction. A classic way to do this is to
define a new function, say g, as follows:

$$g(x) = \text{if halt}(x) = 1 \text{ then loop forever else } 0.$$

Notice that g is computable because we're assuming that "halt" is computable. Therefore g must occur somewhere in the list of computable functions (8.1). In other words, there is some natural number n such that $g = f_n$.
We can obtain a contradiction by studying the situation that occurs when g is
given its own index n as an argument:

$$g(n) = f_n(n).$$

We can find a contradiction by considering the two possible values for
halt(n). First we'll assume halt(n) = 1. In this case the definition of $g(n)$ tells
us that $g(n)$ loops forever. The assumption halt(n) = 1 also tells us—by using
the definition of the halt function—that f_n halts on input n. In other words,
$f_n(n)$ halts. But $g(n) = f_n(n)$. So $g(n)$ halts. So we've proved the following non
sequitur:

If halt(n) = 1, then $g(n)$ loops forever and $g(n)$ halts.

This certainly can't be true. So we'll make the other assumption that halt(n)
= 0. In this case the definition of $g(n)$ tells us that $g(n)$ halts with the value 0.
The assumption halt(n) = 0 also tells us—by using the definition of the halt
function—that f_n does not halt on input n. In other words, $f_n(n)$ does not halt.
But $g(n) = f_n(n)$. So $g(n)$ does not halt. So we've proved the following non sequitur:

If halt(n) = 0, then $g(n)$ halts and $g(n)$ does not halt.

So we obtain a contradiction for the two possible values of halt(n). Therefore
our assumption that the halt function is computable was wrong. So there is
no computable function to tell whether an arbitrary computable function
halts on its own index. Thus there certainly is no computable function that
can tell whether an arbitrary computable function halts on an arbitrary input. Therefore the halting problem is not solvable.   QED.

A restricted form of the halting problem, which is solvable, asks the
question: Is there a computable function that, when given f_n, m, and k, can
tell whether f_n halts on input m in k units of time? Can you see why this
function is computable? We'll leave it as an exercise.

The Total Problem

Can we tell by examining a computable function whether it halts on all inputs? In other words, can we tell whether a computable function is total? For example, we can certainly tell for the functions f and g defined by $f(x) = 4$ and $g(x) =$ if $x > 5$ then $x + 1$ else loop forever.

A general problem concerning computable functions is called the *total problem*, and we'll state it as follows:

> Is there an algorithm to tell whether an arbitrary computable   (8.4)
> function is total?

The answer is no. To prove (8.4), we need the following intermediate result about listing total computable functions:

> There is no effective enumeration of all the total computable   (8.5)
> functions.

Proof: We'll prove (8.5) for the case of natural number functions having a single variable. Suppose, by way of contradiction, that we have an effective enumeration of all the total computable functions:

$$h_0, h_1, h_2, ..., h_n, ...$$

Now define a new function H by diagonalization as follows:

$$H(n) = h_n(n) + 1.$$

Since each h_n is total, it follows that H is total. Since the listing is an effective enumeration, there is an algorithm that when, given n, produces h_n. Therefore $h_n(n) + 1$ can be computed. Thus H is computable. Therefore H is a total computable function that is not in the listing because it differs from each function in the list at the diagonal entries $h_n(n)$.   QED.

Now we'll prove that the answer to (8.4) is no.

Proof: The proof will be indirect. So we'll assume that the answer is yes. In other words, we'll assume that there is some algorithm that can decide whether an arbitrary computable function is total. We'll start by defining a function "total" as follows:

$$total(x) = \text{if } f_x \text{ is a total function then } 1 \text{ else } 0.$$

This function is computable because we're assuming that there is an algorithm to decide whether "f_x is a total function." We will obtain a contradiction by exhibiting an effective enumeration of all total computable functions, which we know can't happen by (8.5). One way to accomplish this is to define the function g as follows:

$g(0)$ is the smallest index k such that total$(k) = 1$.

$g(n + 1)$ is the smallest index k greater than $g(n)$ such that total$(k) = 1$.

Since total is computable and we have an effective enumeration of all the computable functions f_n, it follows that g is computable. Therefore we have an effective enumeration of all the total computable functions, which we can list as follows:

$$f_{g(0)}, f_{g(1)}, f_{g(2)}, ..., f_{g(n)}, ...$$

But this contradicts (8.5). Therefore the function "total" is not computable. Thus there is no algorithm to tell whether an arbitrary computable function is total.   QED.

Other Problems

We'll conclude this section with a few more examples of unsolvable problems. Then we'll have a short discussion about partially solvable problems and solvable problems.

The Equivalence Problem

Can we tell by examining two programs whether they produce the same output when given the same input? Depending on the programs, we might be able to do it. For example, we can certainly tell that the two functions f and g are equal, where $f(x) = x + x$ and $g(x) = 2x$. The *equivalence problem* asks a more general question:

> Does there exist an algorithm that can decide whether   (8.6)
> two arbitrary computable functions produce the same output?

The answer to this question is no. So the equivalence problem is unsolvable. If we restrict the problem to deciding whether an arbitrary computable function is the identity function, the answer is still no. Most proofs of the equivalence problem show that this restricted version is unsolvable.

Post's Correspondence Problem

The problem known as *Post's correspondence problem* was introduced by Post [1946]. An *instance* of the problem can be stated as follows: Given a finite sequence of pairs of strings

$$\langle s_1, t_1 \rangle, ..., \langle s_n, t_n \rangle,$$

is there a sequence of indexes $i_1, ..., i_k$, with repetitions allowed, such that

$$s_{i_1}...s_{i_k} = t_{i_1}...t_{i_k}?$$

For example, let's consider the instance of the problem consisting of the following sequence of pairs, where we'll number the pairs sequentially as 1, 2, 3, and 4:

$$\langle ab, a \rangle, \langle b, bb \rangle, \langle aa, b \rangle, \langle b, aab \rangle.$$

After a little fiddling we can find that the sequence 1, 2, 1, 3, 4 will produce the following equality:

$$abbabaab = abbabaab.$$

For another example, let's consider the instance of the problem described by the following sequence of pairs, which we'll refer to as 1 and 2:

$$\langle ab, a \rangle, \langle b, ab \rangle.$$

This instance of the problem has no solution. To see this, notice that any solution sequence would have to contain an equal number of 1's and 2's to make sure that the two strings have equal length. But this implies that the left side would have twice as many b's than a's and the right side would have twice as many a's than b's. So the strings could not be equal.

Post's correspondence problem asks the following general question:

Is there an algorithm that can decide whether an arbitrary   (8.7)
instance of the problem has a solution?

Post's correspondence problem is unsolvable. At first glance it might seem that the problem is solvable by an algorithm that exhaustively checks sequences of pairs for a desired equality of strings. But if there is no solution for some instance of the problem, then the algorithm will go on checking ever larger sequences for an equality that doesn't exist. So it won't be able to halt and tell us that there is no solution sequence.

Hilbert's Tenth Problem

In 1900, Hilbert stated 23 problems that—at the time—were not solved. The problem known as *Hilbert's tenth problem* can be stated as follows:

> Does a polynomial equation $p(x_1, ..., x_n) = 0$ with integer   (8.8)
> coefficients have a solution consisting of integers?

Of course, we can solve specific instances of the problem. For example, it's easy for us to find integer solutions to the equation

$$2x + 3y + 1 = 0.$$

It's also easy for us to see that there are no integer solutions to the equation

$$x^2 - 2 = 0.$$

In 1970, Matiyasevich proved that Hilbert's tenth problem is unsolvable. So there is no algorithm to decide whether an arbitrary polynomial equation with integer coefficients has a solution of integers.

Turing Machine Problems

There are many unsolvable problems that deal with halting in one way or another and they are often expressed in terms of Turing machines. For example, each of the following problems is unsolvable, where M is an arbitrary Turing machine:

> Does M halt when started on the empty tape?
> Is there an input string for which M halts?
> Does M halt on every input string?

Of course, with a little effort, these problems can also be stated in terms of other computational models. For example, in terms of partial recursive functions, the three problems take the following form, where f is an arbitrary partial recursive function:

> Is $f(0)$ defined?
> Is there a natural number n for which $f(n)$ is defined?
> Is f a total function?

The Busy Beaver Problem

Let's spend a little time discussing a problem from the last chapter about hard-working Turing machines. In Example 8 of Section 7.1 we defined a busy beaver as deterministic Turing machine that writes either Λ or 1 on a tape cell such that it accepts the empty string and, before it halts, it writes the largest number of 1's that can be written by Turing machines that write either Λ or 1 on a tape cell, that accept the empty string, and that have the same number of states.

The *busy beaver function* is the function b with domain the positive integers such that $b(n)$ is the number of 1's that can be written by a busy beaver with n states, not including the halt state. We noted that $b(1) = 1$, $b(2) = 4$, $b(3) = 6$, $b(4) = 13$, and $b(5) \geq 4,098$. We also noted that Rado [1962] proved that the busy beaver function is not computable. In other words, the following problem is unsolvable:

For an arbitrary value of n, what is the value of $b(n)$?

We'll prove that b is not computable by proving four statements, the last of which is the desired result.

1. $b(n + 1) > b(n)$ for all $n \geq 1$.

Proof: If T is a busy beaver with n states, then we can modify T as follows: Replace the Halt state by a state that looks to the right for an empty cell and when it is found, it writes a 1 and then Halts. This new machine has $n + 1$ states and prints one more 1 than T. Therefore a busy beaver with $n + 1$ states prints more 1's than T. Therefore $b(n + 1) > b(n)$.   QED.

2. If f is computable by a Turing machine with k states, then
    $b(n + k) \geq f(n)$ for all $n \geq 1$.

Proof: Let T be the k-state Turing machine that computes f by starting with a tape that contains n 1's and halting with a tape that contains $f(n)$ 1's. For any given n we can modify T by adding n new states at the beginning that write n 1's onto the tape and then transfers to the original start state of T. The modified machine has $n + k$ states and when it is started on the empty tape, it halts with $f(n)$ 1's on the tape. Therefore a busy beaver with $n + k$ states must print at least $f(n)$ 1's on the tape. Therefore we have the desired result $b(n + k) \geq f(n)$.   QED.

3. The composition of two computable functions is computable.

Proof: We'll leave this general result as an exercise.   QED.

4. The busy beaver function b is not computable.

Proof: Suppose, by way of contradiction, that b is computable. Pick the simple computable function g defined by $g(n) = 2n$. Let f be the composition of b with g. That is, let $f(n) = b(g(n)) = b(2n)$. The function f is computable by Statement 3. So we can apply Statement 2 to obtain the result $b(n + k) \geq f(n)$ for all $n \geq 1$. But $f(n) = b(2n)$. So Statement 2 becomes $b(n + k) \geq b(2n)$ for all $n \geq 1$. If we let $n = k + 1$, then we obtain the inequality

$$b(k + 1 + k) \geq b(2(k + 1)),$$

which can be written as $b(2k + 1) \geq b(2k + 2)$. But this inequality contradicts Statement 1. Therefore b is not computable.   QED.

We should note that busy beavers and the busy beaver function can be described with other computational models. For example, Morales-Bueno [1995] uses the Simple programming language to describe busy beavers and to prove that b is not computable.

Partially Solvable Problems

Recall that a decision problem is partially solvable (or partially decidable) if there is an algorithm that halts with the answer yes for those instances of the problem with yes answers, but that may run forever for those instances whose answers are no. Many unsolvable problems are in fact partially solvable. Whenever we can search for a yes answer to a decision problem and be sure that it takes a finite amount of time, then we know that the problem is partially solvable.

For example, the halting problem is partially solvable because for any computable function f_n and any input x we can evaluate the expression $f_n(x)$. If the evaluation halts with a value, then we output yes. We don't care what happens if $f_n(x)$ is undefined or its evaluation never halts.

Another partially solvable problem is Post's correspondence problem. In this case, we can check for a solution by systematically looking at all sequences of length 1, then length 2, and so on. If there is a sequence that gives two matching strings, we'll eventually find it and output yes. Otherwise, we don't care what happens.

The total problem is not even partially solvable. Although we won't prove this fact, we can at least observe that an arbitrary computable function f_n can't be proven total by testing it on every input because there are infinitely many inputs.

Solvable Problems

The things that we really want to deal with are solvable problems. In fact, this book is devoted to presenting ideas and techniques for solving problems. For example, in Chapter 5 we studied several techniques for solving the recognition problem for regular languages. In Chapter 6 we saw that the recognition problem for context-free languages is solvable.

It's also nice to know that most unsolvable problems have specific instances that are solvable. For example, the following problems are solvable:

1. Let $f(x) = x + 1$. Does f halt on input $x = 35$? Does f halt on any input?

2. Is Ackermann's function a total function?

3. Are the following two functions f and g equivalent?

$$f(x) = \text{if } x \text{ is odd then } x \text{ else } x + 1,$$

$$g(x) = \text{if } x \text{ is even then } 2x - x + 1 \text{ else } x.$$

Exercises

1. Show that the composition of two computable functions is computable. In other words, show that if $h(x) = f(g(x))$, where f and g are computable and the range of g is a subset of the domain of f, then h is computable.

2. Show that the following problem is solvable: Is there a computable function that, when given f_n, m, and k, can tell whether f_n halts on input m in k units of time?

3. Show that the following function is computable:

$$h(x) = \text{if } f_x \text{ halts on input } x \text{ then } 1 \text{ else loop forever.}$$

4. Suppose we have the following effective enumeration of all the computable functions that take a single argument:

$$f_0, f_1, f_2, ..., f_n, ...$$

For each of the following functions g, explain what is WRONG with the following diagonalization argument claiming to show that g is a computable function that isn't in the list. "Since the enumeration is effective, there is an algorithm to transform each n into the function f_n. Since each f_n is computable, it follows that g is computable. It is easy to see that g is not in the list. Therefore g is a computable function that isn't in the list."

   a. $g(n) = f_n(n) + 1$.

   b. $g(n) = \text{if } f_n(n) = 4 \text{ then } 3 \text{ else } 4$.

   c. $g(n) = $ if $f_n(n)$ halts and $f_n(n) = 4$ then 3 else 4.

   d. $g(n) = $ if $f_n(n)$ halts and $f_n(n) = 4$ then 3 else loop forever.

5. Show that the problem of deciding whether two DFAs over the same alphabet are equivalent is solvable.

6. For each of the following instances of Post's correspondence problem, find a solution or state that no solution exists.

   a. $\{\langle a, abbbbb\rangle, \langle bb, b\rangle\}$.

   b. $\{\langle ab, a\rangle, \langle ba, b\rangle, \langle a, ba\rangle, \langle b, ab\rangle\}$.

   c. $\{\langle 10, 100\rangle, \langle 0, 01\rangle, \langle 0, 00\rangle\}$.

   d. $\{\langle 1, 111\rangle, \langle 0111, 0\rangle, \langle 10, 0\rangle\}$.

   e. $\{\langle ab, aba\rangle, \langle ba, abb\rangle, \langle b, ab\rangle, \langle abb, b\rangle, \langle a, bab\rangle\}$.

8.2 A Hierarchy of Languages

We now have enough tools to help us describe a hierarchy of languages. In addition to meeting some old friends, we'll also meet some new kids on the block.

The Languages

Starting with the smallest class of languages—the regular languages—we'll work our way up to the largest class of languages—the languages without grammars.

Regular Languages

Regular languages are described by regular expressions and they are the languages that are accepted by NFAs and DFAs. Regular languages are also defined by grammars with productions having the form

$$A \to \Lambda, \quad A \to w, \quad A \to B, \quad \text{or} \quad A \to wB,$$

where A and B are arbitrary nonterminals and w is a nonempty string of terminals. A typical regular language is $\{a^m b^n \mid m, n \in \mathbb{N}\}$.

Deterministic Contex-Free Languages

Deterministic context-free languages are recognized by deterministic PDAs that accept by final state, and they are described by LR(1) grammars. The language $\{a^n b^n \mid n \in \mathbb{N}\}$ is the standard example of a deterministic context-free language that is not regular.

Context-Free Languages

Context-free languages are recognized by PDAs that may be deterministic or nondeterministic. Context-free languages are also defined by grammars with productions having the form $A \to w$, where A is an arbitrary nonterminal and w is an arbitrary string of grammar symbols. The language of palindromes over $\{a, b\}$ is a classic example of a context-free language that is not deterministic context-free.

Context-Sensitive Languages

Context-sensitive languages are defined by grammars having productions of the form $v \to w$, where $1 \leq |v| \leq |w|$. The restriction tells us that Λ cannot occur on the right side of a production. So the empty string can't belong to a context-sensitive language. Given this restriction, we can say that any context-free language that does not contain the empty string is context-sensitive. To see this, we need to recall from Section 6.4 that any context-free language that does not contain the empty string has a grammar without Λ productions. So any production has the form $A \to w$, where $w \neq \Lambda$. This tells us that $|A| \leq |w|$. Therefore the language must be context-sensitive

The language $\{a^n b^n c^n \mid n > 0\}$ is the standard example of a context-sensitive language that is not context-free. For example, here's a context-sensitive grammar for the language:

$$
\begin{aligned}
S &\to abc \mid aAbc \\
A &\to abC \mid aAbC \\
Cb &\to bC \\
Cc &\to cc.
\end{aligned}
$$

If we restrict a Turing machine to a finite tape consisting of the input tape cells together with two boundary cells that may not be changed, and if we allow nondeterminism, then the resulting machine is called a *linear bounded automaton* (LBA). Here's the connection between LBAs and context-sensitive languages:

> The context-sensitive languages coincide with the languages without Λ that are accepted by LBAs.

In Example 2 of Section 7.1 we constructed a Turing machine to recognize the language $\{a^n b^n c^n \mid n \geq 0\}$. In fact the Turing machine that we constructed is an LBA because it uses only the tape cells of the input string. The LBA can be easily modified to reject Λ and thus accept the context-sensitive language $\{a^n b^n c^n \mid n > 0\}$.

An interesting fact about context-sensitive languages is that they can be recognized by LBAs that always halt. In other words,

The recognition problem for context-sensitive languages is solvable.

To see this, suppose we have a context-sensitive grammar with terminal alphabet A. Let $w \in A^*$ with $|w| = n$. Since each production has the form $u \to v$ with $|u| \le |v|$, we can construct all the derivation paths from the start symbol that end in a sentential form of length n. Then simply check to see whether w coincides with any of these sentential forms.

Recursively Enumerable Languages

The most general kind of grammars are the *unrestricted grammars* with productions of the form $v \to w$, where v is any nonempty string and w is any string. So the general definition of a grammar (1.24) is that of an unrestricted grammar. Unrestricted grammars are also called *phrase-structure grammars*. The most important thing about unrestricted grammars is that the class of languages that they generate is exactly the class of languages that are accepted by Turing machines. Although we won't prove this statement, we should note that a proof consists of transforming any unrestricted grammar into a Turing machine and transforming any Turing machine into an unrestricted grammar. The resulting algorithms have the same flavor as the transformation algorithms (12.7) and (12.8) for context-free languages and PDAs.

A language is called *recursively enumerable* if there is a Turing machine that outputs (i.e., enumerates) all the strings of the language. If we assume the Church-Turing thesis, we can replace "Turing machine" with "algorithm." For example, let's show that the language $\{a^n \mid f_n(n) \text{ halts}\}$ is recursively enumerable. We are assuming that the functions f_n are the computable functions that take only single arguments and are enumerated as in (8.1). Here's an algorithm to enumerate the language $\{a^n \mid f_n(n) \text{ halts}\}$:

1. Set $k = 0$.
2. For each pair $\langle m, n \rangle$ such that $m + n = k$ do the following:
   if $f_n(n)$ halts in m steps then output a^n.
3. Increment k, and go to Step 2.

An important fact that we won't prove is that the class of recursively enumerable languages is exactly the same as the class of languages that are accepted by Turing machines. Therefore we have three different ways to say the same thing:

The languages generated by unrestricted grammars are the languages accepted by Turing machines, which are the recursively enumerable languages.

The language $\{a^n \mid f_n(n) \text{ halts}\}$ is a classic example of a recursively enumerable language that is not context-sensitive. The preceding algorithm shows that the language is recursively enumerable. Now if the language were context-sensitive, then it could be recognized by an algorithm that always halts. This means that we would have a solution to the halting problem, which we know to be unsolvable. Therefore $\{a^n \mid f_n(n) \text{ halts}\}$ is not context-sensitive.

Nongrammatical Languages

There are many languages that are not definable by any grammar. In other words, they are not recursively enumerable, which means that they can't be recognized by Turing machines. The reason for this is that there are an uncountable number of languages and only a countable number of Turing machines (we enumerated them all in the last section). Even for the little alphabet $\{a\}$ we know that power($\{a\}^*$) is uncountable. In other words, there are an uncountable number of languages over $\{a\}$.

The language $\{a^n \mid f_n \text{ is total}\}$ is a standard example of a language that is not recursively enumerable. This is easy to see. Again we're assuming that the functions f_n are the computable functions listed in (8.1). Suppose, by way of contradiction, that the language is recursively enumerable. This means that we can effectively enumerate all the total computable functions. But this contradicts (8.5), which says that the total computable functions can't be effectively enumerated. Therefore the language $\{a^n \mid f_n \text{ is total}\}$ is not recursively enumerable.

Summary

Let's summarize the hierarchy that we've been discussing. Each line of Table 8.1 represents a particular class of grammars and/or languages. Each line also contains an example of the class together with the type of machines that will recognize each language of the class. Each line represents a more general class than the next lower line of the table, with the little exception that context-sensitive languages can't contain Λ. The example language given on each line is a classic example of a language that belongs on that line but not on a lower line of the table. The symbols DPDA, TM, and NTM mean deterministic pushdown automaton, Turing machine, and nondeterministic Turing machine. The symbol LBA-Λ stands for the class of LBAs that do not recognize the empty string.

Grammar or Language	Classic Example	Machine
Arbitrary (grammatical or nongrammatical)	$\{a^n \mid f_n \text{ is total}\}$	None
Unrestricted (recursively enumerable)	$\{a^n \mid f_n(n) \text{ halts}\}$	TM or NTM
Context-sensitive	$\{a^n b^n c^n \mid n \geq 1\}$	LBA-Λ
Context-free	Palindromes over $\{a, b\}$	PDA
LR(1) (deterministic context-free)	$\{a^n b^n \mid n \in \mathbb{N}\}$	DPDA
Regular	$\{a^m b^n \mid m, n \in \mathbb{N}\}$	DFA or NFA

Table 8.1

The four grammars—unrestricted, context-sensitive, context-free, and regular—were originally introduced by Chomsky [1956, 1959]. He called them type 0, type 1, type 2, and type 3, respectively.

Exercises

1. Construct a two-tape Turing machine to enumerate all strings in the language $\{a^n b^n c^n \mid n \geq 0\}$. Use the first tape to keep track of n, the number of a's, b's and c's to print for each string. Use the second tape to print the strings, each separated by the symbol #.

2. Find a context-sensitive grammar for the language $\{a^n b^n a^n \mid n > 0\}$.

3. Any context-sensitive grammar can be *extended* to a grammar that accepts one more string, the empty string. Suppose S is the start symbol for a context-sensitive grammar. Pick a new nonterminal T as the new start symbol, and add the two productions $T \rightarrow S \mid \Lambda$. Write an extended context-sensitive grammar for the language of all strings over $\{a, b, c\}$ that contain the same number of a's, b's, and c's.

8.3 Evaluation of Expressions

Much of the practical daily work that occurs in science, mathematics, computer science, and engineering deals with evaluating or transforming expressions of one kind or another. There are some natural questions that arise in dealing with any kind of expression:

How do we evaluate an expression?

Is there more than one way to evaluate an expression?

Can we tell whether two expressions have the same value?

From a computational point of view we're interested in whether there are algorithms to evaluate expressions. If we want to evaluate expressions automatically, then we need to specify some rules for transforming one expression into another.

Let's introduce some terminology. A *transformation rule* is a production of the form

$$E \to F,$$

where E and F are expressions. A transformation rule is also called a *reduction rule* or a *rewrite rule*. We can read $E \to F$ as "E reduces to F" or "E rewrites to F." The word *rewrite* sounds more general than *reduce*. But we'll normally use *reduce* because our goal in evaluating expressions is to *reduce* or *simplify* an expression. The context should take care of any ambiguity resulting from the use of the symbol "$\to$," which is also used for grammar productions, function types, logical implication, and string-processing productions.

We can apply reduction rules to transform expressions by using substitution. For example, suppose G_0 is an expression containing one or more occurrences of a subexpression of the form E, where $E \to F$ is a reduction rule. If G_1 is obtained from G_0 by replacing one or more occurrences of E by F, then we obtain a new transformation from G_0 to G_1, which we'll denote by $G_0 \to G_1$. If we continue the process to obtain G_2 from G_1, and so on, then we obtain a *reduction sequence* that we'll denote as

$$G_0 \to G_1 \to G_2 \to \dots.$$

When we evaluate expressions, we try to find reduction sequences that stop at some desired value.

Where do reduction rules come from? Usually, they come from assumptions (i.e., axioms) about the subject of discussion. An equation $E = F$ always gives rise to two reduction rules $E \to F$ and $F \to E$. Sometimes it may be possible to use only one of the two reduction rules from an equation to evaluate expressions. For example, the equation $\text{succ}(0) = 1$ gives rise to the two rules

$$\text{succ}(0) \to 1 \quad \text{and} \quad 1 \to \text{succ}(0).$$

The first of the two rules, $\text{succ}(0) \to 1$, appears to be more useful in the evaluation expressions.

A sequence of reductions may not always be unique. For example, consider the expression

$$\text{succ}(0) + \text{succ}(\text{succ}(0)).$$

We can evaluate this expression in the following two ways:

$$\text{succ}(0) + \text{succ}(\text{succ}(0)) \to 1 + \text{succ}(\text{succ}(0)) \to 1 + \text{succ}(1),$$
$$\text{succ}(0) + \text{succ}(\text{succ}(0)) \to \text{succ}(0) + \text{succ}(1) \to 1 + \text{succ}(1).$$

Should every reduction sequence for an expression result in the same value? It would be nice, but it's not always the case. For example, suppose we're given the following four reduction rules:

$$a \to b, \quad a \to c, \quad b \to d, \quad b \to a.$$

If there aren't any other rules, then there are distinct reduction sequences that give distinct values. For example, consider the following two reduction sequences that start with the letter a:

$$a \to b \to d,$$
$$a \to c.$$

Are reduction sequences always finite? To see that the answer is no, suppose we have the following funny-looking rule:

$$g(x) \to g(g(x)).$$

Then certainly the expression $g(a)$ has no finite reduction sequence because there is always an occurrence of $g(a)$ that can be replaced by $g(g(a))$. Thus the nth term of the sequence has the expression $g^n(a)$.

For another example, suppose we have the rule

$$f(x) \to \text{if } x = 1 \text{ then } 1 \text{ else } f(x + 1).$$

Then an infinite reduction sequence for $f(1)$ can be given as follows, where we choose to evaluate the rightmost subexpression involving f first:

$$f(1) \to \text{ if } 1 = 1 \text{ then } 1 \text{ else } f(1 + 1)$$
$$\to \text{ if } 1 = 1 \text{ then } 1 \text{ else } (\text{if } 1 + 1 = 1 \text{ then } 1 \text{ else } f(1 + 1 + 1))$$
$$\to$$
$$\vdots$$

On the other hand, if we evaluate the leftmost subexpression first, then we obtain the following finite reduction:

$$f(1) \to \text{if } 1 = 1 \text{ then } 1 \text{ else } f(1 + 1) \to 1.$$

So it isn't always clear how to apply reduction rules. A set of rules has the *Church-Rosser property* if whenever an expression E evaluates—in two different ways—to expressions F and G, then there is an expression H and reductions F to H and G to H. This is certainly a desired property for a set of rules because it guarantees that expressions have unique values whenever their reduction sequences terminate. So a set of reduction rules should have the Church-Rosser property if we want to write an algorithm that uses the rules to evaluate things.

In the remaining paragraphs we'll continue our discussion of reduction rules. First we'll introduce a famous computational model—the lambda calculus—which has the same power as the Turing machine model and whose reduction rules can be efficiently implemented. Then we'll introduce the famous Knuth-Bendix procedure for finding reduction rules.

Lambda Calculus

The *lambda calculus* is a computational model that was invented by Church. A description of it can be found in the book by Church [1941]. As the word "calculus" implies, the *lambda calculus* is a language of expressions together with some transformation rules. After we look at the formal definitions for expressions and transformations, we'll show how the lambda calculus can be used to describe logical notions as well as computable functions.

The wffs of the lambda calculus are usually called *lambda expressions*— or simply *expressions* if the context is clear. They are defined by the following simple grammar, where an identifier is any name that we wish to use:

$$E \to V \mid (E\,E) \mid \lambda V.E$$
$$V \to \text{identifier}.$$

For example, the following expressions are lambda expressions:

$$x$$
$$\lambda x.x$$
$$\lambda x.y$$
$$(\lambda x.x\ y)$$
$$(\lambda x.x\ (\lambda x.y\ a)).$$

Lambda expressions of the form $\lambda x.M$ are called *abstractions*. An abstraction represents a function definition. Lambda expressions of the form $(M\ N)$ are called *applications*. An application $(M\ N)$ represents the application of M to N. To see the analogy with functions as we know them, suppose we have two functions f and g defined by

$$f(x) = a \quad \text{and} \quad g(x) = x.$$

Using lambda calculus notation, we would write f and g as the two lambda expressions

$$\lambda x.a \quad \text{and} \quad \lambda x.x.$$

An expression like $f(g(b))$ would be written as $(\lambda x.a\ (\lambda x.x\ b))$. So lambda calculus allows us to handle functions without giving them specific names.

An occurrence of the variable x in a lambda expression is *bound* if x occurs in a subexpression of the form $\lambda x.M$. Otherwise, the occurrence of x is *free*. For example, in the expression $\lambda x.x$ both occurrences of x are bound. In the expression $\lambda y.x$ the variable y is bound and x is free. In the expression $(\lambda y.(\lambda x.x\ y)\ x)$ the rightmost occurrence of x is free and the other four occurrences of x and y are bound.

When discussing bound and free variables in lambda expressions we can think of λx just the way we think of a quantifier in predicate calculus. For example, in an expression like $\lambda x.M$ we say that M is the *scope* of λx. In terms of scope we could say that an occurrence of x in an expression is bound if it occurs in λx or in the scope of λx. Otherwise, the occurrence of x is free.

We can easily construct the set of free variables for any lambda expression. Let free(E) denote the set of free variables occurring in the expression E. The following three rules can be applied recursively to define free(E) for any lambda expression E:

1. free(x) = $\{x\}$.

2. free($(M\ N)$) = free(M) $\cup$ free(N).

3. free($\lambda x.M$) = free(M) $-$ $\{x\}$.

For example, free($\lambda x.y$) = $\{y\} - \{x\} = \{y\}$, and free($\lambda x.x$) = $\{x\} - \{x\} = \varnothing$. An expression is *closed* if it doesn't have any free variables. In other words, a lambda expression E is closed if free(E) = $\varnothing$. The expression $\lambda x.x$ is closed. Closed lambda expressions are also called *combinators*.

To make a calculus, we need some rules to transform lambda expressions. To do this, we need to discuss substitution of variables. If E is a lambda expression, then the expression obtained from E by replacing all free occurrences of the variable x by the lambda expression N is denoted by

$$E[x/N].$$

In other words, $E[x/N]$ is calculated by replacing all free occurrences of x in E by the expression N. Now we can describe the main reduction rule for applications, which of course is based on the application of a function to its argument. We'll put some restrictions on the rule later. But for now we'll state the rule, called β-reduction, as follows:

$$(\lambda x.M\ N) \rightarrow M[x/N].$$

For example, let's evaluate the application $(\lambda x.x\ a)$:

$$(\lambda x.x\ a) \rightarrow a.$$

So it makes sense to call $\lambda x.x$ the identity function. As another example, we'll evaluate the application $(\lambda x.y\ a)$:

$$(\lambda x.y\ a) \rightarrow y.$$

So it makes sense to call $\lambda x.y$ the constant function that always returns y.

A lambda expression of the form $(\lambda x.M\ N)$ is called a *redex* because it is a reducible expression. An expression is called a *normal form* if it can't be reduced. In other words, a normal form is not a redex, and it doesn't contain any redexes. For example, x, $(y\ a)$, and $\lambda x.y$ are normal forms. But $(x\ (\lambda y.z\ a))$ is not a normal form because it contains the redex $(\lambda y.z\ a)$. We might think that every lambda expression has a normal form because all we have to do is evaluate all the redexes until we can't do it any longer. The next example shows that this process could take a very long time.

EXAMPLE 1 (*An Infinite Loop*). If we apply the function $\lambda x.(x\ x)$ to itself, we get the following infinite chain of reductions:

$$
\begin{aligned}
(\lambda x.(x\ x)\ \lambda x.(x\ x)) \ &\rightarrow (\lambda x.(x\ x)\ \lambda x.(x\ x)) \\
&\rightarrow (\lambda x.(x\ x)\ \lambda x.(x\ x)) \\
&\rightarrow (\lambda x.(x\ x)\ \lambda x.(x\ x)) \\
&\rightarrow \cdots
\end{aligned}
$$

The expression $(\lambda x.(x\ x)\ \lambda x.(x\ x))$ is the smallest lambda expression with no normal form. ◆

In some cases there can be a choice of several expressions to evaluate. For example, consider the following application:

$$(\lambda x.x \ (\lambda y.y \ a)).$$

In this case we have a choice. We can evaluate the application $(\lambda y.y \ a)$ first to obtain the sequence

$$(\lambda x.x \ (\lambda y.y \ a)) \to (\lambda x.x \ a) \to a.$$

A second choice is to evaluate main application $(\lambda x.x \ (\lambda y.y \ a))$ to obtain the sequence

$$(\lambda x.x \ (\lambda y.y \ a)) \to (\lambda y.y \ a) \to a.$$

These examples are instances of two important reduction orders used to evaluate lambda expressions. To introduce them, we need a little terminology. A redex is *innermost* if it doesn't contain any redexes. For example, the expression

$$((\lambda x.\lambda y.y \ (\lambda x.y \ z)) \ (\lambda x.x \ y))$$

has two innermost redexes, $(\lambda x.y \ z)$ and $(\lambda x.x \ y)$. A redex is *outermost* if it is not contained in any redex. For example, the expression $(\lambda x.M \ N)$ is itself an outermost redex. The expression $\lambda x.(\lambda y.(\lambda x.y \ y) \ z)$ has outermost redex $(\lambda y.(\lambda x.y \ y) \ z)$ and innermost redex $(\lambda x.y \ y)$.

The two reduction rules that we've been talking about are called *applicative order reduction* (AOR) and *normal order reduction* (NOR), and they're defined as follows:

AOR: Reduce the leftmost of the innermost redexes first. This is similar to the *call by value* parameter-passing technique. In other words, the argument expression is evaluated prior to the execution of the function body. Two examples of AOR are

$$(\lambda x.x \ (\lambda y.y \ a)) \to (\lambda x.x \ a) \to a,$$

$$(\lambda y.(\lambda x.y \ z) \ w) \to (\lambda y.y \ w) \to w.$$

NOR: Reduce the leftmost of the outermost redexes first. This is similar to the *call by name* parameter-passing technique. In other words, the argument expression is passed to the function without being evaluated.

Evaluation takes place if it is encountered during the execution of the function body. Two examples of NOR are

$$(\lambda x.x \ (\lambda y.y \ a)) \rightarrow (\lambda y.y \ a) \rightarrow a,$$

$$(\lambda y.(\lambda x.y \ z) \ w) \rightarrow (\lambda x.w \ z) \rightarrow w.$$

Does it make any difference which rule we use? Yes, in some cases. But it's nice to know that no matter what rule we use, IF we reach normal forms with both rules, then the normal forms are equal, except possibly for renaming of variables. Here's a classic example.

EXAMPLE 2. A classic example of an application that terminates with NOR but does not terminate with AOR is the following:

$$(\lambda x.\lambda y.y \ (\lambda z.(z \ z) \ \lambda z.(z \ z))).$$

With NOR we get the short reduction sequence

$$(\lambda x.\lambda y.y \ (\lambda z.(z \ z) \ \lambda z.(z \ z))) \rightarrow \lambda y.y.$$

But with AOR we get the infinite reduction sequence

$$(\lambda x.\lambda y.y \ (\lambda z.(z \ z) \ \lambda z.(z \ z))) \rightarrow (\lambda x.\lambda y.y \ (\lambda z.(z \ z) \ \lambda z.(z \ z)))$$
$$\rightarrow (\lambda x.\lambda y.y \ (\lambda z.(z \ z) \ \lambda z.(z \ z)))$$
$$\vdots$$

$\blacklozenge$

Although things may seem OK so far, we need to consider some restrictions in evaluating lambda expressions. A problem can occur when an evaluation causes the number of bound occurrences of some variable to increase. For example, let's consider the following reduction sequence:

$$((\lambda x.\lambda y.(y \ x) \ y) \ x) \rightarrow (\lambda y.(y \ y) \ x) \rightarrow (x \ x).$$

Notice that the first step causes an increase from two to three in the number of bound occurrences of y. The name of a variable should not cause any difference in the evaluation of a function. So in the first expression, we'll rename the bound occurrences of y to z. This gives us the expression

$$((\lambda x.\lambda z.(z \ x) \ y) \ x).$$

We can evaluate this expression as follows:

$$((\lambda x.\lambda z.(z\ x)\ y)\ x) \rightarrow (\lambda z.(z\ y)\ x) \rightarrow (x\ y).$$

So in one case we obtain $(x\ x)$, and in another case we obtain $(x\ y)$, all because we chose to use different variable names for bound variables. We certainly do not wish to conclude that $(x\ x) = (x\ y)$. In fact, this assumption can lead to the fallacy that all lambda expressions are equal! We'll leave this as an exercise.

We can't pick just any name when changing the names of bound variables. For example, it seems clear that $\lambda x.x = \lambda y.y$ and $\lambda x.y = \lambda z.y$. It also seems clear that $\lambda x.y \neq \lambda y.y$ and $\lambda x.\lambda y.x \neq \lambda y.\lambda y.y$. Changing the names of bound variables in a lambda expression is called *α-conversion*. Here it is:

α-Conversion

$\lambda x.M = \lambda y.M[x/y]$ if y is a new variable not occurring in M.

For example, we can apply the rule to get $\lambda x.x = \lambda y.y$ and $\lambda x.y = \lambda z.y$. But $\lambda x.y \neq \lambda y.y$, and $\lambda x.\lambda y.x \neq \lambda y.\lambda y.y$.

Using the terminology of the predicate calculus, we can say that β-reduction can be applied to the expression $(\lambda x.M\ N)$ if "N is free to replace x in M." In other words, the substitution can't introduce any new bound occurrences of variables in $M[x/N]$. We can always ensure that this is the case by making sure that the lambda expression being reduced has disjoint sets of bound and free variables. This can always be accomplished by α-conversion. We'll state the β-reduction rule with this restriction:

β-Reduction

$(\lambda x.M\ N) \rightarrow M[x/N]$ if N is free to replace x in M. This occurs if the
                                                                                     bound variables and the free variables in $\lambda x.M$
                                                                                     are disjoint.

Another nice simplification rule is called *η-reduction*. Here it is:

η-Reduction

$\lambda x.(M\ x) = M$ if x is not free in M.

For example, suppose we have the expression $\lambda x.(\lambda y.x\ x)$. If we let $M = \lambda y.x$, then the expression has the form $\lambda x.(M\ x)$. If we apply the expression M to N, then we obtain the value y as follows:

$$(M\ N) = (\lambda x.y\ N) \rightarrow y.$$

On the other hand, if we apply the expression $\lambda x.(M\,x)$ to N, we also obtain the value y by the following reduction sequence:

$$(\lambda x.(M\,x)\,N) = (\lambda x.(\lambda x.y\,x)\,N) \rightarrow (\lambda x.y\,N) \rightarrow y.$$

In other words, it makes sense to say that $\lambda x.(\lambda x.y\,x) = \lambda x.y$.

Simplifying Things

Lambda expressions are often written without so many parentheses. But we need to make some assumptions in these cases. For example,

$$M\,N \text{ means } (M\,N),$$
$$M\,N\,P \text{ means } ((M\,N)\,P).$$

So in the absence of parentheses, always associate to the left.

We can also simplify the definition of any function that we wish to name. For example, if we wish to define g as the function $g = \lambda x.M$, then we'll write it in simplified form as

$$g\,x = M.$$

If a function has more than one input variable, then we'll list them in order on the left side of the equality. For example, the function $h = \lambda x.\lambda y.M$ will be denoted as follows:

$$h\,x\,y = M.$$

For the lambda calculus, β-reduction and η-reduction both have the Church-Rosser property. That's why they are so important to computation. They always compute the same thing, no matter in what order the rules are applied. The lambda calculus gives us a wide variety of expressions that are familiar to us. Let's look at some elementary data types.

Booleans

We can define true and false as lambda expressions such that the usual logical operations can also be represented by lambda expressions. For example, we'll define true and false as follows:

$$\text{true} = \lambda x.\lambda y.x,$$
$$\text{false} = \lambda x.\lambda y.y.$$

Now we can easily find lambda expressions for the other Boolean operations. For example, we'll define the conditional as follows:

$$\text{if } C \text{ then } M \text{ else } N = C\,M\,N.$$

If this conditional is defined correctly, we should be able to conclude the following two statements:

$$\text{true } M\,N = M,$$

$$\text{false } M\,N = N.$$

These are easily seen to be correct by the following two evaluations:

$$\text{true } M\,N = \lambda x.\lambda y.x\ M\,N = \lambda y.M\,N = M,$$

$$\text{false } M\,N = \lambda x.\lambda y.y\ M\,N = \lambda y.y\ N = N.$$

So the definitions of true and false allow the conditional to act correctly. Notice also that if C is neither true nor false, then the value of $C\,M\,N$ can be an arbitrary expression. The operations of conjunction, disjunction, and negation can all be expressed as conditionals as follows:

$$\text{And } M\,N = M\,N \text{ false,}$$

$$\text{Or } M\,N = M \text{ true } N,$$

$$\text{Not } M = M \text{ false true.}$$

To see that these definitions make sense, we should check the truth tables. For example, we'll compute one line of the truth table for the preceding definition of the And function as follows:

$$\text{And true false = true false false = false.}$$

If we want to expand the expression in lambda notation we obtain the following evaluation, where we've expanded And but have not expanded true and false:

$$
\begin{aligned}
\text{And true false} \ &= \ ((\text{And true}) \text{ false}) \\
&= \ ((\lambda M.\lambda N.((M\,N) \text{ false}) \text{ true}) \text{ false}) \\
&= \ ((\text{false true}) \text{ false}) \\
&= \ \text{false.}
\end{aligned}
$$

In using Boolean values it is sometimes necessary to know whether an expression is true. The function "isTrue" will do the job:

$$\text{isTrue } M = M \text{ true false.}$$

For example, we have the following two evaluations:

$$\text{isTrue true} = \text{true true false} = \text{true,}$$
$$\text{isTrue false} = \text{false true false} = \text{false.}$$

Lists

We can define the usual list operations by using lambda calculus. We'll give definitions for emptyList, the predicate isEmpty, the constructor cons, and the destructors head and tail:

$$\text{emptyList} = \lambda x.\text{true,}$$
$$\text{isEmpty} = \lambda s.(s \; \lambda h.\lambda t \text{ false}),$$
$$\text{cons} = \lambda h.\lambda t.\lambda s. \; (s \; h \; t),$$
$$\text{head} = \lambda x.(x \text{ true}),$$
$$\text{tail} = \lambda x.(x \text{ false}).$$

These list functions should work the way we expect them to. For example, consider the evaluation of the following expression:

$$
\begin{aligned}
\text{head (cons } a \; b \;) \;\; &= \;\; \lambda x.(x \text{ true}) \, (\text{cons } a \; b \;) \\
&\rightarrow \; (\text{cons } a \; b \;) \text{ true} \\
&= \; (\lambda h.\lambda t.\lambda s. \; (s \; h \; t) \, a \; b) \text{ true} \\
&\rightarrow \; \lambda s. \; (s \; a \; b \;) \text{ true} \\
&\rightarrow \; \text{true } a \; b \\
&\rightarrow \; a.
\end{aligned}
$$

Natural Numbers

Now we'll tackle the natural numbers. We want to find lambda expressions to represent the natural numbers and the fundamental operations successor, predecessor, and isZero. We'll start by defining the symbol 0 as the following lambda expression:

$$0 = \lambda x.x.$$

Now we'll define a successor function, which will allow us to represent all the natural numbers. A popular way to define "succ" is as follows:

$$\text{succ } x = \lambda s.(s \text{ false } x).$$

So the formal definition with all variables on the right side looks like

$$\text{succ} = \lambda x.\lambda s.(s \text{ false } x).$$

We have the following representations for the first few natural numbers:

$0 = \lambda x.x,$
$1 = \text{succ } 0 = \lambda s.(s \text{ false } 0),$
$2 = \text{succ } 1 = \lambda s.(s \text{ false } 1) = \lambda s.(s \text{ false } \lambda s.(s \text{ false } 0)),$
$3 = \text{succ } 2 = \lambda s.(s \text{ false } 2) = \lambda s.(s \text{ false } \lambda s.(s \text{ false } \lambda s.(s \text{ false } 0))).$

To test for zero, we can define the "isZero" function as follows:

$$\text{isZero} = \lambda x.(x \text{ true}).$$

For example, we can evaluate the expression (isZero 0) as follows:

$$
\begin{aligned}
(\text{isZero } 0) &= (\lambda x.(x \text{ true}) \ \lambda x.x) \\
&= (\lambda x.x \text{ true}) \\
&= \text{true}.
\end{aligned}
$$

Similarly, the evaluation of the expression (isZero 1) goes as follows:

$$
\begin{aligned}
(\text{isZero } 1) &= (\lambda x.(x \text{ true}) \ (\text{succ } 0)) \\
&\to ((\text{succ } 0) \text{ true}) \\
&= (\lambda s.(s \text{ false } 0) \text{ true}) \\
&\to \text{true false } 0 \\
&\to \text{false}.
\end{aligned}
$$

To compute the predecessor of a nonzero natural number, we can define the "pred" function as follows:

$$\text{pred} = \lambda x.(x \text{ false}).$$

For example, we can compute the value of the expression (pred 1) as follows:

$$\begin{aligned}
(\text{pred } 1) \;&=\; (\lambda x.(x \text{ false}) \; 1) \\
&\to\; 1 \text{ false} \\
&=\; (\text{succ } 0) \text{ false} \\
&=\; (\lambda s.(s \text{ false } 0) \text{ false}) \\
&\to\; \text{false false } 0 \\
&\to\; 0.
\end{aligned}$$

Recursion

From a computational point of view we would like to be able to describe the process of recursion with lambda calculus. For example, suppose we're given the following informal recursive definition of the function f:

$$f(x) = \text{if isZero}(x) \text{ then } 1 \text{ else } h(x, f(\text{pred}(x))).$$

Is there a lambda expression for the function f? Yes. We'll need a special lambda expression called the Y combinator. It looks terrible, but it works. Here's the definition, like it or not:

$$Y = \lambda x.(\lambda y.(x \; (y \; y)) \; \lambda y.(x \; (y \; y))). \tag{8.9}$$

The important point about Y is that it has the following property for any lambda expression E:

$$(Y \, E) = (E \; (Y \, E)).$$

This is easy to verify by using (8.9) as follows:

$$(Y \, E) = (\lambda y.(E \; (y \; y)) \; \lambda y.(E \; (y \; y))) = (E \; (\lambda y.(E \; (y \; y)) \; \lambda y.(E \; (y \; y)))) = (E \; (Y \, E)).$$

Let's see how Y can be used to construct a lambda expression that represents a recursive definition.

EXAMPLE 3. We'll find a lambda expression to represent the function f defined by the following informal recursive definition:

$$f(x) = \text{if isZero}(x) \text{ then } 1 \text{ else } h(x, f(\text{pred}(x))).$$

We start by defining the lambda expression E as follows:

$$E = \lambda f.\lambda x. \text{ if isZero}(x) \text{ then } 1 \text{ else } h(x, f(\text{pred}(x))).$$

Now we define F as the following lambda expression:

$$F = (Y E).$$

The nice thing about F is that $(F x)$ evaluates to $f(x)$. In other words, F is a lambda expression that represents the recursively defined function f. For example, let's evaluate the expression $(F 1)$:

$$
\begin{aligned}
(F 1) \ &= \ ((Y E) 1) \\
&= \ (E (Y E) 1) \\
&= \ (\lambda x. \text{ if isZero}(x) \text{ then } 1 \text{ else } h(x, (Y E)(\text{pred}(x)))) \ 1) \\
&= \ \text{if isZero}(1) \text{ then } 1 \text{ else } h(1, (Y E)(\text{pred}(1))) \\
&= \ h(1, (Y E)(\text{pred}(1))) \\
&= \ h(1, E (Y E) (\text{pred}(1))) \\
&= \ h(1, \lambda x. \text{ if isZero}(x) \text{ then } 1 \text{ else } h(x, (Y E)(\text{pred}(x))) (\text{pred}(1))) \\
&= \ h(1, \text{ if isZero}(\text{pred}(1)) \text{ then } 1 \text{ else } h(x, (Y E)(\text{pred}(\text{pred}(1))))) \\
&= \ h(1, 1).
\end{aligned}
$$

This is the same value that we get by evaluating the expression $f(1)$ using the informal definition. In other words, we have $(F 1) = f(1)$.   ◆

Weak-Head Normal Form

The complexity of evaluation of a lambda expression can often be improved if we delay the evaluation of certain parts of the expression. To be specific, we may wish to delay the evaluation of a lambda expression that does not have all of its arguments. A nice thing about this technique is that it allows us to forget about the renaming problem and α-conversion. Let's describe this more fully.

A lambda expression is said to be in *weak-head normal form* if it doesn't have enough arguments. In other words, a lambda expression is in weak-head normal form if it takes one of the following forms:

$$\lambda x.E,$$
$$(f E_1 \dots E_k), \quad \text{where } f \text{ has arity } n > k.$$

For example, $(+ 2)$ is in weak-head normal form because $+$ needs two arguments. The expression $\lambda x.(\lambda y.z \ w)$ is in weak-head normal form, even though it contains the redex $(\lambda y.z \ w)$.

Let's do an example to see how reduction to weak-head normal form eliminates the need to worry about renaming and α-conversion.

EXAMPLE 4. Suppose we start with the following lambda expression:

$$\lambda x.(\lambda y.\lambda x.(+ x\ y)\ x).$$

This expression is already in weak-head normal form. Suppose we want to reduce it further to its normal form by evaluating all redexes. We'll do this as follows:

$$\lambda x.(\lambda y.\lambda x.(+ x\ y)\ x) \quad = \lambda x.(\lambda y.\lambda z.(+ z\ y)\ x) \qquad \text{(rename with } \alpha\text{-conversion)}$$
$$= \lambda x.\lambda z.(+ z\ x).$$

Notice what happens when we apply the two expressions to 7:

$$(\lambda x.(\lambda y.\lambda x.(+ x\ y)\ x)\ 7) = (\lambda y.\lambda x.(+ x\ y)\ 7) = \lambda x.(+ x\ 7),$$

$$(\lambda x.\lambda z.(+ z\ x)\ 7) = \lambda z.(+ z\ 7).$$

So in either case we obtain the same value. But the intermediate step of renaming by α-conversion is eliminated if we only reduce the lambda expressions to their weak-head normal form. ◆

The lambda calculus is a powerful computational model, equal in power to Turing machines. There are also efficient algorithms to evaluate lambda expressions. These algorithms often delay the evaluation of an expression until it is needed as an argument for the evaluation of some other expression. Thus expressions are reduced to weak-head normal form. Sharing of arguments also occurs, in which only one occurrence of each argument is evaluated. For example, the normal order evaluation of

$$(\lambda x.(f\ x\ x)\ E)$$

first causes the reduction to $(f\ E\ E)$. To evaluate f, both copies of E must be evaluated. A sharing strategy links both occurrences of E and makes only one evaluation. A related technique called *memoization* keeps the results of function calls in a "memo" table. Before a function is applied to an argument, the memo table is searched to see whether it has already been evaluated.

Thus lambda calculus can serve as an intermediate code language for compilers of functional languages. Lambda calculus notation is also useful in evaluating expressions in reasoning systems. For example, in higher-order unification, if the variable F represents a function or predicate, then the two terms $F(a)$ and b can be unified by replacing F by the constant function that returns the value b. This can be concisely written as $\{F/\lambda x.b\}$.

Knuth-Bendix Completion

In this section we'll discuss an important computational technique for creating reduction rules from a given set of axioms. The goal is to construct a set of reduction rules that satisfy the following *completion* property: An equation $s = t$ is derivable from the axioms if and only if s and t can be reduced to the same normal form. The general problem of finding reduction rules that satisfy the completion property is unsolvable. But a technique that works in many cases is called *Knuth-Bendix completion*. It was introduced in the paper by Knuth and Bendix [1970].

We'll start with an introductory example. Suppose that the following two equations hold for all x in some set:

$$g^5(x) = x, \tag{8.10}$$
$$g^3(x) = x.$$

Now suppose we want to evaluate expressions of the form $g^k(x)$ for any natural number k. For example, let's see whether we can use equations (8.10) to evaluate the expression $g(x)$:

$$g(x) = g(g^5(x)) = g^6(x) = g^3(g^3(x)) = g^3(x) = x. \tag{8.11}$$

Therefore the two equations (8.10) imply the following simple equation:

$$g(x) = x. \tag{8.12}$$

The nice thing is that we don't need equations (8.10) any longer because (8.12) will suffice to evaluate $g^k(x)$ for any natural number k as follows:

$$g^k(x) = g^{k-1}(g(x)) = g^{k-1}(x) = \cdots = x.$$

Is it possible to automate the process that obtained the simple equation (8.12) from the two equations (8.10)? The answer is yes in many cases. In fact, the procedure that we're going to present will do even more. It will obtain a set of reduction rules. To see what we mean by this, let's observe some things about evaluation (8.11).

To obtain the equation $g(x) = g(g^5(x))$, we replaced x by $g^5(x)$. In other words, we thought of the equation $g^5(x) = x$ in its symmetric form $x = g^5(x)$. But to obtain the equations

$$g^3(g^3(x)) = g^3(x) = x,$$

we replaced $g^3(x)$ by x. In other words, we used the equation $g^3(x) = x$ as it was written. When we use the equation $g(x) = x$ to evaluate another expression, we always replace $g(x)$ by x. In other words, we use $g(x) = x$ as the reduction rule $g(x) \to x$.

Now let's get busy and discuss a general procedure that can sometimes find reduction rules from a set of equations. As always, we need some terminology. If u is an expression containing a subexpression s, then we can emphasize this fact by writing $u[s]$. For any expression t, we let $u[t]$ denote an expression obtained from $u[s]$ by replacing one occurrence of s by t. For example, if $u = f(g(x), g(x))$, and we wish to emphasize the fact that $g(x)$ is a subexpression of u, then we can write $u[g(x)]$. Then $u[t]$ denotes either $f(t, g(x))$ or $f(g(x), t)$.

We will always assume that there is a well-founded order $\succ$ defined on the expressions under consideration such that the following *monotonic property* holds for all expressions s, t, and $u[s]$ and all substitutions θ:

$$\text{If } s \succ t, \text{ then } u[s] \succ u[t] \text{ and } s\theta > t\theta.$$

For example, suppose we consider the expressions of the form $g^n(x)$ for all variables x and for all $n \in \mathbb{N}$. Suppose further that we define $g^n(x) \succ g^m(x)$ for all $n > m$. This ordering is clearly well-founded and monotonic. Notice that we can't compare two expressions that contain distinct variables. For example, if we wanted to have $g^2(x) \succ g(y)$, then the ordering would no longer be monotonic because a substitution like $\{y/g^2(x)\}$ applied to $g^2(x) \succ g(y)$ gives $g^2(x) \succ g^3(x)$, which contradicts our definition of $\succ$.

If we have expressions that contain different operations or that contain operations that take more than a single argument, then it takes more work to find an ordering that is well-founded and monotonic.

We also need to discuss the *specialization* ordering on expressions, which is denoted by the symbol

$$\rhd.$$

For expressions s and l we write $s \rhd l$ if a subexpression of s is an instance of l but no subexpression of l is an instance of s. For example, $f(x, g(a)) \rhd g(z)$ because the subexpression $g(a)$ of $f(x, g(a))$ is an instance of $g(z)$ by the substitution $\{z/a\}$ and no subexpression of $g(z)$ is an instance of $f(x, g(a))$. Two other examples are $g(g(x)) \rhd g(x)$ and $f(a, x) \rhd a$. In these two cases the empty substitution does the job.

Tradition dictates that we use the double arrow $\leftrightarrow$ in place of $=$ to represent an equation. In other words, the equation $s = t$ will now be written $s \leftrightarrow t$, where s and t are expressions. We assume that $s \leftrightarrow t$ if and only if $t \leftrightarrow s$. The construction technique we're about to describe uses six inference rules. When a pair of the form $\langle E, R \rangle$ appears in an inference rule, E represents a set of equations and R represents a set of reduction rules. An expression of the form $t \rightarrow_R u$ means that t reduces to u by using the rules of R. Here are the six rules of inference:

Delete (Remove a trivial equation):

$$\frac{\langle E \cup \{s \leftrightarrow s\}, R \rangle}{\therefore \ \langle E, R \rangle} .$$

Compose (Replace a rule by a composition):

$$\frac{\langle E, R \cup \{s \rightarrow t\} \rangle, t \rightarrow_R u}{\therefore \ \langle E, R \cup \{s \rightarrow u\} \rangle} .$$

Simplify (Replace equation by a simpler one):

$$\frac{\langle E \cup \{s \leftrightarrow t\}, R \rangle, t \rightarrow_R u}{\therefore \ \langle E \cup \{s \leftrightarrow u\}, R \rangle} .$$

Orient (Turn an equation into a rule):

$$\frac{\langle E \cup \{s \leftrightarrow t\}, R \rangle, s \succ t}{\therefore \ \langle E, R \cup \{s \rightarrow t\} \rangle} .$$

Collapse (Turn a rule into an equation):

$$\frac{\langle E, R \cup \{s \rightarrow t\} \rangle, s \rightarrow_R u \text{ by rule } l \rightarrow r \text{ in } R \text{ with } s \rhd l}{\therefore \ \langle E \cup \{u \leftrightarrow t\}, R \rangle} .$$

Deduce (Add an equation):

$$\frac{\langle E, R \rangle, s \leftarrow_R u \rightarrow_R t}{\therefore \ \langle E \cup \{s \leftrightarrow t\}, R \rangle} .$$

A *completion procedure* starts with the pair $\langle E_0, R_0 \rangle$, where E_0 is the original set of equations and R_0 is a set of reduction rules—most often R_0 will be the empty set—and applies the inference rules to generate a sequence of pairs as follows:

$$\langle E_0, R_0 \rangle, \langle E_1, R_1 \rangle, ..., \langle E_p, R_p \rangle.$$

The goal of such a procedure is to obtain a final pair (E_f, R_f) in which $E_f = \varnothing$ and R_f satisfies the following completion property: An equation $s \leftrightarrow t$ can be derived from the equations E_0 and reduction rules R_0 if and only if s and t can be reduced to the same normal form by the reduction rules R_f.

Let's demonstrate the idea by doing a simple completion procedure for the two equations that we met in (8.10), which we've listed in double arrow form as follows:

$$g^5(x) \leftrightarrow x \quad \text{and} \quad g^3(x) \leftrightarrow x.$$

We'll assume that $g^m(x) \succ g^n(x)$ for any $m > n$. This ordering is well-founded and monotonic. We'll start our completion procedure with the set of two equations and with the empty set of reduction rules. We'll keep applying the inference rules until we can't apply them any longer. Table 8.2 shows the process, where each step follows from the previous step by applying some inference rule:

Step i	Equations E_i	Rules R_i	Inference Rule Used
0	$g^5(x) \leftrightarrow x$ $g^3(x) \leftrightarrow x$	$\varnothing$	
1	$g^5(x) \leftrightarrow x$	$g^3(x) \to x$	Orient
2	$g^2(x) \leftrightarrow x$	$g^3(x) \to x$	Simplify: $g^5(x) \to_R g^2(x)$ by rule $g^3(x) \to x$
3	$\varnothing$	$g^2(x) \to x$ $g^3(x) \to x$	Orient
4	$g(x) \leftrightarrow x$	$g^2(x) \to x$	Collapse: $g^3(x) \to_R g(x)$ by rule $g^2(x) \to x$ with $g^3(x) \rhd g^2(x)$
5	$\varnothing$	$g(x) \to x$ $g^2(x) \to x$	Orient
6	$g(x) \leftrightarrow x$	$g(x) \to x$	Collapse: $g^2(x) \to_R x$ by rule $g(x) \to x$ with $g^2(x) \rhd g(x)$
7	$x \leftrightarrow x$	$g(x) \to x$	Simplify: $g(x) \to_R x$ by rule $g(x) \to x$
8	$\varnothing$	$g(x) \to x$	Delete

Table 8.2

This completion procedure gives us the single reduction rule $g(x) \to x$. As we observed in the opening example, this reduction rule can be used to evaluate any expression of the form $g^k(x)$ to obtain the value x.

Now let's look at a classic example of a completion procedure from Knuth and Bendix [1970]. It starts with the following three equations, which can be used as axioms for a group, where e is the identity:

$$e \cdot x \leftrightarrow x, \tag{8.13}$$
$$x^{-1} \cdot x \leftrightarrow e,$$
$$(x \cdot y) \cdot z \leftrightarrow x \cdot (y \cdot z).$$

The ordering $\succ$ defined on the expressions of this group is a bit complicated. But we'll describe it because it is a nice example of a recursive definition. For an expression s, let

$$n(x, s)$$

denote the number of occurrences of x in s. For an expression s, let $w(s)$ be the sum of $n(e, s)$ and all $n(x, s)$ for variables x in s. For example, if

$$s = (x \cdot e) \cdot (x \cdot y),$$

then

$$w(s) = n(e, s) + n(x, s) + n(y, s) = 1 + 2 + 1 = 4.$$

If s and t are expressions over the group defined by axioms (8.13), then we define $s \succ t$ if either of the following two conditions is satisfied:

1. $w(s) > w(t)$, and $n(s, x) \geq n(t, x)$ for each variable x in t.

2. $w(s) = w(t)$, and $n(s, x) = n(t, x)$ for each variable x in either s or t, and $s \succ t$ matches one of the following patterns, where x^{-n} means that the operation $^{-1}$ is applied n times. For example, $x^{-2} = (x^{-1})^{-1}$.

   $x^{-n} \succ x$ for any variable x and $n \geq 1$.

   $e^{-n} \succ e$ for $n \geq 1$.

   $(a_1 \cdot a_2)^{-1} \succ b_1 \cdot b_2$.

   $a^{-1} \succ b^{-1}$ if $a \succ b$.

   $a_1 \cdot a_2 \succ b_1 \cdot b_2$ if either $a_1 \succ b_1$ or $a_1 = b_1$ and $a_2 \succ b_2$.

For example, condition 1 of the definition tells us that $(x \cdot y) \succ x$. Therefore we can conclude, by condition 2 of the definition, that $(x \cdot y) \cdot z \succ x \cdot (y \cdot z)$.

The inference rules can now be applied to the three equations (8.13) to obtain the following set of reduction rules:

$$e \cdot x \to x$$
$$x \cdot e \to x$$
$$x^{-1} \cdot x \to e$$
$$x \cdot x^{-1} \to e$$
$$e^{-1} \to e$$
$$x^{-1-1} \to x$$
$$y^{-1} \cdot (y \cdot z) \to z$$
$$y \cdot (y^{-1} \cdot z) \to z$$
$$(x \cdot y) \cdot z \to x \cdot (y \cdot z)$$
$$(x \cdot y)^{-1} \to y^{-1} \cdot x^{-1}.$$

In the exercises we'll examine how some of these reduction rules are found. These reduction rules statisfy the completion property. In other words, they can be used to reduce two expressions s and t to the same normal form if and only if the equation $s \leftrightarrow t$ is derivable from the three equations (8.13). For example, to see whether the equation $((x \cdot y^{-1}) \cdot z)^{-1} \leftrightarrow (z^{-1} \cdot y) \cdot x^{-1}$ can be derived from equations (8.13), all we need to do is reduce both expressions to normal form as follows:

$$((x \cdot y^{-1}) \cdot z)^{-1} \to z^{-1} \cdot (x \cdot y^{-1})^{-1} \to z^{-1} \cdot (y^{-1-1} \cdot x^{-1}) \to z^{-1} \cdot (y \cdot x^{-1})$$

and

$$(z^{-1} \cdot y) \cdot x^{-1} \to z^{-1} \cdot (y \cdot x^{-1}).$$

Since the normal forms are equal, we have

$$((x \cdot y^{-1}) \cdot z)^{-1} \leftrightarrow (z^{-1} \cdot y) \cdot x^{-1}.$$

We should remark that it's not always possible to obtain a complete set of reduction rules for a system of equations. In other words, the completion procedure may not terminate, or it may terminate with a set of reduction rules that does not generate the same set of equations as the original equations. Finding a complete set of reduction rules depends heavily on the ordering $\succ$ that must be defined on the expressions under consideration. The presentation that we've given here is based on the collection of papers edited by Aït-Kaci and Nivat [1989]. These papers and the original paper by Knuth and Bendix [1970] contain more detailed discussions about ordering expressions. They also include many applications of the procedure.

Exercises

1. Why is "twice" a good name for the lambda expression $\lambda x.(x\ (x\ y))$?

2. Simplify each of the following lambda expressions.
   a. $(x\ y)[x/\lambda z.z]$.
   b. $(\lambda x.x\ (\lambda y.x\ a))$.
   c. $\lambda x.(\lambda y.x\ x)$.
   d. $\lambda x.(\lambda y.y\ x)$.
   e. $(\lambda x.M)[x/N]$.
   f. $((\lambda x.\lambda y.(y\ x)\ z)\ w)$.

3. For each of the following lambda expressions, answer the question: Is α-conversion needed before β-reduction of the expression? Answer YES or NO.
   a. $(\lambda x.(x\ y)\ \lambda x.y)$.
   b. $(\lambda x.\lambda y.(y\ x)\ y)$.

4. Find a lambda expression of the form $\lambda x.(M\ x)$ that satisfies each of the following properties.
   a. η-reduction may be applied.
   b. η-reduction may NOT be applied.

5. Evaluate the following lambda expression using β-reduction until no more applications can be evaluated:
$$(((\lambda x.\lambda y.\lambda z.(x\ (y\ z))\ \lambda x.x)\ u)\ v).$$

6. Evaluate the following lambda expression in two different ways:
$$(\lambda x.(\lambda y.y\ x)\ \lambda x.(\lambda y.x\ x)).$$
   a. Use normal order reduction.
   b. Use applicative order reduction.

7. Let F be the function defined as follows:
$$F = \lambda x.\lambda y.((\text{Not}\ x)\ \text{true}\ (\text{Not}\ y)).$$

Compute the value of the expression $(F\ \text{true}\ \text{true})$. Do not expand Not, true, and false.

8. Recall that the Y combinator is a lambda expression with the following property for any lambda expression E: $(Y\ E) = (E\ (Y\ E))$. Suppose we define the function F as follows:
$$F = (Y\ g),$$
$$g = \lambda f.\lambda x.((\text{isZero}\ x)\ 1\ (f\ (\text{pred}\ x))).$$

Calculate the value of the expression $(F\ 1)$. Do not expand the functions isZero, 1, and pred.

9. Write down each step in the evaluation of each of the following lambda expressions.

    a. tail (cons $a\ b$).

    b. isEmpty(cons $a\ b$).

    c. isEmpty emptyList.

10. Write down each step in the evaluation of each of the following lambda expressions.

    a. isZero 2.   b. pred 2.

11. Find the value of each of the following lambda expressions, where an n-tuple is defined inductively as

    $$\langle x \rangle = x,$$
    $$\langle x_1, x_2, ..., x_k \rangle = \lambda s.(s\ x_1\ \langle x_2, ..., x_k \rangle).$$

    a. $(\langle a, b, c, d \rangle$ false false true$)$.

    b. $(\langle a, b, c, d, e \rangle$ false false false false$)$.

12. Explain the statement "normal order evaluation is safer than applicative order evaluation."

13. Find the normal form, if it exists, for each of the following lambda expressions.

    a. $(\lambda y.(y\ y)\ \lambda y.(y\ y))$.

    b. $((\lambda x.\lambda y.(x\ y)\ \lambda x.x)\ \lambda y.(y\ y))$.

14. Find the weak-head normal form for each of the following lambda expressions.

    a. $\lambda x.(\lambda y.x\ c)$.

    b. $(\lambda x.x\ \lambda y.(\lambda x.y\ z))$.

15. Prove the following statement: If $(x\ y) = (x\ x)$, then $M = N$ for any lambda expressions M and N.

16. Use a Knuth-Bendix inference rule to replace one of the two reduction rules $f(f(x)) \to x$ and $(x \cdot c) \cdot c \to f(f(x)) \cdot c$.

17. Use the Knuth-Bendix inference rules to find a single reduction rule that is equivalent to the two equations $g^3(x) \leftrightarrow g(x)$ and $g^4(x) \leftrightarrow x$.

18. Given the equations (8.13), use the Knuth-Bendix inference rules to accomplish each of the following tasks. To accomplish a given task, you may use the results of any of the preceding tasks.

a. Replace the equations (8.13) by three reduction rules.

b. Add the reduction rule $y^{-1} \cdot (y \cdot z) \to z$.

c. Add the reduction rule $e^{-1} \cdot x \to x$.

d. Add the reduction rule $(x^{-1})^{-1} \cdot e \to x$.

e. Add the reduction rule $(x^{-1})^{-1} \cdot y \to x \cdot y$.

f. Add the reduction rule $x \cdot e \to x$.

g. Add the reduction rule $e^{-1} \to e$.

h. Add the reduction rule $(x^{-1})^{-1} \to x$.

i. Remove the reduction rule $(x^{-1})^{-1} \cdot e \to x$.

j. Remove the reduction rule $e^{-1} \cdot x \to x$.

k. Remove the reduction rule $(x^{-1})^{-1} \cdot y \to x \cdot y$.

Chapter Summary

Some general problems—such as the halting problem, the total problem, the equivalence problem, and the Post correspondence problem—can't be solved by any machine. The halting problem and Post's correspondence problem are partially solvable. It's often the case that specific instances of unsolvable problems are solvable. For example, we can certainly tell whether f halts on any input x if f is defined by $f(x) = 2x$.

There is a hierarchy of languages extending from the class of regular languages up to the class of languages that have no restrictions on their grammars and finally to the class of languages that may or may not have grammars. All the grammatical languages can be recognized by certain kinds of machines. But the class of languages without grammars can't be recognized by any machine.

From a computational point of view, most of us are interested in finding techniques for solving problems rather than finding problems that can't be solved. So we discussed some general computational techniques for evaluating expressions. The lambda calculus is a computational model—equivalent in power to the Turing machine model—with a small set of reduction rules for evaluating expressions, and these rules can be efficiently implemented. The Knuth-Bendix procedure provides an algorithm for finding reduction rules for expressions that are defined by a set of axioms.

9

Computational Complexity

Remember that time is money.
—Benjamin Franklin (1706–1790)

Time and space are important words in computer science because we want fast algorithms and we want algorithms that don't use a lot of memory. The word "complexity" is used in computer science when we try to compare or classify problems with respect to the amount of time or space that is required by algorithms to solve them. For example, from an informal point of view, we say that problem A is more complex than problem B if any algorithm to solve A takes more time to execute than some algorithm that solves B. We also use "complexity" to compare different algorithms that solve the same problem. For example, an algorithm for a problem is more complex than another algorithm for the same problem if, when both algorithms are given the same input, the first alorithm takes more time to run than the second algorithm.

In this chapter we'll study some fundamental techniques and tools that can be used to analyze algorithms to determine the time or space that they require. Although the study of algorithm analysis is beyond our scope, we'll give some examples to show how the process works. After introducing the idea of an optimal algorithm, we'll discuss the worst case analysis of algorithms. Then we'll see how to compare the growth rates of functions. This will lead us into a discussion about the basics of complexity theory.

Chapter Guide

Section 9.1 introduces the optimal algorithm problem. We'll give a definition for the worst case performance of an algorithm and then we'll analyze a few example algorithms.

465

Section 9.2 presents some techniques for comparing the rates of growth of functions. We'll apply the results to functions that describe the approximate running time of algorithms.

Section 9.3 discusses how decision problems are classified by whether there exist solutions whose execution times are "reasonable." After we clarify the meaning of "reasonable," we'll discuss the complexity classes *P*, *NP*, and *PSPACE* and what it means for a class to be *NP*-complete. Lastly we'll describe complexity from a formal point of view.

9.1   Optimal Algorithms

An important question of computer science is: Can you convince another person that your algorithm is efficient? This takes some discussion. Let's start by stating the following problem.

The Optimal Algorithm Problem

Suppose algorithm *A* solves problem *P*. Is *A* the best solution to *P*?

What does "best" mean? Two typical meanings are *least time* and *least space*. In either case we still need to clarify what it means for an algorithm to solve a problem in the least time or the least space. For example, an algorithm running on two different machines may take different amounts of time. Do we have to compare *A* to every possible solution of *P* on every type of machine? This is impossible. So we need to make a few assumptions in order to discuss the optimal algorithm problem. We'll concentrate on "least time" as the meaning of "best" because time is the most important factor in most computations.

Instead of executing an algorithm on a real machine to find its running time, we'll analyze the algorithm by counting the number of certain operations that it will perform when executed on a real machine. In this way we can compare two algorithms by simply comparing the number of operations of the same type that each performs. If we make a good choice of the type of operations to count, we should get a good measure of an algorithm's performance. For example, we might count addition operations and multiplication operations for a numerical problem. On the other hand, we might choose to count comparison operations for a sorting problem.

The number of operations performed by an algorithm usually depends on the size or structure of the input. The size of the input again depends on the problem. For example, for a sorting problem, "size" usually means the number of items to be sorted. Sometimes inputs of the same size can have different structures that affect the number of operations performed. For example, some sorting algorithms perform very well on an input data set that is all mixed up but perform badly on an input set that is already sorted!

Because of these observations we need to define the idea of a worst case input for an algorithm A. An input of size n is a *worst case input* if, when compared to all other inputs of size n, it causes A to execute the largest number of operations. Now let's get down to business. For any input I we'll denote its size by size(I), and we'll let time(I) denote the number of operations executed by A on I. Then the *worst case function* for A is defined as follows:

$$W_A(n) = \max\{\text{time}(I) \mid I \text{ is an input and size}(I) = n\}.$$

Now let's discuss comparing different algorithms that solve the same problem P. We'll always assume that the algorithms we compare use certain specified operations that we intend to count. If A and B are algorithms that solve P and if $W_A(n) \le W_B(n)$ for all $n > 0$, then we know algorithm A has worst case performance that is better than or equal to that of algorithm B. An algorithm A is *optimal in the worst case* for problem P if, for any algorithm B that exists or ever will exist, the following relationship holds:

$$W_A(n) \le W_B(n) \quad \text{for all } n > 0.$$

How in the world can we ever find an algorithm that is optimal in the worst case for a problem P? The answer involves the following three steps:

1. (Find an algorithm) Find or design an algorithm A to solve P. Then do an analysis of A to find the worst case function W_A.

2. (Find a lower bound) Find a function F such that $F(n) \le W_B(n)$ for all $n > 0$ and for all algorithms B that solve P.

3. Compare F and W_A. If $F = W_A$, then A is optimal in the worst case.

An interesting situation occurs when $F \ne W_A$ in Step 3. This means that $F(n) < W_A(n)$ for some n. In this case there are two possible courses of action to consider:

Try to find a better algorithm than A. In other words, try to find an algorithm C such that $W_C(n) \le W_A(n)$ for all $n > 0$.

Try to find a "better" lower bound than F. In other words, try to find a new function G such that $F(n) \le G(n) \le W_B(n)$ for all $n > 0$ and for all algorithms B that solve P.

We should note that the zero function is always a lower bound, but it's not very interesting because most algorithms take more than zero time. A few problems have optimal algorithms. For the vast majority of problems, optimal algorithms have not yet been found. The examples that follow contain both kinds of problems.

EXAMPLE 1 (*Matrix Multiplication*). We can "multiply" two n by n matrices A and B to obtain the product AB, which is the n by n matrix defined by letting the element in the ith row and jth column of AB be the value of the expression $\sum_{k=1}^{n} A_{ik} B_{kj}$. In other words, for $1 \leq i \leq n$ and $1 \leq j \leq n$ we have

$$(AB)_{ij} = \sum_{k=1}^{n} A_{ik} B_{kj}.$$

For example, let A and B be the following 2 by 2 matrices:

$$A = \begin{bmatrix} a & b \\ c & d \end{bmatrix}, \qquad B = \begin{bmatrix} e & f \\ g & h \end{bmatrix}.$$

The product AB is given by the following 2 by 2 matrix:

$$AB = \begin{bmatrix} ae + bg & af + bh \\ ce + dg & cf + dh \end{bmatrix}.$$

Notice that the computation of AB takes eight multiplications and four additions. The definition of matrix multiplication of two n by n matrices uses n^3 multiplication operations and $n^2(n - 1)$ addition operations.

A known lower bound for the number of multiplication operations needed to multiply two n by n matrices is n^2. Strassen [1969] showed how to multiply two matrices with about $n^{2.81}$ multiplication operations. The number 2.81 is an approximation to the value of $\log_2(7)$. It stems from the fact that a pair of 2 by 2 matrices can be multiplied by using seven multiplication operations. Multiplication of larger-size matrices is broken down into multiplying many 2 by 2 matrices. Therefore the number of multiplication operations becomes less than n^3. This revelation got research going in two camps. One camp is trying to find a better algorithm. The other camp is trying to raise the lower bound above n^2. In recent years, algorithms have been found with still lower numbers. Pan [1978] gave an algorithm to multiply two 70×70 matrices using 143,640 multiplications, which is less than $70^{2.81}$ multiplication operations. Coppersmith and Winograd [1987] gave an algorithm that, for large values of n, uses $n^{2.376}$ multiplication operations. The search goes on for better lower bounds. ◆

EXAMPLE 2 (*Finding the Minimum*). Let's look at an example of an optimal algorithm to find the minimum number in an unsorted list of n numbers. We'll count the number of comparison operations that an algorithm makes between elements of the list. To find the minimal number in a list of n numbers, the minimal number must be compared with the other $n - 1$ numbers. So $n - 1$ is a lower bound on the number of comparisons needed to find the minimum number in a list of n numbers. If we represent the list as an array a indexed from 1 to n, then the following algorithm is optimal because the operation $\leq$ is executed exactly $n - 1$ times.

$$m := a[1];$$
$$\textbf{for } i := 2 \textbf{ to } n \textbf{ do}$$
$$\qquad m := \text{if } m \leq a[i] \text{ then } m \text{ else } a[i]$$
$$\textbf{od}$$

$\blacklozenge$

EXAMPLE 3 (*Simple Sort*). In this example we'll construct a simple sorting algorithm and analyze it to find the number of comparison operations. We'll sort an array a of numbers indexed from 1 to n as follows: Find the smallest element in a, and exchange it with the first element. Then find the smallest element in positions 2 through n, and exchange it with the element in position 2. Continue in this manner to obtain a sorted array. To write the algorithm, we'll use a function "min" and a procedure "exchange," which are defined as follows:

min(a, i, n) is the index of the minimum number among the elements $a[i]$, $a[i + 1]$, ..., $a[n]$. We can easily modify the algorithm in Example 2 to accomplish this task with with $n - i$ comparisons.

exchange($a[i]$, $a[j]$) represents the usual operation of swapping elements and does not use any comparisons.

We can write the sorting algorithm as follows:

$$\textbf{for } i := 1 \textbf{ to } n - 1 \textbf{ do}$$
$$\qquad j := \min(a, i, n);$$
$$\qquad \text{exchange}(a[i], a[j])$$
$$\textbf{od}$$

Now let's compute the number of comparison operations. The algorithm for min(a, i, n) makes $n - i$ comparisons. So as i moves from 1 to $n - 1$, the number of comparison operations moves from $n - 1$ to $n - (n - 1)$. We can easily add up these numbers because they form a simple arithmetic expression as follows:

$$(n - 1) + (n - 2) + \cdots + 1 = \frac{n(n-1)}{2}.$$

The algorithm makes the same number of comparisons no matter what the form of the input array, even if it is sorted to begin with. So any arrangement of numbers is a worst case input. For example, to sort 1000 items it would take 499,500 comparisons, no matter how the items are arranged to begin with.

There are many faster sorting algorithms. For example, an algorithm called "heapsort" takes no more than $2n \log_2 n$ comparisons for its worst case performance. So for 1000 items, heapsort would take a maximum of 20,000 comparisons—quite an improvement over our simple sort algorithm. In Section 9.2 we'll find a good lower bound for comparison sorting algorithms.
♦

Decision Trees

We can often use a tree to represent the decision processes that take place in an algorithm. A *decision tree* for an algorithm is a tree whose nodes represent decision points in the algorithm and whose leaves represent possible outcomes. Decision trees can be useful in trying to construct an algorithm or trying to find properties of an algorithm. For example, lower bounds may equate to the depth of a decision tree.

If an algorithm makes decisions based on the comparison of two objects, then it can be represented by a binary decision tree. Each node in the tree represents a pair of objects to be compared, and each branch from that node represents a path taken by the algorithm based on the comparison. Each leaf can represent an outcome of the algorithm. Many sorting and searching algorithms can be analyzed with decision trees because they perform comparisons. Let's look at some examples to illustrate the idea.

EXAMPLE 4 (*Binary Search*). Suppose we search a sorted list in a binary fashion. That is, we check the middle element of the list to see whether it's the key we are looking for. If not, then we perform the same operation on either the left half or the right half of the list, depending on the value of the key. This algorithm has a nice representation as a decision tree. For example, suppose we have the sorted list containing the first 15 prime numbers:

$$2, 3, 5, 7, 11, 13, 17, 19, 23, 29, 31, 37, 41, 43, 47.$$

Suppose we're given a key K, and we must find whether it is in the list. We don't know in advance whether K is in the list.

The decision tree for a binary search of the list of primes has the number 19 at its root. This represents the comparison of K with 19. If $K = 19$, then we are successful in one comparison. If $K < 19$, then we go to the left child of 19; otherwise we go to the right child of 19. The result is a ternary decision tree in which the leaves are labeled with either S, for successful search, or U, for unsuccessful search. The tree is pictured in Figure 9.1.

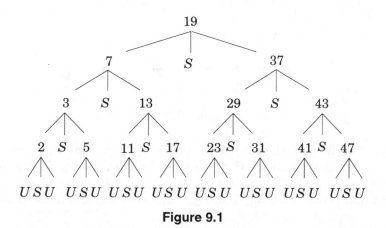

Figure 9.1

It's easy to see in this case that there will be at most four comparisons to find whether K is in the list. So a worst case lower bound for the number of comparisons is 4, which is 1 plus the depth of the binary tree whose nodes are the numbered nodes in Figure 9.1. We know that the minimum depth of a binary tree with n nodes is $\lfloor \log_2 n \rfloor$. So the lower bound for the worst case of a binary search algorithm on a sorted input list of n elements is

$$1 + \lfloor \log_2 n \rfloor. \quad \blacklozenge$$

EXAMPLE 5 (*Weighing Things*). Suppose that we are given eight coins and told to find the heavy coin among the eight with the assumption that they all look alike, and the other seven all have the same weight, and we must use a pan balance. There are two ways to proceed, depending on whether or not we want to consider the possibility that the balance may balance. If the pan never balances, then we will obtain a binary decision tree. Otherwise, we get a ternary decision tree.

Solution 1 (binary tree): Let each internal node of the tree represent the pan balance, with an equal number of coins on each side. If the left side goes down, then the heavy coin is on the left side of the balance. Otherwise, the heavy coin is on the right side of the balance. Each leaf represents one coin that is the heavy coin. Suppose we label the coins with the numbers 1,2, ..., 8. One algorithm's decision tree is pictured in Figure 9.2, where the numbers on either side of a nonleaf node represent the coins on either side of the pan balance.

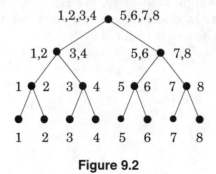

Figure 9.2

This algorithm finds the heavy coin in three weighings. Can we do better?

Solution 2 (ternary tree): Here we allow for the third possibility that the two pans are balanced. So we don't have to use all eight coins on the first weighing. The decision tree in Figure 9.3 shows one solution to the problem.

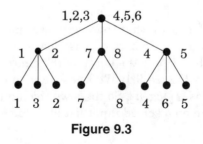

Figure 9.3

Notice that there is no middle branch on the middle subtree, since at this point, one of the coins 7 or 8 must be the heavy one. This algorithm finds the heavy coin in two weighings.

The second solution is an optimal pan balance algorithm for this problem, where we are counting the number of weighings to find the heavy coin. To see this, notice that any one of the eight coins could be the heavy one. Therefore there must be at least eight leaves on any algorithm's decision tree. But a binary tree of depth k can have 2^k possible leaves, so to get eight leaves, we must have $2^k \geq 8$. This implies that $k \geq 3$. But a ternary tree of depth k can have 3^k possible leaves. So to get eight leaves, we must have $3^k \geq 8$, or $k \geq 2$. Therefore 2 is a lower bound for the number of weighings. Since the second solution solves the problem in two weighings, it is optimal.   ◆

EXAMPLE 6. Suppose we have a set of 13 coins in which at most one coin is bad and a bad coin may be heavier or lighter than the other coins. The problem is to use a pan balance to find the bad coin if it exists and say whether it is heavy or light. We'll find a lower bound on the heights of decision trees for pan balance algorithms to solve the problem.

Any solution must tell whether a bad coin is heavy or light. Thus there are 27 possible conditions: no bad coin and the 13 pairs of conditions

$$\langle i\text{th coin light}, i\text{th coin heavy}\rangle.$$

Therefore any decision tree for the problem must have at least 27 leaves. So a ternary decision tree of depth k must satisfy $3^k \geq 27$, or $k \geq 3$. This gives us a lower bound of 3. Now the big question: Is there an algorithm to solve the problem, where the decision tree of the algorithm has depth 3? The answer is no. Just look at the cases of different initial weighings, and note in each case that the remaining possible conditions cannot be distinguished with just two more weighings. Therefore any decision tree for this problem must have depth 4 or more.   ◆

EXAMPLE 7 (*A Worst Case Lower Bound for Comparison Sorting*). Let's find a lower bound for the number of comparison operations performed by any sorting algorithm that sorts by comparing elements in the list to be sorted. Assume that we have a set of n distinct numbers. Since there are $n!$ possible arrangements of these numbers, it follows that any algorithm to sort a list of n numbers has $n!$ possible input arrangements. Therefore any decision tree for a comparison sorting algorithm must contain at least $n!$ leaves, one leaf for each possible outcome of sorting one arrangement. We know that a binary tree of depth d has at most 2^d leaves. So the depth d of the decision tree for any comparison sort of n items must satisfy the inequality

$$n! \leq 2^d.$$

We can solve this inequality for the natural number d by taking logs and using the ceiling function as follows:

$$\log_2 n! \leq d$$
$$\lceil \log_2 n! \rceil \leq d.$$

In other words, $\lceil \log_2 n! \rceil$ is a worst case lower bound for the number of comparisons to sort n items. We'll state it for the record:

Any algorithm that sorts by comparing elements must use at   (9.1)
least $\lceil \log_2 n! \rceil$ comparisons in the worst case to sort n items.

If we calculate $\lceil \log_2 n! \rceil$ by first computing $n!$ and then taking the log and the
floor, then the job is quite difficult for large values of n. But we'll see later in
Section 9.2 that $\lceil \log_2 n! \rceil$ is "approximately" the same as $n \log_2 n$.   ◆

Exercises

1. For the following program, answer each question by giving a formula in
   terms of a natural number n:

   $$i := 0;$$
   while $i < n$ **do**
       for $j := 0$ **to** i **do** S **od**;
       $i := i + 1$
   od

   a. Find the number of times that the assignment statement (:=) is executed during the running of the program.

   b. Modify the program by replacing "$i := i + 1$" by "$i := i + 2$". Then find
   the number of times that the assignment statement (:=) is executed
   during the running of the program.

2. Draw a picture of the decision tree for an optimal algorithm to find the
   maximum number in the list $\langle x_1, x_2, x_3, x_4 \rangle$.

3. Suppose there are 95 possible answers to some problem. For each of the
   following types of decision tree, find a reasonable lower bound for the
   number of decisions necessary to solve the problem.

   a. Binary decision tree.

   b. Ternary decision tree.

   c. Four-way decision tree.

4. Find a nonzero lower bound on the number of weighings necessary for
   any ternary pan balance algorithm to solve the following problem: A set
   of 30 coins contains at most one bad coin, which may be heavy or light. Is
   there a bad coin? If so, state whether it's heavy or light.

5. Find an optimal pan balance algorithm to find a bad coin, if it exists,
   from 12 coins, where at most one coin is bad (i.e., heavier or lighter than
   the others). *Hint:* Once you've decided on the coins to weigh for the root
   of the tree, then the coins that you choose at the second level should be
   the same coins for all three branches of the tree.

6. The expression x^{55} can be evalutated with 54 multiply operations. But it can also be evalutated with nine multiply operations as follows:

$$x^2 = x \cdot x, \quad x^4 = x^2 \cdot x^2, \quad x^8 = x^4 \cdot x^4, \quad x^{16} = x^8 \cdot x^8, \quad x^{32} = x^{16} \cdot x^{16}, \quad x^{48} = x^{32} \cdot x^{16},$$
$$x^{52} = x^{48} \cdot x^4, \quad x^{54} = x^{52} \cdot x^2, \quad x^{55} = x^{54} \cdot x.$$

Find an algorithm to evaluate x^{55} using eight multiply operations.

9.2 Comparing Rates of Growth

Sometimes it makes sense to approximate the number of steps required to execute an algorithm because of the difficulty involved in finding a closed form for an expression or the difficulty in evaluating an expression. To approximate one function with another function, we need some way to compare them. That's where "rate of growth" comes in. We want to give some meaning to statements like "f has the same growth rate as g" and "f has a lower growth rate than g."

For our purposes we will consider functions whose domains and codomains are subsets of the real numbers. We'll examine the asymptotic behavior of two functions f and g by comparing $f(n)$ and $g(n)$ for large positive values of n (i.e., as n approaches infinity).

Big Theta

Let's begin by discussing the meaning of the statement "f has the same growth rate as g." We say that f has the *same growth rate* as g, or f has the *same order* as g, if we can find a number m and two nonzero numbers c and d such that

$$cg(n) \leq f(n) \leq dg(n) \qquad \text{for all } n \geq m. \tag{9.2}$$

In this case we write

$$f(n) = \Theta(g(n)),$$

which is read, "$f(n)$ is *big theta* of $g(n)$." It's easy to verify that the relation "has the same growth rate as" is an equivalence relation. In other words, the following three properties hold for all functions:

$f(n) = \Theta(f(n))$.
If $f(n) = \Theta(g(n))$, then $g(n) = \Theta(f(n))$.
If $f(n) = \Theta(g(n))$ and $g(n) = \Theta(h(n))$, then $g(n) = \Theta(h(n))$.

If $f(n) = \Theta(g(n))$ and we also know that $g(n)$ is positive for all $n \geq m$, then we can divide the inequality (9.2) by $g(n)$ to obtain

$$c \leq \frac{f(n)}{g(n)} \leq d \quad \text{for all } n \geq m.$$

This inequality gives us a better way to think about "having the same growth rate." It tells us that the ratio of the two functions is always within a fixed bound beyond some point. We can always take this point of view for functions that count the steps of algorithms because they are positive valued.

Now let's see whether we can find some functions that have the same growth rate. To start things off, suppose f and g are proportional. This means that there is a nonzero constant c such that $f(n) = cg(n)$ for all n. In this case, definition (9.2) is satisfied by letting $d = c$. Thus we have the following statement:

If two functions f and g are proportional, then $f(n) = \Theta(g(n))$.   (9.3)

EXAMPLE 1. Recall that log functions with different bases are proportional. In other words, if we have two bases $a > 1$ and $b > 1$, then

$$\log_a n = (\log_a b)(\log_b n) \quad \text{for all } n > 0.$$

So we can disregard the base of the log function when considering rates of growth. In other words, we have

$$\log_a n = \Theta(\log_b n). \quad \blacklozenge \quad (9.4)$$

It's interesting to note that two functions can have the same growth rate without being proportional. Here's an example.

EXAMPLE 2. Let's show that $n^2 + n$ and n^2 have the same growth rate. The following inequality is true for all $n \geq 1$:

$$1n^2 \leq n^2 + n \leq 2n^2.$$

Therefore $n^2 + n = \Theta(n^2)$. $\blacklozenge$

The following theorem gives us a nice tool for showing two functions have the same growth rate:

If $\lim\limits_{n\to\infty}\dfrac{f(n)}{g(n)} = c$, where $c \neq 0$ and $c \neq \infty$, then $f(n) = \Theta(g(n))$.   (9.5)

For example, the quotient $(25n^2 + n)/n^2$ approaches 25 as n approaches infinity. Therefore $25n^2 + n = \Theta(n^2)$.

We should note that the limit in (9.5) is not a necessary condition for $f(n) = \Theta(g(n))$. For example, let f and g be defined as follows:

$$f(n) = \text{if } n \text{ is odd then 2 else 4,}$$

$$g(n) = 2.$$

We can write $1g(n) \le f(n) \le 2g(n)$ for all $n \ge 1$. Therefore $f(n) = \Theta(g(n))$. But the quotient $f(n)/g(n)$ alternates between the two values 1 and 2. Therefore the limit of the quotient does not exist. Still the limit test (9.5) will work for the majority of functions that occur in analyzing algorithms.

Approximations can be quite useful for those of us who can't remember formulas that we don't use all the time. For example, we can write the sums from (2.16) in terms of Θ as follows:

$$\sum_{i=1}^{n} i = \Theta(n^2).\tag{9.6}$$

$$\sum_{i=1}^{n} i^2 = \Theta(n^3).\tag{9.7}$$

$$\text{If } a \neq 1, \text{ then } \sum_{i=0}^{n} a^i = \Theta(a^{n+1}).\tag{9.8}$$

$$\text{If } a \neq 1, \text{ then } \sum_{i=0}^{n} ia^i = \Theta(na^{n+1}).\tag{9.9}$$

The first two sums are special cases of the following result:

$$\sum_{i=1}^{n} i^k = \Theta(n^{k+1}).\tag{9.10}$$

EXAMPLE 3. Let's clarify a statement that we made in Example 7 of Section 9.1. We showed that $\lceil \log_2 n! \rceil$ is the worst case lower bound for comparison sorting algorithms. But $\log n!$ is hard to calculate for even modest values of n. We stated that $\lceil \log_2 n! \rceil$ is "approximately" equal to $n \log_2 n$. Now we can make the following statement:

$$\log n! = \Theta(n \log n). \qquad (9.11)$$

To prove this statement, we'll find some bounds on $\log n!$ as follows:

$$
\begin{aligned}
\log n! &= \log n + \log(n-1) + \ldots + \log 1 \\
&\leq \log n + \log n + \ldots + \log n \qquad (n \text{ terms}) \\
&= n \log n.
\end{aligned}
$$

$$
\begin{aligned}
\log n! &= \log n + \log(n-1) + \ldots + \log 1 \\
&\geq \log n + \log(n-1) + \ldots + \log(\lceil n/2 \rceil) \qquad (\lceil n/2 \rceil \text{ terms}) \\
&\geq \log\lceil n/2 \rceil + \ldots + \log\lceil n/2 \rceil \qquad (\lceil n/2 \rceil \text{ terms}) \\
&= \lceil n/2 \rceil \log \lceil n/2 \rceil \\
&\geq (n/2) \log(n/2).
\end{aligned}
$$

So we have the inequality:

$$(n/2)\log(n/2) \leq \log n! \leq n \log n.$$

It's easy to see (i.e., as an exercise) that if $n > 4$, then $(1/2)\log n < \log(n/2)$. Therefore we have the following inequality for $n > 4$:

$$(1/2)(n \log n) \leq (n/2)\log(n/2) \leq \log n! \leq n \log n.$$

In other words, there are nonzero constants 1/2 and 1 and a number 4 such that

$$(1/2)(n \log n) \leq \log n! \leq (1)(n \log n) \quad \text{for all } n > 4.$$

This tells us that $\log n! = \Theta(n \log n)$.   ◆

An important approximation to $n!$ is *Stirling's formula*—named for the mathematician James Stirling (1692–1770)—which is written as follows:

$$n! = \Theta\left(\sqrt{2\pi n}\left(\frac{n}{e}\right)^n \right). \qquad (9.12)$$

Let's see how we can use big theta to discuss the approximate performance of algorithms. For example, the worst case performance of the binary search algorithm is $\Theta(\log n)$ because the actual value is $1 + \lfloor \log_2 n \rfloor$. The worst case performance of a linear sequential search is $\Theta(n)$ because the worst case number of comparisons is n.

For sorting algorithms that sort by comparison the worst case lower bound is $\lceil \log_2 n! \rceil = \Theta(n \log n)$. Many sorting algorithms, like the simple sort algorithm in Section 9.1, have worst case performance of $\Theta(n^2)$. The "dumbSort" algorithm, which constructs a permutation of the given list and then checks to see whether it is sorted, may have to construct all possible permutations before it gets the right one. Thus dumbSort has worst case performance of $\Theta(n!)$. An algorithm called "heapsort" will sort any list of n items using at most $2n \log_2 n$ comparisons. So heapsort is a $\Theta(n \log n)$ algorithm in the worst case.

Little Oh

Now let's discuss the meaning of the statement "f as a lower growth rate than g." We say that f has a *lower growth rate* than g or f has *lower order* than g if

$$\lim_{n \to \infty} \frac{f(n)}{g(n)} = 0. \tag{9.13}$$

In this case we write

$$f(n) = o(g(n)),$$

which can be read, "f is *little oh* of g." When you say, "little oh," think of "lower order."

For example, the quotient n/n^2 approaches 0 as n goes to infinity. Therefore $n = o(n^2)$, and we can say that n has lower order than n^2. For another example, if a and b are positive numbers such that $a < b$, then $a^n = o(b^n)$. To see this, notice that the quotient $a^n/b^n = (a/b)^n$ approaches 0 as n approaches infinity because $0 < a/b < 1$.

For those readers familiar with derivatives, the evaluation of limits can often be accomplished by using L'Hôpital's rule:

$$\text{If } \lim_{n \to \infty} f(n) = \lim_{n \to \infty} g(n) = \infty \quad \text{or} \quad \lim_{n \to \infty} f(n) = \lim_{n \to \infty} g(n) = 0 \tag{9.14}$$

and if f and g are differentiable beyond some point, then

$$\lim_{n \to \infty} \frac{f(n)}{g(n)} = \lim_{n \to \infty} \frac{f'(n)}{g'(n)}.$$

EXAMPLE 4. We'll show that $\log n = o(n)$. Since both n and $\log n$ approach infinity as n approaches infinity, we can apply (9.14) to $(\log n)/n$. Since we can write $\log n = (\log e)(\log_e n)$, it follows that the derivative of $\log n$ is $(\log e)(1/n)$. Therefore we obtain the following equations:

$$\lim_{n \to \infty} \frac{\log n}{n} = \lim_{n \to \infty} \frac{(\log e)(1/n)}{1} = 0.$$

So $\log n$ has lower order than n, and we can write $\log n = o(n)$.   ◆

Let's list a hierarchy of some familiar functions according to their growth rates, where $f(n) \prec g(n)$ means that $f(n) = o(g(n))$:

$$1 \prec \log n \prec n \prec n \log n \prec n^2 \prec n^3 \prec 2^n \prec 3^n \prec n! \prec n^n. \qquad (9.15)$$

This hierarchy can help us compare different algorithms. For example, we would certainly choose an algorithm with running time $\Theta(\log n)$ over an algorithm with running time $\Theta(n)$.

Big Oh and Big Omega

It is often useful to express the fact that f has order less than or equal to g. In terms of Θ and o this means either $f(n) = \Theta(g(n))$ or $f(n) = o(g(n))$. The standard notation for this either-or situation is

$$f(n) = O(g(n)), \qquad (9.16)$$

which we read, "$f(n)$ is *big oh* of $g(n)$." For example, we have $2n + 1 = O(n^2)$ and $300n^2 + n = O(n^2)$. We can define $f(n) = O(g(n))$ without regard to big theta and little oh as follows:

$f(n) = O(g(n))$ means that there are positive numbers c and m (9.17)
such that $|f(n)| \leq c\,|g(n)|$ for all $n \geq m$.

EXAMPLE 5. We'll show that $n^2 = O(n^3)$ and $5n^3 + 2n^2 = O(n^3)$. Since $n^2 \leq 1n^3$ for all $n \geq 1$, it follows that $n^2 = O(n^3)$. Since $5n^3 + 2n^2 \leq 7n^3$ for all $n \geq 1$, it follows that $5n^3 + 2n^2 = O(n^3)$.   ◆

Now let's go the other way. Suppose we want to express the fact that f has order greater than or equal to that of g. In terms of Θ and o this means that either $f(n) = \Theta(g(n))$ or $g(n) = o(f(n))$. The standard notation for this either-or situation is

$$f(n) = \Omega(g(n)), \tag{9.18}$$

which we can read, "$f(n)$ is *big omega* of $g(n)$." For example, $2n^3 = \Omega(n^2)$ and $300n^2 = \Omega(n^2)$. We can define $f(n) = \Omega(g(n))$ without regard to big theta and little oh as follows:

> $f(n) = \Omega(g(n))$ means that there are positive numbers c and m $\qquad$ (9.19)
> such that $|f(n)| \geq c|g(n)|$ for all $n \geq m$.

EXAMPLE 6. We'll show that $n^3 = \Omega(n^2)$ and $3n^2 + 2n = \Omega(n^2)$. Since $n^3 \geq 1n^2$ for all $n \geq 1$, it follows that $n^3 = \Omega(n^2)$. Since $3n^2 + 2n \geq 1n^2$ for all $n \geq 1$, it follows that $3n^2 + 2n = \Omega(n^2)$. ◆

Let's see how we can use the terms that we've defined so far to discuss algorithms. For example, suppose we have constructed an algorithm A to solve some problem P. Suppose further that we've analyzed A and found that it takes $5n^2$ operations in the worst case for an input of size n. This allows us to make a few general statements. First, we can say that the worst case performance of A is $\Theta(n^2)$. Second, we can say that an optimal algorithm for P, if one exists, must have a worst case performance of $O(n^2)$. In other words, an optimal algorithm for P must do no worse than our algorithm A.

Continuing with our example, suppose some good soul has computed a worst case theoretical lower bound of $\Theta(n \log n)$ operations for any algorithm that solves P. Then we can say that an optimal algorithm, if one exists, must have a worst case performance of $\Omega(n \log n)$. In other words, an optimal algorithm for P can do no better than the given lower bound of $\Theta(n \log n)$.

Before we leave our discussion of approximate optimality, let's look at some other ways to use the symbols. The four symbols Θ, o, O, and Ω can also be used to represent terms within an expression. For example, the equation

$$h(n) = 4n^3 + O(n^2)$$

means that $h(n)$ equals $4n^3$ plus a term of order at most n^2. When used as part of an expression, big oh is the most popular of the four symbols because it gives a nice way to concentrate on those terms that contribute the most muscle.

We should also note that the four symbols Θ, o, O, and Ω can be formally defined to represent sets of functions. In other words, for a function g we define the following four sets:

$\mathcal{O}(g)$ is the set of functions of the same order as g;

$o(g)$ is the set of functions of lower order than g;

$O(g)$ is the set of functions of the same order or lower order than g;

$\Omega(g)$ is the set of all functions of the same order or higher order than g.

When set representations are used, we can use an expression like

$$f(n) \in \mathcal{O}(g(n))$$

to mean that f has the same order as g. The set representations also give some nice relationships. For example, we have the following set equalities:

$$O(g(n)) = \mathcal{O}(g(n)) \cup o(g(n)),$$
$$\mathcal{O}(g(n)) = O(g(n)) \cap \Omega(g(n)),$$
$$o(g(n)) = O(g(n)) - \mathcal{O}(g(n)).$$

Exercises

1. Prove that the relation defined by $f(n) = \mathcal{O}(g(n))$ is an equivalence relation.

2. For any constant $k > 0$, prove each of the following statements.
   a. $\log(kn) = \mathcal{O}(\log n)$.
   b. $\log(k + n) = \mathcal{O}(\log n)$.

3. Find an example of an increasing function f such that $f(n) = \mathcal{O}(1)$.

4. Prove the following sequence of orders: $n \prec n \log n \prec n^2$.

5. Find a place to insert the function $\log \log n$ in the sequence (9.15).

6. For each each of the following functions f, find an appropriate place in the sequence (9.15).
   a. $f(n) = \log 1 + \log 2 + \log 3 + \cdots + \log n$.
   b. $f(n) = \log 1 + \log 2 + \log 4 + \cdots + \log 2^n$.

7. For any constant k, show that n^k has lower order than 2^n.

8. For each of the following values of n, calculate the following three numbers: the exact value of $n!$, Stirling's approximation (9.12) for the value of $n!$, and the difference between the two values.
   a. $n = 5$.   b. $n = 10$.

9. Prove the following sequence of orders: $2^n \prec n! \prec n^n$.

10. Let $f(n) = O(h(n))$ and $g(n) = O(h(n))$. Prove each of the following statements.

    a. $af(n) = O(h(n))$ for any real number a.

    b. $f(n) + g(n) = O(h(n))$.

11. We can decide whether an integer $n > 1$ is prime by testing whether n is divisible by 2 or by any odd number from 3 up to $\lfloor \sqrt{n} \rfloor$. Show that this algorithm takes $\Theta(10^{k/2})$ division operations in the worst case, where k is the number of digits in the decimal representation of n.

9.3 Complexity Classes

Some computational problems are impractical because the known algorithms to solve them take too much time or space. In this section we'll make the idea of "too much" more precise by introducing some fundamental complexity classes of problems. The main results of the theory are stated in terms of *decision problems* that ask a question whose answer is either yes or no. So we'll only consider decision problems.

We should note that a computational problem can often be rephrased as a decision problem that reflects the original nature of the problem. For example, the problem of finding the prime factors of a natural number greater than 1 can be rephrased as a decision problem that asks whether a natural number greater than 1 is composite (not prime).

Let's look at another example. The traveling salesman problem is to find the shortest tour of a set of cities that starts and ends at the same city. This problem can be modified to form a decision problem by giving a number B and asking whether there is a tour of the cities that starts and ends at the same city and the length of the tour is less than or equal to B. Here's a more precise statement of the decision version of the traveling salesman problem:

Traveling Salesman Problem

Given a set of cities $\{c_1, ..., c_m\}$, a set of distances $d(c_i, c_j) > 0$ for each $i \neq j$, and a bound $B > 0$, does there exist a tour $\langle v_1, ..., v_m \rangle$ of the m cities (a permutation of the cities) such that

$$d(v_1, v_2) + ... + d(v_{m-1}, v_m) + d(v_m, v_1) \leq B?$$

An *instance* of a decision problem is a specific example of the given part of the problem. For example, an instance I of the traveling salesman problem can be represented as follows:

$$I = \{\langle c_1, c_2, c_3, c_4 \rangle, B = 27, \quad d(c_1, c_2) = 10, \quad d(c_1, c_3) = 5, \quad d(c_1, c_4) = 9,$$
$$d(c_2, c_3) = 6, \quad d(c_2, c_4) = 9, \quad d(c_3, c_4) = 3\}.$$

The *length* of an instance is an indication of the space required to represent the instance. For example, the length of the preceding instance I might be the number of characters that occur between the two braces { and }. Or the length might be some other measure like the number of bits required to represent the instance as an ASCII string. We often approximate the length of an instance. For example, an instance I with m cities contains $m(m - 1)/2$ distances and one bounding relation. We can assume that each of these entities takes more than some constant amount of space. If c is this constant, then the length of I is no more than

$$c(m + 1 + m(m - 1)/2).$$

So we can assume that the length of I is $O(m^2)$.

Sometimes we want more than just a yes or no answer to a decision problem. A *solution* for an instance of a decision problem is a structure that yields a yes answer to the problem. If an instance has a solution, then the instance is called a *yes-instance*. Otherwise the instance is a *no-instance*. For example, the tour $\langle c_1, c_2, c_4, c_3 \rangle$ is a solution for the instance I given previously for the traveling salesman problem because its total distance is 27. But the tour $\langle c_1, c_4, c_3, c_2 \rangle$ is a no-instance because its total distance is 28.

The Class P

Informally, the class P consists of all problems that can be solved in polynomial time. Let's clarify this statement a bit. For our purposes, a *deterministic algorithm* is an algorithm that never makes an arbitrary choice of what to do next during a computation. In other words, each step of the algorithm is uniquely determined. We say that a deterministic algorithm *solves* a decision problem if for each instance of the problem the algorithm halts with the correct answer, yes or no.

Now we can be a bit more precise and say that the class P consists of those decision problems that can be solved by deterministic algorithms that have worst case running times of polynomial order. In short, the class P consists of those decision problems that can be solved by deterministic algorithms of order $O(p(n))$ for some polynomial p. In other words, a decision problem is in the class P if there is a deterministic algorithm A that solves the problem and there is a polynomial p such that for each instance I of the problem we have $W_A(n) \leq p(n)$, where n is the size of I.

There are many familiar problems in the class P. For example, consider the problem determining whether an item can be found in an n-element list. A simple search that compares the item to each element of the list takes at most n comparisons. If we assume that the size of the input is n, then the algorithm solves the problem in time $O(n)$. Thus the problem is in P.

A problem is said to be *tractable* if it is in P and *intractable* if it is not in P. In other words, a problem is intractable if it has a lower bound worst case complexity greater than any polynomial.

The Class NP

Informally, the class NP consists of all problems for which a solution can be checked in polynomial time. Problems in NP can have algorithms that search in a nondeterministic manner for a solution. The stipulation is that a solution path must take no more than polynomial time. Let's clarify things a bit. For our purposes, a *nondeterministic algorithm* for an instance I of a decision problem has two distinct stages as follows:

Guessing Stage: A guess is made at a possible solution S for instance I.

Checking Stage: A deterministic algorithm starts up to supposedly check whether the guess S from the guessing stage is a solution to instance I. This checking algorithm will halt with the answer yes if and only if S is a solution of I. But it may or may not halt if S is not a solution of I.

In theory, the guess at a possible solution S could be made out of thin air. Also in theory, S could be a structure of infinite length so that the guessing stage would never halt. And also in theory, the checking stage may not even consider S.

We say that a nondeterministic algorithm solves a decision problem in polynomial time if there is a polynomial p such that for each yes instance I there is a solution S that when guessed in the guessing stage will lead the checking stage to halt with yes, and the time for the checking stage is less than or equal to $p(n)$, where $n = \text{length}(I)$.

Now we can be a bit more precise and say that the class NP consists of those decision problems that can be solved by nondeterministic algorithms in polynomial time.

Let's consider some relationships between P and NP. The first result is that P is a subset of NP. To see this, notice that any problem π in P has a deterministic algorithm A that solves any instance of π in polynomial time. We can construct a nondeterministic polynomial time algorithm to solve π as follows: For any instance I of π, let the guessing stage make a guess S. Let the checking stage ignore S and run algorithm A on I. This stage will halt with yes or no depending on whether I is a yes instance or not. Therefore π is in *NP*. So we've proven the following simple relationship:

$$P \subset NP. \tag{9.20}$$

So we have a lot of problems—all those in P—that are in *NP*. It is not known whether P and *NP* are equal. In other words, no one has been able to find an *NP* problem that is not in P, which would prove that $P \neq NP$, and no one has been able to prove that all *NP* problems are in P, which would prove that $P = NP$. This problem is one of the foremost open questions of mathematics and computer science.

The traveling salesman problem is an *NP* problem. Let's see why. A guessing stage can guess a tour $\langle v_1, ..., v_m \rangle$ of the m cities. Then the checking stage can check whether

$$d(v_1, v_2) + ... + d(v_{m-1}, v_m) + d(v_m, v_1) \leq B.$$

This check takes $m - 1$ addition operations and one comparison operation. We can assume that each of these operations takes a constant amout of time. Therefore a guess can be checked in time $O(m)$. Since the length of an instance of the traveling salesman problem is $O(m^2)$, it follows that the checking stage takes time $O(\sqrt{n})$, where n is the length of an instance of the problem. So the checking stage can be done in polynomial time (actually better than linear time), it follows that the traveling salesman problem is in *NP*.

It is not known whether the traveling salesman problem is in P. It appears that any deterministic algorithm to solve the problem might have to check all possible tours of m cities. Since each tour begins and ends at the same city, there are $(m - 1)!$ possible tours to check. But $(m - 1)!$ has higher order than any polynomial in m, and thus it also has higher order than any polynomial in m^2. Since the length of an input instance is $O(m^2)$, it follows that the worst case running time of such an algorithm is greater than any polynomial with respect to the length of an input instance.

The Class PSPACE

Now let's look at a class of decision problems that are characterized by the space required by algorithms to solve them. The class *PSPACE* is the set of decision problems that can be solved by algorithms that use no more memory cells than a polynomial in the length of an instance. In other words, a problem is in *PSPACE* if there is an algorithm to solve it and there is a polynomial p such that the algorithm uses no more than $p(n)$ memory cells where n is the length of an instance.

It's easy to see that P and NP are subsets of *PSPACE*. To see this, notice that any step of an algorithm can access at most a fixed finite number of memory cells. If the number of memory cells that be accessed in one step is k, then any algorithm that takes $p(n)$ steps will use at most $kp(n)$ memory cells. If $p(n)$ is a polynomial, then $kp(n)$ is also a polynomial. So we have the following complexity relationships:

$$P \subset NP \subset PSPACE. \tag{9.21}$$

Just as it is not known whether P and NP are equal, it is also not known whether NP and *PSPACE* are equal.

Let's look at a classic example of a *PSPACE* problem. That is, a problem that is in *PSPACE* but for which it is not known whether it is in NP. Before we can state the problem, we need a definition. A *quantified Boolean formula* is a logical expression of the form

$$Q_1 x_1 \, Q_2 x_2 \, ... \, Q_n x_n \, E$$

where $n \geq 1$, each Q_i is either $\forall$ or $\exists$, each x_i is distinct, and E is a wff of the propositional calculus that is restricted to using the variables x_1, ..., x_n, the operations $\neg$, $\wedge$, and $\vee$, and parentheses. For example, the following wffs are quantified Boolean formulas:

$$\exists x \, x,$$
$$\forall x \, \exists y \, \neg \, x \vee y,$$
$$\forall x \, \exists y \, \forall z \, ((x \vee \neg y) \wedge z).$$

A quantified Boolean formula is true if it's value is true over the domain {true, false}. Otherwise it is false. For example, the preceding three formulas have the following values:

$$\exists x \, x \text{ is true,}$$
$$\forall x \, \exists y \, \neg \, x \vee y \text{ is true,}$$
$$\forall x \, \exists y \, \forall z \, ((x \vee \neg y) \wedge z) \text{ is false.}$$

The problem we want to consider is whether a given quantified Boolean formula is true. We'll state the problem as follows:

Quantified Boolean Formula Problem (QBF)

Given a quantified Boolean formula, is it true?

We'll show that *QBF* is in *PSPACE*. An algorithm that tests whether a quantified Boolean formula with n variables is true can proceed to test the formula on all 2^n truth assignments of the n variables. In the worst case, when all n variables are universally quantified, we would have to test all 2^n truth assignments. Although the time required for this algorithm is exponential, the truth assignments can be generated and used to test the formula in a fixed amount of space that is proportional to the length of the given formula. Therefore *QBF* is in *PSPACE*. It is not known whether *QBF* is in *NP*.

Intractable Problems

We haven't yet given an example of an intractable problem (i.e., a problem that is not in P). Of course, any unsolvable problem is intractable because there is no algorithm to solve it. So there is no polynomial time algorithm to solve it. But this isn't very satisfying. So we'll give some real live examples of problems that are intractable.

The first intractable problem involves arithmetic formulas. The problem is to decide the truth of statements in a simple theory about addition of natural numbers. The statements of the theory are expressed as closed wffs of a first-order predicate calculus that uses just + and =. For example, the following formulas are wffs of the theory:

$$\forall x \, \forall y \, (x + y = y + x),$$
$$\exists y \, \forall x \, (x + y = x),$$
$$\forall x \, \forall y \, \exists z \, (\neg \, (x = y) \rightarrow x + z = y),$$
$$\forall x \, \forall y \, \forall z \, (x + (y + z) = (x + y) + z),$$
$$\forall x \forall y \, (x + x = x \rightarrow x + y = y).$$

Each wff of the theory is either true or false when interpreted over the natural numbers. You might notice that one of the preceding example wffs is false and the other four are true. In 1930, Presburger showed that this theory is decidable. In other words, there is an algorithm that can decide whether any wff of the theory is true. The theory has come to be called *Presburger arithmetic*.

Fischer and Rabin [1974] proved that any algorithm to solve the decision problem for Presburger arithmetic must have an exponential lower bound for the number of computational steps. Here's the theorem.

There is a constant $c > 0$ such that for every nondeterministic or deterministic algorithm A that solves the decision problem for Presburger arithmetic, there is a natural number k such that for every natural number $n > k$, there is a wff of length n for which A requires more that $2^{2^{cn}}$ computational steps to decide whether the wff is true.

This statement tells us that the decision problem for Presburger arithmetic is not in *NP*. Therefore it is not in *P*. So it must be intractable.

Now let's look at another problem about Presburger arithmetic that has exponential space complexity. The problem concerns the length of formal proofs in Presburger arithmetic. Fischer and Rabin [1974] proved that any proof system for wffs of Presburger arithmetic contains proofs of exponential length. Here's the theorem.

> There is a positive constant $c > 0$ such that for every formal proof system for Presburger arithmetic, there is a natural number k such that for every natural number $n > k$, there is a true wff of length n for which its shortest formal proof requires more that $2^{2^{cn}}$ symbols.

There is no decision problem mentioned in this theorem. So we don't have a problem to classify. But we can at least conclude that any formal proof system that contains the simple Presburger arithmetic will use a lot of space for some formal proofs.

The second intractable problem involves regular expressions. Recall that the set of *regular expressions* over an alphabet A is defined inductively as follows, where + and · are binary operations and * is a unary operation:

Basis: $\Lambda, \varnothing$, and a are regular expressions for all $a \in A$.

Induction: If R and S are regular expressions, then the following expressions are also regular: $(R), R + S, R{\cdot}S$, and R^*.

For example, here are a few of the infinitely many regular expressions over the alphabet $A = \{a, b\}$:

$$\Lambda, \quad \varnothing, \quad a, \quad b, \quad \Lambda + b, \quad b^*, \quad a + (b{\cdot}a), \quad (a + b){\cdot}a, \quad a{\cdot}b^*, \quad a^* + b^*.$$

Each regular expression represents a regular language. For example, Λ represents the language $\{\Lambda\}$; $\varnothing$ represents the empty language $\varnothing$; $a{\cdot}b^*$ represents the language of all strings that begin with a and are followed by zero or more occurrences of b; and $(a + b)^*$ represents the language $\{a, b\}^*$.

Suppose we extend the definition of regular expressions to include the additional notation $(R)^2$ as an abbreviation for $R{\cdot}R$. For example, we have

$$a{\cdot}a{\cdot}a{\cdot}a{\cdot}a = a{\cdot}((a)^2)^2 = a{\cdot}(a^2){\cdot}(a^2).$$

A *generalized regular expression* is a regular expression that may use this additional notation. Now we're in position to state an intractable problem.

Inequivalence of Generalized Regular Expressions

Given a generalized regular expression R over a finite alphabet A, does the language of R differ from A*.

Here are some examples to help us get the idea:

The language of the expression $(a + b)$* is the same as $\{a, b\}$*.

The language of the expression $\Lambda + (a{\cdot}b)^2 + a$* $+ b$* differs from $\{a, b\}$*.

The language of the expression $\Lambda + (a{\cdot}b)^2 + (a + b)$* is the same as $\{a, b\}$*.

Meyer and Stockmeyer [1972] showed that the problem of inequivalence of generalized regular expressions is intractable. They showed it by proving that any algorithm to solve the problem requires exponential space. So the problem is not in *PSPACE*. Therefore it is not in *NP* and not in *P*. So it is intractable. We should note that the intractablility comes about because we allow abbreviations of the form $(R)^2$. That is, the *inequivalence of regular expressions*, where the abbreviation is not allowed, is in *PSPACE*.

Completeness

Whenever we have a class of things, there is the possibility that some object in the class is a good representative of the class. From the point of view of complexity, we want to find representatives of NP that are connected to the other problems in NP in such a way that if the representative can be solved efficiently, then so can every other problem in NP. This is a bit vague. So let's get down to brass tacks and discuss a mechanism for transforming one problem into another so that an efficient solution for one will automaically give an efficient solution for the other.

A problem A is *polynomially reducible* to a problem B if there is a polynomial time computable function f that maps instances of A to instances of B such that

$$I \text{ is a yes-instance of } A \text{ iff } f(I) \text{ is a yes-instance of } B.$$

This property of f says that yes-instances of A get mapped to yes-instances of B and that no-instances of A get mapped to no-instances of B.

Let's see how we can use this idea to find an efficient algorithm for A from an efficient algorithm for B. Suppose we have found a polynomial time algorithm, say M, to solve B. We'll use M and f to find a polynomial time algorithm that solves A. The algorithm can be described as follows:

Take an arbitrary instance I of problem A. To find out whether I is a yes-instance of A we first construct the instance $f(I)$ of problem B. (There is an efficient algorithm to construct $f(I)$ because f is polynomial time computable.) Then we run algorithm M on the instance $f(I)$. If M finds that $f(I)$ is a yes-instance of B, then it follows from the property of f that I is a yes-instance of A. If M finds that $f(I)$ is a no-instance of B, then it follows from the property of f that I is a no-instance of A. So the efficient algorithm to solve problem A is just the composition of the algorithm M and the algorithm to compute f.

This algorithm solves A and it does it in polynomial time because both the algorithm for B and the algorithm for f are polynomial time algorithms. We'll give an example of polynomial reducibility shortly.

The importance of polynomial reducibility comes into play in discussions about the class *NP*. A decision problem in *NP* is said to be *NP-complete* if every other decision problem in *NP* can be polynomially transformed to it. For example, suppose we could find some problem B in *NP* such that every other problem in *NP* could be polynomially reduced to B. Then it might make sense to concentrate on trying to find an efficient algorithm for B. If we found a deterministic polynomial time algorithm for B, then every problem in *NP* would have a deterministic polynomial time algorithm. In addition to providing us with efficient solutions to many well-known problems, we would also be able to say that *NP* and P are equal.

But we can't start thinking about such things until we know whether there are any *NP*-complete problems. The first example of an *NP*-complete problem is due to Cook [1971]. The problem asks whether a propositional wff in conjunctive normal form is satisfiable. In other words, is there an assignment of truth values to the letters of the formula such that the value of the formula is true? We'll state the problem as follows:

CNF-Satisfiability Problem

Given a propositional wff in conjunctive normal form, is it satisfiable?

For example, $(x \vee y \vee \neg z) \wedge (x \vee z)$ is satisfiable by letting x = true, y = false, and z = false. But $(x \vee y) \wedge (x \vee \neg y) \wedge \neg x$ is not satisfiable because its value is false for any assignments of truth values to x and y.

Cook proved that the CNF-satisfiability problem is *NP*-complete. We'll state the result for the record:

Cook's Theorem

The CNF-satisfiability problem is *NP*-complete.

It's easy to see that CNF-satisfiability is in *NP*. Let the length of a wff be the total number of literals that appear in it. If n is the length of a wff, then the number of distinct variables in the wff is at most n. For example, the length of

$$(x \vee y \vee \neg z) \wedge (x \vee z)$$

is five and the wff has three variables. The guessing stage of a nondeterministic algorithm can produce some assignment of truth values for the variables of the wff. Then the checking stage must check to see whether each fundamental disjunction of the wff is true for the given assignment. Once a literal in some fundamental disjunction is found to be true, then the fundamental disjunction is true. So the checking process can proceed to the next fundamental disjunction. Since there are n literals in the wff, there are at most n literals to check. So the checking stage can be done in $O(n)$ time. Therefore CNF-satisfiability is in *NP*.

Cook proved that CNF-satisfiability is *NP*-complete by showing that any *NP* problem can be polynomially reduced to CNF-satisfiability. The proof is complicated and lengthy. So we won't discuss it. Cook's theorem opened the flood gates for finding other *NP*-complete problems. The reason is that once we have an *NP*-complete problem (e.g., CNF-satisfiability), then to show that some other problem A is *NP*-complete, all we have to do is show that A is in *NP* and then show that some known *NP*-complete problem (e.g., CNF-satisfiability) can be polynomially reduced to A. It follows that any *NP* problem can be polynomially reduced to A by polynomially reducing it to the known *NP*-complete problem that can be polynomially reduced to A. Let's state this result for the record.

If A is an *NP* problem and B is an *NP*-complete problem that is polynomially reducible to A, then A is *NP*-complete.

For example, Cook also proved that a restricted form of CNF-satisfiability is *NP*-complete. The problem is called the *3-satisfiablity problem* because the wffs contain at most three literals in each fundamental disjunction. For example, fundamental disjunctions like

$$(x), \quad (x \vee y), \quad \text{and} \quad (x \vee y \vee z)$$

are allowed. But $(x \vee y \vee z \vee w)$ is not allowed. However, there is no restriction on the number of variables that occur in a restricted expression and there is no limit to the number of fundamental disjunctions that occur. For example, the following expression, which contains five fundamental disjunctions and uses four variables, is OK because each fundamental disjunction has at most three literals:

$$(x \vee \neg y \vee z) \wedge (x \vee \neg y) \wedge (\neg x \vee y \vee w) \wedge (w \vee \neg y) \wedge (x \vee \neg y).$$

Cook proved that the 3-satisfiablity problem is *NP*-complete by showing that CNF-satisfiability can be polynomially reduced to it. Let's state and prove this transformation result.

The 3-satisfiability problem is *NP*-complete.

Proof: The 3-satisfiability problem is in *NP* because it is just a restricted form of the CNF-satisfiability problem, which we know is in *NP*. To show that 3-satisfiability is *NP*-complete, we'll show that CNF-satisfiability can be polynomially reduced to it. The basic idea is to transform each fundamental disjunction that has four or more literals into a conjunctive normal form where each fundamental disjunction has three literals with the property that, for some assignment of truth values to variables, the original fundamental disjunction is true if and only if the replacement conjunctive normal form is true. Here's how the transformation is accomplished. Suppose we have the following fundamental disjunction that contains k literals, where $k \geq 4$:

$$(l_1 \vee l_2 \vee ... \vee l_k).$$

We transform this fundamental disjunction into the following conjunctive normal form, where $x_1, x_2, ..., x_{k-1}$ are new variables :

$$(l_1 \vee l_2 \vee x_1) \wedge (l_3 \vee \neg x_1 \vee x_2) \wedge (l_4 \vee \neg x_2 \vee x_3) \wedge ...$$
$$\wedge (l_{k-2} \vee \neg x_{k-4} \vee x_{k-3}) \wedge (l_{k-1} \vee l_k \vee \neg x_{k-3}).$$

This transformation can be applied to each fundamental disjunction (containing four or more literals) of a conjunctive normal form, resulting in a conjunctive normal form where each each fundamental disjunction has three or fewer literals. For example, the fundamental disjunction

$$(u \vee \neg w \vee x \vee \neg y \vee z)$$

is transformed into

$$(u \vee \neg w \vee x_1) \wedge (x \vee \neg x_1 \vee x_2) \wedge (\neg y \vee z \vee \neg x_2)$$

where x_1 and x_2 are new variables.

The point about the transformation is that there is some assignment to the new variables such that the original fundamental disjunction is true (i.e., one of its literals is true) if and only if the new expression is true. For example, if l_1 = true or l_2 = true, then we can set all the variables x_i to false to make the new expression true. If l_3 = true, then we can set x_1 to true and all the other variables x_i to false to make the new expression true. In general, if l_i = true, then set x_j to true for $j \le i - 2$ and set x_j to false for $j > i - 2$. This will make the new expression true.

Conversely, suppose there is some truth assignment to the variables x_j that makes the new expression is true. Then some literal in the original fundamental disjunction must be true. For example, if x_1 = false, then either l_1 or l_2 must be true. Similarly, if x_{k-3} = true, then either l_{k-1} or l_k must be true. Now assume that x_1 = true and x_{k-3} = false. In this case, there must be an index i, $1 \le i < k - 3$, such that x_i = true and x_{i+1} = false. It follows that l_{i+2} must be true. Therefore some literal must be true, which makes the original fundamental disjunction true.

We need to show that the transformation can be done in polynomial time. An straightforward algorithm to accomplish the transformation applies the definition to each fundamental disjunction that contains four or more literals. If an input wff has length n (i.e., n literals), then there are at most $n/4$ fundamental disjunctions of length four or more. Each of these fundamental disjunctions is transformed into a conjunctive normal form containing at most $3(n - 2)$ literals. Therefore the algorithm constructs at most $3n(n - 2)/4$ literals. Since each new literal can be constructed in a constant amount of time, the algorithm will run in time $O(n^2)$. Therefore the CNF-satisfiability problem can be polynomially reduced to the 3-satisfiablity problem.   QED.

Now we have another *NP*-complete problem. Many *NP*-complete problems have been obtained by exhibiting a polynomial reduction from the 3-satisfiablity problem. No one knows whether the 3-satisfiablity problem is in P. If it were, then we could tell the world that P and NP are the same.

It's natural to wonder about what would happen if we restricted things further and considered the 2-*satisfiablity problem*, where each fundamental disjunction of a conjunctive normal form has at most two literals. It turns out that the 2-satisfiablity problem is in P. In other words, there is a deterministic polynomial time algorithm that solves the 2-satisfiablity problem.

Why hasn't anyone been able to say whether the 3-satisfiablity problem is in P?

We don't know. But we'll look at a deterministic polynomial time algorithm for the 2-satisfiablity problem and discuss why it becomes exponential when extended to the 3-satisfiablity problem.

EXAMPLE 1 (*The 2-Satisfiability Problem is in P*). We'll give a deterministic polynomial time algorithm to solve the 2-satisfiability problem. The algorithm uses the resolution rule for propostions (4.3). Suppose that the input wff has the form

$$C_1 \wedge C_2 \wedge \dots \wedge C_n,$$

where each C_i is a clause (i.e., fundamental disjunction) consisting of either a single literal or the disjunction of two literals. Now we can describe the algorithm. We list the clauses $C_1, C_2, \dots, C_n$ as premises. Then we apply the resolution rule (4.3) to all possible pairs of existing or new clauses until we obtain the empty clause or until no new clauses are obtainable. If we obtain the empty clause, then the original wff is unsatisfiable and we output the answer no. Otherwise the wff is satisfiable and we output the answer yes.

The algorithm is clearly deterministic. Let's discuss why it halts and why it runs in polynomial time. Since each clause has at most two literals, the resolvant of any two clauses contains at most two literals. For example,

> the resolvant of $x \vee y$ and $\neg x \vee z$ is $y \vee z$

and

> the resolvant of $x \vee x$ and $\neg x \vee y$ is y.

Since there are n clauses in the wff, it follows that it has at most $2n$ distinct literals. Since we have the equivalence $x \vee y \equiv y \vee x$, we'll assume that two clauses are identical (not distinct) if they contain the same literals without regard to order. It follows that there are at most $n(2n + 1)$ distinct clauses that contain two literals. There are at most $2n$ distinct clauses consisting of one literal and there is one empty clause. So the algorithm generates at most $2n^2 + 3n + 1$ distinct clauses. Therefore the algorithm will always halt.

We'll leave it as an exercise to show that the number of times that the resolution rule is performed by the algorithm is $O(n^4)$. The algorithm must also spend some time on overhead, like checking to see whether each resolvant is distinct from those that already exist. We'll also leave it as an exercise to show that this checking takes $O(n^6)$ comparisons. So the algorithm runs in polynomial time. Therefore the 2-satisfiability problem is in P.   ◆

The reason that the resolution algorithm for 2-satisfiability runs in polynomial time is that each resolvant has at most two literals. If we were to apply the algorithm to the 3-satisfiability problem, then the number of possible clauses would explode because resolvants might contain up to as many literals as there are in the original wff. For example, notice that

> the resolvant of $x \vee y \vee z$ and $\neg x \vee v \vee w$ is $y \vee z \vee v \vee w$.

So resolvants can get bigger and bigger. If a wff contains n clauses and each clause contains at most three literals, then there are at most $3n$ literals in the wff. If we agree to remove redundant literals from each resolvant, then the maximum number of literals in any resolvant is $3n$. Now we'll count the number of distinct clauses that consist of at most $3n$ literals. Since we're not concerned about the order of occurrence of literals in a clause, it follows that the number of distinct clauses consisting of at most $3n$ literals is equal to the number of subsets of a set with $3n$ elements, which is 2^{3n}. So in the worst case, the algorithm takes exponential time.

On the surface, the 2- and 3-satisfiability problems appear to be similar in difficulty. But after a little analysis, we can see that they appear to be worlds apart. Perhaps someone will eventually use these two problems to help explain whether P and NP are the same or are distinct.

We should mention the notion of NP-hard problems. A problem is NP-*hard* if all NP problems can be polynomially reduced to it. So the difference between NP-complete and NP-hard is that an NP-complete problem must be in NP. An NP-hard problem need not be in NP.

Formal Complexity Theory

Many results in complexity theory are very hard to state and very hard to prove. So practitioners normally try to simplify things as much as possible and formalize things so that statements can be clear and concise, and so that there can be a common means of communicating results. This is done by discussing complexity theory in terms of languages and Turing machines.

We can still discuss any decision problem that we like. But we'll think of each instance of a decision problem as a string over an alphabet of symbols. The set of all yes-instances for the problem forms a language over this alphabet. An algorithm to solve the decision problem will be a Turing machine that recognizes the language of yes-instances.

For example, the problem of deciding whether a natural number $n \geq 2$ is prime can easily be stated as a language recognition problem. We can pick some letter, say a, and define the language

$$L = \{a^n \mid n \text{ is a prime number}\}.$$

Now we can decide whether a natural number $n \geq 2$ is prime by deciding whether a string of two or more a's is in the language L.

Let's get on with things and describe some formal complexity theory. A Turing machine has *time complexity* $t(n)$ if for every input string of length n, it executes at most $t(n)$ instructions before stopping. A language has *time complexity* $t(n)$ if it is accepted by a Turing machine of time complexity $t(n)$. The class *TIME*$(t(n))$ is the set of all languages of time complexity $t(n)$.

If a Turing machine M has time complexity $O(n^k)$ for some natural number k, we say that M has a *polynomial time complexity*. We'll let *DPTIME* be the set of languages that are accepted by deterministic Turing machines in polynomial time. Similarly, we'll let *NPTIME* be the set of languages that are accepted by nondeterministic Turing machines in polynomial time. Since any language accepted by a deterministic Turing machine can also be accepted by a nondeterministic Turing machine—just add a nondeterministic instruction to the deterministic machine—it follows that

$$DPTIME \subset NPTIME. \tag{9.22}$$

Let's see if we can bring space complexity into the discussion. A Turing machine has *space complexity* $s(n)$ if for every input string of length n, it uses at most $s(n)$ tape cells before stopping. A language has *space complexity* $s(n)$ if it is accepted by a Turing machine of space complexity $s(n)$. The class $SPACE(s(n))$ is the set of all languages of space complexity $s(n)$. If a Turing machine M has space complexity $O(n^k)$ for some natural number k, we say that M has a *polynomial space complexity*.

Let $DSPACE(s(n))$ be the set of languages accepted by deterministic Turing machines of space complexity $s(n)$. Let $NSPACE(s(n))$ be the set languages accepted by nondeterministic Turing machines of space complexity $s(n)$. Let *DPSPACE* be the set languages accepted by deterministic Turing machines in polynomial space. Let *NPSPACE* be the set of languages accepted by nondeterministic Turing machines in polynomial space. The nice thing about these classes of languages is the following equality, which we'll discuss in an exercise:

$$DPSPACE = NPSPACE.$$

Because of this equality, we'll use *PSPACE* to denote the common value of these two equal sets. In other words, *PSPACE* is the set of languages that are accepted by either deterministic or nondeterministic Turing machines in polynomial space.

Now let's discuss the connection between the time and space classes. If a Turing machine has time complexity $t(n)$, then it uses n tape cells to store the input string and, since it can access only one tape cell per instruction, it uses at most $t(n)$ more cells during its computation. So the space complexity of the Turing machine is

$$t(n) + n.$$

If $t(n)$ is a polynomial, then $t(n) + n$ is also a polynomial. So if a language is accepted by a nondeterministic Turing machine in polynomial time, then it is also accepted by the same Turing machine in polynomial space. In other words, we can write

$$NPTIME \subset PSPACE. \tag{9.23}$$

We can put (9.22) and (9.23) together to obtain the following fundamental relationships between classes:

$$DPTIME \subset NPTIME \subset PSPACE. \tag{9.24}$$

The class DPTIME is usually denoted by P and the class *NPTIME* is usually denoted by *NP*. This gives us the more popular representation of (9.24) as follows:

$$P \subset NP \subset PSPACE. \tag{9.25}$$

It is widely believed that these containments are proper. But no one has been able to prove or disprove whether either containment is proper. In other words, it is not known whether there is a language in *NP* that is not in *P* and it is not known whether there is a language in *PSPACE* that is not in *NP*. These are among the most important unresolved questions in present day computer science.

Now let's discuss the idea of polynomial reducibility in terms of languages and Turing machines. First, we'll say that a function is polynomial time computable if it can be computed in polynomial time by some Turing machine. Now, we say that a language K over alphabet A is *polynomially reducible* to a language L over alphabet B if there is a polynomial time computable function $f : A^* \to B^*$ such that

$$x \in K \quad \text{if and only if} \quad f(x) \in L.$$

This property of f says that the language K gets mapped by f into the language L and its complement gets mapped by f into the complement of L. In other words, the property can be written as follows:

$$f(K) \subset L \quad \text{and} \quad f(A^* - K) \subset (B^* - L).$$

Let's see how we can use this idea. If we happen to find an efficient Turing machine, say M, that accepts language L, then we can also find an efficient Turing machine that accepts language K. Here's how. Take an arbitrary string $x \in A^*$. To find out whether x is in K we first construct $f(x)$. (There is an efficient Turing machine to construct f because it is polynomial time computable.) Then we run Turing machine M with input $f(x)$. If M accepts $f(x)$, then $f(x) \in L$, which, by the property of f, implies that $x \in K$. If M rejects $f(x)$, then $f(x) \notin L$, which, by the property of f, implies that $x \notin K$. So the efficient Turing machine to accept language K is just the composition of the Turing machine M and the Turing machine to compute f.

The purpose of this section has been to give a very brief introduction to complexity classes. The book by Garey and Johnson [1979] is a good choice to begin further study. Among other good things, it contains a very large list of *NP*-complete problems.

Exercises

1. Transform $(u \vee v \vee w \vee x \vee y \vee z)$ into an equivalent conjunctive normal form where each fundamental disjunction has three literals.

2. The 1-*satisfiability problem* is to determine whether a conjunction of literals is satisfiable. Prove that the 1-satisfiability problem is in P by finding a deterministic polynomial time algorithm to solve it.

3. Show that the worst case complexity for the number of resolution steps required in the resolution algorithm for the 2-satisfiability problem in Example 1 is $O(n^4)$. Then show that the worst case complexity for the number of comparisons that must be made to see whether a resolvant is distinct from those already in existence is $O(n^6)$.

4. For each of the following questions, assume that A is an *NP* problem.

   a. Suppose you prove a theorem showing that a lower bound for the running time of any algorithm to solve A is $\Theta(2^n)$. What would you tell the world?

   b. Suppose you find a deterministic algorithm that solves A in polynomial time. What would you tell the world?

   c. Suppose A is NP-complete and you find a deterministic algorithm that solves A in polynomial time. What would you tell the world?

   d. Suppose you prove that the 3-satisfiablility problem is polynomially reducible to A. What would you tell the world?

5. Let $DSPACE(s(n))$ be the languages accepted by deterministic Turing machines of space complexity $s(n)$. Let $NSPACE(s(n))$ be the set languages accepted by nondeterministic Turing machines of space complexity $s(n)$. Let $DPSPACE$ be the set languages accepted by deterministic Turing machines in polynomial space. Let $NPSPACE$ be the set of languages accepted by nondeterministic Turing machines in polynomial space. There is a theorem that states $NSPACE(n^i) \subset DSPACE(n^{2i})$. Use this result to prove that $DPSPACE = NPSPACE$.

Chapter Summary

This chapter introduces some basic ideas of computational complexity with respect to the worst case running time of algorithms for problems. An optimal algorithm for a problem is usually hard to find because it must perform better than all algorithms that exist or will ever exist.

It often makes sense to find approximations for the functions that describe the number of operations performed by algorithms. We use the rate of growth of a function as a means to compare one function to another. The symbols used for such comparisons are big theta, little oh, big oh, and big omega.

The class P consists of the decision problems that can be solved by deterministic polynomial time algorithms. The class NP consists of the decision problems that can be solved by nondeterministic polynomial time algorithms. The class $PSPACE$ consists of the decision problems that can be solved by polynomial space algorithms. It follows that

$$P \subset NP \subset PSPACE.$$

The question of whether these containments are proper is an important open problem.

Answers to Selected Exercises

Chapter 1

Section 1.1

1. Consider the four statements "if $1 = 1$ then $2 = 2$," "if $1 = 1$ then $2 = 3$," "if $1 = 0$ then $2 = 2$," and "if $1 = 0$ then $2 = 3$." The second statement is the only one that is false.

3. a. 47 is a prime between 45 and 54. **c.** 9 is odd but not prime. Therefore the statement is false.

4. Let $d \mid m$ and $m \mid n$. Then there are integers k and j such that $m = d \cdot k$ and $n = m \cdot j$. Therefore we can write $n = m \cdot j = (d \cdot k) \cdot j = d \cdot (k \cdot j)$, which says that $d \mid n$.

5. a. Let x and y be any two even integers. Then they can be written in the form $x = 2m$ and $y = 2n$ for some integers m and n. Therefore the sum $x + y$ can be written as $x + y = 2m + 2n = 2(m + n)$, which is an even integer.

7. Let $x = 3m + 4$, and let $y = 3n + 4$ for some integers m and n. Then the product $x \cdot y$ has the form $x \cdot y = (3m + 4)(3n + 4) = 9mn + 12m + 12n + 16 = 3(3mn + 4m + 4n + 4) + 4$, which has the same form as x and y.

9. First we'll prove the statement "if x is odd then x^2 is odd." If x is odd, then $x = 2n + 1$ for some integer n. Therefore $x^2 = (2n + 1)(2n + 1) = 4n^2 + 4n + 1 = 2(2n^2 + 2n) + 1$, which is an odd integer. Now we must prove the second statement "if x^2 is odd then x is odd." We'll do it indirectly by proving the contrapositive of the statement, which is "if x is even then x^2 is even." If x is even, then $x = 2n$ for some integer n. Therefore $x^2 = 2n \cdot 2n = 2(2n^2)$, which is even. Therefore the second statement is also true.

Section 1.2

1. a. True. **c.** False. **e.** True. **g.** True.

3. $A = \{x\}$ and $B = \{x, \{x\}\}$.

4. a. $\{\varnothing, \{x\}, \{y\}, \{z\}, \{w\}, \{x, y\}, \{x, z\}, \{x, w\}, \{y, z\}, \{y, w\}, \{z, w\}, \{x, y, z\}, \{x, y, w\}, \{x, z, w\}, \{y, z, w\}, \{x, y, z, w\}$. **c.** $\{\varnothing\}$. **e.** $\{\varnothing, \{\{a\}\}, \{\varnothing\}, \{\{a\}, \varnothing\}\}$.

6. Let $S \in \text{power}(A \cap B)$. Then $S \subset A \cap B$, which says that $S \subset A$ and $S \subset B$. Therefore $S \in \text{power}(A)$ and $S \in \text{power}(B)$, which says that $S \in \text{power}(A) \cap \text{power}(B)$. This proves that $\text{power}(A \cap B) \subset \text{power}(A) \cap \text{power}(B)$. The other containment is similar.

7. No. A counterexample is $A = \{a\}$ and $B = \{b\}$.

8. a. A counterexample is $A = \{a\}$ and $B = \{b\}$. **c.** A counterexample is $A = \{a\}$, $B = \{b\}$, and $C = \{b\}$.

9. a. $[x, y, z]$, $[x, y]$. **c.** $[a, a, a, b, b, c]$, $[a, a, b]$. **e.** $[x, x, a, a, [a, a], [a, a]]$, $[x, x]$.

11. Let A and B be bags, and let m and n be the number of times x occurs in A and B, respectively. If $m \geq n$, then put $m - n$ occurrences of x in $A - B$, and if $m < n$, then do not put any occurrences of x in $A - B$.

13. $\langle x, x, x \rangle$, $\langle x, x, y \rangle$, $\langle x, y, x \rangle$, $\langle y, x, x \rangle$, $\langle x, y, y \rangle$, $\langle y, x, y \rangle$, $\langle y, y, x \rangle$, $\langle y, y, y \rangle$.

14. a. $\{\langle a, a \rangle, \langle a, b \rangle, \langle b, a \rangle, \langle b, b \rangle, \langle c, a \rangle, \langle c, b \rangle\}$. **c.** $\{\langle \, \rangle\}$.
e. $\{\langle a, a \rangle, \langle a, b \rangle, \langle a, c \rangle, \langle b, a \rangle, \langle b, b \rangle, \langle b, c \rangle, \langle c, a \rangle, \langle c, b \rangle, \langle c, c \rangle\}$.

15. a. Show that the two sets are equal by showing that each is a subset of the other. Let $\langle x, y \rangle \in (A \cup B) \times C$. Then either $x \in A$ or $x \in B$, and $y \in C$. So either $\langle x, y \rangle \in A \times C$ or $\langle x, y \rangle \in B \times C$. Thus $\langle x, y \rangle \in (A \times C) \cup (B \times C)$, and we have the containment $(A \cup B) \times C \subset (A \times C) \cup (B \times C)$. For the other containment, let $\langle x, y \rangle \in (A \times C) \cup (B \times C)$. Then either $\langle x, y \rangle \in A \times C$ or $\langle x, y \rangle \in B \times C$, which says that either $x \in A$ or $x \in B$, and $y \in C$. Thus $\langle x, y \rangle \in (A \cup B) \times C$ and we have the containment $(A \times C) \cup (B \times C) \subset (A \cup B) \times C$. The two containments show that the sets are equal.
c. We'll prove that $(A \cap B) \times C = (A \times C) \cap (B \times C)$ by showing that each side is a subset of the other. Since we have $A \cap B \subset A$ and $A \cap B \subset B$, it follows that $(A \cap B) \times C \subset (A \times C) \cap (B \times C)$. Now let $\langle x, y \rangle \in (A \times C) \cap (B \times C)$. Then we have $x \in A \cap B$ and $y \in C$, which implies that $\langle x, y \rangle \in (A \cap B) \times C$. This gives the containment $(A \times C) \cap (B \times C) \subset (A \cap B) \times C$. The two containments show that the sets are equal.

Section 1.3

1. There are eight total functions of type $\{a, b, c\} \to \{1, 2\}$. For example, one function sends all elements of $\{a, b, c\}$ to 1; another function sends all elements of $\{a, b, c\}$ to 2; another sends a and b to 1 and c to 2; and so on.

2. a. O. **c.** $\{x \mid x = 4k + 3 \text{ where } k \in \mathbb{N}\}$. **e.** $\mathbb{N}$.

3. a. -5. **c.** 4.

4. a. 3. **c.** -9.

5. a. $f(\{0, 2, 4\}) = \{0, 2, 4\}$; $f^{-1}(\{0, 2, 4\}) = \mathbb{N}_6$.
c. $f(\{0, 5\}) = \{0, 4\}$; $f^{-1}(\{0, 5\}) = \{0, 3\}$.

6. a. A. **c.** $\{0\}$.

7. a. Eight functions; no injections, six surjections, no bijections, and two with none of the properties. **c.** 27 functions; six satisfy the three properties (injective, surjective, and bijective), 21 with none of the properties.

8. The fatherOf function is not injective because some fathers have more than one child. The fatherOf function is not surjective because there are people who are not fathers.

9. a. Let $f(x) = f(y)$. Then $\dfrac{1}{x+1} = \dfrac{1}{y+1}$, which says that $x = y$, which implies that f is injective. To show that f is surjective, let $y \in (0, 1)$. Solving the equation $\dfrac{1}{x+1} = y$ for x yields $x = \dfrac{1-y}{y}$, which is a positive real number Thus $f(x) = y$, which says that f is surjective. Therefore f is a bijection.

10. a. Let $f(x) = f(y)$. Then $\dfrac{x}{1-x} = \dfrac{y}{1-y}$, which says that $x - xy = y - xy$. Cancelling $-xy$ yields $x = y$, which implies that f is injective. To show that f is surjective, let y be a positive real number. Solving the equation $\dfrac{x}{1-x} = y$ for x yields $x = \dfrac{y}{1+y}$, which is in the interval $(0, 1)$. Thus $f(x) = y$, which says that f is surjective. Therefore f is a bijection.

11. Suppose $(0, 1)$ is countable. Then we can list all the numbers in $(0, 1)$ as r_0, $r_1, r_2, ..., r_n, ...$. Each of these numbers can be represented as an infinite decimal form. (For example, $\frac{1}{2} = 0.50000000...$.) Now we can apply (1.21) to conclude that there is some number in $(0, 1)$ that is not in our listing. This contradiction tells us that $(0, 1)$ is uncountable.

Section 1.4
1. a. $L \cdot M = \{bba, ab, a, abbbba, abbab, abba, bbba, bab, ba\}$.
c. $L^2 = \{\Lambda, abb, b, abbabb, abbb, babb, bb\}$.

2. a. $L = \{b, ba\}$. **c.** $L = \{a, b\}$.

3. a. The statement is true because $A^0 = \{\Lambda\}$ for any language A. **b.** We'll prove the equality $L^* = L^* \cdot L^*$ by showing containment of sets. First we have $L^* = L^* \cdot \{\Lambda\}$ and $L^* \cdot \{\Lambda\} \subset L^* \cdot L^*$. Therefore $L^* \subset L^* \cdot L^*$. Next, if $x \in L^* \cdot L^*$, then $x = y \cdot z$, where $y, z \in L^*$. Then there are natural numbers m and n such that $y \in L^m$ and $z \in L^n$. Therefore $x = y \cdot z$ in L^{m+n}, which is a subset of L^*. Therefore we have the other containment $L^* \cdot L^* \subset L^*$. The equality $L^* = (L^*)^*$ is proved similarly: L^* is a subset of $(L^*)^*$ by definition. For the other way, if $x \in (L^*)^*$, then there is a number n such that $x \in (L^*)^n$. So x is a concatenation of n strings, each one from L^*. So x is a concatenation of n strings, each from some power of L. Therefore $x \in L^*$. Therefore $(L^*)^* \subset L^*$.

4. a. $S \rightarrow DS, D \rightarrow 7, S \rightarrow DS, S \rightarrow DS, D \rightarrow 8, D \rightarrow 0, S \rightarrow D, D \rightarrow 1$. **c.** $S \Rightarrow DS \Rightarrow DDS \Rightarrow DDDS \Rightarrow DDDD \Rightarrow DDD1 \Rightarrow DD01 \Rightarrow D801 \Rightarrow 7801$.

5. a. $S \rightarrow bb \mid bbS$. **c.** $S \rightarrow \Lambda \mid abS$.

6. a. $O \rightarrow D1 \mid D3 \mid D5 \mid D7 \mid D9$, and $D \rightarrow \Lambda \mid D0 \mid D1 \mid D2 \mid D3 \mid D4 \mid D5 \mid D6 \mid D7 \mid D8 \mid D9$.

7. $S \rightarrow \Lambda \mid aSa \mid bSb \mid cSc$.

8. a. $S \rightarrow aSb \mid \Lambda$.
c. $S \rightarrow T \mid C, T \rightarrow a\, Tc \mid b, C \rightarrow BA, B \rightarrow bB \mid \Lambda$, and $A \rightarrow aA \mid \Lambda$.

10. a. The set of all strings of balanced pairs of brackets.

Chapter 2

Section 2.1

1. a. The basis case is the statement $1 \in \text{Odd}$, and the induction case states that if $x \in \text{Odd}$, then $\text{succ}(\text{succ}(x)) \in \text{Odd}$. **c.** Basis: $4, 3 \in S$. Induction: If $x \in S$ then $x + 3 \in S$.

2. a. For the base case, put $\langle\,\rangle \in \text{Even}[A]$. For the induction case, if $L \in \text{Even}[A]$ and $a, b \in A$, then put $\text{cons}(a, \text{cons}(b, L)) \in \text{Even}[A]$.

3. Basis: $\langle\,\rangle, \langle a \rangle, \langle b \rangle \in S$. Induction: If $x \in S$ and $x \neq \langle\,\rangle$, then if $\text{head}(x) = a$ then put $\text{cons}(b, x) \in S$, else put $\text{cons}(a, x) \in S$.

4. Basis: $0, 1 \in B$. Induction: If $x \in B$ and $\text{head}(x) = 1$, then put the following four strings in B: $x \cdot 1 \cdot 0, x \cdot 1 \cdot 1, x \cdot 0 \cdot 1$, and $x \cdot 0 \cdot 0$.

6. a. $B = \{\langle x, y \rangle \mid x, y \in \mathbb{N} \text{ and } x \geq y\}$.

7. a. First definition: Basis: $\langle\langle\,\rangle, \langle\,\rangle\rangle \in S$. Induction: If $\langle x, y \rangle \in S$ and $a \in A$, then $\langle a{::}x, y \rangle, \langle x, a{::}y \rangle \in S$. Second definition: Basis: $\langle\langle\,\rangle, L \rangle \in S$ for all $L \in \text{Lists}[A]$. Induction: If $a \in A$ and $\langle K, L \rangle \in S$, then $\langle a{::}K, L \rangle \in S$. **c.** First definition: Basis: $\langle 0, \langle\,\rangle\rangle \in S$. Induction: If $\langle x, L \rangle \in S$ and $m \in \mathbb{N}$, then $\langle x, m{::}L \rangle$, $\langle \text{succ}(x), L \rangle \in S$. Second definition: Basis: $\langle 0, L \rangle \in S$ for all $L \in \text{Lists}[\mathbb{N}]$. Induction: If $\langle n, L \rangle \in S$ and $n \in \mathbb{N}$, then $\langle \text{succ}(n), L \rangle \in S$.

8. Put $\langle\,\rangle \in E$ and all single-node trees in O as basis cases. For the induction case, consider the following four situations: (1) if $t \in O$ and $a \in A$, then put $\text{tree}(t, a, \langle\,\rangle)$ and $\text{tree}(\langle\,\rangle, a, t)$ in E; (2) if $t \in E$ and $a \in A$, then put $\text{tree}(t, a, \langle\,\rangle)$ and $\text{tree}(\langle\,\rangle, a, t)$ in O; (3) if $s, t \in O$ and $a \in A$, then put $\text{tree}(s, a, t)$ in O; if $s \in O, t \in E$, and $a \in A$, then put $\text{tree}(s, a, t)$ and $\text{tree}(t, a, s)$ in E.

9. a. Basis: $\Lambda \in L(G)$. Induction: If $w \in L(G)$, then put $aaw \in L(G)$.

Section 2.2

1. We'll unfold the leftmost term in each expression:

$$\text{fib}(4) = \text{fib}(3) + \text{fib}(2) = \text{fib}(2) + \text{fib}(1) + \text{fib}(2) = \text{fib}(1) + \text{fib}(0) + \text{fib}(1) + \text{fib}(2)$$
$$= 1 + \text{fib}(0) + \text{fib}(1) + \text{fib}(2) = 1 + 0 + \text{fib}(1) + \text{fib}(2) = 1 + 0 + 1 + \text{fib}(2)$$
$$= 1 + 0 + 1 + \text{fib}(1) + \text{fib}(0) = 1 + 0 + 1 + 1 + \text{fib}(0) = 1 + 0 + 1 + 1 + 0$$
$$= 3.$$

2. Assume lists are not empty. Then "small" can be defined as follows:

$$\text{small}(L) = \quad \text{if tail}(L) = \langle \, \rangle \text{ then head}(L)$$
$$\text{else if head}(L) < \text{small}(\text{tail}(L)) \text{ then head}(L)$$
$$\text{else small}(\text{tail}(L)).$$

3. 1, 1, 2, 2, 3, 4, 4, 4, 5, 6, 7, 7, 8, 8, 8, 8, 9.

6. Modify (2.8) by adding another basis case to return 1 if the input is 1:

$$\text{bin}(x) = \quad \text{if } x = 0 \text{ then } 0$$
$$\text{else if } x = 1 \text{ then } 1$$
$$\text{else cat}(\text{bin}(\text{floor}(x/2), x \bmod 2)).$$

7. a. In(T): **if** $T \neq \langle \, \rangle$ **then** In(left(T)); print(root(T)); In(right(T)) **fi.**

8. a. isMember(x, L) $=$ if $L = \langle \, \rangle$ then false
$$\text{else if } x = \text{head}(L) \text{ then true}$$
$$\text{else isMember}(x, \text{tail}(L)).$$

c. areEqual(K, L) = if isSubset(K, L) then isSubset(L, K) else false.

e. intersect(K, L) $=$ if $K = \langle \, \rangle$ then $\langle \, \rangle$
$$\text{else if isMember}(\text{head}(K), L) \text{ then}$$
$$\text{head}(K) :: \text{intersect}(\text{tail}(K), L)$$
$$\text{else}$$
$$\text{intersect}(\text{tail}(K), L).$$

9. Assume that the product of the empty list $\langle \, \rangle$ with any list is $\langle \, \rangle$. Then define product as follows:

$$\text{product}(A, B) = \quad \text{if } A = \langle \, \rangle \text{ or } B = \langle \, \rangle \text{ then } \langle \, \rangle$$
$$\text{else concatenate the four lists}$$
$$\langle \langle \text{head}(A), \text{head}(B) \rangle \rangle,$$
$$\text{product}(\langle \text{head}(A) \rangle, \text{tail}(B)),$$
$$\text{product}(\text{tail}(A), \langle \text{head}(B) \rangle), \text{ and}$$
$$\text{product}(\text{tail}(A), \text{tail}(B)).$$

10. $f(x) = x - 10$ for $x > 10$ and $f(x) = 1$ for $0 \leq x \leq 10$.

Section 2.3

1. a.   **c.**

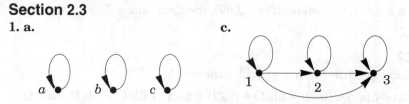

2. a. Symmetric. **c.** Reflexive and transitive.

3. The symmetric and transitive properties are conditional statements. Therefore they are always true for the vacuous cases when their hypotheses are false.

4. a. isGrandchildOf. **c.** isNephewOf.

5. a. {⟨a, a⟩, ⟨b, b⟩, ⟨c, c⟩, ⟨a, b⟩, ⟨b, c⟩}. **c.** {⟨a, b⟩}.
e. {⟨a, a⟩, ⟨b, b⟩, ⟨c, c⟩, ⟨a, b⟩}. **g.** {⟨a, a⟩, ⟨b, b⟩, ⟨c, c⟩}.

6. $r(\varnothing) = \{\langle a, a \rangle \mid a \in A\}$, which is basic equality over A.

7. a. $\varnothing$. **c.** {⟨a, b⟩, ⟨b, a⟩, ⟨b, c⟩, ⟨c, b⟩}.

8. a. $\varnothing$. **c.** {⟨a, b⟩, ⟨b, a⟩, ⟨a, a⟩, ⟨b, b⟩}.

9. a. isAncestorOf. **c.** greater.

10. a. Yes, it's an equivalence relation. The statement "$a + b$ is even" is the same as saying that a and b are both odd or both even. Using this fact, it's easy to prove the three properties.
c. Yes. The statement $ab > 0$ means that a and b have the same sign. Using this fact, it's easy to prove the three properties. Another way is to observe that there is a function "sign" such that $ab > 0$ if and only if sign(a) = sign(b). Thus the relation is a kernel relation, which we know is an equivalence relation.
e. Yes. Check the three properties.

12. R is reflexive and symmetric, but it's not transitive. For example, 2 R 6 and 6 R 12, but 2 $R̸$ 12.

13. a. No. **c.** Yes. **e.** No.

14. a.   **b.**   **c.**

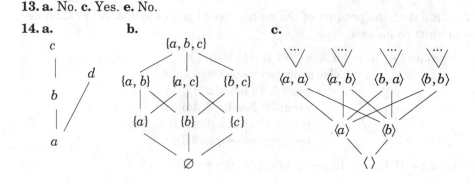

15. a. No tree has fewer than zero nodes. Therefore every descending chain of trees is finite if the order is by the number of nodes. **c.** No list has length less than zero. Therefore every descending chain of lists is finite if the order is by the length of the list.

16. Yes.

Section 2.4

1. a. The equation is true for $n = 1$ because $1^2 = \dfrac{1\,(1 + 1)\,(2 \cdot 1 + 1)}{6}$. So assume that the equation is true for n, and prove that it's true for $n + 1$. Starting with the left side of the equation for $n + 1$, we get

$$1^2 + 2^2 + \ldots + n^2 + (n + 1)^2 \;=\; (1^2 + 2^2 + \ldots + n^2) + (n + 1)^2$$

$$= \frac{n(n + 1)\,(2n + 1)}{6} + (n + 1)^2$$

$$= \frac{(n + 1)\,((n + 1) + 1)\,(2(n + 1) + 1)}{6}.$$

c. The equation is true if $n = 1$ because we get $1 = 1^2$. Next, assume that the equation is true for n, and prove that it's true for $n + 1$. Starting on the left-hand side, we get

$$1 + 3 + \ldots + (2n - 1) + (2(n + 1) - 1) = (1 + 3 + \ldots + (2n - 1)) + (2(n + 1) - 1)$$

$$= n^2 + (2(n + 1) - 1)$$

$$= n^2 + 2n + 1 = (n + 1)^2.$$

2. For $n = 0$ the equation becomes $0 = 1 - 1$. Assume that the equation is true for n. Then the case for $n + 1$ goes as follows:

$$F_0 + F_1 + \ldots + F_n + F_{n+1} = (F_0 + F_1 + \ldots + F_n) + F_{n+1} = F_{n+2} - 1 + F_{n+1} = F_{n+3} - 1.$$

3. a. For $n = 0$ the equation becomes $2 = 3 - 1$. Assume that the equation is true for n. Then the case for $n + 1$ goes as follows:

$$L_0 + L_1 + \ldots + L_n + L_{n+1} = (L_0 + L_1 + \ldots + L_n) + L_{n+1} = L_{n+2} - 1 + L_{n+1} = L_{n+3} - 1.$$

4. For $n = 1$ the equation becomes $a = a$. Assume that the equation is true for n and prove the $n + 1$ case as follows:

$$a + ar + ar^2 + \ldots + ar^{n-1} + ar^n = a\left(\frac{r^n - 1}{r - 1}\right) + ar^n$$

$$= a\left(\frac{r^n - 1 + (r - 1)r^n}{r - 1}\right) = a\left(\frac{r^{n+1} - 1}{r - 1}\right).$$

6. For $n = 1$ the equation becomes $a_1 = (1/2)(a_1 + a_1) = a_1$. Assume that the equation is true for n and prove the $n + 1$ case as follows:

$$a_1 + \ldots + a_n + a_{n+1} = \frac{n}{2}(a_1 + a_n) + a_{n+1}.$$

Now use the fact that there is a constant difference, say c, between each number of the progression (e.g., $a_{n+1} = a_n + c = a_1 + nc$) to transform the last expression into the following expression for the $n + 1$ case:

$$\frac{n+1}{2}(a_1 + a_{n+1}).$$

7. Power($\varnothing$) = $\{\varnothing\}$. So a finite set with 0 elements has 2^0 subsets. Now let A be a set with $|A| = n > 0$, and assume that the statement is true for any set with fewer than n elements. We can write $A = \{x\} \cup B$, where $|B| = n - 1$. So we can write power(A) as the union of two disjoint sets: power(A) = power(B) $\cup \{\{x\} \cup C \mid C \in$ power(B)$\}$. Since $x \notin B$, these two sets have the same cardinality, which by induction is 2^{n-1}. In other words, we have $|\{\{x\} \cup C \mid C \in$ power(B)$\}| = |$power(B)$| = 2^{n-1}$. Therefore $|$power(A)$| = |$power(B)$| + |\{\{x\} \cup C \mid C \in$ power(B)$\}| = 2^{n-1} + 2^{n-1} = 2^n$. Therefore any finite set with n elements has 2^n subsets.

8. a. If $L = \langle x \rangle$, then forward(L) = {print(head(L)); forward(tail(L))} = {print(x); forward($\langle\ \rangle$)} = {print(x)}. We'll use the well-founded ordering based on the length of lists. Let L be a list with n elements, where $n > 1$, and assume that forward is correct for all lists with fewer than n elements. Then forward(L) = {print(head(L)); forward(tail(L))}. Since tail(L) has fewer than n elements, forward(tail(L)) correctly prints out the elements of tail(L) in the order listed. Since print(head(L)) is executed before forward(tail(L)), it follows that forward(L) is correct.

9. a. We can use well-founded induction, where $L \prec M$ if length(L) < length(M). Since an empty list is sorted and sort($\langle\ \rangle$) = $\langle\ \rangle$, it follows that the function is correct for the basis case $\langle\ \rangle$. For the induction case, assume that sort(L) is sorted for all lists L of length n, and show that sort($x :: L$) is sorted. By definition, we have sort($x :: L$) = insert(x, sort(L)). The induction assumption implies that sort(L) is sorted. Therefore insert(x, sort(L)) is sorted by the assumption in the problem. Thus sort($x :: L$)) is sorted.

10. Let $\prec$ denote the lexicographic ordering on $\mathbb{N} \times \mathbb{N}$. Then $\mathbb{N} \times \mathbb{N}$ is a well-ordered set, hence well-founded with least element $\langle 0, 0 \rangle$. We'll use (2.17) to prove that $f(x, y)$ is defined (i.e., halts) for all $\langle x, y \rangle \in \mathbb{N} \times \mathbb{N}$. First we have $f(0, 0) = 0 + 1 = 1$. So $f(0, 0)$ is defined. Thus Step 1 of (2.17) is done. Now to Step 2. Assume that $\langle x, y \rangle \in \mathbb{N} \times \mathbb{N}$, and assume that $f(x', y')$ is defined for all $\langle x', y' \rangle$ such that $\langle x', y' \rangle \prec \langle x, y \rangle$. To finish Step 2, we must show that $f(x, y)$ is defined. The definition of $f(x, y)$ gives us three possibilities:

1. If $x = 0$, then $f(x, y) = y + 1$. Thus $f(x, y)$ is defined.
2   If $x \neq 0$ and $y = 0$, then $f(x, y) = f(x - 1, 1)$. Since $\langle x - 1, 1 \rangle \prec \langle x, y \rangle$, our assumption says that $f(x - 1, 1)$ is defined. Therefore $f(x, y)$ is defined.
3. If $x \neq 0$ and $y \neq 0$, then $f(x, y) = f(x - 1, f(x, y - 1))$. First notice that we have $\langle x, y - 1 \rangle \prec \langle x, y \rangle$. So our assumption says that $f(x, y - 1)$ is defined. Thus the pair $\langle x - 1, f(x, y - 1) \rangle$ is a valid element of $\mathbb{N} \times \mathbb{N}$. Now, since we have $\langle x - 1, f(x, y - 1) \rangle \prec \langle x, y \rangle$ our assumption again applies to say that $f(x - 1, f(x, y - 1))$ is defined. Therefore $f(x, y)$ is defined.

So Steps 1 and 2 of (2.17) have been accomplished for the statement "$f(x, y)$ is defined." Therefore $f(x, y)$ is defined for all natural numbers x and y. QED.

Section 2.5

1. The zero is m because $\min(x, m) = \min(m, x) = m$ for all $x \in A$. The identity is n because $\min(x, n) = \min(n, x) = x$ for all $x \in A$. If $x, y \in A$ and $\min(x, y) = n$, then x and y are inverses of each other. Since n is the largest element of A, it follows that n is the only element with an inverse.

2. The zero is $\varnothing$ and the identity is $\{\Lambda\}$. The only language with an inverse is $\{\Lambda\}$ itself.

3. $S = \{a, f(a), f^2(a), f^3(a), f^4(a)\}$.

4. $\text{monus}(x, 0) = x$, $\text{monus}(0, y) = 0$, $\text{monus}(s(x), s(y)) = \text{monus}(x, y)$, where $s(x)$ denotes the successor of x.

5. $\text{reverse}(L) =$ if $\text{isEmptyL}(L)$ then L
              else $\text{cat}(\text{reverse}(\text{tail}(L)), \langle \text{head}(L) \rangle)$.

8. $f(\Lambda) = \text{length}(\Lambda) = 0$, and if x and y are arbitrary strings in A^*, then $f(\text{cat}(x, y)) = \text{length}(\text{cat}(x, y)) = \text{length}(x) + \text{length}(y) = f(x) + f(y)$.

10. a. $\{(ab)^n b \mid n \in \mathbb{N}\}$. **c.** $\varnothing$. **e.** $\{ba^n \mid n \in \mathbb{N}\}$.

Chapter 3

Section 3.1

1. a. $(A \rightarrow B) \wedge (A \vee B) \equiv (\neg A \vee B) \wedge (A \vee B) \equiv (\neg A \wedge A) \vee B \equiv \text{false} \vee B \equiv B$.
c. $A \wedge B \rightarrow C \equiv \neg(A \wedge B) \vee C \equiv (\neg A \vee \neg B) \vee C \equiv \neg A \vee (\neg B \vee C)$
$\equiv \neg A \vee (B \rightarrow C) \equiv A \rightarrow (B \rightarrow C)$.
e. $A \rightarrow B \wedge C \equiv \neg A \vee (B \wedge C) \equiv (\neg A \vee B) \wedge (\neg A \vee C) \equiv (A \rightarrow B) \wedge (A \rightarrow C)$.

2. a. One of several answers is $A = \text{false}$, $B = \text{true}$, and $C = \text{false}$. **c.** $A = \text{false}$, $B = \text{true}$ or false, and $C = \text{true}$.

3. a. $P \wedge (\neg Q \vee P)$ or P. **c.** $\neg Q \vee P$. **e.** $(\neg P \vee Q) \wedge (\neg P \vee R)$.
g. $(A \vee C \vee \neg E \vee F) \wedge (B \vee C \vee \neg E \vee F) \wedge (A \vee D \vee \neg E \vee F) \wedge (B \vee D \vee \neg E \vee F)$.

4. a. $(P \wedge \neg Q) \vee P$ or P. **c.** $\neg Q \vee P$. **e.** $\neg P \vee (Q \wedge R)$.

5. Let D mean "I am dancing," H mean "I am happy," and M mean "there is a mouse in the house." Then a proof can be written as follows:

1.	$D \rightarrow H$	P
2.	$M \vee H$	P
3.	$\neg H$	P
4.	M	2, 3, DS
5.	$\neg D$	1, 3, MT
6.	$M \wedge \neg D$	4, 5, Conj
	QED	1, 2, 3, 6, CP.

6.   a.

1.	A	P
2.	$\quad B$	P
3.	$\quad A \wedge B$	1, 2, Conj
4.	$B \rightarrow A \wedge B$	2, 3, CP
	QED	1, 4, CP.

c.

1.	$A \vee B \rightarrow C$	P
2.	A	P
3.	$A \vee B$	2, Add
4.	C	1, 3, MP
	QED	1, 2, 4, CP.

e.

1.	$A \vee B \rightarrow C \wedge D$	P
2.	$\quad B$	P
3.	$\quad A \vee B$	2, Add
4.	$\quad C \wedge D$	1, 3, MP
5.	$\quad D$	4, Simp
6.	$B \rightarrow D$	2, 5, CP
	QED	1, 6, CP.

g.

1.	$\neg (A \wedge B)$	P
2.	$B \vee C$	P
3.	$C \rightarrow D$	P
4.	$\quad A$	P
5.	$\quad \neg A \vee \neg B$	1, T
6.	$\quad \neg B$	4, 5, DS
7.	$\quad C$	2, 6, DS
8.	$\quad D$	3, 7, MP
9.	$A \rightarrow D$	4, 8, CP
	QED	1, 2, 3, 9, CP.

i.   1. $A \rightarrow C$ $\qquad\qquad\qquad$ P
        2. $\qquad\quad A \wedge B$ $\qquad\quad$ P
        3. $\qquad\quad A$ $\qquad\qquad$ 2, Simp
        4. $\qquad\quad C$ $\qquad\qquad$ 1, 3, MP
        5. $A \wedge B \rightarrow C$ $\qquad$ 2, 4, CP
        QED $\qquad\qquad\qquad$ 1,5, CP.

7. **a.**   1. A $\qquad\qquad\qquad$ P
        2. $\neg (B \rightarrow A)$ $\qquad$ P for IP
        3. $\neg (\neg B \vee A)$ $\qquad$ 2, T
        4. $B \wedge \neg A$ $\qquad\quad$ 3, T
        5. $\neg A$ $\qquad\qquad\quad$ 4, Simp
        6. $A \wedge \neg A$ $\qquad\quad$ 1, 5, Conj
        QED $\qquad\qquad\quad$ 1, 2, 6, IP.

    c.   1. $\neg B$ $\qquad\qquad\quad$ P
        2. $\neg (B \rightarrow C)$ $\qquad$ P for IP
        3. $\neg (\neg B \vee C)$ $\qquad$ 2, T
        4. $B \wedge \neg C$ $\qquad\quad$ 3, T
        5. B $\qquad\qquad\qquad$ 4, Simp
        6. $\neg B \wedge B$ $\qquad\quad$ 1, 5, Conj
        QED $\qquad\qquad\quad$ 1, 2, 6, IP.

    e.   1. $A \rightarrow B$ $\qquad\qquad\qquad\qquad$ P
        2. $\neg ((A \rightarrow \neg B) \rightarrow \neg A)$ $\quad$ P for IP
        3. $(\neg A \vee \neg B) \wedge A$ $\qquad\quad$ 2, T
        4. A $\qquad\qquad\qquad\qquad\quad$ 3, Simp
        5. $\neg A \vee \neg B$ $\qquad\qquad\quad$ 3, Simp
        6. $\neg B$ $\qquad\qquad\qquad\quad$ 4, 5, DS
        7. $\neg A$ $\qquad\qquad\qquad\quad$ 1, 6, MT
        8. $A \wedge \neg A$ $\qquad\qquad\quad$ 4, 7, Conj
        QED $\qquad\qquad\qquad\qquad$ 1, 2, 8, IP.

    g.   1. $A \rightarrow B$ $\qquad\qquad$ P
        2. $B \rightarrow C$ $\qquad\qquad$ P
        3. $\neg (A \rightarrow C)$ $\qquad$ P for IP
        4. $A \wedge \neg C$ $\qquad\quad$ 3, T
        5. A $\qquad\qquad\qquad$ 4, Simp
        6. $\neg C$ $\qquad\qquad\quad$ 4, Simp
        7. B $\qquad\qquad\qquad$ 1, 5, MP
        8. C $\qquad\qquad\qquad$ 2, 7, MP
        9. $C \wedge \neg C$ $\qquad\quad$ 6, 8, Conj
        QED $\qquad\qquad\quad$ 1, 2, 3, 9, IP.

8. For some proofs we'll use IP in a subproof.

a.

1.	A	P
2.	$\neg (B \to (A \wedge B))$	P for IP
3.	$B \wedge \neg (A \wedge B)$	2, T
4.	B	3, Simp
5.	$\neg (A \wedge B)$	3, Simp
6.	$\neg A \vee \neg B$	5, T
7.	$\neg B$	1, 6, DS
8.	$B \wedge \neg B$	4, 7, Conj
9.	false	8, T
	QED	1, 2, 9, IP.

c.

1.	$A \vee B \to C$	P
2.	A	P
3.	$\neg C$	P for IP
4.	$\neg (A \vee B)$	1, 3, MT
5.	$\neg A \wedge \neg B$	4, T
6.	$\neg A$	5, Simp
7.	$A \wedge \neg A$	2, 6, Conj
	QED	1, 2, 3, 7, IP.

e.

1.	$A \vee B \to C \wedge D$	P
2.	$\neg (B \to D)$	P for IP
3.	$B \wedge \neg D$	2, T
4.	B	3, Simp
5.	$A \vee B$	4, Add
6.	$C \wedge D$	1, 5, MP
7.	$\neg D$	3, Simp
8.	D	6, Simp
9.	$D \wedge \neg D$	7, 8, Conj
	QED	1, 2, 9, IP.

g.

1.	$\neg (A \wedge B)$	P
2.	$B \vee C$	P
3.	$C \to D$	P
4.	$\neg (A \to D)$	P for IP
5.	$A \wedge \neg D$	4, T
6.	$\neg D$	5, Simp
7.	$\neg C$	3, 6, MT
8.	B	2, 7, DS
9.	$B \to \neg A$	1, T
10.	$\neg A$	8, 9, MP
11.	A	5, Simp
12.	$A \wedge \neg A$	10, 11, Conj
	QED	1, 2, 3, 4, 12, IP.

i.
1.	$A \rightarrow (B \rightarrow C)$		P
2.	$\quad B$		P
3.	$\qquad A$		P
4.	$\qquad\quad \neg C$		P for IP
5.	$\qquad\quad B \rightarrow C$		1, 3, MP
6.	$\qquad\quad C$		2, 5, MP
7.	$\qquad\quad C \wedge \neg C$		4, 6, Conj
8.	$\qquad A \rightarrow C$		3, 4, 7, IP
9.	$\quad B \rightarrow (A \rightarrow C)$		2, 8, CP
	QED		1, 9, CP.

k.
1.	$A \rightarrow C$	P
2.	$\quad A$	P
3.	$\quad\quad \neg (B \vee C)$	P for IP
4.	$\quad\quad \neg B \wedge \neg C$	3, T
5.	$\quad\quad C$	1, 2, MP
6.	$\quad\quad \neg C$	4, Simp
7.	$\quad\quad C \wedge \neg C$	5, 6, Conj
8.	$A \wedge B \rightarrow C$	2, 3, 7, IP
	QED	1, 8, CP.

9.   **a.**
1.	$A \vee B$	P
2.	$A \rightarrow C$	P
3.	$B \rightarrow D$	P
4.	$\neg (C \vee D)$	P for IP
5.	$\neg C \wedge \neg D$	4, T
6.	$\neg C$	5, Simp
7.	$\neg A$	2, 6, MT
8.	B	1, 7, DS
9.	D	3, 8, MP
10.	$\neg D$	5, Simp
11.	$D \wedge \neg D$	9, 10, Conj
	QED	1,2, 3, 4, 11, IP.

Section 3.2

1. a. The three occurrences of x, left to right, are free, bound, and bound. The four occurrences of y, left to right, are free, bound, bound, and free.

c. The three occurrences of x, left to right, are free, bound, and bound. Both occurrences of y are free.

2. $\forall x \, p(x, y, z) \rightarrow \exists z \, q(z)$.

3. a. One interpretation has $p(a)$ = true, in which case both $\forall x \, p(x)$ and $\exists x \, p(x)$ are true. Therefore W is true. The other interpretation has $p(a)$ = false, in which case both $\forall x \, p(x)$ and $\exists x \, p(x)$ are false. Therefore W is true.

4. a. Let the domain be the set $\{a, b\}$, and assign $p(a)$ = true and $p(b)$ = false. Finally, assign the constant $c = a$. **c** and **d.** Let $p(x, y)$ = false for all elements x and y in any domain. Then the antecedent is false for both parts (c) and (d). Therefore the both wffs are true for this interpretation. **e.** Let $D = \{a\}$, $f(a) = a$, $y = a$, and let p denote equality.

5. a. Let the domain be $\{a\}$, and let $p(a)$ = true and $c = a$. **c.** Let $D = \mathbb{N}$, let $p(x)$ mean "x is odd," and let $q(x)$ mean "x is even." Then the antecedent is true, but the consequent is false. **e.** Let $D = \mathbb{N}$, and let $p(x, y)$ mean "$y = x + 1$." Then the antecedent $\forall x \, \exists y \, p(x, y)$ is true and the consequent $\exists y \forall x \, p(x, y)$ is false for this interpretation.

6. a. If the domain is $\{a\}$, then either $p(a)$ = true or $p(a)$ = false. In either case, W is true.

7. a. Let $\{a\}$ be the domain of the interpretation. If $p(a, a)$ = false, then W is true, since the antecedent is false. If $p(a, a)$ = true, the W is true, since the consequent is true. **c.** Let $\{a, b, c\}$ be the domain. Let $p(a, a) = p(b, b) = p(c, c)$ = true and $p(a, b) = p(a, c) = p(b, c)$ = false. This assignment makes W false. Therefore W is invalid.

8. a. For any domain D and any element $d \in D$, $p(d) \to p(d)$ is true. Therefore any interpretation is a model. **c.** If the wff is invalid, then there is some interpretation making the wff false. This says that $\forall x \, p(x)$ is true and $\exists x \, p(x)$ is false. This is a contradiction because we can't have $p(x)$ true for all x in a domain while at the same time having $p(x)$ false for some x in the domain. **e.** If the wff is not valid, then there is an interpretation with domain D for which the antecedent is true and the consequent is false. So $A(d)$ and $B(e)$ are false for some elements $d, e \in D$. Therefore $\forall x \, A(x)$ and $\forall x \, B(x)$ are false, contrary to assumption. **g** and **h.** If the antecedent is true for a domain D, then $A(d) \to B(d)$ is true for all $d \in D$. If $A(d)$ is true for all $d \in D$, then $B(d)$ is also true for all $d \in D$ by MP. Thus the consequent is true for D.

9. a. Suppose the wff is satisfiable. Then there is an interpretation that assigns c a value in its domain such that $p(c) \wedge \neg \, p(c)$ = true. Of course, this is impossible. Therefore the wff is unsatisfiable. **c.** Suppose the wff is satisfiable. Then there is an interpretation making $\exists x \, \forall y \, (p(x, y) \wedge \neg \, p(x, y))$ true. This says that there is an element d in the domain such that $\forall y \, (p(d, y) \wedge \neg \, p(d, y))$ is true. This says that $p(d, y) \wedge \neg p(d, y)$ is true for all y in the domain, which is impossible.

10. a. The left side is true for domain D iff $A(d) \wedge B(d)$ is true for all $d \in D$ iff $A(d)$ and $B(d)$ are both true for all $d \in D$ iff the right side is true for domain D. **c.** Assume that the left side is true for domain D. Then $A(d) \to B(d)$ is true for some $d \in D$. If $A(d)$ is true, then $B(d)$ is true by MP. So $\exists x \, B(x)$ is true for D. If $A(d)$ is false, then $\forall x \, A(x)$ is false. So in either case the right side is true for D. Now assume the right side is true for D. If $\forall x\, A(x)$ is true, then $\exists x\, B(x)$ is also true. This means that $A(d)$ is true for all $d \in D$ and $B(d)$ is true for some $d \in D$. Thus $A(d) \to B(d)$ is true for some $d \in D$, which says that the left side is true for D. **e.** $\exists x\, \exists y\, W(x, y)$ is true for D iff $W(d, e)$ is true for some elements $d, e \in D$ iff $\exists y\, \exists x\, W(x, y)$ is true for D.

11. All proofs use an interpretation with domain D.
a. $\forall x\, (C \wedge A(x))$ is true for D iff $C \wedge A(d)$ is true for all $d \in D$ iff C is true in D and $A(d)$ is true for all $d \in D$ iff $C \wedge \forall x\, A(x)$ is true for D.
c. $\forall x\, (C \vee A(x))$ is true for D iff $C \vee A(d)$ is true for all $d \in D$ iff C is true in D or $A(d)$ is true for all $d \in D$ iff $C \vee \forall x\, A(x)$ is true for D.
e. $\forall x\, (C \to A(x))$ is true for D iff $C \to A(d)$ is true for all $d \in D$ iff either C is false in D or $A(d)$ is true for all $d \in D$ iff $C \to \forall x\, A(x)$ is true for D.
g. $\forall x\, (A(x) \to C)$ is true for D iff $A(d) \to C$ is true for all $d \in D$ iff either $A(d)$ is false for some $d \in D$ or C is true in D iff $\exists x\, A(x) \to C$ is true for D.

12. a. $\exists x\, \forall y\, \forall z\, ((\neg p(x) \vee p(y) \vee q(z)) \wedge (\neg q(x) \vee p(y) \vee q(z)))$.
c. $\exists x\, \forall y\, \exists z\, \forall w\, (\neg p(x, y) \vee p(w, z))$.

13. a. $\exists x\, \forall y\, \forall z\, ((\neg p(x) \wedge \neg q(x)) \vee p(y) \vee q(z))$.
c. $\exists x\, \forall y\, \exists z\, \forall w\, (\neg p(x, y) \vee p(w, z))$.

Section 3.3

1. a.

	1.	$\forall x\, p(x)$	P
	2.	$p(x)$	1, UI
	3.	$\exists x\, p(x)$	2, EG
		QED	1, 3, CP.

c.

	1.	$\exists x\, (p(x) \wedge q(x))$	P
	2.	$p(c) \wedge q(c)$	1, EI
	3.	$p(c)$	2, Simp
	4.	$\exists x\, p(x)$	3, EG
	5.	$q(c)$	2, Simp
	6.	$\exists x\, q(x)$	5, EG
	7.	$\exists x\, p(x) \wedge \exists x\, q(x)$	4, 6, Conj
		QED	1, 7, CP.

e.

	1.	$\forall x\, (p(x) \to q(x))$	P
	2.	$\forall x\, p(x)$	P
	3.	$p(x)$	2, UI
	4.	$p(x) \to q(x)$	1, UI
	5.	$q(x)$	3, 4, MP
	6.	$\exists x\, q(x)$	5, EG
	7.	$\forall x\, p(x) \to \exists x\, q(x)$	2, 6, CP
		QED	1, 7, CP.

g. 1. $\exists y \, \forall x \, p(x, y)$ P
    2. $\forall x \, p(x, c)$ 1, EI
    3. $p(x, c)$ 2, UI
    4. $\exists y \, p(x, y)$ 3, EG
    5. $\forall x \, \exists y \, p(x, y)$ 4, UG
       QED   1, 5, CP.

2. a. 1. $\forall x \, p(x)$ P
    2. $\neg \, \exists x \, p(x)$ P for IP
    3. $\forall x \, \neg p(x)$ 2, T
    4. $p(x)$ 1, UI
    5. $\neg \, p(x)$ 3, UI
    6. $p(x) \wedge \neg \, p(x)$ 4, 5, Conj
    7. false   6, T
       QED   1, 2, 7, IP.

c. 1. $\exists y \, \forall x \, p(x, y)$ P
    2. $\neg \, \forall x \, \exists y \, p(x, y)$ P for IP
    3. $\exists x \, \forall y \, \neg p(x, y)$ 2, T
    4. $\forall x \, p(x, c)$ 1, EI
    5. $\forall y \, \neg p(d, y)$ 3, EI
    6. $p(d, c)$ 4, UI
    7. $\neg \, p(d, c)$ 5, UI
    8. $p(d, c) \wedge \neg \, p(d, c)$ 6, 7, Conj
       QED   1, 2, 8, IP.

e. 1. $\forall x \, p(x) \vee \forall x \, q(x)$ P
    2. $\neg \, \forall x \, (p(x) \vee q(x))$ P for IP
    3. $\exists x \, (\neg \, p(x) \wedge \neg \, q(x))$ 2, T
    4. $\neg \, p(c) \wedge \neg \, q(c)$ 3, EI
    5. $\neg \, p(c)$ 4, Simp
    6. $\neg \, \forall x \, p(x)$ 5, UI (contrapositive)
    7. $\neg \, q(c)$ 4, Simp
    8. $\neg \, \forall x \, q(x)$ 7, UI (contrapositive)
    9. $\neg \, \forall x \, p(x) \wedge \neg \, \forall x \, q(x)$ 6, 7, Conj
    10. $\neg \, (\forall x \, p(x) \vee \forall x \, q(x))$ 9, T
    11. false   1, 10, Conj, T
        QED   1, 2, 11, IP.

3. a. Let $D(x)$ mean that x is a dog, $L(x)$ mean that x likes people, $H(x)$ mean that x hates cats, and $a =$ Rover. Then the argument can be formalized as follows:

$$\forall x \, (D(x) \rightarrow L(x) \vee H(x)) \wedge D(a) \wedge \neg \, H(a) \rightarrow \exists x \, (D(x) \wedge L(x)).$$

Proof: 1. $\forall x \, (D(x) \to L(x) \vee H(x))$ P
        2. $D(a)$ P
        3. $\neg \, H(a)$ P
        4. $D(a) \to L(a) \vee H(a)$ 1, UI
        5. $L(a) \vee H(a)$ 2, 4, MP
        6. $L(a)$ 3, 5, DS
        7. $D(a) \wedge L(a)$ 2, 6, Conj
        8. $\exists x \, (D(x) \wedge L(x))$ 7, EG
        QED   1, 2, 3, 8, CP.

c. Let $H(x)$ mean that x is a human being, $Q(x)$ mean that x is a quadruped, and $M(x)$ mean that x is a man. Then the argument is can be formalized as

$$\forall x \, (H(x) \to \neg \, Q(x)) \wedge \forall x \, (M(x) \to H(x)) \to \forall x \, (M(x) \to \neg \, Q(x)).$$

Proof: 1. $\forall x \, (H(x) \to \neg \, Q(x))$ P
       2. $\forall x \, (M(x) \to H(x))$ P
       3. $H(x) \to \neg \, Q(x)$ 1, UI
       4. $M(x) \to H(x)$ 2, UI
       5. $M(x) \to \neg \, Q(x)$ 3, 4, HS
       6. $\forall x \, (M(x) \to \neg \, Q(x))$ 5, UG
          QED   1, 2, 6, CP.

e. Let $F(x)$ mean that x is a freshman, $S(x)$ mean that x is a sophomore, $J(x)$ mean that x is a junior, and $L(x, y)$ mean that x likes y. Then the argument can be formalized as $A \to B$, where

$$A = \exists x \, (F(x) \wedge \forall y \, (S(y) \to L(x, y))) \wedge \forall x \, (F(x) \to \forall y \, (J(y) \to \neg \, L(x, y)))$$

and

$$B = \forall x \, (S(x) \to \neg \, J(x)).$$

Proof: 1. $\exists x \, (F(x) \wedge \forall y \, (S(y) \to L(x, y)))$ P
       2. $\forall x \, (F(x) \to \forall y \, (J(y) \to \neg \, L(x, y)))$ P
       3. $F(c) \wedge \forall y \, (S(y) \to L(c, y))$ 1, EI
       4. $\forall y \, (S(y) \to L(c, y))$ 3, Simp
       5. $S(x) \to L(c, x)$ 4, UI
       6. $S(x)$ P
       7. $L(c, x)$ 5, 6, MP
       8. $F(c) \to \forall y \, (J(y) \to \neg \, L(c, y))$ 2, UI
       9. $F(c)$ 3, Simp
     10. $\forall y \, (J(y) \to \neg \, L(c, y))$ 8, 9, MP
     11. $J(x) \to \neg \, L(c, x)$ 10, UI
     12. $\neg \, J(x)$ 7, 11, MT
     13. $S(x) \to \neg \, J(x)$ 6, 12, CP
     14. $\forall x \, (S(x) \to \neg \, J(x))$ 13, UG
          QED   1, 2, 14, CP.

4. First prove that the left side implies the right side, then the converse.

a.
1.	$\exists x\, \exists y\, W(x, y)$	P
2.	$\exists y\, W(c, y)$	1, EI
3.	$W(c, d)$	2, EI
4.	$\exists x\, W(x, d)$	3, EG
5.	$\exists y\, \exists x\, W(x, y)$	4, EG
	QED	1, 5, CP.

1.	$\exists y\, \exists x\, W(x, y)$	P
2.	$\exists x\, W(x, d)$	1, EI
3.	$W(c, d)$	2, EI
4.	$\exists y\, W(c, y)$	3, EG
5.	$\exists x\, \exists y\, W(x, y)$	4, EG
	QED	1, 5, CP.

c
1.	$\exists x\, (A(x) \vee B(x))$	P
2.	$\neg\, (\exists x\, A(x) \vee \exists x\, B(x))$	P for IP
3.	$\forall x\, \neg\, A(x) \wedge \forall x\, \neg\, B(x)$	2, T
4.	$\forall x\, \neg\, A(x)$	3, Simp
5.	$A(c) \vee B(c)$	1, EI
6.	$\neg\, A(c)$	4, UI
7.	$B(c)$	5, 6, DS
8.	$\forall x\, \neg\, B(x)$	3, Simp
9.	$\neg\, B(c)$	8, UI
10.	$B(c) \wedge \neg\, B(c)$	7, 9, Conj
	QED	1, 2, 10, IP.

1.	$\exists x\, A(x) \vee \exists x\, B(x)$	P
2.	$\neg\, \exists x\, (A(x) \vee B(x))$	P for IP
3.	$\forall x\, (\neg\, A(x) \wedge \neg\, B(x))$	2, T
4.	$\forall x\, \neg\, A(x) \wedge \forall x\, \neg\, B(x)$	3, T Part b)
5.	$\forall x\, \neg\, A(x)$	4, Simp
6.	$\neg\, \exists x\, A(x)$	5, T
7.	$\exists x\, B(x)$	1, 6, DS
8.	$\forall x\, \neg\, B(x)$	4, Simp
9.	$\neg\, \exists x\, B(x)$	5, T
10.	$\exists x\, B(x) \wedge \neg\, \exists x\, B(x)$	7, 9, Conj
	QED	1, 2, 10, IP.

5.
1.	$\forall x\, (\exists y\, (q(x, y) \wedge s(y)) \rightarrow \exists y\, (p(y) \wedge r(x, y)))$	P
2.	$\neg\, (\neg\, \exists x\, p(x) \rightarrow \forall x\, \forall y\, (q(x, y) \rightarrow \neg\, s(y)))$	P for IP
3.	$\neg\, \exists x\, p(x) \wedge \neg\, \forall x\, \forall y\, (q(x, y) \rightarrow \neg\, s(y))$	2, T
4.	$\neg\, \exists x\, p(x)$	3, Simp
5.	$\neg\, \forall x\, \forall y\, (q(x, y) \rightarrow \neg\, s(y))$	3, Simp

6. $\exists x \, \exists y \, (q(x, y) \wedge s(y))$	5, T
7. $\exists y \, (q(c, y) \wedge s(y))$	6, EI
8. $\exists y \, (q(c, y) \wedge s(y)) \rightarrow \exists y \, (p(y) \wedge r(c, y))$	1, UI
9. $\exists y \, (p(y) \wedge r(c, y))$	7, 8, MP
10. $p(d) \wedge r(c, d)$	9, EI
11. $p(d)$	10, Simp
12. $\exists x \, p(x)$	11, EG
13. false	4, 12, 13, T
QED	1, 2, 13, IP.

7. a. Line 2 is wrong because x is free in line 1, which is a premise. Therefore x is flagged on line 1. Thus line 1 can't be used with the UG rule to generalize x. **c.** Line 2 is wrong because $f(y)$ is not free to replace x. That is, the substitution of $f(y)$ for x yields a new bound occurrence of y. Therefore EG can't generalize to x from $f(y)$. **e.** Line 4 is wrong because c already occurs in the proof on line 3.

Section 3.4

1. a. Second. **c.** Fifth. **e.** Third. **g.** Third. **i.** Fourth.

2. a. Here are two possible answers:

$$\exists A \, \exists B \, \forall x \, ((A(x) \rightarrow \neg B(x)) \wedge (B(x) \rightarrow \neg A(x)))$$

or $\exists A \, \exists B \, \forall x \, \neg (A(x) \wedge B(x)).$

3. a. Let S be state and C be city. Then we can write $\forall S \, \exists C \, S(C) \wedge (C = $ Springfield). The wff is second order. **c.** Let $H, R, S, B,$ and A stand for house, room, shelf, book, and author, respectively. Then we can write the statement as $\exists H \, \exists R \, \exists S \, \exists B \, (H(R) \wedge R(S) \wedge S(B) \wedge A(B, \text{Thoreau}))$. The wff is fourth order. **e.** The statement can be expressed as follows:

$$\exists S \, \exists A \, \exists B \, (\forall x \, (A(x) \vee B(x) \rightarrow S(x)) \wedge \forall x \, (S(x)$$
$$\rightarrow A(x) \vee B(x)) \wedge \forall x \, \neg (A(x) \wedge B(x))).$$

The wff is second order.

5. Think of $S(x)$ as $x \in S$. **a.** For any domain D the antecedent is false because S can be the empty set. Thus the wff is true for all domains. **c.** For any domain D the consequent is true because S can be chosen as D. Thus the wff is true for all domains.

6. a. Assume that the statement is false. Then there is some line L containing every point. Now Axiom 3 says that there are three distinct points not on the same line. This is a contradiction. Thus the statement is true. **c.** Let w be a point. By Axiom 3 there is another point $x, x \neq w$. By Axiom 1 there is a line L on x and w. By part (a) there is a point z not on L. By Axiom 1 there is a line M on w and z. Since z is on M and z is not on L, it follows that $L \neq M$.   QED.

7. Here are some sample formalizations.

a. $\forall L \, \exists x \, \neg \, L(x)$.

Proof:
1.	$\neg \, \forall L \, \exists x \, \neg \, L(x)$	P for IP
2.	$\exists L \forall x \, L(x)$	1, T
3.	$\forall x \, l(x)$	2, EI
4.	Axiom 3	
5.	$l(a) \wedge l(b) \rightarrow \neg \, l(c)$	4, EI, EI, EI, Simp, UI
6.	$l(a) \wedge l(b)$	3, UI, UI, Conj
7.	$\neg \, l(c)$	5, 6, MP
8.	$l(c)$	3, UI
9.	false	7, 8, Conj, T
	QED	1, 9, IP.

c. $\forall x \, \exists L \, \exists M \, (L(x) \wedge M(x) \wedge \exists y \, (\neg \, L(y) \wedge M(y)))$. We give two proofs. The first uses part (a), and the second does not.

Proof (using part (a)):
1.	$\neg \, (\forall x \, \exists L \, \exists M \, (L(x) \wedge M(x) \wedge \exists y \, (\neg \, L(y) \wedge M(y))))$	P for IP
2.	$\exists x \, \forall L \, \forall M \, (\neg \, (L(x) \wedge M(x)) \vee \forall y \, (L(y) \vee \neg \, M(y)))$	1, T
3.	$\forall L \, \forall M \, (\neg \, (L(a) \wedge M(a)) \vee \forall y \, (L(y) \vee \neg \, M(y)))$	2, EI
4.	Axiom 3	
5.	$b \neq c \wedge b \neq d \wedge c \neq d \wedge \forall L \, (L(b) \wedge L(c) \rightarrow \neg \, L(d))$	4, EI, EI, EI
6.	$a \neq b$	T
7.	$a \neq b \rightarrow \exists L \, (L(a) \wedge L(b))$	Axiom 1, UI, UI
8.	$\exists L \, (L(a) \wedge L(b))$	6, 7, MP
9.	$l(a) \wedge l(b)$	8, EI
10.	$\forall L \, \exists x \, \neg \, L(x)$	Part (a)
11.	$\exists x \, \neg \, l(x)$	10, UI
12.	$\neg \, l(e)$	11, EI
13.	$a \neq e$	T
14.	$a \neq e \rightarrow \exists L \, (L(a) \wedge L(e))$	Axiom 1, UI, UI
15.	$\exists L \, (L(a) \wedge L(e))$	13, 14, MP
16.	$m(a) \wedge m(e)$	15, EI
17.	$l(a) \wedge m(a)$	9,Simp,16,Simp,Conj
18.	$\neg \, (l(a) \wedge m(a)) \vee \forall y \, (l(y) \vee \neg \, m(y))$	3, UI, UI
19.	$\forall y \, (l(y) \vee \neg \, m(y))$	17, 18, DS
20.	$l(e) \vee \neg \, m(e)$	19, UI
21.	$\neg \, m(e)$	12, 20, DS
22.	false	16, Simp, 21, Conj T
	QED	1, 22, CP.

Proof (without using part (a)):
1.	$\neg \, (\forall x \, \exists L \, \exists M \, (L(x) \wedge M(x) \wedge \exists y \, (\neg \, L(y) \wedge M(y))))$	P for IP
2.	$\exists x \, \forall L \, \forall M \, (\neg \, (L(x) \wedge M(x)) \vee \forall y \, (L(y) \vee \neg \, M(y)))$	1, T

3. $\forall L \ \forall M \ (\neg \ (L(a) \wedge M(\mathrm{a})) \vee \forall \mathrm{y} \ (L(\mathrm{y}) \vee \neg \ M(\mathrm{y})))$ 2, EI, UI, UI
4. Axiom 3
5. $b \neq c \wedge b \neq d \wedge c \neq d \wedge \forall L \ (L(b) \wedge L(c) \rightarrow \neg \ L(d))$ 4, EI, EI, EI
6. $a \neq b$ T
7. $a \neq b \rightarrow \exists L \ (L(a) \wedge L(b))$ axiom 1, UI, UI
8. $\exists L \ (L(a) \wedge L(b))$ 6, 7, MP
9. $l(a) \wedge l(b)$ 8, EI
10. $a \neq c$ T
11. $a \neq c \rightarrow \exists L \ (L(a) \wedge L(c))$ axiom 1, UI, UI
12. $\exists L \ (L(a) \wedge L(c))$ 10, 11, MP
13. $m(a) \wedge m(c)$ 12, EI
14. $a \neq d$ T
15. $a \neq d \rightarrow \exists L \ (L(a) \wedge L(d))$ axiom 1, UI, UI
16. $\exists L \ (L(a) \wedge L(d))$ 15, 16, MP
17. $n(a) \wedge n(d)$ 16, EI
18. $l(a) \wedge m(a)$ 9, Simp, 13, Simp, Conj
19. $\neg \ (l(a) \wedge m(a)) \vee \forall \mathrm{y} \ (l(\mathrm{y}) \vee \neg \ m(\mathrm{y}))$ 3, UI, UI
20. $\forall \mathrm{y} \ (l(\mathrm{y}) \vee \neg \ m(\mathrm{y}))$ 18, 19, DS
21. $l(c) \vee \neg \ m(c))$ 20, UI
22. $l(c)$ 13, Simp, 21, DS
23. $l(a) \wedge n(a)$ 9, Simp, 13, Simp, Conj
24. $\neg \ (l(a) \wedge n(a)) \vee \forall \mathrm{y} \ (l(\mathrm{y}) \vee \neg \ n(\mathrm{y}))$ 3, UI, UI
25. $\forall \mathrm{y} \ (l(\mathrm{y}) \vee \neg \ n(\mathrm{y}))$ 23, 24, DS
26. $l(d) \vee \neg \ n(d)$ 25, UI
27. $l(d)$ 17, Simp, 26, DS
28. $l(b) \wedge l(c)$ 9, Simp, 22, Conj
29. $\forall L \ (L(b) \wedge L(c) \rightarrow \neg \ L(d))$ 5, Simp
30. $l(b) \wedge l(c) \rightarrow \neg \ l(d)$ 29, UI
31. $\neg \ l(d)$ 28, 30, MP
32. false   27, 31, Conj, T
    QED   1, 32, IP.

Section 3.5

1.
    1. $s = v$ P
    2. $t = w$ P
    3. $p(s, t)$ P
    4. $p(v, t)$ 1, 3, EE
    5. $p(v, w)$ 2, 4, EE
    QED   1, 2, 3, 5, CP.

3. We can write $Ux \ A(x)$ as either of the following two wffs:

$$\exists x \ (A(x) \wedge \forall y \ (A(y) \rightarrow x = y)) \quad \text{or} \quad \exists x \ A(x) \wedge \forall x \ \forall y \ (A(x) \wedge A(y) \rightarrow x = y).$$

5. a.
1.	$t = u$	P
2.	$\neg\, p(\ldots t \ldots)$	P
3.	$p(\ldots u \ldots)$	P for IP
4.	$u = t$	1, Symmetric
5.	$p(\ldots t \ldots)$	3, 4, EE
6.	false	2, 5, Conj, T
	QED	1, 2, 3, 6, IP.

c.
1.	$t = u$	P
2.	$p(\ldots t \ldots) \vee q(\ldots t \ldots)$	P
3.	$\neg\, (p(\ldots u \ldots) \vee q(\ldots u \ldots))$	P for IP
4.	$\neg\, p(\ldots u \ldots) \wedge \neg\, q(\ldots u \ldots)$	3, T
5.	$\neg\, p(\ldots u \ldots)$	4, Simp
6.	$\neg\, q(\ldots u \ldots)$	4, Simp
7.	$u = t$	1, Symmetric
8.	$\neg\, p(\ldots t \ldots)$	5, 7, EE from part (a)
9.	$\neg\, q(\ldots t \ldots)$	6, 7, EE from part (a)
10.	$\neg\, p(\ldots t \ldots) \wedge \neg\, q(\ldots t \ldots)$	8, 9, Conj
11.	$\neg\, (p(\ldots t \ldots) \vee q(\ldots t \ldots))$	10, T
12.	false	2, 11, Conj, T
	QED	1, 12, CP.

e.
1.	$x = y$	P
2.	$\forall z\, p(\ldots x \ldots)$	P
3.	$p(\ldots x \ldots)$	2, UI
4.	$p(\ldots y \ldots)$	1, 3, EE
5.	$\forall z\, p(\ldots y \ldots)$	4, UG
	QED	1, 2, 5, CP.

7. a. Proof of $p(x) \rightarrow \exists y\, (x = y \wedge p(y))$:
1.	$p(x)$	P
2.	$\neg\, \exists y\, (x = y \wedge p(y))$	P for IP
3.	$\forall y\, (x \neq y \vee \neg\, p(y))$	2, T
4.	$x \neq x \vee \neg\, p(x)$	3, UI
5.	$x \neq x$	1, 4, DS
6.	$x = x$	EA
7.	false	5, 6, Conj, T
	QED	1, 2, 7, IP.

Proof of $\exists y\, (x = y \wedge p(y)) \rightarrow p(x)$:
1.	$\exists y\, (x = y \wedge p(y))$	P
2.	$x = c \wedge p(c)$	1, EI
3.	$p(x)$	2, EE
	QED	1, 3, IP.

Section 3.6

1.

    1. $\{odd(x + 1)\}\, y := x + 1 \,\{odd(y)\}$ AA

    2. $true \wedge even(x)$ P

    3. $even(x)$ 2, Simp

    4. $odd(x + 1)$ 3, T

    5. $true \wedge even(x) \to odd(x + 1)$ 2, 4, CP

    6. $\{true \wedge even(x)\}\, y := x + 1 \,\{odd(y)\}$ 1, 5, Consequence

    QED.

2. a.

    1. $\{x + b > 0\}\, y := b \,\{x + y > 0\}$ AA

    2. $\{a + b > 0\}\, x := a \,\{x + b > 0\}$ AA

    3. $a > 0 \wedge b > 0 \to a + b > 0$ T

    4. $\{a > 0 \wedge b > 0\}\, x := a \,\{x + b > 0\}$ 2, 3, Consequence

    QED   1, 4, Composition.

3. Use the composition rule (3.43) applied to a sequence of three statements.

a.

    1. $\{temp < x\}\, y := temp \,\{y < x\}$ AA

    2. $\{temp < y\}\, x := y \,\{temp < x\}$ AA

    3. $\{x < y\}\, temp := x \,\{temp < y\}$ AA

    QED   3, 2, 1, Composition.

4. a. First, prove the correctness of the wff $\{x < 10 \wedge x \geq 5\}\, x := 4 \,\{x < 5\}$:

    1. $\{4 < 5\}\, x := 4 \,\{x < 5\}$ AA

    2. $x < 10 \wedge x \geq 5 \to 4 < 5$ T

    3. $\{x < 10 \wedge x \geq 5\}\, x := 4 \,\{x < 5\}$ 1, 2, Consequence

    QED.

Second, prove that $x < 10 \wedge \neg\, (x \geq 5) \to x < 5$. This is a valid wff because $\neg\, (x \geq 5) \equiv x < 5$. Thus the original wff is correct, by the if-then rule.

c. First, prove $\{true \wedge x < y\}\, x := y \,\{x \geq y\}$:

    1. $\{y \geq y\}\, x := y \,\{x \geq y\}$ AA

    2. $true \wedge x < y \to y \geq y$ T

    3. $\{true \wedge x < y\}\, x := y \,\{x \geq y\}$ 1, 2, Consequence

    QED.

Second, prove that $true \wedge \neg\, (x < y) \to x \geq y$. This is a valid wff because $true \wedge \neg\, (x < y) \equiv \neg\, (x < y) \equiv (x \geq y)$. Thus the original wff is correct, by the if-then rule.

5. a. Use the if-then-else rule. Thus we must prove the two statements, $\{true \wedge x < y\}\, max := y \,\{max \geq x \wedge max \geq y\}$ and $\{true \wedge x \geq y\}\, max := x \,\{max \geq x \wedge max \geq y\}$. For example, the first statement can be proved as follows:

1. $\{y \geq x \wedge y \geq y\}$ max $:= y$ $\{$max $\geq x \wedge$ max $\geq y\}$ AA
2.   true $\wedge x < y$ P
3. $x < y$ 2, Simp
4. $x \leq y$ 3, Add
5. $y \geq y$ T
6. $y \geq x \wedge y \geq y$ 4, 5, Conj
7. true $\wedge x < y \rightarrow y \geq x \wedge y \geq y$ 2, 6, CP
8. $\{$true $\wedge x < y \}$ max $:= y$ $\{$max $\geq x \wedge$ max $\geq y\}$ 1, 7, Consequence
    QED.

6. a. The wff is incorrect if $x = 1$.

7. Since the wff fits the form of the while rule, we need to prove the following statement:

$$\{x \geq y \wedge \text{even}(x - y) \wedge x \neq y\} \; x := x - 1; y := y + 1 \; \{x \geq y \wedge \text{even}(x - y)\}.$$

Proof:

1. $\{x \geq y + 1 \wedge \text{even}(x - y - 1)\} \, y := y + 1 \, \{x \geq y \wedge \text{even}(x - y)\}$ AA
2. $\{x - 1 \geq y + 1 \wedge \text{even}(x - 1 - y - 1)\} \, x := x - 1 \{x \geq y + 1 \wedge \text{even}(x - y - 1)\}$ AA
3. $x \geq y \wedge \text{even}(x - y) \wedge x \neq y$ P
4. $x \geq y + 2$ $3, T$
5. $x - 1 \geq y + 1$ $4, T$
6. $\text{even}(x - 1 - y - 1)$ $3, T$
7. $x \geq y \wedge \text{even}(x - y) \wedge x \neq y$
   $\rightarrow x - 1 \geq y + 1 \wedge \text{even}(x - 1 - y - 1)$ 3, 6, CP
   QED   1, 2, 7, Consequence, Composition.

Now the result follows from the while rule.

8. Let Q be the suggested loop invariant. The postcondition is equivalent to $Q \wedge \neg C$, where C is the while loop condition. Therefore the program can be proven correct by proving the validity of the following two wffs:

$$\{Q \wedge C\} \, i := i + 1; \, s := s + i \, \{Q\} \text{ and } \{n \geq 0\} i := 0; s := 0; \, \{Q\}.$$

9. a. Let the well-founded set be $\mathbb{N}$, and define $f : \text{States} \rightarrow \mathbb{N}$ by $f(i, x) = x - i$. If $s = \langle i, x \rangle$, then after the execution of the loop body the state will be $t = \langle i + 1, x \rangle$. Thus $f(s) = x - i$ and $f(t) = x - i - 1$. With these interpretations, (3.48) can be written as follows:

$$i \leq x \wedge i < x \wedge x - i \in \mathbb{N} \rightarrow x - i - 1 \in \mathbb{N} \wedge x - i > x - i - 1.$$

This statement can be proven formally as follows:

Proof: 1. $i \leq x \wedge i < x \wedge x - i \in \mathbb{N}$ P
        2. $i < x$ 1, Simp

3. $x - i > 0$	2, T
4. $x - i - 1 \geq 0$	3, T
5. $x - i > x - i - 1$	T
6. $x - i - 1 \in \mathbb{N} \wedge x - i > x - i - 1$	4, 5, Conj
QED	1, 6, CP.

10. Let P be the set of positive integers, and define $f :$ States $\to P$ by $f(x, y) = x + y$. If $s = \langle x, y \rangle$, then the state after the execution of the loop body will depend on whether $x < y$. If $x < y$, then $t = \langle x, y - x \rangle$, which gives $f(t) = x$. Otherwise, if $x > y$, then $t = \langle x - y, y \rangle$, which gives $f(t) = y$. So in either case, $f(t) < f(s)$ and $f(t) \in P$. This amounts to an informal proof of the statement (3.48):

$$\text{true} \wedge x \neq y \wedge f(s) \in \mathbb{N} \to f(t) \in \mathbb{N} \wedge f(s) > f(t).$$

Chapter 4

Section 4.1

1. a. $(A \vee C \vee D) \wedge (B \vee C \vee D)$.
c. $\forall x\, (\neg p(x, c) \vee q(x))$.
e. $\forall x\, \forall y\, (p(x, y) \vee q(x, y, f(x, y)))$.

2. $p \vee \neg p$ and $p \vee \neg p \vee q \vee q$.

3. a.

1.	$A \vee B$	P
2.	$\neg A$	P
3.	$\neg B \vee C$	P
4.	$\neg C$	P
5.	B	1, 2, R
6.	$\neg B$	3, 4, R
7.	$\square$	5, 6, R.

c.

1.	$A \vee B$	P
2.	$A \vee \neg C$	P
3.	$\neg A \vee C$	P
4.	$\neg A \vee \neg B$	P
5.	$C \vee \neg B$	P
6.	$\neg C \vee B$	P
7.	$B \vee C$	1, 3, R
8.	$B \vee B$	6, 7, R
9.	$\neg A$	4, 8, R
10.	$\neg C$	2, 9, R
11.	$\neg B$	5, 10, R
12.	A	1, 11, R
13.	$\square$	9, 12, R.

4. a. {y/x}. **c.** {y/a}. **e.** {$x/f(a)$, $y/f(b)$, z/b}.

5. a. {$x/f(a, b)$, $v/f(y, a)$, z/y} or {$x/f(a, b)$, $v/f(z, a)$, y/z}. **c.** {$x/g(a)$, $z/g(b)$, y/b}.

6. Make sure the clauses to be resolved have distinct sets of variables. The answers are $p(x) \vee \neg p(f(a))$ and $p(x) \vee \neg p(f(a)) \vee q(x) \vee q(f(a))$.

7. a.

1.	$p(x)$	P
2.	$q(y, a) \vee \neg p(a)$	P
3.	$\neg q(a, a)$	P
4.	$\neg p(a)$	2, 3, R, {y/a}
5.	$\square$	1, 4, R, {x/a}
	QED.	

c.

1.	$p(a) \vee p(x)$	P
2.	$\neg p(a) \vee \neg p(y)$	P
3.	$\square$	1, 2, R, {$x/a, y/a$}
	QED.	

e. Number the clauses 1, 2, and 3. Resolve 2 with 3 by unifying all four of the p atoms to obtain the clause $\neg q(a) \vee \neg q(a)$. Resolve this clause with 1 to obtain the empty clause.

8. a. After negating the statement and putting the result in clausal form, we obtain the following proof:

1.	$A \vee B$	P
2.	$\neg A$	P
3.	$\neg B$	P
4.	B	1, 2, R
5.	$\square$	3, 4, R, QED.

c. After negating the statement and putting the result in clausal form, we obtain the following proof:

1.	$p \vee q$	P
2.	$\neg q \vee r$	P
3.	$\neg r \vee s$	P
4.	$\neg p$	P
5.	$\neg s$	P
6.	$\neg r$	3, 5, R
7.	$\neg q$	2, 6, R
8.	q	1, 4, R
9.	$\square$	7, 8, R, QED.

9. a. After negating the statement and putting the result in clausal form, we obtain the following proof:

1.	$p(x)$	P
2.	$\neg p(y)$	P
3.	$\square$	1, 2, R, $\{x/y\}$ QED.

c. After negating the statement and putting the result in clausal form, we obtain the following proof:

1.	$p(x, a)$	P
2.	$\neg p(b, y)$	P
3.	$\square$	1, 2, R, $\{x/b, y/a\}$ QED.

e. After negating the statement and putting the result in clausal form, we obtain the following proof:

1.	$p(x) \vee q(y)$	P
2.	$\neg p(a)$	P
3.	$\neg q(a)$	P
4.	$q(y)$	1, 2, R, $\{x/a\}$
5.	$\square$	3, 4, R, $\{y/a\}$ QED.

10. a. In first-order predicate calculus the argument can be written as the following wff: $\forall x\, (C(x) \rightarrow P(x)) \wedge \exists x\, (C(x) \wedge L(x)) \rightarrow \exists x\, (P(x) \wedge L(x))$, where $C(x)$ means that x is a computer science major, $P(x)$ means that x is a person, and $L(x)$ means that x is a logical thinker. After negating the wff and transforming the result into clausal form, we obtain the proof:

1.	$\neg C(x) \vee P(x)$	P
2.	$C(a)$	P
3.	$L(a)$	P
4.	$\neg P(z) \vee \neg L(z)$	P
5.	$\neg P(a)$	3, 4, R, $\{z/a\}$
6.	$\neg C(a)$	1, 5, R, $\{x/a\}$
7.	$\square$	2, 6, R, $\{\,\}$ QED.

11. a. Let $D(x)$ mean that x is a dog, $L(x)$ mean that x likes people, $H(x)$ mean that x hates cats, and a = Rover. The argument can be formalized as follows: $\forall x\, (D(x) \rightarrow L(x) \vee H(x)) \wedge D(a) \wedge \neg H(a) \rightarrow \exists x\, (D(x) \wedge L(x))$. After negating the wff and transforming the result into clausal form, we obtain the proof:

1.	$\neg D(x) \vee L(x) \vee H(x)$	P
2.	$D(a)$	P
3.	$\neg H(a)$	P
4.	$\neg D(y) \vee \neg L(y)$	P
5.	$L(a) \vee H(a)$	1, 2, R, $\{x/a\}$
6.	$L(a)$	3, 5, R, $\{\,\}$
7.	$\neg D(a)$	4, 6, R, $\{y/a\}$
8.	$\square$	2, 7, R, $\{\,\}$ QED.

c. Let $H(x)$ mean that x is a human being, $Q(x)$ mean that x is a quadruped, and $M(x)$ mean that x is a man. Then the argument can be formalized as

$$\forall x\, (H(x) \to \neg\, Q(x)) \wedge \forall x\, (M(x) \to H(x)) \to \forall x\, (M(x) \to \neg\, Q(x)).$$

After negating the wff and transforming the result into clausal form, we obtain the proof:

1.	$\neg\, H(x) \vee \neg\, Q(x)$	P
2.	$\neg\, M(y) \vee H(y)$	P
3.	$M(a)$	P
4.	$Q(a)$	P
5.	$H(a)$	2, 3, R, $\{y/a\}$
6.	$\neg\, O(a)$	1, 5, R, $\{x/a\}$
7.	$\square$	4, 6, R, $\{\}$ QED.

e. Let $F(x)$ mean that x is a freshman, $S(x)$ mean that x is a sophomore, $J(x)$ mean that x is a junior, and $L(x, y)$ mean that x likes y. Then the argument can be formalized as $A \to B$, where

$$A = \exists x\, (F(x) \wedge \forall y\, (S(y) \to L(x, y))) \wedge \forall x\, (F(x) \to \forall y\, (J(y) \to \neg\, L(x, y)))$$

and $B = \forall x\, (S(x) \to \neg\, J(x))$. After negating the wff and transforming the result into clausal form, we obtain the proof:

1.	$F(a)$	P
2.	$\neg\, S(x) \vee L(a, x)$	P
3.	$\neg\, F(y) \vee \neg\, J(z) \vee \neg\, L(y, z)$	P
4.	$S(b)$	P
5.	$J(b)$	P
6.	$\neg\, J(z) \vee \neg\, L(a, z)$	1, 3, R, $\{y/a\}$
7.	$\neg\, L(a, b)$	5, 6, R, $\{z/b\}$
8.	$\neg\, S(b)$	2, 7, R, $\{x/b\}$
9.	$\square$	4, 8, R, $\{\}$ QED.

12. a. We need to show that $x(\theta\sigma) = (x\theta)\sigma$ for each variable x in E. First, suppose $x/t \in \theta$ for some term t. If $x = t\sigma$, then $x(\theta\sigma) = x$ because the binding $x/t\sigma$ has been removed from $\theta\sigma$. But since $x/t \in \theta$, it follows that $x\theta = t$. Now apply σ to both sides to obtain $(x\theta)\sigma = t\sigma = x$. Therefore $x(\theta\sigma) = x = (x\theta)\sigma$. If $x \neq t\sigma$, then $x(\theta\sigma) = t\sigma = (x\theta)\sigma$. Second, suppose that $x/t \in \sigma$ and x does not occur as a numerator of θ. Then $x(\theta\sigma) = t = x\sigma = (x\theta)\sigma$. Lastly, if x does not occur as a numerator of either σ or θ, then the substitutions have no effect on x. Thus $x(\theta\sigma) = x = (x\theta)\sigma$.

c. If $x/t \in \theta$, then $x/t = x/t\varepsilon$, so it follows from the definition of composition that $\theta = \theta\varepsilon$. For any variable x we have $x(\varepsilon\theta) = (x\varepsilon)\theta = x\theta$. Therefore we have the desired result $\theta\varepsilon = \varepsilon\theta = \theta$.

e. The proof follows:

$$(A \cup B)\theta = \{E\theta \mid E \in A \cup B\} = \{E\theta \mid E \in A\} \cup \{E\theta \mid E \in B\} = A\theta \cup B\theta.$$

Section 4.2

1. a. isChildOf(x, y) ← isParentOf(y, x).

c. isGreatGrandParentOf(x, y) ← isParentOf(x, w),
isParentOf(w, z),
isParentOf(z, y).

2. a. The following definition will work if $x \neq y$:

isSiblingOf(x, y) ← isParentOf(z, x), isParentOf(z, y).

c. Let s denote isSecondCousinOf. Two possible definitions are

$s(x, y)$ ← isParentOf(z, x), isParentOf(w, y), isCousinOf(z, w)

or

$s(x, y)$ ← isGreatGrandParentOf(z, x), isGreatGrandParentOf(z, y).

3. a.

1.	$p(a, b) \leftarrow$		P
2.	$p(a, c) \leftarrow$		P
3.	$p(b, d) \leftarrow$		P
4.	$p(c, e) \leftarrow$		P
5.	$g(x, y) \leftarrow p(x, z), p(z, y)$		P
6.	$\leftarrow g(a, w)$		P initial goal
7.	$\leftarrow p(a, z), p(z, y)$		5, 6, R, $\theta_1 = \{x/a, w/y\}$.
8.	$\leftarrow p(b, y)$		1, 7, R, $\theta_2 = \{z/b\}$
9.	$\square$		3, 8, R, $\theta_3 = \{y/d\}$ QED.

b.

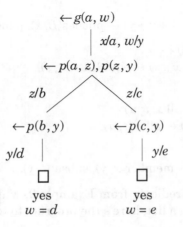

4. a.

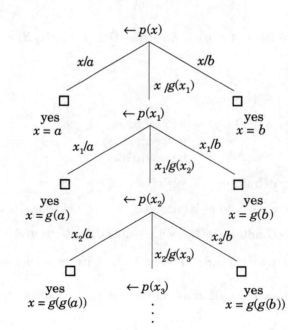

c. $\{g^n(a) \mid n \in \mathbb{N}\}$.

5. a. The program returns the answer yes.

6. a. The symmetric closure s can be defined by the two clause program:

$$s(x, y) \leftarrow r(x, y) \text{ and } s(x, y) \leftarrow r(y, x).$$

7. a.   fib(0, 1) ←
fib(1, 1) ←
fib(x, $y + z$) ← fib($x - 1$, y), fib($x - 2$, z).

c.   pnodes($\langle\ \rangle$, 0) ←
pnodes($\langle L, a, R\rangle$, $1 + x + y$) ← pnodes(L, x), pnodes(R, y).

8. a.   equalLists($\langle\ \rangle$, $\langle\ \rangle$) ←
equalLists($x :: t$, $x :: s$) ← equalLists(t, s).

c.   all(x, $\langle\ \rangle$, $\langle\ \rangle$) ←
all(x, $x :: t$, u) ← all(x, t, u)
all(x, $y :: t$, $y :: u$) ← all(x, t, u).

e.   subset($\langle\ \rangle$, y) ←
subset($x :: t$, y) ← member(x, y), subset(t, y).

g. Using the "remove" predicate from Example 9, which removes one occurrence of an element from a list, here's the program to test for a subbag:

subBag($\langle\ \rangle, y$) ←
subBag($x :: t, y$) ← member(x, y), remove(x, y, w), subBag(t, w).

9. Let the predicate schedule(L, S) mean that S is a schedule for the list of classes L. For example, if L = $\langle$english102, math200$\rangle$, then S is a list of 4-tuples of the form $\langle$name, section, time, place$\rangle$. For the example, S might look like the following:

$\langle\langle$english102, 2, 3pm, ivy238$\rangle$, $\langle$math200, 1,10am, briar315$\rangle\rangle$.

Assume that the available classes are listed as facts of the following form:

class(name, section, time, place) ← .

The following solution will yield one schedule of classes which might contain time conflicts. All schedules can be found by backtracking. If a class cannot be found, a note is made to that effect.

schedule($\langle\ \rangle, \langle\ \rangle$) ←
schedule($x :: y, S$)　← class(x, Sect, Time, Place),
　　　　　　　　　　schedule(y, T),
　　　　　　　　　　cons($\langle x$, Sect, Time, Place$\rangle, T, S$)

schedule($x :: y, \langle$unfillable$\rangle$) ← .

10. Let letters(A, L) mean that L is the list of propositional letters that occur in the wff A. Let replace(p, true, A, B) mean $B = A(p/$true$)$. Then we can start the process for a wff A with the goal ← tautology(A, Answer), where A is a tautology if Answer = true. The initial definitions might go like the following, where capital letters denote variables:

tautology(A, Answer) ← letters(A, L), evaluate(A, L, Answer)

evaluate($A, \langle\ \rangle, Y$)　← value(A, Y)
evaluate($A, H :: T$, Answer)　← replace(H, true, A, B),
　　　　　　　　　　　　replace(H, false, A, C),
　　　　　　　　　　　　value($B \wedge C$, Answer).

When "value" is called, $B \wedge C$ is a proposition containing only true and false terms. The first few clauses for the "replace" predicate might include the following:

replace(X, true, X, true) ←
replace(X, true, $\neg X$, false) ←
replace(X, true, $\neg A, \neg B$) ← replace(X, true, A, B)
replace(X, true, $A \wedge X, B$) ← replace(X, true, A, B)
replace(X, true, $X \wedge A, B$) ← replace(X, true, A, B)
replace(X, true, $A \wedge B, C \wedge D$)　← replace(X, true, A, C),
　　　　　　　　　　　　　　replace(X, true, B, D).

Continue by writing the clauses for the false case and for the other operators ∨ and →. The first few clauses for the "value" predicate might include the following:

$$\text{value}(\text{true}, \text{true}) \leftarrow$$
$$\text{value}(\text{false}, \text{false}) \leftarrow$$
$$\text{value}(\neg \, \text{true}, \text{false}) \leftarrow$$
$$\text{value}(\neg \, \text{false}, \text{true}) \leftarrow$$
$$\text{value}(\neg \, X, Y) \leftarrow \text{value}(X, A), \text{value} \, (\neg A, Y)$$
$$\text{value}(\text{false} \wedge X, \text{false}) \leftarrow$$
$$\text{value}(X \wedge \text{false}, \text{false}) \leftarrow$$
$$\text{value}(\text{true} \wedge X, Y) \leftarrow \text{value}(X, Y)$$
$$\text{value}(X \wedge \text{true}, Y) \leftarrow \text{value}(X, Y)$$
$$\text{value}(X \wedge Y, Z) \leftarrow \text{value}(X, U), \text{value}(Y, V), \text{value}(U \wedge V, Z).$$

Continue by writing the clauses to find the value of expressions containing the operators ∨ and → . The predicate to construct the list of propositional letters in a wff might start off something like the following:

$$\text{letters}(X, \langle X \rangle) \leftarrow \text{atom}(X).$$
$$\text{letters}(X \wedge Y, Z) \leftarrow \text{letters}(X, U), \text{letters}(Y, V), \text{cat}(U, V, Z).$$

Continue by writing the clauses for the other operations.

Chapter 5

Section 5.1

1. a. $\{a, b\}$. **c.** $\{a, \Lambda, b, bb, ..., b^n, ...\}$. **e.** $\{a, b, ab, bc, abb, bcc, ..., ab^n, bc^n, ...\}$.

2. a. $a + b + c$. **c.** $ab^* + ba^*$. **e.** $\Lambda + a(bb)^*$. **g.** $\Lambda + c^*a + bc^*$. **i.** a^*bc^*.

3. $0 + 1(0 + 1)^*$.

4. a. $(aa + ab + ba + bb)^*$. **c.** $(a + b)^*aba(a + b)^*$.

5. a. $(ab)^*$. **c.** $aa^*(a + b)^*$.

6. a. $b + ab^* + aa^*b + aa^*ab^*$
$$= b + ab^* + aa^*(b + ab^*)$$
$$= (\Lambda + aa^*)(b + ab^*)$$
$$= a^*(b + ab^*) \quad \text{(by (5.1), property 5)}.$$

c. By using property 7 of (5.1) the subexpression $(a + bb^*a)^*$ of the left side can be written $(a^*bb^*a)^*a^*$. So the left expression has the following form:

$$ab^*a(a + bb^*a)^*b = ab^*a(a^*bb^*a)^*a^*b.$$

Similarly, the subexpression $(b + a\,a^*b)^*$ of the right side of the original equation can be written as $b*(aa*bb*)*$. So the right expression has the following form:

$$a(b + aa*b)*aa*b = ab*(aa*bb*)*aa*b.$$

So we'll be done if we can show that $ab*a(a*bb*a)*a*b = ab*(aa*bb*)*aa*b$. Since both expressions have $ab*$ on the left end and $a*b$ on the right end, it suffices to show that

$$a(a*bb*a)* = (aa*bb*)*a.$$

But this equation is just an instance of property 8 of (5.1).

7. The proofs follow from corresponding properties of languages given in Chapter 1. See, for example, properties (1.22) and Exercise 3 of Section 1.4.

8. a. $\varnothing$. **c.** $\varnothing$.

9. a. $(b + ab)*(\Lambda + a)$. **c.** $(b + ab + aab + aaab)*(\Lambda + a + aa + aaa)$.

11.a. Let $X = R*S$. Then we can use properties 2, 3, and 5 of (5.1) to write the right side of the equation $X = RX + S$ as follows:

$$RX + S = R(R*S) + S = RR*S + \Lambda S = (RR* + \Lambda)S = R*S = X.$$

c. *Hint*: Assume that A and B are two solutions to the equation so that we have $A = RA + S$ and $B = RB + S$. Try a proof by contradiction by assuming that $A \neq B$. Then there is some string in one of $L(A)$ and $L(B)$ that is not in the other. Say w is the shortest string in $L(A) - L(B)$. Then $w \notin L(S)$ because if it were, then it would also be in $L(B)$. Thus $w \in L(RA)$. Now argue toward a contradiction.

Section 5.2

1. $T(0, a) = T(2, a) = 1, T(0, b) = 0, T(1, a) = T(2, b) = T(3, b) = 3, T(1, b) = T(3, a) = 2$, where 0 is the start state and both 2 and 3 are final states.

2. a. States 0 (start), 1(final), and 2. $T(0, a) = T(0, b) = 1$ and all other transitions go to state 2. **c.** States 0, 1, 2, 3, with start state 0 and final states 0, 1, and 2. $T(0, a) = 1, T(0, b) = 2, T(2, b) = 2$, and all other transisitons go to state 3. **e.** States 0 (start), 1 (final), 2 (final), and 3. $T(0, a) = T(1, b) = 1, T(0, b) = T(2, c) = 2$, and all other transitions go to state 3.

3. States 0 (start), 1, 2, 3, 4 (final), and 5. $T(0, -) = T(0, +) = 1, T(0, d) = T(1, d) = T(2, d) = 2, T(2, .) = 3, T(3, d) = T(4, d) = 4$, and all other transitions go to state 5.

5. a. States 0 (start), 1, 2 (final), 3, and 4 (final). $T(0, a) = \{1\}, T(1, c) = \{2\}, T(0, \Lambda) = T(3, a) = \{3\}, T(3, b) = T(4, c) = \{4\}$, and all other transitions go to $\varnothing$.

c. States 0 (start), 1, 2 (final), and 3. $T(0, a) = \{1\}$, $T(1, b) = \{2\}$, $T(0, \Lambda) = T(3, a) = \{3\}$, $T(3, \Lambda) = \{2\}$, and all other transitions go to $\emptyset$.

6. a.

c.

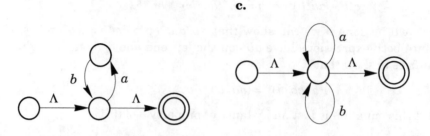

7. The NFA obtained is for $(a + b)*$.

8. Without any simplification we obtain **a.** $ab*a(a + bb*a)*b$. **c.** These two expressions are shown to be equal in the exercises of Section 5.1.

9. If we apply the algorithm by eliminating states 2, 1, and 0 in that order, then we obtain the expression $(ab)*(c + a)$.

11. Let the digits 0 and 1 denote the output of the sensors, where 1 means that traffic is present. The strings 00, 01, 10, and 11 represent the four possible pairs of inputs, where the left digit is the left-turn sensor and the right digit is the north-south traffic sensor. Each state outputs a string of length 3 over the letters

$$G \text{ (green)}, R \text{ (red)}, \text{ and } Y \text{ (yellow)}.$$

In a string of length 3, the left letter denotes the left-turn light, the middle letter denotes the east-west light, and the right letter denotes the north-south light. The start state is 0 with output RGR, which gives priority to traffic on the main east-west highway. A Moore machine to model the behavior of the signals can be written as follows:

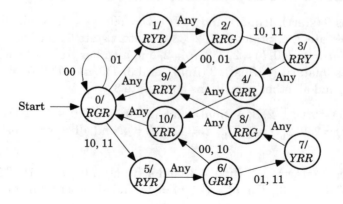

Section 5.3

1. a. The NFA has seven states: 0 (start), 1, 2, 3, 4, 5, and 6 (final). $T(0, \Lambda) =$ $\{1, 3\}$, $T(1, a) = \{2\}$, $T(2, \Lambda) = \{1, 3\}$, $T(3, \Lambda) = \{4, 6\}$, $T(4, b) = \{5\}$, $T(5, \Lambda) = \{4, 6\}$, and all other transitions map to $\emptyset$. **c.** The NFA has ten states: 0 (start), 1, 2, 3, 4, 5, 6, 7, 8, and 9 (final). $T(0, \Lambda) = \{1, 5\}$, $T(1, \Lambda) = \{2, 4\}$, $T(2, a) = \{3\}$, $T(3, \Lambda) = \{2, 4\}$, $T(4, \Lambda) = \{9\}$, $T(5, \Lambda) = \{6, 8\}$, $T(6, b) = \{7\}$, $T(7, \Lambda) = \{6, 8\}$, $T(8, \Lambda) = 9$, and all other transitions map to $\emptyset$.

2. The states are $\{0, 1\}$ (start) and $\{1, 2\}$ (final), and all transitions go to state $\{1, 2\}$.

3. a. $ba^* + aba^* + a^*$ over $A = \{a, b\}$. **c.** States $\{0, 1, 2\}$ (start and final), $\{1, 2\}$ (final), $\{2\}$ (final), and $\emptyset$. $T_D(\{0, 1, 2\}, a) = \{1, 2\}$, $T_D(\{0, 1, 2\}, b) = \{2\}$, $T_D(\{1, 2\}, a) = T_D(\{1, 2\}, b) = T_D(\{2\}, a) = \{2\}$, where the other transitions go to $\emptyset$.

4. a. States $\{0\}$ (start) and $\{0, 1\}$ (final), where $T_D(\{0\}, a) = T_D(\{0, 1\}, a) = \{0, 1\}$.

5. a. The NFA has seven states: 0 (start), 1, 2, 3, 4, 5, and 6 (final). $T(0, \Lambda) =$ $\{1, 3\}$, $T(1, a) = \{2\}$, $T(2, \Lambda) = \{1, 3\}$, $T(3, \Lambda) = \{4, 6\}$, $T(4, b) = \{5\}$, $T(5, \Lambda) = \{4, 6\}$, and all other transitions map to $\emptyset$. The DFA has four states: 0 (start, final), 1 (final), 2 (final), and 3. $T_D(0, a) = T_D(1, a) = 1$, $T_D(0, b) = T_D(1, b) = T_D(2, b) = 2$, $T_D(2, a) = T_D(3, a) = T_D(3, b) = 3$. **c.** The NFA has ten states: 0 (start), 1, 2, 3, 4, 5, 6, 7, 8, and 9 (final). $T(0, \Lambda) = \{1, 5\}$, $T(1, \Lambda) = \{2, 4\}$, $T(2, a) = \{3\}$, $T(3, \Lambda) = \{2, 4\}$, $T(4, \Lambda) = \{9\}$, $T(5, \Lambda) = \{6, 8\}$, $T(6, b) = \{7\}$, $T(7, \Lambda) = \{6, 8\}$, $T(8, \Lambda) = 9$, and all other transitions map to $\emptyset$. The DFA has four states: 0 (start, final), 1 (final), 2 (final), and 3. $T_D(0, a) = T_D(1, a) = 1$, $T_D(0, b) = T_D(2, b) = 2$, $T_D(1, b) = T_D(2, a) = T_D(3, a) = T_D(3, b) = 3$.

7. $T_{\min}([0], a) = T_{\min}([0], b) = T_{\min}([1], b) = [1]$, and $T_{\min}([1], a) = T_{\min}([4], a) = T_{\min}([4], b) = [4]$, where $[0] = \{0\}$, $[1] = \{1, 2, 3\}$, and $[4] = \{4, 5\}$.

8. a. $\{1, 3\}$. **c.** $T_{\min}([0], a) = T_{\min}([1], a) = T_{\min}([2], b) = [1]$, $T_{\min}([0], b) = T_{\min}([2], a) = T_{\min}([4], b) = [2]$, $T_{\min}([1], b) = T_{\min}([4], a) = [4]$.

9. a. The equivalence pairs are $\{0, 2\}$, $\{1, 3\}$, $\{1, 4\}$, $\{3, 4\}$. Therefore the states are $\{0, 2\}$ and $\{1, 3, 4\}$, where $\{0, 2\}$ is the start state and $\{1, 3, 4\}$ is the final state. $T_{\min}([0], a) = T_{\min}([1], a) = [1]$, and $T_{\min}([0], b) = T_{\min}([1], b) = [0]$.

10. a. The NFA has ten states. It transforms into a DFA with two states, both of which are final. The minimum state DFA has the single state 0 (start, final), and $T(0, a) = 0$. **c.** See the answer to Exercise 5a for the seven-state NFA and the four-state DFA. The minimum state DFA has three states, 0 (start, final), 1 (final), and 2. $T_{\min}(0, a) = 0$, $T_{\min}(0, b) = T_{\min}(1, b) = 1$, $T_{\min}(1, a) = T_{\min}(2, a) = T_{\min}(2, b) = 2$.

11. $(a + b)^*$.

Section 5.4

1. a. $S \to a \mid$ **b. c.** $S \to a \mid B, B \to \Lambda \mid bB.$ **e.** $S \to aB \mid bC, B \to \Lambda \mid bB, C \to \Lambda$ $\mid cC.$ **g.** $S \to \Lambda \mid aaS \mid bbS.$ **i.** $S \to cT \mid abU, T \to \Lambda \mid aT \mid bT, U \to cT \mid abU.$

2. a. $S \to a \mid b \mid c.$ **c.** $S \to aB \mid bC, B \to \Lambda \mid bB, C \to \Lambda \mid aC.$ **e.** $S \to \Lambda \mid aB,$ $B \to \Lambda \mid bbB.$ **g.** $S \to \Lambda \mid a \mid cA \mid bC, A \to a \mid cA, C \to \Lambda \mid cC.$ **i.** $S \to aS \mid bC,$ $C \to \Lambda \mid cC.$

3. a. $S \to \Lambda \mid aaS \mid abS \mid baS \mid bbS.$ **c.** $S \to aS \mid bS \mid abaT, T \to \Lambda \mid aT \mid bT.$

4. a. $S \to a \mid Sab.$ **c.** $S \to Tc \mid Sa \mid Sb, T \to \Lambda \mid Tab.$

5. $S \to aS \mid bS \mid aI, I \to bJ, J \to bK, K \to \Lambda.$

7. The case implies that $y = a^i b^j$, where $i > 0$ and $j > 0$. So xy^2z has the form $xa^i b^j a^i b^j z$, which can't be in the language.

8. a. Let $L = \{a^n b a^n \mid n \in \mathbb{N}\}$, and suppose that L is regular. By the first pumping lemma (5.13) there are strings $x, y, z \in \{a, b\}^*, y \neq \Lambda$, such that $xy^k z \in L$ for all $k \geq 0$. For $k = 0$ we have $xz \in L$, which says that b must occur in either x or z. For $k = 1$ we have $xyz \in L$. Therefore y consists of all a's. Therefore xy^2z contains more a's on one side of the b than on the other side. This implies that $xy^2z \notin L$, which is a contradiction. Thus L is not regular.

9. Let L and M be two regular languages. Let A be the union of the alphabets for L and M. By (5.15)(4) we know that the complements $L' = A^* - L$ and $M' = A^* - M$ are regular languages. By (5.15)(1) the union $L' \cup M'$ is regular. Since $L' \cup M' = (L \cap M)'$, one more application of (5.15)(4) tells us that $L \cap M$ is regular.

11. For each state i and letter $a \in A$, create an edge $\langle i, j \rangle$ labled with a in the new DFA if there is a path from i to j in the DFA for L whose labels concatenate to $f(a)$. This new DFA accepts a string w exactly when the original DFA accepts $f(w)$. In other words, the new DFA accepts $f^{-1}(L)$.

12. a. $\{xby \mid x$ and y are strings of length n over $\{a, c\}^*\}.$ **c.** Let $g(a) = a, g(b) = \Lambda,$ and $g(c) = b.$

Chapter 6

Section 6.1

1. a. $S \to aSbb \mid \Lambda.$ **c.** $S \to aSa \mid bSb \mid \Lambda.$ **e.** $S \to aSa \mid bSb \mid a \mid b \mid \Lambda.$

2. a. $S \to A \mid B, A \to aAb \mid \Lambda, B \to aBbb \mid \Lambda.$ **c.** $S \to AS \mid \Lambda, A \to aAb \mid \Lambda.$

Section 6.2

1. a. A PDA for $\{ab^n cd^n \mid n \geq 0\}$ has start state 0 and final state 3 with $\perp$ as the starting stack symbol:

$\langle 0, a, \perp, \text{nop}, 1 \rangle,$
$\langle 1, b, \perp, \text{push}(b), 1 \rangle,$
$\langle 1, b, b, \text{push}(b), 1 \rangle,$
$\langle 1, c, \perp, \text{nop}, 2 \rangle,$
$\langle 1, c, b, \text{nop}, 2 \rangle,$
$\langle 2, d, b, \text{pop}, 2 \rangle,$
$\langle 2, \Lambda, \perp, \text{nop}, 3 \rangle.$

c. A PDA for $\{wcw^R \mid w \in \{a, b\}^*\}$ has start state 0 and final state 2 with $\perp$ as the starting stack symbol.

$\langle 0, a, ?, \text{push}(a), 0 \rangle,$
$\langle 0, b, ?, \text{push}(b), 0 \rangle,$
$\langle 0, c, ?, \text{nop}, 1 \rangle,$
$\langle 1, a, a, \text{pop}, 1 \rangle,$
$\langle 1, b, b, \text{pop}, 1 \rangle,$
$\langle 1, \Lambda, \perp, \text{nop}, 2 \rangle.$

e. A PDA for $\{a^n b^{n+2} \mid n \geq 0\}$ has start state 0 and final state 2 with $\perp$ as the starting stack symbol:

$\langle 0, a, \perp, \text{push}(a), 0 \rangle,$
$\langle 0, a, a, \text{push}(a), 0 \rangle,$
$\langle 0, b, \perp, \text{nop}, 1 \rangle,$
$\langle 0, b, a, \text{nop}, 1 \rangle,$
$\langle 1, b, \perp, \text{nop}, 2 \rangle,$
$\langle 1, b, a, \text{pop}, 1 \rangle.$

2. Let 0 be the start and final state and $\perp$ be the starting stack symbol.

$\langle 0, a, \perp, \text{push}(a), 0 \rangle,$
$\langle 0, a, a, \text{nop}, 0 \rangle,$
$\langle 0, b, \perp, \text{push}(b), 0 \rangle,$
$\langle 0, b, a, \text{push}(b), 0 \rangle,$
$\langle 0, b, b, \text{nop}, 0 \rangle.$

3. a. State 0 is the start state, and both states 0 and 3 are final states with $\perp$ as the starting stack symbol.

$\langle 0, a, \perp, \text{push}(a), 1 \rangle,$
$\langle 1, a, a, \text{push}(a), 1 \rangle,$
$\langle 1, b, a, \text{pop}, 2 \rangle,$
$\langle 2, b, a, \text{pop}, 2 \rangle,$
$\langle 2, \Lambda, \perp, \text{nop}, 3 \rangle.$

4. a. Let the states be 0 and 1, where 0 is the start state and the final state with $\perp$ as the starting stack symbol. The PDA can be represented as follows:

$\langle 0, a, \bot, \langle \text{push}(X), \text{push}(a) \rangle, 1 \rangle$,
$\langle 1, a, a, \langle \text{pop}, \text{push}(X), \text{push}(a) \rangle, 1 \rangle$,
$\langle 1, b, a, \langle \text{pop}, \text{pop} \rangle, 1 \rangle$,
$\langle 1, b, X, \text{pop}, 1 \rangle$,
$\langle 1, \Lambda, \bot, \text{push}(X), 0 \rangle$.

5. Create a new start state s and a new empty stack state e. Then add the following instructions to the PDA of Example 1: $\langle s, \Lambda, Y, \text{push}(X), 0 \rangle$, $\langle 2, \Lambda, X,$ pop, $e \rangle$, $\langle 2, \Lambda, Y, \text{pop}, e \rangle$, $\langle e, \Lambda, X, \text{pop}, e \rangle$, $\langle e, \Lambda, Y, \text{pop}, e \rangle$.

6. Create a new start state s and a new unique final state f. Then add the following instructions to the PDA of Example 2: $\langle s, \Lambda, Y, \text{push}(X), 0 \rangle$, $\langle 0, \Lambda, Y,$ nop, $f \rangle$, $\langle 1, \Lambda, Y, \text{nop}, f \rangle$.

7. a. $\langle 0, a, a, \text{pop}, 0 \rangle$,
$\langle 0, b, b, \text{pop}, 0 \rangle$,
$\langle 0, c, c, \text{pop}, 0 \rangle$,
$\langle 0, \Lambda, S, \langle \text{pop}, \text{push}(c) \rangle, 0 \rangle$,
$\langle 0, \Lambda, S, \langle \text{pop}, \text{push}(b), \text{push}(S), \text{push}(a) \rangle, 0 \rangle$.

8. $S \to X_{01}, X_{01} \to a X_{01} X_{11}, X_{11} \to b, X_{01} \to \Lambda$.

9. a. The set of strings over $\{a, b\}$ containing an equal number of a's and b's such that for any letter in a string the number of b's to its left is less than or equal to the number of a's to its left. **b.** $S \to X_{00}, X_{00} \to \Lambda \mid a A_{00} X_{00}, A_{00} \to b \mid a A_{00} A_{00}$, which can be simplified to $S \to \Lambda \mid aAS, A \to b \mid aAA$. **c.** Yes.

Section 6.3
1. a. $S \to a \mid bA, A \to a \mid ba$. **c.** $S \to aB, B \to aBc \mid b$.

2. An LL(3) grammar: $S \to aA \mid aaB, A \to aA \mid \Lambda, B \to bB \mid \Lambda$. An LL(2) grammar: $S \to aC, C \to A \mid aB, A \to aA \mid \Lambda, B \to bB \mid \Lambda$.

3. a. $S \to aT, T \to bS \mid \Lambda$. The grammar is LL(1).

4. a. $S \to cT, T \to aT \mid bT \mid \Lambda$. The grammar is LL(1).

5. Let the letters $E, R, T, V,$ and F denote procedures. Then define them as follows:

E:	**begin** call T; call R **end**;
R:	**if** lookahead = "+" **then** **begin** match("+"); call T; call R **end;**
T:	**begin** call F; call V **end**;
V:	**if** lookahead = "*" **then** **begin** match("*"); call F; call V **end;**

> F: **if** lookahead $= a$ **then** match(a)
>   **else if** lookahead $=$ "(" **then**
>   **begin** match("("); call E; match(")") **end**
>   **else** error
>   **fi.**

6. a. First(Λ) = {Λ}, First(aSb) = {a}, First(S) = {a, Λ}. Follow(S) = {$\$$, b}. $P[S, a]$ = "$S \to aSb$," and $P[S, b]$ = $P[S, \$]$ = "$S \to \Lambda$." **c.** First(Λ) = {Λ}, First(a) = {a}, First(R) = {+, Λ}, First(V) = {$*$, Λ}, First(F) = First(T) = First(E) = First(FV) = First(TR) = {(, a}, First($*FV$) = {$*$}, First($+TR$) = {+}. Follow(E) = Follow(R) = {), $\$$}, Follow(T) = Follow(V) = {+, $\$$,)}, Follow(F) = {$*$, +,), $\$$}. $P[E, a]$ = $P[E, (]$ = "$E \to TR$," $P[R, +]$ = "$R \to +TR$," $P[R,)]$ = $P[R, \$]$ = "$R \to \Lambda$," $P[T, a]$ = $P[T, (]$ = "$T \to FV$," $P[V, *]$ = "$V \to *FV$," $P[V, +]$ = $P[V,)]$ = $P[V, \$]$ = "$V \to \Lambda$," $P[F, a]$ = "$F \to a$," and $P[F, (]$ = "$F \to (E)$."

7. a. The sentential forms that can occur in a rightmost derivation take the following forms, where $n \geq 0$: aA, ad, $ac^{n+1}A$, $ac^{n+1}d$, bB, bd, $bc^{n+1}B$, and $bc^{n+1}d$. In each case the handle is completely determined without scanning past it. So the grammar is LR(0).

9. The problem lies with the handles defined by the productions $A \to ab$ and $B \to ab$. For example, the input strings ab and abb need one lookahead symbol beyond ab to determine which handle to use. But the strings $aabb$ and $aabbbb$ need three lookahead symbols beyond ab to determine the appropriate handle. Generalizing from these examples, we see that no fixed number of lookahead symbols can suffice to determine which handle to use.

10. a. A table with four states has the following nonblank entries: $P[0, b]$ = "shift 2," $P[0, S]$ = 1, $P[1, a]$ = "shift 3," $P[1, \$]$ = accept, $P[2, a]$ = $P[2, \$]$ = "$S \to b$," and $P[3, a]$ = $P[3, \$]$ = "$S \to Sa$."
c. A table with six states has the following nonblank entries: $P[0, a]$ = "shift 4," $P[0, S]$ = 3, $P[0, A]$ = 1, $P[1, b]$ = "shift 5," $P[1, B]$ = 2, $P[2, \$]$ = "$S \to AB$," $P[3, \$]$ = accept, $P[4, b]$ = "$A \to a$,"and $P[5, \$]$ = "$B \to b$."

Section 6.4

1. a. $S \to aA \mid aBb \mid a \mid ab, A \to aA \mid a, B \to aBb \mid ab$.

2. a. $S \to AR \mid BT \mid c, R \to SA, T \to SB, A \to a, B \to b$.

3. $S \to aABC \mid aBC \mid bC \mid dD \mid d \mid \Lambda, A \to aA \mid a, C \to cC \mid c, D \to dD \mid d, B \to b$.

4. a. Let $z = a^m b^m a^m = uvwxy$. Show that the pumped variables v and x can't contain distinct letters. Then at least one of v and x must have the form a^i or b^i for some $i > 0$. Look at the different cases, and come up with contradictions showing that the pumped string uv^2wx^2y can't be in the language.

c. Let $L = \{a^p \mid p$ is a prime number$\}$, and assume that L is context-free. Let $z = a^p$, where p is a prime number larger than $m + 1$ from (6.19). Let $k = |u| + |w| + |y|$. Since $|vwx| \leq m$ and $|vx| \geq 1$, it follows that $k > 1$. For any $i \geq 0$ we have $|uv^iwx^iy| = k + i(p - k)$. Letting $i = k$, we get the equation $|uv^kwx^ky| = k + k(p - k) = k(1 + p - k)$, which can't be a prime number. This contradicts the requirement that each pumped string must be in L. Therefore L is not context-free.

5. a. $\{xb^ny \mid x$ and y are strings of length n over $\{a, c\}^*\}$.

c. If $\{a^nb^na^n \mid n \in \mathbb{N}\}$ is context-free, then by (6.23), $f^{-1}(\{a^nb^na^n \mid n \in \mathbb{N}\})$ is context-free. So by (6.22) and part (b) we must conclude that $\{a^nb^nc^n \mid n \in \mathbb{N}\}$ is context-free. But this is not the case. So $\{a^nb^na^n \mid n \in \mathbb{N}\}$ can't be context-free.

Chapter 7

Section 7.1

1. Consider the general algorithm that repeatedly cancels the same letter from each end of the input string by replacing its occurrences by Λ. A Turing machine program to accomplish this follows, where the start state is 0.

$\langle 0, a, \Lambda, R, 1 \rangle$	Replace a by Λ.
$\langle 0, b, \Lambda, R, 4 \rangle$	Replace b by Λ.
$\langle 0, \Lambda, \Lambda, S, \text{Halt} \rangle$	It's an even-length palindrome.
$\langle 1, a, a, R, 1 \rangle$	Scan right.
$\langle 1, b, b, R, 1 \rangle$	Scan right.
$\langle 1, \Lambda, \Lambda, L, 2 \rangle$	Found the right end.
$\langle 2, a, \Lambda, L, 3 \rangle$	Replace rightmost a by Λ.
$\langle 2, \Lambda, \Lambda, S, \text{Halt} \rangle$	It's an odd length palindrome.
$\langle 3, a, a, L, 3 \rangle$	Scan left.
$\langle 3, b, b, L, 3 \rangle$	Scan left.
$\langle 3, \Lambda, \Lambda, R, 0 \rangle$	Found left end.
$\langle 4, a, a, R, 4 \rangle$	Scan right.
$\langle 4, b, b, R, 4 \rangle$	Scan right.
$\langle 4, \Lambda, \Lambda, L, 5 \rangle$	Found the right end.
$\langle 5, b, \Lambda, L, 3 \rangle$	Replace rightmost b by Λ.
$\langle 5, \Lambda, \Lambda, S, \text{Halt} \rangle$	It's an odd length palindrome.

3. This machine will remember the current cell, write Λ, and move right to the state that writes the remembered symbol. The start state is 0.

$\langle 0, a, \Lambda, R, 1 \rangle$ Go write an a.
$\langle 0, b, \Lambda, R, 2 \rangle$ Go write a b.
$\langle 0, \Lambda, \Lambda, S, \text{Halt} \rangle$ Done.

$\langle 1, a, a, R, 1 \rangle$ Write an a and go write an a.
$\langle 1, b, a, R, 2 \rangle$ Write an a and go write a b.
$\langle 1, \Lambda, a, S, \text{Halt} \rangle$ Done.

$\langle 2, a, b, R, 1 \rangle$ Write a b and go write an a.
$\langle 2, b, b, R, 2 \rangle$ Write a b and go write a b.
$\langle 2, \Lambda, b, S, \text{Halt} \rangle$ Done.

4. a. The leftmost string is moved right one cell position, overwriting the # symbol. Then the machine scans left and halts with the tape head at the leftmost cell of the number. A Turing machine program with start state 0 follows.

$\langle 0, 1, \Lambda, R, 1 \rangle$ Write Λ and go find #.

$\langle 1, 1, 1, R, 1 \rangle$ Scan right.
$\langle 1, \#, 1, L, 2 \rangle$ Overwrite # with 1.

$\langle 2, 1, 1, L, 2 \rangle$ Scan left.
$\langle 2, \Lambda, \Lambda, R, \text{Halt} \rangle$.

5. a. Complement the number while scanning it left to right. Then add 1. The start state is 0. The machine halts immediately when addition is complete.

$\langle 0, 0, 1, R, 0 \rangle$ Complement while scanning left to right.
$\langle 0, 1, 0, R, 0 \rangle$
$\langle 0, \Lambda, \Lambda, L, 1 \rangle$ Go to add 1.

$\langle 1, 0, 1, S, \text{Halt} \rangle$ No carry.
$\langle 1, 1, 0, L, 1 \rangle$ Carry.
$\langle 1, \Lambda, 1, S, \text{Halt} \rangle$ Carry.

c. Assume that the tape head is at the right end of the input string. The machine will overwrite the input string with the answer and halt with the tape head at the left end of the answer. The start state is 0.

Add the first bit:

$\langle 0, 0, 1, L, 1 \rangle$ Add 1 + 0, no carry.
$\langle 0, 1, 0, L, 2 \rangle$ Add 1 + 1, carry.

Add the second bit with no carry:

$\langle 1, 0, 1, L, 4 \rangle$ Add 1 + 0, done with add, move left.
$\langle 1, 1, 0, L, 3 \rangle$ Add 1 + 1, go to carry state.
$\langle 1, \Lambda, 1, S, \text{Halt} \rangle$ Add 1, done with add.

Add the second bit with carry:

$\langle 2, 0, 0, L, 3 \rangle$	Add $1 + 1 + 0$, go to carry state.
$\langle 2, 1, 1, L, 3 \rangle$	Add $1 + 1 + 1$, go to carry state.
$\langle 2, \Lambda, 0, L, 3 \rangle$	Add $1 + 1$, go to carry state.

Carry state:

$\langle 3, 0, 1, L, 4 \rangle$	Done with add, move to left.
$\langle 3, 1, 0, L, 3 \rangle$	Stay in carry state.
$\langle 3, \Lambda, 1, S, \text{Halt} \rangle$	Done with add.

Move to left end of number:

$\langle 4, 0, 0, L, 4 \rangle$	Move left.
$\langle 4, 1, 1, L, 4 \rangle$	Move left.
$\langle 4, \Lambda, \Lambda, R, \text{Halt} \rangle$	Done with add.

7. Let 0 be the start state and the "noncarry" state. State 1 will be the "carry" state. The tape head for the output tape will always be positioned at a blank cell. The first four instructions perform the normal add with no carry:

$\langle 0, \langle 0, 0, \Lambda \rangle, \langle 0, 0, 0 \rangle, \langle L, L, L \rangle, 0 \rangle$	
$\langle 0, \langle 0, 1, \Lambda \rangle, \langle 0, 1, 1 \rangle, \langle L, L, L \rangle, 0 \rangle$	
$\langle 0, \langle 1, 0, \Lambda \rangle, \langle 1, 0, 1 \rangle, \langle L, L, L \rangle, 0 \rangle$	
$\langle 0, \langle 1, 1, \Lambda \rangle, \langle 1, 1, 0 \rangle, \langle L, L, L \rangle, 1 \rangle$	Go to carry state.

The next instructions copy the extra portion of the longer of the two numbers, if necessary:

$\langle 0, \langle 0, \Lambda, \Lambda \rangle, \langle 0, \Lambda, 0 \rangle, \langle L, L, L \rangle, 0 \rangle$	1st number longer.
$\langle 0, \langle 1, \Lambda, \Lambda \rangle, \langle 1, \Lambda, 1 \rangle, \langle L, L, L \rangle, 0 \rangle$	
$\langle 0, \langle \Lambda, 0, \Lambda \rangle, \langle \Lambda, 0, 0 \rangle, \langle L, L, L \rangle, 0 \rangle$	2nd number longer.
$\langle 0, \langle \Lambda, 1, \Lambda \rangle, \langle \Lambda, 1, 1 \rangle, \langle L, L, L \rangle, 0 \rangle$	
$\langle 0, \langle \Lambda, \Lambda, \Lambda \rangle, \langle \Lambda, \Lambda, \Lambda \rangle, \langle S, S, R \rangle, \text{Halt} \rangle$	Done.

The next four instructions perform the add with carry:

$\langle 1, \langle 0, 0, \Lambda \rangle, \langle 0, 0, 1 \rangle, \langle L, L, L \rangle, 0 \rangle$	Go to noncarry state.
$\langle 1, \langle 0, 1, \Lambda \rangle, \langle 0, 1, 0 \rangle, \langle L, L, L \rangle, 1 \rangle$	
$\langle 1, \langle 1, 0, \Lambda \rangle, \langle 1, 0, 0 \rangle, \langle L, L, L \rangle, 1 \rangle$	
$\langle 1, \langle 1, 1, \Lambda \rangle, \langle 1, 1, 1 \rangle, \langle L, L, L \rangle, 1 \rangle$	

The next instructions add the carry to the extra portion of the longer of the two numbers, if necessary:

$\langle 1, \langle 0, \Lambda, \Lambda \rangle, \langle 0, \Lambda, 1 \rangle, \langle L, L, L \rangle, 0 \rangle$	1st number longer.
$\langle 1, \langle 1, \Lambda, \Lambda \rangle, \langle 1, \Lambda, 0 \rangle, \langle L, L, L \rangle, 1 \rangle$	
$\langle 1, \langle \Lambda, 0, \Lambda \rangle, \langle \Lambda, 0, 1 \rangle, \langle L, L, L \rangle, 0 \rangle$	2nd number longer.
$\langle 1, \langle \Lambda, 1, \Lambda \rangle, \langle \Lambda, 1, 0 \rangle, \langle L, L, L \rangle, 1 \rangle$	
$\langle 1, \langle \Lambda, \Lambda, \Lambda \rangle, \langle \Lambda, \Lambda, 1 \rangle, \langle S, S, S \rangle, \text{Halt} \rangle$	Done.

9.

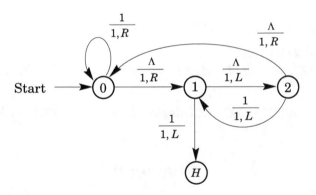

Section 7.2

1. a. $Z := X$; $Z := Z + Y$.

c. Temp $:= X$; **while** Temp $\neq 0$ **do** S; Temp $:= 0$ **od**.

e. $\quad A := X$; $B := Y$; Ans $:= 0$;
  while $A \neq 0$ **do**
   if $B \neq 0$ **then** $A := \text{pred}(A)$; $B := \text{pred}(B)$
   else Ans $:= A$; $A := 0$
   fi
  od.

g. Use the fact that "$X \leq Y$" is equivalent to "$X < Y + 1$," which is equivalent to
"$(Y + 1)$ monus $X \neq 0$."

i. Use the fact that "$X \neq Y$" is equivalent to "absoluteDiff$(X, Y) \neq 0$."

k. $Z := X + Y$; **while** $Z \neq 0$ **do** S; $Z := X + Y$ **od**. A solution that does not use addition can be written:

   $A := 1$;
   while $A \neq 0$ **do**
    if $X \neq 0$ **then**
     S
    else if $Y \neq 0$ **then** S **else** $A := 0$ **fi**
    fi
   od.

2. a. Let $h = 0$ and $g(a, b) = p_1(a, b)$. Then the definition takes the form $\text{pred}(0) = h$ and $\text{pred}(\text{succ}(x)) = g(x, \text{pred}(x))$.

3. a. f is the successor function. **c.** $f(x, y) = $ if $x \leq y$ then $y - x$ else undefined.

5. $\text{LE}(x, y) = \text{sgn}(\text{monus}(\text{succ}(y), x)) = \text{less}(x, \text{succ}(y))$. For example,

$$\text{LE}(1, 2) = \text{sgn}(\text{monus}(3, 1)) = \text{less}(1, 3) = 1,$$
$$\text{LE}(1, 1) = \text{sgn}(\text{monus}(2, 1)) = \text{less}(1, 2) = 1,$$
$$\text{LE}(2, 1) = \text{sgn}(\text{monus}(2, 2)) = \text{less}(2, 2) = 0.$$

6. a. a^i. **c.** a^i.

7. a. $a \to a$. **c.** $* \to \Lambda$. **e.** $Xa \to bX, Xb \to aX, X \to \Lambda$ (halt), $\Lambda \to X$.

8. a. $a \to a$. **c.** $X*Y \to XY$.
e. $aX \to @b\#X, bX \to @a\#X, @X\#aY \to @Xb\#Y, @X\#bY \to @Xa\#Y, @X\# \to X$
(halt).

9. a. $X \to aXa$ and $X \to bXb$ with single axiom Λ. **c.** $X*Y\#Z \to aX*bY\#cZ$ with
axiom $*\#$.

Chapter 8

Section 8.1

1. Since f and g are computable, there are algorithms to compute f and g. An
algorithm to compute $h(x)$ consists of running the algorithm for g on input x.
If the algorithm halts with value $g(x)$, then run the algorithm for f on the input $g(x)$. If this algorithm halts, then output the value $f(g(x))$. If either algorithm fails to halt, then the algorithm for $h(x)$ fails to halt.

3. Since f_x is one of the computable functions, we can compute $h(x)$ by running the algorithm to compute $f_x(x)$. If the algorithm halts, then we'll return
the value $h(x) = 1$. If the algorithm does not halt, then we're still OK, since we
want $h(x)$ to run forever.

4. a. g is not computable because $f_n(n)$ may not be defined. **c.** g is not computable because if $f_n(n)$ does not halt, there is no way to discover the fact and
output the number 4.

5. Given two DFAs over the same alphabet, construct the minimum-state
versions of each DFA. If they have a different number of states, then return
0. If they have the same number of states, then check to see whether the
states of one table can be renamed to obtain the other table. If so, then return
1. Otherwise, return 0.

6. a. The sequence 1, 2, 2, 2, 2, 2 produces the equality $abbbbbbbbbb =$
$abbbbbbbbbb$. **c.** There is no solution. **e.** The sequence 1, 5, 2, 3, 4, 4, 3, 4 will
produce the equality $abababababbabbbabb = abababababbabbbabb$.

Section 8.2

1. Let both tapes be empty at the start. The machine starts by printing 1 on
the first tape and # on the second tape. The 1 indicates $n = 1$, and # separates
the empty string Λ from the next string to be printed. Then it executes the
following loop forever: Scan 1's to the right printing a's; scan 1's to the left
printing b's; scan 1's to the right printing c's; print 1 and # and scan 1's to the
left. The start state is 0, and the tapes are initially blank.

$\langle 0, \langle \Lambda, \Lambda \rangle, \langle 1, \# \rangle, \langle S, R \rangle, 1 \rangle$ Initialize $n = 1$, print #.

$\langle 1, \langle 1, \Lambda \rangle, \langle 1, a \rangle, \langle R, R \rangle, 1 \rangle$ Scan right printing a's.
$\langle 1, \langle \Lambda, \Lambda \rangle, \langle \Lambda, \Lambda \rangle, \langle L, S \rangle, 2 \rangle$ Done with a's.

$\langle 2, \langle 1, \Lambda \rangle, \langle 1, b \rangle, \langle L, R \rangle, 2 \rangle$ Scan left printing b's.
$\langle 2, \langle \Lambda, \Lambda \rangle, \langle \Lambda, \Lambda \rangle, \langle R, S \rangle, 3 \rangle$ Done with b's.

$\langle 3, \langle 1, \Lambda \rangle, \langle 1, c \rangle, \langle R, R \rangle, 3 \rangle$ Scan right printing c's.
$\langle 3, \langle \Lambda, \Lambda \rangle, \langle 1, \# \rangle, \langle L, R \rangle, 4 \rangle$ Done with string,
increment n and print #.

$\langle 4, \langle 1, \Lambda \rangle, \langle 1, \Lambda \rangle, \langle L, S \rangle, 4 \rangle$ Scan left.
$\langle 4, \langle \Lambda, \Lambda \rangle, \langle \Lambda, \Lambda \rangle, \langle R, S \rangle, 1 \rangle$ Go print another string.

3. $T \to \Lambda \mid S, S \to SABC \mid ABC, AB \to BA, BA \to AB, BC \to CB, CB \to BC,$
$AC \to CA, CA \to AC, A \to a, B \to b, C \to c.$

Section 8.3

1. For a function f and argument w we have $((\lambda x.(x\ (x\ y))\ f)\ w) = (f\ (f\ w))$, which applies f twice to w.

2. a. $(x\ y)[x/\lambda z.z] = (\lambda z.z\ y) = y.$ **c.** $\lambda x.(\lambda y.x\ x) = \lambda x.x.$ **e.** $\lambda x.M$, since all occurrences of x are bound.

3. a. No.

4. a. $\lambda x.(y\ x).$

5. $(((\lambda x.\lambda y.\lambda z.(x\ (y\ z))\ \lambda x.x)\ u)\ v) \to ((\lambda y.\lambda z.(\lambda x.x\ (y\ z))\ u)\ v)$
$\to ((\lambda y.\lambda z.(y\ z)\ u)\ v) \to (\lambda z.(u\ z)\ u)\ v) \to (u\ v).$

6. a. $(\lambda x.(\lambda y.y\ x)\ \lambda x.(\lambda y.x\ x)) \to (\lambda y.y\ \lambda x.(\lambda y.x\ x)) \to \lambda x.(\lambda y.x\ x) \to \lambda x.x.$

7. $(F\ \text{true true}) \to (\lambda x.\lambda y.((\text{Not}\ x)\ \text{true}\ (\text{Not}\ y))\ \text{true true})$
$\to (\lambda y.((\text{Not true})\ \text{true}\ (\text{Not}\ y))\ \text{true})$
$\to ((\text{Not true})\ \text{true}\ (\text{Not true})) \to (\text{false true false}) \to \text{false}.$

8. $(F\ 1)$ = $((Y\ g)\ 1)$
= $(g\ (Y\ g)\ 1)$
= $(\lambda x.\ ((\text{isZero}\ x)\ 1\ ((Y\ g)\ (\text{pred}\ x)))\ 1)$
= $((\text{isZero}\ 1)\ 1\ ((Y\ g)\ (\text{pred}\ 1)))$
= $(\text{false}\ 1\ ((Y\ g)\ 0))$
= $((Y\ g)\ 0)$
= $(g\ (Y\ g)\ 0)$
= $(\lambda x.\ ((\text{isZero}\ x)\ 1\ ((Y\ g)\ (\text{pred}\ x)))\ 0)$
= $((\text{isZero}\ 0)\ 1\ ((Y\ g)\ (\text{pred}\ 0)))$
= $(\text{true}\ 1\ ((Y\ g)\ (\text{pred}\ 0)))$
= $1.$

9. a.   tail (cons a b) = $\lambda x.(x$ false) (cons a b)
$\rightarrow$ (cons a b) false
= $(\lambda h.\lambda t.\lambda s.\ (s\ h\ t)\ a\ b)$ false
$\rightarrow$ $\lambda s.\ (s\ a\ b)$ false
$\rightarrow$ false a b
$\rightarrow$ b.

c.   isEmpty emptyList = $\lambda s.(s\ \lambda h.\lambda t.$false) emptyList
$\rightarrow$ emptyList $(\lambda h.\lambda t.$false)
= $\lambda x.$true $(\lambda h.\lambda t.$false)
$\rightarrow$ true.

10. a.   isZero 2 = $(\lambda x.(x$ true) (succ 1))
$\rightarrow$ ((succ 1) true)
= $(\lambda s.(s$ false 1) true)
$\rightarrow$ true false 1
$\rightarrow$ false.

11.a. c.

13. a. No normal form.

14. a. It's already in weak-head normal form.

15. Since $(x\ y) = (x\ x)$, we can form the equation $\lambda y.(x\ y) = \lambda y.(x\ x)$. So for any expression M we have $(\lambda y.(x\ y)\ M) = (\lambda y.(x\ x)\ M)$, which upon evaluation gives $(x\ M) = (x\ x)$. From this equation we can write $\lambda x.(x\ M) = \lambda x.(x\ x)$. Now we can form an equation $(\lambda x.(x\ M)\ \lambda x.x) = (\lambda x.(x\ x)\ \lambda x.x)$, which evaluates to $M = \lambda x.x$. So all expressions are equal to $\lambda x.x$ and thus are equal to each other.

16. Use the compose inference rule to replace the rule $(x \cdot c) \cdot c \rightarrow f(f(x)) \cdot c$ by the rule $(x \cdot c) \cdot c \rightarrow x \cdot c$.

17. Start with $E_0 = \{g^3(x) \leftrightarrow g(x),\ g^4(x) \leftrightarrow x\}$ and $R_0 = \emptyset$. The orient inference rule gives $E_1 = \{g^4(x) \leftrightarrow x\}$ and $R_1 = \{g^3(x) \rightarrow g(x)\}$. The simplify inference rule gives $E_2 = \{g^2(x) \leftrightarrow x\}$ and $R_2 = \{g^3(x) \rightarrow g(x)\}$. The orient inference rule gives $E_3 = \emptyset$ and $R_3 = \{g^3(x) \rightarrow g(x),\ g^2(x) \rightarrow x\}$. The collapse inference rule gives $E_4 = \{g(x) \leftrightarrow g(x)\}$ and $R_4 = \{g^2(x) \rightarrow g(x)\}$. The delete inference rule gives $E_5 = \emptyset$ and $R_5 = \{g^2(x) \rightarrow g(x)\}$.

18. a. Use the orient inference rule to replace the three equations (8.3) by the three reduction rules $e \cdot x \rightarrow x$, $x^{-1} \cdot x \rightarrow e$, and $(x \cdot y) \cdot z \rightarrow x \cdot (y \cdot z)$.
c. The expression $e^{-1} \cdot (e \cdot x)$ can be reduced in two ways: Using a rule from part (a) gives $e^{-1} \cdot (e \cdot x) \rightarrow_R e^{-1} \cdot x$; using the rule from part (b) gives $e^{-1} \cdot (e \cdot x)$ $\rightarrow_R x$. Therefore the deduce inference rule gives the equation $e^{-1} \cdot x \leftrightarrow x$. The orient inference rule replaces this equation with the desired rule $e^{-1} \cdot x \rightarrow x$.
e. The expression $(x^{-1-1} \cdot e) \cdot y$ can be reduced in two ways: Using rules from part (a) gives $(x^{-1-1} \cdot e) \cdot y \rightarrow_R x^{-1-1} \cdot (e \cdot y) \rightarrow_R x^{-1-1} \cdot y$; using the rule from part (d) gives $(x^{-1-1} \cdot e) \cdot y \rightarrow_R x \cdot y$. Therefore the deduce inference rule gives the

equation $x^{-1-1} \cdot y \leftrightarrow x \cdot y$. The orient inference rule replaces this equation with the desired rule $x^{-1-1} \cdot y \rightarrow x \cdot y$.

g. The expression $e^{-1} \cdot e$ can be reduced in two ways: Using a rule from part (a) gives $e^{-1} \cdot e \rightarrow_R e$; using the rule from part (f) gives $e^{-1} \cdot e \rightarrow_R e^{-1}$. Therefore the deduce inference rule gives the equation $e^{-1} \cdot e \leftrightarrow e^{-1}$. The orient inference rule replaces this equation with the desired rule $e^{-1} \cdot e \rightarrow e^{-1}$.

i. We have the reduction $x^{-1-1} \cdot e \rightarrow_R x \cdot e$ by the reduction rule in part (h), where $x^{-1-1} \cdot e \vartriangleright x^{-1-1}$. So the collapse inference rule gives the equation $x \cdot e \leftrightarrow x$. The simplify inference rule with the rule in part (f) replaces this equation with $x \leftrightarrow x$, which is removed by the delete inference rule.

k. We have the reduction $x^{-1-1} \cdot y \rightarrow_R x \cdot y$ by the reduction rule in part (h), where $x^{-1-1} \cdot y \vartriangleright x^{-1-1}$. So the collapse inference rule gives the equation $x \cdot y \leftrightarrow x \cdot y$, which is removed by the delete inference rule.

Chapter 9

Section 9.1

1. a. $1 + n + n(n + 1)/2$.

2.

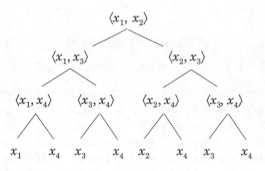

3. a. 7. **c.** 4.

5. There are 25 possibilities. Therefore a ternary pan balance algorithm must make at least three comparisons to solve the problem. One example is

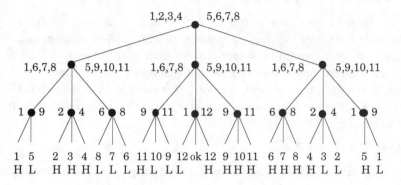

Section 9.2

1. (Reflexive) Since $1f(n) \leq f(n) \leq 1f(n)$, it follows that $f(n) = \Theta(f(n))$ for every function f. (Symmetric) If $f(n) = \Theta(g(n))$, then there are nonzero constants c, d, and m such that $cg(n) \leq f(n) \leq dg(n)$ for all $n \geq m$. Now take the different cases for c and d. For example, we'll do the case for $c > 0$ and $d < 0$. In this case we get $-(1/d)f(n) \leq g(n) \leq (1/c)f(n)$ for all $n \geq m$. Thus $g(n) = \Theta(f(n))$. The other cases for c and d are similar. (Transitive) Assume that $f(n) = \Theta(g(n))$ and $g(n) = \Theta(h(n))$. Then we can write $cg(n) \leq f(n) \leq dg(n)$ for $n \geq m$ and $ah(n) \leq g(n) \leq bh(n)$ for $n \geq k$. Take different cases for a, b, c, and d. For example, if $c > 0$ and $d > 0$, then we have $(ca)h(n) \leq f(n) \leq (bd)h(n)$ for $n \geq \max\{m, k\}$. This says that $f(n) = \Theta(h(n))$.

2. a. The quotient $\log (kn)/\log n$ approaches 1 as n approaches infinity.

3. Let $f(n) = (n - 1)/n$. Then f is increasing, and for all $n \geq 2$ we have the inequality $(1/2){\cdot}1 \leq f(n) \leq 1{\cdot}1$. Therefore $f(n) = \Theta(1)$.

5. $1 \prec \log \log n \prec \log n$.

6. a. $f(n) = \Theta(n \log n)$. Notice that $f(n) = \log(1{\cdot}2{\cdots}n) = \log(n!)$. Now use (9.12) to approximate $n!$ and take the log of Stirlings's formula to obtain $\Theta(n \log n)$.

7. Take limits.

8. a. $5! = 120$; Stirling ≈ 118.02; diff $= 1.98$.

9. In each case, replace $n!$ by Stirling's approximation (9.12). Then take limits

11. The worst case occurs when the algorithm must try to divide n by 2 and by all the odd numbers from 3 up to $\lfloor \sqrt{n} \rfloor$. So there are about $\lfloor \sqrt{n} \rfloor/2$ divisions to perform. If k is the number of digits in the decimal representation of n, then $k = \lfloor \log_{10} n \rfloor + 1$. Solving this equation for n gives the approximation $n = \Theta(10^k)$. So an approximation for the number of divisions is $\Theta(10^{k/2})$.

Section 9.3

1. $(u \vee v \vee x_1) \wedge (w \vee \neg x_1 \vee x_2) \wedge (x \vee \neg x_2 \vee x_3) \wedge (y \vee z \vee \neg x_3)$.

3. In the worst case there would be $2n^2 + 3n + 1$ clauses generated. If we numbered the clauses $C_1, C_2, ..., C_s$, where $s = 2n^2 + 3n + 1$, then in the worst case each clause C_k would be resolved with each of the clauses $C_1, ..., C_{k-1}$. So there would be at most $s(s + 1)/2 = O(n^4)$ resolution steps. Since there are at most $O(n^4)$ resolution steps and at most $O(n^2)$ clauses, it follows that there are at most $O(n^6)$ comparisons to see whether a resolvant is distinct from those clauses already listed.

4. a. $P \neq NP$. **c.** $P = NP$.

5. Any deterministic Turing machine can be thought of as a nondeterministic

Turing machine (that always guesses and checks the right solution). So it follows that $DSPACE \subset NPSPACE$. For the other direction, if $L \in NSPACE$, then $L \in NSPACE(n^i)$ for some i. The given theorem then tells us that $L \in DSPACE(n^{2i})$, which implies that $L \in DSPACE$. Therefore

$$NSPACE \subset DPSPACE.$$

So the two classes are equal.

Bibliography

In addition to the books and papers specifically referenced in this book, we've also included some general references.

Aït-Kaci, H., and M. Nivat, Resolution of Equations in Algebraic Structures. Volume 2: Rewriting Techniques. Academic Press, New York, 1989.

Andrews, P. B., *An Introduction to Mathematical Logic and Type Theory: To Truth Through Proof*. Academic Press, New York, 1986.

Apt, K. R., Ten years of Hoare's logic: A survey—Part 1. *ACM Transactions on Programming Languages and Systems 3* (1981), 431–483.

Brady, A. H., The determination of the value of Rado's noncomputable function $\Sigma(k)$ for four-state Turing macines. *Mathematics of Computation 40* (1983), 647–665.

Brassard, G., and P. Bratley, *Algorithmics: Theory and Practice*. Prentice-Hall, Englewood Cliffs, N. J., 1988.

Chang, C., and R. C. Lee, *Symbolic Logic and Mechanical Theorem Proving*. Academic Press, New York, 1973.

Chomsky, N., Three models for the description of language. *IRE Transactions on Information Theory 2* (1956), 113–124.

Chomsky, N., On certain formal properties of grammar. *Information and Control 2* (1959), 137–167.

Church, A., An unsolvable problem of elementary number theory. *American Journal of Mathematics 58* (1936), 345–363.

Church, A., *The Calculi of Lambda Conversion*. Annals of Mathematical Studies no. 6, Princeton University Press, 1941. Reprinted in 1963 by University Microfilms, Inc., Ann Arbor, Michigan.

Cook, S. A., The complexity of theorem-proving procedures. *Proceedings of the 3rd Annual ACM Symposium on Theory of Computing* (1971), 151–158.

Coppersmith, D., and S. Winograd, Matrix multiplication via arithmetic progressions. *Proceedings of 19th Annual ACM Symposium on the Theory of Computing* (1987), 1–6.

Delong, H., *A Profile of Mathematical Logic*. Addison-Wesley, Reading, Mass., 1970.

Fischer, M. J., and M. O. Rabin, Super-exponential complexity of Presburger arithmetic. *Complexity of Computation*, ed. R. M. Karp. American Mathematical Society, Providence, R. I., 1974, pp. 27–41.

Floyd, R. W., Assigning meanings to programs. *Proceedings AMS Symposium Applied Mathematics, 19*, AMS, Providence R.I., 1967, pp. 19–31.

Garey, M. R., and D. S. Johnson, *Computers and Intractability: A Guide to the Theory of NP-Completeness*. W. H. Freeman, San Francisco, 1979.

Gentzen, G., Untersuchungen uber das logische Schliessen. *Mathematische Zeitschrift 39* (1935), 176–210, 405–431; English translation: Investigation into logical deduction, *The Collected Papers of Gerhard Gentzen*, ed. M. E. Szabo. North-Holland, Amsterdam, 1969, pp. 68–131.

Gödel, K., Die Vollständigkeit der Axiome des logischen Funktionenkalküls. *Monatshefte für Mathematic und Physik 37* (1930), 349–360.

Gödel, K., Über formal unentscheidbare Sätze der Principia Mathematica und verwandter Systeme I. *Monatshefte für Mathematic und Physik 3 8* (1931), 173–198.

Greibach, S. A., A new normal-form theorem for context-free phrase-structure grammars. *Journal of the ACM 12* (1965), 42–52.

Hamilton, A. G., *Logic for Mathematicians*. Cambridge University Press, New York, 1978.

Hein, J. L., A declarative laboratory approach for discrete structures, logic, and computability. *ACM SIGCSE Bulletin 25*, 3 (1993), 19–25.

Hilbert, D., and W. Ackermann, *Principles of Mathematical Logic*. (1938). Translated by Lewis M. Hammond, George G. Leckie, and F. Steinhardt. Edited by Robert E. Luce. Chelsea, New York, 1950.

Hindley, J. R., Combinators and lambda-calculus: A short outline. *Lecture Notes in Computer Science 242*. Springer-Verlag, New York, 1985, pp. 104–122.

Hoare, C.A.R., An axiomatic basis for computer programming. *Communications of the ACM 12* (1969), 576–583.

Hopcroft, J. E., and J. D. Ullman, *Introduction to Automata Theory, Languages, and Computation*. Addison-Wesley, Reading, Mass., 1979.

Kleene, S. C., General recursive functions of natural numbers. *Mathematische Annalen 112* (1936), 727–742.

Kleene, S. C., *Introduction to Metamathematics*. Van Nostrand, New York, 1952.

Kleene, S. C., Representation of events by nerve nets. *Automata Studies*, ed. C. E. Shannon and J. McCarthy. Princeton University Press, Princeton, N. J., 1956, pp. 3–42.

Kleene, S. C., *Mathematical Logic*. John Wiley, New York, 1967.

Knuth, D. E., On the translation of languages from left to right. *Information and Control 8* (1965), 607–639.

Knuth, D. E., *The Art of Computer Programming*. Volume 1: *Fundamental Algorithms*. Addison-Wesley, Reading, Mass., 1968; second edition, 1973.

Knuth, D. E., Two notes on notation. *The American Mathematical Monthly 99* (1992), 403–422.

Knuth, D. E., and P. Bendix, Simple word problems in universal algebras. *Computational Problems in Abstract Algebra*, ed. J. Leech. Pergamon Press, Elmsford, N. Y., 1970, pp. 263–297.

Kurki-Suonio, R., Notes on top-down languages. *BIT 9* (1969), 225–238.

Lewis, P. M., and R. E. Stearns, Syntax-directed transduction. *Journal of the ACM 15* (1968), 465–488.

Lin, S., and T. Rado, Computer studies of Turing machine problems. *Journal of the ACM 12* (1965), 196–212.

Lukasiewicz, J., *Elementary Logiki Matematycznej*. PWN (Polish Scientific Publishers), 1929; translated as *Elements of Mathematical Logic*, Pergamon, Elmsford, N. Y., 1963.

Mallows, C. L., Conway's challenge sequence. *The American Mathematical Monthly 98* (1991), 5–20.

Manna, Z., *Mathematical Theory of Computation*. McGraw-Hill, New York, 1974.

Markov, A. A., The theory of algorithms. *Trudy Math. Inst. Steklov 42* (1954); English translation published in 1962.

Marxen, H., and J. Buntrock. Attacking the Busy Beaver 5. *Bulletin of the European Association for Theoretical Computer Science 40* (1990), 247–251.

Mealy, G. H., A method for synthesizing sequential circuits. *Bell System Technical Journal 34* (1955), 1045–1079.

Mendelson, E., *Introduction to Mathematical Logic*. Van Nostrand, New York, 1964.

Meyer, A. R., and L. J. Stockmeyer, The equivalence problem for regular expressions with squaring requires exponential time. *Proceedings of the 19th Annual Symosium on Switching and Automata Theory* (1972), 125–129.

Minsky, M. L., *Computation: Finite and Infinite Machines*. Prentice-Hall, Englewood Cliffs, N. J., 1967.

Moore, E. F., Gedanken-experiments on sequential machines. *Automata Studies*, ed. C. E. Shannon and J. McCarthy. Princeton University Press, Princeton, N. J., 1956, pp. 129–153.

Morales-Bueno, R., Noncomputability is easy to understand. *Communications of the ACM 38* (1995), 116–117.

Myhill, J., Finite automata and the representation of events. WADD TR-57-624, Wright Patterson AFB, Ohio, 1957, pp. 112–137.

Nagel, E., and J. R. Newman, *Gödel's Proof*. New York University Press, New York, 1958.

Nerode, A., Linear automaton transformations. *Proceedings of the American Mathematical Society 9* (1958), 541–544.

Pan, V., Strassen's algorithm is not optimal. *Proceedings of 19th Annual IEEE Symposium on the Foundations of Computer Science* (1978), 166–176.

Paterson, M. S.; and M. N. Wegman, Linear Unification. *Journal of Computer and Systems Sciences 16* (1978), 158–167.

Paulson, L. C., *Logic and Computation*. Cambridge University Press, New York, 1987.

Post, E. L., Formal reductions of the general combinatorial decision problem. *American Journal of Mathematics 65* (1943), 197–215.

Post, E. L., A variant of a recursively unsolvable problem. *Bulletin of the American Mathematical Society 52* (1946), 246–268.

Rabin, M. O., and D. Scott, Finite automata and their decision problems. *IBM Journal of Research and Development 3* (1959), 114–125.

Rado, T. On noncomputable functions. *Bell System Technical Journal 41* (1962), 877–884.

Robinson, J. A., A machine-oriented logic based on the resolution principle. *Journal of the ACM 12* (1965), 23–41.

Rosenkrantz, D. J., and R. E. Stearns, Properties of deterministic top-down grammars. *Information and Control 17* (1970), 226–256.

Schoenfield, J. R., *Mathematical Logic.* Addison-Wesley, Reading, Mass., 1967.

Schöning, U., *Logic for Computer Scientists.* Birkhauser, Boston, 1989.

Shepherdson, J. C., and H. E. Sturgis, Computability of recursive functions. *Journal of the ACM 10* (1963), 217–255.

Skolem, T., Uber de mathematische logik. *Norsk Matematisk Tidsskrift 10* (1928), 125–142. Translated in ed. Jean van Heijenoort. *From Frege to Godel: A Source Book in Mathematical Logic 1879–1931*, Harvard University Press, Cambridge, Mass., 1967, pp. 508–524.

Snyder, W., and J. Gallier, Higher-order unification revisited: Complete sets of transformations. *Journal of Symbolic Computation 8* (1989), 101–140.

Strassen, V., Gaussian elimination is not optimal. *Numerische Mathematik 13* (1969), 354–356.

Suppes, P., *Introduction to Logic.* Van Nostrand, New York, 1957.

Thompson, K., Regular expression search algorithms. *Communications of the ACM 11* (1968), 419–422.

Turing, A., On computable numbers, with an application to the Entscheidungsproblem. *Proc. London Math. Soc.*, series 2, *42* (1936), 230–265; correction in *43* (1937), 544–546.

Warren, D. S., Memoing for logic programs. *Communications of the ACM 35* (1992), 93–111.

Whitehead, A. N., and B. Russell, *Principia Mathematica.* Cambridge University Press, New York, 1910.

Wos, L., R. Overbeek, E. Lusk, and J. Boyle, *Automated Reasoning: Introduction and Applications.* Prentice-Hall, Englewood Cliffs, N. J., 1984.

Greek Alphabet

A	α	alpha
B	β	beta
Γ	γ	gamma
Δ	δ	delta
E	ε	epsilon
Z	ζ	zeta
H	η	eta
Θ	θ	theta
Ι	ι	iota
K	κ	kappa
Λ	λ	lambda
M	μ	mu
N	ν	nu
Ξ	ξ	xi
O	o	omicron
Π	π	pi
P	ρ	rho
Σ	σ	sigma
T	τ	tau
Y	υ	upsilon
Φ	ϕ	phi
X	χ	chi
Ψ	ψ	psi
Ω	ω	omega

Symbol Glossary

Each symbol or expression is listed with a short definition and the page number where it first occurs. The list is ordered by page number.

$m \mid n$	m divides n with no remainder	2
$x \in S$	x is an element of S	9
$x \notin S$	x is not an element of S	9
...	ellipsis	9
$\varnothing$	the empty set	9
$\mathbb{N}$	natural numbers	10
$\mathbb{Z}$	integers	10
$\mathbb{Q}$	rational numbers	10
$\mathbb{R}$	real numbers	10
$\{x \mid P\}$	set of all x satisfying property P	10
$A \subset B$	A is a subset of B	11
$A \not\subset B$	A is not a subset of B	11
$A \cup B$	A union B	12
$\cup A_i$	union of the sets A_i	12
$A \cap B$	A intersection B	13
$\cap A_i$	intersection of the sets A_i	13
$A - B$	difference: elements in A but not B	14
$A \oplus B$	symmetric difference: $(A - B) \cup (B - A)$	14
A'	complement of A	14
$[a, b, b, a]$	bag, or multiset, of four elements	15
$\langle x, y, x \rangle$	tuple of three elements	15
$\langle \, \rangle$	empty tuple	15
$A \times B$	product of A and B: $\{\langle a, b \rangle \mid a \in A \text{ and } b \in B\}$	16
$\langle \, \rangle$	empty list	16
$\langle x, y, x \rangle$	list of three elements	17

$\mathrm{cons}(h, t)$	list with head h and tail t	17
$\mathrm{Lists}[A]$	lists over A	17
Λ	empty string	18
$|s|$	length of string s	18
A^*	strings over alphabet A	18
$f : A \to B$	function type: f has domain A and codomain B	25
$f(C)$	image of C under f	25
$f^{-1}(D)$	pre-image of D under f	26
$\lfloor x \rfloor$	floor of x: largest integer $\leq x$	26
$\lceil x \rceil$	ceiling of x: smallest integer $\geq x$	27
$a \bmod b$	remainder upon division of a by b	27
$\mathbb{N}_n$	the set $\{0, 1, ..., n - 1\}$	27
$\log_b x = y$	$b^y = x$	27
$f \circ g$	composition of functions f and g	29
f^{-1}	inverse of bijective function f	30
$|S|$	cardinality of S	30
$L \cdot M$	product of languages L and M	38
L^0	the language $\{\Lambda\}$	39
L^n	product of language L with itself n times	39
L^*	closure of language L	39
L^+	positive closure of language L	39
$A \to \alpha$	grammar production	40
$A \to \alpha \mid \beta$	grammar productions $A \to \alpha$ and $A \to \beta$	42
$A \Rightarrow \alpha$	A derives α in one step	43
$A \Rightarrow^+ \alpha$	A derives α in one or more steps	43
$A \Rightarrow^* \alpha$	A derives α in zero or more steps	43
$L(G)$	language of grammar G	44
$h :: t$	list with head h and tail t	55
$a \cdot s$	string with head a and tail s	56
$\mathrm{tree}(L, x, R)$	binary tree with root x and subtrees L and R	59
$\Sigma\, a_i$	sum of the numbers a_i	64
$\Pi\, a_i$	product of the numbers a_i	64
$n!$	n factorial: $n \cdot (n - 1) \cdots 1$	65
$x\, R\, y$	x related by R to y	72
$R \circ S$	composition of binary relations R and S	74
$r(R)$	reflexive closure of R	76
$s(R)$	symmetric closure of R	76
$t(R)$	transitive closure of R	76
R^c	converse of relation R	76
$[x]$	equivalence class of things equivalent to x	78
S/R	partition of S by the equivalence relation R	79

tsr(R)	smallest equivalence relation containing R	80
$\langle A, \preceq \rangle$	reflexive partially ordered set	83
$\langle A, \prec \rangle$	irreflexive partially ordered set	83
$x \prec y$	x is less than y or x is a predecessor of y	83
$x \preceq y$	$x \prec y$ or $x = y$	83
$\langle A; s, a \rangle$	algebra with carrier A and operations s and a	101
$\bar{x}$	complement of Boolean algebra variable x	105
$\neg P$	logical negation of P	119
$P \wedge Q$	logical conjunction of P and Q	119
$P \vee Q$	logical disjunction of P and Q	119
$P \rightarrow Q$	logical conditional: P implies Q	119
$P \equiv Q$	logical equivalence of P and Q	121
$\therefore$	therefore	125
$\exists x$	existential quantifier: there is an x	138
$\forall x$	universal quantifier: for all x	138
$W(x/t)$	wff obtained from W by replacing free x's by t	141
x/t	binding of the variable x to the term t	141
$W(x)$	W contains a free variable x	142
c_x	x is a subscripted variable	163
$\{P\} S \{Q\}$	S is correct for precondition P and postcondition Q	188
$\vdash W$	turnstile to denote W is a theorem	202
$\square$	empty clause: a contradiction	206
$\{x/t, y/s\}$	substitution containing two bindings	214
ε	empty substitution	214
$E\theta$	instance of E: substitution θ applied to E	214
$\theta\sigma$	composition of substitutions θ and σ	215
$C\theta - N$	remove all occurrences of N from clause $C\theta$	221
$R(S)$	resolution of clauses in the set S	223
$\leftarrow A$	logic program goal: is A true?	232
$C \leftarrow$	logic program fact: C is true	233
$C \leftarrow A, B$	logic program conditional: C if A and B	233
$L(M)$	language recognized by machine M	269
a/x	Mealy machine: if a is input, then output x	280
i/x	Moore machine: if in state i, then output x	280
$T(i, a) = j$	deterministic finite automaton transition	284
$T(i, a) = \{j, k\}$	nondeterministic finite automaton transition	287
$\lambda(s)$	lambda closure of state s	295
$T_{min}([s], a) = [T(s, a)]$	minimum-state DFA transition	304
$\langle i, b, C, \text{pop}, j \rangle$	pushdown automaton instruction	327

$\langle A \rightarrow y, p \rangle$	handle of a sentential form	356
$\langle A \rightarrow x \cdot y, d \rangle$	item for LR(1) parsing	363
$\langle i, a, b, L, j \rangle$	Turing machine instruction	383
$\min_y(g(x, y) = 0)$	the minimum y such that $g(x, y) = 0$	408
$x \rightarrow y$	Markov string-processing production	410
$x \rightarrow y$	Post string-processing production	412
$s, t \rightarrow u$	Post system inference rule	414
$f_0, f_1, ..., f_n, ...$	effective enumeration of computable functions	424
$E \rightarrow F$	reduce expression E to F	440
$\lambda x.M$	lambda expression: an abstraction that defines a function	443
$(M\ N)$	lambda expression: the application of M to N	443
$E[x/N]$	expression obtained from E by replacing free x's by N	444
$s \leftrightarrow t$	expressions s and t are equal	456
$t \rightarrow_R u$	t reduces to u by using the rules of R	457
W_A	worst case function for algorithm A	467
$\Theta(f)$	big theta: same growth rate as f	475
$o(f)$	little oh: lower growth rate than f	479
$O(f)$	big oh: same as or lower growth rate than f	480
$\Omega(f)$	big omega: same as or higher growth rate than f	481
P	problems solved in deterministic polynomial time	484
NP	problems solved in nondeterministic polynomial time	485
$PSPACE$	problems solved in polynomial space	486

Index